משנה

ArtScroll Mishnah Series®

A rabbinic commentary to the Six Orders of the Mishnah

Rabbis Nosson Scherman / Meir Zlotowitz

General Editors

the mishnah

ARTSCROLL MISHNAH SERIES / A NEW TRANSLATION WITH A COMMENTARY **YAD AVRAHAM** ANTHOLOGIZED FROM TALMUDIC SOURCES AND CLASSIC COMMENTATORS.

Published by

Mesorah Publications, ltd

THE COMMENTARY HAS BEEN NAMED **YAD AVRAHAM**
AS AN EVERLASTING MEMORIAL AND SOURCE OF MERIT
FOR THE *NESHAMAH* OF
אברהם יוסף ע״ה בן הר״ר אליעזר הכהן גליק נ״י
AVRAHAM YOSEF GLICK ע״ה
WHOSE LIFE WAS CUT SHORT ON 3 TEVES, 5735

FIRST EDITION
First Impression . . . November, 1987

Published and Distributed by
MESORAH PUBLICATIONS, Ltd.
Brooklyn, New York 11223

Distributed in Israel by
MESORAH MAFITZIM / J. GROSSMAN
Rechov Harav Uziel 117
Jerusalem, Israel

Distributed in Europe by
J. LEHMANN HEBREW BOOKSELLERS
20 Cambridge Terrace
Gateshead
TYNE AND WEAR
England NE8 1RP

THE ARTSCROLL MISHNAH SERIES®
SEDER NEZIKIN Vol. II(b): *MAKKOS / SHEVUOS*

ISBN
0-89906-297-0 (hard cover)
0-89906-298-9 (paperback)

Typography by CompuScribe at ArtScroll Studios, Ltd.
1969 Coney Island Avenue / Brooklyn, N.Y. 11223 / (718) 339-1700

Printed in the United States of America by Moriah Offset
Bound by Sefercraft, Quality Bookbinders, Ltd. Brooklyn, N.Y.

Seder Nezikin Vol. II(b):

מסכת מכות

Tractate Makkos

מסכת שבועות

Tractate Shevuos

Translation and anthologized commentary by

Rabbi Avrohom Yoseif Rosenberg

Edited by

Rabbi Gavriel Finkel / Rabbi Yehezkel Danziger

The Publishers are grateful to

TORAH UMESORAH

and

YAD AVRAHAM INSTITUTE

for their efforts in the publication of the

ARTSCROLL MISHNAH SERIES

יהושע אוהב ישראל היה

(ערובין כב:)

This volume is dedicated
to the memory of my son

Joshua Waitman

יהושע יצחק ע״ה בן אברהם מאיר נ״י

שנקטף בדמי ימיו

b. October ***18****, 1968 /* כ״ו תשרי תשכ״ט

d. August 13, 1987 / **י״ח אב, תשמ״ז**

In the formative years of searching and doubt,
he strove for truth and was a magnet for others.
He was a leader, a scholar, a role model,
with a smile for the downcast and a helping hand
for the flounderer.
He would not see bad in people; better to make them good.
No one was lonely or friendless when he was near.

And that is why the shock was so great and the grief
so lasting when he was taken at ***18*** *—*
with so much life and service ahead.
He inspired in life; he inspires still.
Because the memory of the righteous is always alive.

May the study of this Mishnah volume
be a merit for his lustrous soul.

תנצב״ה

הסכמה

RABBI MOSES FEINSTEIN
455 F. D. R. DRIVE
NEW YORK, N. Y. 10002

OREGON 7-1222

משה פיינשטיין
ר"ם תפארת ירושלים
בנוא יארק

בע"ה

הנה ידידי הרב הגאון ר' אברהם יוסף ראזענבערג שליט"א אשר היה מתלמידי החשובים ביותר וגם הרביץ תורה בכמה ישיבות ואצלינו בישיבתנו בסטעטן איילאנד, ובזמן האחרון הוא מתעסק בתרגום ספרי קודש ללשון אנגלית המדוברת ומובנת לבני מדינה זו, וכבר איתמחי גברא בענין תרגום לאנגלית וכעת תרגם משניות לשפת אנגלית וגם לקוטים מדברי רבותינו מפרשי משניות על כל משנה ומשנה בערך, והוא לתועלת גדול להרבה אנשי ממדינה זו שלא התרגלו מילדותם ללמוד המשנה וגם יש הרבה שבעזר השי"ת התקרבו לתורה ויראת שמים כשכבר נתגדלו ורוצים ללמוד שיוכלו ללמוד משניות בנקל בשפה המורגלת להם, שהוא ממזכי הרבים בלמוד משניות וזכותו גדול. ואני מברכו שיצליחהו השי"ת בחבורו זה. וגם אני מברך את חברת ארטסקרול אשר תחת הנהלת הרב הנכבד ידידי מוהר"ר מאיר יעקב בן ידידי הגאון ר' אהרן שליט"א זלאטאוויץ אשר הוציאו כבר הרבה חבורים חשובים לזכות את הרבים וכעת הם מוציאים לאור את המשניות הנ"ל.

ועל זה באתי על החתום בז' אדר תשל"ט בנוא יארק.

נאום משה פיינשטיין

מכתב ברכה

יעקב קמנצקי

RABBI J. KAMENECKI

38 SADDLE RIVER ROAD

MONSEY, NEW YORK 10952

בע"ה

יום ה׳ ערב חג השבועות תשל"ס, פה מאנסי.

כבוד הרבני איש החסד שוע ונדיב מוקיר רבנן מר אלעזר נ"י גליק שלו׳ וברכת כל טוב.

מה מאד שמחתי בהודעי כי כבודו רכש לעצמו הזכות שייקרא ע"ש בנו המנוח הפירוש מבואר על כל ששת סדרי משנה ע"י "ארטסקראל" והנה חברה זו יצאה לה מוניטין בפירושה על תנ"ך, והנה נקוה שכשם שהצליחה בתורה שבכתב כן תצליח בתורה שבע"פ. ובהיות שאותיות "משנה" הן כאותיות "נשמה" לפיכך טוב עשה בכוונתו לעשות זאת לעילוי נשמת בנו המנוח אברהם יוסף ע"ה, ומאד מתאים השם "יד אברהם" לזה הפירוש, כדמצינו במקרא (ש"ב י"ח) כי אמר אין לי בן בעבור הזכיר שמי וגו׳. ואין לך דבר גדול מזה להפיץ ידיעת תורה שבע"פ בקרב אחינו שאינם רגילים בלשון הקדש. וד׳ הטוב יהי׳ בעזרו ויוכל לברך על המוגמר. ויראה רוב נחת מכל אשר אתו כנפש מברכו.

יעקב קמנצקי

מכתב ברכה

YESHIVAT TELSHE | **ישיבת טלז**
Kiryat Telshe Stone | קרית טלז־סטון
Jerusalem, Israel | ירושלים

בע״ה — ד׳ בהעלותך — לבני א״י, תשל״ט — פה קרית טלז, באה״ק

מע״כ ידידי האהובים הרב ר׳ מאיר והרב ר׳ נתן, נר״ו, שלום וברכה נצח!

אחדשה״ט באהבה ויקר,

לשמחה רבה היא לי להודע שהרחבתם גדול עבודתכם בקודש לתורה שבע״פ, בהוצאת המשנה בתרגום וביאור באנגלית, וראשית עבודתכם במס׳ מגילה.

אני תקוה שתשימו לב שיצאו הדברים מתוקנים מנקודת ההלכה, וחזקה עליכם שתוציאו דבר נאה ומתוקן.

בפנותכם לתורה שבע״פ יפתח אופק חדש בתורת ה׳ לאלה שקשה עליהם ללמוד הדברים במקורם, ואלה שכבר נתעשרו מעבודתכם במגילת אסתר יכנסו עתה לטרקלין חדש וישמשו להם הדברים דחף ללימוד המשנה, וגדול יהי׳ שכרכם.

יהא ה׳ בעזרכם בהוספת טבעת חדשה באותה שלשלת זהב של הפצת תורת ה׳ להמוני עם לקרב לב ישראל לאבינו שבשמים בתורה ואמונה טהורה.

אוהבכם מלונ״ח,
מרדכי

מכתב ברכה

RABBI SHNEUR KOTLER
BETH MEDRASH GOVOHA
LAKEWOOD, N. J.

בע״ה

שניאור קוטלר
בית מדרש גבוה
לייקוואוד, נ. דז.

בשורת התרחבות עבודתם הגדולה של סגל חבורת ,,ארטסקרול״, המעתיקים ומפרשים, לתחומי התושבע״פ, לשים אלה המשפטים לפני הציבור כשלחן ערוך ומוכן לאכול לפני האדם [ל׳ רש״י], ולשימה בפיהם — לפתוח אוצרות בשנות בצורת ולהשמיעם בכל לשון שהם שומעים — מבשרת צבא רב לתורה ולימודה [ע׳ תהלים ס״ח י״ב בתרגום יונתן], והיא מאותות ההתעוררות ללימוד התורה, וזאת התעודה על התנוצצות קיום ההבטחה ,,כי לא תשכח מפי זרעו״. אשרי הזוכים להיות בין שלוחי ההשגחה לקיומה וביצועה.

יה״ר כי תצליח מלאכת שמים בידם, ויזכו ללמוד וללמד ולשמור מסורת הקבלה כי בהרקת המים החיים מכלי אל כלי תשתמר חיותם, יעמוד טעמם בם וריחם לא נמר. [וע׳ משאחז״ל בכ״מ ושמרתם זו משנה — וע׳ חי׳ מרן רי״ז הלוי עה״ת בפ׳ ואתחנן] ותהי׳ משנתם שלמה וברורה, ישמחו בעבודתם חברים ותלמידים, ,,ישוטטו רבים ותרבה הדעת״, עד יקויים ,,אז אהפוך אל העמים שפה ברורה וגו׳ ״ [צפני׳ ג׳ ט׳, עי׳ פי׳ אבן עזרא ומצודת דוד שם].

ונזכה כולנו לראות בהתכנסות הגליות בזכות המשניות כל׳ חז״ל עפ״י הכתוב ,,גם כי יתנו בגוים עתה אקבצם״, בגאולה השלמה בב״א.

הכו״ח לכבוד התורה, יום ו׳ עש״ק לס׳ ,,ויוצא פרח ויצץ ציץ ויגמול שקדים״, ד׳ תמוז התשל״ט

יוסף חיים שניאור קוטלר
בלאאמו״ר הגר״א זצוק״ל

מכתב ברכה

ב״ה

ישיבה דפילאדעלפיא

ב״ה

לכבוד ידידי וידיד ישיבתנו, מהראשונים לכל דבר שבקדושה

הרבני הנדיב המפורסם ר׳ אליעזר הכהן גליק נ״י

אחדש״ה באהבה,

בשורה טובה שמעתי שכב׳ מצא את המקום המתאים **לעשות יד ושם** להנציח זכרו **של בנו אברהם יוסף ע״ה** שנקטף בנעוריו. ,,ונתתי להם בביתי ובחומתי יד ושם״. אין לו להקב״ה אלא ד׳ אמות של הלכה בלבד. א״כ זהו בית ד׳ לימוד תורה שבע״פ וזהו המקום לעשות יד ושם לנשמת בנו ע״ה.

נר ד׳ נשמת אדם אמר הקב״ה נרי בידך ונרך בידי. נר מצוה ותורה אור, תורה זהו הנר של הקב״ה וכששומרים נר של הקב״ה שעל ידי הפירוש **,,יד אברהם״** בשפה הלעוזית יתרבה ויתפשט לימוד ושקיעת התורה בבתי ישראל. ד׳ ישמור נשמת אדם.

בנו אברהם יוסף ע״ה נתברך בהמדה שבו נכללות כל המדות, לב טוב והיה אהוב לחבריו. בלמדו בישיבתנו היה לו הרצון לעלות במעלות התורה וכשעלה לארצנו הקדושה היתה מבוקשו להמשיך בלמודיו. ביקוש זה ימצא מלואו על ידי הרבים המבקשים דרך ד׳, שהפירוש **,,יד אברהם״** יהא מפתח להם לים התלמוד.

התורה נקראת ,,אש דת״ ונמשלה לאש ויש לה הכח לפעפע ברזל לפצוץ כוחות האדם, הניצוץ שהאיר בך רבנו הרב שרגא פייוועל מנדלויץ זצ״ל שמרת עליו, ועשה חיל. עכשיו אתה מסייע להאיר נצוצות בנשמות בני ישראל שיעשה חיל ויהא לאור גדול.

תקותי עזה שכל התלמידי חכמים שנדבה רוחם להוציא לפועל מלאכה ענקית זו לפרש המשניות כולה, יצא עבודתם ברוח פאר והדר ויכוונו לאמיתה של תורה ויתקדש ויתרבה שם שמים על ידי מלאכה זו.

יתברך כב׳ וב״ב לראות ולרוות נחת רוח מצאצאיו.

הכו״ח לכבוד התורה ותומכיה עש״ק במדבר תשל״ט

אלי׳ שווי

מכתב ברכה

דוד קאהן

ביהמ״ד גבול יעבץ
ברוקלין, נוא יארק

בס״ד כ״ה למטמונים תשל״ט

כבוד רחימא דנפשאי, עושה ומעשה
ר׳ אלעזר הכהן גליק נטריה רחמנא ופרקיה

שמוע שמעתי שכבר תקעת כפיך לתמוך במפעל האדיר של חברת ארטסקרול — הידוע בכל קצווי תבל ע״י עבודתה הכבירה בהפצת תורה — לתרגם ולבאר ששה סדרי משנה באנגלית. כוונתך להנציח זכר בנך הנחמד אברהם יוסף ז״ל שנקטף באבו בזמן שעלה לארץ הקודש בתקופת התרוממות הנפש ושאיפה לקדושה, ולמטרה זו יכונה הפירוש בשם „**יד אברהם**״; וגם האיר ה׳ רוחך לגרום עילוי לנשמתו הטהורה שעי״ז יתרבה לימוד התורה שניתנה בשבעים לשון, על ידי כלי מפואר זה.

מכיוון שהנני מכיר היטיב שני הצדדים, אוכל לומר לדבק טוב, והנני תקוה שיצליח המפעל הלזה לתת יד ושם וזכות לנשמת אברהם יוסף ז״ל. חזקה על חברת ארטסקרול שתוציא דבר נאה מתוקן ומתקבל מתחת ידה להגדיל תורה ולהאדירה.

והנני מברך אותך שתמצא נוחם לנפשך, שהאבא זוכה לברא, ותשבע נחת — אתה עם רעיתך תחיה — מכל צאצאיכם היקרים אכי״ר

ידידך עז
דוד קאהן

Preface

אָמַר ר׳ יוֹחָנָן: לֹא כָּרַת הקב״ה בְּרִית עִם יִשְׂרָאֵל אֶלָּא עַל־תּוֹרָה שֶׁבְּעַל
פֶּה שֶׁנֶּאֱמַר: ,,כִּי עַל־פִּי הַדְּבָרִים הָאֵלֶּה כָּרַתִּי אִתְּךָ בְּרִית . . .״

R' Yochanan said: The Holy One, Blessed is He, sealed a covenant with Israel only because of the Oral Torah, as it is said [Exodus 34:27]: For according to these words have I sealed a covenant with you ... (Gittin 60b).

With gratitude to Hashem Yisborach *we present the Jewish public with Makkos / Shevuos, the fifth and sixth tractates of* Seder Nezikin. *Following the successful completion of* Moed *and* Nashim, *work is proceeding not only on the rest of* Nezikin *but on the other three other* sedarim *as well. All of this is thanks to the vision and commitment of* MR. AND MRS. LOUIS GLICK. *In their quiet, self-effacing way, they have been a major force for the propagation of Torah knowledge and the enhancement of Jewish life for a generation. The commentary to the mishnayos bears the name* YAD AVRAHAM, *in memory of their son* AVRAHAM YOSEF GLICK ע״ה. *An appreciation of the* niftar *will appear in Tractate* Berachos. *May this dissemination of the Mishnah in his memory be a source of merit for his soul.* תנצב״ה.

By dedicating the ArtScroll Mishnah Series, the Glicks have added a new dimension to their tradition of Torah support. The many study groups in synagogues, schools and offices throughout the English-speaking world are the most eloquent testimony to the fact that thousands of people thirst for Torah learning presented in a challenging, comprehensive, and comprehensible manner.

We are proud and grateful that such venerable luminaries as MARAN HAGAON HARAV YAAKOV KAMINETZKI זצ״ל *and* להבל״ח MARAN HAGAON HARAV MORDECHAI GIFTER שליט״א *have declared that this series should be translated into Hebrew.* Boruch Hashem, *it has stimulated readers to echo the words of King David:* גַּל־עֵינַי וְאַבִּיטָה נִפְלָאוֹת מִתּוֹרָתֶךָ, *Uncover my eyes that I may see wonders of Your Torah (Psalms 119:18).*

May we inject two words of caution:

First, although the Mishnah, by definition, is a compendium of laws, the final halachah does not necessarily follow the Mishnah. The development of halachah proceeds through the Gemara, commentators, codifiers, responsa, and the acknowledged poskim. *Even when our commentary cites the* Shulchan

Aruch, *the intention is to sharpen the reader's understanding of the Mishnah, but not to be a basis for actual practice. In short, this work is meant as a first step in the study of our recorded Oral Law — no more.*

Second, as we have stressed in our other books, the ArtScroll commentary is not meant as a substitute for the study of the sources. While this commentary, like others in the various series, will be immensely useful even to accomplished scholars and will often bring to light ideas and sources they may have overlooked, we strongly urge those who can, to study the classic seforim *in the original. It has been said that every droplet of ink coming from* Rashi's *pen is worthy of seven days' contemplation. Despite the exceptional caliber of our authors, none of us pretends to replace the study of the greatest minds in Jewish history.*

The author of this volume, RABBI AVROHOM YOSAIF ROSENBERG, *is familiar to ArtScroll Mishnah readers from his fine work on many other tractates. His manuscript was edited by* RABBI YEHEZKEL DANZIGER, *Editor-in-Chief of the Mishnah Series, and* RABBI GAVRIEL FINKEL, *of the Talmudical Academy of Adelphia.*

We are also grateful to the staff of Mesorah Publications: RABBI HERSH GOLDWURM, *whose encyclopedic knowledge is always available;* REB SHEAH BRANDER, *who remains a leader in bringing beauty of presentation to Torah literature;* RABBI AVIE GOLD, SHIMON GOLDING, SHMUEL KLAVER, SHEILA TANNENBAUM, YOSEF TIMINSKY, MICHAEL ZIVITZ, LEA FREIER, MRS. ESTHER FEIERSTEIN, MRS. FAIGIE WEINBAUM, MRS. JUDI DICK, MENUCHA MARCUS, ESTIE ZLOTOWITZ, ZISSIE GLATZER, AND CHAVIE GLUCK.

Finally, our gratitude goes to RABBI DAVID FEINSTEIN שליט״א *and* RABBI DAVID COHEN שליט״א, *whose concern, interest, and guidance throughout the history of the ArtScroll Series have been essential to its success.*

Rabbi Nosson Scherman / Rabbi Meir Zlotowitz

ג׳ כסלו תשמ״ח / *November 26, 1986*
Brooklyn, New York

מסכת מכות

Tractate Makkos

Deuteronomy 25:1-4

כִּי־יִהְיֶה רִיב בֵּין אֲנָשִׁים וְנִגְּשׁוּ אֶל־הַמִּשְׁפָּט וּשְׁפָטוּם
וְהִצְדִּיקוּ אֶת־הַצַּדִּיק וְהִרְשִׁיעוּ אֶת הָרָשָׁע. וְהָיָה אִם־בִּן
הַכּוֹת הָרָשָׁע וְהִפִּילוֹ הַשֹּׁפֵט וְהִכָּהוּ לְפָנָיו כְּדֵי רִשְׁעָתוֹ
בְּמִסְפָּר. אַרְבָּעִים יַכֶּנּוּ לֹא יֹסִיף פֶּן יֹסִיף לְהַכֹּתוֹ
עַל־אֵלֶּה מַכָּה רַבָּה וְנִקְלָה אָחִיךָ לְעֵינֶיךָ. לֹא־תַחְסֹם
שׁוֹר בְּדִישׁוֹ.

If there is a dispute between men, they are to come for adjudication and the judges are to judge them; they are to vindicate the righteous party and condemn the wicked one. And it shall be that if the wicked one is liable to lashes; the judge shall cast him down and have him lashed in his presence, according to his wickedness, in the [assigned] number. He is to strike him forty lashes, and may not exceed it; lest he strike him one lash beyond these and your brother be demeaned before your eyes. You may not muzzle an ox during its threshing.

Deuteronomy 19:16-21:

כִּי־יָקוּם עֵד־חָמָס בְּאִישׁ לַעֲנוֹת בּוֹ סָרָה. וְעָמְדוּ
שְׁנֵי־הָאֲנָשִׁים אֲשֶׁר־לָהֶם הָרִיב לִפְנֵי ה׳ לִפְנֵי הַכֹּהֲנִים
וְהַשֹּׁפְטִים אֲשֶׁר יִהְיוּ בַּיָּמִים הָהֵם. וְדָרְשׁוּ הַשֹּׁפְטִים הֵיטֵב
וְהִנֵּה עֵד־שֶׁקֶר הָעֵד שֶׁקֶר עָנָה בְּאָחִיו. וַעֲשִׂיתֶם לוֹ
כַּאֲשֶׁר זָמַם לַעֲשׂוֹת לְאָחִיו וּבִעַרְתָּ הָרָע מִקִּרְבֶּךָ.
וְהַנִּשְׁאָרִים יִשְׁמְעוּ וְיִרָאוּ וְלֹא־יֹסִפוּ לַעֲשׂוֹת עוֹד כַּדָּבָר
הָרָע הַזֶּה בְּקִרְבֶּךָ. וְלֹא תָחוֹס עֵינֶךָ נֶפֶשׁ בְּנֶפֶשׁ עַיִן בְּעַיִן
שֵׁן בְּשֵׁן יָד בְּיָד רֶגֶל בְּרָגֶל.

If a false witness rises up against a person to bear unfounded testimony against him. The two men involved in the controversy shall stand before HASHEM, *before the Kohanim and the judges who will be at that time. And the judges shall inquire thoroughly, and behold the witness is false, he testified falsely against his brother. You shall do to him as he had planned to do to his brother, and you shall remove the evil from your midst. And those remaining shall hear and fear, and they shall not continue to do any such evil thing anymore in your midst. Your eye shall not pity: a life for a life, an eye for an eye, a tooth for a tooth, a hand for a hand, a foot for a foot.*

General Introduction to Makkos

Tractate *Makkos* [also known as *Malkus*], deals with three topics: (1) עֵדִים זוֹמְמִים, *zomemim* [false] witnesses; (2) גָּלוּת, the exile of people who commit murders inadvertently; and (3) מַלְקוּת, the punishment of lashes meted out to one who transgresses one of the Torah's prohibitions. In its way, it concludes the delineation of the laws of judicial procedure and jurisprudence begun in tractate *Sanhedrin*, the preceding volume. The topic which forms the first chapter — the law of the false witnesses — is inserted here by way of continuation of a ruling concerning them stated in the last mishnah of *Sanhedrin*. The other two chapters, which deal with exile and lashes, both of which are closely related to capital punishment, follow in order to complete the matters dealt with in Tractate *Sanhedrin*. Indeed, *Meiri* considers *Makkos* to be a continuation of *Sanhedrin*. *Rambam* (Introduction to the Mishnah), however, maintains that *Makkos* is not a part of *Sanhedrin*, but a distinct tractate by itself. It is juxtaposed with *Sanhedrin*, because lashes, like capital punishment, is a procedure that only the court has the right to administer.

◆§ עֵדִים זוֹמְמִין, Zomemim Witnesses

The law of עֵדִים זוֹמְמִין, *zomemin witnesses* is given in *Deut.* 19:16-21. In these verses the Torah prescribes that witnesses whose testimony has been proven false are to be punished with the very punishment which they planned to have inflicted upon the victim of their plot, whether capital punishment, lashes, or monetary payments. The Torah does not, however, specify the method by which witnesses may be proven false.

If the testimony of two witnesses is contradicted by that of other witnesses — a situation known as הַכְחָשָׁה — there is no reason to accept one set as truthful more so than the other. Even if one version is the testimony of numerous witnesses, while the other version is the testimony of just two witnesses, the law is that we may not favor one over the other. Since the Torah credits the testimony of two witnesses as valid, there is no advantage to testimony coming from a larger number of witnesses. This is the principle of תְּרֵי כְּמֵאָה, *two [witnesses] are the equivalent of a hundred.* Thus, if the testimony of all the witnesses leaves us with two clearly conflicting versions of the events, each suported by at least two witnesses, the impasse can be resolved only by discarding both testimonies.

However, since this does not resolve which set of witnesses is telling the truth, neither set can be said to have been proven false. The Torah's law concerning false witnesses, therefore, cannot be referring to this situation. The Oral Law teaches that the law of *zomemin* applies only to witnesses who have been proven false through a specific process known as הֲזָמָה, *hazamah.* This is when a second set of witnesses state that they saw the first set of witnesses at the time of the alleged incident in a place where they could not have possibly witnessed the incident to which they testify. These latter witnesses make no statement concerning the incident which is the subject of the trial; they merely state that the witnesses who previously gave testimony could not possibly have seen what they claim to have seen . In such a case

the Torah decrees that the discrediting witnesses are to be believed and that the ones they impeach are to be considered proven false. Here too it is irrelevant how many witnesses are in each group, as long as they are at least two. Refutation in this manner is known as הֲזָמָה, *hazamah*, and the witnesses thereby discredited are known as עֵדִים זוֹמְמִין, *zomemim* witnesses. Any other means of refutation (e.g., the victim of an alleged murder personally appearing in the courtroom obviously alive and well), though conclusive in its refutation of the witnesses, does not render them *zomemim* (see mishnah 4).

As noted above, the Torah mandates punishing *zomemim* by inflicting upon them the same punishment they sought to inflict on their victim — be it execution, *malkus*, or monetary payment. There are, however, situations in which the fate they sought to impose upon the victim is somewhat intangible and therefore not subject to an equivalent punishment. In such instances they are punished with *malkus* instead. This unusual type of *hazamah* punishment is discussed in the very first mishnah of the tractate.

There are two major conditions attached to the imposition of the *hazamah* punishment. The first is that the witnesses are not liable to the punishment unless their victim has been convicted by their testimony, but the sentence has not yet been meted out. If they are discredited before the court hands down a guilty verdict, they are not punished. More suprisingly, there is a Scriptural decree that if the sentence has already been carried out and the victim has been executed, they can no longer be punished by the courts for their crime. The rationale for this law, and its details, will be discussed in the commentary. There is also a question whether this exsclusion applies only to executions, or to *malkus* and monetary payments as well. This too will be addressed in the commentary.

The laws of *hazamah* play an important role in the overall laws of testimony. There is a fundamental rule of testimony that any testimony not susceptible to refutation by *hazamah* [עֵדוּת שֶׁאִי אַתָּה יָכוֹל לַהֲזִמָּהּ] is inadmissible. For this reason, witnesses must state very specifically when and where the incident took place (*Sanhedrin* 5:1). Should they be allowed to be vague about the time and place, their testimony would in effect be shielded from the possibility of *hazamah* and would therefore be inadmissible. Similarly, if the very nature of the testimony precludes their being punished for testifying falsely even if they are found to be *zomemin*, such testimony is also inadmissible. [The testimony, however, need not be susceptible to the equivalent punishment; as long as it is at least subject to *malkus*, it is admissible.]

◆§ גָּלוּת, Exile

The second chapter of this tractate deals with the law of exile decreed by the Torah (*Numbers* 35:9-34; *Deut.* 19:1-10) upon one who murders inadvertantly [שׁוֹגֵג]. Since this exile is a form of atonement, it is reserved for those who kill inadvertently but with a measure of negligence. If the killing was the result of complete negligence, it is considered close to being intentional, and too severe a crime to be atoned for the exile. [Rather, punishment is left to the hands of Heaven, as it is in the case of one who murders intentionally but in the absence of witnesses or without proper warning (see below, in regard to *malkus*).] If death resulted from an unforseeable mishap, it is considered completely accidental [אוֹנֵס] and thus exempt from exile. The first two *mishnayos* of this chapter set out the parameters of this rule.

Exile is served in one of six עָרֵי מִקְלָט, *cities of refuge*, set aside for this purpose, or in one of the forty-two Levitical cities. The murderer must remain there until the death of the *Kohen Gadol* who is in office at the time of his sentence. Should he leave the city, he may be killed by the relatives of his victim. Indeed, he may be killed by them even before his trial and sentence to exile. For this reason, anyone committing murder under any circumstance must immediatley flee to a city of refuge (or Levitical city) to escape the vengeance of the גוֹאֵל הַדָּם, *goel hadam*, literally, the avenger of the blood. From there he is brought to court to stand trial and receive his sentence — execution, exile, or exoneration.

◆§ מַלְקוּת, Malkus [Lashes]

מַכּוֹת *[Makkos]*, the Hebrew word from which our tractate takes its name, means *blows*. The Rabbinic term *malkus* (beating) is specifically applied to the punishment of lashes meted out by the courts for the willful transgression of the Torah's negative commandments.

In Torah law, there is no distinction between civil, criminal and religious law. All three of these categories carry with them penalties subject to judicial imposition according to rules of jurisprudence. Not all the Torah's prohibitions are subject to this punishment, however, and even those that are must be violated in certain specific ways before this punishment can actually be imposed.

In general, any negative commandment not subject to one of the four types of court-imposed death penalties spelled out in tractate *Sanhedrin*, is subject to the punishment of *malkus*. Even those subject to כָּרֵת [*kares*], and מִיתָה בִּידֵי שָׁמַיִם [*death at the hands of Heaven*], two types of Divinely imposed premature death [see our commentary to *Sanhedrin* 9:6, p. 169, for the differences between them], are subject to the penalty of *malkus* as well. If *malkus* is inflicted, the transgressor is released from the Divine punishment due him if he has repented; see mishnah 3:15.

In contrast to the rule for prohibitions subject to death penalties, *kares*, or Heavenly death, it is not necessary for the Torah to specify the punishment of lashes for an infraction. Any negative commandment not excepted from *malkus* by one of the rules listed below, automatically carries with it a penalty of *malkus*. [By the same token, transgressions subject to *kares* or Heavenly death do not carry a penalty of *malkus* unless they are admonished against by a negative commandment.] *Rambam (Hil. Sanhedrin* chs. 18, 19) enumerates two hundred and seven negative commandments whose infraction is subject to *malkus*.

The exceptions to the punishment of *malkus* are: (1) A negative commandment followed by a positive commandment that is designed to undo the transgression [לָאו הַנִּתָּק לַעֲשֵׂה]. In the case of these prohibitions, it is understood that the Torah offers the positive commandment as the alternative to lashes. For example, the Torah forbids stealing, but commands a thief to return what he has stolen; therefore, restitution, not *malkus*, is the atonement for stealing.[1] (2) Only negative commandments violated in an active manner are subject to lashes, not prohibitions transgressed through inaction. Thus, there is no *malkus* for leaving over sacrificial meat, for example (see 3:3), — nothing is *done* and lashes are not administered unless one has *committed* a wrong by performing an act. (3)Transgressions whose

---

1. Even these negative commandments may be subject to lashes, however, if the transgressor refuses to perform the positive commandment, or renders it impossible to do so; see commentary at the end of mishnah 3:4.

negative commandment serves as the injunction for a death penalty [לָאו שֶׁנִּתָּן לְאַזְהָרַת מִיתַת בֵּית דִּין]. (4) Negative commandments for whose violation the Torah stipulates monetary compensation. Thus, one who assaults a fellow Jew has violated a negative commandment (*Rambam, Chovel* 5:1), but he is obligated to pay damages instead of receiving *malkus*. (5) A negative commandment which serves as the admonition for several different prohibitions [לָאו שֶׁבִּכְלָלוֹת]. An example of this is the injunction (*Lev.* 19:22): לֹא תֹאכְלוּ עַל־הַדָּם, *You shall not eat over blood*, which the *Gemara* cites as the admonition for several prohibitions (see *Sanhedrin* 63a). (6) A negative commandment that is worded in a positive manner, e.g., the commandment imposed upon the *Kohen Gadol* (*Lev.* 21:13): וְהוּא אִשָּׁה בִבְתוּלֶיהָ יִקָּח, *He shall marry a woman in her virginity*. If a *Kohen Gadol* marries a non-virgin, he transgresses this commandment but does not incur *malkus*. See *Rambam Comm.* 3:1.

Even for transgressing a negative commandment for which there is a penalty of *malkus*, the lashes are not actually imposed unless two proper witnesses testify before the court to having seen the violation. Furthermore, they must have warned the transgressor immediately prior to his commision of the act (see mishnah 3:7). The witnesses must also be rigorously examined in the same fashion as witnesses testifying in a capital case (*Rambam, Hil. Sanhedrin* 16:4).

[א] **כֵּיצַד** הָעֵדִים נַעֲשִׂים זוֹמְמִין? „מְעִידִין אָנוּ בְּאִישׁ פְּלוֹנִי שֶׁהוּא בֶּן־גְּרוּשָׁה," אוֹ „בֶּן־חֲלוּצָה." אֵין אוֹמְרִים יֵעָשֶׂה זֶה בֶּן־גְּרוּשָׁה אוֹ בֶּן־חֲלוּצָה תַּחְתָּיו, אֶלָּא לוֹקֶה אַרְבָּעִים. „מְעִידִין

יד אברהם

Chapter One

1.

It has been explained in the General Introduction that witnesses can be proven false only if other witnesses testify against them that they could not possibly have seen what they claim to have seen since they were elsewhere at that time. Discrediting witnesses by this method is known as הֲזָמָה, *hazamah*, and the witnesses so discredited are known as עֵדִים זוֹמְמִין, *zomemim witnesses*. The Torah (*Deut.* 19:16-21) decrees that witnesses found to be *zomemim* are to be punished by inflicting upon them whatever penalty they sought to impose upon the victim of their scheme.

There are, however, situations in which this cannot be done for one reason or another. Mishnah 1 takes up the question of how the *zomemim* witnesses are to be punished in such cases.

כֵּיצַד הָעֵדִים נַעֲשִׂים זוֹמְמִין? — *How are witnesses punished for hazamah?* [Lit., *how do witnesses become zomemim?*]

I.e., how are those *zomemim* witnesses punished, upon whom the punishment of doing to them as they intended to do to their victim cannot be carried out? (*Rav* from *Gem.* 2a).

„מְעִידִין אָנוּ בְּאִישׁ פְּלוֹנִי שֶׁהוּא בֶּן־גְּרוּשָׁה," — *'We testify regarding so-and-so that he is the son of a divorcee,'*

The witnesses testify against a man known to be a *Kohen* that his mother was divorced in their presence from an earlier husband prior to her marriage to this man's father, a *Kohen*. Since a *Kohen* is prohibited from marrying a divorcee (*Lev.* 21:7), this man, who was subsequently begotten of this illicit union, would be a *chalal*, disqualified *Kohen* (*Rav; Rashi*).

אוֹ „בֶּן־חֲלוּצָה." — *or, 'the son of a chalutzah.'*

Or they testify that the subject's mother received *chalitzah* from her brother-in-law (see below) prior to her marriage to the subject's father, a *Kohen*. Since a *Kohen* is Rabbinically proscribed from marrying a *chalutzah*, the child of this union would Rabbinically have the status of a *chalal* (*Ran; Tos. Yom Tov*).

Others explain that they testify that they heard the man's father say that his son was the son of a divorcee or a *chalutzah*, in which case the father would be believed (*Meiri*; see *Yevamos* 127b).

[When a man dies childless, the Torah commands that his widow marry one of his brothers in fulfillment of the *mitzvah* of *yibum* (levirate marriage). If the brothers refuse to marry her, she must be released from her *yibum*-bond (so that she can be free to remarry) by a procedure known as *chalitzah*. A woman released by *chalitzah* is referred to as a *chalutzah*. Although a *Kohen* is Biblically permitted to marry a *chalutzah*, since she is a widow and not a divorcee, the Rabbis prohibited such a union because of her similarity to a divorcee (see General Introduction to ArtScroll *Yevamos*).

אֵין אוֹמְרִים יֵעָשֶׂה זֶה בֶּן־גְּרוּשָׁה אוֹ בֶּן־חֲלוּצָה תַּחְתָּיו; — *We do not say* [*that*] *this one should be made* [*like*] *the son of a divorcee or the son of a chalutzah in his stead;*

If these witnesses are proven to be false by the process of *hazamah*, and they are

1
1

1. How are witnesses punished for *hazamah?* 'We testify regarding so-and-so that he is the son of a divorcee,' or, 'the son of a *chalutzah.*' We do not say [that] this one should be made [like] the son of a divorcee or the son of a *chalutzah* in his stead; rather, he is flogged forty [lashes]. 'We testify against so-and-so

YAD AVRAHAM

also *Kohanim,* we do not say that their punishment for conspiring to disqualify a *Kohen* from the *Kehunah* (priesthood) is that *they* should in turn be disqualified.

The *Gemara* (2a) derives this ruling from the Torah's stipulation regarding the *zomemim:* וַעֲשִׂיתֶם לוֹ כַּאֲשֶׁר זָמַם לַעֲשׂוֹת, *and you shall do to him as he had planned to do.* Two requirements are hereby set for applying the parallel punishment rule of *hazamah:* (1) *And you shall do to 'him'* — to him and not to his offspring; i.e., the punishment must be limited to the *zomem*-witness alone. (2) *As he had planned to do* — the effect of the witness' punishment must be identical to the effect he planned for his victim. These conditions cannot both be met in the case of our mishnah. Should we render the witness a disqualified *Kohen* in the fullest sense, his children would become disqualified as well, since we are dealing with a hereditary disqualification. Should we disqualify him and not his children, we would not be fulfilling the requirement of punishing the witness exactly as he had planned to do to the defendant, since, in this case, the defendant's offspring would have become disqualified as well.

Some commentators raise the following question. The state of being a *chalal* [disqualified *Kohen*] is not merely a matter of ritual status but carries monetary penalties as well, since a *chalal* does not receive *terumah* or any of the other gifts to which a *Kohen* is normally entitled. The witnesses thus conspired not only to confer the status of *chalal* on the defendant but also to deprive him of the monetary benefits of the priesthood. Although the witnesses cannot be punished by rendering them *chalalim,* as explained above, why are they not at least required to pay their victim for conspiring to deprive him of his *Kohanic* benefits?

One solution offered is that the rule of *hazamah* applies only to a clearly defined penalty, not to one which will require continual assessment. Therefore, the rule of *hazamah* does not apply to this case since the amount of *Kohanic* benefits that the victim is destined to receive is presently indeterminate.

An alternate solution is that the victim's loss of benefits would not have constituted actual damages to him since these benefits may be given to any *Kohen* of the donor's choice and thus this *Kohen* has no claim to them in advance.

A third solution is that in order to apply the law of *hazamah,* it must be applied completely. Since in this case we would only apply it as regards the monetary consequences but not as regards the ritual status of *chalal,* we cannot apply it at all *(Ritva).*[1]

אֶלָּא לוֹקֶה אַרְבָּעִים. — *rather, he is flogged forty* [*lashes*].

[Since we cannot fulfill the usual order of punishment, they receive lashes instead.]

1. It is in order to teach us this additional point that the *Tanna* chose the examples of a son of a divorcee or *chalutzah* to illustrate the principle of *to him and not to his offspring* rather than the otherwise equivalent case of a *mamzer* [child of an incestuous or adulterous union] which is applicable to all Jews and not restricted to *Kohanim.* By citing a case limited to *Kohanim,* he teaches that the witnesses are not required to pay for the loss of benefits which the *Kohen* would have suffered *(Ritva).* Another reason may be that the cases of this mishnah were chosen because they occur more frequently than that of the *mamzer* (ibid.). Again, the *Tanna's* choice of these particular cases may be that this mishnah is connected with the final mishnah in *Sanhedrin,* which deals with the daughter of a *Kohen (Tos. Yom Tov* from *Tosafos).*

אָנוּ בְאִישׁ פְּלוֹנִי שֶׁהוּא חַיָּב לִגְלוֹת.״ אֵין אוֹמְרִים יִגְלֶה זֶה תַּחְתָּיו, אֶלָּא לוֹקֶה אַרְבָּעִים.

„מְעִידִין אָנוּ בְאִישׁ פְּלוֹנִי שֶׁגֵּרַשׁ אֶת־אִשְׁתּוֹ,״ וְלֹא נָתַן לָהּ כְּתֻבָּתָהּ. וַהֲלֹא בֵּין הַיּוֹם וּבֵין לְמָחָר

יד אברהם

Actually he receives only thirty-nine lashes, as will be taught in 3:10. This is also the case throughout the tractate and wherever else the term forty lashes is used to describe the penalty of flogging.

This ruling is indicated in *Deut.* 25:1-3: כִּי־יִהְיֶה רִיב בֵּין אֲנָשִׁים וְנִגְּשׁוּ אֶל־הַמִּשְׁפָּט וּשְׁפָטוּם וְהִצְדִּיקוּ אֶת־הַצַּדִּיק וְהִרְשִׁיעוּ אֶת־הָרָשָׁע. וְהָיָה אִם בִּן־הַכּוֹת הָרָשָׁע וְהִפִּילוֹ הַשֹּׁפֵט וְהִכָּהוּ לְפָנָיו כְּדֵי רִשְׁעָתוֹ בְּמִסְפָּר. אַרְבָּעִים יַכֶּנּוּ ..., *Should there be a quarrel between men, and they approach the tribunal and they judge them, and they vindicate the innocent and condemn the guilty. If the guilty is liable to lashes, the judge shall lay him down and strike him before him according to his wickedness, in number. Forty lashes shall he strike him ...*

Now, it is true that the simple meaning would appear to be that the litigants approach the tribunal and they [the judges] vindicate the innocent [litigant] and condemn the guilty [litigant]. However, according to this interpretation, the entire phrase regarding the vindication of the innocent and condemnation of the guilty seems superfluous to the subject of this passage — the law of flogging. Does vindication of the innocent in any way affect the punishment deserved by the guilty? Let the Torah state simply, *Should there be a quarrel between men and they approach the tribunal and they judge them. If the guilty is liable to lashes the judge shall lay him down and strike him, etc.* This phrase, then, indicates an additional interpretation which accounts for the phrase's inclusion: *They* [the litigants] *approach the tribunal and they* [the vindicating witnesses] *vindicate the innocent* [litigant who was falsely accused by the false witnesses] *and condemn the guilty* [witnesses]. *If the guilty is liable to lashes* [i.e., if it is impossible to fulfill the law of *hazamah*, as in our case] the Torah prescribes the penalty of lashes (*Rav* from *Gem.* 2b; see *Rashi* and *Meiri* ad loc.).

Although, as explained in the introduction to the tractate, the penalty of lashes is prescribed for the transgression of any לָאו, *prohibition*, the fact that the false witnesses transgressed the prohibition of לֹא תַעֲנֶה בְרֵעֲךָ עֵד שָׁקֶר, *You shall not bear false witness against your fellowman* (*Ex.* 20:13), would not be sufficient to make them liable for lashes. The reason is that this general prescription of lashes applies only to prohibitions which are violated by physical action. Since testifying does not constitute a physical action [the movement of the lips during the act of speech is not considered 'action' in this context], there would be no penalty of *malkus* [lashes]. Therefore, the Torah has to specify that the witnesses are indeed to be flogged (*Tos. Yom Tov* from *Gem.* 2b).

Some authorities assert that the penalty of *malkus* is meted out to the witnesses only in the case of the *son of a divorcee*, i.e., if they testify that the *Kohen's* mother was a divorcee, which would disqualify him Biblically from the *Kehunah*. Should they testify that his mother was a *chalutzah*, however, they are not sentenced to *malkus* since they merely sought to disqualify him Rabbinically. Although the mishnah groups them together, this is not to be taken literally, but merely as part of the standard mishnaic idiom of בֶּן־גְּרוּשָׁה וּבֶן־חֲלוּצָה. See 3:1, *Yevamos* 6:3 (*Ramban; Ritva*).

Rambam (*Hil. Eidus* 20:8), however, states explicitly that the mishnah's ruling applies in the case of the *chalutzah* as well. [Since the witnesses' testimony is, nevertheless, false, they have transgressed the negative commandment of

1 that he is liable to exile.' We do not say [that] this one
1 should be exiled in his stead; rather, he is flogged forty [lashes].

'We testify against so-and-so that he divorced his wife,' and he did not give her the *kesubah*. Now, either today or tomorrow he may have to give her the

לֹא תַעֲנֶה בְרֵעֲךָ עֵד שָׁקֶר, *You shall not bear false witness against your fellowman,* and they are thus subject to lashes.]

„מְעִידִין אָנוּ בְאִישׁ פְּלוֹנִי שֶׁהוּא חַיָּב לִגְלוֹת." — *'We testify against so-and-so that he is liable to exile.'*

Witnesses come and testify against a person that he killed someone unintentionally and is, therefore, liable to be exiled to a city of refuge (see below, ch. 2).

This presents some difficulty. Exile is for unintentional murder, but no one can know conclusively what was in the murderer's heart. Accordingly, even after the witnesses' testimony, the murderer can always exempt himself from exile by claiming that he killed intentionally. [This would not expose him to a death penalty, since one cannot be executed on his own admission. Although there are witnesses to the act, they did not warn him, and their testimony, therefore, cannot cause him to be executed (see below, 2:3).]

Tosafos resolve this problem by explaining the mishnah to refer to a case in which they testify that he killed him under such circumstances that make it highly unlikely that the murder was intentional. In such a case, the defendant cannot claim that he killed him intentionally in order to avoid exile. It is also possible that if the defendant does not contest their statement, he is assumed to be an unintentional murderer and would thus have been exiled had the second group of witnesses failed to vindicate him by proving the first group false *(Tos. Yom Tov)*.

אֵין אוֹמְרִים יִגְלֶה זֶה תַּחְתָּיו; — *We do not say [that] this one should be exiled in his stead;*

If these witnesses are found to be false, we do not say that each witness should be exiled instead of the defendant. This ruling is based on the verse describing the punishment of exile for the unintentional murderer *(Deut.* 19:5): הוּא יָנוּס אֶל־אַחַת הֶעָרִים הָאֵלֶּה וָחָי, *He shall flee to one of these cities and live.* The pronoun הוּא, *he*, already evident from the verb's conjugation, denotes the emphatic, thus intimating that *he* must flee — but not witnesses who conspire against him *(Rav* from *Gem.* 2b).

אֶלָּא לוֹקֶה אַרְבָּעִים. — *rather, he is flogged forty [lashes].*

[Instead, each of the false witnesses is flogged forty [i.e., thirty-nine] lashes, as explained above in regard to testimony about the son of a divorcee or *chalutzah*.]

„מְעִידִין אָנוּ בְאִישׁ פְּלוֹנִי שֶׁגֵּרַשׁ אֶת־אִשְׁתּוֹ," וְלֹא נָתַן לָהּ כְּתֻבָּתָהּ. — *'We testify against so-and-so that he divorced his wife,' and he did not give her the kesubah.*

Witnesses testify that a man divorced his wife in their presence on a specific day *(Rav; Rashi)* and did not pay her the *kesubah*. [The *kesubah* is the contract that a husband presents to his wife upon their marriage which specifies his obligations to her and the monetary settlement she will receive in the event of her divorce or becoming widowed.] The husband, however, claims that he never divorced her and is therefore not obligated to pay her *kesubah*. The witnesses were subsequently found to be false *(Rav; Rashi)*.

It is a bit difficult to understand how the witnesses can testify that she did not yet receive her *kesubah*. They can testify only concerning an incident that took place, but how can they testify with certainty that a certain event never took place. In the words of the Talmud: *'We have not seen' is not*

מכות
א/א

סוֹפוֹ לִתֵּן־לָהּ כְּתֻבָּתָהּ. אוֹמְדִין כַּמָּה אָדָם רוֹצֶה לִתֵּן בִּכְתֻבָּתָהּ שֶׁל־זוֹ, שֶׁאִם נִתְאַלְמְנָה אוֹ־נִתְגָּרְשָׁה; וְאִם מֵתָה, יִירָשֶׁנָּה בַּעֲלָהּ.

„מְעִידִין אָנוּ בְאִישׁ פְּלוֹנִי שֶׁהוּא חַיָּב לַחֲבֵרוֹ אֶלֶף זוּז עַל־מְנָת לִתְּנָם לוֹ מִכָּאן וְעַד שְׁלֹשִׁים יוֹם," וְהוּא אוֹמֵר: „מִכָּאן וְעַד עֶשֶׂר שָׁנִים" — אוֹמְדִין כַּמָּה אָדָם רוֹצֶה לִתֵּן וְיִהְיוּ בְיָדוֹ אֶלֶף זוּז, בֵּין נוֹתְנָן

יד אברהם

proof. From *Rav* and *Rashi* it would appear that the witnesses do not testify directly about the *kesubah* obligation but only about the divorce. Thus, her grounds for claiming the *kesubah* is the fact of her divorce, which carries with it an automatic obligation of *kesubah.* Since the husband denies divorcing her, he in effect admits to not having paid the *kesubah,* and their testimony therefore obligates him to pay it. The difficulty involved with this explanation is that they can claim that they thought she had already received her *kesubah* and that their intention was never to obligate him to pay the *kesubah* but only to free her to remarry (see *Sanhedrin* 41a). The mishnah probably means that the witnesses testify that the husband divorced her on a certain date with the stipulation that he pay her *kesubah* in their presence, a condition with which he did not comply. It is, therefore, obvious that they wished to obligate him to pay the *kesubah (Pnei Yehoshua;* cf. *Tif. Yis., Tif. Yaakov, Chiddushei Basra).*

וַהֲלֹא בֵּין הַיּוֹם וּבֵין לְמָחָר סוֹפוֹ לִתֵּן־לָהּ כְּתֻבָּתָהּ. — *Now, either today or tomorrow he may have to* [lit., *he is destined to*] *give her the kesubah.*

The question is what shall they pay? It would be unfair to obligate them to pay the entire amount of her *kesubah,* since her husband may still divorce her or predecease her and be obligated to pay her *kesubah* anyway. Consequently, the witnesses through their collusive testimony did not cause him to pay money he would not have had to pay his wife someday. They did, however, obligate him to pay earlier than he really had to, thereby withholding from him the use of that money during the intervening period *(Rav; Rashi).*

אוֹמְדִין כַּמָּה אָדָם רוֹצֶה לִתֵּן בִּכְתֻבָּתָהּ שֶׁל־זוֹ, — *We* [*therefore*] *assess how much a person would want to give for this* [*woman's*] *kesubah,*

I.e., we assess how much a person would pay the woman to buy the rights to her *kesubah (Rav).*

שֶׁאִם נִתְאַלְמְנָה אוֹ נִתְגָּרְשָׁה; — [*on the chance*] *that she becomes widowed or divorced;*

When a speculator buys the right to collect the *kesubah,* the amount he pays will be much less than the actual amount collectible with the *kesubah.* The reason for this is that he collects only if the husband divorces her or if he dies before she does. If she dies first, he will collect nothing. Thus, he is taking a significant chance of never gaining anything from his buying of the *kesubah (Rav).*

וְאִם מֵתָה, יִירָשֶׁנָּה בַּעֲלָהּ. — *and* [*that*] *if she dies, her husband will inherit her.*

[I.e., if she predeceases her husband, he will inherit all her property, the *kesubah,* the usufructuary property, and the fixed-value property.] In this case, the purchaser will lose the money he paid for the *kesubah.*

This sum which the purchaser pays for the chance of receiving her *kesubah* is the amount the witnesses are obligated to pay *(Rav; Rambam, Hil. Eidus* 21:1). As the *Gemara* (3a) explains: We assess according to the woman and her *kesubah. Rambam* (ibid.) interprets the

1 *kesubah.* We [therefore] assess how much a person
1 would want to give for this [woman's] *kesubah,* [on the chance] that she becomes widowed or divorced; and [that] if she dies, her husband will inherit her.

'We testify against so-and-so that he owes another one thousand *zuz* to be paid between now and thirty days,' and he says, 'Between now and ten years' — we assess how much a person would give so that one thousand *zuz* should be in his possession, [and] instead

YAD AVRAHAM

Gemara to mean that if the woman was sick or old [so that she was likely to die before her husband], or she lives harmoniously with her husband, the price of her *kesubah,* when she sells it, will not equal its price if the woman was well and young, or she did not get along with her husband, because in the latter cases it is more likely that the woman will eventually collect the *kesubah.* Similarly, the consideration of the large *kesubah* is not like that of the small *kesubah.* If her *kesubah* amounts to one thousand *zuz,* it may be sold for a consideration of one hundred, but if it was one hundred, it is not sold for ten but for less. All these factors must be taken into account and determined by judicial assessment.

Others dispute this explanation on the grounds that it was not her rights to the *kesubah* that they sought to confiscate, but his rights. Thus, what she could fetch for the sale of her *kesubah* on the open market is of no consequence. *Rosh,* therefore, explains that the effect of their false testimony would have been to force him to pay his *kesubah* debt now; the court assesses how much a person would be willing to pay for the right to have use of that money until the husband either dies or divorces his wife, while taking into account the possibility that if the wife dies first, the debt need never be repaid. This amount must then be paid by the witnesses to the husband *(Tos. Yom Tov).*

„מְעִידִין אָנוּ בְאִישׁ פְּלוֹנִי שֶׁהוּא חַיָּב לַחֲבֵרוֹ אֶלֶף זוּז עַל־מְנָת לִתְּנָם לוֹ מִכָּאן וְעַד שְׁלֹשִׁים יוֹם," — *'We testify against so-and-so that he owes another* [lit., *his fellowman*] *one thousand zuz to be paid between now and thirty days,'*

[I.e., they testify that on a certain day someone borrowed one thousand *zuz* from another to be repaid by the end of thirty days.]

וְהוּא אוֹמֵר: „מִכָּאן וְעַד עֶשֶׂר שָׁנִים" — *and he says, 'Between now and ten years'* —

[I.e., the borrower claims that the term of the loan was ten years.] The witnesses were subsequently found to be false through the testimony of other witnesses who testified that they were with them elsewhere on the alleged date of the loan. Since the debtor admits to the loan, however, they cannot be held liable for the complete amount of the loan, since the debtor will have to repay it someday anyway *(Rabbeinu Yehonasan).*

This question can only arise with regard to an oral loan. Had the loan been recorded in a document, it would have stated clearly when the loan must be repaid. Even if no term was stated, there would still be no room for dissent, for a loan note that has no set term is interpreted as being payable on demand. Either way the testimony of the witnesses that the term was for thirty days would have no legal bearing whatsoever. Consequently, upon being discredited, they would not have to pay anything *(Meiri).*

אוֹמְדִין כַּמָּה אָדָם רוֹצֶה לִתֵּן וְיִהְיוּ בְיָדוֹ אֶלֶף זוּז, בֵּין נוֹתְנָן מִכָּאן וְעַד שְׁלֹשִׁים יוֹם, בֵּין נוֹתְנָן מִכָּאן וְעַד עֶשֶׂר שָׁנִים. — *we assess how much a person would give so that one thousand zuz should be in his possession,*

מִכָּאן וְעַד שְׁלשִׁים יוֹם, בֵּין נוֹתְנָן מִכָּאן וְעַד עֶשֶׂר שָׁנִים.

[ב] „מְעִידִין אָנוּ בְאִישׁ פְּלוֹנִי שֶׁחַיָּב לַחֲבֵרוֹ מָאתַיִם זוּז," וְנִמְצְאוּ זוֹמְמִין, לוֹקִין וּמְשַׁלְּמִין, שֶׁלֹּא הַשֵּׁם הַמְבִיאוֹ לִידֵי מַכּוֹת מְבִיאוֹ לִידֵי תַשְׁלוּמִין; דִּבְרֵי רַבִּי מֵאִיר. וַחֲכָמִים אוֹמְרִים: כָּל־הַמְשַׁלֵּם אֵינוֹ לוֹקֶה.

יד אברהם

[*and*] *instead of* [*having to*] *repay them within thirty days, to have up to ten years to repay them.*

The apparent meaning is that we assess how much a debtor would give his creditor to extend the term of the loan from thirty days to ten years.

This presents a difficulty, however, since paying for an extension of a loan constitutes taking interest, which the Torah prohibits. Since the debtor could never actually make such a payment, the witnesses did not deprive him of that money, and it therefore makes no sense to sentence the witnesses to pay this amount. Several solutions have been offered to solve this difficulty. One is that we assess how much a creditor would deduct from the loan so that the debtor, who is obliged to repay the loan at the end of ten years, will instead pay it back at the end of thirty days. There is no prohibition against the creditor deducting from his due for early payment. Therefore, that is considered the value of keeping money for that period of time (*Ritva; Mishneh LaMelech*).

Another solution offered is that the witnesses must pay the amount the debtor would pay a third party to persuade the creditor to extend the term of the loan. Since he does not pay the creditor, it is not considered interest (*Rabbeinu Yehonasan*).

Another solution is that we assess how much a debtor would profit by keeping money in his possession for ten years rather than keeping it for only thirty days (*Radbaz*). *Ritva*, however, rejects this solution since the amount of such a hypothetical profit cannot be fixed. Furthermore, preventing one from gaining profit is not considered a damage, and the witnesses should not have to pay for this.

R' Eliezer of Tuch qualifies this mishnah as referring to a debt of hire rather than a loan. He deduces from this mishnah that paying for an extension of payment for a debt of hire is not considered interest (#97 of Responsa related to *Sefer Mishpatim* of *Rambam*). This ruling is, however, not accepted by most authorites. See *Mishneh LaMelech, Hil. Malveh* 7:11; *Responsa Radbaz* 1:84.

2.

„מְעִידִין אָנוּ בְאִישׁ פְּלוֹנִי שֶׁחַיָּב לַחֲבֵרוֹ מָאתַיִם זוּז," — *'We testify against so-and-so that he owes another two hundred zuz,'*

[Two witnesses testify that someone borrowed two hundred *zuz* from another on a specific day in a specific place.]

וְנִמְצְאוּ זוֹמְמִין, — *and they were found to be zomemim,*

[I.e., other witnesses came and testified that the first pair of witnesses were at that very time at a different location, as will be explained in mishnah 4.]

לוֹקִין וּמְשַׁלְּמִין, — *they are flogged and must pay,*

[The false witnesses are flogged for the sin of testifying falsely, and they must

of [having to] repay them within thirty days, to have up to ten years to repay them.

2. 'We testify against so-and-so that he owes another two hundred *zuz*,' and they were found to be *zomemim*, they are flogged and must pay, for it is not the Scriptural verse that makes him liable for lashes that makes him liable for monetary payment; [these are] the words of R' Meir. But the Sages say: Whoever pays is not flogged.

YAD AVRAHAM

pay for plotting to inflict a loss on their victim.]

שֶׁלֹּא הַשֵּׁם הַמְּבִיאוֹ לִידֵי מַכּוֹת מְבִיאוֹ לִידֵי תַשְׁלוּמִין; — *for it is not the Scriptural verse that makes him liable for lashes that makes him liable for monetary payment;*

The witnesses are liable for lashes for transgressing the negative commandment of לֹא תַעֲנֶה בְרֵעֲךָ עֵד שָׁקֶר, *You shall not bear false witness against your fellowman (Exodus* 20:13). In addition they are liable for monetary payment because of the Scriptural verse: וַעֲשִׂיתֶם לוֹ כַּאֲשֶׁר זָמַם לַעֲשׂוֹת לְאָחִיו, *And you shall do to him as he planned to do to his brother.* Since they planned to cause their victim to pay money, they in turn must pay *(Rav; Rashi).*

Should one Scriptural interdict give rise to two potential penalties, it appears from *Rashi* that only one penalty would apply even according to R' Meir. *Tos,* however, differ and explain R' Meir to mean that the negative commandment for which lashes are inflicted is not needed to impose the monetary penalty, because one can be liable to a monetary payment without having infracted a negative commandment. Thus, the negative commandment is construed as a warning that this infraction is punishable by lashes in addition to whatever monetary penalty is imposed by the verse.

דִּבְרֵי רַבִּי מֵאִיר. — *[these are] the words of R' Meir.*

The *Gemara* (4b) explains that R' Meir derives his view from the law of מוֹצִיא שֵׁם רַע, *one who slanders* [his wife] *(Rav).* This refers to the section of the Torah in *Deut.* 22:13-22. A man marries a *naarah* (a girl between the ages of twelve and twelve-and-a-half), assumed to be a virgin, and subsequently accuses her of having committed adultery after their *erusin* (betrothal), bringing witnesses to support his claim. If the witnesses are proven false, the husband is sentenced to lashes and fined one hundred *selas* for defaming his wife. R' Meir derives from this law that for a single act one can be liable to lashes in addition to a monetary payment.

וַחֲכָמִים אוֹמְרִים: כָּל־הַמְשַׁלֵּם אֵינוֹ לוֹקֶה. — *But the Sages say: Whoever pays is not flogged.*

The Sages rule that one cannot suffer the twin punishments of payment and flogging for the same transgression. They base this ruling on the verse said in regard to flogging *(Deut.* 25:2): כְּדֵי רִשְׁעָתוֹ, *according to his wickedness.* Since this is written in the singular, they deduce that one is never punished for more than one wickedness at a time. I.e., if someone, with a single act, commits a sin punishable by lashes and also a sin punishable by a monetary payment, he pays and is not flogged. In their view, the case of the slanderer from which R' Meir derives his ruling is a special Scriptural edict not applicable to other cases *(Gem.* 4b).

Since the Sages do not state that whoever is flogged does not pay, we understand that

[ג] „מְעִידִין אָנוּ בְאִישׁ פְּלוֹנִי שֶׁהוּא חַיָּב מַלְקוּת אַרְבָּעִים," וְנִמְצְאוּ זוֹמְמִים, לוֹקִין שְׁמוֹנִים — מִשּׁוּם: „לֹא תַעֲנֶה בְרֵעֲךָ עֵד שָׁקֶר," וּמִשּׁוּם: „וַעֲשִׂיתֶם לוֹ כַּאֲשֶׁר זָמַם"; דִּבְרֵי רַבִּי מֵאִיר. וַחֲכָמִים אוֹמְרִים: אֵין לוֹקִין אֶלָּא אַרְבָּעִים.

מְשַׁלְּשִׁין בְּמָמוֹן, וְאֵין מְשַׁלְּשִׁין בְּמַכּוֹת. כֵּיצַד?

יד אברהם

preference over monetary payments, since it is the more severe punishment *(Kesubos* 32b).

The halachah is in accordance with the Sages *(Rav; Rambam, Hil. Eidus* 18:1).

they rule that the monetary payment is given preference over the lashes *(Rav* from *Gem.* 4b). *Tos. Yom Tov* makes clear that this rule applies only to *zomemin* witnesses, as derived by the *Gemara.* In other cases, however, the penalty of lashes is given

3.

„מְעִידִין אָנוּ בְאִישׁ פְּלוֹנִי שֶׁהוּא חַיָּב מַלְקוּת אַרְבָּעִים," — *'We testify against so-and-so that he is liable to forty lashes,'*

[I.e., witnesses testify that someone transgressed a negative commandment, for which the penalty is lashes.]

וְנִמְצְאוּ זוֹמְמִים, לוֹקִין שְׁמוֹנִים — *and they were found to be zomemim, they are flogged eighty* [*lashes*] —

[If they were discovered to be liars by the method of *hazamah* delineated below in mishnah 4, they are subjected to twice the usual number of lashes, as explained below.]

מִשּׁוּם: „לֹא תַעֲנֶה בְרֵעֲךָ עֵד שָׁקֶר," — *because of (Exodus 20:13): 'You shall not bear false witness against your neighbor,'*

[Since they testified falsely, they are liable for lashes for transgressing this negative commandment.]

וּמִשּׁוּם: „וַעֲשִׂיתֶם לוֹ כַּאֲשֶׁר זָמַם"; — *and because of (Deut. 19:19): 'And you shall do to him as he planned to do';*

[Since they plotted to have their victim flogged, they are punished accordingly.]

דִּבְרֵי רַבִּי מֵאִיר. — [*these are*] *the words of R' Meir.*

R' Meir asserts that it makes no difference whether the law of *hazamah* cannot be applied (as above mishnah 1), or it can be applied, as in our mishnah. In either case the witnesses are flogged for transgressing the negative commandment against testifying falsely, in addition to being punished with the fate they intended to impose on the victim of their plot *(Rav).*

וַחֲכָמִים אוֹמְרִים: אֵין לוֹקִין אֶלָּא אַרְבָּעִים. — *But the Sages say: They are flogged only forty* [*lashes*].

In keeping with the principle of אֵין עוֹנְשִׁין אֶלָּא אִם־כֵּן מַזְהִירִין, *we do not punish unless we warn,* meaning that whenever the Torah prescribes a punishment for any act, that act must be forewarned by a negative commandment. When violating that commandment the punishment is not the general lashes prescribed for the violation of negative commandments, because the commandment is for the purpose of serving as a warning for the special punishment prescribed for this infraction. In this case, the negative commandment warning the false witnesses, *You shall not bear false witness against your fellowman,* must serve as the warning

1
3

3. 'We testify against so-and-so that he is liable to forty lashes,' and they were found to be *zomemim,* they are flogged eighty [lashes] — because of (*Exodus* 20:13): *You shall not bear false witness against your neighbor,* and because of (*Deut. 19:19*): *And you shall do to him as he planned to do;* [these are] the words of R' Meir. But the Sages say: They are flogged only forty [lashes].

They divide [payments of] money, but they do not divide lashes. How so? [If] they testified against him

YAD AVRAHAM

for the penalty of doing to them as they planned to do to their victim.

It is only when the normal *hazamah* penalty cannot be imposed (as in mishnah 1) that they receive lashes for their transgression. This is based on a separate derivation (*Gem.* 2b). There is, therefore, no additional penalty of lashes for this transgression (*Gem.* 4b).

R' Meir, however, considers the verse (*Deut.* 19:20): וְלֹא־יֹסִפוּ לַעֲשׂוֹת עוֹד, *and they shall no longer continue,* as the warning against false witnesses. Hence, the witnesses do receive lashes for violating the commandment, *You shall not bear false witness* (*Gem.* 5a).

The halachah is in accordance with the Sages (*Rav; Rambam, Hil. Eidus* 18:1).

מְשַׁלְּשִׁין בְּמָמוֹן, — *They divide* [*payments of*] *money,*

False witnesses who are liable to make monetary payments divide the payments according to the number of witnesses. I.e., if there were three witnesses, each one pays one third of the penalty (*Rav; Rashi* 3a). [The word מְשַׁלְּשִׁין derives from שְׁלֹשָׁה, *three,* meaning that each witness pays one third.] Should there be four, they divide the amount into four parts (*Rashi*).

Tos. Yom Tov suggests that the *Tanna* chose a case of three witnesses instead of two because in mishnah 7 it states that three witnesses have the same laws as two; e.g., that the third one is punished equally with the first two, although the verdict could have been delivered without him. Therefore, in order to give an example of this, when the mishnah discusses the division of the monetary payment it is illustrated to show that all three witnesses are equal.

Rashi (3a) also suggests that the word מְשַׁלְּשִׁין does not refer to a case of three witnesses but rather is derived from שָׁלִישׁ, *a third party.* In this case, the *beis din* becomes the third party between the witnesses to divide the fine equally.

וְאֵין מְשַׁלְּשִׁין בְּמַכּוֹת. — *but they do not divide lashes.*

I.e., the witnesses do not share the number of lashes they plotted to inflict on the defendant. Rather, each one is subjected to the full number of lashes. It is only in the previous case involving money that they divide the punishment. Since their money is combined and given to the defendant, he receives the full amount they sought to victimize him. Consequently, it is considered that the witnesses have suffered the penalty they sought to impose. In the case of lashes, however, since the victim receives nothing there is no way of combining their separate lashes. Thus, dividing the lashes would result in each witness receiving thirteen lashes, with no punishment of thirty-nine lashes being meted out to anyone. Therefore, each witness must suffer the complete number of lashes (*Rav; Tos. Yom Tov; Rashi* in explanation of *Gem.* 5a).

הֶעִידוּהוּ שֶׁהוּא חַיָּב לַחֲבֵרוֹ מָאתַיִם זוּז, וְנִמְצְאוּ זוֹמְמִין, מְשַׁלְּשִׁין בֵּינֵיהֶם. אֲבָל אִם הֶעִידוּהוּ שֶׁהוּא חַיָּב מַלְקוּת אַרְבָּעִים, וְנִמְצְאוּ זוֹמְמִין, כָּל־אֶחָד וְאֶחָד לוֹקֶה אַרְבָּעִים.

[ד] **אֵין** הָעֵדִים נַעֲשִׂים זוֹמְמִין עַד־שֶׁיָּזֹמּוּ אֶת־עַצְמָן. כֵּיצַד? אָמְרוּ: „מְעִידִין אָנוּ בְּאִישׁ פְּלוֹנִי שֶׁהָרַג אֶת־הַנֶּפֶשׁ"; אָמְרוּ לָהֶם: „הֵיאָךְ אַתֶּם מְעִידִין, שֶׁהֲרֵי נֶהֱרַג זֶה," אוֹ „הַהוֹרֵג," הָיָה עִמָּנוּ אוֹתוֹ הַיּוֹם בְּמָקוֹם פְּלוֹנִי" — אֵין אֵלּוּ זוֹמְמִין. אֲבָל אָמְרוּ לָהֶם: „הֵיאָךְ אַתֶּם מְעִידִין, שֶׁהֲרֵי אַתֶּם

יד אברהם

כֵּיצַד? הֶעִידוּהוּ שֶׁהוּא חַיָּב לַחֲבֵרוֹ מָאתַיִם זוּז, וְנִמְצְאוּ זוֹמְמִין, מְשַׁלְּשִׁין בֵּינֵיהֶם. — *How so? [If] they testified against him that he owed another two hundred zuz, and they were found to be zomemim, they divide [it] among themselves.*

[I.e., if there were two witnesses, each one must pay one hundred *zuz;* if there were four, each one pays fifty *zuz,* etc., as long as the shares total the full amount.]

אֲבָל אִם הֶעִידוּהוּ שֶׁהוּא חַיָּב מַלְקוּת אַרְבָּעִים, וְנִמְצְאוּ זוֹמְמִין, כָּל־אֶחָד וְאֶחָד לוֹקֶה אַרְבָּעִים. — *But if they testified against him that he was liable to forty lashes, and they were found to be zomemim, each one is flogged forty [lashes].*

[As explained above.]

Later commentators give other reasons why the money can be combined with that given by the other witnesses, while the lashes given each one cannot be combined with the lashes given the others.

Beis Halevi suggests that when one receives thirty-nine lashes, each lash is more painful than the one that preceded it since the body becomes more and more sore with each successive lash. Therefore, the combination of three times thirteen lashes does not equal the suffering the witnesses plotted to inflict on the defendant, since those thirty-nine lashes would have been much more painful than the three sets of thirteen of the three witnesses. Money, however, can be combined, since the whole is equal to the sum of its parts *(Beis Halevi on Chumash,* end of *Beshallach).*

4.

The following mishnah delineates the fundamental rule of *hazamah,* defining when the witnesses are proven completely false — *zomemim* — and thus subject to punishment, and when they are considered merely contradicted by other witnesses but not definitely false.

אֵין הָעֵדִים נַעֲשִׂים זוֹמְמִין עַד־שֶׁיָּזֹמּוּ אֶת־עַצְמָן. — *The witnesses do not become zomemim unless they discredit them personally.*

I.e., they are regarded as definitely false only when the second group of witnesses testifies against them personally. The *hazamah* testimony of the second group need not concern itself whether or not the alleged deed actually took place, as the mishnah proceeds to explain. This is derived from the verse dealing with the law of *hazamah (Deut.* 19:18): וְהִנֵּה עֵד־שֶׁקֶר הָעֵד, *and behold, the witness is false (Rav* from *Gem.* 5a). Since the Torah does not state: עֵדוּת שֶׁקֶר

1 that he owed another two hundred *zuz,* and they were
4 found to be *zomemim,* they divide [it] among themselves. But if they testified against him that he was liable to forty lashes, and they were found to be *zomemim,* each one is flogged forty [lashes].

4. The witnesses do not become *zomemim* unless they discredit them personally. How so? [If] they said, 'We testify against so-and-so that he killed someone'; [and others] said to them, 'How can you testify [so], when this murder victim,' or 'this murderer,' 'was with us on that day in such-and-such a place' — these are not [considered] *zomemim.* But [if] they said to them, 'How can you testify [so], when you were with us on that day

YAD AVRAHAM

הָעֵדוּת, *the testimony is false,* we understand that the refutation deals with the witnesses themselves *(Rambam Comm.).*

כֵּיצַד? — *How so?*

[I.e., in which case are they regarded as *zomemim?*]

אָמְרוּ: „מְעִידִין אָנוּ בְאִישׁ פְּלוֹנִי שֶׁהָרַג אֶת־הַנֶּפֶשׁ״; — *[If] they said, 'We testify against so-and-so that he killed someone';*

[I.e., they testify that Reuven killed Shimon on a certain day in a certain place.]

אָמְרוּ לָהֶם: — *[and others] said to them,*

[I.e., other witnesses said to them.]

„הֵיאַךְ אַתֶּם מְעִידִין, — *'How can you testify* [*so*],

[How can you testify that Reuven murdered Shimon on that day in that place?]

שֶׁהֲרֵי נֶהֱרַג זֶה,״ — *when this murder victim,'*

[I.e., this Shimon about whom you testify was murdered.]

או „הַהוֹרֵג,״ — *or 'this murderer,'*

[Or they say that Reuven, the alleged murderer . . .]

„הָיָה עִמָּנוּ אוֹתוֹ הַיּוֹם בְּמָקוֹם פְּלוֹנִי״ — *'was with us on that day in such-and-such a place'* —

[In both these cases the second witnesses testify that the murder could not have happened as described by the first witnesses since either the villain or victim were seen by them elsewhere at the time the murder was supposed to have taken place.]

אֵין אֵלּוּ זוֹמְמִין. — *these are not* [*considered*] *zomemim.*

Although the second set of witnesses contradict the first, the first witnesses do not become *zomemim.* This is known as עֵדוּת מֻכְחֶשֶׁת, *contradicted testimony,* in which case the law is that *beis din* rejects both groups of witnesses completely *(Rambam Comm.),* for we do not know which is the false group and which is the truthful one *(Rambam, Hil. Eidus* 18:2).

אֲבָל אָמְרוּ לָהֶם: — *But* [*if*] *they said to them,*

[I.e., if the second group of witnesses said to the first.]

„הֵיאַךְ אַתֶּם מְעִידִין, — *'How can you testify* [*so*],

[I.e., how can you testify that Reuven committed a murder at that time.]

שֶׁהֲרֵי אַתֶּם הֱיִיתֶם עִמָּנוּ אוֹתוֹ הַיּוֹם בְּמָקוֹם פְּלוֹנִי,״ — *when you were with us on that day in such-and-such a place,'*

הֱיִיתֶם עִמָּנוּ אוֹתוֹ הַיּוֹם בְּמָקוֹם פְּלוֹנִי,״ הֲרֵי אֵלּוּ זוֹמְמִין, וְנֶהֱרָגִין עַל־פִּיהֶם.

[ה] **בָּאוּ** אֲחֵרִים וְהִזִּימוּם, בָּאוּ אֲחֵרִים וְהִזִּימוּם, אֲפִלּוּ מֵאָה, כֻּלָּם יֵהָרְגוּ. רַבִּי יְהוּדָה אוֹמֵר: אִסְטָסִית הִיא זוֹ, וְאֵינָהּ נֶהֱרֶגֶת אֶלָּא כַּת הָרִאשׁוֹנָה בִּלְבָד.

יד אברהם

I.e., you were with us in location B at the very time you claimed Reuven murdered Shimon in location A *(Tos. Yom Tov)*.

הֲרֵי אֵלּוּ זוֹמְמִין, — *these are* [*considered*] *zomemim,*

[The first witnesses are deemed refuted. Since the latter witnesses testify concerning the first pair themselves, not concerning the testimony, the Torah rules that we believe the second pair completely and the first not at all, as explained above.]

The mishnah in *Sanhedrin* (5:1) says that witnesses must state the exact hour the event took place. Their testimony is considered collusive only if location B is at least one hour's journey from location A. In the case they identified the day but not the hour, point B must be at least one day's journey from point A, otherwise their testimony is not considered refuted since it is possible that the witnesses were in both places on the same day *(Gem. 5a)*.

וְנֶהֱרָגִין עַל־פִּיהֶם. — *and they are executed by their testimony.*

It is the Torah's decree that we inflict upon the discredited witnesses that which they plotted to inflict upon their victim, even the death penalty.

However, no such penalty is decreed by the Torah for witnesses whose falsity is discovered by any method other than witnesses. Thus, even if the alleged murder victim appears in the flesh, the witnesses are punished only with מַכַּת מַרְדּוּת, *disciplinary lashes*, a Rabbinically instituted punishment, but not by the imposition of the penalty they sought to inflict *(Rambam, Hil. Eidus* 18:6).

5.

The following mishnah is a continuation of the preceding one.

בָּאוּ אֲחֵרִים — [*If*] *others came*

If, after the first witnesses were discredited, other witnesses came forth and gave the same testimony as the original pair, namely, that they saw Reuven kill Shimon *(Rashi)*.

וְהִזִּימוּם, — *and they discredited them,*

I.e., the same witnesses who had refuted the first group, refuted also this second group by saying that they were also with them in a different location on that day *(Rashi)*.

בָּאוּ אֲחֵרִים וְהִזִּימוּם, — [*and still*] *others came, and they discredited them* [*too*],

[I.e., a third pair came and testified the same as the first, that Reuven killed Shimon, and the same pair refuted them as well.]

אֲפִלּוּ מֵאָה, — *even one hundred,*

Even if one hundred groups of witnesses came one after the other and testified as the first witnesses had testified, and the same group discredited all of them by testifying about each of the

1 in such-and-such a place,' these are [considered]
5 *zomemim*, and they are executed by their testimony.

5. [If] others came and they discredited them, [and still] others came, and they discredited them [too], even one hundred, all of them are executed. R' Yehudah says: This is a group of plotters, and only the first group is executed.

YAD AVRAHAM

one hundred groups that they could not have witnessed this happening because they were with us elsewhere on that day *(Rav).*

כֻּלָּם יֵהָרְגוּ. — *all of them are executed.*

All one hundred groups of witnesses testifying about the murder are considered *zomemim* on the basis of the testimony of the single group of discrediting witnesses, and in consequence, all one hundred are put to death for their false testimony *(Rambam Comm.).*

רַבִּי יְהוּדָה אוֹמֵר: אִסְטָסִית הִיא זוֹ, — *R' Yehudah says: This is a group of plotters,*

R' Yehudah maintains that the testimony of this pair is suspect. It looks as if they decided to discredit all those who come to testify against the accused, and we do not believe them *(Rav; Rashi).*

Another explanation has a reading of אִסְטָסִים, *a [kettle of] dye*, meaning: Are these witnesses a kettle of dye, which stains everything that touches it? *(Rav* from *Rambam Comm.; Rif).* According to this reading, the word derives from אִסְטִיס, *isatis*, a source of blue dye (see comm. to *Sheviis* 7:1).

וְאֵינָהּ נֶהֱרֶגֶת אֶלָּא כַּת הָרִאשׁוֹנָה בִּלְבָד. — *and only the first group is executed.*

R' Yehudah holds that once the testimony of the first group has been proven false, we do not accept any further testimony against the accused in regard to this matter. Therefore, even if it happened that *beis din* did accept the testimony of another pair of witnesses, and they too were discredited, they are not punished by death, since *beis din* would not have executed the accused on their testimony *(Rav, Rambam Comm.).*

According to this, R' Yehudah does not exempt the later groups of witnesses from the death penalty because the discrediting group is suspect, but because their testimony was never of any consequence in the first place (since the accused could not have been convicted by their testimony in any case). It is therefore a bit difficult to understand why R' Yehudah mentions that they are plotters, since that has no bearing on their being exempt from punishment. To resolve this, *Tos. Yom Tov* explains that R' Yehudah is personally of the opinion that the witnesses are not killed because their testimony is of no value. However, he mentions the fact that they are plotters in response to the Sages, arguing that even according to the Sages, who accept the testimony of all subsequent witnesses, they should still not be killed because they are being discredited by plotters.

The halachah is in accordance with the Sages *(Rav, Rambam, Hil. Eidus* 18:3, 20:6).

6.

The following mishnah explains that if the witnesses were discredited either before the verdict was rendered or after the punishment was already meted out to the accused perpetrators, they are not punished. They are only considered *zomemin* if they were refuted after the verdict was handed down but before it was carried out.

[ו] **אֵין** הָעֵדִים זוֹמְמִין נֶהֱרָגִין עַד־שֶׁיִּגָּמֵר הַדִּין. שֶׁהֲרֵי הַצְּדוּקִין אוֹמְרִים: עַד־שֶׁיֵּהָרֵג, שֶׁנֶּאֱמַר: ,,נֶפֶשׁ תַּחַת נָפֶשׁ.״ אָמְרוּ לָהֶם חֲכָמִים: וַהֲלֹא כְבָר נֶאֱמַר: ,,וַעֲשִׂיתֶם לוֹ כַּאֲשֶׁר זָמַם לַעֲשׂוֹת לְאָחִיו״ — וַהֲרֵי אָחִיו קַיָּם וְאִם־כֵּן, לָמָּה נֶאֱמַר: ,,נֶפֶשׁ תַּחַת נָפֶשׁ?״ יָכוֹל מִשָּׁעָה שֶׁקִּבְּלוּ עֵדוּתָן, יֵהָרְגוּ; תַּלְמוּד לוֹמַר: ,,נֶפֶשׁ תַּחַת נָפֶשׁ״ — הָא אֵינָן נֶהֱרָגִין עַד־שֶׁיִּגָּמֵר הַדִּין.

יד אברהם

אֵין הָעֵדִים זוֹמְמִין נֶהֱרָגִין — *Zomemim witnesses are not executed*

[I.e., witnesses who testified that someone committed an act punishable by capital punishment and who were later discredited by the process of *hazamah.*]

עַד־שֶׁיִּגָּמֵר הַדִּין. — *unless the verdict had been delivered.*

They are not liable to the penalty for *hazamah* unless the accused had already been convicted by their testimony before they were discredited *(Rav; Rashi).*

שֶׁהֲרֵי הַצְּדוּקִין אוֹמְרִים: עַד־שֶׁיֵּהָרֵג, — *For the Sadducees say: Unless he has been executed,*

[The Sadducees, a heretical sect in Mishnaic times who accepted only the Written Law as they understood it but denied the Oral Law, ruled that *zomemim* witnesses are executed only if the accused was already put to death prior to their being discredited.]

שֶׁנֶּאֱמַר: ,,נֶפֶשׁ תַּחַת נָפֶשׁ.״ — *as it is said: 'A life for a life.'*

[I.e., if a life has been taken, they are punished by having their life taken away from them; otherwise not.]

In the standard editions, נֶפֶשׁ תַּחַת נָפֶשׁ is the verse quoted. This is an error, however, since that verse is found in *Exodus* 24:18, in the section dealing with the injuries inflicted on a pregnant woman, and it has no connection with our topic. The correct reading would seem to be נֶפֶשׁ בְּנֶפֶשׁ, which is the verse found in the section dealing with *zomemim* witnesses *(Tos. Yom Tov; Rashi; Hagahos HaGra; Sifre).*

אָמְרוּ לָהֶם חֲכָמִים: — *The Sages said to them:*

[I.e., the Sages said to the Sadducees.]

וַהֲלֹא כְבָר נֶאֱמַר: ,,וַעֲשִׂיתֶם לוֹ כַּאֲשֶׁר זָמַם לַעֲשׂוֹת לְאָחִיו״ — וַהֲרֵי אָחִיו קַיָּם! — *Has it not already stated (Deut. 19:21): 'And you shall do to him as he planned to do his brother' — indicating that his brother is still alive!*

Since the Torah refers to the accused as *his brother* even at the time the witnesses are to be punished, it would appear that he is still alive at that time *(Tos. Yom Tov* from *Rashi; Tif. Yis.).*

Ritva, citing *Lev.* 9:4 and *Deut.* 25:7, maintains that a dead brother is also still called a brother. He concludes, therefore, that the proof is from the expression כַּאֲשֶׁר זָמַם, *as he planned to do,* indicating that his plan did not come to fruition as yet *(Tos. R' Akiva).*

The difficulty raised by *Ritva* — that brothers are referred to as brothers even after their death — can be resolved by drawing a distinction between blood brothers and people referred to as brothers because they share a common obligation to keep *mitzvos.* In the former they do indeed remain brothers forever. However in the latter they can only be considered brothers as long as they share this common obligation. After the death of one person, when he is no longer required to perform *mitzvos,* they can no longer be considered brothers. Therefore, since the brothers referred to in our case are spiritual

6. *Zomemim* witnesses are not executed unless the verdict had been delivered. For the Sadducees say: Unless he had been executed, as it is said: *A life for a life.* The Sages said to them: Has it not already stated *(Deut.* 19:21): *And you shall do to him as he planned to do his brother* — indicating that his brother is still alive! If so, why does it say, *A life for a life?* Because it might be thought that from the time their testimony is accepted, they may be executed; [the Torah] therefore states: *A life for a life* — [to teach] that they are not executed unless a verdict has been issued.

YAD AVRAHAM

ones, they could not be called brothers if one of them had been executed, thus proving the contention of the Sages that the penalty meted out to *zomemim* witnesses is only before the verdict was carried out *(R' Eliyahu Guttmacher; Rashash* to *Sanhedrin* 10a).

וְאִם־כֵּן, לָמָּה נֶאֱמַר: „נֶפֶשׁ תַּחַת נֶפֶשׁ״? — *If so, why does it say, 'A life for a life'?*

[I.e., since the witnesses are liable for merely plotting, why does the Torah frame their punishment in terms of *a life for a life?*]

יָכוֹל מִשָּׁעָה שֶׁקִּבְּלוּ עֵדוּתָן, יֵהָרְגוּ; — *Because it might be thought that from the time their testimony is accepted, they may be executed;*

[I.e., on the basis of the expression, כַּאֲשֶׁר זָמַם לַעֲשׂוֹת, *as he planned to do,* it might be mistakenly concluded that false witnesses are executed if they were discredited immediately upon the acceptance of their testimony, even before the accused was convicted.]

תַּלְמוּד לוֹמַר: „נֶפֶשׁ תַּחַת נֶפֶשׁ״ — הָא אֵינָן נֶהֱרָגִין עַד־שֶׁיִּגָּמֵר הַדִּין. — *[the Torah] therefore states: 'A life for a life' — [to teach] that they are not executed unless a verdict has been issued.*

By adding the phrase, *a life for a life,* the Torah makes clear that although the accused has not yet been executed [by their testimony], his life has at least been made forfeit by it — i.e., he has been convicted. Since once a death penalty has been handed down the convict is considered legally dead in regard to many laws — e.g., if someone kills him he is exempt — their false testimony may in a sense be construed as having taken a life *(Tos. Yom Tov).*

Although the mishnah deals solely with capital cases, the *Gemara* explains that the same is true as regards witnesses testifying that one is liable to lashes or exile. In these cases too the witnesses are not punished unless the accused was first convicted and they were then discredited. If they were discredited before the verdict was delivered, they are not liable.

The *Gemara* states further that in the event the sentence had already been carried out prior to the discrediting of the witnesses, the witnesses are not punished. Although logic would dictate that they should certainly be punished in this case — since if they are punished for merely planning, they should surely be punished for having succeeded in executing their plans — the *Gemara* teaches us that we cannot sentence anyone to a punishment by dint of such a *kal vachomer* conclusion. Therefore, since the Torah does not explicitly decree the death penalty for such an event, we cannot impose it logically.

Although this appears contrary to common sense, it has been rationalized by various commentators. *Ramban,* in his commentary on the Torah, explains

[ז] „עַל־פִּי שְׁנַיִם עֵדִים אוֹ שְׁלֹשָׁה עֵדִים יוּמַת הַמֵּת.״ אִם מִתְקַיֶּמֶת הָעֵדוּת בִּשְׁנַיִם, לָמָּה פָּרַט הַכָּתוּב בִּשְׁלֹשָׁה? אֶלָּא לְהַקִּישׁ שְׁלֹשָׁה לִשְׁנַיִם: מַה־שְּׁלֹשָׁה מַזִּימִין אֶת־הַשְּׁנַיִם, אַף הַשְּׁנַיִם יָזֹמּוּ אֶת־הַשְּׁלֹשָׁה. וּמִנַּיִן אֲפִילוּ מֵאָה? תַּלְמוּד לוֹמַר: „עֵדִים.״ רַבִּי שִׁמְעוֹן אוֹמֵר: מַה־שְּׁנַיִם אֵינָן נֶהֱרָגִין עַד־שֶׁיִּהוּ שְׁנֵיהֶם זוֹמְמִין, אַף שְׁלֹשָׁה

יד אברהם

that God guides the judges in their judgment and does not allow them to err. A person who has been put to death through the testimony of false witnesses was doubtless guilty of other sins for which he deserved to die. Therefore, although their testimony was false, the Torah does not have them punished for having caused the death of their victims since they probably were not innocent.

Another reason given is that since they plotted to have their victim executed in cold blood, not as a murderer who kills another in the heat of a quarrel, they do not deserve to have their sin expiated by suffering the death penalty at the hands of *beis din*. Rather, they are doomed to suffer for it in the Hereafter, a more severe penalty *(Meiri* from *Geonim; Kesef Mishneh, Hil. Eidus* 20:2).

Still another rationale offered is that the Torah wished to avoid the disgrace that would come to *beis din* for executing an innocent person. Therefore, no capital punishment was prescribed for the *zomemim* in this case *(Meiri; Abarbanel* on Torah, quoting *Rav Chisdai).*

In the case of lashes, *Rambam (Hil. Eidus* 20:2) rules that the witnesses are punished even if the accused was already flogged. *Radbaz* deduces that *Rambam* must have interpreted the mishnah literally, i.e., that the accused, being called a brother, must be living. Since, in the case of lashes, he is living even after he has been flogged, there is no objection to his already having been dealt his punishment.

This ruling would be consistent with the rationales offered above. The notion that God would not allow the *beis din* to execute an innocent man, and he must therefore have been guilty of another crime, can be readily understood to apply to execution, not lashes. Similarly, the idea that death is not enough to expiate for the grave sin of causing a man to be executed unlawfully applies only to the death penalty. In the case of lashes, however, their sin can surely be expiated through lashes *(Kesef Mishneh).*

Ravad, however, differs with *Rambam*, and rules that lashes follow the same rule as capital cases. Just as in the latter the witnesses are exempt if the accused was already executed, so too with lashes the witnesses are exempt if the accused has already been dealt his lashes. [He apparently explains the mishnah as *Ritva* does, that the witnesses are punished only if they have done nothing more than plot, not if they succeeded. This applies to lashes as well as capital punishment.]

In the case of monetary payments, many authorities rule that the witnesses are punished even if the accused has already paid. *Rambam* (ad loc.), consistent with his view in regard to lashes, applies the same ruling to monetary payments as well. *Tos. (Bava Kamma* 4b), however, give two reasons for differentiating between monetary matters and all other types of punishments: (1) Since money can always be returned, its payment, in a sense, is never regarded as having been done; (2) we may punish by *kal vachomer* in monetary matters.

1 7. By *the testimony of two witnesses or three wit-*
7 *nesses shall the one who is to die be put to death*
(Deut. 17:6). Now if the testimony may be established by two, why did Scripture specify *by three?* It is to compare three to two: Just as three can discredit two, so two can discredit three. How do we know that [this is true] even [for] one hundred? To teach [this] it states: *witnesses.* R' Shimon says: Just as two are not executed unless both are proved *zomemim,* so three are not

YAD AVRAHAM

Therefore, even if the deed is regarded as done, we can punish the witnesses on the basis of logical conclusion: If the Torah punishes for planning a misdeed, it surely punishes where the deed was actually accomplished.

7.

„עַל־פִּי שְׁנַיִם עֵדִים אוֹ שְׁלֹשָׁה עֵדִים יוּמַת הַמֵּת." — *'By the testimony of two witnesses or three witnesses shall the one who is to die be put to death' (Deut. 17:6).*

[This verse teaches how many witnesses are required when establishing a fact in *beis din.* The question arises . . .]

אִם־מִתְקַיֶּמֶת הָעֵדוּת בִּשְׁנַיִם, לָמָּה פָּרַט הַכָּתוּב בִּשְׁלֹשָׁה? — *Now if the testimony may be established by two, why did Scripture specify 'by three'?*

[What is the necessity of mentioning three witnesses?]

אֶלָּא לְהַקִּישׁ שְׁלֹשָׁה לִשְׁנַיִם: — *It is to compare three to two:*

[To teach that the law governing the testimony of three witnesses is identical to the law governing two.]

In view of the way this statement is subsequently explained in the mishnah it would appear more accurate to read: לְהַקִּישׁ שְׁנַיִם לִשְׁלֹשָׁה, *to compare two to three,* since we are making two witnesses as effective as three *(Tos. Yom Tov).* This is indeed *Rosh's* reading *(Rishon LeTzion).*

מַה־שְּׁלֹשָׁה מְזִימִין אֶת־הַשְּׁנַיִם, — *Just as three can discredit two,*

I.e., there is nothing surprising in the fact that three can discredit two since they outnumber them *(Tos. Yom Tov* from *Nimmukei Yosef).*

אַף הַשְּׁנַיִם יָזֹמּוּ אֶת־הַשְּׁלֹשָׁה. — *so two can discredit three.*

[A group consisting of two witnesses can similarly discredit by *hazamah* a group consisting of three witnesses.]

וּמִנַּיִן אֲפִילוּ מֵאָה? — *How do we know that [this is true] even [for] one hundred?*

I.e., how do we know that two can refute even one hundred witnesses testifying to the contrary? *(Rav; Tif. Yis.).*

תַּלְמוּד לוֹמַר: „עֵדִים." — *To teach* [*this*] *it states: 'witnesses.'*

In the verse: *By the testimony of two witnesses or three witnesses,* the repetition of the word *witnesses* is seemingly superfluous. It is added to teach that any number of witnesses beyond the minimum — whether three or more — are treated the same as two witnesses.

רַבִּי שִׁמְעוֹן אוֹמֵר: מַה־שְּׁנַיִם אֵינָן נֶהֱרָגִין עַד־שֶׁיְּהוּ שְׁנֵיהֶם זוֹמְמִין, — *R' Shimon says: Just as two are not executed unless both are proved zomemim,*

[I.e., if only one witness was discredited by *hazamah* (by having been observed elsewhere), but not the other, he is not punished. Only if both have been proved *zomemim* can either be punished.] This is derived from the fact that when prescribing the punishment for *zomemim* witnesses the Torah states:

אֵינָן נֶהֱרָגִין עַד־שֶׁיִּהְיוּ שְׁלָשְׁתָּן זוֹמְמִין. וּמִנַּיִן אֲפִילוּ מֵאָה? תַּלְמוּד לוֹמַר: „עֵדִים."

רַבִּי עֲקִיבָא אוֹמֵר: לֹא בָא הַשְּׁלִישִׁי אֶלָּא לְהַחְמִיר עָלָיו וְלַעֲשׂוֹת דִּינוֹ כַּיּוֹצֵא בָאֵלּוּ. וְאִם־כֵּן עָנַשׁ הַכָּתוּב לַנִּטְפָּל לְעוֹבְרֵי עֲבֵרָה כְּעוֹבְרֵי עֲבֵרָה, עַל־אַחַת כַּמָּה וְכַמָּה יְשַׁלֵּם שָׂכָר לַנִּטְפָּל לְעוֹשֵׂי מִצְוָה כְּעוֹשֵׂי מִצְוָה!

יד אברהם

וְהִנֵּה עֵד־שֶׁקֶר הָעֵד, *And behold the witness was false.* The *Gemara* explains that as a general rule, whenever the Torah uses the expression *witness* in the singular, it nevertheless refers to two witnesses [a set of witnesses] unless the verse states explicitly otherwise. Therefore, in our verse when it states *behold the witness was false* the meaning is both witnesses were proved false *(Rav; Rashi* from *Sotah* 2b).

אַף שְׁלֹשָׁה אֵינָן נֶהֱרָגִין עַד שֶׁיִּהְיוּ שְׁלָשְׁתָּן זוֹמְמִין. — *so three are not executed unless the three of them are proved zomemim.*

In a case in which three witnesses testified against the defendant, if only two of the three witnesses were proven *zomemim* they are not executed. Even though the testimony of these two witnesses would have been sufficient to convict the accused, and the testimony of the third was therefore unnecessary, nevertheless we learn from this verse that none of the witnesses can be punished until all are proven *zomemim (Rashi).*

They are considered one group only if each witness testified immediately following the preceding one, i.e. within the time it takes to say שָׁלוֹם עָלֶיךָ רַבִּי, *Peace upon you, my master.* Any witness testifying after a longer interval has elapsed is not considered a part of the group and he need not be found a *zomem* for the others to be executed *(Rav).* Should the initial two witnesses be separated by such an interval, however, they would still be considered one group *(Tos. Yom Tov* from *Rashi). Tos.* and *Rambam* differ, as will be discussed in mishnah 8 *(Tos. Yom Tov).*

According to R' Shimon, we indeed compare three witnesses to two. As we will discuss further, the *Tanna Kamma* subscribes to R' Shimon's derivation. It may be, therefore, that to accommodate this ruling too in his own, he chose to formulate the earlier one in terms of comparing three to two, although the first comparison was actually of two to three. We thereby solve the difficulty raised by *Tos. Yom Tov* [see above, s.v. אלא להקיש שלשה לשנים] *(Shoshannim LeDavid).*

וּמִנַּיִן אֲפִילוּ מֵאָה? — *How do we know that [this is true] even [for] one hundred?*

[I.e., how do we know that even if one hundred witnesses testify against the defendant, that none of them may be executed unless the entire group of one hundred witnesses is proved *zomemim?*]

תַּלְמוּד לוֹמַר: „עֵדִים." — *To teach [this] it states: 'witnesses.'*

[The word עֵדִים, being superfluous [see above], teaches us that no matter how many witnesses testify, as long as they are one group, they are not executed until all are proved *zomemim.*]

רַבִּי עֲקִיבָא אוֹמֵר: לֹא בָא הַשְּׁלִישִׁי אֶלָּא לְהַחְמִיר עָלָיו — *R' Akiva says: The third witness is mentioned only for the purpose of dealing stringently with him*

I.e., the Torah did not mention the third witness for the reasons stated above. It is obvious that two can discredit three; since the word of two people is acceptable for any kind of testimony, there is no reason why they should not be able to discredit a larger group. Similarly, it is obvious that three are not executed until all three are proved

1
7

executed unless the three of them are proved *zomemim*. How do we know that [this is true] even [for] one hundred? To teach [this] it states: *witnesses.*

R' Akiva says: The third witness is mentioned only for the purpose of dealing stringently with him and to make his sentence the same as these. Now if Scripture punished one who joined transgressors like the transgressors [themselves], how much more will it reward the one who joins those who perform a *mitzvah* the same as those who perform the *mitzvah!*

YAD AVRAHAM

zomemim, since they compose one group *(Tos. Yom Tov* from *Rashi).*

Thus, the reason the Torah mentioned the third witness must be to teach us that he is dealt with and punished as severely as the first two. Although the accused would have been sentenced on the basis of the first two witnesses' testimony even without his testimony, since he added his testimony to theirs, we do not exempt him from punishment *(Rav; Rashi).*

[In the mishnah printed with the *Gemara*, the word לְהָקֵל, *to deal leniently*, is added to the text: *The third one was not mentioned for the purpose of dealing leniently with him but for the purpose of ...* This refers to R' Shimon's ruling that the Torah mentions the third witness to teach us that the *zomemim* witnesses are not executed until all three are proven false.]

וְלַעֲשׂוֹת דִּינוֹ כַּיּוֹצֵא בָאֵלּוּ. — *and to make his sentence the same as these.*

I.e., to punish him just as we punish the first two witnesses, whose testimony was essential in convicting the defendant, as explained above *(Rav; Tif. Yis.).*

וְאִם־כֵּן עָנַשׁ הַכָּתוּב לַנִּטְפָּל לְעוֹבְרֵי עֲבֵרָה כְּעוֹבְרֵי עֲבֵרָה, — *Now if Scripture punished one who joined transgressors like the transgressors* [*themselves*],

[We see that the testimony of the third witness was inconsequential in the sentencing of the defendant; yet, since he joined the transgressors — the first two witnesses — he shares their fate.]

עַל־אַחַת כַּמָּה וְכַמָּה יְשַׁלֵּם שָׂכָר לַנִּטְפָּל לְעוֹשֵׂי מִצְוָה כְּעוֹשֵׂי מִצְוָה! — *how much more will it reward the one who joins those who perform a mitzvah the same as those who perform the mitzvah!*

We find that the reward for those who perform *mitzvos* is much more extensive than the retribution meted out to the sinners. An example of this principle can be learned from *Exodus* 20:5, 34:7. There it states that *Hashem* bestows the reward of the fathers on thousands of generations, whereas retribution is visited upon four generations. If we understand 'thousands' in its minimum sense to mean two thousand, we find that *Hashem's* beneficence is 500 times as great as his retribution. Therefore, one who joins those performing *mitzvos* can surely look forward to a great reward *(Rashi* ad loc.; *Riva* 23a).

It is not clear whether the three *Tannaim* mentioned in the mishnah agree with each other, with each *Tanna* stressing a different point, or whether each *Tanna* argues with the other two. *Rambam (Comm.)* understands all three to agree on all points, each one accepting the ruling of his colleagues. *Nimmukei Yosef*, however, quotes *Riva* who says that R' Akiva differs with R' Shimon and holds that the third witness is mentioned to teach us to deal stringently with him and punish him along with the first two; the first two, however, are punished even if the third one is not discredited. He quotes *Ri ibn Gias* who goes further and explains that according to R' Akiva, even if the third witness was not personally discredited, he is punished along

[ח] **מַה־שְּׁנַיִם,** נִמְצָא אֶחָד מֵהֶן קָרוֹב אוֹ־פָסוּל, עֵדוּתָן בְּטֵלָה, אַף שְׁלֹשָׁה, נִמְצָא אֶחָד מֵהֶן קָרוֹב אוֹ־פָסוּל, עֵדוּתָן בְּטֵלָה. מִנַּיִן אֲפִילוּ מֵאָה? תַּלְמוּד לוֹמַר: „עֵדִים."

אָמַר רַבִּי יוֹסֵי: בַּמֶּה דְבָרִים אֲמוּרִים? בְּדִינֵי נְפָשׁוֹת; אֲבָל בְּדִינֵי מָמוֹנוֹת, תִּתְקַיֵּם הָעֵדוּת בַּשְּׁאָר. רַבִּי אוֹמֵר: אֶחָד דִּינֵי מָמוֹנוֹת וְאֶחָד דִּינֵי נְפָשׁוֹת, בִּזְמַן שֶׁהִתְרוּ בָהֶן. אֲבָל בִּזְמַן שֶׁלֹּא הִתְרוּ בָהֶן —

יד אברהם

with the first two. This is learned from the fact that the mishnah says he is punished for *joining the transgressors,* indicating that his transgression was not proven. If he was himself discredited, he is punished for being a transgressor in his own right.

8.

The following mishnah does not deal with the laws of *hazamah,* but is a continuation of R' Akiva's interpretation of the aforementioned verse. He states another way in which three witnesses are comparable to two *(Tos. Yom Tov* from *Nimmukei Yosef).*

מַה־שְּׁנַיִם, — *Just as* [*with*] *two,*

[I.e., just as two witnesses.]

In the mishnah printed with the *Gemara,* the reading is וּמַה, thus connecting it to the preceding mishnah *(Shoshannim LeDavid).*

נִמְצָא אֶחָד מֵהֶן קָרוֹב — [*if*] *one of them is found* [*to be*] *a kinsman*

[A witness who is related to another witness or to either one of the litigants is disqualified. In *Sanhedrin* 3:4, the mishnah delineates which kinsmen are disqualified to be witnesses.]

אוֹ־פָסוּל, — *or a disqualified* [*witness*],

[I.e., one disqualified to testify because of his sins. See *Sanhedrin* 3:3, *Rosh Hashanah* 1:8.]

עֵדוּתָן בְּטֵלָה, — *their testimony is void,*

If one of two witnesses is disqualified, the testimony is surely void, since there is only one remaining witness *(Beis David; Tos. Chadashim;* see *Tos. Yom Tov, Rashash).*

אַף שְׁלֹשָׁה, נִמְצָא אֶחָד מֵהֶן קָרוֹב אוֹ־פָסוּל, עֵדוּתָן בְּטֵלָה. — *so too* [*with*] *three,* [*if*] *one of them is found* [*to be*] *a kinsman or a disqualified* [*witness*], *their testimony is void.*

[I.e., if a group of three witnesses testified and one of the witnesses was disqualified because of kinship or general ineligibility, the testimony of the entire group becomes void. Although the testimony of this third witness was not required, once he becomes a witness, his invalidation voids the testimony of the entire group.]

מִנַּיִן אֲפִילוּ מֵאָה? — *How do we know that* [*this is so*] *even* [*for*] *a hundred?*

[How do we know that even if only one out of a group of one hundred witnesses is found to be a kinsman or a disqualified witness, the testimony of all of them is nevertheless void?]

תַּלְמוּד לוֹמַר: „עֵדִים." — *To teach* [*this*] *it states: 'witnesses.'*

[From here we deduce that even many witnesses are counted as two, and that if even one of them is disqualified, the testimony of all is void.]

אָמַר רַבִּי יוֹסֵי: בַּמֶּה דְבָרִים אֲמוּרִים? — *Said R' Yose: In regard to what is this said?*

8. Just as [with] two, [if] one of them is found [to be] a kinsman or a disqualified [witness], their testimony is void, so too [with] three, [if] one of them is found [to be] a kinsman or a disqualified [witness], their testimony is void. How do we know that [this is so] even [for] a hundred? To teach [this] it states: '*witnesses.*'

Said R' Yose: In regard to what is this said? In regard to capital cases; but in regard to civil cases, the testimony is established through the remaining [witnesses]. Rabbi says: Both in civil cases and in capital cases, but only if they warned them. But if they did not warn them —

YAD AVRAHAM

[I.e., in which case do we say that the disqualification of one witness voids the testimony of the entire group?]

בְּדִינֵי נְפָשׁוֹת; אֲבָל בְּדִינֵי מָמוֹנוֹת, תִּתְקַיֵּם הָעֵדוּת בַּשְּׁאָר. — *In regard to capital cases; but in regard to civil cases, the testimony is established through the remaining [witnesses].*

Although the same rules of jurisprudence generally apply to both capital and monetary cases, the Torah *(Num.* 35:25) states an additional rule in regard to capital cases: וְהִצִּילוּ הָעֵדָה, *and the congregation shall save,* meaning: there are times when *beis din* must look for ways to exonerate the defendant. This teaches that there are rules of judicial procedure favoring the defendant that apply to capital cases that do not apply to civil cases *(Rav; Rashi).* R' Yose sees the rule voiding the testimony of a large group of witnesses because of the disqualification of one of them to be one of these special leniencies and therefore applicable only to capital, and not civil, cases.

Tosafos (6a) explain R' Yose's rationale to be that in monetary cases, even if there were only two witnesses and one became disqualified, the testimony of the remaining witness is not entirely void, since in monetary matters one witness is sufficient to make the defendant liable to an oath. Consequently, when deriving the rule for three witnesses from that of two, it makes sense to say that if in a civil case there were three and one was disqualified, we can still convict the defendant through the testimony of the remaining two witnesses. In capital cases, however, if there were originally two witnesses and one was disqualified, the testimony is completely void since a single witness is useless when dealing with corporal punishment. Therefore, when deriving the rule for three witnesses, we conclude that if there were three and one was disqualified we void the entire testimony.

רַבִּי אוֹמֵר: — *Rabbi says:*

This refers to R' Yehudah HaNassi ['the Prince'] (135-219 C.E.), redactor of the Mishnah, who was reverently referred to as *Rabbi,* teacher par excellence, and *Rabbeinu HaKadosh,* our Holy Teacher.

אֶחָד דִּינֵי מָמוֹנוֹת וְאֶחָד דִּינֵי נְפָשׁוֹת, — *Both in civil cases and in capital cases,*

Rabbi disputes R' Yose's view that the disqualification of an entire set of witnesses because of the disqualification of one of them is restricted to capital cases. In Rabbi's view, this rule applies to both capital and civil cases *(Tif. Yis.)* with the following proviso:

בִּזְמַן שֶׁהִתְרוּ בָהֶן. — *but only if they warned them.*

In transgressions punishable by corporal punishment [e.g. lashes or death], the courts do not administer the punishment unless the perpetrator was warned of the

מַה יַּעֲשׂוּ שְׁנֵי אַחִין שֶׁרָאוּ בְּאֶחָד שֶׁהָרַג אֶת־הַנֶּפֶשׁ?

[ט] **הָיוּ** שְׁנַיִם רוֹאִין אוֹתוֹ מֵחַלּוֹן זֶה, וּשְׁנַיִם רוֹאִין אוֹתוֹ מֵחַלּוֹן זֶה, וְאֶחָד מַתְרֶה בּוֹ בָּאֶמְצַע — בִּזְמַן שֶׁמִּקְצָתָן רוֹאִין אֵלּוּ אֶת־אֵלּוּ, הֲרֵי אֵלּוּ עֵדוּת אַחַת; וְאִם לָאו, הֲרֵי אֵלּוּ שְׁתֵּי עֵדֻיּוֹת. לְפִיכָךְ אִם־נִמְצֵאת אַחַת מֵהֶן זוֹמֶמֶת, הוּא

יד אברהם

consequences of his sin. In such cases, the testimony of the entire set is void only if the disqualified witness took part in warning the accused *(Rav; Rashi)*. By doing so, he demonstrates his intent to serve as a witness, and thus becomes one of the set of witnesses to the transgression from the moment of its commission. Accordingly, his subsequent disqualification invalidates the testimony of the entire set.

However, if when he saw the crime he did not intend to testify in court, he does not become classified as one of the set of witnesses to the act. Consequently, even though he later decides to testify, his disqualification does not affect the other witnesses *(Tos. 6a)*.

If the disqualified witness warned the perpetrator, but claims he never intended to testify, we do not believe him and the testimony is void *(Tif. Yis.)*.

אֲבָל בִּזְמַן שֶׁלֹּא הִתְרוּ בָהֶן — *But if they did not warn them* —

I.e., if the disqualified witness did not warn the perpetrator and did not intend to be a witness to this act at the time of its commission, the testimony of the other witnesses does not become void because of him *(Rav; Rashi)*.

מַה־יַּעֲשׂוּ שְׁנֵי אַחִין שֶׁרָאוּ בְּאֶחָד שֶׁהָרַג אֶת־הַנֶּפֶשׁ? — *what should two brothers do who saw someone commit a murder?*

I.e., if they together with a third party saw someone commit a murder *(Tos. Yom Tov from Rashi)*. Since the disqualification of kinship applies even to witnesses related to each other, if the rule were otherwise and two brothers were among a group of people who witnessed a murder, they would inevitably cause the testimony of the entire group to be voided and let the murderer go free. However, since the rule is that only those witnesses who intended to testify and warned the perpetrator are numbered among the group, these kinsmen can avoid this undesirable consequence by refraining from any intention to become witnesses. Lacking the intention of testifying, they will not void the entire group *(Nimmukei Yosef)*.

Tosafos are of the opinion that even if he intended to testify, a kinsman voids the entire group only if he actually testifies. In that case the two brothers can readily avoid voiding the testimony of the entire group by both not coming to testify. However, a problem might still arise if one brother was not aware that the other brother had testified. Therefore there must still be a mechanism for insuring that the testimony of two brothers should not invalidate everyone's testimony and allow a killer to go free *(Tos. Yom Tov* from *Tos.)*.

In monetary cases, the judges ascertain the intent of the disqualified persons by asking them if their intention in coming to court is merely to observe the proceedings or if their intention is to testify *(Gem. 6a)*. Should they reply the latter, it is evident that they intended to testify from the very beginning, and they therefore disqualify the entire group *(Rashi)*. *Tosafos*, citing *Rabbeinu Chaim Cohen*,

what should two brothers do who saw someone commit a murder?

9. [If] two saw him from this window, and two saw him from that window, and one in the middle warned him — if some of them saw each other, then they are one set of witnesses; if not, they are two sets of witnesses. Therefore, if one of them is found to be

YAD AVRAHAM

explain that the judges pose the question to the qualified witnesses (not the disqualified ones). If they reply that they came to court to testify along with the disqualified persons, the entire group is invalidated. But if they reply that they came merely to observe, they are not considered a group with the disqualified ones and their testimony is therefore valid.

9.

The following mishnah discusses whether people observing a crime from different locations are nevertheless considered one group of witnesses or whether they are considered two groups.

הָיוּ שְׁנַיִם רוֹאִין אוֹתוֹ מֵחַלּוֹן זֶה, וּשְׁנַיִם רוֹאִין אוֹתוֹ מֵחַלּוֹן זֶה, — *[If] two saw him from this window, and two saw him from that window,*

[I.e., two witnesses witnessed the murder by looking out of one window, while two others saw the same crime from another window.]

וְאֶחָד מַתְרֶה בוֹ בָאֶמְצַע — *and one in the middle warned him —*

I.e., there was another person standing between the two windows who, although he could not see the murder, was nevertheless aware of the crime about to take place. He proceeded to warn the would-be perpetrator, and both groups of witnesses clearly heard the warning. This is a valid warning, although the one issuing the warning did not witness the crime and the witnesses did not actually see the person giving the warning (*Tos. Yom Tov* from *Tos.*).

בִּזְמַן שֶׁמִּקְצָתָן רוֹאִין אֵלּוּ אֶת־אֵלּוּ, — *if some of them saw each other,*

If at least one of the witnesses belonging to one group saw one of the witnesses belonging to the other group, or if one of the witnesses in each group saw the one giving the warning, or the one giving the warning saw them (*Tos. Yom Tov* from *Tos.* 6b; *Rambam, Hil. Eidus* 4:1).

הֲרֵי אֵלּוּ עֵדוּת אַחַת; — *then they are one set of witnesses;*

All four witnesses are considered one group. Therefore, if one of them is found to be a kinsman or a disqualified witness, the entire testimony is void. Similarly, if one group is discredited by *hazamah*, they are not put to death until the other group is also discredited (*Tos.* 6b).

וְאִם לָאו, — *if not,*

I.e., if they did not see each other, nor did they see the one giving the warning (*Tos. Yom Tov* from *Tos.*).

הֲרֵי אֵלּוּ שְׁתֵּי עֵדֻיּוֹת. — *they are two sets of witnesses.*

[The two pairs of witnesses who saw the crime from the two windows are considered two distinct groups of witnesses, since there is nothing to link them together.]

לְפִיכָךְ אִם־נִמְצֵאת אַחַת מֵהֶן זוֹמֶמֶת, — *Therefore, if one of them is found to be zomemim,*

[I.e., if other witnesses come and say to

מכות
א/י

וָהֵן נֶהֱרָגִין, וְהַשְּׁנִיָּה פְּטוּרָה. רַבִּי יוֹסֵי אוֹמֵר: לְעוֹלָם אֵין נֶהֱרָגִין עַד שֶׁיְּהוּ פִּי שְׁנֵי עֵדָיו מַתְרִין בּוֹ, שֶׁנֶּאֱמַר: „עַל־פִּי שְׁנַיִם עֵדִים.״ דָּבָר אַחֵר: „עַל פִּי שְׁנַיִם עֵדִים״ — שֶׁלֹּא תְהֵא סַנְהֶדְרִין שׁוֹמַעַת מִפִּי הַתֻּרְגְּמָן.

[י] **מִי־שֶׁנִּגְמַר** דִּינוֹ וּבָרַח, וּבָא לִפְנֵי אוֹתוֹ בֵּית דִּין, אֵין סוֹתְרִים אֶת־

יד אברהם

one of these pairs, 'How can you testify that you saw this event in such-and-such a place when you were with us in another place at that time!']

הוּא וָהֵן נֶהֱרָגִין, — *both he and they are executed,*

Both the defendant and the *zomemim* witnesses are executed.

The witnesses are executed since they were found to be *zomemim (Rav)*. Since they constitute a separate set of witnesses, they can be executed even though the other pair of witnesses have not been found to be *zomemim*. By the same token, the other pair's testimony is not voided by their disqualification. Consequently, the defendant is executed by dint of the testimony of the remaining group of witnesses.

Although, in fact, the defendant was found guilty of murder, the *zomemim* witnesses are, nevertheless, liable. Since at the time of their testimony, he had not yet been sentenced to death, they were falsely testifying to convict an innocent man. Therefore, they are liable *(Gem.* 5a).

וְהַשְּׁנִיָּה פְּטוּרָה. — *and the second* [*set*] *is exempt.*

If the second pair was not discredited, it is obvious that they are exempt *(Tif. Yis.)*. Thus, the mishnah must be referring to a case in which the second group was also found to be *zomemim*, but after the defendant had already been executed. As explained above (mishnah 6), witnesses are liable to execution for their false testimony only if they attempted to execute the defendant, not if they actually succeeded in having him executed *(Tos. Yom Tov* from *Nimmukei Yosef)*.

רַבִּי יוֹסֵי אוֹמֵר: לְעוֹלָם אֵין נֶהֱרָגִין עַד שֶׁיְּהוּ פִּי שְׁנֵי עֵדָיו מַתְרִין בּוֹ, — *R' Yose says: They are not executed unless his two witnesses warn him,*

[R' Yose disputes a fundamental assumption of the *Tanna Kamma's* ruling. In his view, the warning is valid only when it is given by both the witnesses testifying against the defendant. Thus, there is no question of their being made into a single group by virtue of the person issuing the warning.]

The *Tanna Kamma*, however, rules that anyone can deliver the warning, even one who does not witness the crime. To make this point, the *Tanna Kamma* illustrated his case in which two groups become one by dint of some of one group seeing some of the other by choosing an instance in which the person delivering the warning did not see the crime being committed *(Tos.* 6b).

שֶׁנֶּאֱמַר: „עַל־פִּי שְׁנַיִם עֵדִים.״ — *as it is said (Deut. 17:6): 'By the testimony* [lit. *mouth*] *of two witnesses.'*

R' Yose explains the verse to mean that every component necessary to prosecute the defendant — both the warning and testimony — must come from the witnesses *(Tos. Yom Tov* from *Nimmukei Yosef)*. The halachah is in accordance with the *Tanna Kamma (Rambam, Hil. Eidus* 4:1).

zomemim, both he and they are executed, and the second [set] is exempt. R' Yose says: They are not executed unless his two witnesses warn him, as it is said (*Deut.* 17:6): *By the testimony of two witnesses.* Another explanation: *By the testimony of two witnesses* — that a *sanhedrin* should not hear [testimony] from the mouth of an interpreter.

10. [If] one was sentenced and fled, and then came before that very same court, they do not

YAD AVRAHAM

דָּבָר אַחֵר: „עַל־פִּי שְׁנַיִם עֵדִים" — שֶׁלֹּא תְהֵא סַנְהֶדְרִין שׁוֹמַעַת מִפִּי הַתֻּרְגְּמָן. — *Another explanation: 'By the testimony of two witnesses' — that a sanhedrin should not hear [testimony] from the mouth of an interpreter.*

[I.e., another interpretation of the verse, *By the testimony* [lit. *mouth*] *of two witnesses*, is that *beis din* must hear and understand the testimony from the mouth of the witnesses and not through an interpreter.]

Several reasons have been given for this halachah. *Rashi (Sanhedrin* 17a) explains that the interpreter is actually a witness relaying information to *beis din* which he received from the other witnesses — in effect, hearsay testimony. Since the rule is that witnesses can only testify about events they themselves saw, interpreters are invalid.

Radvaz (vol. I, 331) gives the reason that if the testimony is submitted through an interpreter, it will be impossible to discredit the testimony by *hazamah* and punish the witnesses for it, since the witnesses can always deny that that was what they said. Consequently, the law of *hazamah* cannot be inflicted upon them and, as explained above, testimony immune to *hazamah* is not admissable.

Nimmukei Yosef reasons that the interpreter may distort the testimony of the witnesses. Moreover, if the judges cannot communicate with the witnesses, they cannot examine them as thoroughly.

Although the mishnah deals only with the witnesses, *Rambam (Hil. Sanhedrin* 21:7) applies this halachah to the litigants as well, ruling that the litigants must present their claims to the judges without the aid of an interpreter. *Ritva* quotes *Rabbeinu Meir Halevi*, who subscribes to this view and, indeed, this is the decision of *Tur, Choshen Mishpat* 17, and *Shulchan Aruch* 17:6. *Bach* rules that Biblically this ruling applies only to capital cases. The Rabbis, however, applied it to civil cases as well.

Ritva quotes others who rule that the mishnah applies only to witnesses, not to litigants. *Radvaz* (vol. 1, 331) also rules that this halachah applies only to witnesses. He claims that even *Rambam* follows this reasoning. His application to litigants is merely Rabbinical. Therefore, if it is impossible to judge the litigants without the aid of an interpreter, even *Rambam* agrees that it is permissible. Indeed, it was common practice to judge immigrants from Italy or Turkey with the aid of an interpreter, since there were no Rabbinic judges in the Ashkenazic lands who understood those languages.

10.

מִי־שֶׁנִּגְמַר דִּינוֹ וּבָרַח, — [*If*] *one was sentenced and fled,*

He fled the local *beis din* before they had time to execute him *(Rabbeinu Yehonasan).*

וּבָא לִפְנֵי אוֹתוֹ בֵּית דִּין, — *and then came before that very same court,*

He was recognized in the place to which he had fled and brought back before the same *beis din* that had origi-

דִּינוֹ. כָּל־מָקוֹם שֶׁיַּעַמְדוּ שְׁנַיִם וְיֹאמְרוּ: „מְעִידִין אָנוּ בְּאִישׁ פְּלוֹנִי שֶׁנִּגְמַר דִּינוֹ בְּבֵית דִּינוֹ שֶׁל־פְּלוֹנִי, וּפְלוֹנִי וּפְלוֹנִי עֵדָיו,״ הֲרֵי זֶה יֵהָרֵג.

סַנְהֶדְרִין נוֹהֶגֶת בָּאָרֶץ וּבְחוּצָה לָאָרֶץ. סַנְהֶדְרִין הַהוֹרֶגֶת אֶחָד בַּשָּׁבוּעַ נִקְרֵאת חָבְלָנִית. רַבִּי אֶלְעָזָר בֶּן־עֲזַרְיָה אוֹמֵר: אֶחָד לְשִׁבְעִים שָׁנָה. רַבִּי טַרְפוֹן וְרַבִּי עֲקִיבָא אוֹמְרִים: אִלּוּ הָיִינוּ בְסַנְהֶדְרִין, לֹא נֶהֱרַג אָדָם מֵעוֹלָם. רַבָּן שִׁמְעוֹן בֶּן־גַּמְלִיאֵל אוֹמֵר:

יד אברהם

nally sentenced him. The same ruling would be in effect even if this *beis din* is now located in a different city *(Meiri).*

.אֵין סוֹתְרִים אֶת־דִּינוֹ — *they do not overturn his sentence.*

I.e., they do not retry his case, but carry out the sentence.

The *Gemara* (7a) explains that the same would be true if he was brought in front of another *beis din* in a different city. The mishnah's implication that there is a distinction between the original *beis din* and a different one applies only if he was originally tried in the Diaspora and fled from there to Eretz Yisrael. In such a case, if he is brought before a new court he is retried, because there is a possibility that the merit of his being in Eretz Yisrael will cause a new court to find grounds to exonerate him. However, if he is brought to justice before the same court, even if it had in the meantime relocated from the Diaspora to Eretz Yisrael, he is not retried. The same *beis din* will find it exceedingly difficult to see things differently than before. It therefore makes no sense to retry him in front of the same *beis din (Tos. Yom Tov; Rambam, Hil. Sanhedrin* 13:8).

כָּל־מָקוֹם שֶׁיַּעַמְדוּ שְׁנַיִם וְיֹאמְרוּ: „מְעִידִין אָנוּ בְּאִישׁ פְּלוֹנִי שֶׁנִּגְמַר דִּינוֹ בְּבֵית דִּינוֹ שֶׁל־פְּלוֹנִי, — *Wherever two stand up and declare, 'We testify concerning so-and-so that he was sentenced in so-and-so's court,*

I.e., if he fled from Eretz Yisrael to the Diaspora, or even from one city in Eretz Yisrael to another, and witnesses testified in another *beis din* that he was sentenced to death in such-and-such a *beis din (Tos. Yom Tov* from *Gem.* 7a).

,״וּפְלוֹנִי וּפְלוֹנִי עֵדָיו — *and so-and-so and so-and-so were his witnesses,'*

They must testify who the witnesses were on whose testimony the defendant was convicted. This must be done so that in the event that they are false other witnesses may be able to refute or contradict them *(Tos. Yom Tov).*

.הֲרֵי זֶה יֵהָרֵג — *he is executed.*

He is executed only in a case of murder. In other capital cases, however, the perpetrator is not executed unless the witnesses who testified at his original trial are present. This is because in regard to all capital cases except murder the Torah states that the witnesses must be the first to participate in his execution, which is possible only if they are present *(Rambam, Hil. Sanhedrin* 13:7 from *Sanhedrin* 45b).

.סַנְהֶדְרִין נוֹהֶגֶת בָּאָרֶץ וּבְחוּצָה לָאָרֶץ — *A sanhedrin functions both in the Holy Land and outside the Holy Land.*

The mishnah now delineates some of the rules governing the minor *sanhedrin,* composed of twenty-three duly ordained judges. This ordination, known as *semichah,* was bestowed only in Eretz Yisrael. Once someone received such ordination, however, he was qualified to

1 10 overturn his sentence. Wherever two stand up and declare, 'We testify concerning so-and-so that he was sentenced in so-and-so's court, and so-and-so and so-and-so were his witnesses,' he is executed.

A *sanhedrin* functions both in the Holy Land and outside the Holy Land. A *sanhedrin* that executes once in a septenary is called a destroyer. R' Elazar ben Azariah says: Once in seventy years. R' Tarfon and R' Akiva say: Had we been on a *sanhedrin*, a person would never have been executed. Rabban Shimon ben Gamliel

YAD AVRAHAM

judge cases of fines, cases of lashes, and even capital cases, not only in Eretz Yisrael, but also in the Diaspora *(Rav)*.

The *Gemara* (7a) derives from the Biblical passages concerning the establishment of courts that in Eretz Yisrael there is a requirement to establish courts in every province and in every city; outside the Holy Land, we are only required to establish courts in each province, but not in every city.

According to this reading, the mishnah tells us that there is an obligation for the *sanhedrin* to function outside the Holy Land. *Rambam's* reading of the *Gemara*, however, is: 'Outside the Holy Land, you are not required to establish courts, neither in every province nor in every city.' Accordingly, the mishnah teaches that if we establish a *sanhedrin*, although we are not required to do so, it is empowered to function the same as the *sanhedrin* in Eretz Yisrael *(Meiri)*. See *Rambam, Hil. Sanhedrin* 1:2.

A *sanhedrin* may function either in the Holy Land or in the Diaspora only when the Great Sanhedrin of seventy-one members is established in the *Lishkas HaGazis* (Chamber of Hewn Stone) in the Temple Court. Otherwise, the lesser *sanhedrins* have no power to try capital cases. See *Tos. Yom Tov, Ritva, Meiri.*

The *Gemara (Sanhedrin* 41a) relates that forty years prior to the destruction of the Temple, the Great Sanhedrin left its place in the Temple since murder became prevalent, and the *sanhedrin* was unable to judge all the murderers *(Rashi* ad loc.).

סַנְהֶדְרִין הַהוֹרֶגֶת אֶחָד בַּשָּׁבוּעַ — *A sanhedrin that executes once in a septenary*

I.e., one person in seven years *(Rav)*.

נִקְרֵאת חוֹבְלָנִית. — *is called a destroyer.*

They should have judged slowly and carefully and sought ways of exonerating the defendant *(Rav)*.

רַבִּי אֶלְעָזָר בֶּן־עֲזַרְיָה אוֹמֵר: אֶחָד לְשִׁבְעִים שָׁנָה. — *R' Elazar ben Azariah says: Once in seventy years.*

The meaning of this is uncertain. It is not clear whether R' Elazar ben Azariah means that such a *sanhedrin* is deemed a destructive one, or whether he means to say that this is a reasonable number of executions *(Tos. Yom Tov* from *Gem.* 7a). In either case, the mishnah's intention is that the judges of a capital case should strive to find ways of exonerating the defendant. However, should there be no way to do so, they must execute even a thousand *(Rambam Comm.)*.

רַבִּי טַרְפוֹן וְרַבִּי עֲקִיבָא אוֹמְרִים: אִלּוּ הָיִינוּ בְּסַנְהֶדְרִין, לֹא נֶהֱרַג אָדָם מֵעוֹלָם. — *R' Tarfon and R' Akiva say: Had we been on a sanhedrin, a person would never have been executed.*

I.e., had they lived when the *sanhedrins* tried capital cases, they would have examined the witnesses with questions designed to raise doubts which would be virtually impossible to resolve. In murder cases, for example, they would have asked the witnesses if they saw whether the murdered man was healthy

אַף הֵן מַרְבִּין שׁוֹפְכֵי דָמִים בְּיִשְׂרָאֵל.

[א] **אֵלּוּ** הֵן הַגּוֹלִין: הַהוֹרֵג נֶפֶשׁ בִּשְׁגָגָה. הָיָה מְעַגֵּל בְּמַעְגִּילָה, וְנָפְלָה עָלָיו וַהֲרָגַתּוּ; הָיָה מְשַׁלְשֵׁל בְּחָבִית, וְנָפְלָה עָלָיו וַהֲרָגַתּוּ; הָיָה

יד אברהם

or whether he was a *treifah;* i.e., whether he was suffering from an injury which would cause him to die within twelve months. Such a person is deemed legally dead in many respects, and his murderer would be exempt from the penalty of execution. Even if the victim's body was subsequently examined and found not to have such injuries, R' Tarfon and R' Akiva would suggest that perhaps there was a hole in the place where the sword was thrust, and the murdered man was, in reality, a *treifah.* In cases of adultery, they would raise similar questions, which the witnesses would be equally incapable of resolving with certainty *(Rav* from *Gem.* 7a).

Legally, the court is not obligated to consider such possibilities but may rely on the fact that the great majority of people are not *treifos.* Nevertheless, R' Akiva and R' Tarfon would have asked enough of these and similar-type questions that the witnesses would most often have ended up contradicting one another and thereby invalidating their testimony *(Tos. Yom Tov* from *Tos.* 7a).

They were not concerned with the possibility that someone would be executed for profaning the Sabbath or worshipping idols since those sins were unusual *(Tos. Yom Tov* from *Tos.).*

רַבָּן שִׁמְעוֹן בֶּן־גַּמְלִיאֵל אוֹמֵר: אַף הֵן מַרְבִּין שׁוֹפְכֵי דָמִים בְּיִשְׂרָאֵל. — *Rabban Shimon ben Gamliel says: They too would have increased* [*the number of*] *murderers in Israel.*

Since they would seek ways of exonerating the murderers, they would not eliminate the murderers, who would then continue to commit more murders *(Rav).* Furthermore, they would eliminate criminals' fear of retribution, thereby increasing the number of people willing to commit murder *(Rashi).*

Rabban Shimon ben Gamliel was especially concerned with murder more than other crimes because murder, in contrast to adultery, is both sinful against God and destructive to people *(Tos. Yom Tov).*

Chapter 2

This chapter deals with one who murders unintentionally. Generally speaking, the law is that he must go into exile in one of the cities designated for this purpose. These cities were known as עָרֵי מִקְלָט, *cities of refuge.* He must remain there until the death of the *Kohen Gadol* (High Priest), at which time he may return. If he strays out of the refuge city for any reason, the גוֹאֵל הַדָּם [*goel hadam*], lit. *avenger of the blood,* i.e., the closest kinsman to the victim, may kill him in revenge.

Rambam (Hil. Rotzeach 6:1-4) explains that there are three categories of unintentional murders, each with different laws governing it.

(1) There is one who kills completely unintentionally, concerning whom the Torah says *(Ex.* 21:13): *Who did not lie in wait.* The law regarding him is that he go into exile in one of the refuge cities and be saved.

(2) There is another who kills unintentionally in a manner that is almost an accident. A most unusual circumstance occurs, one that the murderer could not have foreseen, which results in the death of the victim. In this case the law states that he is

says: They too would have increased [the number of] murderers in Israel.

1. These are the ones who are exiled: One who kills a person inadvertently. [If] he was pushing out with a roller, and it fell upon him and killed him; [or if] he was letting down a cask, and it fell upon him and killed him; [or if] he was descending a ladder, and he fell upon him and killed him — he is exiled. But if he was

YAD AVRAHAM

exempt even from exile, it being considered tantamount to an accident. Should the *goel hadam* (avenger of blood) kill this murderer, he is himself liable to death.

(3) The third category is one who kills unintentionally, yet in a manner that is almost willful. This is a case in which the murder occurred through negligence or in circumstances that anyone could have foreseen, and precautions should therefore have been taken to avoid the accident. Such negligent homicide is too severe a crime to be atoned for by exile, and the law of exile therefore does not apply to him. Since the murder was not deliberate, however, he cannot be executed. He is, nevertheless, subject to vengeance at the hand of the *goel hadam*, and he must take precautions to guard his own life.

1.

אֵלּוּ הֵן הַגּוֹלִין: — *These are the ones who are exiled:*

The following are considered unintentional murderers who are exiled to the refuge cities *(Tif. Yis.)*.

הַהוֹרֵג נֶפֶשׁ בִּשְׁגָגָה. — *One who kills a person inadvertently.*

[As it is written *(Num.* 35:11): *They shall be refuge cities for you, and a murderer who killed someone unwittingly shall flee there.* The mishnah now delineates the types of unintentional killers who are sentenced to be exiled.]

הָיָה מְעַגֵּל בְּמַעְגִּילָה, — *[If] he was pushing out with a roller,*

This was a smooth round stone *(Rav)* or flat block of wood *(Rashi)* that was used to smooth down the tar or mud which was spread over the roof to waterproof it *(Rashi)* or to make it glisten *(Rambam Comm.)*. *Rashi* explains that the roofs in those days were flat. Consequently, they would have to make the tar smooth and slope slightly so that the rain would run off. This they would do by means of a thick smooth block of wood, which the roofer would push downward toward the edge of the roof, then pull back up toward himself [in the center of the roof], repeating the operation until the roof became smooth (see *Meiri)*. The act of pushing out [towards the roof's edge] is called מְעַגֵּל, literally *rolling*, while the act of pulling it back is called מוֹשֵׁךְ, *drawing* (see mishnah 2).

וְנָפְלָה עָלָיו וַהֲרָגַתּוּ; — *and it fell upon him and killed him;*

[I.e., as the roofer was pushing out, the roller suddenly slipped from his hand and fell off the roof, killing his neighbor who was standing below.]

הָיָה מְשַׁלְשֵׁל בְּחָבִית, — *[or if] he was letting down a cask,*

I.e., he was lowering a cask from the roof by means of a rope *(Rashi)*.

וְנָפְלָה עָלָיו וַהֲרָגַתּוּ; — *and it fell upon him and killed him;*

The rope slipped out of his hand and the cask fell, killing the one standing

יוֹרֵד בְּסֻלָּם, וְנָפַל עָלָיו וַהֲרָגוֹ — הֲרֵי זֶה גוֹלֶה. אֲבָל אִם־הָיָה מוֹשֵׁךְ בַּמַּעְגִּילָה, וְנָפְלָה עָלָיו וַהֲרָגַתּוּ; הָיָה דוֹלֶה בֶחָבִית וְנִפְסַק הַחֶבֶל, וְנָפְלָה עָלָיו וַהֲרָגַתּוּ; הָיָה עוֹלֶה בַסֻּלָּם, וְנָפַל עָלָיו וַהֲרָגוֹ — הֲרֵי זֶה אֵינוֹ גוֹלֶה. זֶה הַכְּלָל: כָּל־שֶׁבְּדֶרֶךְ יְרִידָתוֹ, גוֹלֶה; וְשֶׁלֹּא בְדֶרֶךְ יְרִידָתוֹ, אֵינוֹ גוֹלֶה.

יד אברהם

below (*Tos. Yom Tov* from *Gem.* 7a).

However, if the rope snapped, he would not be liable for exile according to Rabbi, who rules further in the mishnah that if the iron flies off an axe handle during wood-chopping and kills someone, the perpetrator is exempt. The rope tearing is analogous to the iron slipping off the handle (ibid.).

הָיָה יוֹרֵד בְּסֻלָּם, וְנָפַל עָלָיו וַהֲרָגוֹ — [*or if*] *he was descending a ladder, and he fell upon him and killed him* —

I.e., if the person was descending a ladder and fell off it, killing the person down below with his body (*Rashi*).

הֲרֵי זֶה גוֹלֶה. — *he is exiled.*

[These three are all examples of cases in which an unintentional murderer must go into exile.]

Each of these three examples adds an additional point. Had the mishnah taught only the case of the roofer, we might have attributed his decree of exile to the fact that he should have been more cautious not to let his roller fall. However, one lowering a cask was surely trying to be careful that the rope should not slip, since he does not want his cask to break. Nevertheless, the mishnah teaches that he is liable to exile. The third case goes one step further by teaching that even one descending a ladder, who can be assumed to have exercised great caution for his own well-being, is held accountable if he falls and kills someone, and he too must be exiled (*Tos. Yom Tov* from *Tos.* 7a).

אֲבָל אִם־הָיָה מוֹשֵׁךְ בַּמַּעְגִּילָה, וְנָפְלָה עָלָיו וַהֲרָגַתּוּ; — *But if he was drawing back the roller, and it fell upon him and killed him;*

I.e., if the roofer was pulling the tool upward toward himself when it slipped out of his hand, killing his neighbor (*Rav; Rashi*).

הָיָה דוֹלֶה בֶחָבִית וְנִפְסַק הַחֶבֶל, וְנָפְלָה עָלָיו וַהֲרָגַתּוּ; — [*or if*] *he was hoisting up the cask and the rope broke, and it fell upon him and killed him;*

[I.e., the rope attached to the cask broke, causing the cask to roll down and hit his neighbor.]

הָיָה עוֹלֶה בַסֻּלָּם וְנָפַל עָלָיו וַהֲרָגוֹ — [*or if*] *he was ascending the ladder, and he fell upon him and killed him* —

[I.e., as he was ascending the ladder, he slipped and fell upon his neighbor, killing him.]

הֲרֵי זֶה אֵינוֹ גוֹלֶה. — *he is not exiled.*

The above occurrences are considered accidental rather than unintentional acts, being that they are unusual. Consequently, there is no exile [see preface] (*Rambam, Hil. Rotzeach* 6:12).

זֶה הַכְּלָל: כָּל־שֶׁבְּדֶרֶךְ יְרִידָתוֹ, — *This is the rule: For* [*any death which occurs*] *in the course of descent,*

[If he kills someone in the course of his own descent or while moving an object or implement in a downward motion.]

גוֹלֶה; — *he is exiled;*

This is based on (*Num.* 35:23): וַיַּפֵּל עָלָיו וַיָּמֹת, *and he cast it upon him and he died,* meaning that he cast it upon him in the course of falling. The mishnah uses the word כָּל, *any* death through a downward motion, to include the case of one who kills during a downward mo-

2 drawing back the roller, and it fell upon him and killed
1 him; [or if] he was hoisting up the cask and the rope
broke, and it fell upon him and killed him; [or if] he was
ascending the ladder, and he fell upon him and killed
him — he is not exiled. This is the rule: For [any death
which occurs] in the course of descent, he is exiled; but
for [one which occurs] not in the course of descent, he is
not exiled.

tion initiated for the purpose of raising something (*Rav* from *Gem.* 7b). *Rashi* gives an example of one who picks up an axe. In doing so, he bends forward in order to be able to apply greater thrust to his backward swing of the axe. If in his bending forward, he inadvertently kills someone, he is sentenced to exile. Although his downward motion was for the purpose of raising his hand with the axe, this is nevertheless a descending motion, and he is therefore sentenced to exile (*Tos. Yom Tov*).

וְשֶׁלֹּא בְדֶרֶךְ יְרִידָתוֹ, — *but for* [*one which occurs*] *not in the course of descent,*

This includes one who raises an axe and swings it over his back, then lifts it to bring it down in front of him with greater force. Should he kill someone while raising the axe in order to bring it down, he is not sentenced to exile. Although he raised it with the intention of bringing it down, it is nevertheless an upward motion (*Tos. Yom Tov*).

אֵינוֹ גוֹלֶה. — *he is not exiled.*

Rambam (*Hil. Rotzeach* 6:12) rationalizes this halachah with the following reasoning: Since it is common for descending objects to cause damage, because it is the nature of heavy objects to fall quickly, it behooves a person to be especially careful to see that everything is in proper order during the descent. If he did not exercise greater caution he must go into exile. However, when engaged in an upward motion, in which he is exerting force in the opposite direction from that of gravity, it is deemed an accident (*Meiri*).

Lechem Shamayim questions this distinction, since it is the nature of objects to fall and damage regardless of the original direction of their motion. Accordingly, he reasons that when the person or the object is going down, the one holding it has his sights trained below, and he must therefore watch that it should not fall down. But, when he or the object is going up, he is occupied with looking upward and cannot be expected to watch that it should not fall down. Consequently, in such cases, it is deemed almost an accident, and there is no exile.

◆§ The Torah's Woodchopping Accident

In the section dealing with the laws of the unintentional murderer, the Torah illustrates the law by depicting a scene in which two people enter a forest to chop wood, and the axe-head of one of them flies off its handle and kills the other. The wording is as follows: וַאֲשֶׁר יָבֹא אֶת־רֵעֵהוּ בַיַּעַר לַחְטֹב עֵצִים וְנִדְּחָה יָדוֹ בַגַּרְזֶן לִכְרֹת הָעֵץ וְנָשַׁל הַבַּרְזֶל מִן־הָעֵץ וּמָצָא אֶת־רֵעֵהוּ וָמֵת, הוּא יָנוּס אֶל־אַחַת הֶעָרִים־הָאֵלֶּה וָחָי., *And whoever comes with his fellowman into the forest to chop wood, and his hand swings the axe to chop the tree, and the iron flies from the wood and finds his fellowman and he dies, he shall flee to one of these cities and live* (*Deut.* 19:5).

As the mishnah explains, there is a controversy whether the Torah speaks of the iron slipping off the handle and hitting the other person, or whether it speaks of the iron chopping into the tree and causing a chip to fly with such force that it kills the other person.

נִשְׁמַט הַבַּרְזֶל מִקַּתּוֹ וְהָרַג — רַבִּי אוֹמֵר: אֵינוֹ גוֹלֶה; וַחֲכָמִים אוֹמְרִים: גוֹלֶה. מִן־הָעֵץ הַמִּתְבַּקֵּעַ — רַבִּי אוֹמֵר: גוֹלֶה; וַחֲכָמִים אוֹמְרִים: אֵינוֹ גוֹלֶה.

[ב] **הַזּוֹרֵק** אֶבֶן לִרְשׁוּת הָרַבִּים וְהָרַג, הֲרֵי זֶה גוֹלֶה. רַבִּי אֱלִיעֶזֶר בֶּן יַעֲקֹב אוֹמֵר: אִם־מִכְּשֶׁיָּצָאתָה הָאֶבֶן מִיָּדוֹ, הוֹצִיא הַלָּז אֶת־רֹאשׁוֹ וְקִבְּלָהּ, הֲרֵי זֶה פָּטוּר. זָרַק אֶת־הָאֶבֶן לַחֲצֵרוֹ

יד אברהם

נִשְׁמַט הַבַּרְזֶל מִקַּתּוֹ וְהָרַג — *Should the iron fly off its handle and kill —*

I.e., if one was chopping wood, and suddenly the axe-head slipped off the handle which was thrust into it, killing someone *(Rav)*.

This must refer to a case in which the axe-blade slipped off when the wielder was bringing it down. Otherwise, everyone would rule it accidental, as in the previous cases in the mishnah *(Rabbeinu Yehonasan)*.

רַבִּי אוֹמֵר: אֵינוֹ גוֹלֶה; — *Rabbi says: He is not exiled;*

Rabbi explains וְנָשַׁל, *fly off*, as a transitive verb. Thus he translates the verse to mean *and the iron makes fly from the tree*, i.e., that the axe-blade causes chips to fly, and one of these chips hits his companion, killing him. It does not, in his view, refer to the axe-blade slipping off the handle *(Rav* from *Gem.* 7b). Where the axe-blade did fly off, it would be considered negligence, since obviously the axe-blade was loose and that is something which should have been checked. In that case, he would not be liable to exile because exile would not be sufficient to expiate his sin *(Rabbeinu Chananel; Meiri)*.

On the other hand, if he checked the axe-blade and found it to be secure and it still came loose and killed, it would be deemed an unforseeable accident and again exile would not be prescribed *(Rabbeinu Yehonasan)*.

וַחֲכָמִים אוֹמְרִים: גוֹלֶה. — *but the Sages say: He is exiled.*

According to them, the word וְנָשַׁל is an intransitive verb, meaning that the iron axe-head flies off the handle to kill the other person *(Rav* from *Gem.* 7b). This in their opinion is not deemed negligence, since sometimes the blade appears to be fastened securely although, in fact, it is not *(Meiri)*.

מִן־הָעֵץ הַמִּתְבַּקֵּעַ — *From the tree that is being chopped —*

I.e., if a chip flies from the tree that is being felled *(Rashi)*.

Others explain that the axe-blade slipped off because of the impact against the tree that was being chopped, whereas the preceding case deals with the axe-blade flying off the handle while it was being swung *(Rabbeinu Chananel; Meiri; Rambam, Hil. Rotzeach* 6:15, according to extant editions).

רַבִּי אוֹמֵר: גוֹלֶה; — *Rabbi says: He is exiled;*

[As explained above, *Rabbi* explains וְנָשַׁל as a transitive verb, meaning that the iron caused a chip to fly from the tree. Therefore, the slayer is exiled.]

וַחֲכָמִים אוֹמְרִים: אֵינוֹ גוֹלֶה. — *but the Sages say: He is not exiled.*

The Sages judge this an indirect consequence of his act and rule that exile is prescribed only when murder was the direct result of his act, albeit unintentional (Rav; Rambam, Hil. Rotzeach 6:15). Meiri adds that some explain that it is considered an unforseeable accident, and he is therefore exempt from exile.

Should the iron fly off its handle and kill — Rabbi says: He is not exiled; but the Sages say: He is exiled. From the tree that is being chopped — Rabbi says: He is exiled; but the Sages say: He is not exiled.

2. [If] one throws a stone into a public domain and kills, he is exiled. R' Eliezer ben Yaakov says: If, after the stone left his hand, the other one put his head out and received the blow, he is exempt. [If] he threw a stone into his own yard and killed — if the victim had

YAD AVRAHAM

2.

הַזּוֹרֵק אֶבֶן לִרְשׁוּת הָרַבִּים וְהָרַג, הֲרֵי זֶה גוֹלֶה. — *[If] one throws a stone into a public domain and kills, he is exiled.*

The *Gemara* (8a) qualifies the term *public domain* in this mishnah as not referring to an ordinary one, i.e., a place frequented by many people. Throwing a stone where one will almost certainly encounter people and may kill someone is close to being an intentional murder, and this sin cannot be expiated with exile. The mishnah deals with one who throws a stone into a dung heap used as a latrine, mostly at night. However, occasionally someone sits there by day. Should he throw a stone by day and hit someone sitting there, he is exiled. Since people usually do not use the dung heap during the day, it is not akin to an intentional murder. However, since occasionally it is frequented even by day, it is not judged an unforseeable accident, but rather an inadvertent slaying (*Rav* from *Gem.* 8a).

Should this dung heap not be used by the general populace at all, even if there is an individual who occasionally uses it, the killer is not sentenced to exile, since it would then be considered an accident (*Tos.; Rambam, Hil. Rotzeach* 6:7).

Tif. Yis. questions the ruling of this mishnah on the grounds that a stone is thrown upwards. According to the rule established in the previous mishnah, therefore, the perpetrator should not be exiled. He answers that the mishnah speaks of a case in which the stone killed its victim while falling. [This is difficult since that is true in all cases mentioned in mishnah 1, yet the murderer is exempt if he released the cask or a roller while raising them even though they fell down and killed the victim. Rather, the solution would seem to be that only in the case in which the object fell without the intention of the one who dropped it, do we require that it happen in a downward motion. In our case, however, he cast the stone intentionally and his deed is adjudged inadvertent only because he was unaware of the presence of the victim. In this instance, there is no difference whether the stone was cast upwards or downwards. Moreover, although he cast the stone upward, he was fully aware that it would later fall downward, unlike the cases in mishnah 1.]

רַבִּי אֱלִיעֶזֶר בֶּן־יַעֲקֹב אוֹמֵר: אִם מִכְּשֶׁיָּצְאתָה הָאֶבֶן מִיָּדוֹ, הוֹצִיא הַלָּז אֶת־רֹאשׁוֹ וְקִבְּלָהּ, הֲרֵי זֶה פָּטוּר. — *R' Eliezer ben Yaakov says: If, after the stone left his hand, the other one put his head out and received the blow, he is exempt.*

Since the victim was not in the line of the throw when the killer released the rock, he is not exiled. This ruling is derived from the words וּמָצָא אֶת־רֵעֵהוּ, *and finds his fellowman,* meaning that the neighbor was already there, and the axe-head [or wood-chip] found him, not that he came later and caused the axe-head to find him (*Rav* from *Gem.* 8a).

זָרַק אֶת־הָאֶבֶן לַחֲצֵרוֹ וְהָרַג — *[If] he threw a stone into his own yard and*

וְהָרַג — אִם־יֵשׁ רְשׁוּת לַנִּזָּק לִכָּנֵס לְשָׁם, גּוֹלֶה, וְאִם לָאו, אֵינוֹ גוֹלֶה; שֶׁנֶּאֱמַר: „וַאֲשֶׁר יָבֹא אֶת־רֵעֵהוּ בַיַּעַר" — מָה הַיַּעַר רְשׁוּת לַנִּזָּק וְלַמַּזִּיק לִכָּנֵס לְשָׁם. יָצָא חֲצַר בַּעַל הַבַּיִת, שֶׁאֵין רְשׁוּת לַנִּזָּק וְלַמַּזִּיק לִכָּנֵס לְשָׁם. אַבָּא שָׁאוּל אוֹמֵר: מַה חֲטָבַת עֵצִים רְשׁוּת; יָצָא הָאָב הַמַּכֶּה אֶת־בְּנוֹ, וְהָרַב הָרוֹדֶה אֶת־תַּלְמִידוֹ, וּשְׁלִיחַ בֵּית־דִּין.

יד אברהם

killed —

[I.e., he killed a person who had entered his yard.]

אִם־יֵשׁ רְשׁוּת לַנִּזָּק לִכָּנֵס לְשָׁם, גּוֹלֶה, — *if the victim had a right to enter there, he is exiled,*

I.e., since the owner of the courtyard had given him permission to enter he should have exercised greater caution before throwing the stone *(Rav).*

וְאִם לָאו, אֵינוֹ גוֹלֶה; — *but if not, he is not exiled;*

[I.e., if the victim had no permission to enter the courtyard, the rock-thrower is exempt from exile *(Rambam, Hil. Rotzeach* 6:11).]

שֶׁנֶּאֱמַר: „וַאֲשֶׁר יָבֹא אֶת־רֵעֵהוּ בַיַּעַר" — מָה הַיַּעַר רְשׁוּת לַנִּזָּק וְלַמַּזִּיק לִכָּנֵס לְשָׁם; — *as it is said (Deut. 19:5): 'And whoever comes with his fellowman into the forest' — [it must be] like the forest, which is a place into which [both] the victim and the assailant have permission to enter.*

[I.e., if he kills there he goes to exile. We derive from this example in the Torah that only when slaying in similar circumstances, viz., in a place in which both have permission to be, is one liable to exile.]

The word וְלַמַּזִּיק, *and the assailant,* appears superfluous. It is added to avoid the impression that if the assailant has permission to enter, he is exempt, since the victim should have watched himself. The *Tanna,* therefore, emphasizes that it is incumbent upon the assailant to be cautious at all times *(Tos. Yom Tov).*

יָצָא חֲצַר בַּעַל הַבַּיִת, שֶׁאֵין רְשׁוּת לַנִּזָּק וְלַמַּזִּיק לִכָּנֵס לְשָׁם. — *This excludes the courtyard of the householder, into which the victim and the assailant may not* [*both*] *enter.*

[The verse quoted above excludes a householder who inadvertently killed someone who had entered his courtyard without permission.]

In some editions, the word וְלַמַּזִּיק is omitted from this clause *(Meiri;* see *Kol HaRemez; Beis David).*

אַבָּא שָׁאוּל אוֹמֵר: — *Abba Shaul says:*

[Abba Shaul now expounds on the next words in the verse, לַחְטֹב עֵצִים, *to chop wood.*]

מַה חֲטָבַת עֵצִים רְשׁוּת; — [*It must be*] *like chopping wood,* [*which is*] *an optional act.*

I.e., he can either enter the forest to chop wood or he can desist; it is entirely up to him *(Rav* from *Gem.).*

The mishnah, printed with the *Gemara,* includes three more words, אַף כָּל־רְשׁוּת, *so all* [*matters*] *must be optional.* [The intention is that by illustrating the laws of exile with a case of chopping wood the Torah teaches us that only when engaged in an optional activity is one liable to exile.]

יָצָא — *This excludes*

[I.e., this excludes from the law of exile] anyone who kills inadvertently in

2 a right to enter there, he is exiled, but if not, he is not
2 exiled; as it is said (*Deut.* 19:5): *And whoever comes with his fellowman into the forest* — [it must be] like the forest, which is a place into which [both] the victim and the assailant have permission to enter. This excludes the courtyard of the householder, into which the victim and the assailant may not [both] enter. Abba Shaul says: [It must be] like chopping wood, [which is] an optional act. This excludes the father who hits his son, and the teacher who chastises his pupil, and the agent of the court.

YAD AVRAHAM

the process of performing a *mitzvah*, as follows (*Rav*).

הָאָב הַמַּכֶּה אֶת־בְּנוֹ, — *the father who hits his son,*

I.e., when the purpose is chastisement (*Rashi*). According to the conclusion of the *Gemara*, the father is exempt if he hits his son either to teach him Torah, a trade, or to chastise him for improper behavior, since it is a a *mitzvah* for him to do so.

וְהָרַב הָרוֹדֶה אֶת־תַּלְמִידוֹ, — *and the teacher who chastises his pupil,*

Here the term רוֹדֶה, *chastises*, is used since the teacher may not hit him for any reason other than to teach him Torah. Since it is a *mitzvah* to teach someone else's son Torah, he may hit him if he does not learn properly; but since it is not a *mitzvah* for someone other than the father to teach him a trade, he is not permitted to hit for that purpose.

וּשְׁלִיחַ בֵּית־דִּין. — *and the agent of the court.*

Rashi explains that this refers to the agent of *beis din* who metes out the lashes to one who was sentenced to be flogged. If the person being flogged should die while being flogged, the flogger is exempt from exile because he is performing a *mitzvah*. Although *beis din* obviously erred in their assessment of how many lashes the defendant could tolerate (see below, 3:10), since he intended to fulfill a *mitzvah* the agent is exempt from exile (*Rabbeinu Yehonasan*).

Rambam (*Hil. Rotzeach* 5:6) explains that the agent of the court refers to the marshal who compels the people summoned to court to appear before the *beis din*. If they refuse to appear, the agent may hit them until they comply. Should they die under his blows, the agent is exempt from exile.

Meiri prefers *Rambam's* interpretation because the agent administering the lashes assessed by *beis din* would be exempt whether he was performing a *mitzvah* or not, since the death was completely accidental. *Ramban*, however, agrees with *Rabbeinu Yehonasan*, explaining that although these three are listed together, the reasons for their exemption from exile vary. Whereas the father and the teacher are exempt because they are performing a *mitzvah*, the agent of *beis din* is absolved because the death was accidental.

3.

The previous mishnayos have detailed the various liabilities and exemptions from exile based on the nature of the act which caused the death or various circumstances attendant upon it. The following mishnah discusses those that derive from the identity of the victim or his murderer.

[ג] **הָאָב** גּוֹלֶה עַל־יְדֵי הַבֵּן, וְהַבֵּן גּוֹלֶה עַל־יְדֵי הָאָב. הַכֹּל גּוֹלִין עַל־יְדֵי יִשְׂרָאֵל, וְיִשְׂרָאֵל גּוֹלִין עַל־יְדֵיהֶן, חוּץ מֵעַל־יְדֵי גֵר תּוֹשָׁב. וְגֵר תּוֹשָׁב אֵינוֹ גוֹלֶה אֶלָּא עַל־יְדֵי גֵר תּוֹשָׁב. הַסּוּמָא אֵינוֹ גוֹלֶה; דִּבְרֵי רַבִּי יְהוּדָה. רַבִּי מֵאִיר אוֹמֵר: גּוֹלֶה.

יד אברהם

הָאָב גּוֹלֶה עַל־יְדֵי הַבֵּן, — *A father is exiled as a result of his son,*

If a father kills his son inadvertently — when he is not hitting him to teach him Torah, a trade, or to chastise him to improve his ways *(Rav).*

The *Gemara* (8b) explains that if the son has already mastered a trade and the father hits him while teaching him a second trade, the father is liable to exile, there being no *mitzvah* to learn an additional trade.

וְהַבֵּן גּוֹלֶה עַל־יְדֵי הָאָב. — *and a son is exiled as a result of his father.*

[A son is exiled for killing his father inadvertently.]

הַכֹּל גּוֹלִין עַל־יְדֵי יִשְׂרָאֵל, — *All are exiled as a result of an Israelite,*

Anyone who kills a regular Jew inadvertently is sentenced to exile for his death. This ruling is meant to include even Cutheans and Canaanite slaves *(Rav* from *Gem.* 8b).

The Cutheans were one of the nations brought by the Assyrian king, Shalmanesser, to settle the part of Eretz Yisrael left desolate by the exile of the Ten Tribes *(II Kings* 17:24-41). [The term was later used to describe all the alien peoples resettled by the Assyrians in Israel. Because they lived primarily in Samaria, they became known to secular history as the Samaritans.] An outbreak of attacks by lions motivated them to convert to Judaism out of fear that they were being punished for not observing the religion of the land, but bècause their basis for conversion was not a true commitment to Judaism, considerable dispute arose among the Sages regarding its validity (see *Kiddushin* 75b). Later, in Talmudic times, they were discovered worshiping the image of a dove on Mt. Gerizim, whereupon the Rabbis designated them totally non-Jewish. In Mishnaic times, however, they were still classified as Jews according to many, including evidently the *Tanna* of this mishnah. Since in later times it was decided that they were gentiles, this ruling would not apply to them according to the halachah.

Canaanite slave is the generic name applied to non-Jewish slaves belonging to Jewish masters.[1] Canaanite slaves are obligated to keep all the commandments which women are obligated to keep. Since in order to become a Canaanite slave they must also undergo מִילָה, *circumcision,* and טְבִילָה, *immersion* — the other two basic elements of conversion — they are in a status akin to Jews, and are therefore granted asylum in the refuge cities, should they inadvertently kill an Jew. The same is true if a Jew kills one of them.

וְיִשְׂרָאֵל גּוֹלִין עַל־יְדֵיהֶן, — *and Israelites are exiled as a result of them,*

I.e., should a Jew inadvertently kill a Cuthean or a Canaanite slave, he is exiled *(Tif. Yis.* from *Gem.* 8b).

חוּץ מֵעַל־יְדֵי גֵר תּוֹשָׁב. — *with the excep-*

1. This term is used to distinguish them from *Hebrew slaves,* Jews who have fallen into servitude. Hebrew slaves are considered full Jews in every respect and are actually indentured servants, not slaves.

2 **3.** A father is exiled as a result of his son, and a son is
3 exiled as a result of his father. All are exiled as a result of an Israelite, and Israelites are exiled as a result of them, with the exception of a resident alien. A resident alien is exiled only as a result of a resident alien.

A blind person is not exiled; [these are] the words of R' Yehudah. R' Meir [however] says: He is exiled.

YAD AVRAHAM

tion of a resident alien.

The *resident alien* is a non-Jew who lives in Israel and who has accepted upon himself the observance of the seven Noachide commandments (*Avodah Zarah* 64b). As regards the law of exile, he is treated in certain respects like a non-Jew, viz., that if he kills a Jew, he is not afforded the sanctuary or the atonement of the refuge cities, but is put to death. In other respects, however, he is treated differently from a gentile, viz., if one resident alien kills another, he must flee to one of the refuge cities.

Although the literal translation means: *except as a result of a resident alien, Rav* explains this to mean that a resident alien is not exiled if he kills an Israelite, but is put to death. *Tos. Yom Tov* quotes many authorities who read: חוץ מִגֵּר תּוֹשָׁב, a reading which better lends itself to this interpretation.

Concerning a Jew who kills a resident alien, *Rambam* rules that he is exiled (*Comm.* and *Hil. Rotzeach* 5:3). *Ritva* reasons that since we are required to sustain them in their time of need, there is surely a liability of exile on their account. *Ravad* (ad loc.) and *Ramah*, quoted by *Ritva*, however, rule that if a Jew kills a resident alien, he is exempt.

וְגֵר תּוֹשָׁב אֵינוֹ גוֹלֶה אֶלָּא עַל־יְדֵי גֵר תּוֹשָׁב. — *A resident alien is exiled only as a result of a resident alien.*

We derive this from (*Num.* 35:15): וְלַגֵּר וְלַתּוֹשָׁב בְּתוֹכָם, *and for the alien and the resident among them.* The *Gemara* explains this to mean that if a resident alien kills another resident alien, he is sentenced to exile.

Rambam (ad loc.) rules that if a resident alien kills a Canaanite slave, or a Canaanite slave kills a resident alien, the slayer is exiled. *Kesef Mishneh* is at a loss for *Rambam's* source.

הַסּוּמָא אֵינוֹ גוֹלֶה; דִּבְרֵי רַבִּי יְהוּדָה. — *A blind person is not exiled; [these are] the words of R' Yehudah.*

[I.e., a blind person who killed inadvertently is not exiled.]

This is derived from the verse (*Num.* 35:23): בְּלֹא רְאוֹת, [*If he killed*] *without seeing,* meaning that in this instance he did not see, but ordinarily he is able to see. This excludes the blind man, who never sees (*Rav, Tos. Yom Tov* from *Gem., Rashi* 9b).

Rambam (*Hil. Rotzeach* 6:14) classifies the blind man's slaying as akin to an accidental slaying.

רַבִּי מֵאִיר אוֹמֵר: גּוֹלֶה. — *R' Meir [however] says: He is exiled.*

R' Meir reasons that actually there are two verses which would seem to exclude a blind man. One is בְּלֹא רְאוֹת, as explained above. The other is (*Deut.* 19:4) בִּבְלִי־דַעַת, *without knowledge* [i.e., one who was in this particular case without knowledge, not one who is generally unaware]. There is a general rule of hermeneutics that whenever there are two verses which would seem to exclude the same thing, they are actually intended to include it. Therefore, R' Meir includes the blind man in the law of exile (*Tos. Yom Tov* from *Gem.* 9b). The halachah, however, is in accordance with R' Yehudah (*Rav; Rambam, Hil. Rotzeach* 6:14).

הַשּׂוֹנֵא אֵינוֹ גוֹלֶה. רַבִּי יוֹסֵי בַּר־יְהוּדָה אוֹמֵר: הַשּׂוֹנֵא נֶהֱרָג מִפְּנֵי שֶׁהוּא כְמוּעָד. רַבִּי שִׁמְעוֹן אוֹמֵר: יֵשׁ שׂוֹנֵא גוֹלֶה וְיֵשׁ שׂוֹנֵא שֶׁאֵינוֹ גוֹלֶה. זֶה הַכְּלָל: כָּל־שֶׁהוּא יָכוֹל לוֹמַר לְדַעַת הָרַג, אֵינוֹ גוֹלֶה; וְשֶׁלֹּא לְדַעַת הָרַג, הֲרֵי זֶה גוֹלֶה.

[ד] **לְהֵיכָן** גּוֹלִין? לְעָרֵי מִקְלָט: לְשָׁלֹשׁ שֶׁבְּעֵבֶר הַיַּרְדֵּן, וּלְשָׁלֹשׁ שֶׁבְּאֶרֶץ כְּנַעַן, שֶׁנֶּאֱמַר: ,,אֵת שְׁלֹשׁ הֶעָרִים תִּתְּנוּ מֵעֵבֶר

יד אברהם

הַשּׂוֹנֵא אֵינוֹ גוֹלֶה. — *An enemy is not exiled.*

An enemy is defined in this case as anyone who did not speak to another for three days out of enmity for him. If he then killed him unintentionally he is not exiled *(Rav; Rambam, Hil. Rotzeach* 6:10).

The cities of refuge do not afford him any asylum since he is assumed to have killed his victim almost intentionally. This is derived from the verse *(Num.* 35:23): וְהוּא לֹא אוֹיֵב לוֹ, *and he is not his enemy (Rav; Rambam, Hil. Rotzeach* 6:10). His sin is therefore too grave to be expiated by exile.

Tos. Yom Tov points out that this is similar to the enemy who is disqualified from testifying against the one to whom he has not spoken for three days, as in *Sanhedrin* 3:5.

רַבִּי יוֹסֵי בַּר־יְהוּדָה אוֹמֵר: הַשּׂוֹנֵא נֶהֱרָג מִפְּנֵי שֶׁהוּא כְמוּעָד. — *R' Yose bar Yehudah says: An enemy is executed because he is considered forewarned.*

[I.e., he is put to death by *beis din* since the murder is considered to have been carried out intentionally.] Although he was not warned by the witnesses before the killing, and the rule is that a person is not executed by *beis din* unless he was forewarned, in this case it is not necessary since it is as though he was warned. The reason is that in R' Yose bar Yehudah's opinion the witnesses' pre-crime warning is necessary only to ascertain that the crime was committed intentionally, which can be assumed in this case *(Tif. Yis.* from *Gem.* 9a).

רַבִּי שִׁמְעוֹן אוֹמֵר: יֵשׁ שׂוֹנֵא גוֹלֶה וְיֵשׁ שׂוֹנֵא שֶׁאֵינוֹ גוֹלֶה. — *R' Shimon says: Some enemies are exiled and some enemies are not exiled.*

I.e., there are some cases in which an enemy slays his rival unintentionally, in which his action may be assumed to have been close to intentional, as the previous *Tanna* ruled. There are, however, other cases in which even an enemy cannot be assumed to have committed the murder intentionally and he would then be exiled *(Rabbeinu Yehonasan).*

זֶה הַכְּלָל: כָּל־שֶׁהוּא יָכוֹל לוֹמַר לְדַעַת הָרַג, אֵינוֹ גוֹלֶה; — *This is the rule: Anyone concerning whom it can be said [that] he killed intentionally, is not exiled;*

An example of this is the person tarring his roof and the roller slips out of hand, falling on his enemy and killing him. Although this is generally judged an unintentional slaying, for which the killer is exiled (mishnah 1), since this killer was an enemy of his victim, we suspect that he intentionally let the roller slip out of his hand *(Tos. Yom Tov* from *Gem.* 9b).

Similarly, a person letting down a cask with a rope who had it slip out of his hand and fall on his enemy and kill him

2 An enemy is not exiled. R' Yose bar Yehudah says:
4 An enemy is executed because he is considered forewarned. R' Shimon says: Some enemies are exiled and some enemies are not exiled. This is the rule: Anyone concerning whom it can be said [that] he killed intentionally, is not exiled; but [if it is clear] that he killed unintentionally, he is exiled.

4. Where are they exiled? To the cities of refuge: to the three on the other side of the Jordan, and to the three in the land of Canaan, as it is said (*Num.* 35:14):

would not be exiled (*Rabbeinu Yehonasan*).

וְשֶׁלֹּא לָדַעַת הָרַג, הֲרֵי זֶה גוֹלֶה. — *but [if it is clear] that he killed unintentionally, he is exiled.*

I.e., if it is certain that he killed unintentionally, e.g., if he was letting down a cask with a rope, and the rope broke, causing the cask to fall upon his enemy and kill him. Such an accident is considered unlikely to have been intentional (*Tos. Yom Tov* from *Gem.* 9b).

The halachah follows the opinion of the anonymous *Tanna,* that an enemy is neither exiled nor executed (*Rambam, Rotzeach* 6:10).

4.

לְהֵיכָן גּוֹלִין? לְעָרֵי מִקְלָט: — *Where are they exiled? To the cities of refuge:*

[The unwitting murderers who are liable to exile are exiled to one of the six refuge cities designated for this purpose. These cities were regular cities, inhabited by the Levites (see *Joshua* ch. 19, and *I Chronicles* ch. 6).]

לְשָׁלֹשׁ שֶׁבְּעֵבֶר הַיַּרְדֵּן, — *to the three on the other side of the Jordan,*

I.e., Betzer in the territory of Reuven, Ramoth in Gilead in the territory of Gad, and Golan in Bashan in the territory of the half-tribe of Menasheh (*Gem.* 9b from *Deut.* 4:43, *Joshua* 20:8).

וּלְשָׁלֹשׁ שֶׁבְּאֶרֶץ כְּנַעַן, — *and to the three in the land of Canaan,*

I.e., to the primary area of Eretz Yisrael, which lay west of the Jordan. These three were: Hebron in the territory of Judah, Shechem in the mountain region of Ephraim, and Kedesh in the mountain region of Naftali (*Gem.* 9b from *Joshua* 20:7).

The two sets of cities were located parallel to one another. Hebron was parallel to Betzer; Shechem was parallel to Ramoth; Kedesh was parallel to Golan (*Gem.* ibid.).

[Betzer was located southwest of Aroer at the same latitude as Hebron. Ramoth Gilead is identified as the city called Kalet Alrabet on one of the highest peaks of Mount Gilead to the north of Wadi Zerki (Yabok). Golan's location is not known exactly; it is however believed to be Jaulan, north of the Yarmuk.]

The *Gemara* (9b) attributes the uneven distribution of cities of refuge [there were nine-and-a-half tribes living in Eretz Yisrael proper, while only two-and-a-half tribes lived on the east bank] to the fact that there were more murderers in Gilead.

[This does not mean that murder was rampant in the Trans-Jordan, only that its rate of occurrence was disproportion-

לַיַּרְדֵּן וְאֵת שְׁלֹשׁ הֶעָרִים תִּתְּנוּ בְּאֶרֶץ כְּנָעַן, וגו׳.״ עַד שֶׁלֹּא נִבְחֲרוּ שָׁלֹשׁ שֶׁבְּאֶרֶץ יִשְׂרָאֵל, לֹא הָיוּ שָׁלֹשׁ שֶׁבְּעֵבֶר הַיַּרְדֵּן קוֹלְטוֹת, שֶׁנֶּאֱמַר: „שֵׁשׁ עָרֵי מִקְלָט תִּהְיֶינָה״ — עַד־שֶׁיִּהְיוּ שֶׁשְׁתָּן קוֹלְטוֹת כְּאֶחָד.

[ה] **וּמְכֻוָּנוֹת** לָהֶן דְּרָכִים מִזּוֹ לָזוֹ, שֶׁנֶּאֱמַר: „תָּכִין לְךָ הַדֶּרֶךְ וְשִׁלַּשְׁתָּ, וגו׳.״ וּמוֹסְרִין לָהֶן שְׁנֵי תַלְמִידֵי חֲכָמִים שֶׁמָּא יַהַרְגֶנּוּ

יד אברהם

ately higher there than in the rest of the land.]

The question arises, however, why would more murderers in the Trans-Jordan require that there be a greater concentration of cities of refuge? These cities were designed to protect an individual who committed an *unintentional murder*, not a *deliberate* one.

Tosafos answer on the basis of a principle of Divine justice which the *Gemara* (10b) expresses: An individual who deliberately murders another without witnesses will ultimately die through an accidental murder. *Tosafos*, therefore, assert that the disproportionate number of murderers in the Trans-Jordan were people who murdered intentionally, but without witnesses. God therefore arranged for them to be killed inadvertently, and thus there was a need for a greater proportion of cities of refuge (see *Maharsha*).

Ramban (Numbers 35:14) maintains that although these people committed intentional murders, they feigned having killed accidentally. It was therefore necessary to have a greater proportion of cities of refuge, since it was not possible to determine who indeed was telling the truth.

Gur Aryeh (Numbers 35:14) explains that since Gilead was a land where intentional murder was frequent, life was not valued so highly. It therefore became a place where more accidental murders occurred as well, since people were less sensitive to the necessity of being careful in regard to another's life.

Maharsha suggests that there was a need for these cities for those individuals who committed intentional murders as well, since both intentional and unintentional murders fled to the cities of refuge before their trial (see mishnah 6).

שֶׁנֶּאֱמַר: „אֵת שְׁלֹשׁ הֶעָרִים תִּתְּנוּ מֵעֵבֶר לַיַּרְדֵּן וְאֵת שְׁלֹשׁ הֶעָרִים תִּתְּנוּ בְּאֶרֶץ כְּנָעַן, וגו׳.״ — *as it is said (Num. 35:14): 'Three of the cities you shall place on the other side of the Jordan, and three of the cities you shall place in the land of Canaan,' etc.*

These were the six primary cities of refuge. In fact, however, the forty-two cities given to the Levites *(Num.* 35:6) also served as cities of refuge. The difference between the primary six and the additional forty-two is that the six cities protected the unintentional murderers from vengeance by the *goel hadam* whether or not he intended the city to protect him, whereas the forty-two cities of the Levites protected him only if protection was his intention for moving there *(Rav, Tos. Yom Tov* from *Gem.* 10a).

Minchas Chinuch (502) interprets *Rashi* (10a) to mean that the additional forty-two Levitical cities which served as auxiliary cities of refuge protected the unintentional murderer only if, at the time he entered the city, he intended that the city to protect him. However, if he entered without such intention, either by not being aware of its power or by being transported into the city while asleep or unconscious, and he later decided to take advantage of the city's protection, it would not afford him protection.

עַד־שֶׁלֹּא נִבְחֲרוּ שָׁלֹשׁ שֶׁבְּאֶרֶץ יִשְׂרָאֵל, לֹא הָיוּ שָׁלֹשׁ שֶׁבְּעֵבֶר הַיַּרְדֵּן קוֹלְטוֹת, — *As long as*

Three of the cities you shall place on the other side of the Jordan, and three of the cities you shall place in the land of Canaan, etc. As long as the three in Eretz Yisrael were not yet chosen, the three on the other side of the Jordan did not afford refuge, as it is said (*Num.* 35:13): *They shall be six cities of refuge* — until all six of them afford refuge simultaneously.

5. Direct roads were laid out from one to another, as it is said (*Deut.* 19:3): *Prepare the way for yourself and divide . . . in three places, etc.* They would appoint for them two Torah scholars so that he should not kill

YAD AVRAHAM

the three in Eretz Yisrael were not yet chosen, the three on the other side of the Jordan did not afford refuge,

[The three cities of refuge on the east side of the Jordan were designated by Moshe prior to the crossing into Eretz Yisrael, as stated in *Deut.* 4:41-43. However, they did not actually afford refuge until the three cities in Eretz Yisrael were also formally established.]

שֶׁנֶּאֱמַר: „שֵׁשׁ עָרֵי מִקְלָט תִּהְיֶינָה" — עַד־שֶׁיִּהְיוּ שֶׁשְּׁתָּן קוֹלְטוֹת כְּאֶחָד. — *as it is said (Num. 35:13): 'They shall be six cities of refuge' — until all six of them afford refuge simultaneously.*

[I.e., the Torah teaches that they do not begin to function as refuge cities until there are six of them.]

Moshe, who was not destined to cross into Canaan, nevertheless designated them even though they served no purpose until some time later. In doing so he said, 'Since [the opportunity to do] a *mitzvah* has come my way, let me fulfill it' (*Tos. Yom Tov* from *Gem.* 10a).

5.

וּמְכֻוָּנוֹת לָהֶן דְּרָכִים מִזּוֹ לָזוֹ, — *Direct roads were laid out from one to another,*

The roads were constructed in such a manner that from any city there was a direct road leading to one of the refuge cities. Signs were posted at every crossroads, upon which the word מִקְלָט [*refuge*] was inscribed, to direct the murderer in his flight to a city of refuge (*Rav* from *Gem.* 10b).

שֶׁנֶּאֱמַר: „תָּכִין לְךָ הַדֶּרֶךְ וְשִׁלַּשְׁתָּ, וְגוֹ'." — *as it is said (Deut. 19:3): 'Prepare the way for yourself and divide . . . in three places,' etc.*

I.e., you shall prepare the road to facilitate travel upon it (*Tos. Yom Tov* from *Gem.* 10b).

Rambam (*Hil. Rotzeach* 8:5) elaborates: 'The *beis din* are required to see that the roads leading to the cities of refuge are direct and to repair and widen them. They must remove all obstacles and obstructions from them, leaving neither mound, valley, nor stream, but they must make a bridge over it so as not to hinder the fleeing slayer, as it is said: *Prepare the way for yourself.* The width of the road to the refuge cities must be no less than thirty-two cubits.'

וּמוֹסְרִין לָהֶן שְׁנֵי תַלְמִידֵי חֲכָמִים שֶׁמָּא יַהַרְגֶנּוּ בַּדֶּרֶךְ, — *They would appoint for them two Torah scholars so that he should not kill him on the way,*

The following mishnah teaches that all murderers initially run to the refuge cities for safety. *Beis din* would then send for the murderer to appear in court so that it could try him and decide on a

בַּדֶּרֶךְ, וִידַבְּרוּ אֵלָיו. רַבִּי מֵאִיר אוֹמֵר: אַף הוּא מְדַבֵּר עַל־יְדֵי עַצְמוֹ, שֶׁנֶּאֱמַר: „וְזֶה דְּבַר הָרֹצֵחַ.״

[ו] **רַבִּי** יוֹסֵי בַר־יְהוּדָה אוֹמֵר: בַּתְּחִלָּה, אֶחָד שׁוֹגֵג וְאֶחָד מֵזִיד מַקְדִּימִין לְעָרֵי מִקְלָט, וּבֵית דִּין שׁוֹלְחִין וּמְבִיאִין אוֹתוֹ מִשָּׁם. מִי שֶׁנִּתְחַיֵּב מִיתָה בְּבֵית דִּין, הֲרָגוּהוּ, וְשֶׁלֹּא נִתְחַיֵּב

יד אברהם

proper punishment. If he deserved execution, he was executed; if he indeed deserved exile, they sent him back to the city of refuge. Our mishnah teaches that if he was found to deserve exile, *beis din* appointed two Torah scholars to escort him back to the city of refuge, so that the *goel hadam* should not kill him on the way (*Tos. Yom Tov* from *Rambam, Hil. Rotzeach* 5:8).

וִידַבְּרוּ אֵלָיו. — *and they would speak to him.*

I.e., the two Torah scholars should protect the murderer by speaking to the *goel hadam*. They say to him, 'Do not behave like a murderer; the incident occurred inadvertently' (*Gem.* 10b).

The Sages prescribed sending Torah scholars to appeal to his reason and conscience, rather than sending along bodyguards to physically protect him from the vengeance of the *goel hadam*, because violence begets violence and they feared that he would organize a band of stronger men and overpower them (*Tif. Yis.*).

רַבִּי מֵאִיר אוֹמֵר: אַף הוּא מְדַבֵּר עַל־יְדֵי עַצְמוֹ, — *R' Meir says: He, too, should speak for himself,*

[According to our reading, *he too*, R' Meir concurs with the Sages that they appoint two Torah scholars to speak for him. He differs only insofar as he requires the murderer to speak for himself in addition to the intervention of the Torah scholars.] *Rav*, however, explains that R' Meir means that there is no need for the two Torah scholars to speak for him; he argues for himself. Obviously, *Rav* did not have our reading, but one which omitted the word אַף, *too*. His reading was: הוּא מְדַבֵּר עַל־יְדֵי עַצְמוֹ, *He would speak for himself*. *Rambam*, too, in his *Comm.*, explains R' Meir in this manner, and the *baraisa* in the *Gemara* appears to support this reading (*Tos. Yom Tov*).

שֶׁנֶּאֱמַר: „וְזֶה דְּבַר הָרֹצֵחַ.״ — *as it is said* (*Deut.* 19:4): *'And this is the matter* [lit. *word*] *of the murderer.'*

[In the simple meaning of the verse, the word דְּבַר, literally *word*, is taken in the sense of *matter*, i.e., this is the law of the murderer. However, since the literal meaning is *word*, the Rabbis interpret it exegetically to mean that the murderer is obligated to speak up. This intimates that the murderer should speak for himself.]

The Rabbis, however, replied to R' Meir that the intervention of others is more efficacious than the pleading of the one involved (*Tos. Yom Tov* from *Gem.* 10b).

This explanation follows the editions of the mishnah which omit the word אַף, *too*, thus explaining that the Sages assert that we send two Torah scholars to speak for the murderer, while R' Meir maintains that the two Torah scholars are not necessary; rather he speaks on his own behalf. To rebut this argument, the Sages replied that the presence of the scholars is necessary because the intervention of others is more efficacious. According to our editions, however, R' Meir concurs with the Sages that the two Torah scholars speak for him. He differs only insofar as he requires the murderer to speak for himself as well. Accordingly, the reply that the intervention of others is more efficacious is no rebuttal, since R' Meir agrees

him on the way, and they would speak to him. R' Meir says: He, too, should speak for himself, as it is said (*Deut.* 19:4): *And this is the matter of the murderer.*

6. R' Yose bar Yehudah says: To begin with, both the unintentional and the intentional [murderers] hasten to the cities of refuge, and the court summons and brings him from there. Whoever is found by the court to be liable to the death penalty they execute, and whoever is found not to be liable to the death penalty

YAD AVRAHAM

that the presence of the two Torah scholars is necessary. *Ritva*, therefore, quotes his teachers, who explain the Sages' reply to be that the verse וְזֶה דְּבַר הָרֹצֵחַ, *this is the word of the murderer*, which R' Meir cites as support for his view, teaches many other things, as below (mishnah 8), and it thus need not be taken as teaching the lesson that R' Meir ascribes to it.

The halachah is not in accordance with R' Meir *(Rav; Rambam, Hil. Rotzeach* 5:8).

Some rule that the Torah scholars admonish the citizens of the cities of refuge not to denigrate the unintentional murderer, since the murder was unintentional *(Meiri)*.

6.

רַבִּי יוֹסֵי בַּר־יְהוּדָה אוֹמֵר: בַּתְּחִלָּה, — *R' Yose bar Yehudah says: To begin with,*

I.e., the judgment of every murderer begins by ... *(Tos. Yom Tov* from *Rashi* on *Gem.; Tif. Yis.)*.

אֶחָד שׁוֹגֵג וְאֶחָד מֵזִיד מַקְדִּימִין לְעָרֵי מִקְלָט, — *both the unintentional and the intentional* [*murderer*] *hasten to the cities of refuge,*

[I.e., all murderers, whether they killed intentionally or unintentionally, initially flee to the cities of refuge.]

This ruling is stated in the Torah *(Deut.* 19:11): וְכִי־יִהְיֶה אִישׁ שֹׂנֵא לְרֵעֵהוּ וְאָרַב לוֹ וְקָם עָלָיו וְהִכָּהוּ נֶפֶשׁ וָמֵת וְנָס אֶל־אַחַת הֶעָרִים הָאֵל, *Now should a man be an enemy to his neighbor, and lie in wait for him and waylay him and strike him a mortal blow and he die, he shall flee to one of these cities (Tos. Yom Tov* from *Rashi* on *Gem.; Sifre* ad loc.).

וּבֵית דִּין שׁוֹלְחִין וּמְבִיאִין אוֹתוֹ מִשָּׁם. — *and the court summons and brings him from there.*

I.e., the *beis din* of the city in which the victim was killed had the murderer returned to the city for trial *(Meiri; Rambam, Hil. Rotzeach* 5:7).

מִי שֶׁנִּתְחַיֵּב מִיתָה בְּבֵית דִּין, הֲרָגוּהוּ, — *Whoever is found by the court to be liable to the death penalty they execute,*

[I.e., if he killed before witnesses after having been warned, he is put to death.]

The *baraisa* derives this from *(Deut.* 19:12): וְנָתְנוּ אֹתוֹ בְּיַד גֹּאֵל הַדָּם וָמֵת, *and they shall deliver him into the hands of the avenger of the blood, and he shall die* (10b). The intention is that he is delivered to the *beis din* to execute the will of the *goel hadam*, viz., to put him to death *(Meiri)*. Others rule that he was literally delivered into the hands of the *goel hadam*, whose *mitzvah* it was to dispatch him. Should the *goel hadam* refuse or should he be unable to do so, or if there is no *goel hadam*, the murderer is executed by *beis din (Rambam, Hil. Rotzeach* 1:2).

וְשֶׁלֹּא נִתְחַיֵּב מִיתָה, — *and whoever is found not to be liable to the death*

מכות
ב/ו

מִיתָה, פְּטָרוּהוּ. מִי שֶׁנִּתְחַיֵּב גָּלוּת, מַחֲזִירִין אוֹתוֹ לִמְקוֹמוֹ, שֶׁנֶּאֱמַר: „וְהֵשִׁיבוּ אוֹתוֹ הָעֵדָה אֶל־עִיר מִקְלָטוֹ, וגו׳.״

אֶחָד מָשׁוּחַ בְּשֶׁמֶן הַמִּשְׁחָה, וְאֶחָד הַמְרֻבֶּה בִבְגָדִים, וְאֶחָד שֶׁעָבַר מִמְּשִׁיחָתוֹ — מַחֲזִירִין אֶת־הָרוֹצֵחַ. רַבִּי יְהוּדָה אוֹמֵר: אַף מְשׁוּחַ מִלְחָמָה מַחֲזִיר אֶת־הָרוֹצֵחַ. לְפִיכָךְ אִמּוֹתֵיהֶן שֶׁל־כֹּהֲנִים

יד אברהם

penalty,

[I.e., if he is found to be innocent.]

.פְּטָרוּהוּ — *they free.*

[I.e., he is neither executed nor exiled, but set free.]

[This apparently refers to one who killed accidentally or almost accidentally, and is therefore freed even from exile. Should he kill almost intentionally or with negligence, although he cannot be executed or exiled, he is, according to *Rambam (Hil. Rotzeach* 6:4), subject to the vengeance of the *goel hadam,* who may kill him wherever he meets him.]

,מִי שֶׁנִּתְחַיֵּב גָּלוּת — *Whoever is found liable to exile,*

[I.e., if it was determined that he killed unintentionally, and fit the various criteria for exile delineated above.]

מַחֲזִירִין אוֹתוֹ לִמְקוֹמוֹ, שֶׁנֶּאֱמַר: „וְהֵשִׁיבוּ אוֹתוֹ הָעֵדָה אֶל־עִיר מִקְלָטוֹ, וְגו׳.״ — *they return to his place, as it is said (Num. 35:25): 'And the congregation shall return him to his city of refuge,' etc.*

[I.e., they would send him back to the city of refuge to which he had fled originally.]

It was on this trip that *beis din* sent two Torah scholars to escort the murderer and speak on his behalf to the *goel hadam.* Since it has already been ascertained that he killed inadvertently, they can appeal to the *goel hadam* not to kill him. On his way to the *beis din* for his trial, however, they cannot possibly plead his innocence, since it has not yet been determined *(Tos. Yom Tov,* mishnah 5). On this trip, therefore, they must provide him with bodyguards *(Nassan Piryo).*

The verse ends with the statement that the murderer must remain in exile until the death of the *Kohen Gadol.* Therefore, as a continuation, the mishnah proceeds to delineate which *Kohanim Gedolim* release the murderer from his exile upon their death.

,אֶחָד מָשׁוּחַ בְּשֶׁמֶן הַמִּשְׁחָה — *Whether [the Kohen Gadol] was one anointed with the anointment oil,*

The Torah *(Exodus* 30:22-33) commands that a special blend of oils and spices be prepared to be used for anointing the Tabernacle vessels and new *Kohanim Gedolim.* This method of inaugurating new *Kohanim Gedolim* persisted until the reign of King Yoshiah, when the cruse of anointing oil was hidden by him *(Rashi),* along with the Ark of the Tablets and other Temple artifacts, to prevent their capture by gentiles *(Tif. Yis.* from *Yoma* 52b).

,וְאֶחָד הַמְרֻבֶּה בִבְגָדִים — *or one [inaugurated by donning] the additional vestments,*

These are the *Kohanim Gedolim* who served from Yoshiah's reign until the destruction of the First Temple, and those who served throughout the Second Temple. During these periods, the *Kohen Gadol* was inaugurated by wearing the vestments of the *Kohen Gadol,* which were more numerous [*additional*] than those of the ordinary *Kohen (Rav; Rashi).*

2 they free. Whoever is found liable to exile, they return to
6 his place, as it is said (*Num.* 35:25): *And the congregation shall return him to his city of refuge, etc.*

Whether [the *Kohen Gadol*] was one anointed with the anointment oil, or one [inaugurated by donning] the additional vestments, or one who has stepped down from his position — [his death] allows the murderer to return. R' Yehudah says: Even [the death of] the *Kohen* Anointed for Battle allows the murderer to return.

YAD AVRAHAM

Ritva contends that according to the *Gemara* (11b), the *Kohen Gadol* anointed with the anointment oil and the *Kohen Gadol* wearing the additional vestments could both have served during the same period in history. He therefore explains that the mishnah deals with a *Kohen Gadol* who journeyed far from Jerusalem and was detained or was captured there. To take his place, another *Kohen Gadol* was appointed. This *Kohen Gadol* was not anointed, however, since we do not anoint two *Kohanim Gedolim* at the same time. Accordingly, his initiation into the *Kehunah Gedolah* is only by performing the service in the Temple wearing the four extra vestments reserved for the *Kohen Gadol*, as in *Yoma* 7:5 (cf. *Tos. Shantz* and *Tos., Nazir* 47b).

— וְאֶחָד שֶׁעָבַר מִמְּשִׁיחָתוֹ — *or one who has stepped down from his position* [lit. *from his anointment*] —

If the *Kohen Gadol* experienced a seminal emission on Yom Kippur, thereby becoming *tamei* and unfit to perform the Temple service for that day [which only a *Kohen Gadol* may perform], another *Kohen Gadol* is appointed in his stead to perform the Yom Kippur service. When the first *Kohen Gadol* recovers, he is reinstated, and the substitute becomes one who is no longer serving as an anointed *Kohen Gadol* (*Tos. Yom Tov*).

מַחֲזִירִין אֶת־הָרוֹצֵחַ. — [*his death*] *allows the murderer to return.*

I.e., if one of these dies, even if the other two are still alive, the murderer is allowed to return to his home (*Rav* from *Gem.* 11b).

This ruling is derived from the fact that the Torah repeats the law that the murderer returns home upon the death of the *Kohen Gadol* three times (*Rav* from *Gem.* 11a).

רַבִּי יְהוּדָה אוֹמֵר: אַף מְשׁוּחַ מִלְחָמָה — *R' Yehudah says: Even* [*the death of*] *the Kohen Anointed for Battle*

In *Deut.* 20:1-10 the Torah teaches that prior to leaving for battle the armies of Israel were to be addressed by a *Kohen* specially designated for this purpose. [See the verses and *Sotah* 8:1 for the text of his charge.] This *Kohen* was especially anointed for this task and was consequently known as the *Kohen Anointed for Battle* (*Rashi*).

מַחֲזִיר אֶת־הָרוֹצֵחַ. — *allows the murderer to return.*

[I.e., he too is classified as the equivalent of a *Kohen Gadol* in this respect, so that upon his death the murderer is permitted to leave the city of refuge and return home.]

R' Yehudah bases his ruling on *Deut.* 35:23, where the return of the murderer upon the death of the *Kohen Gadol* is mentioned a fourth time, thus referring to a fourth *Kohen Gadol* whose passing would release the murderer. The *Tanna Kamma*, however, does not count this as alluding to another *Kohen Gadol*, since the word גָּדוֹל, *Gadol*, is not mentioned (*Rav* from *Gem.* 11a). He considers it, therefore, as a reference to one of the three *Kohanim Gedolim* already mentioned (*Tos. Yom Tov* from *Gem.* ad loc.).

מְסַפְּקוֹת לָהֶן מִחְיָה וּכְסוּת, כְּדֵי שֶׁלֹּא יִתְפַּלְּלוּ עַל־בְּנֵיהֶן שֶׁיָּמוּתוּ.

מִשֶּׁנִּגְמַר דִּינוֹ, מֵת כֹּהֵן גָּדוֹל, הֲרֵי זֶה אֵינוֹ גוֹלֶה. אִם עַד־שֶׁלֹּא נִגְמַר דִּינוֹ, מֵת כֹּהֵן גָּדוֹל, וּמִנּוּ אַחֵר תַּחְתָּיו, וּלְאַחַר מִכֵּן נִגְמַר דִּינוֹ, חוֹזֵר בְּמִיתָתוֹ שֶׁל־שֵׁנִי.

[ז] **נִגְמַר** דִּינוֹ בְּלֹא כֹהֵן גָּדוֹל, הַהוֹרֵג כֹּהֵן גָּדוֹל, וְכֹהֵן גָּדוֹל שֶׁהָרַג, אֵינוֹ יוֹצֵא

יד אברהם

The halachah is in accordance with the *Tanna Kamma (Rav; Rambam, Hil. Rotzeach* 8:9).

לְפִיכָךְ, — *Therefore,*

[Since unintentional murderers return from exile upon the death of the *Kohen Gadol.*]

אִמּוֹתֵיהֶן שֶׁל־כֹּהֲנִים — *the mothers of the Kohanim*

[I.e., the mothers of the *Kohanim Gedolim.*]

מְסַפְּקוֹת לָהֶן מִחְיָה וּכְסוּת, כְּדֵי שֶׁלֹּא יִתְפַּלְּלוּ עַל־בְּנֵיהֶן שֶׁיָּמוּתוּ. — *would supply them with food and clothing, so that they should not pray for their sons to die.*

[I.e., they would supply food and clothing to the exiled murderers living in the cities of refuge to induce them not to pray for their sons' (the *Kohanim Gedolim)* early death to release them from exile.]

It would seem from this that their prayers for the death of the *Kohen Gadol* might be heeded. The reason for this is that the *Kohen Gadol* is somewhat at fault for the inadvertent death of the victim, and thus the murderer's exile. Had he prayed with the proper devotion for the welfare of the nation such incidents would not occur *(Rav* from *Gem.* 11b).

מִשֶּׁנִּגְמַר דִּינוֹ, מֵת כֹּהֵן גָּדוֹל, — *[If,] after his sentence was passed, the Kohen Gadol died,*

I.e., if the *Kohen Gadol* died after the sentence of exile was passed but before the murderer actually went into exile *(Rav).*

הֲרֵי זֶה אֵינוֹ גוֹלֶה. — *he is not exiled.*

Once he is sentenced it is considered as though he is already exiled. Therefore, he is freed from his exile upon the death of the *Kohen Gadol (Rav).*

Tos. Yom Tov questions this explanation since this concept, that the passing of the sentence is tantamount to its being implemented, is not found anywhere else. He therefore explains that it is not the exile that expiates the sin but rather the death of the *Kohen Gadol.* This can be seen by the fact that the death of the *Kohen Gadol* releases him regardless of how long a stay he had endured. We can therefore understand that just as the demise of the *Kohen Gadol* can atone for his sin while the murderer is in exile, it can also atone for his sin immediately after sentencing *(Tos. Yom Tov).*

Interestingly, *Meiri* states the same reason as *Rav,* adding that although the murderer was not actually punished by being exiled, the anticipation of his exile humbled him to the extent that his sin was expiated by his humbling in conjunction with the death of the *Kohen Gadol.* [This solves the difficulty raised by *Tos. Yom Tov* as well.]

אִם עַד־שֶׁלֹּא נִגְמַר דִּינוֹ, מֵת כֹּהֵן גָּדוֹל, וּמִנּוּ אַחֵר תַּחְתָּיו, — *If the Kohen Gadol died before his sentence was passed, and they appointed another one in his stead,*

2
7

Therefore, the mothers of the *Kohanim* would supply them with food and clothing, so that they should not pray for their sons to die.

[If,] after his sentence was passed, the *Kohen Gadol* died, he is not exiled. If the *Kohen Gadol* died before his sentence was passed, and they appointed another one in his stead, and then his sentence was passed, he returns upon the death of the second one.

7. [If] his sentence was passed without a *Kohen Gadol*, [or if] he killed a *Kohen Gadol*, or [if] a *Kohen Gadol* killed, he never leaves there. He may not leave

YAD AVRAHAM

[I.e., the *Kohen Gadol* died before the murderer was sentenced to exile and another *Kohen Gadol* was appointed in his place.]

וּלְאַחַר מִכֵּן נִגְמַר דִּינוֹ, — *and then his sentence was passed,*

[I.e., after the appointment of the new *Kohen Gadol, beis din* sentenced him to exile.]

חוֹזֵר בְּמִיתָתוֹ שֶׁל־שֵׁנִי. — *he returns upon the death of the second one.*

This is based on *(Num.* 35:25): *And he shall dwell therein until the death of the Kohen Gadol whom he anointed with the holy oil.* The *Gemara* takes this to refer to the *Kohen Gadol* who was anointed in his time, i.e., when he became a murderer [meaning when he was revealed as a murderer] *(Gem.* 11b, *Rashi).*

Although this one was not a *Kohen Gadol* at the time of the slaying, he is still held accountable for not praying that the murderer be acquitted *(Gem.* ad loc.).

7.

נִגְמַר דִּינוֹ בְּלֹא כֹהֵן גָּדוֹל, — *[If] his sentence was passed without a Kohen Gadol,*

[This continues the case begun at the end of the last mishnah.] If, when the *beis din* sentenced him to exile, a new *Kohen Gadol* had not yet been appointed . . . *(Rav).*

הַהוֹרֵג כֹּהֵן גָּדוֹל, — *[or if] he killed a Kohen Gadol,*

[I.e., he killed the *Kohen Gadol* unintentionally] and no *Kohen Gadol* was appointed prior to his sentencing *(Tos. Yom Tov* from *Rambam, Hil. Rotzeach* 7:10; *Ritva, Meiri,* quoting *Rashi).*

וְכֹהֵן גָּדוֹל שֶׁהָרַג, — *or [if] a Kohen Gadol killed,*

This also refers to a case in which no *Kohen Gadol* was appointed until after the sentence was passed *(Tos. Yom Tov* from *Rambam, Hil. Rotzeach* 7:10; *Ritva, Meiri,* quoting *Rashi).*

אֵינוֹ יוֹצֵא מִשָּׁם לְעוֹלָם. — *he never leaves there.*

An unintentional murderer's sentence is tied to the lifespan of the *Kohen Gadol* serving at the moment of his sentencing. Consequently, if there is no *Kohen Gadol* at the time of his sentencing, there is no one whose death can release him from exile *(Rashi, Sanhedrin* 18b).

Others rule that in the last two cases, murders involving the *Kohen Gadol,* even if another *Kohen Gadol* is appointed prior to sentencing he may not leave the city of refuge upon the death of that *Kohen Gadol.* One who kills a *Kohen Gadol,* or a *Kohen Gadol* who kills, is guilty of a sin so great that it can

מִשָּׁם לְעוֹלָם. וְאֵינוֹ יוֹצֵא לֹא לְעֵדוּת מִצְוָה, וְלֹא לְעֵדוּת מָמוֹן, וְלֹא לְעֵדוּת נְפָשׁוֹת. וַאֲפִילוּ יִשְׂרָאֵל צְרִיכִים לוֹ, וַאֲפִילוּ שַׂר־צְבָא יִשְׂרָאֵל כְּיוֹאָב בֶּן־צְרוּיָה, אֵינוֹ יוֹצֵא מִשָּׁם לְעוֹלָם, שֶׁנֶּאֱמַר: „אֲשֶׁר נָס שָׁמָּה" — שָׁם תְּהֵא דִירָתוֹ; שָׁם תְּהֵא מִיתָתוֹ; שָׁם תְּהֵא קְבוּרָתוֹ.

כְּשֵׁם שֶׁהָעִיר קוֹלֶטֶת, כָּךְ תְּחוּמָהּ קוֹלֵט. רוֹצֵחַ

יד אברהם

never be expiated, and he must therefore remain in exile until his own death *(Ritva)*.

Rabbeinu Yehonasan follows this latter view but explains the reason to be that if one kills a *Kohen Gadol*, he has destroyed his own atonement, and he may therefore never leave the city. Should the *Kohen Gadol* commit a murder, since he himself is a *Kohen Gadol*, we do not consider the death of another *Kohen Gadol* appropriate to free him from the refuge city. Thus, he can leave the city only once he himself dies, so that his body may be buried in his ancestral plot.

וְאֵינוֹ יוֹצֵא — *He may not leave there*

I.e., all those exiled to a city of refuge may not leave even for the following reasons *(Tif. Yis.; Rambam, Hil. Rotzeach* 7:8). This is true both for those who may never come out of exile, as well as those who need only remain there until the demise of the *Kohen Gadol* *(Meiri)*.

Rabbeinu Chananel, however, disputes this and states that the following ruling applies only to those who may never leave the city of refuge, viz., the one whose sentence was passed without a *Kohen Gadol*, one who killed a *Kohen Gadol*, or a *Kohen Gadol* who killed. The one who may leave upon the demise of the *Kohen Gadol* may leave in the following cases as well.

לֹא לְעֵדוּת מִצְוָה, — *either for testimony related to a mitzvah,*

I.e., to testify concerning the sighting of the new moon *(Rav; Tif. Yis.)*. Neither may he go out to fulfill any *mitzvah* such as the pilgrimage to Jerusalem on the Three Festivals *(Tif. Yis.)*. *Rambam (Hil. Rotzeach* 7:8) adds: even to save a life with his testimony or to save someone from marauders, or from a river, a fire, or from a collapsed building.

Many commentators ask why it is not incumbent upon the murderer to leave in order to save a life. Since saving a life supersedes all *mitzvos* of the Torah, it should supersede the *mitzvah* of staying in the city of refuge as well. They reply that since he is jeopardizing his own life by leaving the city, because the moment he leaves the city the *goel hadam* is free to kill him, he is not required to jeopardize his own life to save another's. This is true even though the danger to the exile is doubtful while the danger to the other is imminent *(Einayim LaMishpat)*.

וְלֹא לְעֵדוּת מָמוֹן, וְלֹא לְעֵדוּת נְפָשׁוֹת. — *for testimony related to monetary cases, or for testimony related to capital cases.*

I.e., not only may he not go out to testify for a *mitzvah*, which is of lesser importance, but he may not even go out to testify in monetary cases, for which one normally bears a sin if he does not testify, as in *Lev.* 5:1. Furthermore, not only may he not go out to testify in monetary matters but even in capital cases, which are of graver importance, he may still not leave the city *(Ritva)*.

וַאֲפִילוּ יִשְׂרָאֵל צְרִיכִים לוֹ, — *Even if Israel needs him,*

Some editions read: even if *all* Israel needs him *(Rabbeinu Chananel; Rambam, Hil. Rotzeach* 7:8; *Meiri)*.

וַאֲפִילוּ שַׂר צְבָא יִשְׂרָאֵל כְּיוֹאָב בֶּן־צְרוּיָה, —

2 there either for testimony related to a *mitzvah*, for
7 testimony related to monetary cases, or for testimony related to capital cases. Even if Israel needs him, even if he is the general of the army of Israel like Yoav the son of Tzeruyah, he may never leave there, as it is said (*Num.* 35:25): *Who fled there — there* shall be his dwelling; *there* shall be his death; *there* shall be his burial.

Just as the city affords refuge, so its boundaries afford refuge. [If] a murderer went out of the boundary, and

YAD AVRAHAM

even if he is the general of the army of Israel like Yoav the son of Tzeruyah,

I.e., even if Israel needs him to lead them in war, because he is a great general like Yoav the son of Tzeruyah, who was King David's general (*Rambam, Hil. Rotzeach* 7:8).

אֵינוֹ יוֹצֵא מִשָּׁם לְעוֹלָם, — *he may never leave there,*

I.e., until the demise of the *Kohen Gadol* (*Tos. Yom Tov* from *Rambam, Hil. Rotzeach* 7:8); or if he is one of those who do not leave even upon the death of the *Kohen Gadol*, he never goes out at all (*Meiri*).

שֶׁנֶּאֱמַר: „אֲשֶׁר נָס שָׁמָּה"— — *as it is said (Num. 35:25): 'Who fled there' —*

This phrase is found three times in the Torah (*Num.* 35:11,25,26), to teach us three things, as follows (*Meiri* from *Tosefta* 2:2).

שָׁם תְּהֵא דִירָתוֹ; — *'there' shall be his dwelling;*

[I.e., he must always stay in the city.] *Shoshannim LeDavid* explains this to mean that he should dwell in the city proper, not on its outskirts.

שָׁם תְּהֵא מִיתָתוֹ; — *'there' shall be his death;*

I.e., even if the climate in the city is detrimental to his health and could cause his untimely death, he may not leave (*Tif. Yis.*).

שָׁם תְּהֵא קְבוּרָתוֹ. — *'there' shall be his burial.*

If he dies in the city of refuge, he must be buried there and cannot be taken to his ancestral plot. Similarly, if he dies before arriving at the city of exile, his remains are taken there for burial. Once the *Kohen Gadol* dies, however, he may be disinterred and reburied in his ancestral plot (*Gem.* 11b; *Rambam, Hil. Rotzeach* 7:3).

Although the cities of refuge were not permitted to be used for burial of the Levites who resided there, the unintentional murderers were buried there (*Gem.* 12a).

כְּשֵׁם שֶׁהָעִיר קוֹלֶטֶת, כָּךְ תְּחוּמָהּ קוֹלֵט. — *Just as the city affords refuge, so its boundaries afford refuge.*

The area of two thousand cubits surrounding the city on all sides is the boundary of the city. [Its most prominent application is in regard to the distance one may walk on the Sabbath; see General Introduction to ArtScroll *Eruvin* p. 10.] This two-thousand-cubit area affords refuge the same as the city proper. The moment the murderer enters the two-thousand-cubit area he is protected, and if the *goel hadam* should kill him there, he is liable as though he had slain him within the city (*Meiri*).

Even though these outskirts afford refuge, he must live in the city proper. This is learned from the words וְיָשַׁב בָּהּ, *and he shall dwell in it*, meaning that he must dwell in the city proper, not in its outskirts. The implication of this is that only dwelling there is prohib-

שֶׁיָּצָא חוּץ לַתְּחוּם, וּמְצָאוֹ גוֹאֵל הַדָּם – רַבִּי יוֹסֵי הַגְּלִילִי אוֹמֵר: מִצְוָה בְּיַד גּוֹאֵל הַדָּם, וּרְשׁוּת בְּיַד כָּל־אָדָם. רַבִּי עֲקִיבָא אוֹמֵר: רְשׁוּת בְּיַד גּוֹאֵל הַדָּם, וְכָל־אָדָם אֵין חַיָּבִין עָלָיו.

אִילָן שֶׁהוּא עוֹמֵד בְּתוֹךְ הַתְּחוּם וְנוֹפוֹ נוֹטֶה חוּץ לַתְּחוּם, אוֹ עוֹמֵד חוּץ לַתְּחוּם וְנוֹפוֹ נוֹטֶה לְתוֹךְ הַתְּחוּם, הַכֹּל הוֹלֵךְ אַחַר הַנּוֹף.

הָרַג בְּאוֹתָהּ הָעִיר, גּוֹלֶה מִשְּׁכוּנָה לִשְׁכוּנָה;

יד אברהם

ited, but the area does afford refuge *(Tos. Yom Tov).*

רוֹצֵחַ שֶׁיָּצָא חוּץ לַתְּחוּם, וּמְצָאוֹ גוֹאֵל הַדָּם – *[If] a murderer went out of the boundary, and the goel hadam encountered him —*

[I.e., if he leaves the city and goes beyond the two thousand cubits surrounding the city, where the *goel hadam* spots him.]

רַבִּי יוֹסֵי הַגְּלִילִי אוֹמֵר: מִצְוָה בְּיַד גּוֹאֵל הַדָּם, — *R' Yose HaGlili says: It is an obligation upon the goel hadam* [*to kill him*],

[I.e., it is incumbent upon the *goel hadam* to avenge the blood of his relative by killing the murderer.] This is based on *(Num.* 35:27): וְרָצַח גֹּאֵל הַדָּם אֶת־הָרֹצֵחַ, *the avenger of the blood shall murder the murderer (Tos. Yom Tov* from *Gem.* 12a).

וּרְשׁוּת בְּיַד כָּל־אָדָם. — *and it is optional for anyone else.*

[I.e., it is permissible, but not incumbent, for anyone else to kill him.]

רַבִּי עֲקִיבָא אוֹמֵר: רְשׁוּת בְּיַד גּוֹאֵל הַדָּם, — *R' Akiva says: It is optional for the goel hadam,*

R' Akiva explains וְרָצַח to mean *and he murders,* meaning he may murder, since Scripture does not use the construct יִרְצַח, which would unequivocally mean *he shall murder (Tos. Yom Tov* from *Gem.* 12a).

וְכָל־אָדָם אֵין חַיָּבִין עָלָיו. — *and anyone else is not liable for him.*

The Torah, when referring to the murderer states: אֵין לוֹ דָּם, *he is without blood.* This expression indicates that no one is liable for killing him. They are, however, forbidden to do so. On the other hand, once he leaves the refuge, the *goel hadam* is granted permission by the Torah to kill him if he is so inclined *(Rav; Ritva; Meiri).*

Tos. Yom Tov asks why one is not liable for the killing if it is forbidden to kill him. He explains that since the *goel hadam* has the option to kill him, he is already considered a dead man, designated by the Torah as אֵין לוֹ דָּם, *without blood.* Therefore, others are also exempt for killing him, even though they are forbidden to do so.

The halachah is in accordance with R' Akiva. However, this is only if the murderer leaves the city intentionally. Should he leave unintentionally, whoever kills him is himself liable to execution *(Rav* from *Gem.* 12a). The reason is that the crime of leaving the city of refuge should not be judged more severely than the actual murder. Just as one is executed only for an intentional murder and is exiled for an inadvertent one, so too for leaving the refuge city intentionally he may be put to death, while for leaving it accidentally he should be exiled [i.e., returned to his exile] *(Tos. Yom Tov* from *Gem.* 12a). However, *Rambam (Hil. Rotzeach* 5:11) understands the *Gemara's* conclusion to be that if the murderer leaves the city

2 the *goel hadam* encountered him — R′ Yose HaGlili
7 says: It is an obligation upon the *goel hadam* [to kill him], and it is optional for anyone else. R′ Akiva says: It is optional for the *goel hadam,* and anyone else is not liable for him.

[If] a tree was standing within the boundary and its branches extended beyond the boundary, or it was standing beyond the boundary and its branches extended into the boundary, everything follows the branches.

[If] he killed in that city, [he] is exiled from section to

accidentally, whoever kills him is liable only to exile. Only if someone should kill him within the city's boundaries is he himself liable to execution. This view is shared by *Meiri* (see *Tif. Yaacov).*

אִילָן שֶׁהוּא עוֹמֵד בְּתוֹךְ הַתְּחוּם וְנוֹפוֹ נוֹטֶה חוּץ לַתְּחוּם, — *[If] a tree was standing within the boundary and its branches extended beyond the boundary,*

[I.e., it was standing near the boundary of a city of refuge with its branches extending out beyond the boundary.]

אוֹ עוֹמֵד חוּץ לַתְּחוּם וְנוֹפוֹ נוֹטֶה לְתוֹךְ הַתְּחוּם, — *or it was standing beyond the boundary and its branches extended into the boundary,*

[I.e., into the two thousand cubits around the city of refuge. The question now is whether the area beneath the tree is considered part of the city's boundary, affording refuge to the murderer who stands beneath it.]

הַכֹּל הוֹלֵךְ אַחַר הַנּוֹף. — *everything follows the branches.*

The *Gemara* (12b) explains the mishnah to mean that we follow the branches as well as the trunk, and that they are included within the boundary either way. Should the tree stand within the boundary with its branches stretching beyond the boundary, as soon as the murderer stands under the branches, the city gives him refuge and he may not be killed. In this case, the branches follow the trunk. In the event that tree stands outside the boundary with its branches stretching into the boundary, the trunk follows the branches so that the murderer is safe if he reaches the trunk *(Rav* from *Gem.* 12b).

The reason the *Tanna* phrases this ruling in terms of *follows the branches* is because this is the novel part of his ruling. In regard to most legal matters, the branches follow the trunk. Accordingly, the *Tanna* tells us that in regard to refuge, the trunk also follows the branches, i.e., when it affords greater protection that way *(Tos. Yom Tov* from *Rashi* 12b).

הָרַג בְּאוֹתָהּ הָעִיר, — *[If] he killed in that city,*

I.e., if a murderer who fled to a city of refuge killed someone unintentionally while in that refuge city *(Tos. Yom Tov* from *Rashi).*

גּוֹלֶה מִשְּׁכוּנָה לִשְׁכוּנָה; — *[he] is exiled from section to section;*

I.e., he is exiled to another section within that same city, since he is not permitted to leave the city because of the first murder *(Rashi).* The *Gemara* (12b) bases this ruling on the wording of the verse *(Num.* 35:28): כִּי בְעִיר מִקְלָטוֹ יֵשֵׁב, *For in his city of refuge he shall remain,* meaning even if it has already afforded him refuge and he becomes liable to exile

וּבֶן־לֵוִי גּוֹלֶה מֵעִיר לְעִיר.

[ח] **כַּיּוֹצֵא** בוֹ, רוֹצֵחַ שֶׁגָּלָה לְעִיר מִקְלָטוֹ, וְרָצוּ אַנְשֵׁי הָעִיר לְכַבְּדוֹ, יֹאמַר לָהֶם: „רוֹצֵחַ אֲנִי.״ אָמְרוּ לוֹ: „אַף־עַל־פִּי־כֵן,״ יְקַבֵּל מֵהֶן, שֶׁנֶּאֱמַר: „וְזֶה דְּבַר הָרֹצֵחַ.״

מַעֲלִים הָיוּ שָׂכָר לַלְוִיִּם; דִּבְרֵי רַבִּי יְהוּדָה. רַבִּי מֵאִיר אוֹמֵר: לֹא הָיוּ מַעֲלִים לָהֶן שָׂכָר.

יד אברהם

again, it must still remain his city of refuge (*Tos. Yom Tov* from *Gem.* 12b).

וּבֶן־לֵוִי — *but a Levite*

I.e., a Levite residing in a city of refuge who killed someone inadvertently (*Tos. Yom Tov* from *Rashi*). [As explained above, the cities of refuge were given to the Levites to live in.]

גּוֹלֶה מֵעִיר לְעִיר. — *is exiled from city to city.*

Since he was never exiled to this city, he may leave it. He is therefore exiled to another of the Levitical cities (*Tos. Yom Tov* from *Rashi*).

8.

כַּיּוֹצֵא בוֹ, — *Similarly,*

This mishnah has no connection at all with the preceding one. It is therefore very peculiar that this mishnah begins with the word *similarly* (*Meiri*). Indeed, in *Tosefta* (2:2), *Yalkut Shimoni, Deut.* 19:4, *Meiri, Rabbeinu Yehonasan,* as well as in the Munich manuscript, it is omitted. There are many theories to account for its being included in the standard editions of the Mishnah and the Talmud. *Ritva* explains the connection in the following manner. The preceding mishnah dealt with the Levite who is exiled from city to city although his own city is also a city of refuge. This is in order to instill in him a feeling of humility. To this our mishnah adds that similarly, a murderer who goes into exile in a city of refuge must act humbly, and if the people wish to honor him, he must refuse that honor (see below).

Tos. Yom Tov theorizes that although these words are not relevant to our mishnah, they appear here in order to standardize the text of this mishnah with the identical mishnah in *Sheviis* (10:8), in the context of which this is relevant [see there].

In the Naples edition of the Mishnah, these words appear at the end of the preceding mishnah: A Levite is exiled from one city to a similar city. This version is shared by *Kos HaYeshuos* and *Meleches Shlomo.*

Others conjecture that this mishnah is connected to mishnah 5 in which R' Meir derives from the verse: וְזֶה דְּבַר הָרֹצֵחַ, *And this is the matter* [lit. *word*] *of the murderer,* that the murderer speaks for himself in pleading with the *goel hadam* to spare his life. Similarly, we derive from that verse that the murderer must speak to the people of the city and refuse the honor they wish to bestow upon him (*Tif. Yis.; Beis Pinchas*).

רוֹצֵחַ שֶׁגָּלָה לְעִיר מִקְלָטוֹ, וְרָצוּ אַנְשֵׁי הָעִיר לְכַבְּדוֹ, — *a murderer who went into exile in his city of refuge, and the people of the city wished to honor him,*

I.e., they wish to honor him because of his wisdom (*Rabbeinu Yehonasan*).

יֹאמַר לָהֶם: „רוֹצֵחַ אֲנִי.״ — *he should say to them, 'I am a murderer.'*

I am not worthy of such honor since this incident occurred to me (*Rabbeinu Yehonasan*).

2 section; but a Levite is exiled from city to city.

8 **8.** Similarly, a murderer who went into exile in his city of refuge, and the people of the city wished to honor him, he should say to them, 'I am a murderer.' [If] they said to him, 'Even so,' he may accept [the honor] from them, as it is said (*Deut.* 19:4): *And this is the matter of the murderer.*

They would pay rent to the Levites; [these are] the words of R' Yehudah. R' Meir says: They would not pay them rent.

YAD AVRAHAM

Meiri writes that he must publicize that he is humbled and saddened by the misfortune that occurred through him.

אָמְרוּ לוֹ: „אַף־עַל־פִּי־כֵן," — *[If] they said to him, 'Even so,'*

I.e., should the people of the city reply to the murderer that they nevertheless wish to honor him *(Rabbeinu Yehonasan).*

יְקַבֵּל מֵהֶן, — *he may accept* [*the honor*] *from them,*

He need not insist on declining the honor *(Rabbeinu Yehonasan).*

שֶׁנֶּאֱמַר: „וְזֶה דְּבַר הָרֹצֵחַ." — *as it is said (Deut. 19:4): 'And this is the matter* [lit. *word*] *of the murderer.'*

I.e., a mere word is sufficient. [He need not refuse the honor they wish to bestow upon him.] *(Tos. Yom Tov; Rabbeinu Yehonasan).*

Tosefta (2:2) states, however: 'You have only the first word.' [The apparent meaning is that the singular דְּבַר, *the word of*, implies that the murderer need decline but once and that suffices. After that, he may accept the honor they wish to bestow upon him.]

מַעֲלִים הָיוּ שָׂכָר לַלְוִיִּם; — *They would pay rent to the Levites;*

There were forty-two cities scattered throughout Israel which did not belong to the tribe in whose boundaries they were, but which were reserved for the Levites (see *Joshua* ch. 19; *I Chronicles* ch. 6). These forty-two Levitical cities also served as cities of refuge. If the murderer sought refuge in one of these cities he must pay rent to the owner of the house in which he resides *(Rav; Meiri; Rambam Comm.). Rashi* explains that the [neighboring] cities would pay rent to the Levites for the murderers' use of their houses. *Tos.* explain this to refer to the payment of taxes to the Levites for the use of their city.

דִּבְרֵי רַבִּי יְהוּדָה. — *[these are] the words of R' Yehudah.*

This law applies only in the case of the forty-two cities. However, in the six principal cities of refuge, even R' Yehudah rules that they need not pay the rent to the Levite inhabitants of those cities. The reason for this is that the Torah states concerning the six cities *(Num.* 35:12): וְהָיוּ לָכֶם הֶעָרִים לְמִקְלָט, *And the cities shall be for you as refuge.* The word לָכֶם, *for you,* indicates that you shall have the cities for all your necessities. Therefore, you do not have to pay for the use of these cities. Concerning the forty-two Levitical cities, however, the Torah states *(Num.* 35:6): וַעֲלֵיהֶם תִּתְּנוּ אַרְבָּעִים וּשְׁתַּיִם עִיר, *and in addition to them you shall place forty-two cities.* They resemble the six only insofar as they afford refuge to the murderers, but not for other necessities. Therefore, rent must be paid to the Levites for their use *(Tos. Yom Tov* from *Gem.* 12b).

רַבִּי מֵאִיר אוֹמֵר: לֹא הָיוּ מַעֲלִים לָהֶן שָׂכָר. — *R' Meir says: They would not pay them*

וְחוֹזֵר לִשְׂרָרָה שֶׁהָיָה בָהּ; דִּבְרֵי רַבִּי מֵאִיר. רַבִּי יְהוּדָה אוֹמֵר: לֹא הָיָה חוֹזֵר לִשְׂרָרָה שֶׁהָיָה בָהּ.

[א] **וְאֵלּוּ** הֵן הַלּוֹקִין: הַבָּא עַל־אֲחוֹתוֹ, וְעַל־אֲחוֹת אָבִיו, וְעַל־אֲחוֹת אִמּוֹ, וְעַל־אֲחוֹת אִשְׁתּוֹ; וְעַל־אֵשֶׁת אָחִיו, וְעַל־אֵשֶׁת אֲחִי

יד אברהם

rent.

R' Meir maintains that the forty-two cities resembled the six principal cities of refuge in all respects. Just as the six belonged to Israel for all their necessities, so did the forty-two Levitical cities *(Tos. Yom Tov* from *Gem.* 12b).

The halachah is not in accordance with R' Meir *(Rav; Rambam, Hil. Rotzeach* 8:10).

וְחוֹזֵר לִשְׂרָרָה שֶׁהָיָה בָהּ; — *He returns to the office he had previously occupied;*

I.e., if he was a *Nasi* or the head of the *beis din,* he may resume that office after being released from his exile by the death of the *Kohen Gadol (Tos. Yom Tov* from *Rashi).*

דִּבְרֵי רַבִּי מֵאִיר. — *[these are] the words of R' Meir.*

R' Meir compares the exiled murderer to the Hebrew slave, who, after being freed, is restored to the office he had occupied previously *(Tos. Yom Tov* from *Gem.* 13a).

רַבִּי יְהוּדָה אוֹמֵר: לֹא הָיָה חוֹזֵר לִשְׂרָרָה שֶׁהָיָה בָהּ. — *R' Yehudah says: He would not return to the office he had occupied.*

R' Yehudah bases this on the verse *(Lev.* 25:41): *And he shall return to his family, and to the heritage of his forefathers he shall return.* This verse refers to a Hebrew slave who returns home when the year of *Yovel* arrives. R' Yehudah understands the phrase *to his family* to imply a limitation — he returns only to his family, but not to the honorable position occupied by his forefathers. R' Meir contends that since the verse adds the words *to the heritage of his forefathers,* it means that he should occupy the same honorable position they occupied. By exegesis, these *Tannaim* derive that the same applies to the exiled murderer who returns home after the death of the *Kohen Gadol;* R' Meir rules that he returns to his office and R' Yehudah rules that he does not. *Rambam (Comm.* and *Hil. Rotzeach* 7:14) states: Although atonement was effected for him, he never returns to the high office he previously occupied. He is deposed from his honor for the rest of his life because this grave misfortune came about through him.

Chapter 3

As has been learned previously, the penalty for transgressing a negative precept is *malkus,* lashes. *Rambam (Hil. Sanhedrin* chs. 18, 19) notes the three classes of negative commandments for which the penalty is lashes: those for which there is a penalty of כָּרֵת, *kares,* a Divinely imposed premature death; מִיתָה בִידֵי שָׁמַיִם, those for which the penalty is death by the hands of Heaven [for the difference between this and *kares,* see *Yad Avraham* comm. to *Sanhedrin* 9:6, p. 169]; and ordinary negative precepts. In all of these cases, the penalty is only for trangressions involving action. Those that are transgressed passively are not punishable by lashes. The sum total of all negative precepts for which the penalty is lashes is two hundred and seven.

Although theoretically all negative precepts punishable by *kares* [as well as those punishable by death at the hands of Heaven] are also punishable by lashes, in actual

3 He returns to the office he had previously occupied;
1 [these are] the words of R' Meir. R' Yehudah says: He would not return to the office he had occupied.

1. These are the ones who incur the penalty of lashes: One who cohabits with his sister, his father's sister, his mother's sister; his wife's sister; his brother's

YAD AVRAHAM

practice the sinner does not necessarily receive both punishments. Lashes are imposed only in the case of one who willfully transgressed after being warned by witnesses that the act he was about to perform was prohibited *(Rambam, Hil. Sanhedrin* 16:4). Since lashes are a judicially imposed punishment, the court cannot act without the proper testimony of witnesses. In the absence of witnesses or a proper warning, the offender cannot receive lashes. Nevertheless, he can still receive *kares*. Since in the eyes of Heaven it is clear whether his violation was willful or not, the testimony of witnesses is irrelevant.] On the other hand, the penalty of *kares* can be forgiven with proper repentance and atonement, which the Heavenly tribunal accepts.[1] Lashes, however, will still be imposed by the human courts *(Tos. Yom Tov;* see mishnah 15).

Although our chapter commences with the words אֵלּוּ הֵן הַלּוֹקִין, *these are the ones who incur the penalty of lashes,* the *Tanna's* intention is not to delineate all those subject to this penalty. Rather, he lists only those whose penalty is not obvious. Thus, he lists the transgressions subject to *kares,* since their liability to lashes is a matter of controversy among *Tannaim (Gem.* 13b), and those whose negative commandment is obscure and must be derived by one of the hermeneutic methods by which the Torah is expounded. The commentary will explain the reason for the listing of each of the transgressions mentioned in the mishnah *(Rav; Rashi).*

וְאֵלּוּ הֵן הַלּוֹקִין: — *These are the ones who incur the penalty of lashes:*

[I.e., these are the sinners who are subject to thirty-nine lashes — known as *malkus* — as below in mishnah 10.]

הַבָּא עַל־אֲחוֹתוֹ, וְעַל־אֲחוֹת אָבִיו, וְעַל־אֲחוֹת אִמּוֹ, — *One who cohabits with his sister, his father's sister, his mother's sister,*

[All these are incestuous relationships subject to *kares,* as stated in *Leviticus* 20:17, 19; thus they are subject to *malkus* as well. These women are prohibited regardless of whether they are sisters by the same father, the same mother, or both.]

וְעַל־אֲחוֹת אִשְׁתּוֹ; — *his wife's sister;*

This prohibition, stated in *Leviticus* 18:18, is punishable by *kares (Leviticus* 18:29), and therefore *malkus* as well. The prohibition is applicable only during the wife's lifetime. After her death, her husband is permitted to marry her sister *(Yevamos* 4:13).

Although the prohibition of intimacy with one's brother's wife precedes the prohibition of taking two sisters in *Lev.* 18, the *Tanna* reverses the order here in the mishnah to keep the prohibitions of sisters in one series and the prohibitions of wives in another series *(Lechem Shamayim).*

וְעַל־אֵשֶׁת אָחִיו, — *his brother's wife,*

[I.e., if his brother divorced her or died, leaving her a widow, she is nevertheless prohibited to him by reason of kinship. The prohibition, for which the penalty of

1. It is for this reason that the double punishment of both *kares* and lashes does not violate the principle that a perosn who incurs two punishments is subjected only to the more severe of them, not both (see above, 1:2). Since it is within the transgressor's power to free himself of the penalty of *kares* by repenting, this case does not fall within the double punishment rule *(Tos. Yom Tov* from *Gem.* 13b).

אָבִיו, וְעַל־הַנִּדָּה; אַלְמָנָה לְכֹהֵן גָּדוֹל, גְּרוּשָׁה וַחֲלוּצָה לְכֹהֵן הֶדְיוֹט, מַמְזֶרֶת וּנְתִינָה לְיִשְׂרָאֵל, בַּת־יִשְׂרָאֵל לְנָתִין וּלְמַמְזֵר.

אַלְמָנָה וּגְרוּשָׁה, חַיָּבִין עָלֶיהָ מִשּׁוּם שְׁנֵי שֵׁמוֹת;

יד אברהם

malkus is incurred, is stated in *Leviticus* 18:16, and the penalty of *kares* in verse 29. (The only exception to this is where the brother dies childless and *yibum* — marriage to her husband's brother — is mandated. See *Deut.* 25:5-10 and Tractate *Yevamos.*)]

וְעַל־אֵשֶׁת אֲחִי אָבִיו, — *his father's brother's wife,*

[If his father's brother dies or divorces his wife, she remains forbidden to him by this prohibition under penalty of *kares.* The prohibition is found in *Leviticus* 18:14, and the penalty of *kares* in verse 29, together with the penalty of *kares* for other acts of incest.]

וְעַל־הַנִּדָּה; — *or with a menstruant;*

[I.e., a woman who has menstruated and has not yet purified herself by immersion in a *mikveh* after waiting the prescribed number of days. Cohabitation with her is prohibited under penalty of *kares,* and it is immaterial whether she was still menstruating at the time the cohabitation takes place. The prohibition of intimacy with a menstruant is stated in *Leviticus* 18:19, and it applies whether she is married or single *(Rama, Yoreh Deah* 183:1). The penalty of *kares* is found in 20:18.]

This concludes the list of forbidden cohabitations subject to *malkus* as a result of the *kares* penalty. As mentioned above, these sinners are listed because the *Tanna* wishes to teach that although all these sins are punishable by *kares,* they are also punishable by *malkus (Rav; Rashi).*

אַלְמָנָה לְכֹהֵן גָּדוֹל, — *a widow to a Kohen Gadol,*

[The mishnah now begins a list of unions prohibited by a negative commandment which are punishable only by *malkus,* not *kares.*]

A *Kohen Gadol* is forbidden to cohabit with or marry a widow *(Rambam, Hil. Sanhedrin* 19:4, 153), and the penalty for doing so is *malkus.* The prohibition is stated in *Leviticus* 21:14. The reason this is listed in the mishnah will be explained further.

גְּרוּשָׁה וַחֲלוּצָה לְכֹהֵן הֶדְיוֹט, — *a divorcee or a chalutzah to an ordinary Kohen,*

The prohibition to a *Kohen* of marrying a divorcee is stated in *Leviticus* 21:7.[1] The prohibition to a *Kohen* of a *chalutzah* — a widow who had been subject to the *yibum* requirement but who was freed from it by the ceremony of *chalitzah* (see *Deut.* 25:7-10, and above, comm. to 1:1) — is not mentioned explicitly in the Torah. The *Gemara (Kiddushin* 78a) derives it from the same verse as the divorcee. From the seeming superfluity of the word וְאִשָּׁה, *and a woman,* the Rabbis learned to include *chalutzah* in this prohibition. *Rashi* and *Rav* appear to hold that this prohibition is Biblical, as explained further. *Tosafos, Ramban* and *Ritva* point out, however, that the *Gemara* qualifies this derivation as an *asmachta,* a Biblical support for a Rabbinical enactment. Therefore, if a *Kohen* cohabits with a *chalutzah,* he is not liable to the regular *malkus* but rather to מַכַּת מַרְדּוּת *[makkas mardus],*

1. *Rambam (Isurei Biah* 17:2) rules that in contrast to the *Kohen Gadol*-widow prohibition, a *Kohen* does not incur lashes for cohabiting with a divorcee unless he married her, but not for a promiscuous union. *Ravad* disputes this and considers the divorcee prohibition identical to that of the widow.

3 wife, his father's brother's wife, or with a menstruant; a
1 widow to a *Kohen Gadol,* a divorcee or a *chalutzah* to an
ordinary *Kohen,* a *mamzeress* or a Nesinite to an Israelite, an Israelitess to a Nesinite or to a *mamzer.*

For a widow and a divorcee, one is liable for two [negative] commandments; for a divorcee and a

YAD AVRAHAM

blows dealt for rebellion or disobedience of Rabbinic legislation.

There are various views concerning the severity of *makkas mardus. Aruch* and *Rambam* (*Comm.* and *Nazir* 4:3) rule that *makkas mardus* is inflicted upon the sinner without a specific number and without assessment of his ability to endure. It is inflicted according to what *beis din* deems necessary to uphold their enactments. Similar to this is *Ran's* view at the end of this tractate, that he is whipped according to what the judges deem necessary at that time. *Ran* (to *Rif, Kesubos* 80a) states that a sinner who continues to defy the Rabbinic authority is beaten until he repents or until he dies. Should he, however, have merely infracted a Rabbinic enactment, it is unlikely that he should be punished so severely.

Rivash (responsum 90) rules that he is dealt thirty-nine blows, the same as Biblical lashes, but they are milder.

Others rule that *makkas mardus* consists of thirteen lashes, one-third of the *malkus* of the Torah (*Magen Avraham* 496:2; *Tashbetz* 2:51).

מַמְזֶרֶת — *a mamzeress*

A *mamzeress* (fem. of *mamzer*) is the product of an illicit union punishable by *kares* or execution by the courts (see *Yevamos* 4:13), or the child of a *mamzer.* She is forbidden to marry anyone but a *mamzer,* a convert, or a freed slave (*Even Haezer* 4:22, 24). The prohibition on marrying a *mamzeress* is stated in *Deut.* 23:3.

וּנְתִינָה לְיִשְׂרָאֵל, — *or a Nesinite to an Israelite,*

I.e., a girl of the Gibeonites whom Joshua allowed to convert to Judaism. נְתִינָה, *Nesinah* (fem. of *Nasin*), means *appointed one.* They were given this appellation because they were appointed, or subjected, by Joshua to be wood-cutters and water-drawers for the Temple services (*Joshua* 9:27). It is forbidden for a regular Jew to marry them because of the negative precept of (*Deut.* 7:3): וְלֹא תִתְחַתֵּן בָּם, *And you shall not make marriages with them* (the seven Canaanite nations enumerated two verses earlier), the Gibeonites being of one of the nations of Canaan. For transgressing this *mitzvah,* the one who marries a Nesinite is subject to *malkus (Rav).*

There is, however, a dispute whether the Biblical negative commandment not to marry descendants of the seven Canaanite nations applies after they have converted to Judaism or only in their non-Jewish state. *Rashi (Kesubos* 29a), who there seems to follow this latter view, therefore explains the prohibition to marry a Nesinite as a Rabbinical enactment by the court of King David. See *Tosafos* (ibid. s.v. אלו נערות) who dispute this. *Rashi* in our tractate seems to contradict his view there as well. See *Ritva* here.

בַּת־יִשְׂרָאֵל לְנָתִין וּלְמַמְזֵר. — *an Israelitess to a Nesinite or to a mamzer.*

[I.e., a Jewish woman who marries a Nesinite or *mamzer.* The above-mentioned are the prohibited unions punishable by *malkus.*]

In all the above cases, the penalty of *malkus* applies to both the man and the woman *(Rambam, Hil. Isurei Biah* 17:5).

אַלְמָנָה וּגְרוּשָׁה, חַיָּבִין עָלֶיהָ מִשּׁוּם שְׁנֵי שֵׁמוֹת; — *For a widow and a divorcee, one is liable for two [negative] commandments;*

If a *Kohen Gadol* cohabits with a woman who was widowed from one husband and then divorced from another, he is liable to two sets of *malkus (Rav).*

The order of these events is critical. This is because there is a general rule that

גְרוּשָׁה וַחֲלוּצָה, אֵינוֹ חַיָּב אֶלָּא מִשֵּׁם אֶחָד בִּלְבָד.

[ב] **הַטָּמֵא** שֶׁאָכַל אֶת־הַקֹּדֶשׁ, וְהַבָּא אֶל־הַמִּקְדָּשׁ טָמֵא; וְהָאוֹכֵל חֵלֶב, וְדָם, וְנוֹתָר, וּפִגּוּל, וְטָמֵא; הַשּׁוֹחֵט וְהַמַּעֲלֶה בַּחוּץ;

יד אברהם

אֵין אִסּוּר חָל עַל אִסּוּר, *One prohibition cannot take effect on another* (*Kiddushin* 77b). This means that when a series of prohibitions come to bear on a specific object, once it is prohibited by one prohibition, the later prohibitions cannot take effect on it. As a result, someone who transgresses with it is liable only to the punishment of the first prohibition. Accordingly, once a woman is prohibited to a *Kohen Gadol* by being a divorcee, she cannot become additionally prohibited to him by then becoming a widow. The reverse, however, is possible because of the exception to this rule for an אִסּוּר מוֹסִיף, *a more extensive prohibition*, i.e., a second prohibition which includes more people in it than the first. By taking effect in regard to those not yet prohibited, it takes effect in regard to those already prohibited as well. Thus, since only a *Kohen Gadol* is prohibited from marrying a widow, whereas a divorcee is prohibited to every *Kohen*, where she was first a widow and subsequently became a divorcee, thereby becoming forbidden to all *Kohanim*, the *Kohen Gadol* would be liable twice (*Rav; Rashi*).

גְרוּשָׁה וַחֲלוּצָה, — *for a divorcee and a chalutzah,*

I.e., a *Kohen* marries a woman who was first divorced by one husband and then widowed from her second husband under circumstances warranting *yibum*. She was then released from *yibum* through *chalitzah* (*Rav; Rashi*).

אֵינוֹ חַיָּב אֶלָּא מִשֵּׁם אֶחָד בִּלְבָד. — *he is liable for but one [negative] commandment.*

I.e., he is liable only for transgressing the divorcee prohibition (*Rav*).

[Every *chalutzah* is perforce a widow, but as was explained above, the widow prohibition cannot take effect on a woman already forbidden to him as a divorcee. This leaves only the *chalutzah* prohibition to consider.]

We have already noted above that *Rav* and *Rashi* rule that the prohibition of a *chalutzah* to a *Kohen* is Biblical. Therefore, if a *Kohen* marries a *chalutzah*, he is subjected to *malkus*. Should he marry a woman who was both divorced and received *chalitzah*, however, there is no additional penalty for the *chalutzah*. Since the *chalutzah* prohibition is derived from the same clause that prohibits marrying a divorcee, it is as though he marries a woman who was twice divorced, for which he is subject to only one set of lashes (*Rabbeinu Yehonasan*).

Tosafos, however, along with many other authorities, rule that the prohibition of a *chalutzah* is Rabbinical, the violation of which is punishable only by *makkas mardus*. Accordingly, the lesson of the mishnah is that if a *Kohen* is intimate with a woman who is divorced as well as being a *chalutzah*, and is subjected to *malkus* because of that transgression, he is not additionally subjected to *makkas mardus* as well. Some authorities understand this as a general rule that, whenever one is subjected to *malkus*, he is automatically exempt from *makkas mardus* for committing any Rabbinical transgression simultaneously (*Mishneh LaMelech, Isurei Biah* 17:7; *Minchas Chinuch* 428).

Others, however, understand this to apply only in this case, since, Rabbinically, a *chalutzah* is judged as a divorcee. Therefore, there is no additional penalty if the woman is already a divorcee. In other cases, however,

chalutzah, he is liable for but one [negative] commandment.

2. A [person who is] *tamei* who eats holy [foods], one who enters the Temple while *tamei;* one who eats fat, blood, leftover [sacrificial meat], *piggul,* or

YAD AVRAHAM

in which the Rabbinical transgression is not related to the Biblical transgression, the penalty of *malkus* does not exempt him from *makkas mardus (Pri Megadim, Introduction to Orach Chaim* 1:28; *Shoshannas HaAmakim* 9; *Tif. Yis.* ad loc.; *Rabbeinu Yehonasan).*

The cases of the widow and the divorcee were included in the mishnah to teach the rule of double liability *(Rav).*

2.

After completing his listing of the forbidden unions punishable by *malkus* (lashes), the *Tanna* resumes his enumeration of those transgressions punishable by *kares* for which one is liable to *malkus* as well, again ending with a list of ordinary negative commandments for which there is only a liability of *malkus.*

הַטָּמֵא שֶׁאָכַל אֶת־הַקֹּדֶשׁ, — *A [person who is] tamei who eats holy [foods],*

A person contaminated with *tumah* is forbidden to partake of sacrifical meat or other hallowed foods, e.g., the remainder of a *minchah* or the loaves of a thanksgiving offering (see *Shevuos* ch. 2). This sin is punishable by *kares* (as in *Lev.* 7:20). The admonition against this is not stated explicitly. The *Gemara* (14b) derives it from (*Lev.* 12:4): בְּכָל־קֹדֶשׁ לֹא־תִגָּע, *She shall touch no holy foods.* The *Gemara* interprets this to mean that a woman who has just given birth [the subject of that passage] may not eat any hallowed foods [as a result of her state of *tumah*]. Since the verse continues, וְאֶל־הַמִּקְדָּשׁ לֹא תָבֹא, *and she shall not enter the Temple,* a transgression punishable by *kares,* the admonition stated at the beginning of the verse is likewise referring to a transgression punishable by *kares* — viz., eating holy foods while in a state of *tumah (Tos. Yom Tov* from *Gem.* 14b).

As noted in the General Introduction, in order for there to be a punishment of *malkus,* there must be a Scriptural admonition warning against the act, in addition to the statement of punishment *(Gem.* 13b).

וְהַבָּא אֶל־הַמִּקְדָּשׁ טָמֵא; — *one who enters the Temple while tamei;*

As already stated above, this is punishable by *kares (Num.* 19:13). The admonition is stated in *Num.* 5:3: וְלֹא יְטַמְּאוּ אֶת־מַחֲנֵיהֶם, *And they shall not contaminate their camps (Gem.* 14b).

וְהָאוֹכֵל חֵלֶב, וְדָם, — *one who eats fat, blood,*

Both the admonition against eating fat [i.e., the specific fats prohibited by the Torah, generally those reserved for sacrifice on the altar in a sacrificial animal; see *Rambam, Hil. Maachalos Asuros* 7:5], and blood and the penalty of *kares* are stated in *Lev.* 7:22-27 *(Tos. Yom Tov).*

וְנוֹתָר, — *leftover [sacrificial meat],*

Meat of sacrifices that was left over beyond the time allotted for their consumption must be burned. This is stated in *Exodus* 29:34: וְשָׂרַפְתָּ אֶת־הַנּוֹתָר בָּאֵשׁ לֹא יֵאָכֵל כִּי־קֹדֶשׁ הוּא, *and you shall burn the leftover in fire; it shall not be eaten for it is holy (Tos. Yom Tov; Rashi).* The penalty for eating leftover sacrificial foods is *kares (Lev.* 19:8). This transgression is punishable by *malkus* as well since the admonition is expressed as a negative commandment.

וְהָאוֹכֵל חָמֵץ בְּפֶסַח; וְהָאוֹכֵל וְהָעוֹשֶׂה מְלָאכָה בְּיוֹם הַכִּפּוּרִים; וְהַמְפַטֵּם אֶת־הַשֶּׁמֶן, וְהַמְפַטֵּם אֶת־הַקְּטֹרֶת, וְהַסָּךְ בְּשֶׁמֶן הַמִּשְׁחָה; וְהָאוֹכֵל נְבֵלוֹת, וּטְרֵפוֹת, שְׁקָצִים, וּרְמָשִׂים.

יד אברהם

וּפִגּוּל, — *piggul,*

Piggul [lit. *abomination*] is the term used by the Torah *(Lev.* 7:18) to describe a sacrifice disqualified in the following manner: During his performance of any of the four blood services (slaughter, receiving the blood, transporting it to the altar, and throwing it against the side of the altar), the *Kohen* had the intent of eating its meat, or burning its sacrificial parts on the altar, after the time allotted by the Torah. For example, if someone received the blood of a *shlamim* (peace-offering) with the intention of eating its meat for three days (rather than the prescribed two), the offering is *immediately* disqualified and its consumption is prohibited even though the intention was never carried out.]

The admonition against eating *piggul* is the same as that against eating leftover sacrificial foods: *It shall not be eaten for it is holy.* The intention is that anything that is holy, once it becomes disqualified, may not be eaten under penalty of *kares (Tos. Yom Tov* from *Rashi).*

וְטָמֵא; — *or [sacrificial foods which have become] tamei;*

This is prohibited by the negative commandment *(Lev.* 7:19): וְהַבָּשָׂר אֲשֶׁר יִגַּע בְּכָל־טָמֵא לֹא יֵאָכֵל, *And meat which touches anything tamei shall not be eaten (Tos. Yom Tov* from *Rashi),* but it does not entail *kares (Rambam, Hil. Sanhedrin* 19:4).

הַשּׁוֹחֵט וְהַמַּעֲלֶה בַחוּץ; — *one who slaughters [a sacrificial animal] or offers [it] up outside [the Temple];*

Should one offer up a sacrificial animal outside the Temple, he transgresses the negative commandment *(Deut.* 12:13): הִשָּׁמֶר לְךָ פֶּן־תַּעֲלֶה עֹלֹתֶיךָ בְּכָל־מָקוֹם אֲשֶׁר תִּרְאֶה, *Beware lest you offer your burnt-offerings in any place that you see.* The word הִשָּׁמֶר, *beware,* is always interpreted by the Sages as a negative commandment.

The above verse refers to the offering of the sacrifice — i.e., burning its fats or meat on an altar outside the Temple. The admonition against slaughtering sacrificial animals outside the Temple Court is not stated explicitly in the Torah. In *Zevachim* (106a), some derive it from *Lev.* 17:7, while others derive it from an analogous expression found both in the case of one who slaughters outside the Temple and one who offers the sacrifice outside the Temple *(Tos. Yom Tov; Rashi).*

Both of these transgressions are punishable by *kares (Lev.* 17:4,9).

וְהָאוֹכֵל חָמֵץ בְּפֶסַח; — *one who eats chametz on Pesach;*

This is prohibited by *(Ex.* 13:3): וְלֹא יֵאָכֵל חָמֵץ, *and chametz shall not be eaten (Tos. Yom Tov).* This is punishable by *kares (Exodus* 12:15).

וְהָאוֹכֵל וְהָעוֹשֶׂה מְלָאכָה בְּיוֹם הַכִּפּוּרִים; — *one who eats or performs work on Yom Kippur;*

Both of these transgressions are punishable by *kares (Lev.* 23:29f*).* The admonition against performing work is expressed clearly in *Lev.* 23:28: וְכָל־מְלָאכָה לֹא תַעֲשׂוּ בְּעֶצֶם הַיּוֹם הַזֶּה, *and you shall do no work on this very day,* thus imposing the penalty of *malkus.* There is, however, no explicit *negative* commandment prohibiting eating on Yom Kippur.

The Rabbis (*Yoma* 81a) derive this from the fact that the Torah calls Yom Kippur, *Sabbath.* Yom Kippur, therefore, assumes an admonition the same as the Sabbath *(Tos. Yom Tov).*

3 [sacrificial foods which have become] *tamei;* one who
2 slaughters [a sacrificial animal] or offers [it] up outside
[the Temple]; one who eats *chametz* on Pesach; one who
eats or performs work on Yom Kippur; one who
compounds [anointing] oil, compounds incense, or
anoints himself with the anointing oil; one who eats
neveilos, treifos, abominable creatures, and crawling
things.

YAD AVRAHAM

וְהַמְפַטֵּם אֶת־הַשֶּׁמֶן, — *one who compounds [anointing] oil,*

In order for the *Mishkan* (Tabernacles) and its vessels and the *Kohanim* to attain their hallowed state, they had to be anointed with anointing oil. The ingredients, as well as the exact measurements, for the make-up of this oil are given in *Exodus* 30. The mishnah teaches that one who compounds the oil according to the exact components prescribed by the Torah is liable for lashes, as well as *kares.*

The prohibition against this act is stated in *Ex.* 30:32: וּבְמַתְכֻּנְתּוֹ לֹא תַעֲשׂוּ כָּמֹהוּ, *and in its proportion you shall not make anything like it (Tos. Yom Tov* from *Rashi).*

וְהַמְפַטֵּם אֶת־הַקְּטֹרֶת, — *compounds incense,*

[I.e., one who compounds incense with the same components and proportions as the incense burnt in the *Mishkan* and the Temple.] The prohibition of this act is found in *Ex.* 30:37: וְהַקְּטֹרֶת אֲשֶׁר תַּעֲשֶׂה בְּמַתְכֻּנְתָּהּ לֹא־תַעֲשׂוּ לָכֶם, *And the incense that you shall make, you shall not make in its proportion for yourselves (Tos. Yom Tov* from *Rashi).*

This sin is also punishable by *kares (Ex.* 30:38).

וְהַסָּךְ בְּשֶׁמֶן הַמִּשְׁחָה; — *or anoints himself with the anointing oil;*

I.e., he anoints himself with the anointing oil compounded by Moses *(Rav; Rashi).* This was the only anointing oil ever made. It was miraculously preserved and will be discovered again when revealed in Messianic times (*Tos. Yom Tov* from *Kerisos* 5b).

This act is prohibited by the negative commandment (*Ex.* 30:32): עַל־בְּשַׂר אָדָם לֹא יִיסָךְ, *It shall not be anointed on the flesh of man (Tos. Yom Tov* from *Rashi).* Both compounding anointing oil and anointing oneself with the original anointing oil is punishable by *kares (Ex.* 30:33).

[All those enumerated in mishnah 2 up to this point are punishable by *kares,* except eating sacrificial meat which has become *tamei* (see *Rambam, Hil. Sanhedrin* 19:4, 53). From this point on the mishnah continues with transgressions whose penalty is only *malkus,* not *kares.*]

וְהָאוֹכֵל נְבֵלוֹת, — *one who eats neveilos,*

This is prohibited in *Deut.* 14:21: לֹא תֹאכְלוּ כָל־נְבֵלָה, *You shall not eat any carcass (Tos. Yom Tov). [Neveilah* includes any animal or fowl that dies or is killed in any manner other than the manner of slaughtering — *shechitah* — prescribed by the halachah.]

וּטְרֵפוֹת, — *treifos,*

Rambam defines *treifah* as being an animal with an internal fault precluding it from living more than twelve months (*Hil. Maachalos Asuros* 4:8). The eating of a *treifah* is proscribed by *Ex.* 22:30: וּבָשָׂר בַּשָּׂדֶה טְרֵפָה לֹא תֹאכֵלוּ, *and flesh torn in the field you shall not eat (Tos. Yom Tov).*

שְׁקָצִים, — *abominable creatures,*

This listing includes all creatures referred to by the Torah or the Rabbis as *abominations,* viz., all prohibited species that multiply through the union of male and female. This includes unkosher fish

אָכַל טֶבֶל, וּמַעֲשֵׂר רִאשׁוֹן שֶׁלֹּא נִטְּלָה תְרוּמָתוֹ, וּמַעֲשֵׂר שֵׁנִי וְהֶקְדֵּשׁ שֶׁלֹּא נִפְדּוּ. כַּמָּה יֹאכַל מִן־הַטֶּבֶל וִיהֵא חַיָּב? רַבִּי שִׁמְעוֹן אוֹמֵר: כָּל־שֶׁהוּא. וַחֲכָמִים אוֹמְרִים: כְּזַיִת. אָמַר לָהֶם רַבִּי שִׁמְעוֹן: אֵין

יד אברהם

and sea creatures, such as seals, frogs, and the like; unkosher birds; insects such as flies, mosquitos, and bees; reptiles, and rodents. It may even include unkosher animals, for although the Torah does not refer to them as abominations, the Rabbis do *(Tos. Yom Tov; Tif. Yis.)*.

וּרְמָשִׁים. – *and crawling things.*

These are creatures that seem to reproduce spontaneously, e.g., from dung or rotting carcasses. This includes also those that spawn from fruits and other foods. Once they emerge to crawl upon the earth, they are prohibited *(Tos. Yom Tov; Tif. Yis.)*.

These negative commandments are mentioned here because the end of the mishnah discusses ants, which are in the category of שְׁקָצִים, *abominations (Tif. Yis.)*

אָכַל טֶבֶל, – *One who eats tevel* [lit. *if one ate tevel*],

[The Torah mandates that before the produce of Eretz Yisrael may be eaten, various portions of it must be separated to be given to the *Kohen*, Levite, the poor, and a portion to be taken to Jerusalem and eaten there. (The last two do not both apply in the same year, but follow a periodic schedule.) Before these separations are made, the produce is forbidden for eating and is known as *tevel*.]

The admonition against eating *tevel* is (*Lev.* 22:15): וְלֹא יְחַלְּלוּ אֶת־קָדְשֵׁי בְּנֵי יִשְׂרָאֵל אֵת אֲשֶׁר־יָרִימוּ לַה׳, *And they shall not profane the hallowed things of the children of Israel, which they shall separate for* HASHEM. The future tense indicates that the sanctity is derived from the yet unseparated hallowed parts of the produce, which is destined to be separated *(Rav; Rashi* from *Sanhedrin* 83a).

In addition to the penalty of *malkus* for disobeying this admonition, there is a penalty of מִיתָה בִּידֵי שָׁמַיִם, *death by the hands of Heaven (Sanhedrin* 83a), i.e. premature death.

וּמַעֲשֵׂר רִאשׁוֹן שֶׁלֹּא נִטְּלָה תְרוּמָתוֹ, – *or maaser rishon from which terumah was not separated,*

The first portion separated from the crop is known as *terumah* and is given to a *Kohen*. Following that, one-tenth of the crop is separated and given to a Levite. This portion is known as *maaser rishon*, the first tithe. Before eating it, however, the Levite must also in turn give one-tenth of this *maaser* to a *Kohen*. This is known as the *terumah* of the *maaser*.

Should one eat the *maaser* prior to the separation of its *terumah*, he is liable to death at the hands of Heaven, just like one who eats *tevel*. We derive this from *Numbers* 18:27: וְנֶחְשַׁב לָכֶם תְּרוּמַתְכֶם כַּדָּגָן מִן־הַגֹּרֶן וְכַמְלֵאָה מִן־הַיָּקֶב, *And your terumah shall be counted to you as grain from the threshing-floor and as the fullness of the winepress.* From here the Rabbis deduce that just as grain from the threshing-floor is *tevel* until the tithes are separated from it, so too *maaser rishon* is *tevel* until its *terumah* is separated from it *(Rav; Tos. Yom Tov)*.

וּמַעֲשֵׂר שֵׁנִי וְהֶקְדֵּשׁ שֶׁלֹּא נִפְדּוּ. — *or maaser sheni or consecrated objects which were not redeemed.*

[After separating the first tithe to give to a Levite *(maaser rishon)*, the owner of the produce must separate yet another ten percent of what remains to take to Jerusalem and eat there. This second tithe

3 One who eats *tevel*, or *maaser rishon* from which
2 *terumah* was not separated, or *maaser sheni* or consecrated objects which were not redeemed. How much must he eat of *tevel* to be liable? R' Shimon says: Any amount. The Sages [,however,] say: The bulk of an olive. Said R' Shimon to them: Do you not concur with me

YAD AVRAHAM

is known as *maaser sheni*.[1] However, since hauling large amounts of produce to Jerusalem can prove cumbersome, the Torah provided for the redemption of the produce for money, which then assumes the *maaser sheni* sanctity from the produce. The produce in turn may now be eaten anywhere, while the money is taken to Jerusalem where it is used to buy food which is eaten there. Eating unredeemed *maaser sheni* outside of Jerusalem is forbidden and punishable by *malkus*.]

Actually, the transgression of eating *maaser sheni* outside of Jerusalem is stated more explicitly in mishnah 3. Accordingly, the *Gemara* (19b) explains that the mishnah here refers to *maaser sheni* that is *tamei*, which may not be eaten in its state of sanctity at all, even in Jerusalem. The only way it may be eaten is by redeeming the produce to remove its *maaser sheni* sanctity. Thus, as long as it is unredeemed, it is forbidden *(Rav)*.

One is subject to *malkus* for eating *maaser sheni* that is *tamei* only if he does so in Jerusalem (*Tos. Yom Tov* from *Rambam Comm.)*.

The admonition against eating הֶקְדֵּשׁ, *consecrated objects* (foods), belonging to the Temple is not stated explicitly in the Torah. [The mishnah in this context refers to foodstuffs which have been consecrated for their value, i.e., to be sold by the Temple treasury, with the proceeds going into its coffers. It does not refer to sacrificial foodstuffs, which may not be redeemed.] Several explanations are offered for the penalty of *malkus*. *Rashi* and *Rav* hold that it is derived from *terumah* through an analogous wording. Therefore, just as eating *terumah* is prohibited by a negative commandment, so too is eating hallowed foods. *Rambam* (*Hil. Me'ilah* 1:3) derives it from *Deut.* 12:17: לֹא תוּכַל לֶאֱכֹל בִּשְׁעָרֶיךָ . . . וְכָל־נְדָרֶיךָ אֲשֶׁר תִּדֹּר, *You may not eat in your cities ... and all your vows which you shall vow*, which the Sages interpret as referring to eating a burnt-offering. The same prohibition applies to eating or deriving benefit from objects hallowed for the Temple.

כַּמָּה יֹאכַל מִן־הַטֶּבֶל וִיהֵא חַיָּב? — *How much must he eat of tevel to be liable?*

[I.e., how much must he eat to be punishable by *malkus?*]

רַבִּי שִׁמְעוֹן אוֹמֵר: כָּל־שֶׁהוּא. — *R' Shimon says: Any amount.*

[I.e., even a minute quantity makes him liable to *malkus*. Although one is generally not liable to *malkus* for eating a forbidden food unless he consumes a *kezayis* of it (the volume of an olive), R' Shimon considers him liable in this case for even one kernel. The reason follows below.]

וַחֲכָמִים אוֹמְרִים: כְּזַיִת. — *The Sages [however] say: The bulk of an olive.*

[I.e., he is liable only if he eats the volume of an olive, but if he eats less than that volume, he is exempt.]

אָמַר לָהֶם רַבִּי שִׁמְעוֹן: אֵין אַתֶּם מוֹדִים לִי בְּאוֹכֵל נְמָלָה כָּל־שֶׁהוּא שֶׁהוּא חַיָּב? — *Said*

1. The *maaser sheni* tithe is given only in the first, second, fourth and fifth years of the seven-year *Shemittah* cycle. In the third and sixth years it is replaced by *maaser ani*, the tithe for the poor. In the seventh year — *Shemittah* — crops may not be raised, and what grows wild is exempt from all tithes.

אַתֶּם מוֹדִים לִי בְּאוֹכֵל נְמָלָה כָּל־שֶׁהוּא שֶׁהוּא חַיָּב? אָמְרוּ לוֹ: מִפְּנֵי שֶׁהִיא כִבְרִיָּתָהּ. אָמַר לָהֶן: אַף חִטָּה אַחַת כִּבְרִיָּתָהּ.

[ג] **הָאוֹכֵל** בִּכּוּרִים עַד שֶׁלֹּא קָרָא עֲלֵיהֶן, קָדְשֵׁי קָדָשִׁים חוּץ לַקְּלָעִים,

יד אברהם

R' Shimon to them: Do you not concur with me concerning one who eats an ant of any size that he is liable?

R' Shimon cites as proof of his position the law that one who eats an ant is liable for transgressing the negative commandment of eating a swarming thing (*Lev.* 11:41), even though it is less than the volume of an olive. Even the Sages agree that this is so (*Rav; Rashi*).

The *Gemara* (16b) states that if one eats an ant, he transgresses five negative commandments.

אָמְרוּ לוֹ: מִפְּנֵי שֶׁהִיא כִבְרִיָּתָהּ. — *They replied: Because it is as it was created.*

The Sages replied that the law concerning an ant is not applicable to *tevel* and similar prohibitions, because the liability for eating an ant is for eating a *complete* ant — just as it was when it was created, without even one limb missing (*Rabbeinu Yehonasan*).

אָמַר לָהֶן: אַף חִטָּה אַחַת כִּבְרִיָּתָהּ. — *He replied: One wheat kernel, too, is as it was created.*

[R' Shimon replied to the Sages that a kernel of *tevel* is also a whole creation, with nothing missing from it (*Rabbeinu Yehonasan*).

The halachah is in accordance with the Sages (*Rav*).

Tosafos (*Chullin* 96a) explain the position of the Sages to be that the concept of כִּבְרִיָּתָהּ, *as it was when it was created,* applies only if the Torah prohibits a specific item, e.g., גִּיד הַנָּשֶׁה, *the hip sinew,* or a non-kosher bird, implying that this is prohibited regardless of its size, provided it is whole. As regards *tevel,* too, had the Torah prohibited *a kernel of tevel,* one would be liable for eating even one kernel, although it is smaller than the volume of an olive. Since the Torah prohibited *tevel,* however, not *a kernel of tevel,* one is liable only for eating the usual amount, viz., the volume of an olive.

Although one does not receive *malkus* for eating less than a *kezayis* of forbidden foods, it is still forbidden to eat even the least amount of a forbidden food. The *Gemara* (*Yoma* 73b, 74a), however, records a dispute between R' Yochanan and Reish Lakish as to whether the consumption of less than the prescribed amounts is Biblically or Rabbinically forbidden. The halachah follows R' Yochanan that it is Biblically forbidden (*Rambam, Hil. Shvisas HeAsar* 2:3).

3.

This mishnah continues the list of transgressions punishable by *malkus,* lashes.

הָאוֹכֵל בִּכּוּרִים עַד־שֶׁלֹּא קָרָא עֲלֵיהֶן, — *One who eats bikkurim before the recital over them,*

The Torah prescribes that the first fruits of the land — *bikkurim* — be brought to the Temple, where the owner recites the Biblical section specified by the Torah for this occasion — אֲרַמִּי אֹבֵד אָבִי, *The Aramean sought to destroy my father* (*Deut.* 26:5-10). After the conclusion of this recital, he lays the *bikkurim* before the Altar and leaves the Temple.

3
3 concerning one who eats an ant of any size that he is liable? They replied: Because it is as it was created. He replied: One wheat kernel, too, is as it was created.

3. One who eats *bikkurim* before the recital over them, [or who eats] *kodshei kodashim* outside

YAD AVRAHAM

The *bikkurim* are then the property of the *Kohen.*

The mishnah rules that if the *Kohen* ate them before the recital, he is liable to *malkus.* However, if the *Kohen* ate them after the recital he is not liable *(Rav; Rambam Comm.).*

The wording of this explanation presents a difficulty. By stating 'after the recital he is not liable,' *Rav* and *Rambam* would seem to indicate that he is actually forbidden to eat the fruits even after the recital, but that he is not liable to *malkus* if he does. That is obviously not so, since after the recital the *Kohen* may certainly eat the fruits. *Meleches Shlomo* explains that the intention is that although the *bikkurim* are to be laid before the Altar, that act is not essential, and if it is omitted, the *Kohen* would not be liable for eating the fruits. *Shoshannim LeDavid* explains that although the sacrifice accompanying the *bikkurim* was not yet offered up (see *Bikkurim* 3:5), the *Kohen* is not liable. *Rav* would thus read: If the *Kohen* ate the *bikkurim* before the recital, he is liable. If, however, he ate them after the recital, but prior to being put before the Altar or before the sacrifice was offered on the Altar, he is not liable although he certainly should not eat the fruits at that point.

The mishnah follows R' Akiva, who rules that the recital is essential. The Sages, however, rule that laying the *bikkurim* before the Altar is essential, but that recital is not. The halachah is in accordance with the Sages. Therefore, if one eats the *bikkurim* before the recital, he is not subject to *malkus;* but if he eats them prior to placing them before the Altar, he is. The penalty is imposed only if the *bikkurim* were eaten after being brought into the city of Jerusalem. Should they be eaten prior to being brought into the city, there is no penalty of *malkus* [although it is forbidden] *(Rav; Rambam Comm.* and *Hil. Sanhedrin* 19:4,64, *Hil. Bikkurim* 3:3). *Rash* to *Bikkurim* 2:1, as well as *Rashi* and *Tosafos* here (18b), rule that the penalty is imposed only if the *bikkurim* were brought into the Temple court.

קָדְשֵׁי קָדָשִׁים — [*or who eats*] *kodshei kodashim* [lit. *most-holy offerings*]

I.e., the meat of a חַטָּאת, *sin-offering,* or an אָשָׁם, *guilt-offering (Gem.* 18a). If one eats of their meat outside the Temple Courtyard (see below), he is liable to *malkus.*

Sacrifices fall into two categories: *kodshei kodashim,* most-holy offerings; these include the burnt-offering (עוֹלָה), sin-offering or guilt-offering; and *kodshim kalim,* sacrifices of lesser holiness; these include the peace-offering (שְׁלָמִים) and thanksgiving-offering (תּוֹדָה). The meat of the *kodshei kodashim* offerings must be eaten within the Temple Courtyard, while those of *kodashim kalim* may be eaten any place within the walls of Jerusalem. The above does not refer to a burnt-offering since its meat is burnt on the Altar, not eaten *(Zevachim* 5:1,2).

חוּץ לַקְּלָעִים, — *outside the curtains,*

I.e., if a *Kohen* eats it outside the walls of the Temple Courtyard. These walls are referred to as curtains, because it was curtains which originally enclosed the Courtyard in the *Mishkan* [Tabernacle], Israel's first Temple, in the desert.

Tos. (Bava Kamma 94b) state that R' Yehudah HaNasi did not compose the Mishnah but only arranged it, the *mishnayos* having existed before his time. *Tif. Yis.* cites *Moed Katan* 11a, where the *Gemara* states that a certain mishnah preceded Yochanan *Kohen Gadol,* who lived some three hundred years before R' Yehudah HaNasi. Cf. *Kelim* 30:4, where we have proof that the entire

קָדָשִׁים קַלִּים וּמַעֲשֵׂר שֵׁנִי חוּץ לַחוֹמָה, הַשּׁוֹבֵר אֶת־הָעֶצֶם בְּפֶסַח הַטָּהוֹר — הֲרֵי זֶה לוֹקֶה אַרְבָּעִים. אֲבָל הַמּוֹתִיר בְּטָהוֹר, וְהַשּׁוֹבֵר בְּטָמֵא, אֵינוֹ לוֹקֶה אַרְבָּעִים.

יד אברהם

tractate *Kelim* was already arranged in R' Yose's time. Also, in *Avodah Zarah* 14b, we find that Abraham had a tractate *Avodah Zarah* composed of four hundred chapters. It appears, therefore, that the Mishnah was already composed in R' Yehudah HaNasi's time, many mishnayos even in their wording. He divided them into chapters and arranged their sequence. It has been suggested that any mishnah in which there is no controversy appears in its original language, as it was given over by Moshe. For this reason, we recite the chapter אֵיזֶהוּ מְקוֹמָן (*Zevachim* ch. 5) every day; since there is no controversy in it, its language is the original language given over by Moshe as he received it from God. In both that chapter and ours, the walls of the Temple Court are referred to as *curtains*, since in Moshe's time, there were only curtains around the courtyard of the *Mishkan* (*Tif. Yis.*; cf. *Yad Avraham* comm. to *Pesachim* 1:1).

קָדָשִׁים קַלִּים — *kodashim kalim* [lit. *offerings of lesser holiness*]

I.e., if one eats the meat of a peace-offering or a thanksgiving-offering outside the walls of Jerusalem; see below (*Rav*).

The admonition against eating *kodshei kodashim* outside the curtains and *kodashim kalim* outside the walls of Jerusalem is derived from (*Deut.* 12:17): *You may not eat in your cities*, etc. In that verse, all kinds of sacrifices are mentioned, which the Torah proscribes eating 'in your cities.' Eating any sacrifice outside the place prescribed for it is deemed 'eating in the cities' (*Rav; Rambam Comm.*).

וּמַעֲשֵׂר שֵׁנִי — *or maaser sheni*

As explained in the preceding mishnah [s.v. מעשר שני], *maaser sheni* (second tithe) may not be eaten outside of Jerusalem [unless it was redeemed] (*Rav* from *Gem.* 19b).

חוּץ לַחוֹמָה, — *outside the wall,*

I.e., if he ate *maaser sheni* or *kodashim kalim* outside the walls of Jerusalem, he is punished with *malkus*. The prohibition in regard to the *kodashim kalim* has been given above. The *malkus* in regard to *maaser sheni* is for transgressing the negative commandment of (*Deut.* 12:17): לֹא תוּכַל לֶאֱכֹל בִּשְׁעָרֶיךָ מַעְשַׂר דְּגָנְךָ וְתִירֹשְׁךָ וְיִצְהָרֶךָ, *You may not eat in your cities the tithe of your corn, your wine, or your oil.* This teaches that the *maaser sheni* (second tithe) may not be eaten in any of the cities, but only within the walls of Jerusalem.

The penalty of *malkus* applies only once the *maaser* was brought into Jerusalem; if he then takes it out and eats it he is liable. Should he eat it anywhere in Eretz Yisrael prior to its being brought into Jerusalem, there is no penalty. This is derived from the following verse: . . . לִפְנֵי ה׳ אֱלֹהֶיךָ תֹּאכְלֶנּוּ, *But before HASHEM your God you shall eat it.* In this context Scripture decrees: *You may not eat in your cities . . .* (*Rav* from *Gem.* 19b). This indicates that only once it was *before HASHEM*, meaning in Jerusalem, then *you may not eat in your cities.* Nevertheless, it is prohibited to eat it outside of Jerusalem by the implication of the positive commandment [since the Torah commands to eat it in Jerusalem].

הַשּׁוֹבֵר אֶת־הָעֶצֶם בְּפֶסַח הַטָּהוֹר — [*or*] *one who breaks the bone of a Pesach-offering that is tahor —*

[He has transgressed the Torah's command in reference to the *Pesach*-offering, *nor shall you break a bone in it* (*Exodus* 12:10). This prohibition applies only to a *Pesach*-offering that is *tahor* and fit to eat but not to one that is *tamei*, as the mishnah will explain below.]

Chinuch (*Mitzvah* 16) suggests that the reason for this prohibition is that it is not the custom of kings and princes to break and

3 the curtains, *kodashim kalim* or *maaser sheni* outside
3 the wall, [or] one who breaks the bone of a *Pesach*-offering that is *tahor* — incurs the penalty of forty [lashes]. But one who leaves over [meat] of one that is *tahor*, or who breaks [a bone] of one that is *tamei*, does not incur the penalty of forty [lashes].

YAD AVRAHAM

gnaw at bones. This is a habit only of the poor who lack sufficient food and gnaw at bones to assuage their hunger. Therefore, we, who proclaim that on this day we became *a kingdom of priests and a holy people* (*Exodus* 19:6), should deport ourselves in a manner befitting princes.

הֲרֵי זֶה לוֹקֶה אַרְבָּעִים. — *he incurs the penalty of forty* [*lashes*].

[In each of these cases, the sinner has transgressed a negative commandment of the Torah, and is, therefore, subject to thirty-nine lashes.]

◆§ Exceptions to the Penalty of Malkus

The mishnah now discusses a case in which *malkus* is not inflicted for violation of a negative commandment. Although the Torah prohibits one to leave over sacrificial meat past the deadline designated for its eating, one who does so is not punished by *malkus*. The *Gemara* (*Pesachim* 84a) offers two reasons for this: (a) Whenever a negative commandment is followed by a positive commandment that is designed to undo the transgression [לָאו הַנִּתָּק לַעֲשֵׂה], the logical assumption is that the Torah offers the positive commandment as the alternative to lashes. For example, the Torah forbids stealing, but commands a thief to return what he has stolen; therefore, restitution, not *malkus*, is the atonement for stealing. In the case of leaving over sacrificial meat, the Torah commands that leftover meat be burnt; thus, burning the meat substitutes for *malkus*. (b) Only for an active violation of a negative commandment is one liable to lashes. But leaving over sacrificial meat is a passive act — nothing is *done*, and lashes are not administered unless one has *committed* a wrong by performing an act.

אֲבָל הַמּוֹתִיר בַּטָּהוֹר, — *But one who leaves over* [*meat*] *of one that is tahor*,

Although it is forbidden to leave meat past the time when it must be eaten, one who does so is not liable to *malkus*. The negative transgression, *you shall let nothing of it remain till morning* (*Exodus* 12:10), is followed by the compensatory commandment, *that which remains until morning you shall burn in fire* (ibid.). The general rule is that when an affirmative command follows a negative command [לָאו הַנִּתָּק לַעֲשֵׂה], it is regarded as the remedy for the transgression, and there is no punishment for the transgression. Additionally, R' Yaakov (*Pesachim* 84a) is of the opinion that the reason he is absolved is because the prohibition was violated passively — not with an act — and there is a principle that one is not flogged for a transgression involving no action (*Rav* from *Gem.* 16a, *Pesachim* 84a). See General Introduction.

The mishnah states the exemption from *malkus* in terms of an offering that is *tahor*, but the same would certainly apply to one that is *tamei*.[1] The law is framed in terms of a *tahor* to teach that even a *tahor* is exempt from *malkus*, in contrast to the exemption which follows, which applies for a *tamei* (*Tzlach Pesachim* 28a).

וְהַשּׁוֹבֵר בַּטָּמֵא, אֵינוֹ לוֹקֶה אַרְבָּעִים. — *and one who breaks* [*a bone*] *of one that is tamei does not incur the penalty of forty* [*lashes*].

[The prohibition on breaking a bone

1. *Tzlach* (*Pesachim* 28a; see *Noda BiYehudah, Yoreh Deah* 2:13) states that it is nevertheless forbidden to leave over even a *tamei*. This is disputed by *Minchas Chinuch* (*Mitzvah* 7).

[ד] **הַנּוֹטֵל** אֵם עַל־הַבָּנִים — רַבִּי יְהוּדָה אוֹמֵר: לוֹקֶה, וְאֵינוֹ מְשַׁלֵּחַ. וַחֲכָמִים אוֹמְרִים: מְשַׁלֵּחַ, וְאֵינוֹ לוֹקֶה. זֶה הַכְּלָל: כָּל־מִצְוַת לֹא תַעֲשֶׂה שֶׁיֶּשׁ־בָּהּ קוּם עֲשֵׂה אֵין חַיָּבִין עָלֶיהָ.

יד אברהם

of the *Pesach*-offering does not apply to one that was invalidated by becoming *tamei.*] The *Gemara (Pesachim* 84a) infers this from the verse *neither shall you break a bone in it.* The emphasis on the term *in it* teaches that only in *it*, a valid, uncontaminated offering, is one forbidden to break a bone, but one may do so with one which has become *tamei (Rav).*

Based on this derivation, the halachically accepted view (R' Yosef's) reasons that even when it is permitted to offer and eat of a *Pesach*-offering that has become *tamei* — in a case in which the majority of the public was *tamei* (see *Pesachim* 7:5) — its bones *may* be broken (see *Rambam, Hil. Korban Pesach* 10:1).

See *Pesachim* 7:10 that according to the halachically accepted opinion even breaking the bones of a *Pesach*-offering that was *tamei* incurs punishment, if the *tumah* occurred after the offering had already been permitted for consumption, i.e., after its blood had been thrown on the Altar.

4.

The following mishnah deals with the *mitzvah* of שִׁלּוּחַ הַקֵּן, *sending away the nest,* which prohibits taking a mother bird together with her young. In the Torah, we read *(Deut.* 22:6f): כִּי יִקָּרֵא קַן־צִפּוֹר לְפָנֶיךָ בַּדֶּרֶךְ בְּכָל־עֵץ אוֹ עַל־הָאָרֶץ אֶפְרֹחִים אוֹ בֵיצִים וְהָאֵם רֹבֶצֶת עַל־הָאֶפְרֹחִים אוֹ עַל־הַבֵּיצִים לֹא־תִקַּח הָאֵם עַל־הַבָּנִים: שַׁלֵּחַ תְּשַׁלַּח אֶת־הָאֵם וְאֶת־הַבָּנִים תִּקַּח־לָךְ לְמַעַן יִיטַב לָךְ וְהַאֲרַכְתָּ יָמִים — *If a bird's nest chance to be before you on the road, on any tree, or on the ground, with young ones or eggs, and the mother bird is sitting upon the young or on the eggs, you shall not take the mother bird while on the young. You shall send away the mother, and the young you may take for yourself; in order that it may be well with you, and you shall prolong your days.*

Whether the negative commandment of *you shall not take the mother while on the young* is לָאו הַנִּתָּק לַעֲשֵׂה, *a negative commandment rectified by a positive commandment* [i.e., a negative commandment whose transgression can be undone by performance of a positive commandment], is a point in question. The verse may be explained to mean that you shall not take the mother bird, but if you do, you can make amends by sending her away. According to this interpretation, the positive commandment is given to rectify the violation of the negative commandment, and there is therefore no penalty of lashes imposed for the violation, as explained in the previous mishnah. However, it may be simply explained to mean that you may not take the mother bird; rather, send her away. In this case *send her away* is not a separate positive commandment given to remedy the violation, but rather a delineation of the proper procedure to be followed in the first place. According to this view, the transgressor incurs the penalty of lashes, since the Torah does not prescribe a procedure for rectifying the violation.

הַנּוֹטֵל אֵם עַל־הַבָּנִים — [*If*] *one takes a mother* [*bird*] *while on her young* —

[I.e., if one takes the mother bird from a nest while she is sitting on her young, thereby transgressing the negative commandment of *you shall not take the*

4. [If] one takes a mother [bird] while on her young — R' Yehudah says: He incurs the penalty of lashes, and he need not send [her] away. The Sages [,however,] say: He must send [her] away, and he does not incur the penalty of lashes. This is the rule: Any negative commandment that has in it a positive commandment bears no liability.

YAD AVRAHAM

mother bird while on the young.]

רַבִּי יְהוּדָה אוֹמֵר: לוֹקֶה, וְאֵינוֹ מְשַׁלֵּחַ. — *R' Yehudah says: He incurs the penalty of lashes, and he need not send* [*her*] *away.*

R' Yehudah understands שַׁלֵּחַ, *send away,* to be a positive command to send away the mother bird from the very beginning. Although it is written after לֹא־תִקַּח, *you shall not take,* the intention is that you shall not take her, but rather send her away before taking her young. Hence, this is not a negative commandment rectified by a positive commandment (*Rav, Rashi* from *Chullin* 14a).

Rambam (Comm.) explains that R' Yehudah is of the opinion that for any negative commandment, even one rectified by a positive *mitzvah,* there is a penalty of lashes. See *Pnei Yehoshua* to *Makkos* 16, who reconciles *Rambam* with *Gemara (Chullin* 141a).

וַחֲכָמִים אוֹמְרִים: מְשַׁלֵּחַ, וְאֵינוֹ לוֹקֶה. — *The Sages* [*,however,*] *say: He must send* [*her*] *away, and he does not incur the penalty of lashes.*

They hold that שַׁלֵּחַ, *send away,* means that one must send away the mother bird after taking her. Consequently, this is a negative commandment rectified by a positive commandment, for which there is no penalty of *malkus* (*Rav; Rashi*).

The halachah is in accordance with the Sages (*Rav; Rambam, Shechitah* 13:1).

זֶה הַכְּלָל: כָּל־מִצְוַת לֹא תַעֲשֶׂה שֶׁיֶּשׁ־בָּהּ קוּם עֲשֵׂה — *This is the rule: Any negative commandment that has in it a positive commandment*

I.e., any *mitzvah* concerning which the Torah states that if one transgresses that particular negative commandment he must make amends by fulfilling a positive commandment, e.g., the case of sending away the mother bird, in which the Torah prohibits taking her, but then gives a positive commandment of sending her away to make amends for transgressing the negative. Another example would be the negative commandment not to go into a debtor's house to extract security from him. Should one do it, the Torah gave him the opportunity to make amends by returning the pledge [*Deut.* 24:10,13] (*Rav* from *Gem.* 16a).

אֵין חַיָּבִין עָלֶיהָ. — *bears no liability* [lit. *one is not liable for it*].

[I.e., the transgressor does not incur the penalty of *malkus* for transgressing the negative commandment since he can rectify it by fulfilling the positive commandment.]

Should he neglect to fulfill the positive commandment, however, he does incur *malkus.* The *Gemara* (15a,b) cites a major dispute concerning what constitutes neglect in fulfilling the *mitzvah.* R' Yochanan is of the opinion that as long as it is still possible to fulfill the *mitzvah,* the transgressor does not receive *malkus.* Furthermore, in order to be subject to lashes, the transgressor must actively nullify the possibility of performing the positive commandment, for example, by killing the mother bird and thereby making it impossible ever to send her away. Thus, in R' Yochanan's view, imposition of *malkus* in the case of a negative commandment rectified by a positive one is dependent on בִּטְּלוֹ וְלֹא בִטְּלוֹ, *nullifying it* [the positive commandment] *and not nullifying it.* If the

[ה] **הַקּוֹרֵחַ** קָרְחָה בְּרֹאשׁוֹ, וְהַמַּקִּיף פְּאַת רֹאשׁוֹ, וְהַמַּשְׁחִית פְּאַת זְקָנוֹ,

יד אברהם

bird should merely die a natural death, the transgressor would not be subject to *malkus*, since it was not he who removed the possibility of rectifying his violation. In this view, the full prohibition is seen to be the transgression of the negative commandment to the extent that it can no longer be rectified. Thus, the violation of this prohibition is not complete until the transgressor also nullifies the opportunity to undo his violation (*Rashi* 15a).

Reish Lakish, however, considers the criterion for *malkus* in such cases to be whether the transgressor *fulfills it* [the positive commandment] *or does not fulfill it* [קִימוֹ וְלֹא קִיְּמוֹ]. I.e., once he is brought to court for his transgression, he is warned by the judges to rectify his violation by performing the positive commandment or suffer *malkus*. At that point, he must fulfill the positive commandment immediately, and if he fails to do so, he receives the lashes (*Rashi* ibid.; cf. *Tos.*). In this view, the negative commandment is seen as standing on its own, without reference to the positive commandment. The positive commandment merely affords the transgressor the opportunity to escape the penalty for his sin by rectifying his violation; the transgression itself, however, is complete regardless of whether the sinner performs the positive command or not (*Rashi*).

Following the general rule that the halachah follows R' Yochanan in his disputes with Reish Lakish, the criterion for *malkus* in negative commandments rectified by positive commandments is *nullification or non-nullification*. Thus, one who takes the mother bird with her young is not liable to lashes unless he then kills the mother bird (*Kesef Mishneh, Hil. Sanhedrin* 16:4).

This ruling follows *Rashi's* reading of the *Gemara*. However, *Rabbeinu Chananel, Rif*, and *Rambam* (*Hil. Sanhedrin* 16:4; see *Kesef Mishneh*) had in the texts of their *Gemara* a reversal of the positions of R' Yochanan and Reish Lakish, with R' Yochanan making the criterion *fulfillment and non-fulfillment* while Reish Lakish is the one who defines it as *nullification and non-nullification*. Accordingly, the halachah would be that if he was warned by the court to rectify his violation immediately and he failed to do so, he receives *malkus* (*Rif, Rambam* ibid.). *Rav*, too, follows this view and therefore states that even if the bird died naturally — thereby making it impossible for him ever to fulfill the positive commandment of sending her away — he is also liable to *malkus* (*Tos. R' Akiva Eiger*).

5.

The mishnah proceeds to enumerate other negative commandments punishable by *malkus*. In all these cases, there is a ruling that is not self-evident, such as the multiple penalties prescribed in this mishnah (*Rav*).

הַקּוֹרֵחַ קָרְחָה בְּרֹאשׁוֹ, — *One who makes a bald spot on his head,*

I.e., one who makes a bald spot on his head by tearing out his hair in mourning for a dead person. The Torah prohibits such mourning practices (*Deut.* 14:1): וְלֹא תָשִׂימוּ קָרְחָה בֵּין עֵינֵיכֶם לָמֵת, *and you shall not make a bald spot between your eyes for the dead*. This same prohibition is stated regarding *Kohanim* in *Leviticus* 21:5, where the wording is: לֹא יִקְרְחוּ קָרְחָה בְּרֹאשָׁם, *they shall not make a bald spot on their head*. In that context the Torah does not specify that the prohibition applies only if the bald spot is made in anguish over the death of a beloved one. Nevertheless, the *Gemara* (20a) derives that just as Israelites are admonished against making bald spots on their head only if it is done for the dead, so too

3
5 **5.** One who makes a bald spot on his head, or who rounds the corner of his head, or who destroys the corner of his beard, or who inflicts [upon himself] a

YAD AVRAHAM

Kohanim are admonished against this act only if done for that purpose. The minimum size of the bald spot for which one incurs the penalty of *malkus* is the size of a bean (*Rav* from *Gem.* 20b).

וְהַמַּקִּיף פְּאַת רֹאשׁוֹ, — *or who rounds the corner of his head,*

I.e., who cuts off the hair of his temples from behind his ear to his forehead (*Rav* from *Gem.* 20b). He is liable for transgressing the negative commandment of (*Lev.* 19:27): לֹא תַקִּפוּ פְּאַת רֹאשְׁכֶם, *You shall not round the corner of your head.* Since there is no hair behind the ears, nor on the forehead, cutting the hair off the temples so that it will even the line with the back of the ear and with the forehead is prohibited. The corners of the head extend down to the place where the lower jaw is hinged to the upper jaw. The hair of this part of the head is therefore known as *pe'os*, literally, *corners* (*Tos. Yom Tov* from *Rivan*).[1]

Where one cuts another's *pe'os* both transgress this commandment (*Gem.* 20b). This ruling is based on the plural form of the verb תַקִּפוּ in the Scriptural prohibition (*Rivan* 20b; *Tos. Shevuos* 3a). Another interpretation is that the causative sense of the verb may be explained to mean, 'You shall not allow to be rounded' (*Rivan*).

There is, however, a difference between the standard for liability for the cutter and the one to whom it is being done. The cutter is always liable, whereas the one whose hair is being cut is liable only if he inclines his head in such a way as to enable the cutter to do his work (*Gem.* 20b). Should he stay still and not help the cutter, he does not incur *malkus*, although he too has committed a sin. The reason for this is that, as we have seen in the last mishnah, one does not incur lashes for transgressing a prohibition passively. Consequently, the person receiving the haircut must physically assist in the transgression in some way in order to be liable for the penalty (*Ritva; Tos., Shevuos* 3a; *Tur Yoreh Deah* 181; *Shulchan Aruch* 181:4).

[The forbidden method of removing *pe'os* will be discussed further in the mishnah.]

Women are not forbidden to shave the hair of their temples. The prohibition on cutting off the temple hair is grouped together with the prohibition of shaving the beard (*Lev.* 19:27); from this the *Gemara* (*Kiddushin* 35b) derives that whoever is excluded from the prohibition of shaving the beard is similarly excluded from the prohibition on cutting off the hair of the temples. Since women are biologically excluded from the former, they are also legally excluded from the latter.

Nevertheless, *Rambam* (*Hil. Avodas Kochavim* 12:2) states that though women are permitted to shave their own temples, they are forbidden to shave the temples of a man. They are exempted in this case only from the penalty of *malkus* but not from the prohibition itself (ibid. 12:5). *Ravad*, however, considers this prohibition only Rabbinic, not Biblical. *Tur* (*Yoreh Deah* 181) cites the opinion of *Semag* that there is no prohibition at all attached to her.

וְהַמַּשְׁחִית פְּאַת זְקָנוֹ, — *or who destroys the corner of his beard,*

I.e., who shaves it off. He is liable for transgressing the negative commandment of (*Lev.* 19:27): וְלֹא תַשְׁחִית אֵת פְּאַת

1. *Rambam* (*Hil. Avodas Kochavim* 12:6) states that as long as one leaves at least forty hairs on the temple (or according to *Tur's* version, four hairs; see *Kesef Mishneh*), one has not violated this prohibition. *Beis Yosef* (*Yoreh Deah* 181), however, cites the opinion of *Semag* and *Nimmukei Yosef* (quoting *Avi Haezri*) that cutting off completely even two hairs of the temple is punishable by *malkus*. This latter view is accepted as the halachah (*Shulchan Aruch Yoreh Deah* 181:9).

וְהַשּׂוֹרֵט שְׂרִיטָה אַחַת עַל־הַמֵּת — חַיָּב. שָׂרַט שְׂרִיטָה אַחַת עַל־חֲמִשָּׁה מֵתִים, אוֹ חָמֵשׁ שְׂרִיטוֹת עַל־מֵת אֶחָד — חַיָּב עַל־כָּל־אַחַת וְאַחַת.

עַל־הָרֹאשׁ: שְׁתַּיִם — אַחַת מִכָּאן וְאַחַת מִכָּאן. וְעַל־הַזָּקָן — שְׁתַּיִם מִכָּאן וּשְׁתַּיִם מִכָּאן, וְאַחַת

יד אברהם

זְקָנֶךָ, *and you shall not destroy the corner of your beard.*

In this case, too, both the shaver and the shaved transgress this negative commandment, and if the person being shaved assists in the operation, he too incurs the penalty of lashes, as above (*Tif. Yis.* from *Rambam, Avodas Kochavim* 12:7).

Although this prohibition is worded with a singular verb form, which would indicate that only the shaver is liable, nevertheless, since the negative commandment addressed to the *Kohanim* in *Lev.* 21:5: לֹא יְגַלְּחוּ, *they shall not shave*, is indeed worded in the plural, it includes both the shaver and the shaved (*Tos., Shevuos* 3a).

וְהַשּׂוֹרֵט שְׂרִיטָה אַחַת עַל־הַמֵּת — *or who inflicts* [*upon himself*] *a single gash over someone who died —*

I.e., if one lacerates his skin either with his fingernails or with a knife (*Gem.* 21a) out of anguish over a loved one who has died (*Rivan*), he transgresses the negative commandment of (*Lev.* 19:28): וְשֶׂרֶט לָנֶפֶשׁ לֹא תִתְּנוּ בִּבְשַׂרְכֶם, *and a scratch for a* [*dead*] *person you shall not put in your flesh.*

[The expression שְׂרִיטָה אַחַת, *a single gash*, is used to introduce the following ruling governing one who makes five scratches for one dead person.]

One incurs *malkus* only if he inflicts gashes in his flesh in anguish over the loss of a beloved one. Should he do so because of another loss, e.g., his house collapsed, or his ship sank, he does not incur the penalty of lashes (*Gem.* 20b).

Beis Yosef (*Yoreh Deah* 180) rules that not only is there no penalty, it is actually permissible. *Bach*, however, prohibits it (ad loc.).

The *Gemara* (*Sanhedrin* 68b) relates that after the passing of R' Eliezer, R' Akiva came upon his bier between Caesarea and Lod. Seeing his teacher's bier, R' Akiva began beating his flesh until blood flowed to the ground. Finally, he began his eulogy. [He said,] 'My father, my father! The chariots of Israel and its riders! I have many coins, but I have no moneychanger to change them for me!' [I have many questions to ask, but I have no one to whom I can ask them (*Rashi*).] Some authorities deduce from this episode that only gashing or cutting is prohibited. Striking, however, is permissible, even if it results in bleeding (*Ramban, Toras HaAdam* p. 89, ed. Mossad Harav Kook; *Ritva*).

Others object to this leniency, explaining instead that R' Akiva caused his flesh to bleed not for the passing of R' Eliezer per se, but for the vast store of Torah knowledge that had been lost with R' Eliezer's passing. For that reason the *Gemara* relates his eulogy, to demonstrate that he had beaten his flesh because of the loss of a Torah authority who could be approached with many questionable points of halachah (*Tos., Sanhedrin* 68b; *Rosh*, end of *Moed Katan; Tur Yoreh Deah* 180; cf. *Tos., Yevamos* 13b).

חַיָּב. — *he is liable.*

[I.e., one who commits any of the four violations listed here incurs the penalty of *malkus.*]

שָׂרַט שְׂרִיטָה אַחַת עַל־חֲמִשָּׁה מֵתִים, אוֹ חָמֵשׁ שְׂרִיטוֹת עַל־מֵת אֶחָד — [*If*] *he inflicted one gash over five people who died, or five gashes over one person who died —*

[I.e., he made one gash in his flesh in anguish over five persons who died, or five gashes over one death.]

חַיָּב עַל־כָּל־אַחַת וְאַחַת. — *he is liable for each one.*

I.e., he incurs the penalty of *malkus* for each person as well as for each gash. Therefore, in the first instance he is liable

3 single gash over someone who died — he is liable. [If] he
5 inflicted one gash over five people who died, or five gashes over one person who died — he is liable for each one.

On the head: two — one on each side. On the beard — two on each side and one below. R' Eliezer says: If he

to five sets of *malkus*, one for each person whose death prompted him to gash himself. In the second case, he is flogged five times, once for each gash.

The mishnah in *Nazir* states that if a *nazir* drinks wine after being duly warned he is liable to *malkus*. Even if he proceeds to drink five cups of wine after that warning, he still incurs only one set of *malkus*. However, if he is warned between each cup, he is liable to a separate set of *malkus* for each cup. This seems to contradict the law that although he was warned but once, and all five gashes were inflicted together, he incurs the penalty of five sets of *malkus*. Indeed, the ruling in our mishnah is a special law learned from the expression וְשֶׂרֶט לָנֶפֶשׁ, *and a gash for a person*, which implies liability for each gash and for each person (*Rav* from *Gem.* 20b). This implication is derived from the use by the Torah of the singular noun שֶׂרֶט, *a gash*, in defining this prohibition, rather than the verb form לֹא תִשְׂרְטוּ בִּבְשַׂרְכֶם, *you shall not scratch your flesh* (*Tos. Yom Tov* from *Rivan*). The liability for each dead person is derived from Scripture's choice of the word לָנֶפֶשׁ, *for a person*, instead of the word לָמֵת, *for the dead*, as it appears in the negative commandment forbidding making a bald spot (*Tos. Yom Tov*).

עַל־הָרֹאשׁ: שְׁתַּיִם — *On the head: two* —

I.e., for rounding the corners of the hair of his head (i.e., shaving off the temples) he incurs two sets of *malkus*.

אַחַת מִכָּאן וְאַחַת מִכָּאן. — *one on each side* [lit. *one from here and one from here*].

I.e., one for cutting off the right corner and one for cutting off the left corner, each corner being a separate transgression (*Rav*).

The head is composed of two parts: the place where the hair grows, and the face and the beard. These two parts are joined at the temple, and this spot is therefore called the פֵּאָה, *corner*, of the head.

One incurs the penalty of two series of lashes even if he shaves off both *pe'os* at once, and even if he was warned only once. Since there are two *pe'os*, the warning לֹא תַקִּיפוּ, *Don't round*, is considered as applying to each act of removal separately (*Tos. Yom Tov* from *Rivan*).

וְעַל־הַזָּקָן — שְׁתַּיִם מִכָּאן, וּשְׁתַּיִם מִכָּאן, וְאַחַת מִלְּמַטָּה. — *On the beard — two on each side* [lit. *two on this side, two on that side*], *and one below.*

[I.e., for shaving off the beard, the transgressor incurs five sets of *malkus* for destroying the five corners of the beard — two on the right side of the face, and two on the left, and one on the chin. This prohibition refers to shaving them off with a razor, as will be discussed below.]

The *Gemara* does not clarify the exact location of the five corners of the beard. There are, therefore, a number of opinions as to which places are meant. Because of the many opinions, observant Jews do not shave any part of their beards with a razor (*Yoreh Deah* 181:11).

The major opinions are as follows:

(1) The two corners of the lower jaw, the two bones of the upper jaw just below the temples, and the chin (*Rashi*, as quoted by *Nimmukei Yosef*, *Rosh*, and *Rashbam*; *Rambam Comm.*, *Hil. Avodas Kochavim* 12:7; *Rivan*; *Rav*).

(2) The two ends of the upper jawbone on each side and the chin (*Rashi*, *Shevuos* 3a; *Rashi*, *Lev.* 19:27).

(3) The two upper jaws, the two ends of the mustache, and the chin (*Rabbeinu*

מִלְמַטָּה. רַבִּי אֱלִיעֶזֶר אוֹמֵר: אִם־נְטָלוֹ כֻלּוֹ כְּאַחַת, אֵינוֹ חַיָּב אֶלָּא אַחַת. וְאֵינוֹ חַיָּב עַד־שֶׁיִּטְּלֶנּוּ בְּתַעַר. רַבִּי אֱלִיעֶזֶר אוֹמֵר: אֲפִילוּ לִקְטוֹ בְמַלְקֵט אוֹ־בְרְהִיטְנִי, חַיָּב.

יד אברהם

Chananel, as quoted by *Rosh, Rashbam,* and *Nimmukei Yosef).*

Some believe that *Rabbeinu Chananel's* view is that the fifth corner extends to the Adam's apple *(Tur).* See *Taz* 181:3. It must be noted that according to *Rabbeinu Chananel,* even the mustache may not be shaven with a razor since its two ends represent two corners of the beard *(Taz* ad loc.).

רַבִּי אֱלִיעֶזֶר אוֹמֵר: אִם־נְטָלוֹ כֻלּוֹ כְּאַחַת, אֵינוֹ חַיָּב אֶלָּא אַחַת. — *R' Eliezer says: If he removed it all at once, he is liable only once.*

[I.e., if he removed the entire beard at once, he receives only one set of *malkus,* despite having cut off all five corners.] R' Eliezer maintains that since there is but one negative commandment governing the five corners of the beard, it is as if one would eat many olive-sized pieces of prohibited food after having received one warning, for which he receives only one set of lashes *(Rav).* The *Tanna Kamma,* however, rules that since the Torah uses the singular פְּאַת, *the corner of,* it is as if the Torah had said, 'Do not destroy this corner and this corner,' etc., five times. Therefore, he is liable for destroying each corner separately, as in the case of the bald spot and the gash *(Tos. Yom Tov; Rivan).*

As mentioned above, these negative commandments are discussed because of the multiple penalties for each of them. These are: the many sets of *malkus* incurred for making gashes in one's flesh, according to both the number of gashes and the number of dead persons for whom the transgressor makes these gashes; also, the multiple penalties for rounding the corners of the head and destroying the corners of the beard. The sin of making bald spots on the head because of anguish over a death is also mentioned since one is liable for making many bald spots at once, e.g., if he applies a depilatory cream to his five fingers and places them on his head, thereby removing the hair in five places at once *(Gem.* 20b).

וְאֵינוֹ חַיָּב עַד־שֶׁיִּטְּלֶנּוּ בְּתַעַר. — *He is not liable unless he removes it with a razor.*

[One does not incur the penalty of *malkus* for removing the corner of his beard unless he does so by using a razor.]

The Scriptural interdict of removing the beard is worded, וְלֹא תַשְׁחִית אֵת פְּאַת זְקָנֶךָ, *and you shall not destroy the corner of your beard (Lev.* 19:27). This identical interdict appears in *Lev.* 21:5 in regard to *Kohanim.* There it is worded, וּפְאַת זְקָנָם לֹא יְגַלֵּחוּ, *and the corner of their beard they shall not shave.* In the one commandment the prohibition is characterized with the word *destroy* whereas in the other the verb *shave* is used. Since the Oral Tradition teaches that both interdicts apply to both *Kohanim* and Israelites, it is clear that the interdict is limited to an implement which simultaneously shaves and destroys; one which is customarily used to shave the beard and one which destroys — i.e., cuts off the hair at the skin. The scissors, although customarily used for trimming the beard, does not destroy it, since it does not cut close to the skin. A tweezer or a plane, although it pulls out the hair close to the skin, is not customarily used for shaving the beard. The only implement the Sages could find that fits both qualifications was the razor, customarily used for shaving, and cutting very close to the skin *(Rav* from *Gem.* 21a). Accordingly, one may trim his beard with a scissors. However, one must take care not to cut at skin-level with the lower blade

3 removed it all at once, he is liable only once. He is not
5 liable unless he removes it with a razor. R' Eliezer says:
Even if he plucked it with a tweezer or with a plane, he
is liable.

by itself, since cutting in that manner is tantamount to cutting with a razor (*Yoreh Deah* 181:10; *Rama*).

Among Jews who shaved their beards, it was customary to permit using a depilatory powder, which, although removing the hair at skin-level, is not considered a direct action of shaving off the hair. One must, however, be careful not to remove the paste with an iron implement, since this would resemble shaving. Rather, a wooden one or one made of bone was used (*Tif. Yis.*). *Noda BiYehudah* (vol. 2, *Yoreh Deah* 81) also permits the use of the powder, basing his permissibility on the fact that although it destroys the hair, it is not the customary manner of shaving. He also cautions not to remove the paste with a knife, rather by hand. Since some hair may be left even after the powder has removed most of it, cutting with a knife against the skin is tantamount to using a razor.

Some authorities rule that the prohibition in the mishnah requiring that the implement be both one that destroys and one customarily used for shaving is only referring to the penalty of *malkus*. Concerning permissibility, however, one may not remove the beard, even with a scissor if he trims close to the face as with a razor (*Chinuch, Mitzvah* 252).[1]

These rulings apply only to shaving the beard. With regard to cutting the *pe'os*, however, it is forbidden to cut them close to the head even with a scissor. In the context of *pe'os*, destruction is not mentioned. Therefore, even if one does not cut off the hair as close as he would with a razor, it is prohibited. The hair must be sufficiently long so that it can be grasped between the fingers (*Rosh; Tos., Shevuos* 2b and others). *Rambam* (*Hil. Avodas Kochavim* 12:6), however, equates the two. Because of this controversy, we adopt the stringent view and refrain from removing the *pe'os* close to the head even with a scissor (*Yoreh Deah* 181:3).

רַבִּי אֱלִיעֶזֶר אוֹמֵר: אֲפִילוּ לְקָטוֹ בְמַלְקֵט אוֹ־בִּרְהִיטְנִי, — *R' Eliezer says: Even if he plucked it with a tweezer or with a plane,*

This translation follows *Rav*.

Sefer Hazikaron, Lev. 21:5 identifies these implements as a tweezer and small scissor. He quotes *Rashi* (*Kiddushin* 35b), who identifies them both as planes, distinguishing only between the use of the two. The former is a plane used by sword makers to smooth the sheath of the sword, and the latter as a plane used by shield makers to smooth the shield. He questions, however, why the mishnah would use the word לְקָטוֹ, *plucked*, to describe the removal of hair with a plane.

חַיָּב. — *he is liable.*

R' Eliezer believes that these implements are customarily used for shaving the hair. Therefore, they fit into the category of shaving and destruction (*Gem.* 21a). The halachah is not in accordance with R' Eliezer (*Rav; Rambam, Hil. Avodas Kochavim* 12:7; *Yoreh Deah* 180:10).

6.

The following mishnah discusses the penalty for כְּתֹבֶת קַעֲקַע, *tattoo marks*, in one's skin. The Torah states (*Lev.* 19:28): וּכְתֹבֶת קַעֲקַע לֹא תִתְּנוּ בָּכֶם אֲנִי ה', *and you shall not make tattoo marks in yourselves; I am* HASHEM. This is accomplished by pricking the

1. In modern times, questions have arisen over the use of electric shavers. The *Chofetz Chaim* in his *Likkutei Halachos* to this mishnah prohibits the use of electric razors that shave too close to the skin. The common practice permitting the use of most electric shavers is based on the ruling of *R' Moshe Feinstein z''l.*

[ו] **הַכּוֹתֵב** כְּתֹבֶת קַעֲקַע: כָּתַב וְלֹא קִעֲקַע, קִעֲקַע וְלֹא כָתַב — אֵינוֹ חַיָּב, עַד שֶׁיִּכְתֹּב וִיקַעֲקַע בִּדְיוֹ, וּבִכְחוֹל, וּבְכָל־דָּבָר שֶׁהוּא רוֹשֵׁם. רַבִּי שִׁמְעוֹן בֶּן־יְהוּדָה מִשּׁוּם רַבִּי שִׁמְעוֹן אוֹמֵר: אֵינוֹ חַיָּב עַד־שֶׁיִּכְתֹּב שָׁם הַשֵּׁם, שֶׁנֶּאֱמַר: „וּכְתֹבֶת קַעֲקַע לֹא תִתְּנוּ בָּכֶם אֲנִי ה׳.״

יד אברהם

flesh and inserting a coloring agent, such as ink or dye, thereby leaving an indelible impression in the skin. [This was the custom of the pagans, who would mark themselves for their idolatry, implying that they were slaves to it and marked for its worship (*Rambam, Hil. Avodas Kochavim* 12:11).]

הַכּוֹתֵב כְּתֹבֶת קַעֲקַע: — *One who makes a tattoo* [lit. *one who writes a skin-prick writing*]:

I.e., he makes a series of small incisions in his flesh in the form of letters and then fills them with dye or ink (*Rav; Rambam, Hil. Avodas Kochavim* 12:11). *Rivan,* however, explains that the procedure was first to write with dye on top of the skin and then to make the pricks so that the dye would penetrate under the skin (see below).

The mishnah does not make clear whether the Biblical interdict includes only writing letters or if it includes also making any marks on the skin. *Rabbeinu Yehonasan, Rabbeinu Yehudah Almedari, Semak* (*Mitzvah* 72) and *Chinuch* (*Mitzvah* 257) rule that there is no penalty of *malkus* unless one writes a letter. *Ravad* and *Rash* to *Sifra,* however, state explicitly that one is liable even if he does not write letters. This would also appear to be the view of *Meiri,* who states as the basis for this prohibition the custom of the pagans to make a picture of their deity, implying that making pictures is also counted in the interdict of tattooing.

כָּתַב וְלֹא קִעֲקַע, — [*If*] *he wrote but did not prick* [*it into the skin*],

I.e., he wrote on his skin with ink or dye but did not insert it under his skin by making incisions (*Rav*).

קִעֲקַע וְלֹא כָתַב — — [*or*] *he pricked* [*the skin*] *but did not write* —

I.e., if he made incisions with a knife or needle but did not fill them with dye (*Rav*).

Others explain the wording here in the opposite manner. כָּתַב denotes making the shapes in the skin with a knife. קִעֲקַע denotes marking the skin by inserting the dye or ink (*Semag, Mitzvah* 61; *Chinuch, Mitzvah* 257; *Rambam, Hil. Avodas Kochavim* 12:11). Accordingly, we would render: *If he wrote* [with a knife] *but did not mark* [with dye], [*or*] he marked [with dye] *but did not write* [with a knife] —

אֵינוֹ חַיָּב, — *he is not liable,*

[I.e., he does not incur the penalty of lashes.]

עַד שֶׁיִּכְתֹּב וִיקַעֲקַע — *unless he writes and pricks* [*it into the skin*]

I.e., unless he writes with ink or dye on the skin and imbeds it under the skin by pricking (*Rav*). According to *Rambam, Semag,* and *Chinuch,* the intention is that he makes the incision and also fills it in with ink.

Tosafos (*Gittin* 20b), following one opinion in our *Gemara* (21a), rule that though the Biblical prohibition aplies only if he writes and pricks it into the skin, it is nevertheless Rabbinically forbidden to do even one of them. The halachah, however, is that in the absence of both conditions, it is completely

3
6

6. One who makes a tattoo: [If] he wrote but did not prick [it into the skin], [or] he pricked [the skin] but did not write — he is not liable, unless he writes and pricks [it into the skin] with ink, or with blue dye, or with anything that makes a mark. R' Shimon ben Yehudah says in the name of R' Shimon: He is not liable unless he writes a name there, as it is said *(Lev.* 19:28): *And you shall not make tattoo marks in yourselves; I am* HASHEM.

YAD AVRAHAM

permissible *(Beis Yosef, Yoreh Deah* 180).

The mishnah's wording here seems to indicate that the writing was done before the pricking, since otherwise the mishnah should have stated עַד שֶׁיְּקַעֲקַע וְיִכְתֹּב, *unless he pricks and writes.* This would bear out *Rivan's* explanation of the procedure. *Rav,* who previously explained the procedure to be reversed, notes this difficulty and explains that the mishnah follows the expression of the Torah, כְּתֹבֶת קַעֲקַע, literally, *writing of skin-pricks.* The intention, however, is that the pricking preceded the writing. This is also the opinion of *Rabbeinu Yehudah Almadari* and *Nimmukei Yosef.*

As mentioned above, *Rambam* and others also explain that the incision is made first, but they explain that the incision is referred to by the *Tanna* as *writing.* Consequently, the mishnah can be explained literally without any difficulty. In practice, both methods of tattooing are equally prohibited *(Bach, Shach, Yoreh Deah* 180).

בִּדְיוֹ, — *with ink,*

[This is black, as in *Megillah* 2:2 *(Tif. Yis).*]

וּבְכָחוֹל, — *or with blue dye,*

[This was a substance commonly used in eye treatments.]

וּבְכָל־דָּבָר שֶׁהוּא רוֹשֵׁם. — *or with anything that makes a mark.*

I.e., with any dye that leaves a mark *(Meiri).*

The liability is on the one who makes the tattoo. The person being tattooed is not liable unless he assists in some way *(Rambam, Hil. Avodas Kochavim* 12:11).

רַבִּי שִׁמְעוֹן בֶּן־יְהוּדָה מִשּׁוּם רַבִּי שִׁמְעוֹן אוֹמֵר: — *R' Shimon ben Yehudah says in the name of R' Shimon:*

[I.e., in the name of R' Shimon ben Yochai. See comm. to *Shevuos* 1:5.]

אֵינוֹ חַיָּב עַד־שֶׁיִּכְתֹּב שֵׁם הַשֵּׁם, — *He is not liable unless he writes a name there,*

I.e., he does not incur the penalty of lashes unless he writes in the incision the name of a pagan deity *(Rav* from *Gem.* 21a).

Meiri explains that R' Shimon rules that he is not liable unless he tattoos a picture of that deity.

שֶׁנֶּאֱמַר: „וּכְתֹבֶת קַעֲקַע לֹא תִתְּנוּ בָּכֶם אֲנִי ה׳.״ — *as it is said (Lev. 19:28): 'And you shall not make tattoo marks in yourselves; I am* HASHEM.'

It is as though God states: Do not make on yourselves the name of any pagan deity for I am HASHEM, and you shall not accept any deity as sharing that status with Me *(Rav).*

The halachah is not in accordance with R' Shimon *(Rav; Rambam Comm.; Nimmukei Yosef). Rif,* however, decides in accordance with R' Shimon.

According to the *Tanna Kamma* that one is liable for any tattoo, even one not related to idolatry, the reason for the Torah interdiction of this act is not apparent. *Rivan* and *Ritva* indeed state that it is a decree of Scripture, meaning that there is no apparent reason for this *mitzvah. Rambam,* however, as mentioned above, attributes this to the pagan custom of the marking themselves for their idols *(Hil. Avodas Kochavim* 12:11). Accordingly, we must explain that the Torah wished to distance us from pagan customs [even when these do not exactly mirror their practices] *(Chinuch, Mitzvah* 257).

[ז] **נָזִיר** שֶׁהָיָה שׁוֹתֶה בַּיַּיִן כָּל־הַיּוֹם אֵינוֹ חַיָּב אֶלָּא אַחַת. אָמְרוּ לוֹ: „אַל־תִּשְׁתֶּה, אַל־תִּשְׁתֶּה,״ וְהוּא שׁוֹתֶה — חַיָּב עַל־כָּל־אַחַת וְאַחַת.

[ח] **הָיָה** מִטַּמֵּא לְמֵתִים כָּל־הַיּוֹם, אֵינוֹ חַיָּב אֶלָּא אַחַת. אָמְרוּ לוֹ: „אַל־תִּטַּמֵּא, אַל־תִּטַּמֵּא,״ וְהָיָה מִטַּמֵּא — חַיָּב עַל־כָּל־אַחַת וְאַחַת.

יד אברהם

7.

The following three *mishnayos* deal with the *mitzvos* of the *nazir*. A *nazir* is one who has adopted a vow of *nezirus*, a legal state which prohibits him (1) to drink wine or eat grapes or any products of the grapevine, (2) to contaminate himself with the *tumah* of a dead body, and (3) to cut his hair (*Numbers* ch. 6). This mishnah deals with a *nazir's* repeated violation of the prohibition on drinking wine and the number of sets of *malkus* incurred for these infractions.

נָזִיר שֶׁהָיָה שׁוֹתֶה בַּיַּיִן כָּל־הַיּוֹם — *A nazir who drank wine all day*

I.e., he drank enough to incur several sets of lashes, but he was warned only once (*Rav* from *Gem.* 20b; *Nazir* 6:4).

The amount of wine a *nazir* must drink to be liable is a *reviis*, quarter-*log*. The conversion of this ancient measure into modern measures is a matter of controversy. Opinions range from 3.3 to 5.3 fluid ounces.

.אֵינוֹ חַיָּב אֶלָּא אַחַת — *is liable only once.*

I.e., he incurs only one set of thirty-nine lashes for the wine he drank immediately after the warning (*Rav*). For transgressing a negative commandment one receives the punishment of *malkus* only if he was previously warned and only if the transgression followed immediately upon the completion of the warning. Where the interval between warning and transgression was longer than the time it takes to say the words שָׁלוֹם עָלֶיךָ רַבִּי, *Peace upon you, my teacher*, he is not liable, because an interlude of this duration separates the transgression from the warning. Within this time span, however, it is as though the one who warns him has not yet finished speaking (see above 1:7), and the transgression is therefore seen as following immediately upon the warning. This is known as תּוֹךְ כְּדֵי דִבּוּר, *within the time necessary for speech* (see *Rav, Nazir* 4:1). Just as in capital cases, the perpetrator is liable only if he committed the crime within this interval of the warning, so it is in the case of lashes (see *Rambam, Hil. Sanhedrin* 12:2, 16:1). [See further, comm. to ArtScroll *Nazir* 6:4.]

Accordingly, *Rav* states that the liability is not for any of the wine drunk during the day, but only for the wine drunk immediately following the warning (*Tos. Yom Tov*).

If, however, the *nazir* had before him a cup holding several measures of wine, and he was warned that he would be liable to several sets of *malkus* for drinking the entire cup, he becomes liable to all those sets of lashes for consuming the entire cup, provided he does so within the interval of greeting one's teacher (*Rav* from *Yerushalmi*).

Rambam (*Hil. Nezirus* ch. 5) omits this ruling. *Tif. Yis.* reasons that he does so because it is unusual for one to drink many quarter-*logs* within this short period.

7. A *nazir* who kept drinking wine all day is liable only once. [If] they said to him, 'Do not drink, do not drink,' and he kept drinking — he is liable for each one.

8. [I]f] he kept contaminating himself with corpses all day, he is liable only once. [If] they said to him, 'Do not contaminate yourself! Do not contaminate yourself!,' and he kept contaminating himself — he is liable for each one.

YAD AVRAHAM

Ri (cited by *Ritva),* however, states that if he commenced to transgress within that interval, and continues drinking uninterrupted, he is liable to several sets of *malkus,* even though the total time elapsed is far longer than the greeting of a teacher.

אָמְרוּ לוֹ: „אַל־תִּשְׁתֶּה, אַל־תִּשְׁתֶּה,״ וְהוּא שׁוֹתֶה — *[If] they said to him, 'Do not drink, do not drink,' and he kept drinking* —

I.e., they warned him before each drink of wine *(Rav, Nazir* 6:4; *Rambam, Hil. Nezirus* 5:10; *Rivan, Gem.* 20b).

חַיָּב עַל־כָּל־אַחַת וְאַחַת. — *he is liable for each one.*

[He incurs thirty-nine lashes for each drink equalling a *reviis.*]

8.

The following mishnah deals with the other two interdicts governing the *nazir,* viz., the prohibition to contaminate himself with *tumah* through contact with a corpse and the prohibition to shave the hair of his head. Just as in the preceding mishnah, the topic here is the number of sets of lashes inflicted upon him for the infraction of these interdicts. In conjunction with this, the mishnah deals with the interdict against wearing *kilayim,* or *shatnez,* clothing composed of wool and linen, prohibited by the Torah in *Lev.* 19:19 and *Deut.* 22:11.

הָיָה מִטַּמֵּא לְמֵתִים כָּל־הַיּוֹם, — *[If] he kept contaminating himself with corpses all day,*

I.e., if a *nazir* or a *Kohen (Tif. Yis.)* kept coming in contact with human corpses all day after having been warned only once not to do so. Although the first contact rendered him *tamei* for seven days, it is nevertheless forbidden for him to come into further contact with a human corpse *(Rambam, Hil. Nezirus* 5:16).

אֵינוֹ חַיָּב אֶלָּא אַחַת. — *he is liable only once.*

[He is liable only for the initial contamination which took place immediately after the warning. See above, mishnah 7.]

אָמְרוּ לוֹ: „אַל־תִּטַּמֵּא, אַל־תִּטַּמֵּא,״ וְהָיָה מִטַּמֵּא – חַיָּב עַל־כָּל־אַחַת וְאַחַת. — *[If] they said to him, 'Do not contaminate yourself! Do not contaminate yourself!,' and he kept contaminating himself — he is liable for each one.*

If after the initial warning he contaminated himself and then after separating himself from the corpse, he was again warned not to contaminate himself, but he nevertheless contaminated himself again, he is liable a second time. He is liable for each contamination following each separate warning *(Tif. Yis.).*

Rambam (Nezirus 5:17) rules that even if a *nazir* touches several corpses,

הָיָה מְגַלֵּחַ כָּל־הַיּוֹם, אֵינוֹ חַיָּב אֶלָּא אַחַת. אָמְרוּ לוֹ: „אַל־תְּגַלַּח, אַל־תְּגַלַּח,״ וְהוּא מְגַלֵּחַ — חַיָּב עַל־כָּל־אַחַת וְאַחַת.

הָיָה לָבוּשׁ בְּכִלְאַיִם כָּל־הַיּוֹם, אֵינוֹ חַיָּב אֶלָּא אַחַת. אָמְרוּ לוֹ: „אַל־תִּלְבַּשׁ, אַל־תִּלְבַּשׁ,״ וְהוּא פּוֹשֵׁט וְלוֹבֵשׁ — חַיָּב עַל־כָּל־אַחַת וְאַחַת.

יד אברהם

[I.e., because he was warned only once.]

אָמְרוּ לוֹ: „אַל־תְּגַלַּח, אַל־תְּגַלַּח,״ וְהוּא מְגַלֵּחַ — חַיָּב עַל־כָּל־אַחַת וְאַחַת. — *[If] they said to him, 'Do not shave! Do not shave!,' and he kept shaving — he is liable for each one.*

I.e., if they warned him before shaving each hair, he incurs the penalty of lashes for each hair *(Rambam, Hil. Nezirus* 5:13).

הָיָה לָבוּשׁ בְּכִלְאַיִם כָּל־הַיּוֹם, — *[If] he kept wearing kilayim all day,*

I.e., if anyone at all (not necessarily a *nazir)* was wearing a garment composed of a combination of wool and linen *(Tos. Yom Tov* from *Rivan)*, thereby transgressing the commandment, לֹא תִלְבַּשׁ שַׁעַטְנֵז צֶמֶר וּפִשְׁתִּים יַחְדָּו, *you shall not clothe yourself with shatnez, wool and linen together (Deut.* 22:11).

[*Kilayim* is a general word for the various admixtures that the Torah forbids, such as planting different species together or grafting them, or interbreeding different species of animals, or wearing a garment composed of both wool and linen.]

אֵינוֹ חַיָּב אֶלָּא אַחַת. — *he is liable only once.*

[I.e., for the initial donning of the garment. See below.]

אָמְרוּ לוֹ: „אַל־תִּלְבַּשׁ, אַל־תִּלְבַּשׁ,״ וְהוּא פּוֹשֵׁט וְלוֹבֵשׁ — — *[If] they said to him, 'Do not wear it! Do not wear it!,' and he kept taking it off and putting it on —*

and he was warned before each contact, he is liable for each one only if he separated from one corpse and then, following the second warning, touched another one (or the same one again). If he did not separate, but held on despite repeated warnings, he is liable only once.

Ravad (ibid.), however, rules that even for repeated touchings and warnings he is liable only once. The rule of the mishnah that there is liability for each warning is when he became *tamei* in different ways following each warning, e.g., after the initial warning he touched it and after the second warning he came into a tent containing a corpse. [Corpse-contaminated *tumah* is transmitted via an *ohel*, i.e., by being under the same roof with it.] This controversy is based on the *Gemara's* discussion in *Nazir* 42b (see *Lechem Mishneh* ibid.). However, *Mishneh LaMelech (Eivel* 3:1) states that *Ravad's* view is rejected by 'all the Sages of Israel' *(Tos. Yom Tov)*.

As a general rule whenever the mishnah states *he is liable only once* that refers only to the punishments of *beis din;* as far as Heavenly retribution is concerned he is punished for each infraction of the law *(Tos. Yom Tov Nazir* 6:4, *Rambam Comm.)*.

הָיָה מְגַלֵּחַ כָּל־הַיּוֹם, — *[If] he kept shaving all day,*

This does not mean that he continued shaving all day but rather that the *nazir* continued shaving until he had shaved off all the hair of his head *(Rambam, Hil. Nazir* 5:13).

אֵינוֹ חַיָּב אֶלָּא אַחַת. — *he is liable only once.*

3
8

[If] he kept shaving all day, he is liable only once. [If] they said to him, 'Do not shave! Do not shave!,' and he kept shaving — he is liable for each one.

[If] he kept wearing *kilayim* all day, he is liable only once. [If] they said to him, 'Do not wear it! Do not wear it!,' and he kept taking it off and putting it on — he is liable for each one.

YAD AVRAHAM

If, after taking off the garment, he was warned a second time not to put it on, and he nevertheless proceeded to clothe himself in it again, he incurs another set of *malkus*. In fact, he need not take it off completely to be liable a second *malkus*. Even if he removes part of the garment, e.g., from around his head, and after being warned puts it on again, he is liable to a separate set of thirty-nine lashes (*Rav; Rambam, Hil. Kilayim* 5:11). Furthermore, the *Gemara* (21b) adds that even if he did not actually remove the garment at all but merely wore it long enough so that he could have removed it and reclothed himself, he is also liable, if he was warned in the interim (*Rav; Rambam* ad loc.; *Meiri*).

.חַיָּב עַל־כָּל־אַחַת וְאַחַת — *he is liable for each one.*

There is a separate liability for each time he put on the garment or for each time he wrapped his head in it, as explained above. Also, if he wore it for an interval during which there was sufficient time to don the garment a number of times and indeed, he was warned a number of times, he is liable for each warning (*Rav* from *Gem.* 21b).

In view of the halachah that one does not incur lashes for transgressing a negative commandment in which no action is involved, it is difficult to understand how we can rule that he is liable for remaining clothed with the forbidden garment, since wearing the garment without removing it and redonning it does not involve any action.

Two solutions are given for this problem. One is that since it was possible to remove the garment, and he did not, it is adjudged as though he put it on (*Ritva* quoting *Tos.*). *Nimmukei Yosef*[1] explains that since the transgression commenced with an action, that of putting on the garment, and now the wearer could have taken it off, his failure to remove it is connected to and considered an extension of the initial act. The transgression is therefore regarded as if it were accomplished through an action (*Tos. Yom Tov*).

Although each of these four cases deals with multiple penalties due to multiple warnings, the *Tanna* found it necessary to state each one. The first case, that of the *nazir* drinking wine, teaches us that even if he drank the wine without stopping between gulps, since he was warned for each quarter-*log*, he is liable for each one. The second case, that of the *nazir* contaminating himself by contact with a corpse, teaches us that although the *nazir* is already *tamei*, he is liable for further contamination. The third case, that of the *nazir* shaving his head, teaches us that he is liable not only for shaving off all his hair, but even for shaving off one hair. The fourth case, that of the man wearing *shatnez*, teaches us that he is liable although he performed no new action, but merely neglected to take off the forbidden garment (*Tif. Yis.*).

1. The commentary to the *Rif* on *Makkos* was originally attributed to *Ran*, but is now generally accepted to be *Nimmukei Yosef*. *Tos. Yom Tov*, however, refers to this commentary as *Ran*.

[ט] **יֵשׁ** חוֹרֵשׁ תֶּלֶם אֶחָד וְחַיָּב עָלָיו מִשּׁוּם שְׁמוֹנָה לָאוִין: הַחוֹרֵשׁ בְּשׁוֹר וַחֲמוֹר וְהֵן מֻקְדָּשִׁים, בְּכִלְאַיִם בַּכֶּרֶם, וּבַשְּׁבִיעִית, וְיוֹם טוֹב, וְכֹהֵן וְנָזִיר בְּבֵית הַטֻּמְאָה. חֲנַנְיָא בֶּן־חֲכִינַאי אוֹמֵר:

יד אברהם

9.

The following mishnah teaches that it is possible for one to perform one act and to incur many penalties of *makkos* for it. This is when the commission of this act involves the infraction of numerous negative commandments *(Meiri).*

יֵשׁ חוֹרֵשׁ תֶּלֶם אֶחָד וְחַיָּב עָלָיו מִשּׁוּם שְׁמוֹנָה לָאוִין: — *There is [a case in which] one plows a furrow and is liable on its account for eight negative commandments:*

There is a possibility of one plowing a furrow and incurring the penalty of several sets of *malkus.* This occurs when the plowing infracts eight prohibitions and he was warned that by committing this one act he is transgressing all these negative commandments *(Rav).* They are as follows:

הַחוֹרֵשׁ בְּשׁוֹר וַחֲמוֹר — *One who plows with an ox and a donkey*

To plow with an ox and donkey (or any two species) yoked together transgresses the Torah's prohibition *(Deut.* 22:10): לֹא תַחֲרֹשׁ בְּשׁוֹר וּבַחֲמֹר יַחְדָּו, *You shall not plow with an ox and a donkey together.* This is the first negative commandment *(Tif. Yis.).*

וְהֵן מֻקְדָּשִׁים, — *which are consecrated,*

I.e., the ox was consecrated to be used for a sacrifice *(Rav),* such as a firstborn [which is automatically consecrated] *(Rivan, Tos.* from *Gem.* 22a), and the donkey (which cannot serve as a sacrifice) was owned by the Temple treasury. For working with the ox, he transgresses *(Deut.* 15:19): לֹא תַעֲבֹד בִּבְכֹר שׁוֹרֶךָ, *you shall not work with the firstborn of your ox,* which includes working with any consecrated animal. For working with the donkey, he transgresses the negative commandment of *me'ilah,* misuse of Temple funds for personal benefit. Hence, we have the second and the third negative commandments *(Rav).*

Others explain that the donkey mentioned here also refers to a firstborn, which may not be used for work unless first redeemed with a lamb [*Exodus* 13:13] *(Rivan).*[1] *Tosafos* (21b), however, dispute the view that there are lashes for working with an unredeemed firstborn donkey (even if it is forbidden to do so). At the same time, various statements of the *Gemara* (22a) as to the type of negative commandments reckoned by the mishnah seem to negate the explanation that the mishnah refers to a donkey consecrated to the Temple treasury.

Tosafos and *Rambam Comm.,* however, reckon the consecration to account for only the second negative commandment; see below.

Tosafos, in fact, consider the possibility that the term *consecrated* refers only to the ox and not the donkey, since its consecration as a firstborn is in any case irrelevant to the topic of this mishnah, as explained above.

בְּכִלְאַיִם בַּכֶּרֶם, — *with kilayim in a vineyard,*

The Torah *(Deut.* 22:9) forbids sowing mingled seeds in a vineyard: *You shall not sow your vineyard with mingled seeds.* The *Gemara (Chullin* 136b) qualifies this to mean that it is forbidden to sow wheat kernels, barley kernels, and

1. There is a dispute between the *Tannaim* R' Yehudah and R' Shimon whether it is forbidden to derive benefit from an unredeemed firstborn donkey *(Bechoros* 9b). *Rivan* asserts that the mishnah follows the view of R' Yehudah that it is forbidden.

9. There is [a case in which] one plows a furrow and is liable on its account for eight negative commandments: One who plows with an ox and a donkey which are consecrated, with *kilayim* in a vineyard, and during the Sabbatical year, and on a Festival, and [he is] a *Kohen* and a *nazir* in a *tumah*-contaminated place. Chananya ben Chachinai says: Also one who was

YAD AVRAHAM

grape seeds all together. In the case of our mishnah, the three varieties of seeds were lying on the ground and, as he plowed over them, he covered them with earth, thereby sowing them in the soil. Although he does not actually cast them into the ground, he is nevertheless adjudged as sowing since he covers them with earth. The prohibition of sowing *kilayim* constitutes the fourth negative commandment being transgressed with this single act of plowing *(Rav)*.

Rambam and *Tosafos*, as mentioned above, do not count a negative commandment for working with the donkey. Accordingly, they count another negative commandment in the matter of the mingled seeds — viz., sowing two species of seeds in a field. That interdict is found in *Lev.* 19:19: שָׂדְךָ לֹא תִזְרַע כִּלְאָיִם, *you shall not sow your field with mingled seeds.* Since he covers the wheat and barley kernels by plowing, in addition to the grape seeds, he is regarded as having violated the prohibition on sowing mingled seeds in a field, in addition to the one on mingling seeds with a vineyard. Consequently, we have four negative commandments *(Rav, Tos. Yom Tov; see Tos., Pesachim* 47a, and *Tif. Yis., Boaz* 8).

וּבַשְּׁבִיעִית, — *and during the Sabbatical year,*

The Sabbatical [*Shemittah*] year occurs every seventh year and prohibits, among other things, tilling the soil of Eretz Yisrael. Concerning this year the Torah states *(Lev.* 25:4): וּבַשָּׁנָה הַשְּׁבִיעִת שַׁבַּת שַׁבָּתוֹן יִהְיֶה לָאָרֶץ שַׁבָּת לַה׳ שָׂדְךָ לֹא תִזְרָע, *But in the seventh year there shall be a Sabbath of rest for the land, a Sabbath to HASHEM; you shall not sow your field,* thereby prohibiting sowing by a negative commandment *(Rav)*. Plowing in this manner, i.e., covering the seeds, is a *toladah,* a secondary labor derived from the primary labor of sowing *(Tos. Yom Tov* from *Rashi, Pesachim* 47b). Thus we have accounted for five separate commandments *(Tif. Yis.;* cf. *Rashash, Pesachim* 47b).

וְיוֹם טוֹב, — *and on a Festival,*

This is an infraction of the negative commandment on performing labor on a Festival: כָּל־מְלֶאכֶת עֲבֹדָה לֹא תַעֲשׂוּ, *you shall not do any labor of work* [*Num.* 28:18] *(Rav)*. This is the sixth negative commandment *(Tif. Yis.)*.

The *Tanna* does not list plowing on the Sabbath since that is a capital offense, and the negative commandment serving as an admonition against a capital sin bears no penalty of lashes, as explained in the General Introduction *(Tos. Yom Tov* from *Rashi, Pesachim* 47b).

וְכֹהֵן וְנָזִיר בְּבֵית הַטֻּמְאָה. — *and* [*he is*] *a Kohen and a nazir in a tumah-contaminated place.*

I.e., in a cemetery. By entering a cemetery as he plows, he transgresses two negative commandments, one prohibiting a *Kohen* from becoming *tamei* by contact with a corpse and the other prohibiting the *nazir* from becoming *tamei* in this manner. The former is *Lev.* 21:1: לְנֶפֶשׁ לֹא יִטַּמָּא בְּעַמָּיו, *He shall not contaminate himself to a dead person within his people.* The latter is in *Num.* 6:6: כָּל־יְמֵי הַזִּירוֹ לַה׳ עַל־נֶפֶשׁ מֵת לֹא יָבֹא, *All the days that he keeps himself a nazir unto HASHEM, he shall not ap-*

אַף הַלּוֹבֵשׁ כִּלְאַיִם. אָמְרוּ לוֹ: אֵינוֹ הַשֵּׁם. אָמַר לָהֶם: אַף לֹא הַנָּזִיר הוּא הַשֵּׁם.

[י] **כַּמָּה** מַלְקִין אוֹתוֹ? אַרְבָּעִים חָסֵר אַחַת, שֶׁנֶּאֱמַר: „בְּמִסְפָּר אַרְבָּעִים״ — מִנְיָן שֶׁהוּא סָמוּךְ לְאַרְבָּעִים. רַבִּי יְהוּדָה אוֹמֵר: אַרְבָּעִים שְׁלֵמוֹת הוּא לוֹקֶה. וְהֵיכָן הוּא לוֹקֶה אֶת־הַיְתֵרָה?

יד אברהם

proach any dead person (Rav; Rambam Comm.; Rivan).

[These are the seventh and eighth negative commandments.]

חֲנַנְיָא בֶּן־חֲכִינַאי אוֹמֵר: אַף הַלּוֹבֵשׁ כִּלְאַיִם. — *Chananya ben Chachinai says: Also one who was wearing kilayim.*

I.e., it is possible to add yet another negative commandment, viz., that the plower was wearing *shatnez* while plowing *(Rav).*

אָמְרוּ לוֹ: אֵינוֹ הַשֵּׁם. — *They said to him: This is not for that reason.*

The Sages replied to Chananya ben Chachinai that this commandment cannot be counted since the transgression of the negative commandment against wearing *kilayim* is not connected in any way with the plowing but is merely incidental *(Rav; Rivan).*

אָמַר לָהֶם: אַף לֹא הַנָּזִיר הוּא הַשֵּׁם. — *He replied to them: Neither is nazir for that reason.*

[Chananya ben Chachinai replied to the Sages that by the same token the negative commandment of the *nazir* in the cemetery should not be counted, since it too is unrelated to plowing, and is just as readily violated without plowing, by merely walking there. Since that prohibition is nevertheless enumerated, so too should wearing *shatnez* be counted *(Rav; Rivan).* [Chananya also means his objection to include the negative commandment of the *Kohen,* which is similarly not related to plowing, but to entering the contaminated area *(Rivan).*]

The *Tanna Kamma,* however, does include these two negative commandments since one cannot plow with oxen without following them and the plowshare wherever they go. It is therefore somewhat related to the plowing, whereas wearing the *kilayim* is completely incidental *(Rav).*

10.

The Torah states *(Deut.* 25:2,3): וְהָיָה אִם־בִּן הַכּוֹת הָרָשָׁע וְהִפִּילוֹ הַשֹּׁפֵט וְהִכָּהוּ לְפָנָיו כְּדֵי רִשְׁעָתוֹ בְּמִסְפָּר. אַרְבָּעִים יַכֶּנּוּ לֹא יֹסִיף ..., *And it shall be that if the wicked one is sentenced to lashes, that the judge shall make him fall and strike him before him according to his wickedness in number. Forty [lashes] he shall strike him; he shall not add ...* There is a controversy among the *Tannaim* in the following mishnah as to how to explain this Scriptural passage.

כַּמָּה מַלְקִין אוֹתוֹ? — *How many lashes do we give him?*

[I.e., how many lashes do we inflict upon one who is sentenced to receive *malkus?*]

אַרְבָּעִים חָסֵר אַחַת, — *Forty less one,*

I.e., thirty-nine; the forty lashes mentioned in the Torah, less one *(Tif. Yis.; Tos. Yom Tov, Shabbos* 7:2).

שֶׁנֶּאֱמַר: „בְּמִסְפָּר אַרְבָּעִים״ — — *as it is said (Deut. 25:2,3): 'in the number of forty'*

As quoted above, verse 2 of this

3 wearing *kilayim*. They said to him: This is not for that
10 reason. He replied to them: Neither is *nazir* for that reason.

10. How many lashes do we give him? Forty less one, as it is said (*Deut*. 25:2,3): *in the number of forty* — the number that is close to forty. R' Yehudah says: He is flogged with the full forty lashes. Where is the

YAD AVRAHAM

passage ends with the words: כְּדֵי רִשְׁעָתוֹ בְּמִסְפָּר, *according to his wickedness in number*. Verse 3 commences with the words: אַרְבָּעִים יַכֶּנּוּ, *Forty* [*lashes*] *he shall strike him*. The *Tanna Kanna* treats this exegetically as though it were one verse, reading: בְּמִסְפָּר אַרְבָּעִים, *in the number of forty* (*Rivan*).

מִנְיָן שֶׁהוּא סָמוּךְ לְאַרְבָּעִים. — *the number that is close to forty.*

I.e., the number that causes forty to be counted immediately after it, viz., thirty-nine. Had the Torah stated: אַרְבָּעִים בְּמִסְפָּר, *forty in number*, it would have been interpreted literally to mean that the person sentenced to be flogged would receive exactly forty lashes. However, since the Torah states: בְּמִסְפָּר אַרְבָּעִים, *in the number of forty*, the intention is that he is to receive the number related to forty [but not forty], i.e., the number immediately preceding it, viz. thirty-nine (*Rav; Rivan* from *Gem*. 22b).

Many editions read: מִנְיָן שֶׁהוּא סוֹכֵם אֶת־הָאַרְבָּעִים, *the number that counts forty*, meaning the number that causes forty to be counted after it. This appears to be the reading of *Rivan, Semag*, and *Nimmukei Yosef*. Our reading appears to be erroneous (*Rishon LeTzion* from *Lechem Mishneh, Hil. Sanhedrin* 17:1). This reading appears also in the commentaries of *Rabbeinu Yehonasan, Ritva, Rabbeinu Yehudah Almedari*, and *Meiri*.

According to *Rav* and *Rivan*, the Rabbis did not decrease the number of lashes prescribed by the Torah. They merely explained that the Scriptural passage should not be understood literally, but should be expounded in the above manner to mean thirty-nine. *Rambam*, however, explains the mishnah differently. Were the Torah to state: אַרְבָּעִים בְּמִסְפָּר, *forty in number*, it would be obligatory to inflict forty lashes on the guilty party regardless of his ability to endure them. Since, however, the Torah states: בְּמִסְפָּר, *in number*, and then: אַרְבָּעִים, *forty*, the intention is that the Sages were to assess each person to determine the amount of lashes he could endure (see next mishnah). That is the intention of בְּמִסְפָּר, *in number*. The word אַרְבָּעִים, *forty*, is the maximum amount which can be inflicted upon the guilty party even if he could endure many more. Since the Torah authorized the Rabbis to assess the guilty party and empowered them to decrease the number of lashes as they saw fit, they decided to enact a safeguard and decrease the maximum number of lashes to thirty-nine, so that, even if by miscount another lash were to be added, the offender will have received no more than the forty he really deserved (*Rambam Comm.; Hil. Sanhedrin* 17:1, *Lechem Mishneh* ad loc.). [Consequently, if the attendant inflicts forty lashes instead of thirty-nine, according to *Rav* and *Rivan*, he is himself liable to lashes for transgressing the negative commandment of לֹא יֹסִיף, *he shall not add* (see below, mishnah 14). According to *Rambam*, however, he is not liable.]

רַבִּי יְהוּדָה אוֹמֵר: אַרְבָּעִים שְׁלֵמוֹת הוּא לוֹקֶה. — *R' Yehudah says: He is flogged with the full forty lashes.*

[R' Yehudah understands the passage literally.]

וְהֵיכָן הוּא לוֹקֶה אֶת־הַיְתֵרָה? — *Where is the*

בֵּין כְּתֵפָיו.

[יא] **אֵין** אוֹמְדִין אוֹתוֹ אֶלָּא בְמַכּוֹת הָרְאוּיוֹת לְהִשְׁתַּלֵּשׁ. אֲמָדוּהוּ לְקַבֵּל אַרְבָּעִים, לָקָה מִקְצָת, וְאָמְרוּ שֶׁאֵינוֹ יָכוֹל לְקַבֵּל אַרְבָּעִים, פָּטוּר. אֲמָדוּהוּ לְקַבֵּל שְׁמוֹנֶה־עֶשְׂרֵה, מִשֶּׁלָּקָה

יד אברהם

extra one inflicted?

Since mishnah 11 states that the amount of lashes assessed by *beis din* must always be divisible by three, one third of which is inflicted on his chest and two thirds on the back (see mishnah 13), the question arises as to where the fortieth lash is inflicted *(Rav).*

בֵּין כְּתֵפָיו. — *Between his shoulders.*

R' Yehudah bases his view on *(Zechariah* 13:6): *What are these wounds between your hands? And he will say: Which I was struck in the house of those who love me.* R' Yehudah understands this as an allusion to the extra lash dealt the offender between his shoulders by the courts. The false prophet was stricken with these wounds by the Sanhedrin because of their love for him and their desire to set him straight. The Sages, however, explain this verse as an allusion to the blows inflicted on the young students for not learning or for misbehaving. Thus, it has no bearing on court-imposed lashes *(Tos. Yom Tov* from *Gem.* 22b).

The midrash states: Lashes are beloved for they atone for sins, as it is said: כְּדֵי רִשְׁעָתוֹ, *the lashes are worthy* (כְּדָאִי) *to atone for his wickedness.* Lashes are beloved for they endear man to his Father in heaven, as it is said: *And he will say to him, 'What are these wounds between your hands?' And he will say: 'Which I was struck in the house of those who love me.'* These lashes caused me to love my Father in heaven *(Midrash Hagadol; Midrash Tannaim, Deut.* 25:3). [This is apparently in agreement with R' Yehudah's interpretation of the verse in *Zechariah.*]

The halachah is not in accordance with R' Yehudah *(Rambam, Hil. Sanhedrin* 17:1).

11.

We have already explained in the preceding mishnah that the maximum any offender is flogged is thirty-nine lashes, even if he is hale and hearty and able to endure more. Should he be unable to endure thirty-nine lashes, however, *beis din* must assess and inflict only as many lashes as he can endure, so that he not die from the lashes. From the fact that the Torah specifies that the court may not add to the prescribed number of lashes, the Rabbis deduced that, if necessary, the court may decrease the number of lashes *(Rav).*

According to *Rambam* quoted above, the mishnah has already mentioned the halachah of assessing the offender prior to the imposition of the lashes. This procedure is derived from the word בְּמִסְפָּר, *with a number (Shoshannim LeDavid).* In his commentary on this mishnah, *Rambam* is more explicit. He states as follows:

'You should know that *Hashem's* statement: *Forty* [*lashes*] *he shall strike him,* does not mean that he incurs the penalty of exactly forty lashes; rather, the meaning is that the limit of the punishment is forty and no more. That is the intention of the statement, *he shall not add.* And they flog him less than forty according to his

extra one inflicted? Between his shoulders.

11. They may not assess him with any but lashes that may be divided by three. [If] they assessed him [to be able] to endure forty [lashes, and] he was flogged some of them, and they then said that he was unable to endure forty, he is exempt. [If] they assessed him [to be able] endure eighteen [lashes, but] after being flogged,

YAD AVRAHAM

endurance, lest he die. That is the intention of His statement: *according to his wickedness.* It is as though He stated: According to his strength for his wickedness' *(Rambam Comm.,* ed. Kafich).

אֵין אוֹמְדִין אוֹתוֹ — *They may not assess him*

Before being subjected to the punishment of lashes, the offender was evaluated by the court to determine whether he was medically fit to receive the full number of lashes without dying from them. If it was decided that he was not, they must set a lower number for his punishment *(Rav).* In doing so, they do not necessarily assess the full number they estimate he can tolerate.

אֶלָּא בְמַכּוֹת הָרְאוּיוֹת לְהִשְׁתַּלֵּשׁ. — *with any but lashes that may be divided by three.*

[The total number of lashes assessed must be a number divisible by three. If the assessment comes to a number indivisible by three, it is reduced to the next number that is divisible by three.] E.g., if the offender was assessed to be able to endure just twenty lashes, he is given only eighteen *(Rambam).* This is because the lashes must be inflicted one third in the front and two thirds on the back, as will be explained in mishnah 13 *(Rabbeinu Yehonasan).* Although the same could be achieved by raising the number by one, since it is incumbent upon *beis din* to safeguard his life, they may only flog him eighteen lashes *(Rambam, Hil. Sanhedrin* 17:2).

אֲמָדוּהוּ לְקַבֵּל אַרְבָּעִים, — *[If] they assessed him [to be able] to endure forty [lashes],*

I.e., actually thirty-nine but the *Tanna* uses the wording of the Torah *(Rav).*

לָקָה מִקְצָת, וְאָמְרוּ שֶׁאֵינוֹ יָכוֹל לְקַבֵּל אַרְבָּעִים, — *[and] he was flogged some of them, and they then said that he was unable to endure forty,*

I.e., after being dealt a portion of the lashes, the court became aware of his weakened condition and decided that he cannot endure more than the number he has already received *(Rambam, Hil. Sanhedrin* 17:2).

פָּטוּר. — *he is exempt.*

[He is exempt from the remainder of his sentence, and does not receive any more lashes even after he recuperates.]

This applies only if they began flogging him before realizing that his health had deteriorated and that their assessment was now too high. Since he has already been disgraced at this point, he is let off without further punishment. However, if *beis din* noticed before the flogging began that he was in a weakened state, they do not decrease their initial assessment, but wait for him to recover his strength and flog him at a later date *(Rivan).*

אֲמָדוּהוּ לְקַבֵּל שְׁמוֹנֶה־עֶשְׂרֵה, — *[If] they assessed him [to be able] to endure eighteen [lashes],*

Eighteen is used only by way of example, but the same would be true for twelve, nine or any number divisible by three *(Meiri).*

מכות ג/יב

אָמְרוּ שֶׁיָּכוֹל הוּא לְקַבֵּל אַרְבָּעִים, פָּטוּר. עָבַר עֲבֵרָה שֶׁיֵּשׁ־בָּהּ שְׁנֵי לָאוִין: אֲמָדוּהוּ אֹמֶד אֶחָד, לוֹקֶה וּפָטוּר; וְאִם לָאו, לוֹקֶה, וּמִתְרַפֵּא, וְחוֹזֵר וְלוֹקֶה.

[יב] **כֵּיצַד** מַלְקִין אוֹתוֹ? כּוֹפֵת שְׁתֵּי יָדָיו עַל־הָעַמּוּד הֵילָךְ וְהֵילָךְ, וְחַזַּן הַכְּנֶסֶת אוֹחֵז בִּבְגָדָיו — אִם נִקְרְעוּ, נִקְרָעוּ, וְאִם נִפְרְמוּ, נִפְרְמוּ — עַד־שֶׁהוּא מְגַלֶּה אֶת־לִבּוֹ; וְהָאֶבֶן נְתוּנָה

יד אברהם

מִשֶּׁלָּקָה אָמְרוּ שֶׁיָּכוֹל הוּא לְקַבֵּל אַרְבָּעִים, — *[but] after being flogged, they said that he was able to endure forty,*

After they flogged him the lesser number of lashes that they initially assessed him to be able to endure, they realized that he was healthy enough to endure the entire thirty-nine *(Meiri).*

פָּטוּר. — *he is exempt.*

I.e., he does not receive more than the original assessment *(Meiri; Rambam, Hil. Sanhedrin* 17:2). However, if they noticed his improved state of health before the flogging began, they may add to the initial assessment *(Rivan).*

עָבַר עֲבֵרָה שֶׁיֵּשׁ־בָּהּ שְׁנֵי לָאוִין: — *[If] one committed a transgression consisting of two negative commandments:*

For example, he plowed with an ox and a donkey and, with his plowing, he covered mingled seeds in a vineyard (as in mishnah 9) *(Rivan).*

אֲמָדוּהוּ אֹמֶד אֶחָד, לוֹקֶה וּפָטוּר; — *if they assessed him with one assessment, he is flogged and he is exempt;*

I.e., they assessed him for both sets of *malkus* at once and found him to be able to withstand the thirty-nine lashes required for the first set of *malkus* plus some of the lashes required by the second offense. For example, they assessed him to be able to endure forty-two lashes *(Rav* from *Gem.* 22b). In that case, the extra three lashes are counted towards the second set of *malkus (Tos. Yom Tov* from *Rivan).* Whenever he can endure a number of lashes divisible by three in addition to the thirty-nine lashes he incurs for the first sin, they assess him for both series of lashes together and he receives the entire forty-two lashes or more at one time and is exempt from receiving any other lashes for the second sin *(Meiri).*

וְאִם לָאו, — *otherwise,*

I.e., if they assessed him and discovered that he could endure only forty-one lashes, two more than the initial thirty-nine, he cannot be given both sets of lashes at once, since the minimum amount of lashes that must be administered are three. Consequently, *beis din* will punish him for each transgression separately *(Tos. Yom Tov* from *Rivan).*

לוֹקֶה, — *he is flogged,*

I.e., he is flogged with thirty-nine lashes, or less, if he cannot endure thirty-nine for one transgression *(Rambam, Hil. Sanhedrin* 17:4).

וּמִתְרַפֵּא, — *allowed to recover,*

[He is then given time to recover from the lashes he received.]

וְחוֹזֵר וְלוֹקֶה. — *and flogged again.*

After recuperating, *beis din* assesses

3 they said that he was able to endure forty, he is exempt.
12 [If] one committed a transgression consisting of two negative commandments: if they assessed him with one assessment, he is flogged and is exempt; otherwise, he is flogged, allowed to recover, and flogged again.

12. How do they flog him? He binds his two hands on the post on either side, and the attendant of the congregation seizes his garments — if they tear, they tear, and if they split open, they split open — until he bares his chest; and the stone is placed behind him. The

YAD AVRAHAM

him again for the second transgression and he is flogged again *(Rambam, Hil. Sanhedrin* 17:4).

The same procedure is followed if he is liable to any number of sets of *malkus (Rambam Comm.; Meiri).*

12.

כֵּיצַד מַלְקִין אוֹתוֹ? — *How do they flog him?*

[I.e., how do we administer lashes?]

כּוֹפֵת שְׁתֵּי יָדָיו עַל־הָעַמּוּד — *He binds his two hands on the post*

The agent of the *beis din* binds the hands of the one to be flogged on an upright post thrust into the ground, high enough to lean on *(Rav).* It should be one and a half to two cubits high. The sinner leans on it with his hands hanging down, and they are bound to the sides of the post *(Tos. Yom Tov* from *Rivan).*

הֵילָךְ וְהֵילָךְ, — *on either side,*

[I.e., one hand on each side of the post.]

וְחַזַּן הַכְּנֶסֶת — *and the attendant of the congregation* [lit. *assembly place*]

I.e., the court attendant *(Rav),* the agent of the *beis din.* The word חַזָּן as used in the mishnah and the *Gemara* has several meanings, all of which revolve around the concept of one whose duty it is to oversee things. Thus it denotes the one who attends to all the synagogue's needs [similar to the *shamash* of today] *(Rav* to *Sotah* 7:7). *Tos. Yom Tov* (to *Shabbos* 1:3) cites *Aruch* who traces this word to the root חוה, *to see.* In this manner it is also used to denote a teacher (ibid.), since he must oversee the students, and it is in this sense that it came to be used later for the one who leads the congregational prayers.

אוֹחֵז בִּבְגָדָיו — *seizes his garments* —

He grasps the garment of the one to be flogged at the collar and pulls it down over his body *(Ritva). Meiri* explains that he pulls the garment upward over his head.

אִם נִקְרְעוּ, נִקְרָעוּ, וְאִם נִפְרְמוּ, נִפְרָמוּ — *if they tear, they tear, and if they split open, they split open* —

I.e., he need not exercise caution to prevent the garments from tearing *(Meiri).*

Rav explains the term נִקְרַע, *to tear,* as referring to the fabric, while נִפְרְמוּ, *to rip open,* means at the seam. *Rav (Sotah* 1:5) quotes two other explanations: one that פְּרִימָה denotes tearing to a greater extent than קְרִיעָה. It could thus be rendered as *tattered.* The other is that קְרִיעָה is in the length and פְּרִימָה is from the side. The first is *Rashi's* and the second is *Rambam's (Tos. Yom Tov).*

עַד־שֶׁהוּא מְגַלֶּה אֶת־לִבּוֹ; — *until he bares his chest;*

I.e., until he bares his chest as well as his back. This is derived from the verse dealing with lashes where the Torah

מֵאַחֲרָיו. חַזַּן הַכְּנֶסֶת עוֹמֵד עָלֶיהָ וּרְצוּעָה שֶׁל־עֵגֶל בְּיָדוֹ, כְּפוּלָה אֶחָד לִשְׁנַיִם וּשְׁנַיִם לְאַרְבָּעָה, וּשְׁתֵּי רְצוּעוֹת עוֹלוֹת וְיוֹרְדוֹת בָּהּ.

[יג] **יָדָהּ** טֶפַח, וְרָחְבָּהּ טֶפַח, וְרֹאשָׁהּ מַגַּעַת עַל־פִּי כְרֵסוֹ. וּמַכֶּה אוֹתוֹ שְׁלִישׁ מִלְּפָנָיו וּשְׁתֵּי יָדוֹת מִלְּאַחֲרָיו; וְאֵינוֹ מַכֶּה אוֹתוֹ לֹא

יד אברהם

states: *and he shall strike him* — i.e., **him** and not his garments. Therefore, he must bare his chest and back (*Rambam, Hil. Sanhedrin* 16:8; *Ritva* from *Sifre, Deut.* 25:2).

וְהָאֶבֶן נְתוּנָה מֵאַחֲרָיו. — *and the stone is placed behind him.*

The stone on which the person administering the flogging stands is placed behind the one who is being flogged (*Rav; Rivan*). It was not placed exactly behind him, but rather to the side of his back, so that he should be able to flog him across his shoulders. The *Tanna* states that it is placed behind him to indicate that it is placed out of his view, so that he not be additionally frightened by the sight of the court attendant brandishing the whip over him. To cause him this unnecessary anguish would be an infraction of the commandment (*Lev.* 19:18): וְאָהַבְתָּ לְרֵעֲךָ כָּמוֹךָ, *you shall love your neighbor as yourself*. This *mitzvah* is taken by the *Gemara* (*Sanhedrin* 45a) to apply even to minimizing the pain of those being executed (*Tif. Yis.*).

חַזַּן הַכְּנֶסֶת עוֹמֵד עָלֶיהָ — *The attendant of the congregation stands upon it*

This position enables him to bring the whip down with force upon the person being flogged (*Tif. Yis.*).

וּרְצוּעָה שֶׁל־עֵגֶל בְּיָדוֹ, כְּפוּלָה אֶחָד לִשְׁנַיִם וּשְׁנַיִם לְאַרְבָּעָה, — *with a calfskin strap in his hand, doubled one into two and two into four,*

Rav explains that this strap was actually composed of four calfskin straps sewn one upon the other. *Rivan*, however, explains that there were only two straps, with each one doubled so that they appeared as four. *Meiri*, however, understands it to have been one very long strap folded over twice to form four.

The use of calfskin straps is derived from the juxtaposition of the negative commandment prohibiting the muzzling of an ox that is threshing with the law of flogging in *Deut.* 25:3,4 (*Gem.* 23a).

The ruling that the whip should be doubled is based on an exegesis of the word וְהִפִּילוֹ, *and he shall make him fall*, expounded as though written וְהִכְפִּילוֹ, *and he shall double it* (*Tos. Yom Tov* from *Yerushalmi*).

וּשְׁתֵּי רְצוּעוֹת עוֹלוֹת וְיוֹרְדוֹת בָּהּ. — *with two [other] straps running up and down in it.*

I.e., with two narrow thongs of donkey-hide running up and down it (*Rav* from *Gem.* 23a).

Rivan explains that there were holes in the calfskin straps through which the donkey-hide thongs were drawn in a stitch-like manner. The expression *running up and down it* refers to the stitching process, in which the donkey-hide thong is first pushed through the front of the calfskin strap [down] and then pulled through the next hole to the front of the strap [up] (*Meiri*).

Another explanation is that there were holes in the calfskin straps and the donkeyskin thongs were each inserted through the hole of one of the calfskin thongs. They were tied on the inside of the fold with a bow, thus allowing the

attendant of the congregation stands upon it with a calfskin strap in his hand, doubled one into two and two into four, with two [other] straps running up and down in it.

13. Its handle should be a handbreadth, its width a handbreadth, and its tip should reach his navel. He strikes one-third [of the lashes] in the front and two-thirds in the back; and he does not strike him either

YAD AVRAHAM

thongs to be lengthened or shortened according to the breadth of the back of the one to be flogged. The expression *running up and down* refers to the straps being lengthened or shortened (*Meiri*).

The ruling to make these straps of donkey-hide is based on (*Isaiah* 1:3): יָדַע שׁוֹר קֹנֵהוּ וַחֲמוֹר אֵבוּס בְּעָלָיו, *The ox knows its master and the donkey the manger of its owner*. Let the one who knows the manger of its owner come and visit retribution upon the one who does not know the manger of his owner (*Rav* from *Gem.* 23a).

13.

The following mishnah is a continuation of the procedure to be followed for administering lashes.

יָדָהּ טֶפַח, — *Its handle should be a handbreadth,*

I.e., the handle of the whip from which the straps hang is a handbreadth long (*Rav; Tos. Yom Tov* from *Rivan*).

וְרָחְבָּהּ טֶפַח, — *its width a handbreadth,*

I.e., the width of the calfskin strap is a handbreadth (*Rav; Rivan*).

וְרֹאשָׁהּ מַגַּעַת עַל־פִּי כְרֵסוֹ. — *and its tip should reach his navel* [lit. *on top of his stomach*].

I.e., the whip should be sufficiently long so that when it is brought down across his back, the end of it should reach around to his navel (*Rav, Rambam Comm.*). *Rivan*, however, renders this as *the edge of his stomach*, i.e., when the back ends and the stomach begins.

For this reason, the handle had a hole in it, so that the straps could be lengthened or shortened according to the size of each particular person (*Rav; Rambam Comm.*).

וּמַכֶּה אוֹתוֹ שְׁלִישׁ מִלְּפָנָיו — *He strikes one-third* [*of the lashes*] *in the front*

[One-third of the lashes were struck across the front of the guilty party.] According to *Rivan*, these were struck on the stomach. According to *Rav*, they were struck on the chest, between the nipples (*Rav* from *Rambam Comm.* and *Hil. Sanhedrin* 16:9).

וּשְׁתֵּי יָדוֹת מִלְּאַחֲרָיו; — *and two-thirds in the back;*

The lashes struck on the back were opposite the ones given in the front. Thus, according to *Rivan*, they were struck across the back, while according to *Rambam* and *Rav*, they were given on the shoulders, one third on each shoulder.

The *Gemara* (23a) derives this from the verse (*Deut.* 25:2): וְהִכָּהוּ לְפָנָיו כְּדֵי רִשְׁעָתוֹ, *and he shall strike him before him according to his wickedness.* The word כְּדֵי רִשְׁעָתוֹ, *according to his wickedness*, used in the singular in conjunction with לְפָנָיו, *in the front*, implies that he is to be flogged one count, i.e., one third of wickedness in the front and two counts of wickedness or two

עוֹמֵד וְלֹא יוֹשֵׁב, אֶלָּא מֻטֶּה, שֶׁנֶּאֱמַר: „וְהִפִּילוֹ הַשֹּׁפֵט.” וְהַמַּכֶּה מַכֶּה בְיָדוֹ אַחַת בְּכָל־כֹּחוֹ.

[יד] **וְהַקּוֹרֵא** קוֹרֵא: „אִם־לֹא תִשְׁמֹר לַעֲשׂוֹת, וְגוֹ׳,” „וְהִפְלָא ה׳ אֶת מַכֹּתְךָ וְאֵת מַכּוֹת, וְגוֹ׳,” וְחוֹזֵר לִתְחִלַּת הַמִּקְרָא. „וּשְׁמַרְתֶּם אֶת־דִּבְרֵי הַבְּרִית הַזֹּאת, וְגוֹ׳,” וְחוֹתֵם: „וְהוּא רַחוּם יְכַפֵּר עָוֹן, וְגוֹ׳,” וְחוֹזֵר לִתְחִלַּת הַמִּקְרָא.

וְאִם מֵת תַּחַת יָדוֹ, פָּטוּר. הוֹסִיף לוֹ עוֹד רְצוּעָה

יד אברהם

thirds on the back *(Rav).*

וְאֵינוֹ מַכֶּה אוֹתוֹ לֹא עוֹמֵד וְלֹא יוֹשֵׁב, אֶלָּא מֻטֶּה, — *and he does not strike him either standing or sitting, but bent over,*

[I.e., the one who is being flogged cannot be standing or sitting, but must be bent over.] As explained above, he leans over the post around which his hands are bound *(Tif. Yis.* to mishnah 12).

שֶׁנֶּאֱמַר: „וְהִפִּילוֹ הַשֹּׁפֵט.” — *as it is said (Deut. 28:2): 'And the judge shall make him fall.'*

[This indicates that he must strike him when he is bent over.]

וְהַמַּכֶּה מַכֶּה בְיָדוֹ אַחַת — *The flogger strikes with one hand*

I.e., he raises the whip with both hands, but brings it down with one one *(Rav; Tif. Yis.* from *Gem.* 23a).

בְּכָל־כֹּחוֹ. — *with all his might.*

This is based on the words מַכָּה רַבָּה, *a great beating,* implying that the court attendant should bring down the whip with all his might *(Rav; Tos. Yom Tov* mishnah 14, emending *Rivan).*

14.

וְהַקּוֹרֵא קוֹרֵא: — *The reader reads:*

While the lashes are administered one of the judges reads aloud the following Scriptural selections slowly and deliberately *(Rav).*

The obligation to recite these selections is based on the verse *(Lev.* 19:20): בִּקֹּרֶת תִּהְיֶה, which the Rabbis expound as though it read: בִּקְרִיאָה תְּהֵא, *with recitation she shall be (Rav* from *Kerisus* 11a).

„אִם־לֹא תִשְׁמֹר לַעֲשׂוֹת,” וְגוֹ׳, — *(Deut. 28:58ff): 'If you do not observe to do,' etc.*

The rest of the words of this verse are: אֶת־כָּל־דִּבְרֵי הַתּוֹרָה הַזֹּאת הַכְּתֻבִים בַּסֵּפֶר הַזֶּה לְיִרְאָה אֶת־הַשֵּׁם הַנִּכְבָּד וְהַנּוֹרָא הַזֶּה אֵת ה׳ אֱלֹהֶיךָ, *all the words of this Torah, which are written in this Book, to fear this honored and awesome Name,* H*ASHEM your God.*

„וְהִפְלָא ה׳ אֶת־מַכֹּתְךָ וְאֵת מַכּוֹת, וְגוֹ׳,” — *'*H*ASHEM shall make wondrous your plagues and the plagues of,' etc.,*

The remainder of the verse reads: זַרְעֶךָ מַכּוֹת גְּדֹלֹת וְנֶאֱמָנוֹת וָחֳלָיִם רָעִים וְנֶאֱמָנִים, *your seed, great and persistent plagues and evil and lingering sicknesses.*

וְחוֹזֵר לִתְחִלַּת הַמִּקְרָא. — *and he goes back to the beginning of the verses.*

I.e., if the court attendant has not yet completed the lashes, the judge reciting the verses repeats them until the lashes have been completed *(Rambam Comm.;*

3 standing or sitting, but bent over, as it is said (*Deut.*
14 25:2): *And the judge shall make him fall.* The flogger strikes with one hand with all his might.

14. The reader reads *(Deut. 28:58ff): If you do not observe to do, etc.,* HASHEM *will make wondrous your plagues and the plagues of, etc.,* and he goes back to the beginning of the verses. *And you shall observe the words of this covenant, etc.* (*Deut.* 29:8) and he concludes (*Psalms* 78:38): *But He, the Merciful One, is forgiving of iniquity, etc.,* and he goes back to the beginning of the verses.

If he died under his hand, he is exempt. [If] he added

YAD AVRAHAM

Hil. Sanhedrin 16:11).

„וּשְׁמַרְתֶּם אֶת־דִּבְרֵי הַבְּרִית הַזֹּאת, וְגוֹ׳,״ — *'And you shall observe the words of this covenant,' etc. (Deut.* 29:8)

The remainder of the verse reads: וַעֲשִׂיתֶם אֹתָם לְמַעַן תַּשְׂכִּילוּ אֵת כָּל־אֲשֶׁר תַּעֲשׂוּן, *and you shall perform them in order that you prosper in all that you do.*

Although this segment appears in extant editions of the mishnah and the *Gemara,* it does not appear in *Yerushalmi* or in *Rambam Hil. Sanhedrin* 16:11 *(Tos. Yom Tov).* Those who do include this passage delete the preceding piece about repeating the two verses *(Tif. Yis.).* [Since according to this version he has not yet completed the recitation, there is no reason to repeat what he has already recited.]

וְחוֹתֵם: — *and he concludes (Psalms 78:38):*

[I.e., he concludes the reading with the following verse.]

„וְהוּא רַחוּם יְכַפֵּר עָוֹן, וְגוֹ׳,״ — *'But He, the Merciful One, is forgiving of iniquity,' etc.,*

The verse completed reads: וְלֹא־יַשְׁחִית וְהִרְבָּה לְהָשִׁיב אַפּוֹ וְלֹא־יָעִיר כָּל־חֲמָתוֹ, *and does not destroy, frequently He withdraws His anger, not arousing His entire rage.*

This verse consists of thirteen words which, when repeated three times, equal thirty-nine words, corresponding to the thirty-nine lashes administered by *beis din (Orach Chaim* 607:6, *Beur HaGra* 18).

The verse is recited on weekday evenings before the *Maariv* prayer, since that was the time that transgressors were usually flogged *(Abudraham* from *Sefer HaManhig).* [Apparently, these authorities had our reading in the mishnah.]

וְחוֹזֵר לִתְחִלַּת הַמִּקְרָא. — *and he goes back to the beginning of the verses.*

[If he completed the recitation before the court attendant completed administering the lashes, he repeats the reading. This identical phrase appeared earlier in the mishnah. As noted there, there are differing versions of the correct text of this mishnah and where this phrase is to be placed. Those who place it here delete it above. The standard editions of the Mishnah, however, record both versions, and for this reason it has been included in our text as well.]

וְאִם מֵת תַּחַת יָדוֹ, — *If he died under his hand,*

[If the one who was flogged died at the hands of the one administering the lashes.]

פָּטוּר. — *he is exempt.*

אַחַת, וָמֵת – הֲרֵי זֶה גּוֹלֶה עַל־יָדוֹ. נִתְקַלְקֵל בֵּין בְּרֶעִי בֵּין בְּמַיִם, פָּטוּר. רַבִּי יְהוּדָה אוֹמֵר: הָאִישׁ בְּרֶעִי, וְהָאִשָּׁה בְּמַיִם.

[טו] **כָּל־** חַיָּבֵי כְרֵיתוּת שֶׁלָּקוּ נִפְטְרוּ יְדֵי כְרִיתָתָם, שֶׁנֶּאֱמַר: „וְנִקְלָה אָחִיךָ לְעֵינֶיךָ" – כְּשֶׁלָּקָה, הֲרֵי הוּא כְאָחִיךָ; דִּבְרֵי רַבִּי חֲנַנְיָא בֶּן־גַּמְלִיאֵל. אָמַר רַבִּי חֲנַנְיָא בֶּן־גַּמְלִיאֵל: מָה אִם הָעוֹבֵר עֲבֵרָה אַחַת נוֹטֵל נַפְשׁוֹ עָלֶיהָ, הָעוֹשֶׂה מִצְוָה אַחַת, עַל אַחַת כַּמָּה וְכַמָּה שֶׁתִּנָּתֵן

יד אברהם

[Through his extreme fright at what is about to happen to him, he lost control of his bodily functions and soiled himself.]

בֵּין בְּרֶעִי בֵּין בְּמַיִם, פָּטוּר. — *either with excrement or with urine, he is exempt.*

This is based on (*Deut.* 25:3): וְנִקְלָה אָחִיךָ לְעֵינֶיךָ, *and your brother shall be dishonored before your eyes* [by being flogged]. By soiling himself he has been dishonored, even without the lashes, and he is therefore exempt from them (*Rav; Rivan; Rambam, Hil. Sanhedrin* 17:5).

רַבִּי יְהוּדָה אוֹמֵר: הָאִישׁ בְּרֶעִי, וְהָאִשָּׁה בְּמַיִם. — *R' Yehudah says: A man with excrement, and a woman with urine.*

In R' Yehudah's opinion, a man is exempted from the lashes only if he soils himself by defecating, while a woman is exempted even by urine. Since a woman is more sensitive to shame, she is dishonored even by suffering this lesser shame (*Rav*).

The halachah is not in accordance with R' Yehudah (*Rav; Rambam, Hil. Sanhedrin* 17:5).

The court attendant administering the flogging is exempt from exile for killing him accidentally, since he struck him with permission (*Rav*). This follows the rule established above in mishnah 2:2 (*Tos. Yom Tov* from *Rivan*).

הוֹסִיף לוֹ עוֹד רְצוּעָה אַחַת, וָמֵת – הֲרֵי זֶה גּוֹלֶה עַל־יָדוֹ. — [*If*] *he added one more blow, and he died — he is exiled because of him.*

I.e., if the one administering the flogging inadvertently added one blow to the amount assessed by *beis din*, and he died because of the extra lash, he is exiled for killing him inadvertently (*Rav*).

Were he to intentionally inflict more than the assessed number, although he did not mean for him to die, he would nevertheless be considered an intentional murderer and would not be exiled (*Tos. Yom Tov*).

נִתְקַלְקֵל — [*If*] *he soiled himself* [lit. *deteriorated*]

15.

כָּל־חַיָּבֵי כְרֵיתוּת שֶׁלָּקוּ — *All those liable to kares who were flogged*

[As we learned in mishnah 1, negative commandments liable to *kares* are punishable by lashes as well.]

נִפְטְרוּ יְדֵי כְרִיתָתָם, — *become exempt from their kares,*

After being flogged, they become exempt from *kares*, if they have repented (*Rav; Rambam Comm.*). [As taught in *Yoma* 86a, sins punishable by *kares* cannot be atoned for merely by repen-

one more blow, and he died — he is exiled because of him. [If] he soiled himself either with excrement or with urine, he is exempt. R′ Yehudah says: A man with excrement, and a woman with urine.

15. All those liable to *kares* who were flogged become exempt from their *kares*, as it is said (*Deut.* 25:3): *And your brother be dishonored before your eyes* — once he has been flogged, he is as your brother; [these are] the words of R′ Chanania ben Gamliel. Said R′ Chanania ben Gamliel: Now if one who commits one transgression forfeits his soul thereby, one who performs one *mitzvah*, how much more should his soul be

YAD AVRAHAM

tance and Yom Kippur. Such sins require suffering as well to be eradicated. The flogging serves the purpose, if accompanied by repentance.]

שֶׁנֶּאֱמַר: „וְנִקְלָה אָחִיךָ לְעֵינֶיךָ" – כְּשֶׁלָּקָה, הֲרֵי הוּא כְּאָחִיךָ; — *as it is said (Deut. 25:3): 'And your brother be dishonored before your eyes' — once he has been flogged, he is as your brother;*

I.e., after suffering his punishment he is restored to his former status. R′ Chanania understands this as including those liable to *kares* (*Rambam, Hil. Sanhedrin* 17:7).

This idea is expressed dramatically by *Sifre:* Said R′ Chanania ben Gamliel: Scripture constantly refers to him wicked, as it is said: *And it shall be if the wicked one is sentenced to lashes.* But when he has been flogged, Scripture calls him *your brother,* as it is said: *And your brother be dishonored.* A Jew who has sinned has never lost his status of brotherhood, for, an Israelite, although he has sinned, is nevertheless an Israelite. Since in this case the Torah calls him a brother only after being flogged, it is obvious that Scripture is referring to a sinner who has lost his status of brotherhood. This is one who has transgressed a sin punishable by *kares.* Yet, after being flogged, he is restored to his status of brotherhood and need not suffer *kares* (*Toledos Adam*).

דִּבְרֵי רַבִּי חֲנַנְיָא בֶּן־גַּמְלִיאֵל. — [*these are*] *the words of R′ Chanania ben Gamliel.*

The halachah is in accordance with R′ Chanania ben Gamliel (*Rambam, Hil. Sanhedrin* 17:7).

The law expounded in this mishnah led to a great controversy in the period following the expulsion from Spain. The Marranos, having lived as Christians under the threat of the Inquisition, sought to receive lashes in order to atone for the sins they had committed, some of which were punishable by *kares.* Since only a duly ordained Sanhedrin can sentence and administer lashes, and the true *semichah* (ordination) had long-since lapsed [see General Introduction to ArtScroll *Sanhedrin*], there was a movement to reinstate the *semichah* ordination of judges for the Sanhedrin. This caused a great controversy, which finally resulted in the abandonment of the project.

אָמַר רַבִּי חֲנַנְיָא בֶּן־גַּמְלִיאֵל: — *Said R′ Chanania ben Gamliel:*

R′ Chanania teaches that the reward to be reaped for the fulfillment of a *mitzvah* can be inferred from the penalty for transgressing them (*Rav*).

מָה אִם הָעוֹבֵר עֲבֵרָה אַחַת נוֹטֵל נַפְשׁוֹ עָלֶיהָ, — *Now if one who commits one transgression forfeits his soul thereby,*

I.e., he loses his soul by transgressing sins punishable by *kares;* see *Meiri* and *Meleches Shlomo.*

לוֹ נַפְשׁוֹ. רַבִּי שִׁמְעוֹן אוֹמֵר: מִמְּקוֹמוֹ הוּא לָמֵד, שֶׁנֶּאֱמַר: „וְנִכְרְתוּ הַנְּפָשׁוֹת הָעֹשֹׂת, וְגוֹ׳.״ וְאוֹמֵר: „אֲשֶׁר יַעֲשֶׂה אֹתָם הָאָדָם וָחַי בָּהֶם.״ הָא כָּל־הַיּוֹשֵׁב וְלֹא עָבַר עֲבֵרָה נוֹתְנִין לוֹ שָׂכָר כְּעוֹשֶׂה מִצְוָה. רַבִּי שִׁמְעוֹן בַּר רַבִּי אוֹמֵר: הֲרֵי הוּא אוֹמֵר: „רַק חֲזַק לְבִלְתִּי אֲכֹל הַדָּם כִּי הַדָּם הוּא הַנָּפֶשׁ, וְגוֹ׳.״ וּמָה אִם הַדָּם, שֶׁנַּפְשׁוֹ שֶׁל־אָדָם קָצָה מִמֶּנּוּ, הַפּוֹרֵשׁ מִמֶּנּוּ מְקַבֵּל שָׂכָר, גָּזֵל וַעֲרָיוֹת, שֶׁנַּפְשׁוֹ שֶׁל־אָדָם מִתְאַוָּה לָהֶן וּמְחַמַּדְתָּן, הַפּוֹרֵשׁ מֵהֶן עַל־אַחַת כַּמָּה וְכַמָּה שֶׁיִּזְכֶּה לוֹ, וּלְדוֹרוֹתָיו, וּלְדוֹרוֹת דּוֹרוֹתָיו, עַד־סוֹף כָּל־הַדּוֹרוֹת.

[טז] **רַבִּי** חֲנַנְיָא בֶּן עֲקַשְׁיָא אוֹמֵר: רָצָה הַקָּדוֹשׁ בָּרוּךְ הוּא לְזַכּוֹת אֶת־יִשְׂרָאֵל; לְפִיכָךְ הִרְבָּה לָהֶם תּוֹרָה וּמִצְוֹת, שֶׁנֶּאֱמַר: „ה׳ חָפֵץ לְמַעַן צִדְקוֹ, יַגְדִּיל תּוֹרָה וְיַאְדִּיר.״

יד אברהם

kares, which we have been discussing up until now. Furthermore, from there we shall see that merely abstaining from a sin is adjudged as though he had performed a *mitzvah (Rav).*

שֶׁנֶּאֱמַר: „וְנִכְרְתוּ הַנְּפָשׁוֹת הָעֹשֹׂת, וְגוֹ׳.״ — *as it is said (Lev. 18:29): 'And the souls that do them shall be cut off,' etc.*

[This verse refers to the punishment of *kares* for those who engage in incest and other sins enumerated in that section.]

וְאוֹמֵר: „אֲשֶׁר יַעֲשֶׂה אֹתָם הָאָדָם וָחַי בָּהֶם.״ — *And it [also] states (ibid. v. 5): 'Which a man shall do and live by them.'*

Earlier in the same chapter, the Torah enjoins us to the abstinence from incest by stating: *You shall heed My statutes and laws, which a man shall do and live by them; I am* HASHEM.

הָא כָּל־הַיּוֹשֵׁב וְלֹא עָבַר עֲבֵרָה נוֹתְנִין לוֹ שָׂכָר כְּעוֹשֶׂה מִצְוָה. — *This means that whoever*

הָעוֹשֶׂה מִצְוָה אַחַת, עַל אַחַת כַּמָּה וְכַמָּה שֶׁתִּנָּתֵן לוֹ נַפְשׁוֹ. — *one who performs one mitzvah, how much more should his soul be granted him!*

This derivation is based on the principle that the Divine standard for reward far surpasses the Divine standard of retribution, as explained above in the commentary to mishnah 1:7, s.v. על אחת כמה וכמה.

Rav cites a second explanation of R' Chanania ben Gamliel's statement which has it refer not to the reward of *mitzvos* in general but specifically to the reward for accepting the punishment of *malkus* as just and deserved. Giving *malkus* where it is warranted is a *mitzvah.*

רַבִּי שִׁמְעוֹן אוֹמֵר: מִמְּקוֹמוֹ הוּא לָמֵד, — *R' Shimon says: It is derived from its place,*

I.e., we need not infer the reward for *mitzvos* from the retribution for sins; rather, we can derive it from the section of the Torah dealing with the penalty of

granted him! R′ Shimon says: It is derived from its place, as it is said (*Lev.* 18:29): *And the souls that do them shall be cut off, etc.* And it [also] states (ibid. v. 5): *Which a man shall do and live by them.* This means that whoever sits and refrains from committing a transgression is rewarded like one who performs a *mitzvah.* R′ Shimon the son of Rabbi says: It states (*Deut.* 12:23): *Only be steadfast not to eat the blood, for the blood is the life.* Now if for blood, from which a person recoils, one who abstains from it is rewarded, theft and immorality, which a person desires and covets, how much more will one who abstains from them merit for himself, his children, and his grandchildren, until the end of all the generations!

16. R′ Chanania ben Akashia says: The Holy One, Blessed is He, wished to confer merit upon Israel; therefore He gave them Torah and *mitzvos* in abundance, as it is said: *HASHEM desired for the sake of its [Israel′s] righteousness, that the Torah be expanded and strengthened (Isaiah* 42:21).

YAD AVRAHAM

sits and refrains from committing a transgression is rewarded like one who performs a mitzvah.

This teaches us that if one subdues his temptation and abstains from sinning in order to fulfill the commandment of his Creator, his reward is that his soul be given him, as Scripture states: *And live by them.* I.e., the Torah states that his reward shall be that *he shall live by them,* meaning his soul will live on eternally *(Rav).*

רַבִּי שִׁמְעוֹן בַּר רַבִּי אוֹמֵר: — *R′ Shimon the son of Rabbi says:*

[I.e., R′ Shimon the son of R′ Yehudah HaNasi. R′ Shimon brings yet another Scriptural proof that there is reward for abstaining from sin.]

הֲרֵי הוּא אוֹמֵר: „רַק חֲזַק לְבִלְתִּי אֲכֹל הַדָּם כִּי הַדָּם הוּא הַנָּפֶשׁ, וְגו׳.״ — *It states (Deut. 12:23): Only be steadfast not to eat the blood, for the blood is the life.′*

The Torah forbids eating the blood of an animal *(Deut.* 12:23).

וּמָה אִם הַדָּם, שֶׁנַּפְשׁוֹ שֶׁל־אָדָם קָצָה מִמֶּנּוּ, — *Now if for blood, from which a person recoils,*

[I.e., a person has a natural aversion to eating blood.]

הַפּוֹרֵשׁ מִמֶּנּוּ מְקַבֵּל שָׂכָר, — *one who abstains from it is rewarded,*

I.e., he is rewarded for not eating it, as the Torah states in the conclusion to that section *(Deut.* 12:28): לְמַעַן יִיטַב לְךָ וּלְבָנֶיךָ אַחֲרֶיךָ עַד־עוֹלָם, *in order that it be good for you and for your children forever.*

גָּזֵל וַעֲרָיוֹת, שֶׁנַּפְשׁוֹ שֶׁל־אָדָם מִתְאַוָּה לָהֶן וּמְחַמַּדְתָּן, הַפּוֹרֵשׁ מֵהֶן עַל־אַחַת כַּמָּה וְכַמָּה שֶׁיִּזְכֶּה לוֹ, וּלְדוֹרוֹתָיו, וּלְדוֹרוֹת דּוֹרוֹתָיו, עַד סוֹף כָּל־הַדּוֹרוֹת. — *theft and immorality,*

which a person desires and covets, how much more will one who abstains from them merit for himself, his children, and his grandchildren, until the end of all the generations!

All the more so that if one abstains from committing sins which involve physical pleasure, for which a person has a natural inclination *(Rambam Comm.)*, he will surely merit great reward.

16.

רַבִּי חֲנַנְיָא בֶּן עֲקַשְׁיָא אוֹמֵר: רָצָה הַקָּדוֹשׁ בָּרוּךְ הוּא לְזַכּוֹת אֶת־יִשְׂרָאֵל; — *R' Chanania ben Akashia says: The Holy One, Blessed is He, wished to confer merit upon Israel;*

[I.e., He wished to increase their reward for the observance of the *mitzvos.*]

לְפִיכָךְ הִרְבָּה לָהֶם תּוֹרָה וּמִצְוֹת, — *therefore He gave them Torah and mitzvos in abundance,*

I.e., the Torah stated many admonitions against eating abominable creatures, crawling things, and carrion, although people abstain from them in any case. God's purpose was only to increase their reward, for, since it is a *mitzvah* to abstain from them, they are rewarded for keeping a *mitzvah (Rav; Rivan).*

Another explanation is that it is a fundamental principle of the Torah that in order to merit eternal life in the World to Come a person must fulfill at least one *mitzvah* properly with complete devotion to *Hashem.* This *mitzvah* must be performed without incorporating in it any personal interest in the observance, intending it only to fulfill God's will with love. Therefore, God gave us an abundance of *mitzvos* so that every person should, in his lifetime, observe at least one *mitzvah* perfectly and thereby merit eternal life *(Rambam Comm.).*

שֶׁנֶּאֱמַר: „ה׳ חָפֵץ לְמַעַן צִדְקוֹ — *as it is said (Isaiah 42:21): 'HASHEM desired for the sake of its [Israel's] righteousness,*

I.e., to make Israel righteous with abundant reward *(Tos. Yom Tov; Tif. Yis.).*

יַגְדִּיל תּוֹרָה וְיַאְדִּיר.״ — *that the Torah be expanded and strengthened.'*

Therefore, Hashem expanded the Torah, and strengthened it with many admonitions in order to reinforce them, thereby conferring much reward upon Israel for their observance. As Scripture states *(Psalms* 31:20): *How abundant is Your goodness which You have treasured for Your reverent ones (Tif. Yis.).*

סליקא לה מסכת מכות

מסכת שבועות

Tractate Shevuos

ויקרא ה:א־י

וְנֶפֶשׁ כִּי־תֶחֱטָא וְשָׁמְעָה קוֹל אָלָה וְהוּא עֵד אוֹ רָאָה אוֹ יָדָע אִם־לוֹא יַגִּיד וְנָשָׂא עֲוֹנוֹ. אוֹ נֶפֶשׁ אֲשֶׁר תִּגַּע בְּכָל־דָּבָר טָמֵא אוֹ בְנִבְלַת חַיָּה טְמֵאָה אוֹ בְּנִבְלַת בְּהֵמָה טְמֵאָה אוֹ בְּנִבְלַת שֶׁרֶץ טָמֵא וְנֶעְלַם מִמֶּנּוּ וְהוּא טָמֵא וְאָשֵׁם. אוֹ כִי יִגַּע בְּטֻמְאַת אָדָם לְכֹל טֻמְאָתוֹ אֲשֶׁר יִטְמָא בָּהּ וְנֶעְלַם מִמֶּנּוּ וְהוּא יָדַע וְאָשֵׁם. אוֹ נֶפֶשׁ כִּי תִשָּׁבַע לְבַטֵּא בִשְׂפָתַיִם לְהָרַע אוֹ לְהֵיטִיב לְכֹל אֲשֶׁר יְבַטֵּא הָאָדָם בִּשְׁבֻעָה וְנֶעְלַם מִמֶּנּוּ וְהוּא־יָדַע וְאָשֵׁם לְאַחַת מֵאֵלֶּה. וְהָיָה כִי־יֶאְשַׁם לְאַחַת מֵאֵלֶּה וְהִתְוַדָּה אֲשֶׁר חָטָא עָלֶיהָ. וְהֵבִיא אֶת־אֲשָׁמוֹ לַה׳ עַל חַטָּאתוֹ אֲשֶׁר חָטָא נְקֵבָה מִן־הַצֹּאן כִּשְׂבָּה אוֹ־שְׂעִירַת עִזִּים לְחַטָּאת וְכִפֶּר עָלָיו הַכֹּהֵן מֵחַטָּאתוֹ. וְאִם לֹא תַגִּיעַ יָדוֹ דֵּי שֶׂה וְהֵבִיא אֶת־אֲשָׁמוֹ אֲשֶׁר חָטָא שְׁתֵּי תֹרִים אוֹ־שְׁנֵי בְנֵי־יוֹנָה לַה׳ אֶחָד לְחַטָּאת וְאֶחָד לְעֹלָה. וְהֵבִיא אֹתָם אֶל הַכֹּהֵן וְהִקְרִיב אֶת־אֲשֶׁר לַחַטָּאת רִאשׁוֹנָה וּמָלַק אֶת־רֹאשׁוֹ מִמּוּל עָרְפּוֹ וְלֹא יַבְדִּיל. וְהִזָּה מִדַּם הַחַטָּאת עַל־קִיר הַמִּזְבֵּחַ וְהַנִּשְׁאָר בַּדָּם יִמָּצֵה אֶל־יְסוֹד הַמִּזְבֵּחַ חַטָּאת הוּא. וְאֶת־הַשֵּׁנִי יַעֲשֶׂה עֹלָה כַּמִּשְׁפָּט וְכִפֶּר עָלָיו הַכֹּהֵן מֵחַטָּאתוֹ אֲשֶׁר־חָטָא וְנִסְלַח לוֹ.

שמות כ:ז

לֹא תִשָּׂא אֶת־שֵׁם־ה׳ אֱלֹהֶיךָ לַשָּׁוְא כִּי לֹא יְנַקֶּה ה׳ אֵת אֲשֶׁר־יִשָּׂא אֶת־שְׁמוֹ לַשָּׁוְא.

ויקרא יט:יב

וְלֹא־תִשָּׁבְעוּ בִשְׁמִי לַשָּׁקֶר וְחִלַּלְתָּ אֶת־שֵׁם אֱלֹהֶיךָ אֲנִי ה׳.

במדבר ל:ג

אִישׁ כִּי־יִדֹּר נֶדֶר לַה׳ אוֹ־הִשָּׁבַע שְׁבֻעָה לֶאְסֹר אִסָּר עַל־נַפְשׁוֹ לֹא יַחֵל דְּבָרוֹ כְּכָל־הַיֹּצֵא מִפִּיו יַעֲשֶׂה.

Leviticus 5:1-10

Should a person sin and hear the voice of adjuration, and he is a witness, having either seen or known; if he does not tell, he shall bear his iniquity. Or if a person touches anything which is tamei, whether the carcass of a contaminating wild animal, or the carcass of a contaminating domesticated animal, or the carcass of a contaminating sheretz, but it escapes his awareness and he is tamei and becomes guilty. Or if he touches a human tumah, in whatever manner of tumah he becomes contaminated, but it escapes his awareness and he becomes aware, and he becomes guilty. Or if a person should swear, pronouncing with his lips to do bad or to do good, whatever it is that a man shall pronounce in an oath, and it escapes him; and he then becomes aware of it, and he becomes guilty to one of these. It shall be that if someone becomes guilty in one of these matters, he is to confess that in which he had sinned. And he is to bring his guilt-offering to HASHEM *for the sin that he had committed, a female of the flock, a sheep or a goat, for a sin-offering; and the Kohen shall have afforded him atonement from his sin. But if he cannot afford a sheep or goat, then he is to bring as his guilt-offering for having sinned two turtledoves or two young pigeons for* HASHEM, *one as a sin-offering and one as a burnt-offering; he is to bring them to the Kohen, who is to bring first the one that is designated as a sin-offering; he is to pinch through its head from the back of its neck, but should not sever it. He is to sprinkle from the blood of the sin-offering against the wall of the Altar, and the remainder of the blood should be squeezed out at the base of the Altar; it is a sin-offering. And he is to make the second one an burnt-offering according to the law; and the Kohen shall have afforded him atonement from the sin he has committed and it shall be forgiven him.*

Exodus 20:7

You shall not take the Name of HASHEM, *your God, in a vain oath; for* HASHEM *will not absolve the one who takes His Name in a vain oath.*

Leviticus 19:12

You shall not swear in My Name falsely, and thereby desecrate the Name of your God; I am HASHEM.

Numbers 30:3

A man who shall utter a vow to HASHEM *or swear an oath, to bind some prohibition upon himself, he shall not profane his word; all that comes forth from his mouth he shall do.*

General Introduction to Shevuos

One of the greatest forces in human existence is the power of speech. Indeed, it is one of the most salient and unique features of the human species, the 'living spirit' marking the dividing line between man and animal (see *Targum* to *Genesis* 2:7).

The Torah recognizes the enormous power of human speech with a host of laws regulating it. Even beyond that, however, the Torah assigns to it the power to create — through the instruments of oaths and vows — new and legally binding conditions, whose effect is to add to the obligations and restrictions of an individual or the community at large

There are several types of such legal declarations: *neder* (vow; see tractate *Nedarim*), *Shevuah* (oath), *nezirus* (a specific form of oath prohibiting consumption of wine, contact with dead bodies, and cutting one's hair; see tractate *Nazir*), and *hedkesh* (consecration of animals as sacrifices or of property to the Temple treasury; see tractate *Zevachim*).[1]

Tractate *Shevuos* deals primarily with the topic of oaths. In common with the *neder* and the *nezirus*, the *shevuah*, oath, can create a prohibition for a person to engage in a certain activity, as well as an obligation to perform one. However, in addition to this, the Torah establishes the oath as an instrument to attest to the truth of a statement. In keeping with this, the Torah places heavy penalties on one who swears a false oath.

There are four basic types of Biblical oaths: (1) שְׁבוּעַת בִּטּוּי, *an oath of utterance;* (2) שְׁבוּעַת שָׁוְא, *a vain oath;* (3) שְׁבוּעַת הָעֵדוּת, *an oath of testimony;* and (4) שְׁבוּעַת הַפִּקָּדוֹן, *an oath of deposit* (*Meiri*).

◆§ שְׁבוּעַת בִּטּוּי, Oath of Utterance

שְׁבוּעַת בִּטּוּי, *an oath of utterance,* is an oath swearing either to perform a deed at some future time or not to perform one. In this form, it creates new obligations upon the oath-taker to live up to the terms of his oath — either to do what he has sworn to do or to refrain from doing what he has sworn not to do.

There are certain limitations on this form of oath, the primary of which is that such an oath cannot take effect upon another, identical oath or against something decreed by the Torah. The parameters of this limitation, and the exceptions to it, are dealt with in chapter 3.

There is also a second category of oath of utterance, namely, an oath concerning a past incident, e.g., swearing that one did or did not perform a certain act in the past. In this form, the oath is not a legal instrument binding him to some course of action, since whatever has happened, has happened. Rather, it is a legal instrument binding him to the truth of his statement, by means of which he attests to the truth of his declaration. This category of oath is also dealt with in chapter 3.

Should he fail to fulfill his oath, or should it prove false, he has transgressed the admonition (*Lev.* 19:12): וְלֹא תִשָּׁבְעוּ בִשְׁמִי לַשָּׁקֶר, *You shall not swear in My Name*

1. There are also other instances in which declarations effect legal changes, e.g., *terumah,* the oral separation of a portion of the crop of *Eretz Yisrael* to be given to a *kohen.* This imparts a level of sanctity which has various legal consequences; however, the power to declare something *terumah* arises out of the obligation to give *terumah,* not out of the intitiative of the declarer.

falsely (Rambam, Hil. Shevuos 1:3).[1] [Additionally, in the case of his failure to keep his oath concerning the future he is also guilty of violating the admonition not to profane his word (*Numbers* 30:3) (*Kesef Mishneh* ibid.).] For an intentional transgression, he is punished by מַלְקוּת, *lashes,* (see tractate *Makkos*). For an unintentional transgression, the transgressor must bring a חַטָּאת, *sin-offering.*[2]

In this case, the sin-offering is a קָרְבָּן עוֹלֶה וְיוֹרֵד, *a variable sin-offering,* i.e., one whose quality depends upon the monetary resources of the sinner. If the sinner is affluent, he must bring a female sheep or goat for his sacrifice. Should he be poor, he is required to bring only two turtledoves or two young pigeons, one as a sin-offering, the other as a burnt-offering. If he is very poor and cannot afford even two turtledoves or pigeons, he may bring instead a tenth of an *ephah* of fine flour for a מִנְחָה, *minchah* [flour-offering]. This is discussed in *Lev.* 5:4-10.

⸎ שְׁבוּעַת שָׁוְא, Vain Oath

שְׁבוּעַת שָׁוְא, *a vain oath,* is similar to an oath of utterance, in that it too ostensibly binds a person to the truth of a certain statement, or to the performance (or non-performance) of a certain future act. However, in contrast to the oath of utterance, it concerns matters which are either obviously impossible or else

---

1. There are three negative commandments prohibiting false oaths and vows. They are as follows: (1) לֹא תִשָּׂא אֶת־שֵׁם ה׳ אֱלֹקֶיךָ לַשָּׁוְא, *You shall not take the Name of Hashem, Your God, in a vain oath (Exodus* 20:7); (2) וְלֹא תִשָּׁבְעוּ בִשְׁמִי לַשָּׁקֶר, *You shall not swear by My Name falsely (Lev.* 19:12); (3) לֹא יַחֵל דְּבָרוֹ, *He shall not profane his word (Numbers* 30:3). The *Gemara* (20b, 21a) cites a controversy between Rav Dimi and Ravin as to which injunctions apply to oaths concerning past occurences, and which to oaths made in regard to future acts. Rav Dimi's view is that if one swears concerning the future — for example 'I will eat,' or 'I will not eat,' — and he does not keep his word, he transgresses the negative commandment of *you shall not swear by My Name falsely.* [Additionally, he transgresses the negative commandment of *he shall not profane his word,* which applies to both oaths and vows.] If he swears falsely concerning a past occurence, he trangresses the commandment, *you shall not take the Name of Hashem, your God, in a vain oath.* [In Rav Dimi's view, it is a vain oath because it was false from the moment it was uttered, in contrast to an oath in regard to the future, which may yet prove to be true.] If he makes a vow (*neder*), however, and does not keep it, he trangresses only the commandment, *he shall not profane his word.*

Ravin's view is that if he swears falsely concerning a past occurrence he is guilty of a false oath, not a vain one. Thus, he trangresses, *you shall not swear by My Name falsely.* If he swears to do or not to do a particular act and he does not fulfill his oath, he trangresses, *he shall not profane his word.* Only if he swears concerning a thing which is obviously false or impossible does he trangress the prohibition, *you shall not take the Name of Hashem, your God, in a vain oath.*

Rambam (Hil. Shevous 1:3) rules that whether one swears falsely concerning a past occurence, or whether he fails to live up to his oath ocncerning a future course of action, he trangresses the admonition, *you shall not swear by My Name falsely.* This seems not to conform either with the view of Rav Dimi or of Ravin. *Kesef Mishneh* explains that *Rambam* understood Ravin's dispute of Rav Dimi to be only in regard to oaths about the past, maintaining that they are false oaths, not vain ones. His assertion that the violation of an oath in regard to the future trangresses the injunction *he shall not profane his word* is not meant to dispute Rav Dimi's position that he is liable for a false oath, but is meant to emphasize that he is also liable for *profaning his word,* a point not explicitly made by Rav Dimi. *Rambam* thus follows the view of Ravin; see *Kesef Mishneh* at length.

2. Generally, a sin-offering is brought only for one who transgresses a prohibition which, if done intentionally, is punishable by *kares* or execution. The sin-offering for a false oath is an exception to the general rule.

self-evident. As such, it is a pointless, or *vain oath*. It is thus distinguished from the false oath, which concerns matters which though they have proven to be false, *might* have been true.

There are essentially four classes of vain oaths: (a) An oath which is obviously false, e.g., swearing that a stone is gold; (b) one which is self-evident, e.g., that a stone is a stone; (c) an oath to transgress a commandment of the Torah, either positive or negative; (d) an oath to do something impossible, e.g., to climb to the heavens.[1]

In all these cases, the one who swears transgresses the third of the Ten Commandments: לֹא תִשָּׂא אֶת־שֵׁם ה׳ אֱלֹהֶיךָ לַשָּׁוְא, *You shall not take the Name of* HASHEM, *your God, in a vain oath*. Should one be guilty of a deliberate infraction of this prohibition, he incurs the penalty of lashes. However, there is no penalty for unintentional transgression.

◆§ שְׁבוּעַת הָעֵדוּת, Oath of Testimony

שְׁבוּעַת הָעֵדוּת, *an oath of testimony*, is an oath made by a potential witness in response to someone's demand that he testify on his behalf regarding a monetary matter. In response to this demand, the witness denies any knowledge of the matter, swearing to that effect. If he later confesses that he indeed had knowledge of the testimony which would have enabled the person to win his monetary claim, he is liable to a קָרְבָּן עוֹלֶה וְיוֹרֵד, *a variable sin-offering*, for his false oath.[2] This is discussed in *Lev*. 5:1: וְנֶפֶשׁ כִּי תֶחֱטָא וְשָׁמְעָה קוֹל אָלָה וְהוּא עֵד אוֹ רָאָה אוֹ יָדָע אִם־לוֹא יַגִּיד וְנָשָׂא עֲוֹנוֹ, *And should a person sin and hear the voice of an oath, and he is a witness, having either seen or known — if he does not tell, he shall bear his iniquity*. [There is no penalty for a mistaken denial, however, since if he did not remember any testimony at the time he was pressed to testify, his oath denying that he knew anything was, in fact, true. His subsequent recall of the events does not retroactively make his oath false (see 4:2).] This category of oath is the subject of chapter 4.

◆§ שְׁבוּעַת הַפִּקָּדוֹן, Oath of Deposit

שְׁבוּעַת הַפִּקָּדוֹן, *an oath of deposit*, is an oath made by a person to deny another person's claim against him for money. The claim may be for any type of obligation, whether one incurred by stealing, borrowing, accepting a deposit, finding a lost article and not returning it, or the like. Should he later confess his guilt, he must return the principal, adding an additional fifth to the total sum. In addition, he must bring a ram for an אָשָׁם, *guilt-offering*.[3] This is stated by the Torah in *Lev*. 5:20-26, and is discussed by the mishnah in chapter 6.

The remainder of this tractate discusses the oaths which are imposed by the courts on a litigant in a civil case. In essence, these oaths are forms of שְׁבוּעַת הַפִּקָּדוֹן, *oath of deposit*. The last three chapters, however, delineate the conditions under which they are imposed, while chapter 6 primarily discusses the liability for swearing this oath falsely, even for one who swore voluntarily.

◆§ Court-Imposed Oaths

According to Biblical law, there are only three types of oaths imposed by *beis din*: (1) שְׁבוּעַת מוֹדֶה בְּמִקְצָת, *the oath of one who admits part of the claim lodged against*

1. These last two are really the same. The reason swearing to transgress a Torah commandment is considered a vain oath is because it is like swearing to do the impossible.

2. Generally, a sin-offering is brought only for unintentional transgressions. This is one of the rare instances for which a sin-offering is brought for a deliberate transgression.

3. This too is an exception to the rule that sin-offerings are for unintentional transgressions.

him, (2) שְׁבוּעַת הַשּׁוֹמְרִים, *the oath of a shomer* (guardian) who claims exemption for loss of the deposit entrusted to him, or (3) שְׁבוּעַת עֵד אֶחָד, *the single witness oath,* i.e., the oath a defendant in a monetary case must swear to contradict the testimony of a single witness who testifies against him. Chapter 6 of our tractate deals with the oath of מוֹדֶה בְּמִקְצָת, *the one who admits part of the claim,* while chapter 8 deals with the שְׁבוּעַת הַשּׁוֹמְרִים, *oath of the shomer.*

All Biblical oaths are oaths imposed on the defendant, and they take the form of allowing the defendant to swear that he is telling the truth and thereby exempt himself from the claim lodged against him. There are cases, however, in which the Rabbis saw fit to institute an oath on the plaintiff to enable him to collect on his claim even without proof. They also instituted oaths to require various categories of people who manage other people's property to have to swear in certain circumstances that they did not abuse their trusts (see below, 7:8). These oaths are known as שְׁבוּעַת הַמִּשְׁנָה, *a mishnaic oath,* and they are discussed in the chapter 7.

There is also a post-mishnaic oath, known as שְׁבוּעַת הֶסֵּת, *shevuas hesses.* This oath is imposed on a defendant who denies a claim completely, as will be explained in chapter 6. Since this oath was first initiated in Talmudic times *(Gem.* 40b; *Rambam, Hil. Toein* 1:3), the mishnah never refers to it.

◆§ Personal and Adjured Oaths

There are two mechanisms by which a person's declaration becomes an oath. The first is by framing it in the language of an oath — 'I swear . . . ' Such a personal oath is referred to by the mishnah as *an oath by his own mouth,* i.e., a personal oath. The second is by making the declaration in response to the adjuration of another. For example, if a litigant charges his counterpart with an oath to affirm his denial of a claim, and the latter responds to this adjuration by repeating his denial, the denial is considered an oath even though no oath was actually uttered by the respondent. This type of oath is referred to by the mishnah as *adjured by others.*

There is actually a third method by which a declaration becomes an oath. As taught in mishnah 3:10, an adjured oath can become binding by a response of 'Amen,' without a repetition of the denial. However, the oath resulting from such a response is treated as a personal oath, not an adjured oath.

❦ ❦ ❦

In concluding this introduction, we must take note of the great severity attached to the crime of swearing falsely. The *Gemara* (39a) states that when the commandment, *You shall not take the Name of HASHEM, your God, in a vain oath,* was given at Sinai, the entire world trembled. In contrast to other sins, for which there can be atonement without retribution, that commandment makes clear that the sin of a false oath is so severe that retribution can never be completely avoided. Furthermore, not only does retribution come to him, but it comes in some measure even to his family and to the world at large. So great is the odium of swearing falsely that both the plaintiff and the defendant in the matter are tainted by their involvement in a court-imposed oath over money (*Gem.* 39b). This and more was included in the admonition read by the judges to the one about to swear.

In earlier times, the prohibition against swearing falsely was held in such awe by the masses that even those who were considered untrustworthy in their financial dealings could, in the opinion of some authorities, be trusted in their oaths. Stealing was considered the lesser crime. [This matter is discussed in greater length in the commentary to mishnah 7:4.] May the study of this tractate serve to bolster the meticulous observance of these laws.

שבועות [א] **שְׁבוּעוֹת** שְׁתַּיִם שֶׁהֵן אַרְבַּע. יְדִיעוֹת הַטֻּמְאָה שְׁתַּיִם שֶׁהֵן אַרְבַּע. יְצִיאוֹת הַשַּׁבָּת שְׁתַּיִם שֶׁהֵן אַרְבַּע. מַרְאוֹת נְגָעִים

א/א

יד אברהם

Chapter 1

Mishnah 1 introduces the topic of שְׁבוּעַת בִּטּוּי, *the oath of utterance,* then immediately goes off on a tangent and then resumes this discussion in chapter 3. [This form of digression is found throughout the Mishnah.] The mishnah formulates a general description of the law of the oath of utterance which aptly describes several otherwise unrelated laws as well. The mishnah then proceeds to list the other laws defined by this formulation and digresses to discuss the one of them which is linked to the oath of utterance by its inclusion in the same Scriptural passage *(Lev.* ch. 5) and the same variable sin-offering (*Gem.* 3a).[1]

1.

שְׁבוּעוֹת שְׁתַּיִם — *Oaths are of two* [*types*]

I.e., two types of oaths of utterance are mentioned explicitly in the Torah *(Lev.* 5:4) as requiring a sin-offering for their violation: אוֹ נֶפֶשׁ כִּי תִשָּׁבַע לְבַטֵּא בִשְׂפָתַיִם לְהָרַע אוֹ לְהֵיטִיב, *Or if a person swears by uttering with his lips, to do bad or to do good* ... The *bad* and *good* referred to in this verse are not meant literally. Rather, any negative oath such as 'I will not eat' is referred to as bad since he deprives himself; a positive one such as 'I will eat' is referred to as good. Both 'I will' and 'I will not' express an oath concerning the future. These are the only types of oaths mentioned explicitly in the Torah *(Rav, Rashi* from 3:1).

שֶׁהֵן אַרְבַּע. — *which are* [*in reality*] *four.*

I.e., we derive from the verse that one is also obligated to bring a sacrifice if he swears concerning an event that occurred in the past, e.g., that he ate, when in fact he did not eat, or that he did not eat, when in fact he did. This is discussed in greater detail below, in mishnah 3:1 *(Rav).* Thus, the phrase *two which are four* means: *Two:* good and bad, i.e., 'I will and I will not' in the future; *which are four:* good and bad concerning the past (*Rav, Rashi* from 3:1).

יְדִיעוֹת הַטֻּמְאָה שְׁתַּיִם — *Awareness of tumah is of two* [*types*]

One who is *tamei* (ritually unclean) is forbidden to eat hallowed food (e.g., the meat of sacrifices) or to enter the Temple. This part of the mishnah deals with one who inadvertently violated this prohibition.

The *Tanna* refers to *(Lev.* 5:2ff): אוֹ נֶפֶשׁ אֲשֶׁר תִּגַּע בְּכָל-דָּבָר טָמֵא אוֹ בְנִבְלַת חַיָּה טְמֵאָה אוֹ בְּנִבְלַת בְּהֵמָה טְמֵאָה אוֹ בְּנִבְלַת שֶׁרֶץ טָמֵא וְנֶעְלַם מִמֶּנּוּ וְהוּא טָמֵא וְאָשֵׁם. אוֹ כִי יִגַּע בְּטֻמְאַת אָדָם לְכֹל טֻמְאָתוֹ אֲשֶׁר יִטְמָא בָּהּ וְנֶעְלַם מִמֶּנּוּ וְהוּא יָדַע וְאָשֵׁם. — *Or if a person touches anything which is tamei, whether the carcass of a contaminating wild animal or the carcass of a contaminating domesticated animal or the carcass of a contaminating sheretz, but it escapes his awareness and he is tamei and becomes guilty. Or if he touches a human tumah, in whatever manner of tumah he becomes contaminated, but it escapes his awareness and he becomes aware, and he becomes guilty.*

In this section the Torah refers to one

1. It is for this reason that the Mishnah presents this list here rather than in *Shabbos* 1:1 or *Negaim* 1:1 — the two other places where this formulation is used. Since the subject of *awareness of tumah* (see below) is linked to the *oath of utterance,* the Mishnah presents it for discussion here. Having done so, it completes the rest of the list here as well (*Gem.* 3a).

1
1

1. Oaths are of two [types] which are [in reality] four. Awareness of *tumah* is of two [types] which are [in reality] four. Transfers on the Sabbath are of two [types] which are [in reality] four. Appearances of the

YAD AVRAHAM

who unintentionally violates the strictures pertaining to hallowed things either by entering the hallowed precincts of the Temple or by eating hallowed foods while in a state of *tumah* contamination. The passage explicitly deals with only two ways of transgressing this commandment — he forgot his *tumah* and either ate hallowed food or entered the Temple. For this unintentional violation, he is required to bring a variable sin-offering *(Rav; Rashi* from 2:1).

.שֶׁהֵן אַרְבַּע — *which are* [*in reality*] *four.*

The above verse can be understood to include two other accidental violations for which one would also be required to bring the same sacrifice. That is, where he is aware of his *tumah* but forgets that the food he is eating is hallowed or that the ground upon which he is walking is part of the Temple.

Some commentators point out that even though the mishnah mentions only four types of accidental transgressions, there is actually a fifth, viz., that he is aware that he is *tamei,* and also remembers that the food is hallowed; however, he forgets that the Torah prohibits a contaminated person from eating hallowed food *(Beer Yaakov* ch. 3). However, from *Rambam* it seems that in the above case he does not bring a variable sin-offering *(Rambam, Hil. Shegagos* 11:1).

יְצִיאוֹת הַשַּׁבָּת — *Transfers on the Sabbath*

The interdict of transferring an article from a private domain to a public domain on the Sabbath is derived from *(Ex.* 36:6): *And Moses commanded, and they proclaimed throughout the camp, saying: Let no man or woman do any work for the offering of the Sanctuary; and the people were restrained from bringing (Rav).* The *Gemara (Shabbos* 96b) explains that Moses was in the camp of the Levites, a public domain. He ordered the people to cease their work for the *Mishkan,* understood to mean the work of bringing the finished products from the private domains of the camp of the Israelites into the public domain of the camp of the Levites. This is evidenced by the fact that the verse states clearly, *and the people were restrained from bringing,* indicating that the work referred to was the bringing.

שְׁתַּיִם — *are of two* [*types*]

The transfers prohibited expressly by the Torah are from a private domain to a public one; this consists of two types. A man is standing outside a house and the owner is inside. The owner places something into the man's hand, or the man extends his hand into the private domain and takes something from the owner's hand, taking it out into the public domain *(Rav* from *Gem.* 3a). In both these instances one person performs both the removal from one domain and the setting down in the other, without which one would not be liable according to Torah law.

This is known as הוֹצָאָה, *hotzaah,* carrying out of a private domain into a public domain. In each of these cases, the one performing the transfer is liable to death should he commit the transgression willfully in the presence of witnesses after having been warned. Should he do so willfully but without being warned, or without witnesses, he is liable to *kares,* Divinely imposed premature death. If done inadvertently, he is required to bring a sin-offering.

.שֶׁהֵן אַרְבַּע — *which are* [*in reality*] *four.*

From the two expressly described in the Torah, two others can be inferred — namely, transferring from a public domain to a private domain in these same two manners. This happens when the man standing outside extends his hand

שְׁנַיִם שֶׁהֵם אַרְבָּעָה.

[ב] **כָּל** שֶׁיֶּשׁ־בָּהּ יְדִיעָה בַּתְּחִלָּה וִידִיעָה בַּסּוֹף, וְהֶעְלֵם בֵּינָתַיִם, הֲרֵי זֶה בְּעוֹלֶה וְיוֹרֵד.

יד אברהם

into the private domain and places something into the hand of the owner, or when the owner extends his hand into the public domain, takes something from the man's hand and brings it into the private domain, placing it down there (*Rav* from *Gem.* 3a). This is known as הַכְנָסָה, *hachnassah,* taking from a public domain into a private domain. Since the Torah objects to transferring from a private domain to a public one, it stands to reason that the same objection applies to transferring from a public to a private domain (*Rav* from *Gem.* 3a, *Shabbos* 96b).

In these cases, too, the one performing the transfer is liable to the same punishment as someone who transfers from a private to a public domain.

מַרְאוֹת נְגָעִים שְׁנַיִם — *Appearances of the* [*tzaraas*] *affliction are of two* [*types*]

The two afflictions mentioned in the Torah (*Lev.* ch. 13) are called בַּהֶרֶת, *baheres,* and שְׂאֵת, *se'eis* (*Rav* from *Gem.* 5b). A *tzaraas* affliction is a type of discoloration of the skin which is treated by the Torah as a source of *tumah* if it is of certain shades of white [and meets certain other criteria]. The *Gemara* identifies the *baheres* as being as bright as snow, while the *se'eis* resembles white wool, which is slightly darker than snow.

These two colors, snow- and wool-white are actually categories since snow-white includes numerous shades as does wool-white, all of which are *tamei* (*Tos. Yom Tov* to *Negaim* 1:1).

שֶׁהֵם אַרְבָּעָה. — *which are* [*in reality*] *four.*

I.e., each one of these appearances has a *toladah,* subdivision, called סַפַּחַת, *sapachas*[1] in the Torah.

The Torah, in mentioning the different types of *tzaraas,* lists them in the following order: *se'eis, sapachas, baheres* (*Lev.* 13:2). Since *sapachas,* meaning auxiliary, is inserted between the *se'eis* and *baheres* we learn that both the *se'eis* and *baheres* have a *toladah,* a subsidiary (*Gemara* 6b).

The *toladah* of *baheres* (snow-white) resembles the lime (plaster) of the הֵיכָל, *Sanctuary.* The *toladah* of the *se'eis* (fleece-white) resembles the inner membrane of an egg (*Gem.* 5b, 6a). In summation: there are four shades of *negaim* described in descending degrees of brightness: snow-white, fleece-white, lime-white and egg-membrane-white.

2.

Since the laws pertaining to the knowledge of *tumah* contamination are not very numerous, the Mishnah discusses them first, subsequently returning to explain the laws of oaths which are far more numerous. The matters of the Sabbath and the *tzaraas* afflictions are not delineated here at all, since each one has a tractate devoted exclusively to it, viz., *Shabbos* and *Negaim* (*Rav* from *Gem.* 3a; *Rashi*).

כָּל — *Whenever*

I.e., any case of one entering the Temple or eating hallowed things while *tamei* (*Rav; Rashi*).

1. The word *sapachas,* with reference to *I Samuel* 2:36 סְפָחֵנִי נָא, has the meaning of being something subsidiary, auxiliary to something else; hence a subsidiary shade of white.

1 [*tzaraas*] affliction are of two [types] which are [in
2 reality] four.

2. Whenever there is awareness in the beginning and awareness at the end, and unawareness in between, he is liable to a variable [sin-]offering. [If] there

YAD AVRAHAM

שֶׁיֵּשׁ־בָּהּ יְדִיעָה בַתְּחִלָּה — *there is awareness in the beginning*[1]

I.e., before coming into contact with the Temple, he was aware that he had become *tamei* by touching, for example, the carcass of a *sheretz* [one of the eight creeping creatures listed in *Lev.* 11:29,30] *(Rav).*

Rav follows *Rambam (Shegagos* 11:1; but see *Lechem Mishneh* there), who rules according to the view cited in the *Gemara* (5a) that *awareness in the beginning* occurs only when he was actually aware of his *tumah* before eating the hallowed foods or entering the Temple. There is, however, an alternate view in the *Gemara* that contends that to be considered awareness in the beginning it is sufficient if he knew that he had touched a carcass even though he was unaware of its ability to impart *tumah (Rashi* 5a*).* Since he undoubtedly once learned that law in his school days, even though he has now completely forgotten this information, it is adjudged as *awareness in the beginning (Tos. Yom Tov;* see *Shoshanim LeDavid).* However, if a person had grown up among the gentiles and never learned Torah in his youth, the above would not apply *(Tos. Yom Tov* from *Gem.* ad loc.).

וִידִיעָה בַסּוֹף, — *and awareness at the end,*

After he had eaten the hallowed food or lingered in the Temple in a state of *tumah,* he became aware that he had transgressed the laws of *tumah (Rav; Rashi).*

וְהֶעְלֵם בֵּינְתַיִם, — *and unawareness in between,*

I.e., when he ate the hallowed things or entered the Temple he had forgotten that he was *tamei,* or that this food was hallowed, or that this was the Temple *(Rav; Rashi).*

הֲרֵי זֶה בְּעוֹלֶה וְיוֹרֵד. — *he is liable to a variable* [*sin-*]*offering* [lit. *an ascending and descending sacrifice*].

[He is obligated to offer a variable sin-offering to atone for his unwitting transgression of the Temple or hallowed-food sanctity laws. Only if his transgression was both preceded and followed by knowledge of his *tumah* is he liable for a sin-offering for violating the sancity law during his intervening period of forgetfulness.]

A *variable sin-offering* is a sacrifice whose cost varies, ascending for the wealthy man and descending for the poor man. The wealthy man must bring a female sheep or goat for a sin-offering. The poor man who cannot afford an animal brings a pair of birds. If he is too poor to afford even that, he need bring only a flour-offering, consisting of a tenth of an *ephah* of fine flour. This is known as מִנְחַת חוֹטֵא, *the sinner's flour-offering (Rav; Rashi).*

After teaching us the atonement for one who had knowledge in the beginning and end, the mishnah now proceeds to delineate the atonement for this sin where either the knowledge preceding or following the sin was lacking.

1. The only time awareness in the beginning is a pre-condition to bringing an atonement is where he unintentionally ate hallowed foods or entered the Temple while *tamei.* For all other unintentional transgressions for which one is required to bring a sacrifice, no awareness before the act is required *(Rambam, Hil. Shegagos* 11:1).

יֵשׁ בָּהּ יְדִיעָה בַּתְּחִלָּה וְאֵין בָּהּ יְדִיעָה בַּסּוֹף, שָׂעִיר הַנַּעֲשֶׂה בִפְנִים וְיוֹם הַכִּפּוּרִים תּוֹלֶה עַד שֶׁיִּוָּדַע לוֹ וְיָבִיא בְעוֹלֶה וְיוֹרֵד.

[ג] **אֵין** בָּהּ יְדִיעָה בַּתְּחִלָּה, אֲבָל יֵשׁ בָּהּ יְדִיעָה בַּסּוֹף, שָׂעִיר הַנַּעֲשֶׂה בַחוּץ וְיוֹם הַכִּפּוּרִים מְכַפֵּר, שֶׁנֶּאֱמַר: „מִלְּבַד חַטַּאת הַכִּפֻּרִים." עַל־מַה שֶּׁזֶּה מְכַפֵּר, זֶה מְכַפֵּר. מָה הַפְּנִימִי אֵין

יד אברהם

יֵשׁ בָּהּ יְדִיעָה בַּתְּחִלָּה וְאֵין בָּהּ יְדִיעָה בַּסּוֹף — *[If] there was awareness in the beginning but there was no awareness at the end,*

[I.e., he was aware of his *tumah* and the status of the food before he ate it, or he was aware of his *tumah* and the status of the building before he entered it, but he forgot it at the time of his eating or entry, and subsequently never became aware of his misdeed. Thus, he can never bring a personal sin-offering in atonement.]

שָׂעִיר הַנַּעֲשֶׂה בִפְנִים — *the he-goat which is sacrificed inside*

The he-goat sacrificed on Yom Kippur, whose blood is sprinkled in the Holy of Holies by the *Kohen Gadol (Rav)*.

On Yom Kippur, three he-goats were sacrificed: (1) The he-goat sacrificed inside; i.e., the one whose blood was sprinkled between the staves of the Ark (*Yoma* 5:4); (2) the one which was sent to Azazel (*Yoma* 6); (3) the he-goat sacrificed outside, on the altar in the *Azarah*. This he-goat was one of the *mussafim* [additional sacrifices] of the Festivals, as delineated in *Num.* 29:11.

וְיוֹם הַכִּפּוּרִים — *and Yom Kippur*

I.e., the day itself, as in *Lev.* 23:28: כִּי יוֹם כִּפֻּרִים הוּא, *for it is a day of atonements,* meaning that the day itself atones, independent of any sacrifice (*Tos. Yom Tov; Tif. Yis.* from *Rashi* to mishnah 2).

תּוֹלֶה עַד שֶׁיִּוָּדַע לוֹ וְיָבִיא בְעוֹלֶה וְיוֹרֵד. — *suspend [punishment], until he becomes aware of it and brings a variable [sin-] offering.*

I.e., they protect him from suffering due him for his sin until he becomes aware of his transgression and can offer his personal sin-offering in atonement (*Rav* from *Gem.* 8b).

Here we are faced with an obvious question. Why does the mishnah find it necessary to mention that both the he-goat and Yom Kippur together suspend punishment? Since the he-goat is brought only on Yom Kippur, by saying that the he-goat suspends, Yom Kippur is included. *Tif. Yis.* quotes the *Gemara* in *Yoma* 85b that Yom Kippur atones and suspends only for those individuals who have faith and believe that Yom Kippur atones for sins. Therefore the mishnah stresses that the he-goat itself is insufficient to suspend punishment; he requires also the atonement of Yom Kippur. Consequently, if this person has no faith that Yom Kippur can atone for inadvertent sins, his punishment would not be suspended.

3.

This mishnah is a continuation of the preceding one. It delineates the atonement for one who was initially unaware either of his *tumah*, or of the status of the food he was about to eat, or the area he was about to enter. He became aware of it only after the sin was committed. Since he was unaware at the beginning, he is also not liable for a sacrifice.

1 was awareness in the beginning but there was no
3 awareness at the end, the he-goat which is sacrificed inside and Yom Kippur suspend [punishment] until he becomes aware of it and brings a variable [sin-]offering.

3. [If] there was no awareness in the beginning, but there was awareness at the end, the he-goat which is sacrificed outside and Yom Kippur atone, as it is said (*Num.* 29:11): *Aside from the sin-offering of the atonements*. For what this one atones, this one atones.

YAD AVRAHAM

אֵין בָּהּ יְדִיעָה בַּתְּחִלָּה, — [*If*] *there was no awareness in the beginning,*

I.e., he was never aware of his *tumah*. Therefore, he will never be liable for a sacrifice, since such liability is contingent on knowledge of *tumah* prior to the sin (*Rav; Rashi*).

As mentioned in the previous mishnah, there is another view that explains *awareness in the beginning* to mean he was aware of the law of *tumah* sometime in his childhood. They will have to explain having no awareness to mean that he was captured by gentiles in his early childhood, and never learned that one becomes contaminated by touching a dead *sheretz* (*Tos. Yom Tov* from *Gem.* 5a). The same would also apply if he knew the law but was unaware of his contact with the carcass of the *sheretz* (*Tos.* 14b).

אֲבָל יֵשׁ בָּהּ יְדִיעָה בַּסּוֹף, — *but there was awareness at the end,*

I.e., after he had eaten or entered the Temple, he became aware that he had been *tamei* at the time.

According to the alternate view presented above, he became aware that one who touches a dead *sheretz* becomes *tamei*, and he now realizes that he sinned (*Tif. Yis.*).

שָׂעִיר הַנַּעֲשֶׂה בַּחוּץ — *the he-goat which is sacrificed outside*[1]

I.e., the he-goat which is sacrificed on the outer altar among the *mussafim* of Yom Kippur (*Rav; Tif. Yis.*).

וְיוֹם הַכִּפּוּרִים — *and Yom Kippur*

I.e., the day itself atones, as the Torah states (*Lev.* 23:28): *For it is a day of atonements* (*Tos. Yom Tov* from *Rashi*).

מְכַפֵּר, — *atone,*

However, they atone only with a sincere repentance (*Meiri*). In this instance they accomplish a final atonement, not merely a temporary suspension of his punishment, and he needs no further sacrifice (*Tif. Yis.*).

שֶׁנֶּאֱמַר: „מִלְּבַד חַטַּאת הַכִּפֻּרִים." — *as it is said: 'Aside from the sin-offering of the atonements.'*

The Torah says regarding the he-goat which is sacrificed outside: *one he-goat for a sin-offering, aside from the sin-offering of the atonements*. I.e., there is an obligation to offer a he-goat for a sin-offering on the outer altar, aside from the sin-offering whose blood is brought inside the Holy of Holies. The Torah mentions them together in the same verse to equate them in the following manner (*Rav; Rashi*).

עַל־מַה שֶּׁזֶּה מְכַפֵּר, זֶה מְכַפֵּר. מָה הַפְּנִימִי אֵין מְכַפֵּר אֶלָּא עַל־דָּבָר שֶׁיֵּשׁ־בּוֹ יְדִיעָה, — *For what this one atones, this one atones. Just as the inner one atones only for a*

1. There were two altars in the Temple, one in the *Heichal* (Sanctuary), and one in the *Azarah* (Courtyard). The inner altar was used primarily for incense offerings, the outer for all other sacrifices. There were a very few exceptions, the inner he-goat of Yom Kippur among them, in which blood was sprinkled on the inner altar. The he-goat mentioned here was one of many *mussaf* sacrifices whose blood was sprinkled on the outer altar.

מְכַפֵּר אֶלָּא עַל־דָּבָר שֶׁיֶּשׁ־בּוֹ יְדִיעָה, אַף הַחִיצוֹן אֵין מְכַפֵּר אֶלָּא עַל־דָּבָר שֶׁיֶּשׁ־בּוֹ יְדִיעָה.

[ד] **וְעַל־** שֶׁאֵין בָּהּ יְדִיעָה לֹא בַתְּחִלָּה וְלֹא בַסּוֹף, שְׂעִירֵי הָרְגָלִים וּשְׂעִירֵי רָאשֵׁי חֳדָשִׁים מְכַפְּרִים; דִּבְרֵי רַבִּי יְהוּדָה. רַבִּי שִׁמְעוֹן אוֹמֵר: שְׂעִירֵי הָרְגָלִים מְכַפְּרִין, אֲבָל לֹא שְׂעִירֵי רָאשֵׁי חֳדָשִׁים. וְעַל מַה שְּׂעִירֵי רָאשֵׁי חֳדָשִׁים מְכַפְּרִין? עַל־הַטָּהוֹר שֶׁאָכַל אֶת־הַטָּמֵא. רַבִּי מֵאִיר

יד אברהם

case in which there was awareness,

I.e., just as the he-goat whose blood is sprinkled in the Holy of Holies atones for sins which were committed with incomplete knowledge — in this case, without awareness after the sin *(Rav; Rashi).*

אַף הַחִיצוֹן אֵין מְכַפֵּר אֶלָּא עַל־דָּבָר שֶׁיֶּשׁ־בּוֹ יְדִיעָה. — *so the outer one atones only for a case in which there was awareness.*

[The outer one also atones for those unintentional sins for which there was incomplete knowledge: in this case the one who had no awareness in the beginning, but had awareness at the end. However, as stated previously, there is one basic difference between them. Whereas the inner one merely suspends punishment temporarily, the outer one accomplishes a complete atonement.]

4.

וְעַל־שֶׁאֵין בָּהּ יְדִיעָה לֹא בַתְּחִלָּה וְלֹא בַסּוֹף, — *For one in which there was no awareness either in the beginning or at the end,*

[I.e., for the sin of contaminating the Temple or its hallowed things for which he had no knowledge of his *tumah* or of their state of sanctity whatsoever, either before or after (see mishnah 2 and 3).]

The *Gemara* (9b) questions whether the term *no awareness at the end* refers only to one who will never become aware of his transgression [e.g., if he became *tamei* when no witnesses were present, so that there is no way he can be informed of his mistake], or whether it refers even to a case in which people saw him become *tamei* so that ultimately he may become aware of his *tumah*. According to the first possibility, this latter case is classified as knowledge at the end and it is the he-goat sacrificed outside that atones. The conclusion of the *Gemara* is interpreted by different commentators in opposite manners, based on variant readings. According to *Rabbeinu Channanel*, it applies only in the first case. *Ri Migash*, however, quotes a reading according to which it applies in both cases. This is similar to our reading. *Meiri* also quotes both readings.

שְׂעִירֵי הָרְגָלִים — *the he-goats of the Festivals*

Each of the three Festivals has a he-goat for a sin-offering as part of its *mussaf* sacrifice. These sacrifices are enumerated in *Numbers* 28:16 — 29:38 *(Rav).*

וּשְׂעִירֵי רָאשֵׁי חֳדָשִׁים — *and the he-goats of Rosh Chodesh*

[I.e., the he-goats sacrificed on Rosh Chodesh for sin-offerings as part of its *mussaf*, as in *Numbers* 28:15.]

מְכַפְּרִים; — *atone;*

[I.e., the above sin-offerings of he-goats atone for sins in which there was neither prior nor subsequent knowledge.]

Tif. Yis. explains that the he-goat of Rosh Chodesh atones for the *tumah* that occurred between a Festival and Rosh Chodesh, of which he became aware before the next

1 Just as the inner one atones only for a case in which
4 there was awareness, so the outer one atones only for a case in which there was awareness.

4. For one in which there was no awareness either in the beginning or at the end, the he-goats of the Festivals and the he-goats of Rosh Chodesh atone; [these are] the words of of R' Yehudah. R' Shimon says: The he-goats of the Festivals atone, but not the he-goats of Rosh Chodesh. And for what do the he-goats of Rosh Chodesh atone? For a person who is *tahor* who ate [a sacrifice which was] *tamei*. R' Meir says: The atonement

YAD AVRAHAM

Festival. It is therefore necessary to have the atonement of the he-goat of Rosh Chodesh. *Tif. Yaacov* points out that this explanation would be valid only according to those authorities who interpret *no awareness at the end* to mean no possibility of knowledge. However, according to the other interpretation, the explanation of *Tif. Yis.* is not valid. See above, s.v. ולא בסוף.

דִּבְרֵי רַבִּי יְהוּדָה. — [*these are*] *the words of R' Yehudah.*

R' Yehudah bases his view on the verse dealing with the he-goat of Rosh Chodesh, which reads: וּשְׂעִיר עִזִּים אֶחָד לְחַטָּאת לַה', *And one he-goat as a sin-offering to* HASHEM. The words *to* HASHEM are seemingly superfluous, unless we understand their meaning to be that it atones for sins known only to HASHEM, namely those of which the sinner had no knowledge either before or after. He reasons that the he-goats of the Festivals atone for the same type of inadvertency since they are compared to the he-goat of Rosh Chodesh by the conjunctive *vav* of וּשְׂעִיר, '*And*' *one he-goat*, which joins them (*Rav* from *Gem.* 9b).

Tos. Yom Tov remarks that though the *Gemara* considers this derivation, the *Gemara* (10a) concludes that R' Yehudah derives this from the verse at the close of the portion of the Torah that discusses the *mussaf* sacrifices of all the different holidays (*Num.* 29:39). The Torah closes the passage with the verse אֵלֶּה תַּעֲשׂוּ לַה' בְּמוֹעֲדֵיכֶם, *These shall you do* [bring] *on your holy days.* אֵלֶּה is an inclusive word, to say that all *mussaf* sacrifices have a common purpose, namely to atone for a sin in which he had no knowledge either before or after.

רַבִּי שִׁמְעוֹן אוֹמֵר: שְׂעִירֵי הָרְגָלִים מְכַפְּרִין, — *R' Shimon says: The he-goats of the Festivals atone,*

[I.e., the he-goats of the Festivals do indeed atone for one who had no knowledge of his contamination either before or after eating hallowed things or entering the Temple.]

אֲבָל לֹא שְׂעִירֵי רָאשֵׁי חֳדָשִׁים. — *but not the he-goats of Rosh Chodesh.*

[These he-goats atone for other sins in his view.]

וְעַל־מַה שְׂעִירֵי רָאשֵׁי חֳדָשִׁים מְכַפְּרִין? עַל־הַטָּהוֹר שֶׁאָכַל אֶת־הַטָּמֵא. — *And for what do the he-goats of Rosh Chodesh atone? For a person who is tahor who ate* [*a sacrifice which was*] *tamei.*

[Whereas the Festival sin-offering atones for a *tumah*-contaminated person who ate hallowed food, the Rosh Chodesh sin-offering atones for an uncontaminated person who ate hallowed food which had become contaminated with *tumah.*] R' Shimon draws an analogy between the he-goat of Rosh Chodesh and the צִיץ, the gold plate worn on the forehead of the *Kohen Gadol.* Just as the latter atones for *tumah*-contami-

שבועות
א/ד

אוֹמֵר: כָּל־הַשְּׂעִירִים כַּפָּרָתָן שָׁוָה — עַל־טֻמְאַת מִקְדָּשׁ וְקָדָשָׁיו. הָיָה רַבִּי שִׁמְעוֹן אוֹמֵר: שְׂעִירֵי רָאשֵׁי חֳדָשִׁים מְכַפְּרִין עַל־הַטָּהוֹר שֶׁאָכַל אֶת־הַטָּמֵא; וְשֶׁל־רְגָלִים מְכַפְּרִין עַל־שֶׁאֵין בָּהּ יְדִיעָה לֹא בַתְּחִלָּה וְלֹא בַסּוֹף; וְשֶׁל־יוֹם הַכִּפּוּרִים מְכַפֵּר עַל־שֶׁאֵין בָּהּ יְדִיעָה בַּתְּחִלָּה אֲבָל יֶשׁ־בָּהּ יְדִיעָה בַּסּוֹף. אָמְרוּ לוֹ: מַהוּ שֶׁיִּקְרְבוּ זֶה בָזֶה? אָמַר לָהֶם: יִקְרָבוּ. אָמְרוּ לוֹ: הוֹאִיל וְאֵין כַּפָּרָתָן שָׁוָה, הֵיאַךְ קְרֵבִין זֶה בָזֶה? אָמַר לָהֶן: כֻּלָּן בָּאִין לְכַפֵּר עַל־טֻמְאַת מִקְדָּשׁ וְקָדָשָׁיו.

יד אברהם

nated fat, blood, and flesh offered upon the altar, so the he-goat of Rosh Chodesh atones for contaminated meat eaten by the *Kohanim* (*Tos. Yom Tov* from *Gem.* 9b).

רַבִּי מֵאִיר אוֹמֵר: כָּל־הַשְּׂעִירִים כַּפָּרָתָן שָׁוָה — *R' Meir says: The atonement of all the he-goats is alike* —

I.e., all the he-goats of the *mussafim* — viz., those of the Festivals, Rosh Chodesh, and the he-goat that is sacrificed on the outer altar on Yom Kippur — effect atonement for the same transgressions (*Rav; Rashi; Tif. Yis.*).

עַל־טֻמְאַת מִקְדָּשׁ וְקָדָשָׁיו. — *for the tumah of the Temple and its hallowed things.*

They all atone for the one who either had no knowledge in the beginning but had knowledge at the end, or the one who had no knowledge either in the beginning or at the end, as well as for the person who is *tahor* who ate of a *tumah*-contaminated sacrifice. The reason for having a number of sacrifices to atone for the same sin is in order to atone for the *tumah* which occurred in the interim between one *mussaf* and the next. However, even R' Meir agrees that the he-goat which is sacrificed inside on *Yom Kippur* effects the suspension of punishment for one who had knowledge in the beginning but not at the end (*Rav; Rashi; Tif. Yis.* from *Gem.* 8b).

הָיָה רַבִּי שִׁמְעוֹן אוֹמֵר: שְׂעִירֵי רָאשֵׁי חֳדָשִׁים מְכַפְּרִין עַל־הַטָּהוֹר שֶׁאָכַל אֶת־הַטָּמֵא; וְשֶׁל־רְגָלִים מְכַפְּרִין עַל־שֶׁאֵין בָּהּ יְדִיעָה לֹא בַתְּחִלָּה וְלֹא בַסּוֹף; וְשֶׁל־יוֹם הַכִּפּוּרִים מְכַפֵּר עַל־שֶׁאֵין בָּהּ יְדִיעָה בַּתְּחִלָּה אֲבָל יֶשׁ־בָּהּ יְדִיעָה בַּסּוֹף. — *R' Shimon was wont to say: The he-goats of Rosh Chodesh atone for a person who is tahor who ate [a sacrifice] that is tamei; those of the Festivals atone for one who had no awareness either in the beginning or at the end; and the one of Yom Kippur atones for one who had no awareness in the beginning but had awareness at the end.*

This statement is merely a reiteration of what R' Shimon said previously. It is nevertheless repeated in anticipation of the subsequent query of the Sages (*Rav; Rashi*).

אָמְרוּ לוֹ: — *They said to him:*

[The Sages said to R' Shimon. From the substance of their question it is evident that these Sages followed the view of R' Meir; see below.]

מַהוּ שֶׁיִּקְרְבוּ זֶה בָזֶה? — *May one be sacrificed for another?*

If a he-goat was set aside to be sacrificed as a *mussaf* on Yom Kippur, a Festival, or Rosh Chodesh, and it was lost and then found after the occasion for which it had been set aside had passed,

1 of all the he-goats is alike — for the *tumah* of the
4 Temple and its hallowed things. R' Shimon was wont to say: The he-goats of Rosh Chodesh atone for a person who is *tahor* who ate [a sacrifice] that is *tamei;* those of the Festivals atone for one who had no awareness either in the beginning or at the end; and the one of Yom Kippur atones for one who had no awareness in the beginning but had awareness at the end. They said to him: May one be sacrificed for another? He replied: They may be sacrificed. They said to him: Since their atonement is not alike, how can they be sacrificed one for another? He said to them: All of them come to atone for the *tumah* of the Temple and its hallowed things.

YAD AVRAHAM

can it now be used for the *mussaf* of the next Rosh Chodesh or Festival *(Rav; Rashi)?*

אָמַר לָהֶם: יִקְרְבוּ. — *He replied: They may be sacrificed.*

[R' Shimon replied to the Sages that indeed they may be sacrificed as the *mussaf* of a subsequent Festival or Rosh Chodesh.]

אָמְרוּ לוֹ: הוֹאִיל וְאֵין כַּפָּרָתָן שָׁוָה, הֵיאַךְ קְרֵבִין זֶה בָזֶה? — *They said to him: Since their atonement is not alike, how can they be sacrificed one for another?*

[There is a rule that a sin-offering that was set aside to atone for one sin cannot be used even by the same person to atone for a different sin. For example, for unintentionally eating the forbidden fat of an animal one has to bring a sin-offering. One must also bring a sin-offering to atone for drinking the blood of an animal. If a person ate the forbidden fat and set aside an animal to be used as a sacrifice to atone for that sin, and he then drank the blood of an animal in error, he cannot use that animal to atone for the latter sin.]

Based on this, these Sages sought to establish the view of R' Meir and refute the view of R' Shimon. According to R' Meir's view, that the outer he-goat of Yom Kippur and that of the Festivals and Rosh Chodesh all effect the same atonement, it indeed follows that one that was set aside for Yom Kippur and lost, may subsequently be sacrificed on Rosh Chodesh. According to R' Shimon, however, how can the he-goat which was designated to atone for one who had no knowledge in the beginning but had knowledge at the end, be sacrificed on a Festival to atone for one who had knowledge neither in the beginning nor at the end; or on Rosh Chodesh, to atone for a person who was *tahor* who ate a contaminated sacrifice *(Rav; Rashi* from *Gem.* 12a)?

Actually, R' Meir could have posed the same question to R' Yehudah, who rules that the he-goat which is sacrificed on Yom Kippur on the outer altar atones for one who had no knowledge in the beginning but had knowledge at the end, whereas the he-goats of the Festivals and of Rosh Chodesh atone for one who had knowledge neither in the beginning nor at the end. However, according to R' Shimon, the question is of greater difficulty since he rules that each he-goat has a distinct atonement *(Tos. Yom Tov;* see *Gem.* 12a for an alternate explanation; *Tos. R' Akiva).*

אָמַר לָהֶן: כֻּלָּן בָּאִין לְכַפֵּר עַל־טֻמְאַת מִקְדָּשׁ וְקָדָשָׁיו. — *He said to them: All of them come to atone for the tumah of the*

[ה] רַבִּי שִׁמְעוֹן בֶּן־יְהוּדָה אוֹמֵר מִשְּׁמוֹ: שְׂעִירֵי רָאשֵׁי חֳדָשִׁים מְכַפְּרִין עַל־הַטָּהוֹר שֶׁאָכַל אֶת־הַטָּמֵא. מוּסִיף עֲלֵיהֶם שֶׁל־רְגָלִים, שֶׁמְּכַפְּרִין עַל־הַטָּהוֹר שֶׁאָכַל אֶת־הַטָּמֵא וְעַל־שֶׁאֵין בָּהּ יְדִיעָה לֹא בַתְּחִלָּה וְלֹא בַסּוֹף. מוּסִיף עֲלֵיהֶן שֶׁל־יוֹם הַכִּפּוּרִים, שֶׁהֵן מְכַפְּרִין עַל־הַטָּהוֹר שֶׁאָכַל אֶת־הַטָּמֵא, וְעַל־שֶׁאֵין בָּהּ יְדִיעָה לֹא בַתְּחִלָּה וְלֹא בַסּוֹף, וְעַל־שֶׁאֵין בָּהּ יְדִיעָה בַתְּחִלָּה אֲבָל יֵשׁ־בָּהּ יְדִיעָה בַסּוֹף. אָמְרוּ לוֹ: מַהוּ שֶׁיִּקְרְבוּ זֶה בָזֶה? אָמַר לָהֶם: הֵן. אָמְרוּ לוֹ: אִם כֵּן, יִהְיוּ שֶׁל־יוֹם הַכִּפּוּרִים קְרֵבִין בְּרָאשֵׁי חֳדָשִׁים, אֲבָל הֵיאַךְ

יד אברהם

Temple and its hallowed things.

R' Shimon replied to the Sages that even though they atone for different variations of transgressing the sanctity of the Temple and its hallowed things they all actually atone for the same transgression, namely for the *tumah* of the Temple and its hallowed things. Consequently, they may be offered one in lieu of the other *(Rav; Rashi).*

5.

רַבִּי שִׁמְעוֹן בֶּן־יְהוּדָה אוֹמֵר מִשְּׁמוֹ: — *R' Shimon ben Yehudah says in his name:*

I.e., R' Shimon ben Yehudah says in the name of R' Shimon. When R' Shimon is mentioned in the mishnah without his father's name, it is R' Shimon ben Yochai *(Rav; Rashi).*

Prior to his flight from the Romans, when he was confined to a cave, he was known merely as R' Shimon. Following his emergence from the cave twelve or thirteen years later, several other *Tannaim* with the name of Shimon were flourishing, viz., R' Shimon ben Elazar, R' Shimon ben Yehudah, R' Shimon ben Menasya. Therefore, from that time on he was called 'ben Yochai' to distinguish him from the others *(Ben Yochai, Shaar* 1, quoted in footnotes of *Rav Pe'alim,* pp. 55f).

[R' Shimon ben Yehudah has a different version of the view of R' Shimon and the give and take between him and the Sages.]

שְׂעִירֵי רָאשֵׁי חֳדָשִׁים מְכַפְּרִין עַל־הַטָּהוֹר שֶׁאָכַל אֶת־הַטָּמֵא. — *The he-goats of Rosh Chodesh atone for a person who was tahor who ate a contaminated* [*sacrifice*].

I.e., who inadvertently ate the meat of a *tumah*-contaminated sacrifice, which is forbidden for consumption *(Meiri).*

מוּסִיף עֲלֵיהֶם שֶׁל־רְגָלִים, — *Those of the Festivals surpass them*

[The he-goat sin-offerings of the Festivals effect another atonement in addition to the one effected by the he-goats of Rosh Chodesh.]

שֶׁמְּכַפְּרִין עַל־הַטָּהוֹר שֶׁאָכַל אֶת־הַטָּמֵא וְעַל־שֶׁאֵין בָּהּ יְדִיעָה לֹא בַתְּחִלָּה וְלֹא בַסּוֹף. — *in that they atone for a person who is tahor who ate a contaminated* [*sacrifice*] *and for one who had no awareness either in the beginning or at the end.*

[In addition to atoning for one who inadvertently ate a *tumah*-contaminated sacrifice, the he-goat sin-offering of the Festivals also atones for one who was *tamei* who entered the Temple or ate

1
5

5. R' Shimon ben Yehudah says in his name: The he-goats of Rosh Chodesh atone for a person who was *tahor* who ate a contaminated [sacrifice]. Those of the Festivals surpass them in that they atone for a person who is *tahor* who ate a contaminated [sacrifice] and for one who had no awareness either in the beginning or at the end. Those of Yom Kippur surpass them in that they atone for a person who was *tahor* who ate a contaminated [sacrifice], and for one who had no awareness either in the beginning or at the end, and for one who had no awareness in the beginning but had awareness at the end. They said to him: May one be sacrificed for another? He said to them: Yes. They said to him: If so, those of Yom Kippur may be sacrificed on Rosh Chodesh, but how can those of

YAD AVRAHAM

hallowed things in a state of *tumah*, being unaware of his condition both before and after committing the sin. Thus, its powers of atonement are greater than that of the Rosh Chodesh offering.]

מוֹסִיף עֲלֵיהֶן שֶׁל־יוֹם הַכִּפּוּרִים, שֶׁהֵן מְכַפְּרִין — *Those of Yom Kippur surpass them in that they atone*

[The he-goat which is sacrificed outside on Yom Kippur surpasses both the he-goat of Rosh Chodesh and the he-goat of Festivals in its power of atonement.]

עַל־הַטָּהוֹר שֶׁאָכַל אֶת־הַטָּמֵא, — *for a person who was tahor who ate a contaminated [sacrifice],*

[The he-goat of Yom Kippur atones for a *tahor* who ate of a contaminated sacrifice in common with both the he-goats of Rosh Chodesh and the Festivals.]

וְעַל־שֶׁאֵין בָּהּ יְדִיעָה לֹא בַתְּחִלָּה וְלֹא בַסּוֹף, — *and for one who had no awareness either in the beginning or at the end,*

[I.e., in common with the he-goats of the Festivals.]

וְעַל־שֶׁאֵין בָּהּ יְדִיעָה בַּתְּחִלָּה אֲבָל יֶשׁ־בָּהּ יְדִיעָה בַסּוֹף. — *and for one who had no awareness in the beginning but had awareness at the end.*

[In addition to the atonements produced by the other he-goat sacrifices, it also atones for one who had knowledge after the fact, though not before.]

אָמְרוּ לוֹ: מַהוּ שֶׁיִּקְרְבוּ זֶה בָזֶה? — *They said to him: May one be sacrificed for another?*

[The Sages asked R' Shimon whether a he-goat designated for the *mussaf* sacrifice of Yom Kippur which was lost and replaced by another only to be found again may be sacrificed for the *mussaf* of Rosh Chodesh or on a Festival. This is in effect the same question cited in the previous version of the dispute; see above, mishnah 4, s.v. מהו שיקרבו זה בזה.]

אָמַר לָהֶם: הֵן. — *He said to them: Yes.*

[That is, they may replace each other.]

אָמְרוּ לוֹ: אִם כֵּן, יִהְיוּ שֶׁל־יוֹם הַכִּפּוּרִים קְרֵבִין בְּרָאשֵׁי חֳדָשִׁים, — *They said to him: If so, those of Yom Kippur may be sacrificed on Rosh Chodesh,*

[The mishnah stated before that the he-goat of Yom Kippur effects its atonement in addition to atoning for what the Rosh Chodesh he-goat atones. Therefore,

שבועות א/ו

שֶׁל־רָאשֵׁי חֳדָשִׁים קְרֵבִין בְּיוֹם הַכִּפּוּרִים לְכַפֵּר כַּפָּרָה שֶׁאֵינָהּ שֶׁלָּהּ? אָמַר לָהֶן: כֻּלָּן בָּאִין לְכַפֵּר עַל־טֻמְאַת מִקְדָּשׁ וְקָדָשָׁיו.

[ו] **וְעַל־** זְדוֹן טֻמְאַת מִקְדָּשׁ וְקָדָשָׁיו, שָׂעִיר הַנַּעֲשֶׂה בִּפְנִים וְיוֹם הַכִּפּוּרִים מְכַפְּרִין. וְעַל־שְׁאָר עֲבֵרוֹת שֶׁבַּתּוֹרָה, הַקַּלּוֹת וְהַחֲמוּרוֹת, הַזְּדוֹנוֹת וְהַשְּׁגָגוֹת, הוֹדַע וְלֹא הוֹדַע, עֲשֵׂה וְלֹא תַעֲשֶׂה, כְּרֵתוֹת וּמִיתוֹת בֵּית דִּין — שָׂעִיר הַמִּשְׁתַּלֵּחַ מְכַפֵּר.

יד אברהם

we can readily understand that the he-goat of Yom Kippur may be used to replace the he-goat of Rosh Chodesh.]

אֲבָל הֵיאָךְ שֶׁל־רָאשֵׁי חֳדָשִׁים קְרֵבִין בְּיוֹם הַכִּפּוּרִים לְכַפֵּר כַּפָּרָה שֶׁאֵינָהּ שֶׁלָּהּ? — *but how can those of Rosh Chodesh be sacrificed on Yom Kippur to effect an atonement which does not belong to them* [lit. *it*]*?*

[I.e., if the he-goat of Rosh Chodesh was lost and discovered in time to be sacrificed on Yom Kippur, how may it be sacrificed as a *mussaf* of Yom Kippur when it was originally designated to atone only for an uncontaminated person who ate a contaminated sacrifice, not to atone for one who ate hallowed things or entered the Temple in a state of *tumah?*]

אָמַר לָהֶן: כֻּלָּן בָּאִין לְכַפֵּר עַל־טֻמְאַת מִקְדָּשׁ וְקָדָשָׁיו. — *He said to them: They all come to atone for the tumah* [*transgression*] *of the Temple and its hallowed things.*

Although they vary in the details of the transgressions for which they atone, they all atone for basically the same sin — the *tumah* of the Temple and its hallowed things. Therefore they can be interchanged *(Tif. Yis.)*.

6.

Up until this point, the mishnah discussed the atonement for the inadvertent contamination of the Temple or its hallowed things. The following mishnah discusses the atonement for one who entered the Temple intentionally while in a state of *tumah*, or deliberatley ate hallowed things while in that state.

This mishnah does not specifically follow the view of R' Shimon mentioned in the preceding mishnah, but is an anonymous mishnah, agreed to by all *(Rav; Rashi)*.

וְעַל־זְדוֹן טֻמְאַת מִקְדָּשׁ וְקָדָשָׁיו, — *For the deliberate tumah* [*transgression*] *of the Temple and its hallowed things,*

[I.e., if one deliberately entered the Temple or ate hallowed things, knowing that he was *tamei*.]

שָׂעִיר הַנַּעֲשֶׂה בִּפְנִים — *the he-goat which is sacrificed inside*

[As explained above in mishnah 2, this is the he-goat whose blood was sprinkled in the Holy of Holies by the *Kohen Gadol* on Yom Kippur.]

וְיוֹם הַכִּפּוּרִים — *and Yom Kippur*

[I.e., the day itself, as explained in, mishnah 2.]

מְכַפְּרִין. — *atone.*

This is derived from the verse *(Lev.* 16:16): וְכִפֶּר עַל־הַקֹּדֶשׁ מִטֻּמְאֹת בְּנֵי יִשְׂרָאֵל וּמִפִּשְׁעֵיהֶם לְכָל־חַטֹּאתָם, *And he shall atone for the holy place from the tumah-contaminations of the children of Israel and from their rebellions, for all their*

1 Rosh Chodesh be sacrificed on Yom Kippur to effect an
6 atonement which does not belong to them? He said to
them: They all come to atone for the *tumah* of the
Temple and its hallowed things.

6. For the deliberate *tumah* of the Temple and its hallowed things, the he-goat which is sacrificed inside and Yom Kippur atone. For other transgressions of the Torah, whether light or grave, willful or unintentional, of which he was aware and of which he was unaware, positive commandments and negative commandments, those liable to *kares* and capital sins — the he-goat which was sent away [to *Azazel*] atones.

YAD AVRAHAM

sins. The word פְּשָׁעִים, *rebellions,* denotes deliberate sins, indicating that the he-goat which was sacrificed inside atoned for deliberate sins as well as inadvertent ones (*Rav* from *Gem.* 12b).

This is in addition to suspending punishment temporarily for those who entered the Temple with awareness of *tumah* in the beginning but not at the end, as in mishnah 2 (*Tif. Yis.*).

This is true only if the perpetrator was not warned. Had he been warned prior to committing the transgression, his sin would be expiated only by lashes (*Tif. Yis.*).

וְעַל־שְׁאָר עֲבֵרוֹת שֶׁבַּתּוֹרָה, — *For other transgressions of the Torah,*

[I.e., for anyone guilty of transgressing any other commandment of the Torah.]

הַקַּלּוֹת וְהַחֲמוּרוֹת, — *whether light or grave,*

I.e., both for light and grave sins (*Rav* from *Gem.* 12b). [See further in this mishnah for a clarification of light and grave sins.]

הַזְּדוֹנוֹת וְהַשְּׁגָגוֹת, — *willful or unintentional,*

I.e., whether he committed these sins willfully or unintentionally (*Rav* from *Gem.* 12b).

הוֹדַע וְלֹא הוֹדַע, — *of which he was aware and of which he was unaware,*

This refers to the unintentional sins. *Aware* means that he became aware of the possibility that a sin was committed, e.g., he ate of the forbidden fats, assuming that it was the permissible type, and later became aware that it may have been the type for which the Torah decrees *kares.* If the suspicion never entered his mind, however, that would be an example of *unaware* (*Rav* from *Gem.* 12b).

The word *aware* cannot be explained to mean that he realized that he committed a sin, since then he would be liable to bring a sin-offering even after the atonement of Yom Kippur, as the mishnah states in *Kereisos* 6:4 (*Tos. Yom Tov* from *Rashi* 12b). Thus, the *Gemara* (12b) must explain it to refer to the awareness of *possible* guilt. Since he became aware only of the possibility that a sin was committed, he is liable to an אָשָׁם תָּלוּי, *guilt-offering brought in cases of doubt,* from which he becomes exempt after Yom Kippur.

עֲשֵׂה וְלֹא תַעֲשֶׂה, — *positive commandments and negative commandments,*

These are the *light* commandments mentioned above (*Rav* from *Gem.* 12b).

כְּרֵתוֹת וּמִיתוֹת בֵּית דִּין — *those liable to kares and capital sins —*

These are the *grave* sins mentioned above (*Rav* from *Gem.* 12b).

שָׂעִיר הַמִּשְׁתַּלֵּחַ מְכַפֵּר. — *the he-goat which was sent away* [*to Azazel*] *atones.*

This was the he-goat over which the

[ז] **אֶחָד** יִשְׂרָאֵלִים, וְאֶחָד כֹּהֲנִים, וְאֶחָד כֹּהֵן מָשׁוּחַ. מַה בֵּין יִשְׂרְאֵלִים לַכֹּהֲנִים וּלְכֹהֵן מָשׁוּחַ? אֶלָּא שֶׁדַּם הַפָּר מְכַפֵּר עַל־הַכֹּהֲנִים עַל־טֻמְאַת מִקְדָּשׁ וְקָדָשָׁיו. רַבִּי שִׁמְעוֹן אוֹמֵר: כְּשֵׁם שֶׁדַּם הַשָּׂעִיר הַנַּעֲשֶׂה בִפְנִים מְכַפֵּר עַל־יִשְׂרָאֵל, כָּךְ

יד אברהם

Kohen Gadol confessed the sins of the people on Yom Kippur and which was then taken out of Jerusalem and pushed off the side of a mountain. See *Yoma* chapters 4 and 6, where the ritual of sending out the he-goat is delineated.

The *Gemara* (12b, 13a) cites the opinion of Rabbi that the mishnah refers to the case of one who did not repent. Even in that case, Yom Kippur and the he-goat which was sent to *Azazel* would atone for all sins, with the exception of three extremely grave sins, viz., denying the existence of *HASHEM*, speaking derogatorily against the Torah, and breaking the covenant of circumcision. If one is guilty of any of these three sins, the *Azazel* he-goat and Yom Kippur atone only with repentance. According to the Sages, however, Yom Kippur does not atone for any sins unless the sinner repents. Should he fail to repent, the he-goat is of no benefit to him since a sacrifice brought without the proper intent is not pleasing to *HASHEM;* as it states (*Prov.* 21:27): זֶבַח רְשָׁעִים תּוֹעֵבָה, *The sacrifice of the wicked is an abomination.* According to Rabbi, this verse applies only to the rest of the year (*Tos. Yom Tov* from *Gem.* 13a; see *Ritva*).

Rambam (*Hil. Teshuvah* 1:2) rules that if the sinner does not repent, the he-goat that is sent away atones only for the light transgressions. He also states that false and vain oaths are counted among the grave transgressions and are not provided with atonement unless the sinner repents. The difficulty with this opinion is that *Rambam* seems consistent neither with Rabbi nor with the Sages. To reconcile this ruling with the *Gemara,* see *Lechem Mishneh* ad loc. See also *Yad Avraham* comm. to ArtScroll *Yoma* 9:8,9.

7.

The following mishnah is a continuation of the previous one, delineating the atonements afforded the *Kohanim* for their sins, both light and grave, which they committed willfully without being warned, as well as their atonement for contaminating the Temple and its hallowed things.

In this mishnah, there is mention of the *bull of Aaron,* a sacrifice paid for by the *Kohen Gadol* himself, the blood of which was sprinkled in the Holy of Holies along with that of the he-goat. Before slaughtering this bull, the *Kohen Gadol* would confess twice, as in *Yoma* 3:8, 4:2. The purpose of these confessions is discussed here, as well as the atonement effected by the sprinkling of its blood.

אֶחָד יִשְׂרָאֵלִים, וְאֶחָד כֹּהֲנִים, וְאֶחָד כֹּהֵן מָשׁוּחַ. — [*This applies*] *equally to Israelites, Kohanim, and the Anointed Kohen.*

[*Anointed Kohen* is another name for the *Kohen Gadol.*] The he-goat sent to *Azazel* atones for *Kohanim* as well as for Israelites for all sins other than contaminating the Temple and its hallowed things (*Rav; Tif. Yis.* from *Gem.* 13b).

This is derived from the verse (*Lev.* 16:33): וְכִפֶּר אֶת־מִקְדַּשׁ הַקֹּדֶשׁ ... וְעַל הַכֹּהֲנִים וְעַל־כָּל־עַם הַקָּהָל יְכַפֵּר, *And he shall atone for the most holy place ... and for the Kohanim and for the entire people of the congregation he shall atone.* The implication is that the *Kohanim* as well as the entire populace of Israel share a common atonement (*Gem.* 13b). This cannot refer to sins of contaminating the

1
7 **7.** [This applies] equally to Israelites, *Kohanim,* and the Anointed *Kohen.* What is the difference between Israelites, *Kohanim* and the Anointed *Kohen?* Only that the blood of the bull atones for the *Kohanim* for the *tumah* of the Temple and its hallowed things. R' Shimon says: Just as the blood of the he-goat which is sacrificed inside atones for Israel, so the blood of the bull

YAD AVRAHAM

Temple and its hallowed things with *tumah,* since for these transgressions the he-goat that is sacrificed inside atones for the Israelites, while the bull of Aaron atones for the *Kohanim,* as will be explained below. Therefore, it must be referring to the he-goat sent to *Azazel* which atones for all other sins equally for *Kohanim* and Israelites.

מַה בֵּין יִשְׂרְאֵלִים לַכֹּהֲנִים וּלְכֹהֵן מָשׁוּחַ? — *What is the difference between Israelites, Kohanim, and the anointed Kohen?*

I.e., the only difference between Israelites, *Kohanim,* and the *Kohen* [*Gadol*] in regard to atonement is the following *(Rav).*

אֶלָּא שֶׁדַּם הַפָּר מְכַפֵּר עַל־הַכֹּהֲנִים עַל־טֻמְאַת מִקְדָּשׁ וְקָדָשָׁיו. — *Only that the blood of the bull atones for the Kohanim for the tumah* [*transgression*] *of the Temple and its hallowed things.*

All that is atoned for Israelites by either the he-goat that is sacrificed inside (see mishnah 2), or the one sacrificed outside (see mishnah 3), is atoned for *Kohanim* by the bull of Aaron which is sacrificed on Yom Kippur. Thus, the bull of Aaron suspends punishment for those *Kohanim* who had awareness in the beginning but not at the end, and atones for their deliberate *tumah* violations of the Temple and its hallowed things (mishnah 6) [both functions of the he-goat sacrificed inside]. It also atones for *Kohanim* who transgressed without awareness in the beginning [the function of the outside he-goat] *(Rav; Rashi).*

Rashi deletes the word דַּם, *the blood of.* His reading is: שֶׁהַפָּר, *that the bull (Tos. Yom Tov). Rashi's* reading is based on the *Gemara* (14a) which explains that the bull atones for certain sins even before it is slaughtered and for other sins when its blood is sprinkled.[1] The first confession over the bull atones for the *Kohen Gadol* and his household, in order that he be forgiven before becoming an emissary to atone for the people. The second confession and the sprinkling of the blood atone on behalf of the *Kohanim* for those sins for which the he-goat sacrificed inside and the he-goat sacrificed outside atone for Israelites, the former by the confession and the latter by the sprinkling of the blood.

רַבִּי שִׁמְעוֹן אוֹמֵר: — *R' Shimon says:*

R' Shimon differs with R' Yehudah, who rules that the he-goat that is sent away to *Azazel* atones for the *Kohanim* as well as the Israelites for all sins other than the contamination of the Temple and its hallowed things *(Rashi).* He argues as follows:

כְּשֵׁם שֶׁדַּם הַשָּׂעִיר הַנַּעֲשֶׂה בִפְנִים מְכַפֵּר עַל־יִשְׂרָאֵל, — *Just as the blood of the he-goat which is sacrificed inside atones for Israel,*

I.e., just as you (R' Yehudah) agree that the blood of the he-goat which is sacrificed inside atones for Israel for the *tumah* violations of the Temple and its

1. See *Yoma* 3:8 that the *Kohen Gadol* said a confession over the bull and then left it and went on to other rituals. Later (4:2) it states he came back to his bull, confessed a second time and slaughtered it and sprinkled its blood in the Holy of Holies.

דַּם הַפָּר מְכַפֵּר עַל־הַכֹּהֲנִים; כְּשֵׁם שֶׁוִּדּוּיוֹ שֶׁל־שָׂעִיר הַמִּשְׁתַּלֵּחַ מְכַפֵּר עַל־יִשְׂרָאֵל, כָּךְ וִדּוּיוֹ שֶׁל־פָּר מְכַפֵּר עַל־הַכֹּהֲנִים.

[א] **יְדִיעוֹת** הַטֻּמְאָה שְׁתַּיִם שֶׁהֵן אַרְבַּע. נִטְמָא וְיָדַע, וְנֶעֶלְמָה מִמֶּנּוּ הַטֻּמְאָה, וְזָכוּר אֶת־הַקֹּדֶשׁ; נֶעֱלַם מִמֶּנּוּ הַקֹּדֶשׁ, וְזָכוּר אֶת־הַטֻּמְאָה; נֶעֶלְמוּ מִמֶּנּוּ זֶה וָזֶה, וְאָכַל

יד אברהם

As mentioned above, R' Yehudah reasons that the first confession over the bull is for the *Kohen Gadol* and his household, so that he already have attained his personal forgiveness before atoning for the nation. The second confession and the sprinkling of the blood atone, respectively, for the *Kohanim* for that which the he-goat which is sacrificed inside and the he-goat which is sacrificed outside atone for Israel *(Tos. R' Akiva* from *Gem.* 14a).

R' Shimon accounts for R' Yehudah's verse in *Lev.* 16:33 mentioned in the comm. in the beginning of this mishnah to mean that the *Kohanim* are afforded atonement the same as the Israelites, but not necessarily with the same sacrifice. R' Shimon bases his view on the Torah's expression: שְׁנֵי הַשְּׂעִירִם, *the two he-goats,* comparing the he-goat which is sent away to the he-goat which is sacrificed inside. Just as the he-goat which is sacrificed inside atones only for Israel, not for the *Kohanim,* so the he-goat which is sent away to *Azazel* atones only for Israel, not for the *Kohanim.* R' Yehudah maintains that the comparison is merely to teach that they be alike in color, height, and price [see *Yoma* 6:1] *(Tos. Yom Tov* from *Gem.* 13b).

hallowed things without any confession [since there is no confession said over the he-goat that is sacrificed inside, only over the one sent away to *Azazel*] *(Rav; Rashi).*

כָּךְ דַּם הַפָּר מְכַפֵּר עַל־הַכֹּהֲנִים; — *so the blood of the bull atones for the Kohanim;*

So too the blood of the bull atones for the *Kohanim* for their *tumah* violations of the Temple and its hallowed things without any confession *(Rav; Rashi).*

כְּשֵׁם שֶׁוִּדּוּיוֹ שֶׁל־שָׂעִיר הַמִּשְׁתַּלֵּחַ מְכַפֵּר עַל־יִשְׂרָאֵל, — *just as the confession over the he-goat which is sent away* [to *Azazel*] *atones for Israel,*

I.e., it atones for Israel for sins other than the *tumah* violations of the Temple and its hallowed things *(Tif. Yis.).*

כָּךְ וִדּוּיוֹ שֶׁל־פָּר מְכַפֵּר עַל־הַכֹּהֲנִים. — *so the confession of the bull atones for the Kohanim.*

I.e., since the confession is not necessary to atone for the *tumah* sins of the Temple and its hallowed things, it would be superfluous, were it not meant to atone for the *Kohanim* for all other sins. Hence, we deduce that the *Kohanim* have no involvement with the atonement of the he-goat which is sent away *(Rav; Rashi).*

Chapter 2

1.

The principle topic of this tractate is the subject of oaths, as noted above. However, the *Tanna* completes the subject of knowledge of *tumah* before discussing the matter of oaths, since the former has fewer details and fills but two chapters, while the laws

2
1

atones for the *Kohanim;* just as the confession over the he-goat which is sent away [to *Azazel*] atones for Israel, so the confession of the bull atones for the *Kohanim.*

1. Awareness of *tumah* is of two [types] which are [in reality] four. [If] one became *tamei* and was aware of it, and [afterwards] the *tumah* escaped his awareness, but he remembered the hallowed thing; [or awareness of] the hallowed thing escaped him, but he remembered the *tumah;* [or] both escaped his [aware-

YAD AVRAHAM

of oaths occupy six.

After digressing to discuss the various communal sin-offerings which atone for the desecration of the Temple and its hallowed things through *tumah* in instances in which no private sacrifice is in order, the mishnah now resumes its explanation of the clause in the first mishnah of this tractate: *The awareness of tumah is of two types which are in reality four.*

.יְדִיעוֹת הַטֻּמְאָה שְׁתַּיִם שֶׁהֵן אַרְבַּע — *Awareness of tumah is of two* [*types*] *which are* [*in reality*] *four.*

[I.e., there are two cases discussed openly in the Torah, in which a person's interaction with the holy while in a state of *tumah* contamination renders him liable for an atonement sacrifice. This occurs when one had knowledge of his state of *tumah* which then escaped his memory, and he either ate hallowed foods or entered the Temple in that state of *tumah.* This leads to two other cases of liability, not mentioned explicitly in the Torah, but derived by the Rabbis from these verses, as will be explained further in the mishnah. See above 1:1.]

,נִטְמָא וְיָדַע — [*If*] *one became tamei and was aware of it,*

I.e., if one became *tamei* and knew of it at the time or subsequently became aware of it *(Rav; Rashi).*

In addition to the awareness of *tumah,* one must also have awareness of the status of the food as being hallowed or the status of the locale as the Temple, in order to become liable to a sin-offering *(Tos. Yom Tov* from *Rambam, Hil. Shegagos* 11:1; see *Lechem Mishneh).*

As explained above (1:2), many commentators rule that, as long as one is aware that he touched a *sheretz,* for example, and he once learned the Torah law that one becomes *tamei* by contact with a *sheretz,* even though he has since forgotten it, it can still be regarded as original knowledge of *tumah.* He need not have been aware that he was actually *tamei (Tos. Yom Tov* from *Tos.).*

,וְנֶעְלְמָה מִמֶּנּוּ הַטֻּמְאָה — *and* [*afterwards*] *the tumah escaped his awareness,*

[I.e., he subsequently forgot that he was *tamei.*]

;וְזָכוּר אֶת־הַקֹּדֶשׁ — *but he remembererd the hallowed thing;*

[I.e., he was aware that the food he was about to eat was hallowed. This case involving eating hallowed things after having forgotten his state of *tumah* is the first one of the two transgressions explicitly mentioned in the Torah.]

;נֶעְלַם מִמֶּנּוּ הַקֹּדֶשׁ, וְזָכוּר אֶת־הַטֻּמְאָה — [*or awareness of*] *the hallowed thing escaped him, but he remembered the tumah;*

[I.e., the reverse of the previous situation — he forgot that the food was hallowed, but he remembered that he was *tamei.* This is the first of the two cases inferred but not explicitly stated by the Torah.]

,נֶעְלְמוּ מִמֶּנּוּ זֶה וָזֶה — [*or*] *both escaped his*

אֶת־הַקֹּדֶשׁ וְלֹא יָדַע, וּמִשֶּׁאָכַל יָדַע — הֲרֵי זֶה בְּעוֹלֶה וְיוֹרֵד. נִטְמָא וְיָדַע, וְנֶעֶלְמָה מִמֶּנּוּ הַטֻּמְאָה, וְזָכוּר אֶת־הַמִּקְדָּשׁ; נֶעְלַם מִמֶּנּוּ הַמִּקְדָּשׁ, וְזָכוּר אֶת־הַטֻּמְאָה; נֶעֶלְמוּ מִמֶּנּוּ זֶה וָזֶה, וְנִכְנַס לַמִּקְדָּשׁ וְלֹא יָדַע, וּמִשֶּׁיָּצָא יָדַע — הֲרֵי זֶה בְּעוֹלֶה וְיוֹרֵד.

[ב] **אֶחָד** הַנִּכְנָס לָעֲזָרָה וְאֶחָד הַנִּכְנָס לְתוֹסֶפֶת הָעֲזָרָה, שֶׁאֵין מוֹסִיפִין עַל־הָעִיר

יד אברהם

[*awareness*],

[He forgot both that he was *tamei* and that the food was hallowed.]

וְאָכַל אֶת־הַקֹּדֶשׁ וְלֹא יָדַע, — *and he ate hallowed things being unaware,*

[I.e., when he ate the hallowed things, he was unaware of the *tumah* or of the status of the food, or of both.]

וּמִשֶּׁאָכַל יָדַע — *and he became aware after he ate* —

[He later became aware of his state of *tumah* or of the status of the food he had eaten and realized that he had sinned.] He is not liable unless he regained awareness of his transgression (*Rambam, Hil. Shegagos* 11:1; see *Rashi* 4a s.v. ונעלם ונעלם שני פעמים and *Tos.* 4b).

הֲרֵי זֶה בְּעוֹלֶה וְיוֹרֵד. — *he is* [*required to bring*] *a variable* [*sin-*]*offering.*

[For having inadvertently violated the prohibition on eating hallowed foods while in a state of *tumah*, the transgressor must bring a variable sin-offering in atonement. As explained in the introduction to the tractate, this is a sliding-scale sacrifice, the cost and type of the offering being according to the affluence of the sinner.]

נִטְמָא וְיָדַע, וְנֶעֶלְמָה מִמֶּנּוּ הַטֻּמְאָה, וְזָכוּר אֶת־הַמִּקְדָּשׁ; — [*If*] *one became tamei and was aware of it, and* [*afterwards*] *the tumah escaped his* [*awareness*], *but he remembered the Temple;*

[This case of *tumah* involving the Temple (rather than hallowed things) is the second of the two cases mentioned explicitly in the Torah. Here, too, he forgot his *tumah* but remembered that the locale he was about to enter was the Temple.]

נֶעְלַם מִמֶּנּוּ הַמִּקְדָּשׁ, וְזָכוּר אֶת־הַטֻּמְאָה; — [*or awareness of*] *the Temple escaped him, but he remembered the tumah;*

[I.e., he forgot that the locale he was entering was a part of the Temple, but was aware of his state of *tumah* when he entered the Temple. This is the second inferred case.]

נֶעֶלְמוּ מִמֶּנּוּ זֶה וָזֶה, — [*or*] *both of them escaped his awareness,*

[He forgot both that he was *tamei* and that this place was part of the Temple grounds.]

וְנִכְנַס לַמִּקְדָּשׁ וְלֹא יָדַע, — *and he entered the Temple being unaware,*

[He entered the Temple without knowing that he was *tamei*, or that this was the Temple, or both.]

וּמִשֶּׁיָּצָא יָדַע — *and he became aware after he came out, he became aware* —

[After leaving the Temple, he became aware that he had entered it while in a state of *tumah*. Here again he is not liable unless he regained awareness after the sin.]

הֲרֵי זֶה בְּעוֹלֶה וְיוֹרֵד. — *he is* [*required to bring*] *a variable* [*sin-*]*offering.*

[For having violated the prohibition on entering the Temple confines in a state of *tumah*, he is obligated to bring this sacrifice in atonement.]

ness], and he ate hallowed things being unaware, and he became aware after he ate — he is [required to bring] a variable [sin-]offering. [If] one became *tamei* and was aware of it, and [afterwards] the *tumah* escaped his awareness, but he remembered the Temple; [or awareness of] the Temple escaped him, but he remembered the *tumah;* [or] both of them escaped his [awareness], and he entered the Temple being unaware, and he became aware after he came out — he is [required to bring] a variable [sin-]offering.

2. Both the one who enters the Courtyard and the one who enters the addition to the Courtyard [are

YAD AVRAHAM

The *Gemara* (14b) explains that the two cases written explicitly in the Torah are those in which the sinner forgot that he was *tamei*. In one case, he partook of hallowed food, while in the other, he entered the Temple in a state of unawareness.

The other two cases, which are derived from the Torah, but not written explicitly, are those in which the sinner forgets that the meat he wishes to eat is sacrificial meat, or that the place he wishes to enter is the Temple. In each of these cases, too, he must have had knowledge both preceding the state of unawareness and following it. These two types of knowledge bring the total to four. Thus the mishnah lists two groups, each consisting of an *av*, primary case — forgetting the *tumah*, and a *toladah*, derivative — forgetting the object *(Tif. Yis.)*.

The two cases, in which he forgets both his state of *tumah* and the status of the food or of the place he is entering, are not counted, since those cases are merely combinations of the cases already counted *(Tos. Yom Tov)*. Although the sin was committed because of his unawareness, the mishnah refers to the sin as *awareness of tumah* since there is no liability unless awareness preceded the unawareness *(Rav)*.

Actually, one is not liable to bring a variable sin-offering unless there was knowledge both preceding and following the sin. That being so, why does the mishnah say: *Awareness . . . is two which are four,* when in reality it is four which are eight, since each case requires two awarenesses.

One solution offered is that the mishnah does not count the awareness following the sin, since that is a prerequisite to bringing a sin-offering for any type of transgression. Thus, only the awareness before the sin, which is a requirement found exclusively in regard to this sin-offering, is dealt with by this mishnah *(Tos. Yom Tov* from *Gem.* 14b).

An alternative solution given is that, on the contrary, the mishnah counts only the final awareness, which completes the liability to a sin-offering, not the initial awareness, which is only the first step in the process.

2.

The following mishnah delineates the boundaries of the Temple with regard to where a person may not enter when he is in a state of *tumah.*

אֶחָד הַנִּכְנָס לָעֲזָרָה וְאֶחָד הַנִּכְנָס לְתוֹסֶפֶת הָעֲזָרָה, — *Both the one who enters the Courtyard and the one who enters the addition to the Courtyard* [*are liable*];

The halachah of the previous mishnah applies whether he entered the original

וְעַל־הָעֲזָרוֹת אֶלָּא בְמֶלֶךְ, וְנָבִיא, וְאוּרִים וְתֻמִּים, וּבְסַנְהֶדְרִין שֶׁל־שִׁבְעִים וְאֶחָד, וּבִשְׁתֵּי תוֹדוֹת

area of the Temple Courtyard[1] or whether he entered an area added to the Courtyard at a later time *(Rav; Rashi).* In either case, his inadvertent transgression of the *tumah* prohibition renders him liable to a sin-offering. If he does so deliberately, he is subject to *kares* [*Kelim* 1:8] *(Tos. Yom Tov).*

The *Gemara* (14b and *Sanhedrin* 2a) states: The Sanhedrin has the power to enlarge the *Azarah* by consecrating an area adjacent to the *Azarah,* thereby giving it the identical status; also [it has the power] to enlarge the city of Jerusalem by consecrating the nearby land, thus giving it the status of the city proper. This can be done in any generation, when deemed necessary by the Sanhedrin, provided that they follow the procedure stipulated in this mishnah *(Rambam, Hil. Beis HaBechirah* 6:11).

Adjacent to the eastern wall of the *Azarah* was the *Ezras Nashim,* Women's Court. The latter did not have the same status as the former. If one entered the Women's Court in a state of *tumah* he would not be liable to *kares* or sin-offering. However, many years after the Temple was built, King Yehoshaphat enhanced the sanctity of the Women's Court, bestowing upon it the identical status as the *Azarah* itself. Consequently, if a person who was *tamei* were to enter the Women's Court he would be liable to *kares.* Some commentaries maintain that the addition to the Courtyard referred to in this mishnah is the Women's Court after the innovation of Yehoshaphat *(Tif. Yis.).*

Others strongly oppose equating our mishnah with Yehoshaphat's enactment, since, according to their view, Yehoshaphat's sanctification only had the status of a Rabbinic enactment and was thus not the type of addition with which our mishnah is dealing *(Tiferes Yaakov).*

שֶׁאֵין מוֹסִיפִין עַל־הָעִיר — *for they do not add to the city*

I.e., to Jerusalem *(Tif. Yis.).* [The city of Jerusalem possessed sanctity and the extension of the city's limits required an extension of the area of sanctification as well. This sanctity was relevant to various laws, such as the eating of *offerings of lesser holiness* which could be eaten anywhere in Jerusalem; see *Zevachim* 5:7. Thus, expansion of the city was a religious matter, not merely a civic one.]

וְעַל־הָעֲזָרוֹת — *or to the courtyards*

I.e., to any of the courtyards in the Temple, to expand their allotted areas *(Meiri).*

Since adding to the Courtyard requires following the procedure described below, the added areas thereby gain the same degree of sanctity as the original Courtyard. Consequently, one entering the added areas while in a state of *tumah* would be equally liable to one entering the original area of the Courtyard *(Rav; Rashi).*

אֶלָּא בְמֶלֶךְ, וְנָבִיא, וְאוּרִים וְתֻמִּים, וּבְסַנְהֶדְרִין שֶׁל־שִׁבְעִים וְאֶחָד, — *except with a king, a prophet, the Urim V'Tumim, and a Sanhedrin of seventy-one,*

[The approval and participation of these people and institutions is a prerequisite for the expansion of the status of holiness to the added areas (see below).] This is based on the verse *(Ex.* 25:9): כְּכֹל אֲשֶׁר אֲנִי מַרְאֶה אוֹתְךָ אֵת תַּבְנִית הַמִּשְׁכָּן וְאֵת תַּבְנִית כָּל־כֵּלָיו וְכֵן תַּעֲשׂוּ — *According to all that I show you, the pattern of the*

1. The Temple (as well as the *Mishkan)* consisted of three sections: The *Azarah* [referred to in the *Mishkan* (Tabernacle) as *chatzer;* lit. *yard*]; the *Heichal,* the Holy; and *Kodesh HaKodashim,* the Holy of Holies. The *Azarah* was where the slaughtering of sacrifices and their offering on the Altar took place. Any Jew free of *tumah* was able to enter the first eleven cubits of the *Azarah.* The rest of the *Azarah* was reserved for *Kohanim* only. The *Heichal* housed the *Menorah, Shulchan* and the Inner (Golden) Altar. The Holy of Holies contained the Holy Ark, wherein were kept the Two Tablets received by Moshe at Mt. Sinai.

2 liable]; for they do not add to the city or to the Temple
2 courtyards except with a king, a prophet, the *Urim*
V'Tumim, and a Sanhedrin of seventy-one, with two
thanksgiving offerings, and with song. The *beis din*

YAD AVRAHAM

Tabernacle and the pattern of all its utensils, and so shall you do. The final clause appears superfluous. The *Gemara* (23a) explains that the phrase *so shall you do* refers to the future. Any time you build a Temple or an addition to an existing one, it must be consecrated in the same manner as the *Mishkan* (Tabernacle) was sanctified. Just as the *Mishkan* was sanctified by Moshe, who served as both king and prophet, and through his brother Aaron, who as *Kohen Gadol* was attired with the *Choshen* containing the *Urim V'Tumim,* as well as in the presence of the Sanhedrin of seventy-one, so too any subsequent additions require all these (*Rav* from *Gem.* 15a).

There are several opinions as to the precise nature of the *Urim V'Tumim. Rashi* says that they were a slip of parchment upon which the שֵׁם הַמְפוֹרָשׁ, *Ineffable four-letter Name* of HASHEM was written. This was the power that lit up the letters on the breastplate of the *Kohen Gadol,* providing Divine guidance to those making enquiries of it. [For other opinions, see ArtScroll *Yoma* p. 141.]

That Moshe was a king, as well as a prophet, is learned from the verse (*Deut.* 33:5): וַיְהִי בִישֻׁרוּן מֶלֶךְ, *And he was a king in Yeshurun* (*Rambam Comm.* from *Seder Olam,* ch. 7, *Zevachim* 102a).

Tosafos question the requirement of *Urim V'Tumim* since the *Urim V'Tumim* could not have been consulted in the construction of the *Mishkan.* Only a *Kohen* may use the *Urim V'Tumim* and the *Mishkan* was constructed before Aaron was made a *Kohen.* [The *Kehunah* was bestowed on Aaron during the seven days of the *Milluim,* inauguration.] (*Tos. Yom Tov*).

Ritva suggests that during the seven days of *Milluim,* when Moshe served as *Kohen Gadol,* he wore the *Urim V'Tumim.* Therefore, even though the *Urim V'Tumim* was not actually consulted, it was, nevertheless, present at the consecration. Thus in the future, the *Urim V'Tumim* is also required (cf. *Rambam, Beis HaBechirah* 6:11).

An alternate solution is that, although the *Mishkan* was constructed without consulting the *Urim V'Tumim,* establishing the site for the *Mishkan* each time required the guidance of the *Urim V'Tumim* (*Lechem Shamayim*).

We find two conflicting explanations concerning the requirement of Sanhedrin. *Rashi* and *Rav* explain that this is derived from the institution of the seventy elders [who, together with Moshe, constituted a Sanhedrin of seventy-one]. This is also the view of *Rambam* in his commentary both here and to *Sanhedrin* 1:5. *Rashi* and *Rav* to *Sanhedrin,* however, explain that Moshe himself was the equivalent of the Sanhedrin of seventy-one members. On the surface, this second explanation seems more understandable, since we do not find the appointment of a Sanhedrin of seventy elders until *Numbers* 11:16, at which time the *Mishkan* was already in existence. According to the first explanation we must say that the seventy elders mentioned in *Exodus* 24:9 as the elders of the congregation were designated for every sacred occasion, on the order of the Sanhedrin appointed later in *Numbers* 11:16. These are the Sanhedrin referred to in this mishnah (*Tos. Yom Tov*).

וּבִשְׁתֵּי תוֹדוֹת — *with two thanksgiving offerings,*

I.e., the breads of two thanksgiving offerings (*Rav*). A thanksgiving offering consists of an animal to be sacrificed, along with forty loaves of bread, thirty of which are unleavened and ten leavened. They carried the leavened bread from these offerings around the outside of the entire perimeter of the area which was to be sanctified (*Rav* following *Rashi* 15b). According to *Tosafos,* however, they were carried within the boundary of the area which was to be sanctified (*Tos. R' Akiva*). *Meiri* asserts that only one leavened loaf from each of the two thanksgiving offerings was

שבועות ב/ב

וּבְשִׁיר. וּבֵית דִּין מְהַלְּכִין, וּשְׁתֵּי תוֹדוֹת, אַחֲרֵיהֶם, וְכָל־יִשְׂרָאֵל אַחֲרֵיהֶם. הַפְּנִימִית נֶאֱכֶלֶת, וְהַחִיצוֹנָה נִשְׂרֶפֶת. וְכָל־שֶׁלֹּא נַעֲשָׂה בְּכָל־אֵלּוּ — הַנִּכְנָס לְשָׁם אֵין חַיָּבִין עָלֶיהָ.

יד אברהם

borne, not all ten of them.

From the description of the consecration which took place in the time of Nehemiah, the *Gemara* derives that only the breads of the thanksgiving offerings were used, not the animals. In *Nehemiah* (12:31) it states: וָאַעֲמִידָה שְׁתֵּי תוֹדֹת גְּדוֹלֹת, *And I set up two large thanksgiving offerings.* The *Gemara* reasons that since the size of the offering is immaterial, the word *large* must refer to the largest part of the offering. The offering was brought with forty loaves of bread, thirty unleavened and ten leavened. The *Kohen* took an *ephah* of flour, divided it and used half for the thirty unleavened ones and the other half for the leavened. It therefore follows that the leavened loaves were surely larger than the unleavened ones. Since the loaves represented the largest part of the offering, they were the ones borne in the procession.

The *Gemara* reasons that just as the consecration of additions to Jerusalem takes place through the procession of sacrifices that become disqualified when carried out of the city, so additions to the Courtyard are consecrated by the procession of sacrifices which become disqualified when carried out of the Courtyard. This is established as meaning the remnants of a *minchah* [flour-offering], i.e., the part of a *minchah* remaining after the *Kohen* has taken a handful to sacrifice on the Altar. Therefore, the verse in *Nehemiah* which states that sanctification took place with the breads of the thanksgiving offering is referring only to the consecration of Jerusalem and its additions. The *Azarah* and its additions were consecrated with the remnants of a *minchah.*

וּבְשִׁיר. — *and with song.*

The song of the thanksgiving offering was accompanied by harps, lyres, and cymbals which were played at every corner and at every large stone in Jerusalem *(Gem.* 15b).

According to *Rashi,* the song was Psalm 100: מִזְמוֹר לְתוֹדָה, *A Song of Thanksgiving.* According to *Rav* and *Rambam* (from *Gem.*) they would recite psalm 30: מִזְמוֹר שִׁיר־חֲנֻכַּת הַבַּיִת לְדָוִד אֲרוֹמִמְךָ ה׳ כִּי דִלִּיתָנִי ... — *A song with musical accompaniment for the inauguration of the Temple by David. I will exalt You,* HASHEM, *for You have raised me up from the depths ...*

Upon concluding psalm 30, they would recite psalm 91, known in the Talmud as שִׁיר שֶׁל־פְּגָעִים, *the Song of the Demons,* because we read in verse 7 of that psalm that thousands and tens of thousands of demons will fall. Others call it שִׁיר שֶׁל־נְגָעִים, *the Song of the Plagues,* as we read, *nor will any plague come near your tent* (v. 10). This psalm was recited in order to cleanse the hitherto unsanctified area of all impure and evil forces. When plagues and demons are expelled, sanctity can be introduced *(Maharsha; Toras Chayim).*

Rashi explains that this psalm was recited by Moses at the dedication of the *Mishkan.* It was, therefore, chosen as the psalm to be recited at the dedication of any area, whether an addition to the Temple or Holy City.

Tosafos explain that this psalm was recited because it conveys the opposition and harassment suffered by the Jews upon their return from Babylon when they strove to rebuild the Temple.

The *Gemara* states the whole psalm was not recited, only up to the middle of verse 9. According to *Tosafos'* explanation this is readily understandable since the remainder of the psalm does not deal with the persecution suffered by the nation at the hands of its enemies. However, according to *Rashi,* the reason for ending in the middle of the psalm is not apparent. *Ritva* explains that sixty

2 walked with [the] two thanksgiving offerings, after
2 them, and all Israel after them. The inner one was eaten,
and the outer one was burnt. Any [addition] not made with all these — whoever enters therein is not liable for it.

YAD AVRAHAM

words were recited, corresponding to the *sixty mighty men surrounding the bed of Solomon* (*Song* 3:7). According to *Rashi*, these are the sixty myriads of Israelites eligible to go to war, who surrounded the *Mishkan*.

They would then continue with psalm 3, which also refers to the oppression and derision heaped upon Israel by their adversaries prior to the construction of the Second Temple.

Rav and *Rambam* omit these final two psalms, obviously following the view of *Tosafos* that they were recited only because of the opposition suffered by the Jews prior to building the Second Temple. Therefore, at any subsequent time there was no point in reciting them (*Tos. Yom Tov*).

וּבֵית דִּין מְהַלְּכִין, וּשְׁתֵּי תוֹדוֹת, אַחֲרֵיהֶם. — *The beis din walked, with* [*the*] *two thanksgiving offerings, after them,*

The *Gemara* explains this to mean that the *beis din* walked behind the *Kohanim* carrying the loaves.

Tif. Yis. explains the wording of the mishnah to mean that *beis din* walked after the loaf carriers who followed the Levites who sang the psalms.

וְכָל־יִשְׂרָאֵל אַחֲרֵיהֶם. — *and all Israel after them.*

I.e., after the Sanhedrin. They walked in this order until they reached the end of the area they wished to sanctify (*Meiri; Tif. Yis.*).

הַפְּנִימִית נֶאֱכֶלֶת, וְהַחִיצוֹנָה נִשְׂרֶפֶת. — *The inner one was eaten, and the outer one was burnt.*

I.e., the inner loaf (or loaves; see above) was eaten immediately at the conclusion of the procession, while the outer one was burnt (*Meiri*).

In the *Gemara* (15b) the Rabbis differ concerning the placement of the *Kohanim* carrying the two thanksgiving offerings. One opinion is that they marched side by side, with the one closer to the wall being called the inner one, and the one farther from the wall referred to as the outer one. Another opinion is that they marched behind each other, with the one closer to the *beis din* being called the inner one.

The *Gemara* can find no reason for the distinction between the two loaves that would account for the inner being eaten while the outer is burnt. Since both were carried into territory not yet sanctified with the sanctity of Jerusalem, they should both be deemed unfit (by reason of having left their area of sanctity), [1] and both should be burnt. The conclusion is that this was a prophetically instituted procedure (*Tos. Yom Tov*).

וְכָל־שֶׁלֹּא נַעֲשָׂה בְּכָל־אֵלּוּ — *Any* [*addition*] *not made with all these —*

[I.e., any addition made without one or more of these components, such as a king, a prophet, *Urim V'Tumim*, or Sanhedrin.]

הַנִּכְנָס לְשָׁם אֵין חַיָּבִין עָלֶיהָ. — *whoever enters therein is not liable for it.*

Whoever enters that area in a state of *tumah* (*Tif. Yis.*), is not liable to a variable sin-offering if he entered inadvertently, or to *kares* if he entered intentionally. Since the area was never properly sanctified, it did not achieve the

1. Any hallowed food upon leaving the area within which it must be eaten is rendered unfit and must be burned. Thus, sacrifices that are *Kodshei Kodashim* (most holy), which must be eaten in the *Azarah* (main Courtyard), become unfit when taken out even to the Women's Court. Likewise, *Kodashim Kallim* (offerings of lesser holiness), which may be eaten throughout Jerusalem, become unfit upon leaving the walls of Jerusalem.

[ג] **נִטְמָא** בָּעֲזָרָה, וְנֶעֶלְמָה מִמֶּנּוּ הַטֻּמְאָה, וְזָכוּר אֶת־הַמִּקְדָּשׁ; נֶעְלַם מִמֶּנּוּ הַמִּקְדָּשׁ, וְזָכוּר לַטֻּמְאָה; נֶעְלַם מִמֶּנּוּ זֶה וָזֶה — וְהִשְׁתַּחֲוָה אוֹ שֶׁשָּׁהָה בִּכְדֵי הִשְׁתַּחֲוָאָה, בָּא לוֹ בָּאֲרֻכָּה, חַיָּב; בַּקְּצָרָה, פָּטוּר. זוֹ הִיא מִצְוַת עֲשֵׂה

יד אברהם

level of sanctity for which the Torah's penalties are imposed.

The *Gemara* (16a) explains that since all the components are necessary for sanctifying any additional area, Nehemiah's sanctification of Jerusalem (related in *Nehemiah* 12:30), would be invalid since the inauguration of the Second Temple lacked both a king and the *Urim V'Tumim.* The *Gemara* therefore concludes that when Solomon sanctified Jerusalem and the First Temple, they remained in that hallowed state permanently, even after the destruction. There was consequently no real necessity for Nehemiah's sanctification; he did so merely as a symbol (*Rav* from *Gem.* 16a).

According to another view, only one of the above components is required. Those who subscribe to this view hold that Solomon's consecration served only until the destruction of the Temple and the exile. Later, Nehemiah reconsecrated the Temple and the city with those components of the ceremony available to him at that time. See *Eduyos* 8:6.

Rambam rules that Solomon's consecration of the Temple and Jerusalem remained forever, whereas the holiness of the rest of the land terminated when the nation went into exile (*Rambam, Hil. Beis HaBechirah* 6:15).

Lechem Shamayim points out that since according to the first view the consecration of the Second Temple was of no consequence, it is obvious that no addition could have actually been made either to Jerusalem or the Temple Courtyard throughout the Second Temple era.

3.

The mishnah has heretofore dealt with one who inadvertently entered the Temple Courtyard in a state of *tumah.* The following mishnah deals with one who contracted *tumah* while in the Courtyard.

נִטְמָא בָּעֲזָרָה, — [*If*] *one became tamei in the Courtyard,*

I.e., he entered the Temple Courtyard while *tahor,* and contracted *tumah* there by coming in contact with some source of *tumah* (*Meiri*). At the time, he was aware that he had contracted *tumah* (*Rav*).

As above (mishnah 1:2), *Tos. Yom Tov* notes that according to many authorities the knowledge with regard to contracting *tumah* which he gained in his school days suffices to be considered knowledge of *tumah* in this respect, and as long as he knows that he had touched a *sheretz,* he need not have known that he had in fact become *tamei.*

The punishment of *kares* for one who enters the Temple while *tamei* is written twice in the Torah. One verse teaches the liability for *kares* for one who enters while *tamei;* the other for one who became *tamei* while in the Temple (*Tos. Yom Tov* from *Tos.*).

וְנֶעֶלְמָה מִמֶּנּוּ הַטֻּמְאָה, וְזָכוּר אֶת־הַמִּקְדָּשׁ; — *and the tumah escaped his memory, though he remembered the Temple;*

I.e., he forgot his contaminated state (*Tif. Yis.*), but was aware that he was in a consecrated area.

נֶעְלַם מִמֶּנּוּ הַמִּקְדָּשׁ, וְזָכוּר לַטֻּמְאָה; — [*or, the fact that it was*] *the Temple escaped his memory, though he remembered the tumah;*

[I.e., he forgot that he was in a consecrated area though he was still

2
3

3. [If] one became *tamei* in the Courtyard, and the *tumah* escaped his memory, though he remembered the Temple; [or, the fact that it was] the Temple escaped his memory, though he remembered the *tumah;* [or] both escaped his memory — and he prostrated himself, or stayed long enough to prostrate himself, [or if] he went out by a longer way, he is liable; by the shortest way, he is exempt. This is the positive

YAD AVRAHAM

aware that he had contracted *tumah.*]

נֶעְלַם מִמֶּנּוּ זֶה וָזֶה — [*or*] *both escaped his memory —*

[I.e., he forgot both that he had contracted *tumah* and that he was in a consecrated area.]

וְהִשְׁתַּחֲוָה— *and he prostrated himself*

After becoming *tamei* in the Temple and forgetting either that he was in the Temple, or that he had just become *tamei,* or both, he prostrated himself toward the Sanctuary *(Rav* from *Gem.* 16b). He is liable for the act of prostrating himself in a hallowed place while *tamei* *(Rashi* ad loc.).

אוֹ שֶׁשָּׁהָה בִּכְדֵי הִשְׁתַּחֲוָאָה, — *or stayed long enough to prostrate himself,*

Prostrating oneself in the Temple Courtyard facing away from the Sanctuary is not considered a proper prostration. Therefore, if he prostrated himself while *tamei,* facing outward *(Rav* from *Gem.* 16b) toward the east *(Rashi* ad loc.), he cannot be held liable for prostrating while *tamei.* He is liable only if he stayed as long as it would take an average person to properly prostrate himself. Should he stay that long without prostrating himself at all, he is similarly liable *(Tos. Yom Tov; Tif. Yis.).*

The *Gemara* teaches that the amount of time it takes an average person to bow is the period required to recite, in a deliberate fashion [not quickly and not slowly], the second half of the verse *II Chron.* 7:3: וַיִּשְׁתַּחֲווּ וְהוֹדוֹת לַה׳ כִּי טוֹב כִּי לְעוֹלָם חַסְדּוֹ *and they prostrated themselves and thanked* HASHEM *for He is good, for His lovingkindness endures forever (Rav; Rambam Comm.; Tif. Yis.* from *Gem.* ad loc.).

בָּא לוֹ בַאֲרֻכָּה, — [*or if*] *he went out by a longer way,*

If there were two ways to exit the Temple Courtyard after becoming *tamei,* one a short, direct way, the other a longer, roundabout way, and he chose the longer one, he is liable even if he did not stay long enough to prostrate himself *(Rav).* Even if he ran out this longer way so fast that his exit took no longer than it would have taken had he walked the shorter route at an average pace, he is still liable *(Tos. R' Akiva* from *Gem.* 17a).

חַיָּב; — *he is liable;*

I.e., in any of these cases, if his transgression was intentional, he is liable to *kares;* if it was unintentional, he is liable to a variable sin-offering *(Rambam, Hil. Bias Mikdash* 3:22).

בִּקְצָרָה, — *by the shortest way,*

If he did not prostrate himself facing the Temple after becoming *tamei,* nor tarry long enough to prostrate himself, and he left the Courtyard by the shortest route *(Rav; Tif. Yis.).*

פָּטוּר. — *he is exempt.*

[In the case in which he was aware of the *tumah* and the Temple, the term *exempt* refers to *kares* and lashes. If he was unaware of them, *exempt* means not having to bring a sin-offering.] This holds true even if he walked out slowly, taking short steps, and his exit took all day. As long as he went by the most direct route and did not stop walking, he

שֶׁבַּמִּקְדָּשׁ, שֶׁאֵין חַיָּבִין עָלֶיהָ.

[ד] **וְאֵיזוֹ** הִיא מִצְוַת עֲשֵׂה שֶׁבַּנִּדָּה, שֶׁחַיָּבִין עָלֶיהָ? הָיָה מְשַׁמֵּשׁ עִם־הַטְּהוֹרָה, וְאָמְרָה לוֹ: ,,נִטְמֵאתִי," וּפֵרַשׁ מִיָּד, חַיָּב, מִפְּנֵי שֶׁיְּצִיאָתוֹ הֲנָאָה לוֹ כְּבִיאָתוֹ.

[ה] **רַבִּי** אֱלִיעֶזֶר אוֹמֵר: ,,הַשֶּׁרֶץ ... וְנֶעְלַם מִמֶּנּוּ" — עַל־הֶעְלֵם שֶׁרֶץ חַיָּב, וְאֵינוֹ

יד אברהם

is exempt *(Tos. R' Akiva; Tif. Yis.* from *Gem.* 17a).

זוֹ הִיא מִצְוַת עֲשֵׂה שֶׁבַּמִּקְדָּשׁ, שֶׁאֵין חַיָּבִין עָלֶיהָ. — *This is the positive commandment concerning the Temple, for which there is no liability.*

This mishnah in tractate *Horayos* discusses the law of the sin-offering which is sacrificed when the Sanhedrin issues an erroneous ruling and the majority of the community sins by following their ruling [פַּר הֶעְלֵם דָּבָר]. In connection with this, mishnah 2:4 there states an exception to that obligation: *They* [the Sanhedrin] *are not liable for the positive and negative commandment of the Temple.* Although the mishnah there clearly refers to the prohibition for a *tamei* to enter the Temple, it is not immediately clear what the positive commandment is, since this prohibition is framed as a negative commandment.

This is the point addressed by the mishnah here: The case of a person becoming *tamei* in the Temple and being commanded to leave by the shortest route is the case ofthe positive command in regard to the prohibition of *tumah* in the Temple. This positive commandment is stated in *Num.* 5:2: וִישַׁלְּחוּ מִן־הַמַּחֲנֶה ... *And they shall send out of the camp* ... [every person contaminated with a level of *tumah* which would prohibit him from entering] *(Rav; Rashi;* see *Shoshanim LeDovid).*

Should the Sanhedrin erroneously rule that one who contracted *tumah* while in the Temple Courtyard may go out by a long way, they are not liable to bring a sin-offering for their erroneous ruling *(Rav* from *Gem.* 17b). This is so because the above sacrifice is brought only when the erroneous ruling resulted in a transgression whose atonement is a *fixed* sin-offering. However, in the case of *tumah,* a variable sin-offering is brought, thereby ruling out the Sanhedrin's sacrifice.

4.

The following mishnah continues to elaborate the statement of the mishnah in *Horayos* 2:4. In connection with the statement explained at the end of the previous mishnah, the mishnah in *Horayos* adds *but they* [the Sanhedrin] *are liable for the positive and negative commandment of the menstruant.*

וְאֵיזוֹ הִיא מִצְוַת עֲשֵׂה שֶׁבַּנִּדָּה, שֶׁחַיָּבִין עָלֶיהָ? — *Now which is the positive commandment concerning the menstruant, for which there is liability?*

[A menstruating woman is prohibited by a negative commandment from engaging in conjugal relations. The mishnah now asks which is the positive commandment concerning the menstruant for which the Sanhedrin is held liable.]

The mishnah in *Horayos* sets this case

commandment concerning the Temple, for which there is no liability.

4. Now what is the positive commandment concerning the menstruant, for which there is liability? [If] one was cohabiting with a woman who was *tahor*, and she said to him, 'I have become *tamei,*' and he withdrew immediately, he is liable, because his exit is as pleasurable to him as his entry.

5. R' Eliezer says: *A sheretz ... and it escaped his awareness (Lev.* 5:2) — he is liable for forget-

YAD AVRAHAM

in contrast to the case in regard to the Temple cited in the previous mishnah for which they are not liable. It is thus clear that the transgression in regard to a menstruant with which we are concerned in our mishnah is one which is similar to that concerning the Temple; viz., in which the *tumah* occurred after a legitimate entry *(Rav)*.

הָיָה מְשַׁמֵּשׁ עִם־הַטְּהוֹרָה, — *[If] one was cohabiting with a woman who was tahor,*

Thus, in this case also, his entry was permissible *(Rav)*.

וְאָמְרָה לוֹ: „נִטְמֵאתִי," — *and she said to him, 'I have become tamei,'*

I.e., she felt the onset of a menstrual flow during the cohabitation and informed her husband of this *(Rav)*.

וּפֵרַשׁ מִיָּד, — *and he withdrew immediately,*

Not wishing to transgress the *niddah* prohibition, he withdrew immediately, while still in a state of erection *(Rav; Rashi; Tif. Yis.)*.

חַיָּב, מִפְּנֵי שֶׁיְּצִיאָתוֹ הֲנָאָה לוֹ כְּבִיאָתוֹ. — *he is liable, because his exit is as pleasurable to him as his entry.*

I.e., he is liable to *kares*, or, if done unintentionally, to the sin-offering mandated for one who cohabits with a *niddah* [menstruant] *(Rambam, Hil. Isurei Biah* 4:11). This is because his withdrawal from her in a state of erection affords him the pleasure of forbidden relations. Therefore, he must remain passive until his erection passes and withdraw with a *membrum mortum*. This is the *positive commandment concerning the menstruant woman (Rav* from *Gem.* 18a).

This law is derived from the verse *(Lev.* 15:24): וּתְהִי נִדָּתָהּ עָלָיו, *And her menstrual state shall be upon him,* meaning that there is a case in which she should remain with him even in her menstrual state *(Tos. Yom Tov* from *Gem.* 18b). Should the Sanhedrin err in this ruling and teach that he withdraw immediately, they are liable to the sin-offering for an erroneous ruling *(Rav)*.

There are actually numerous instances wherein the Sanhedrin is required to bring the sin-offering; however, the mishnah brings this example since it is the only one comparable to the previous mishnah where his entry was permissible *(Tif. Yis.)*.

5.

רַבִּי אֱלִיעֶזֶר אוֹמֵר: „הַשֶּׁרֶץ . . . וְנֶעְלַם מִמֶּנּוּ" — *R' Eliezer says: 'A sheretz ... and it escaped his awareness' (Lev.* 5:2) —

In stating the obligation for a sin-offering for entering the Temple in *tumah*, the Torah states: *Or a person who*

חַיָּב עַל־הֶעְלֵם מִקְדָּשׁ. רַבִּי עֲקִיבָא אוֹמֵר: „וְנֶעְלַם מִמֶּנּוּ וְהוּא טָמֵא" — עַל־הֶעְלֵם טֻמְאָה חַיָּב, וְאֵינוֹ חַיָּב עַל־הֶעְלֵם מִקְדָּשׁ. רַבִּי יִשְׁמָעֵאל אוֹמֵר: „וְנֶעְלַם," „וְנֶעְלַם," שְׁתֵּי פְעָמִים — לְחַיֵּב עַל־הֶעְלֵם טֻמְאָה וְעַל־הֶעְלֵם מִקְדָּשׁ.

יד אברהם

touches any thing which is tamei, or the carcass of a wild animal which is contaminated, or the carcass of a domesticated animal which is contaminated, or the carcass of a sheretz which is contaminated, but it escaped his awareness, and he is tamei and becomes guilty. R' Eliezer questions the necessity of specifying the specific forms of *tumah,* such as *sheretz,* since they are included in the earlier general statement of *anything which is tamei.* From this seeming redundancy, and the juxtaposition of the words *sheretz* and *it escaped his awareness,* R' Eliezer deduces the following rule *(Rav; Tif. Yis.* from *Gem.* 18b). [*Sheretz* is any of the eight species of creeping creatures listed in *Lev.* 11:29, 30 whose carcasses are a source of *tumah.*]

עַל־הֶעְלֵם שֶׁרֶץ חַיָּב, — *he is liable for forgetting* [lit. *for losing his awareness of*] *the sheretz,*

We learned previously that one is liable to a variable sin-offering only if he was aware of his *tumah,* forgot it, and then, after the transgression, reminded himself again. R' Eliezer states that by specifying *sheretz,* the Torah teaches that it is not sufficient to remember afterwards that somehow he had become *tamei.* Rather, he must be aware of the specific category of *tumah* he contracted — whether it is the *tumah* of a *sheretz* or of an animal carcass, etc.

וְאֵינוֹ חַיָּב עַל הֶעְלֵם מִקְדָּשׁ. — *but he is not liable for forgetting the Temple.*

[Similarly, R' Eliezer deduces that the Torah makes him liable only for the transgression resulting from his forgetting that he was *tamei — forgetting the sheretz* — not for one resulting from his forgetting that he was entering the Temple. Thus, if he remembered that he had contracted *tumah* from a *sheretz,* but forgot that the confines he was entering were of the Temple, he is not liable to a sacrifice.]

רַבִּי עֲקִיבָא אוֹמֵר: „וְנֶעְלַם מִמֶּנּוּ וְהוּא טָמֵא" — *R' Akiva says: 'And it escaped his awareness, and he was tamei' (ibid.)* —

[R' Akiva disputes R' Eliezer's exposition of the verse and cites the second part of the verse to teach the following:]

עַל־הֶעְלֵם טֻמְאָה חַיָּב, — *he is liable for forgetting the tumah,*

From the juxtaposition of the words *it escaped his awareness, and he was tamei,* R' Akiva infers that he need only have known that he was *tamei* to be liable to a variable sin-offering, but need not have been aware of the precise origin of his contamination (*Rav* from *Gem.* 18b).

R' Akiva reasons that since the Torah must specify contamination with the carcass of a beast or with the carcass of cattle for different reasons, it states also the contamination of a *sheretz,* even though it is superfluous *(Tos. Yom Tov* from *Gem.* 19a).

וְאֵינוֹ חַיָּב עַל־הֶעְלֵם מִקְדָּשׁ. — *but he is not liable for forgetting the Temple.*

In this R' Akiva concurs with R' Eliezer, that one is not liable for a variable sin-offering for a transgression resulting from his forgetting that the area he enters is consecrated, only for one resulting for forgetting his state of *tumah* *(Rav* from *Gem.* 18b).

2 ting the *sheretz,* but he is not liable for forgetting the
5 Temple. R' Akiva says: *And it escaped his awareness,*
and he was tamei' (ibid.) — he is liable for forgetting the *tumah,* but he is not liable for forgetting the Temple. R' Yishmael says: [The words] *And it escaped his awareness, and it escaped his awareness, (Lev.* 5:23) [are stated] twice — to make [one] liable both for forgetting the *tumah* and for forgetting the Temple.

YAD AVRAHAM

רַבִּי יִשְׁמָעֵאל אוֹמֵר: „וְנֶעְלַם," „וְנֶעְלַם," שְׁתֵּי פְּעָמִים — *R' Yishmael says: [The words] 'And it escaped his awareness,' 'and it escaped his awareness,' (Lev.* 5:2,3) *[are stated] twice* —

[R' Yishmael points out that the word וְנֶעְלַם, *and it escaped his awareness,* appears both in verse 2 and in verse 3. He therefore deduces that the Torah's intention is as follows:]

— לְחַיֵּב עַל־הֶעְלֵם טֻמְאָה וְעַל־הֶעְלֵם מִקְדָּשׁ. *to make [one] liable both for forgetting the tumah and for forgetting the Temple.*

[Regardless of which one he forgot, if he transgresses as a result, he is liable for the sacrifice. Thus, the view presented throughout these first two chapters was that of R' Yishmael,] and the halachah is in accordance with his view *(Rav; Rambam Comm. and Hil. Shegagos).*

Chapter 3

Chapter 3 resumes the discussion of the שְׁבוּעַת בִּטּוּי, *oath of utterance,* begun in 1:1, and also takes up the topic of the שְׁבוּעַת שָׁוְא, *vain oath.*

An oath of utterance is an oath concerning a course of action or the refraining from it. It is subdivided into two parts, one dealing with the future, the other with the past. When one swears to do something in the future, or not to do something, his oath creates an obligation to do, or an interdiction not to do, what was sworn. Should he fail to adhere to the terms of his oath, he has profaned his word and transgressed the commandment *(Num.* 30:3): לֹא יַחֵל דְּבָרוֹ, *he shall not profane his word.* By not adhering to his oath, he has also made a lie of it. Thus, he also transgresses the commandment וְלֹא־תִשָּׁבְעוּ בִשְׁמִי לַשָּׁקֶר, *And you shall not swear by My Name falsely [Lev.* 19:12] *(Rambam, Hil. Shevuos* 1:3; see *Kesef Mishneh).*[1]

The second category of this oath concerns a past action, such as: 'I ate,' or 'I did not eat.' Should that oath prove to be false, he has transgressed only the commandment *(Lev.* 19:12): וְלֹא־תִשָּׁבְעוּ בִשְׁמִי לַשָּׁקֶר, *And you shall not swear by My Name falsely.* Since it concerns something in the past, it cannot obligate him in any proposed action.

Generally, one who violates a negative commandment is punished by lashes. However, a negative commandment which is transgressed passively, through inaction rather than action, is not punishable by lashes. Speech is not considered an action. Therefore, most transgressions involving speech, e.g., bearing false witness, slander, etc., are not punishable by lashes. The transgression of an oath is an exception and is punished by lashes.

1. *Rambam's* ruling that even in the case of an oath regarding the future, the transgressor is guilty of a false oath, seems at variance with the *Gemara's* conclusion (20b, 21a). Nevertheless, his view is shared by *Chinuch (Mitzvah* 235) and *Smag (Negative Mitzvah* 239); this matter has been discussed in a fn. to the General Introduction. Even *Rambam* agrees that one does not receive lashes for a fake oath regarding the future. See *Kesef Mishneh* and *Lechem Mishneh.*

[א] שְׁבוּעוֹת שְׁתַּיִם, שֶׁהֵן אַרְבַּע: „שְׁבוּעָה שֶׁאֹכַל," וְ„שֶׁלֹּא אֹכַל"; „שֶׁאָכַלְתִּי," וְ„שֶׁלֹּא אָכַלְתִּי." „שְׁבוּעָה שֶׁלֹּא אֹכַל," וְאָכַל כָּל־שֶׁהוּא, חַיָּב; דִּבְרֵי רַבִּי עֲקִיבָא. אָמְרוּ לוֹ לְרַבִּי עֲקִיבָא: הֵיכָן מָצִינוּ בְּאוֹכֵל כָּל־שֶׁהוּא שֶׁהוּא חַיָּב, שֶׁזֶּה חַיָּב? אָמַר לָהֶן רַבִּי עֲקִיבָא: וְכִי הֵיכָן מָצִינוּ בִּמְדַבֵּר וּמֵבִיא קָרְבָּן, שֶׁזֶּה מְדַבֵּר וּמֵבִיא קָרְבָּן?

יד אברהם

1.

שְׁבוּעוֹת שְׁתַּיִם, שֶׁהֵן אַרְבַּע — *Oaths are of two [types], which are [in reality] four:*

[I.e., two types of oaths are mentioned explicitly in the Torah — viz., those pertaining to the future. There are two more which are derived from them — viz., oaths concerning the past, for a total of four.]

„שְׁבוּעָה שֶׁאֹכַל," וְ„שֶׁלֹּא אֹכַל"; — *'I swear that I will eat,' or ['I swear] that I will not eat;'*

[These are cited by way of example of oaths concerning future action.] Both these oaths in regard to the future are stated explicitly in the Torah *(Lev. 5:4):* אוֹ נֶפֶשׁ כִּי תִשָּׁבַע לְבַטֵּא בִשְׂפָתַיִם לְהָרַע אוֹ לְהֵיטִיב, *Or if a person swears by uttering with his lips to do bad or to do good. To do bad* denotes an oath to refrain from a proper human activity, e.g., not to eat. It is referred to as doing bad because it involves mortification of the body. Similarly, *to do good* denotes an oath to engage in a proper human activity, e.g., to eat, which involves benefit to the body *(Rav, Rashi* here and above 1:1).

„שֶׁאָכַלְתִּי," וְ„שֶׁלֹּא אָכַלְתִּי." — *'[I swear] that I ate,' or '[I swear] that I did not eat.'*

These two oaths regarding the past are derived from the extension of the verse, as R' Akiva will explain in mishnah 5 *(Rav; Rashi; Tos. Yom Tov).*

„שְׁבוּעָה שֶׁלֹּא אֹכַל," וְאָכַל כָּל־שֶׁהוּא, חַיָּב; דִּבְרֵי רַבִּי עֲקִיבָא. — *[If he said,] 'I swear that I will not eat,' and he ate a minute quantity, he is liable; [these are] the words of R' Akiva.*

[I.e., if someone swears, 'I will not eat today,' and he violated his oath by eating a small amount, he is liable even though he ate less than a *kezayis,* the volume of an olive. This is in contrast to the general rule of Torah law which is that whenever the Torah mandates something in regard to the act of eating, the minimum amount is a *kezayis.* This is true both in regard to positive and negative commandments. For example, one does not fulfill the *mitzvah* to eat *matzah* on Pesach until he eats at least a *kezayis* of it. Similarly, one is not liable for the punishment of lashes for eating the arious foods forbidden by the Torah unless he consumed at least a *kezayis* (although it is forbidden by a lesser prohibition to eat even smaller amounts).]

In the case of an oath, however, R' Akiva is of the opinion that one is liable to lashes or to a variable sin-offering even if he ate less than a *kezayis,* indeed even for a minute amount. R' Akiva believes that when people use the term 'eating,' they mean even a minute quantity. Thus, when he swore not to eat, he meant to prohibit by that oath even the smallest amount of food *(Rav).* This is based on a

3
1

1. Oaths are of two [types], which are [in reality] four: 'I swear that I will eat,' or '[I swear] that I will not eat;' '[I swear] that I ate,' or '[I swear] that I did not eat.'

[If he said,] 'I swear that I will not eat,' and he ate a minute quantity, he is liable; [these are] the words of R' Akiva. They said to R' Akiva: Where do we find that one who eats a minute quantity is liable, that this one should be liable? R' Akiva said to them: Where do we find one speaking and bringing a sacrifice, that this one speaks and brings a sacrifice?

YAD AVRAHAM

principle in regard to the laws of *nedarim* (vows), that the gauge used in interpreting the scope of a vow or oath is the meaning of the words in popular usage, not necessarily their Biblical meaning *(Nedarim* 30b, 49a; see *Yad Avraham* comm. to ArtScroll *Nedarim* 3:6, 6:1). Therefore, since the colloquial sense of the word 'eat' refers to even the smallest amount of food, R' Akiva is of the opinion that by eating it he has profaned his oath *(Tif. Yis.,* see *Tos. R' Akiva Eiger).*

אָמְרוּ לוֹ לְרַבִּי עֲקִיבָא: הֵיכָן מָצִינוּ בְּאוֹכֵל כָּל־שֶׁהוּא שֶׁהוּא חַיָּב, שֶׁזֶּה חַיָּב? — *They said to R' Akiva: Where do we find that one who eats a minute quantity is liable, that this one should be liable?*

The Sages dispute R' Akiva and contend that, as a rule, a person does not vow to abstain on conditions more stringent than those imposed by the Torah. Therefore, since in the Torah eating forbidden food is punishable only in the volume of an olive, it is probable that he meant this in his vow as well *(Tos.* 21b).

However, if he explicitly states in his oath that he will not eat even a minute quantity, even the Sages agree that he violates his oath with less than a *kezayis.* Similarly, if when making the vow he used the term I will not 'taste' (instead of 'eat'), then the reference is to any quantity *(Tos. Yom Tov* from *Gem.* 21b, 22b).

אָמַר לָהֶן רַבִּי עֲקִיבָא: וְכִי הֵיכָן מָצִינוּ בִּמְדַבֵּר וּמֵבִיא קָרְבָּן, שֶׁזֶּה מְדַבֵּר וּמֵבִיא קָרְבָּן? — *R' Akiva said to them: Where do we find one speaking and bringing a sacrifice, that this one speaks and brings a sacrifice?*

R' Akiva responds to the Sages' objection by pointing out that nowhere else do we find an instance of one pronouncing a prohibition on an article, which results in his having to bring a sacrifice for transgressing his own pronouncement. From this it is evident that the law of oaths is a unique law in that the liability for it is for transgressing his own words. Since R' Akiva's opinion is that in common usage eating implies even less than an olive, he is liable even for the smallest amount *(Rav; Rashi; Tif. Yis.).*

We do, however, find instances in which a person who commits a transgression with his speech *is* required to bring a sacrifice, e.g., the oath of the witnesses (explained in chapter 4), and the blasphemer who, according to R' Meir (with whom R' Akiva is in concurrence), are liable to a sacrifice (see *Kerisos* 1:1). Upon reflection, however, we find that those cases are not comparable to an oath of utterance, since in those cases the utterance itself constitutes the sin (the false testimony, the curse), whereas with an oath of utterance it is the act of transgressing the vow which is forbidden; his words merely make the act a forbidden one.

We find also that the *nazir* brings a sacrifice at the conclusion of his *nezirus,*

„שְׁבוּעָה שֶׁלֹּא אֹכַל," וְאָכַל וְשָׁתָה, אֵינוֹ חַיָּב אֶלָּא אַחַת. „שְׁבוּעָה שֶׁלֹּא אֹכַל וְשֶׁלֹּא אֶשְׁתֶּה," וְאָכַל וְשָׁתָה, חַיָּב שְׁתַּיִם.

[ב] „**שְׁבוּעָה** שֶׁלֹּא אֹכַל" — וְאָכַל פַּת חִטִּין, וּפַת שְׂעוֹרִין, וּפַת כֻּסְמִין, אֵינוֹ חַיָּב אֶלָּא אַחַת. „שְׁבוּעָה שֶׁלֹּא אֹכַל פַּת חִטִּין, וּפַת שְׂעוֹרִין, וּפַת כֻּסְמִין" — וְאָכַל, חַיָּב עַל־כָּל אַחַת וְאַחַת.

יד אברהם

which is something he pronounced upon himself. This sacrifice, however, is brought in order to permit the *nazir* to drink wine, not to atone for a sin, making the oath mentioned in our mishnah the sole instance where a sin-offering is brought for consuming food forbidden by a self-imposed prohibition (*Tos. Yom Tov* from *Gem.* 22a, *Tos.* ad loc.).

The halachah is not in accordance with R' Akiva. Rather, one is liable only if he eats an olive-sized piece, unless he specifies that he will not eat even the smallest quantity, or that he will not taste, in which case he is liable to a sacrifice for any amount (*Gem.* 22a).

Although there is no penalty for eating less than an olive-sized piece, most authorities rule that it is not permissible, but is governed by the same prohibition as eating a small amount of other forbidden foods (*Rambam, Hil. Shevuos* 4:1; *Ran*). This is the principle that any amount of non-kosher food is forbidden by the Torah (חֲצִי שִׁיעוּר אָסוּר מִן הַתּוֹרָה) — and it is only the penalty of lashes or other punishment which cannot be applied unless a *kezayis* was consumed (see *Yoma* 73b, 74a).

„שְׁבוּעָה שֶׁלֹּא אֹכַל", וְאָכַל וְשָׁתָה, — *'I swear that I will not eat', and he ate and drank,*

I.e., he forgot his oath and ate and drank repeatedly during a single period of forgetfulness (*Rav; Rashi*).

[If one violates one of the Torah's laws several times in one spell of forgetfulness, although he is liable for each individual transgression, he is obligated to bring only one sin-offering to atone for all of them upon becoming aware of his mistake. If, however, he transgressed two different laws in one period of unawareness, he brings two sin-offerings.

For example, if he forgot that it is forbidden to write on the Sabbath and he wrote an entire page, he brings only one offering. If he forgot the injunction against writing and planting and he performed both, he is liable to two sin-offerings.]

אֵינוֹ חַיָּב אֶלָּא אַחַת — *he is liable only once.*

Since drinking is included in the expression 'eating,' he is liable to only one sin-offering since it is tantamount to eating twice during one period of forgetfulness (*Rav* from *Gem.* 22b).

The *Gemara* bases the principle that drinking is included in the expression 'eating' on the verse dealing with the redemption of the second tithe, in which the Torah specifies wine among the various foodstuffs which may be purchased with the redemption money. The Torah concludes (*Deut.* 14:26): וְאָכַלְתָּ שָּׁם, *And you shall eat* [*the foodstuffs*] *there* [*in Jerusalem*]. This shows that drinking wine is referred to by the verse as eating.

This basis is not entirely satisfactory since this merely proves that drinking is included in the term 'eating' in Torah terminology. Oaths, however, are dependent upon the usages of the spoken language. The *Gemara*, therefore, offers the additional proof that when one says to his friend, 'Let us sit down to eat,' it is

3 'I swear that I will not eat,' and he ate and drank, he
2 is liable only once. [But if he said,] 'I swear that I will not eat and that I will not drink,' and he ate and drank, he is liable twice.

2. 'I swear that I will not eat' — and he ate wheat bread, barley bread, and spelt bread, he is liable only once. [But if he said,] 'I swear that I will eat neither wheat bread, nor barley bread, nor spelt bread' — and he ate, he is liable for each one.

YAD AVRAHAM

understood that they will eat and drink, showing that even in popular usage, drinking is included in the term 'eating' *(Tos. Yom Tov* from *Gem.* 23a, *Ran).*

„שְׁבוּעָה שֶׁלֹּא אֹכַל וְשֶׁלֹּא אֶשְׁתֶּה", — *[But if he said,] 'I swear that I will not eat and that I will not drink,'*

This is deemed as two separate oaths, one prohibiting eating and one prohibiting drinking *(Rav; Rashi).*

וְאָכַל וְשָׁתָה, — *and he ate and drank,*

[I.e., even in a single period of forgetfulness.]

חַיָּב שְׁתַּיִם — *he is liable twice.*

I.e., he is liable for each oath, as is indeed the reading found in some editions: חַיָּב עַל־כָּל־אֶחָד וְאֶחָד, *he is liable for each one (Meleches Shlomo).*

This raises a question. Since drinking is included in the expression 'eating', it would appear that when he swore not to eat, that oath would include drinking. Therefore, when he subsequently swore not to drink, that second oath should not have taken effect since his first oath had already prohibited drinking and one cannot prohibit by oath something already prohibited by a previous oath (see below, mishnah 7). Thus, he should only be liable once!

The *Gemara* (23a) answers that since he immediately followed his oath not to eat with another one not to drink, he indicated clearly that with his first oath he meant only to prohibit himself from eating, not from drinking *(Rav).*

2.

„שְׁבוּעָה שֶׁלֹּא אֹכַל" — וְאָכַל פַּת חִטִּין, וּפַת שְׂעוֹרִין, וּפַת כֻּסְמִין, — *'I swear that I will not eat' — and he ate wheat bread, barley bread, and spelt bread,*

He ate these three varieties of bread within one period of forgetfulness *(Meiri).*[1]

אֵינוֹ חַיָּב אֶלָּא אַחַת. — *he is liable only once.*

Since he included them all in one statement — *'I will not eat'*, they are all treated as part of a single oath. Thus, by eating the different types of bread he is actually transgressing the same oath a number of times during one period of forgetfulness. He is therefore obligated to bring only one sin-offering *(Meiri).*

„שְׁבוּעָה שֶׁלֹּא אֹכַל פַּת חִטִּין, וּפַת שְׂעוֹרִין, וּפַת כֻּסְמִין" — *[But if he said,] 'I swear that I will eat neither wheat bread, nor barley bread, nor spelt bread' —*

In this case, he specifies the various types of bread he will not eat *(Meiri).*

וְאָכַל — *and he ate,*

I.e., he ate from each of these types of bread *(Rambam Comm.).*

חַיָּב עַל־כָּל אַחַת וְאַחַת. — *he is liable for each one.*

Since he repeated the word *bread* with

1. The same ruling would apply to a deliberate violation if he ate all three with one warning. In this case it would be relevant to how many sets of lashes he would be liable *(Meiri).*

[ג] „שְׁבוּעָה שֶׁלֹּא אֶשְׁתֶּה" — וְשָׁתָה מַשְׁקִין הַרְבֵּה, אֵינוֹ חַיָּב אֶלָּא אַחַת.
„שְׁבוּעָה שֶׁלֹּא אֶשְׁתֶּה יַיִן וְשֶׁמֶן וּדְבַשׁ" — וְשָׁתָה, חַיָּב עַל־כָּל אַחַת וְאַחַת.

[ד] „שְׁבוּעָה שֶׁלֹּא אֹכַל" — וְאָכַל אֳכָלִים שֶׁאֵינָן רְאוּיִן לַאֲכִילָה, וְשָׁתָה מַשְׁקִין שֶׁאֵינָן רְאוּיִן לִשְׁתִיָּה, פָּטוּר.
„שְׁבוּעָה שֶׁלֹּא אֹכַל" — וְאָכַל נְבֵלוֹת, וּטְרֵפוֹת, שְׁקָצִים, וּרְמָשִׂים, חַיָּב. רַבִּי שִׁמְעוֹן פּוֹטֵר.

יד אברהם

each type, we assume that he definitely intended to give each one the status of an individual oath *(Rav)*. We therefore understand the declaration, 'I will not eat,' to be a separate oath for each type of food specified *(Meiri)*. Should his intention have been merely to specify that these three breads be prohibited as part of one oath, he should have said, 'I will not eat wheat bread, nor barley, nor spelt', without repeating the word *bread* each time *(Rav* from *Gem.* 23b).

Actually, he could also have said, 'bread of wheat, barley and spelt', to express his inclusion of all three in a single oath. However, that would have been misleading since that expression could be construed to mean that he would not eat a bread made of a combination of these three grains *(Tos. R' Akiva* from *Gem.* ad loc.).

3.

„שְׁבוּעָה שֶׁלֹּא אֶשְׁתֶּה" — וְשָׁתָה מַשְׁקִין הַרְבֵּה, — *'I swear that I will not drink' — and he drank many beverages,*

[I.e., in one period of forgetfulness.]

אֵינוֹ חַיָּב אֶלָּא אַחַת. — *he is liable only once.*

[Since the one oath 'I will not drink' includes all types of beverages under one heading, he is liable to only one sin-offering.]

„שְׁבוּעָה שֶׁלֹּא אֶשְׁתֶּה יַיִן וְשֶׁמֶן וּדְבַשׁ" — וְשָׁתָה, — *[But if he said,] 'I swear that I will drink neither wine, nor oil, nor honey' — and he drank,*

[I.e., he drank all three of these liquids. *Oil* refers to olive oil.]

חַיָּב עַל־כָּל אַחַת וְאַחַת. — *he is liable for each one.*

This oath is considered in reality three separate oaths, and he is therefore separately liable for violating each one.

The *Gemara* (23b), however, notes that these words could just as well indicate a single oath prohibiting just these three beverages — indeed had he wished to make such an oath he could not have said anything else. Consequently, the *Gemara* qualifies the mishnah as referring to a case in which someone is urging him to drink wine, oil, and honey, and he refuses to do so, swearing to reinforce his refusal. If he intended only one general oath he should have said, 'I swear that I will not drink with you,' and no more. It would then be obvious that he means not to drink any of these three liquids *(Rav* from *Gem.* 23b). Since he specified each item, he means each to be a separate oath — 'I will not drink wine,' 'I will not drink oil,' etc.

3. 'I swear that I will not drink' — and he drank many beverages, he is liable only once. [But if he said,] 'I swear that I will drink neither wine, nor oil, nor honey' — and he drank, he is liable for each one.

4. 'I swear that I will not eat' — and he ate foods that are unfit to eat or drank beverages that are unfit to drink, he is exempt.

'I swear that I will not eat' — and he ate *neveilos, treifos,* abominable creatures, or crawling things, he is liable. R' Shimon exempts [him].

YAD AVRAHAM

4.

„שְׁבוּעָה שֶׁלֹּא אֹכַל" — וְאָכַל אֳכָלִים שֶׁאֵינָן רְאוּיִן לַאֲכִילָה, וְשָׁתָה מַשְׁקִין שֶׁאֵינָן רְאוּיִן לִשְׁתִיָּה, פָּטוּר. — *'I swear that I will not eat' — and he ate foods that are unfit to eat or drank beverages that are unfit to drink, he is exempt.*

E.g., he ate earth *(Rashi* 24a). We assume that a person using the word *eat* in an oath has in mind to interdict only foods and beverages that are fit for human consumption *(Ran).*

However, should he swear explicitly not to eat earth, he is liable for its consumption *(Gem.* 22b).

The *Gemara* questions the minimum amount of earth punishable. On the one hand, since he words his oath with the term 'eating,' which is usually reserved for an olive-sized amount (see above, mishnah 1, the opinion of the Sages), it would make sense to assume that here also the minimum is an olive-sized amount. On the other hand, since earth is in any case not edible, there is no difference between eating an olive-sized amount and the smallest quantity. The question remains unresolved. Consequently, no penalty is meted out, nor is a sacrifice brought, for eating less than an olive-sized amount *(Rambam, Hil. Shevuos* 5:8).

„שְׁבוּעָה שֶׁלֹּא אֹכַל" — וְאָכַל נְבֵלוֹת, וּטְרֵפוֹת, שְׁקָצִים, וּרְמָשִׂים, — *'I swear that I will not eat' — and he ate neveilos, treifos, abominable creatures, or crawling things,*

I.e., he ate things prohibited by the Torah. For the definition of שְׁקָצִים, *abominable creatures,* and רְמָשִׂים, *crawling things,* see *Makkos* 3:2.

חַיָּב. — *he is liable.*

Since these foods are, in fact, edible, except for the Torah's prohibition of them, they are included in the term *eat.* They are therefore included in the terms of the oath *(Rav).* The *Gemara* (22b) likens the Torah's prohibitions of them to a lion crouched over the foods, preventing them from being eaten. Though such foods cannot be eaten, practically speaking, this in no way detracts from their being classified as edible foods *(Rashi).*

However, granting that forbidden foods are classified as edibles, there is still a problem in their being included in this oath. Above (comm. to the end of mishnah 1, s.v. חיב שתים) we learned that an oath does not take effect on something already prohibited by an oath. For this reason, the *Gemara* (23b) asks how an oath can take effect in regard to foods prohibited by the Torah, when it is considered as if all Israel had sworn at Mount Sinai not to eat these forbidden foods. [And if the oath not to eat does *not* include forbidden foods, his consumption of them would not constitute a violation of his oath.]

שבועות ג/ד

אָמַר: "קוֹנָם אִשְׁתִּי נֶהֱנֵית לִי אִם אָכַלְתִּי הַיּוֹם," וְהוּא אָכַל נְבֵלוֹת, וּטְרֵפוֹת, שְׁקָצִים, וּרְמָשִׂים, הֲרֵי אִשְׁתּוֹ אֲסוּרָה.

יד אברהם

The *Gemara* (24a, as understood by *Rashi*) concludes that a non-specific oath such as 'I will not eat' is an example of an אִסּוּר כּוֹלֵל, *an inclusive prohibition*, viz., one which includes both things heretofore permissible and things already prohibited. This type of prohibition constitutes a technical exception to the rule concerning double oaths. Since the new prohibition takes effect in regard to the previously permissible things, it takes effect in regard to the prohibited things as well. Consequently, since the oath prohibited him from eating permissible foods, it also prohibited him from eating forbidden foods, and his consumption of them constitutes a violation of his oath.

There is a rule that one is not liable for transgressing an oath of utterance unless it oath can be sworn both in the positive and in the negative (see mishnah 6). For example, the oath, 'I swear that I will eat bread,' can render one liable since one also has the option to swear not to eat it (*Gem.* 24a). However, in our case, one cannot swear in the positive to eat these forbidden foods since the Torah bars him from doing so. How then can one be liable for the oath not to eat them?

Rashi (24a) replies that since one can swear that he will eat, and fulfill the oath by eating permissible foods, this oath meets the qualification of the positive and negative formulation. Thus, he is liable even if he eats prohibited foods, such as *neveilos*, *treifos*, abominable creatures, and crawling things.

The commentary has to this point followed the view of *Rashi*. *Tosafos*, however, explain the mishnah differently. They contend that forbidden foods are legally regarded as foods unfit for eating, and in the same class as earth. Consequently, if one makes a general unqualified oath not to eat, that would not include forbidden foods, just as earth is excluded, and if he ate them he would *not* be liable for a sin-offering for violating his oath. This is included in the mishnah's first ruling concerning inedible foods.

The second ruling of the mishnah, which holds him liable for eating forbidden foods, deals with one who swears explicitly not to eat *neveilos* (for example). This is the equivalent of one who swears not to eat earth, which, as explained above, makes him liable for eating earth. However, should his oath specify only *neveilos*, the oath would have no bearing since they are already interdicted by the Torah, as explained above. Accordingly, *Tos.* explain that the mishnah must refer to a case in which he specifically coupled his oath on *neveilos* with an oath on kosher foods. I.e., he said, 'I will eat neither *neveilos* nor kosher foods.' Such an oath constitutes an inclusive prohibition (as explained above) and causes the oath to take effect in regard to the forbidden foods as well.

As regards the requirement of the possibility of the oath being sworn in both the positive and the negative sense, which is apparently lacking here since he cannot swear that he will eat both *neveilos* and kosher foods, *Tosafos* suggest that it is possible to swear to eat decayed *neveilos*, which are permissible, being no longer fit for human consumption.[1]

.רַבִּי שִׁמְעוֹן פּוֹטֵר — *R' Shimon exempts [him].*

R' Shimon does not subscribe to the principle of the *inclusive prohibition*. Therefore, the oath does not include forbidden foods (*Rav* from *Gem.* 24a).

The halachah is not in accordance with R' Shimon *(Rav; Rambam Comm.)*.

1. *Rav* seems to incorporate elements of both *Rashi's* and *Tosafos'* explanation into his own and there is some question as to which opinion he actually follows. See *Tos. Yom Tov* and *Tos. R' Akiva Eiger*.

3 [If] he said, *'Konam* that my wife derive pleasure
4 from me if I have eaten today,' and he had eaten
neveilos, treifos, abominable creatures, or crawling
things, his wife is forbidden.

YAD AVRAHAM

◆§ Neder, Konam

If a person wishes to deprive himself of the benefit of a particular object, he can make it Biblically forbidden to himself by means of a נֶדֶר, *neder* (loosely translated, *vow;* pl. *nedarim).* This is a type of declaration, recognized by the Torah as a binding vow, which imparts a prohibited status to an object relative to that person. If, for example, a person says: 'The benefit of this bread is forbidden me like an offering,' it would be prohibited for him to eat or otherwise benefit from the bread. He can also prohibit that which is his to others (but not someone else's property to anyone but himself).

Generally, the formula of a *neder* involves declaring something to be forbidden like a sacrifice. [See *Yad Avraham* to ArtScroll *Nedarim* pp. 20, 24 for an explanation.] When referring to a sacrifice — קָרְבָּן, *korban,* in Hebrew — one may substitute colloquial equivalent terms. The most popular of these substitutes seems to have been the term *konam.*

אָמַר: ,,קוֹנָם אִשְׁתִּי נֶהֱנֵית לִי — *[If] he said, 'Konam that my wife derive pleasure from me*

He pronounced a *neder* upon himself forbidding his wife from deriving pleasure from him. This cannot be referring to all pleasures, since a husband is bound to provide his wife with food and clothing, as well as conjugal relations. Thus, the mishnah must mean that he prohibits other pleasures which he is not obligated to bestow upon her *(Tos. Yom Tov).*

אִם אָכַלְתִּי הַיּוֹם,, — *if I have eaten today,'*

[I.e., he makes his *neder* conditional on his having eaten that day.]

וְהוּא אָכַל נְבֵלוֹת, וּטְרֵפוֹת, שְׁקָצִים, וּרְמָשִׂים, — *and he had eaten neveilos, treifos, abominable creatures, or crawling things.*

The only things he had eaten that day were these forbidden foods.

The mishnah must also be speaking of a case in which he was aware that he had eaten at the time of his *neder*. Otherwise, this would fit into the category of unwitting *nedarim,* as in *Nedarim* 3:2, and the *neder* would be invalid even though the condition was fulfilled *(Tos. Yom Tov). Rosh* in *Nedarim* explains the concept of unwitting *nedarim* to be that if at the time of the declaration he mistakenly thought that he had not eaten or drunk, then he never intended for his *neder* to create any prohibitions. Furthermore, from his addition of the conditional clause 'If I have eaten today,' it is clear that he never intended to effect a *neder.* It is, therefore, not binding. Thus, although he subsequently remembers that he *did* eat or drink, no prohibition results.

הֲרֵי אִשְׁתּוֹ אֲסוּרָה. — *his wife is forbidden.*

Since he had, in fact, eaten food, the *neder* is valid even according to R' Shimon. Although R' Shimon previously exempted the consumption of forbidden foods from the violation of an oath on eating, this was not because the consumption of forbidden foods is not considered eating, but because an oath cannot take effect upon something already prohibited, even (in his view) when it is done through an *inclusive prohibition (Rav).* [Thus, it has no bearing in this case in which the issue is the fulfillment of the condition triggering the *neder*, not the effectiveness of the oath itself.]

[ה] **אֶחָד** דְּבָרִים שֶׁל־עַצְמוֹ וְאֶחָד דְּבָרִים שֶׁל־אֲחֵרִים; וְאֶחָד דְּבָרִים שֶׁיֵּשׁ בָּהֶן מַמָּשׁ וְאֶחָד דְּבָרִים שֶׁאֵין בָּהֶן מַמָּשׁ. כֵּיצַד? אָמַר: „שְׁבוּעָה שֶׁאֶתֵּן לְאִישׁ פְּלוֹנִי,‟ וְ„שֶׁלֹּא אֶתֵּן‟; „שֶׁנָּתַתִּי, וְ„שֶׁלֹּא נָתַתִּי‟; „שֶׁאִישַׁן,‟ וְ„שֶׁלֹּא אִישַׁן‟; „שֶׁיָּשַׁנְתִּי‟, וְ„שֶׁלֹּא יָשַׁנְתִּי‟; „שֶׁאֶזְרֹק צְרוֹר לַיָּם,‟ וְ„שֶׁלֹּא אֶזְרֹק‟; „שֶׁזָּרַקְתִּי,‟ וְ„שֶׁלֹּא זָרַקְתִּי‟. רַבִּי יִשְׁמָעֵאל אוֹמֵר: אֵינוֹ חַיָּב אֶלָּא עַל־הֶעָתִיד לָבֹא, שֶׁנֶּאֱמַר: „לְהָרַע אוֹ לְהֵיטִיב.‟ אָמַר לוֹ רַבִּי עֲקִיבָא:

יד אברהם

5.

The following mishnah begins to delineate the scope of oaths of utterance, paying particular attention to the dispute between R' Akiva and R' Yishmael, whether one is liable for an oath of utterance concerning the past.

אֶחָד דְּבָרִים שֶׁל־עַצְמוֹ — *[The law applies] both to matters pertaining to himself*

I.e., matters pertaining only to himself, such as 'I will eat,' or 'I will not eat' *(Tif. Yis.)*.

וְאֶחָד דְּבָרִים שֶׁל־אֲחֵרִים; — *as well as to matters pertaining to others;*

I.e., an oath regarding one's actions towards someone else, e.g., an oath to give a gift or not to give, as will be explained further in the mishnah. Although Scripture states: לְהָרַע אוֹ לְהֵיטִיב, *to do bad or to do good*, which means that one is liable for an oath to do bad or good to himself, it also includes doing bad or good to others *(Meiri)*.

וְאֶחָד דְּבָרִים שֶׁיֵּשׁ בָּהֶן מַמָּשׁ וְאֶחָד דְּבָרִים שֶׁאֵין בָּהֶן מַמָּשׁ. — *and to both matters of substance and matters lacking substance.*

Matters lacking substance are of two kinds: one concerning things completely intangible, such as an oath regarding sleep; the other, actions which afford no benefit, such as casting a pebble into the sea, as below *(Rav; Rashi)*.

Since the oath places an obligation or an interdict upon the person pronouncing it, it is irrelevant whether it deals with a tangible or an intangible object *(Meiri)*. Cf. ArtScroll *Nedarim* p. 33, s.v. שְׁבוּעָה.

כֵּיצַד? — *How so?*

[What would be an example of an oath of utterance as it applies to others and to matters lacking substance?]

אָמַר: „שְׁבוּעָה שֶׁאֶתֵּן לְאִישׁ פְּלוֹנִי,‟ וְ„שֶׁלֹּא אֶתֵּן‟; — *[If] he said, 'I swear that I will give to so-and-so,' or 'that I will not give';*

[This is an example of an oath pertaining to others.]

In a case in which the intended recipient is a poor man, the oath to give him a gift has no effect since he is obligated in any case to give him charity, and an oath pronounced on something which one is obligated to do by a *mitzvah* is of no consequence. This mishnah deals with an oath to give a gift to a wealthy person, to whom there is no *mitzvah* to give money *(Tos. Yom Tov* from *Gem.* 25a).

„שֶׁנָּתַתִּי,‟ וְ„שֶׁלֹּא נָתַתִּי‟; — *[or] 'that I gave,' or 'that I did not give';*

[I.e., he swore an oath pertaining to others concerning a past action, viz., that he gave a gift to a certain person, or that he did not give.]

5. [The law applies] both to matters pertaining to himself as well as to matters pertaining to others; and to both matters of substance and matters lacking substance. How so? [If] he said, 'I swear that I will give to so-and-so,' or 'that I will not give'; [or] 'that I gave,' or 'that I did not give'; 'that I will sleep,' or 'that I will not sleep'; 'that I slept,' or 'that I did not sleep'; 'that I will cast a pebble into the sea,' or 'that I will not cast'; [or] 'that I have cast,' or 'that I have not cast.' R' Yishmael says: He is liable only for [oaths concerning] the future. As it states (*Lev.* 5:4): *To do bad or to do good.*

YAD AVRAHAM

„שֶׁאִישַׁן," וְ„שֶׁלֹּא אִישַׁן"; — *'that I will sleep,' or 'that I will not sleep';*

This is something intangible, but is nevertheless interdicted by an oath. Cf. *Nedarim* 2:1 (*Tos. Yom Tov*).

Should he say, 'I swear that I will not sleep for three days,' he would be immediately liable for lashes. Since it is impossible to stay awake for three consecutive days, this oath is adjudged a vain oath [שְׁבוּעַת שָׁוְא] for which one receives lashes (see mishnah 8). Since the oath does not take effect as an oath of utterance, he may sleep immediately. The mishnah, therefore, must be qualified as referring to a case in which he explicitly swears not to sleep for some period less than three days (*Gem.* 25a).

Should he make an unqualified statement, 'I swear that I will not sleep,' we assume the intention is that he will never sleep, which is surely a vain oath (*Rama, Yoreh Deah* 236:4). However, should he state that he meant only to abstain from sleep for one day, he is believed, and the oath takes effect (*Shach, Yoreh Deah* 236:1, quoting *Bach*).

„שֶׁיָּשַׁנְתִּי," וְ„שֶׁלֹּא יָשַׁנְתִּי"; — *'that I slept,' or 'that I did not sleep';*

This is the past case of the preceding oath, and is also an oath dealing with the intangible (*Tif. Yis.*).

„שֶׁאֶזְרֹק צְרוֹר לַיָּם," וְ„שֶׁלֹּא אֶזְרֹק"; „שֶׁזָּרַקְתִּי," וְ„שֶׁלֹּא זָרַקְתִּי." — *'that I will cast a pebble into the sea,' or 'that I will not cast'*; [or] *'that I have cast,' or 'that I have not cast.'*

These are also considered matters lacking substance, since they involve actions which afford no benefit, as mentioned above (*Tif. Yis.*).

רַבִּי יִשְׁמָעֵאל אוֹמֵר: אֵינוֹ חַיָּב אֶלָּא עַל־הֶעָתִיד לָבֹא. — *R' Yishmael says: He is liable only for* [*oaths concerning*] *the future.*

R' Yishmael disagrees with the mishnah at the beginning of our tractate, which states *oaths are of two* [*types*], *which are* [*in reality*] *four,* meaning two pertaining to events in the future and two concerning the past. In his view one is liable to a sin-offering only for transgressing an oath pertaining to the future (*Tif. Yis.* from *Gem.* 4a).

However, an oath concerning the past is still considered an oath, even according to R' Yishmael, and if it was deliberately false he is liable to lashes. He merely states that the only oath for which one is liable to a variable sin-offering (for an inadvertent transgression of the oath of utterance) is one concerning the future, not one concerning the past (*Gem.* 3b).

שֶׁנֶּאֱמַר: „לְהָרַע אוֹ לְהֵיטִיב." — *As it states (Lev. 5:4): 'To do bad or to do good.'*

[As was previously explained (1:1), *to do bad* means swearing to refrain from doing something, while *to do good* refers to an oath to perform an act. Both the

שבועות
ג/ו

אִם־כֵּן, אֵין לִי אֶלָּא דְבָרִים שֶׁיֵּשׁ בָּהֶן הֲרָעָה וַהֲטָבָה; דְּבָרִים שֶׁאֵין בָּהֶן הֲרָעָה וַהֲטָבָה מִנַּיִן? אָמַר לוֹ: מֵרִבּוּי הַכָּתוּב. אָמַר לוֹ: אִם רִבָּה הַכָּתוּב לְכָךְ, רִבָּה הַכָּתוּב לְכָךְ.

[ו] **נִשְׁבַּע** לְבַטֵּל אֶת־הַמִּצְוָה, וְלֹא בִטֵּל, פָּטוּר; לְקַיֵּם וְלֹא קִיֵּם, פָּטוּר. שֶׁהָיָה

יד אברהם

oaths are expressed in the future tense. From this R' Yishmael derives that one is liable only for an oath concerning the future.]

אָמַר לוֹ רַבִּי עֲקִיבָא: אִם־כֵּן, אֵין לִי אֶלָּא דְבָרִים שֶׁיֵּשׁ בָּהֶן הֲרָעָה וַהֲטָבָה; — *Said R' Akiva to him: If so, we* [lit. *I*] *know only of things pertaining to doing bad or good;*

[If you interpret the verse literally, as referring only to what is stated explicitly, then we can only derive from it that one is liable to bring a sin-offering for an oath to do good or bad, for example, to eat or to refrain from eating, since that is the strict sense of the text.]

דְּבָרִים שֶׁאֵין בָּהֶן הֲרָעָה וַהֲטָבָה מִנַּיִן? — [*but*] *how do we know of things not pertaining to doing bad or good?*

[How would you derive the liability for an oath that does not involve those factors? Since even R' Yishmael agrees that the law applies to these other cases, it is clear that the verse is not to be taken quite so restrictively.]

אָמַר לוֹ: מֵרִבּוּי הַכָּתוּב. — *He said to him: From the extension of the verse.*

R' Yishmael replied to R' Akiva that these other oaths may be derived from the continuation of the verse: לְכֹל אֲשֶׁר יְבַטֵּא הָאָדָם בִּשְׁבֻעָה, *for anything that a person utters in an oath.* The generalization implied by the term *for anything that a person utters* teaches us to include oaths other than those pertaining to doing bad or good (*Rav* from *Gem.* 26a).

אָמַר לוֹ: אִם רִבָּה הַכָּתוּב לְכָךְ, רִבָּה הַכָּתוּב לְכָךְ. — *He said to him: If the verse extended it in that regard, the verse extended it in this regard* [*as well*].

R' Akiva replied to R' Yishmael that if the generalization implied in the verse extends the liability of oaths of utterance to include even those not pertaining to doing bad or good, it should also extend the liability to include oaths pertaining to the past (*Rav*).

The *Gemara* (26a) explains that R' Yishmael and R' Akiva disagree concerning the method of expounding the verse. R' Akiva subscribes to the method of hermeneutical exposition known as רִבּוּי וּמִעוּט, *amplification and limitation;* R' Yishmael subscribes to the counter-method known as כְּלָל וּפְרָט, *generalization and specification.*[1] R' Akiva explains the verse as amplifying, limiting, and again amplifying. According to this

1. According to the hermeneutic principle, כְּלָל וּפְרָט אֵין בַּכְּלָל אֶלָּא מַה שֶּׁבַּפְּרָט, where a general proposition is followed by the enumeration of particulars which are already comprehended in the general proposition, the scope of the proposition is limited to the items specified. If it is then followed by a second כְּלָל, another general proposition, this second כְּלָל renders the specific cases mentioned as examples, and the proposition then applies to all things which are similar to the specific cases. Other *Tannaim* interpret Scriptural phrases according to the rule of רִבּוּי מִיעוּט וְרִבּוּי. The rule is similar, differing only in what is included in the מִיעוּט, the limiting case. Here the מִיעוּט, *limitation,* is restricted to what is expressly listed plus one other similar example, and is not to be taken as a general example to exclude all other items that are similar.

3
6 Said R' Akiva to him: If so, we know only of things pertaining to doing bad or good; [but] how do we know of things not pertaining to doing bad or good? He said to him: From the extension of the verse. He said to him: If the verse extended it in that regard, the verse extended it in this regard [as well].

6. [If] one swore to annul a *mitzvah*, and did not annul it, he is exempt; to fulfill [a *mitzvah*] and he

method, the amplification of the basic law teaches us to include in it all cases which fit the general guidelines of the law while the limitation inserted in the verse excludes but one thing. Thus, the verse concerning oaths of utterances, which states: או נֶפֶשׁ כִּי תִשָּׁבַע לְבַטֵּא בִשְׂפָתַיִם, *Or if a person swear by uttering with his lips*, is a רִבּוּי, *amplification*, followed by the מִעוּט, *limitation*, לְהָרַע או לְהֵיטִיב, *to do bad or to do good*. [This limits the general category of oaths to oaths to refrain from or to require some form of action.] This is in turn followed by the clause: לְכֹל אֲשֶׁר יְבַטֵּא הָאָדָם בִּשְׁבֻעָה, *for anything that a person utters in an oath*. This is again a רִבּוּי, *amplification*, expanding the laws of this verse to all kinds of oaths, both future and past. Following the hermeneutical system of amplification, limitation, and amplification, we therefore include both future and past in the rules of oaths of utterance and exclude only one type of oath — an oath pertaining to a *mitzvah*, as the following mishnah will explain.

R' Yishmael, however, interprets the verse according to the method of כְּלָל וּפְרָט וּכְלָל, *generalization, specification and generalization* [substituting *generalization* for R' Akiva's *amplification*, etc.]. According to this method, the generalization can only include that which is similar to the specification — in this case, oaths that are neither good nor bad — but not things which are completely dissimilar to the specification. Thus, the liability is limited to oaths pertaining to the future, not those pertaining to the past.

The halachah is in accordance with R' Akiva *(Rav; Rambam Comm.* and *Hil. Shevuos* 1:2).

6.

נִשְׁבַּע לְבַטֵּל אֶת־הַמִּצְוָה, — *[If] one swore to annul a mitzvah,*

I.e., he made an oath not to fulfill a positive *mitzvah*, such as putting on *tefillin*, or to transgress a negative one, such as writing on the Sabbath *(Tif. Yis.)*.

וְלֹא בִטֵּל, — *and did not annul it,*

[I.e., he fulfilled the positive *mitzvah*, or refrained from transgressing the negative one, thereby violating his oath.]

פָּטוּר; — *he is exempt;*

He is exempt from the penalties of transgressing an oath of utterance because such an oath is not considered an oath of utterance. This is based on the Torah's specification that in order to qualify as an oath of utterance it must be an oath *to do bad or to do good*. The intention is that he is liable only if the oath is about something objectively beneficial or detrimental. Eating is beneficial to the body, while not eating is detrimental, since one mortifies his body by abstaining from food. This reasoning applies only in the case of optional matters. In the case of a *mitzvah*, however, if one swears to eat forbidden food, it is on the one hand an oath to do good

שבועות
ג/ו

בַּדִּין שֶׁיְּהֵא חַיָּב, כְּדִבְרֵי רַבִּי יְהוּדָה בֶּן־בְּתֵירָא. אָמַר רַבִּי יְהוּדָה בֶּן־בְּתֵירָא: מָה אִם הָרְשׁוּת, שֶׁאֵינוֹ מֻשְׁבָּע עָלֶיהָ מֵהַר סִינַי, הֲרֵי הוּא חַיָּב עָלֶיהָ; מִצְוָה, שֶׁהוּא מֻשְׁבָּע עָלֶיהָ מֵהַר סִינַי, אֵינוֹ דִין שֶׁיְּהֵא חַיָּב עָלֶיהָ? אָמְרוּ לוֹ: לֹא! אִם אָמַרְתָּ בִּשְׁבוּעַת הָרְשׁוּת, שֶׁכֵּן עָשָׂה בָהּ לָאו כְּהֵן. תֹּאמַר בִּשְׁבוּעַת מִצְוָה, שֶׁלֹּא עָשָׂה בָהּ לָאו כְּהֵן? שֶׁאִם נִשְׁבַּע לְבַטֵּל וְלֹא בִטֵּל, פָּטוּר.

יד אברהם

[He is exempt, however, only from oath-related penalties, but he is subject to whatever penalties apply to one who transgresses the *mitzvah* which was the subject of his oath.]

Meiri, however, rules that although an oath to fulfill a *mitzvah* is not deemed a vain oath at the time of its pronouncement, should he transgress it, it becomes a vain oath retroactively. [His reasoning is probably that, since the purpose of the oath was to inspire him to fulfill the commandment, if he neglected it, the oath turns out to have been of no value. It therefore becomes a vain oath retroactively. This is a unique view.] *Rambam (Hil. Shevuos* 5:16) may also follow *Meiri's* view, though his wording is ambiguous and subject to other interpretations (see *Radbaz* ad loc.).

שֶׁהָיָה בַדִּין שֶׁיְּהֵא חַיָּב, — *For it might have been inferred that he be liable,*

I.e., it would be possible to infer from a קַל וָחֹמֶר [*kal vachomer*], *a conclusion inferred from a lenient law to a strict one,* that he be liable for transgressing an oath of utterance even for failing to keep an oath to fulfill a *mitzvah (Rav).*

כְּדִבְרֵי רַבִּי יְהוּדָה בֶּן־בְּתֵירָא: — *as is the opinion of R' Yehudah ben Beseira:*

R' Yehudah ben Beseira indeed rules that he is liable, for he infers it from a *kal vachomer,* as follows *(Rav; Rashi):*

אָמַר רַבִּי יְהוּדָה בֶּן־בְּתֵירָא: מָה אִם הָרְשׁוּת, — *Said R' Yehudah ben Beseira: If for an optional matter,*

[I.e., if one swears to perform an optional matter and fails to perform it.]

since it benefits his body; at the same time, however, it is an oath to do bad, since he is inflicting harm on his soul. Conversely, should he swear not to eat *chametz* on Pesach, although he is depriving his body of the *chametz* — an oath to do bad — at the same time he is benefiting his soul by abstaining from forbidden food, the *to do good* aspect of the oath. Therefore, the penalty of transgressing an oath of utterance applies neither to an oath to annul a *mitzvah* nor to an oath to fulfill a *mitzvah (Tos. Yom Tov* from *Rambam Comm.* from *Gem.* 27a).

However, though he is not liable for an oath of utterance, he is nevertheless liable for swearing a vain oath, since he swore about something which is impossible [see mishnah 8] *(Rav).*

לְקַיֵּם וְלֹא קִיֵּם, — *to fulfill* [*a mitzvah*] *and he did not fulfill* [*it*],

I.e., if one swore to fulfill either a positive *mitzvah* or a negative one *(Tif. Yis.),* and he did not abide by his oath and did not fulfill the *mitzvah.*

פָּטוּר. — *he is exempt.*

In this case, he is entirely exempt, not only from the penalty due for transgressing an oath of utterance, but also from the penalty for a vain oath. Although the oath does not take effect, it is not considered swearing in vain, since swearing to fulfill a *mitzvah* in order to urge himself on is considered meritorious *(Tif. Yis.; Meiri* to *Nedarim* 8a).

3 did not fulfill [it], he is exempt. For it might have been
6 inferred that he be liable, as is the opinion of R′ Yehudah ben Beseira. Said R′ Yehudah ben Beseira: If for an optional matter, concerning which he was not adjured from Mount Sinai, he is liable; [then] for a *mitzvah,* concerning which he is adjured from Mount Sinai, is it not certain that he should be liable? They said to him: No! If you say this as regards an optional oath, it is because [Scripture] has made negative equal to positive in that regard. Will you say this in the case of an oath to fulfill a *mitzvah,* in which [Scripture] did not make negative equal to positive? For if he swears to annul it and does not annul it, he is exempt.

YAD AVRAHAM

שֶׁאֵינוֹ מֻשְׁבָּע עָלֶיהָ מֵהַר סִינַי, הֲרֵי הוּא חַיָּב עָלֶיהָ; — *concerning which he was not adjured from Mount Sinai, he is liable;*

[Before he pronounced this oath upon himself the Torah did not adjure him to perform this optional matter. Nevertheless, once he swears an oath of utterance to do it he is liable if he does not adhere to it.]

מִצְוָה, שֶׁהוּא מֻשְׁבָּע עָלֶיהָ מֵהַר סִינַי, אֵינוֹ דִין שֶׁיְּהֵא חַיָּב עָלֶיהָ? — *[then] for a mitzvah, concerning which he is adjured from Mount Sinai, is it not certain that he should be liable?*

[I.e., if one swears to keep a *mitzvah* which he was commanded by God at Mount Sinai to perform, he should most certainly be liable if he does not fulfill it. If the Torah commands a man to keep his oath concerning mundane matters, then surely the Torah would expect him to be true to his vow when it involves a *mitzvah.*]

אָמְרוּ לוֹ: לֹא! אִם אָמַרְתָּ בִּשְׁבוּעַת הָרְשׁוּת, שֶׁכֵּן עָשָׂה בָהּ לָאו כְּהֵן. — *They said to him: No! If you say this as regards an optional oath, it is because [Scripture] has made negative equal to positive in that regard.*

I.e., the Sages reject R′ Yehudah ben Beseira's reasoning because it is more reasonable to assume that the Scriptural edict on oaths of utterance — *to do bad or do good* — applies only to optional matters, where one has the option either to do them or not to do them *(Rav).*

תֹּאמַר בִּשְׁבוּעַת מִצְוָה, שֶׁלֹּא עָשָׂה בָהּ לָאו כְּהֵן? שֶׁאִם נִשְׁבַּע לְבַטֵּל וְלֹא בִטֵּל, פָּטוּר. — *Will you say this in the case of an oath to fulfill a mitzvah, in which [Scripture] did not make negative equal to positive? For if he swears to annul it and does not annul it, he is exempt.*

I.e., the option to do or not to do does not apply to oaths concerning the *mitzvos.* Even R′ Yehudah ben Beseira agrees that only an oath to conform with the Biblical command [e.g., *to perform a mitzvah*] is valid [since it reinforces the Biblical command], but not an oath to violate a *mitzvah.*[1] For example, if one swears not to take a *lulav* or not to sit in a *sukkah,* and he does take the *lulav* or sit in the *sukkah,* he is exempt from any penalty for violating his oath even according to R′ Yehudah ben Beseira. Thus,

1. Since there is no *kal vachomer* to make him liable for an oath to annul what he was adjured on Mount Sinai, even R′ Yehudah ben Beseira concurs with the Sages that he is exempt from the penalty of the oath of utterance *(Tos. Yom Tov).*

[ז] „שְׁבוּעָה שֶׁלֹּא אֹכַל כִּכָּר זוֹ"; „שְׁבוּעָה שֶׁלֹּא אֹכְלֶנָּה," „שְׁבוּעָה שֶׁלֹּא אֹכְלֶנָּה" — וַאֲכָלָהּ, אֵינוֹ חַיָּב אֶלָּא אַחַת. זוֹ הִיא שְׁבוּעַת בִּטּוּי שֶׁחַיָּבִין עַל־זְדוֹנָהּ מַכּוֹת, וְעַל־שִׁגְגָתָהּ קָרְבָּן עוֹלֶה וְיוֹרֵד. שְׁבוּעַת שָׁוְא, חַיָּבִין עַל־זְדוֹנָהּ מַכּוֹת, וְעַל־שִׁגְגָתָהּ פָּטוּר.

יד אברהם

when making an oath in regard to the performance of the *mitzvah* of *sukkah* or *lulav*, even R' Yehudah ben Beseira would agree that the only valid oath would be an oath to perform the *mitzvah*. However, since the Torah states: לְהָרַע אוֹ לְהֵיטִיב, *to do bad or to do good*, the Sages reason that one is not liable for an oath unless it is possible to make an oath to the contrary. Since in this case, an oath to the contrary is a vain oath and does not take effect, oaths concerning *mitzvos* do not conform to the provisions of the verse and are thus excluded from the law of *oaths of utterance*. Consequently, one is not liable for transgressing the oath to keep the *mitzvah* (*Rav; Rashi*).

The halachah follows the view of the Sages (*Rav; Rambam Comm., Hil. Shevuos* 5:16).

Some authorities rule that he is exempt only from bringing a sin-offering. However, the oath is valid and by violating his oath he transgresses the negative *mitzvah* of (*Num.* 30:3): לֹא יַחֵל דְּבָרוֹ, *he shall not profane his word*, for which there is a penalty of lashes (*Ran, Nedarim* 8a). Others rule that the oath does not take effect at all. Accordingly, he does not transgress this negative *mitzvah* and there is no penalty at all (*Ramban, Milchamos Hashem* at end of chapter; comm. on *Chumash, Num.* 30:3).

7.

The following mishnah deals with one who prohibits on himself an act many times by swearing repeatedly.

„שְׁבוּעָה שֶׁלֹּא אֹכַל כִּכָּר זוֹ"; — *'I swear that I will not eat this loaf';*

[If one states, 'I swear that I will not eat this loaf,' we assume his intention to be that he will not eat an amount of it considered eating, viz., an olive-sized piece (see above, mishnah 1).] His specifying *this loaf* is not to say that he is liable only if he eats the entire loaf; rather, he means to indicate that his interdiction concerns only this particular loaf, but that he may partake of any other (*Tos. Yom Tov* from *Kesef Mishneh, Hil. Shevuos* 3:9, quoting *Ritva*).

„שְׁבוּעָה שֶׁלֹּא אֹכְלֶנָּה," „שְׁבוּעָה שֶׁלֹּא אֹכְלֶנָּה" — *'I swear that I will not eat it'; 'I swear that I will not eat it'* —

[After uttering the first oath, he swore another oath not to eat it and then repeated it. In contrast to the first oath, the wording 'I will not eat *it*' indicates that he is liable only for eating the entire loaf.]

וַאֲכָלָהּ, — *and he ate it,*

[I.e., he eats the entire loaf.]

אֵינוֹ חַיָּב אֶלָּא אַחַת. — *he is liable only once.*

[I.e., he is liable only for transgressing the initial oath. Since the first oath he swore prohibited him from eating even an olive-sized piece of the loaf, it obviously prohibits him from eating the entire loaf as well. Therefore, the second oath has no effect, since it forbids something already interdicted by the first oath, and as we learned above, an oath cannot take effect upon something already prohibited by a previous oath.]

However, if he should first swear 'I will not eat it,' and then swear 'I will not eat this loaf,' he would be liable twice.

7. 'I swear that I will not eat this loaf'; 'I swear that I will not eat it'; 'I swear that I will not eat it' — and he ate it, he is liable only once. This is the oath of utterance for which one is liable for its willful transgression to [a penalty of] lashes, and for its inadvertent transgression to a variable [sin-]offering. [For] a vain oath, one is liable for its willful transgression to [a penalty of] lashes, and for its inadvertent transgression, one is exempt.

YAD AVRAHAM

This is because the first oath prohibits him only from eating the entire loaf, while the second oath prohibits him from eating even an olive-sized piece. Since the second oath adds to the interdiction of the first one, both oaths are valid. Consequently, if he eats an olive-sized piece, he transgresses the second oath. When he completes eating the entire loaf, he transgresses the first oath, and is, therefore, liable to two sets of lashes *(Rav; Tif. Yis.* from *Gem.* 27b).

Actually, to teach us the rule that one oath cannot take effect upon something already forbidden by another oath, it would have been sufficient to state two oaths. Nevertheless, the *Tanna* mentions a third one in order to teach us that subsequent oaths do not become null and void but are merely suspended. Should he have the first oath annulled by a sage, the second one takes effect. Should he have the second oath annulled as well, the third one takes effect. Annulment of an oath by a sage (or a panel of three laymen) nullifies it retroactively and it is thus as though the first oath never existed. Consequently, the second oath becomes effective retroactively *(Rav* from *Gem.* 27b according to *Rashi).* See *Nedarim* 2:1 for details of annulling a *neder* or oath.

Tos. maintain that the third oath is indeed superfluous and favor the variant reading in which it does not appear. They maintain that even to teach us that the second oath is suspended, the *Tanna* did not need to mention a third oath. We can infer this from the expression: אֵינוֹ חַיָּב אֶלָּא אַחַת, *he is liable but once.* Since the *Tanna* could have stated: חַיָּב אַחַת, *he is liable once,* but instead stated: *he is liable 'but' once,* his intention is that there is but one actual liability; yet the other oath is not completely void, inasmuch as it may take effect if the first one is annulled.

זוֹ הִיא שְׁבוּעַת בִּטּוּי שֶׁחַיָּבִין עַל־זְדוֹנָהּ מַכּוֹת, וְעַל־שִׁגְגָתָהּ קָרְבָּן עוֹלֶה וְיוֹרֵד. — *This is the oath of utterance for which one is liable for its willful transgression to [a penalty of] lashes, and for its inadvertent transgression to a variable sin-offering* [lit. *ascending and descending sacrifice*].

I.e., all the mishnayos in this chapter up to this point dealt with the oath of utterance for which an intentional transgression brings a penalty of lashes, and an inadvertent one requires a variable sin-offering for atonement *(Meiri).*

By using the term *this is the oath,* the mishnah seems to indicate that there is a type of oath of utterance for which there is no penalty of lashes. This occurs if one swears to eat and violates his oath and does not eat. Since his transgression involves no action but occurs passively, there can be no penalty meted out by the *beis din (Tos. Yom Tov* from *Gem.* 21b).

שְׁבוּעַת שָׁוְא, — *[For] a vain oath,*

[The definition of this will be delineated in the following mishnah.]

חַיָּבִין עַל־זְדוֹנָהּ מַכּוֹת, — *one is liable for its willful transgression to [a penalty of] lashes,*

[I.e., for transgressing the negative commandment of *(Ex.* 20:7): לֹא תִשָּׂא אֶת־שֵׁם ה׳ אֱלֹהֶיךָ לַשָּׁוְא, *You shall not take the Name of HASHEM, your God, in a vain oath.*]

וְעַל־שִׁגְגָתָהּ, פָּטוּר. — *and for its inadvertent transgression, one is exempt.*

[ח] **אֵיזוֹ** הִיא שְׁבוּעַת שָׁוְא? נִשְׁבַּע לְשַׁנּוֹת אֶת־הַיָּדוּעַ לָאָדָם — אָמַר עַל־הָעַמּוּד שֶׁל־אֶבֶן שֶׁהוּא שֶׁל־זָהָב, וְעַל־הָאִישׁ שֶׁהוּא אִשָּׁה, וְעַל־הָאִשָּׁה שֶׁהִיא אִישׁ. נִשְׁבַּע עַל־דָּבָר שֶׁאִי אֶפְשָׁר: „אִם לֹא רָאִיתִי גָמָל שֶׁפּוֹרֵחַ בָּאֲוִיר״;

יד אברהם

[In contrast to the law for oaths of utterance, there is no sacrifice mandated by the Torah to atone for the inadvertent violation of the vain oath.]

8.

The following mishnah delineates the various types of vain oaths.

There are four types of vain oaths: (1) Swearing to something which is obviously false, e.g., that a piece of stone is gold; (2) swearing to something which is obviously true, e.g., that a piece of stone is stone; (3) swearing to transgress a *mitzvah*, e.g., not to put on *tefillin;* (4) swearing to do the impossible, e.g., to climb up to the heavens *(Rambam, Hil. Shevuos* 1:4-7). These four oaths are vain because they are pointless. The first two are so obviously true or false that it is preposterous to swear about them. [For this reason, the first category is classified a vain oath, not a false one. In the case of a false oath, the swearer is imparting some information, albeit false, whereas in a vain oath no information whatsoever is imparted *(Tif. Yis.).*] The last two are impossible and thus equally pointless.

אֵיזוֹ הִיא שְׁבוּעַת שָׁוְא? — *What is a vain oath?*

[I.e., what is the vain oath mentioned in the preceding mishnah, for which one is liable to lashes for a willful transgression and exempt for an inadvertent one?]

נִשְׁבַּע לְשַׁנּוֹת אֶת־הַיָּדוּעַ לָאָדָם — *One* [*who*] *swears to contradict* [lit. *to alter*] *what is known to man —*

[I.e., if he makes an oath which is known to people to be false.] This applies only if the oath concerns something known to at least three persons to be contrary to the facts *(Rambam Comm.* from *Gem.* 29a). Otherwise, it is a false oath *(Rashi, Gem.* 29a) and he is guilty of transgressing the negative commandment of *(Lev.* 19:12): וְלֹא־תִשָּׁבְעוּ בִשְׁמִי לַשָּׁקֶר, *And you shall not swear by My Name falsely.*

אָמַר עַל־הָעַמּוּד שֶׁל־אֶבֶן שֶׁהוּא שֶׁל־זָהָב, — [*for example,*] *he said concerning a pillar of stone that it is of gold,*

[I.e., he made an oath concerning this. This is an example of a patently false fact.]

Bach (236) asserts that if at the time of his oath the true nature of the pillar was unknown to all, then his oath is false, not vain. However, if subsequently it became known that the pillar is stone, then his oath becomes vain retroactively and he is punished accordingly.

The *Tanna* states only the example of a vain oath in which he swears that the pillar of stone is gold, not the reverse, because gold pillars are rare [and the *Tanna* generally does not discuss rare situations] *(Tos. Yom Tov).*

וְעַל־הָאִישׁ שֶׁהוּא אִשָּׁה, וְעַל־הָאִשָּׁה שֶׁהִיא אִישׁ. — *concerning a man that he is a woman, or concerning a woman that she is a man.*

I.e., he swears that a certain person is a woman, and it is known to three persons that he is a man *(Bach, Yoreh Deah* 236; *Shach,* 236:10).

Although the mishnah does not make explicit mention of this, *Yerushalmi* (3:8) includes another category of vain oaths, viz., if one swears to *affirm* something generally known. An example is given of one who swears that two equals two.

8. What is a vain oath? One [who] swears to contradict what is known to man — [for example,] he said concerning a pillar of stone that it is of gold, concerning a man that he is a woman, or concerning a woman that she is a man. One [who] swears concerning something that is impossible: [for example,] 'If I did not see a camel flying through the

Yerushalmi goes so far as to include someone who, upon seeing rain falling, swears that fruit will be cheap, which is the obvious result of an abundant crop. This is quoted by *Beis Yosef (Yoreh Deah* 236) and *Taz* (236:8) as halachah. [This is the second category of vain oaths listed in the preface to this mishnah.]

Rambam qualifies this ruling by stating: It is known to the sages, the savants, and the scientists, that the sun is one hundred and seventy times as large as the earth. If one of the populace swore that the sun is larger than the earth, he does not incur the penalty of lashes because of a vain oath. Although the matter is so, this is not known to the general population, but only to the great sages, and he is not liable unless he swears concerning a thing known to three persons of the general populace, e.g., that a man is a man or a stone a stone. Similarly, if he swore that the sun is smaller than the earth, he does not incur the penalty of lashes, although this is certainly untrue, since it is not known to all people, and it is not analogous to one who swears concerning a man that he is a woman *(Hil. Shevuos* 5:22).

נִשְׁבַּע עַל־דָּבָר שֶׁאִי אֶפְשָׁר: — *One [who] swears concerning something that is impossible:*

[This is the third category of vain oaths.]

„אִם לֹא רָאִיתִי גָמָל שֶׁפּוֹרֵחַ בָּאֲוִיר"; — *[for example,] 'If I did not see a camel flying through the air';*

I.e., he swore an oath that all the fruit in the world be prohibited to him if he did not see a camel flying through the air *(Rav* from *Gem.* 29a).

Some of the commentators question this ruling. It would appear that this should be an oath of utterance rather than a vain oath, because the oath itself — *not to eat fruit* — is not vain; it is the condition upon which it hinges that is vain. Since he obviously did not see a camel flying through the air, all the fruit in the world should indeed be forbidden to him. *Tos. Yom Tov* cites two views on this matter. *Ran (Nedarim* 24b) maintains that the person surely had no intention to produce a prohibition, for had he intended to do so, he would not have added this impossible condition. Obviously, then, his aim was to confirm that he saw a camel flying through the air. He merely added that all the fruits be prohibited to make his statement more forceful. Accordingly, this is a vain oath. This view is shared by *Ravad (Hil. Shevuos* 3:5). Thus, the same ruling applies if he says, 'One fruit should be forbidden to me if I did not see a camel flying through the air.'

Tos. and *Rosh*, both here and in *Nedarim*, explain that, indeed, it should be an oath of utterance, and all the fruit in the world should be prohibited. The reason it is not prohibited, and the oath is deemed a vain oath, is that it falls under the category of something impossible, since it is impossible to live without eating any fruit [Fruit in this context includes all produce.] Although he did not say that all fruit should be prohibited forever, since he did not qualify his statement, it is interpreted to mean that it is prohibited forever, because we cannot project our own time limit into his words. Since it is impossible to go forever without fruit, it is deemed a vain oath. Accordingly, the *Tanna* could have taught us this ruling by saying, 'If a man makes an oath prohibiting himself from eating any fruit,' without the stipulation about the flying camel. The *Tanna*, however, wishes to teach the additional lesson that we do not assume that he saw a huge bird and dubbed it a camel. We learn here that we do not try to divine his thoughts, but rather judge his oath by the universally accepted meaning of his utterance.

שבועות
ג/ח

וְ,,אִם לֹא רָאִיתִי נָחָשׁ כְּקוֹרַת בֵּית הַבַּד". אָמַר לָעֵדִים: ,,בּוֹאוּ וְהַעִידוּנִי," ,,שְׁבוּעָה שֶׁלֹּא נְעִידָךְ". נִשְׁבַּע לְבַטֵּל אֶת־הַמִּצְוָה, שֶׁלֹּא לַעֲשׂוֹת סֻכָּה, וְשֶׁלֹּא לִטּוֹל לוּלָב, וְשֶׁלֹּא לְהָנִיחַ תְּפִלִּין. זוֹ הִיא שְׁבוּעַת שָׁוְא שֶׁחַיָּבִין עַל־זְדוֹנָהּ מַכּוֹת, וְעַל־שִׁגְגָתָהּ פָּטוּר.

יד אברהם

וְ,,אִם לֹא רָאִיתִי נָחָשׁ כְּקוֹרַח בֵּית הַבַּד"; — *or, 'If I did not see a snake like the beam of an olive press';*

I.e., in the shape of the beam of an olive press, and in its form. However, should he swear that he saw a snake as thick as a beam, it would not be a vain oath, since this is possible *(Rav* from *Gem.* 29b).

There are various opinions regarding the unique shape of this beam. *Rashi* explains that it is full of incisions. Thus, he is actually saying that he saw a speckled snake. Although many snakes have spots, the *Gemara* explains that he swore that its back was speckled, whereas a snake is speckled only on its throat.

Tos. (Nedarim 25a) question the connection of the speckles to the beam of an olive press. They therefore explain the *Gemara* to mean that the beam is flat, or wide *(Rosh,* ibid.), but not round. Therefore, he is actually swearing that he saw a snake with a flat back, whereas snakes are known to be flat on their bellies, not on their backs. (See *Ran* and *Rambam Comm.* to *Nedarim* 3:2 for other explanations.)

אָמַר לָעֵדִים: ,,בּוֹאוּ וְהַעִידוּנִי," — *One [who] said to witnesses, 'Come and testify for me,'*

[For example, if two bystanders saw that he lent money to someone, and the creditor later asked them to testify on his behalf that this loan had taken place.]

,,שְׁבוּעָה שֶׁלֹּא נְעִידָךְ." — *[and they replied,] 'We swear that we will not testify for you.'*

I.e., although we know the testimony, we swear that we will not testify for you *(Rambam, Hil. Shevuos* 5:15). This is considered a vain oath since it is an oath to annul a *mitzvah,* abrogating the Torah's obligation to testify when one is in possession of testimony which may benefit someone else. This is stated in *Lev.* 5:1: אִם־לוֹא יַגִּיד וְנָשָׂא עֲוֹנוֹ, *If he does not testify, he shall bear his iniquity (Rav).* As we have seen in the preface, this is one of the categories of vain oaths.

Rav and *Rashi* label this an impossible oath *(Tos. Yom Tov).* [*Rashi,* apparently, groups these two types of oaths into one category, viz., the oath to annul a *mitzvah* and the oath to do the impossible, both being inconceivable.]

נִשְׁבַּע לְבַטֵּל אֶת־הַמִּצְוָה: — *One [who] swears to annul a mitzvah:*

According to *Rav* and *Rashi* above, this clause is an explanation of the preceding rule. If they swear, 'We will not testify,' it is a vain oath since its effect is the annulment of a *mitzvah.* The *Tanna* now proceeds to give other examples of oaths to annul a *mitzvah.*

However, from *Rambam (Hil. Shevuos* 5:15), it seems that the previous case of the mishnah may also be understood to include an oath that he will not (in the future) know any testimony favorable to him. This is considered a vain oath, since he has no control over the events he may some day witness. Hence, the clause in the mishnah, 'We swear that we will not testify for you,'

3 air'; or, 'If I did not see a snake like the beam of an olive
8 press'. One [who] said to witnesses, 'Come and testify
for me,' [and they replied,] 'We swear that we will not
testify for you.' One [who] he swears to annul a
mitzvah: [for example,] not to make a *succah,* not to
take a *lulav,* or not to put on *tefillin.* These are the vain
oaths for which one is liable to [a penalty of] lashes for
their willful transgression, and for whose inadvertent
transgression one is exempt.

YAD AVRAHAM

has a double meaning: (1) that we will not know any testimony, which is impossible, and (2) that we will not testify to what we already know, which is an oath to annul a *mitzvah.* Accordingly, the *Tanna* places this case apart from the other oaths to annul a *mitzvah,* since it is not specifically an oath to annul a *mitzvah (Tos. Yom Tov).*

שֶׁלֹּא לַעֲשׂוֹת סֻכָּה, — *[for example,] not to make a succah,*

The word *succah,* without any qualifications refers, in common usage, to the *succah* of the Festival of Succos. Therefore, this is an oath to annul a *mitzvah.*

However, should one swear not to eat matzah, the oath is binding as an oath of utterance, since the term matzah does not necessarily refer to the matzah used for the *mitzvah* on the *seder* night but to any unleavened bread. Once the oath takes effect forbidding him to consume matzah during the year as a whole, it also takes effect in regard to the matzah of the *seder.* This falls under the principle of אִסּוּר כּוֹלֵל, *an inclusive prohibition* (see above, mishnah 4, s.v. חיב), including both the matzah of the *mitzvah* along with ordinary matzah *(Ran).* [Accordingly, he must have the oath annulled in order to be able to perform the *mitzvah.*]

Should he specify, 'I swear that I will not eat *matzah* on the eve of Pesach,' it would be an oath to annul a *mitzvah,* and he is liable to lashes for a vain oath *(Meleches Shlomo* from *Yerushalmi; Rif; Rosh).*

According to *Tur* 236, even in the case of *succah,* as long as he does not specify that he means the *succah* of the Festival, the oath includes both the *mitzvah* and optional *succah* (hut), and is, therefore, not a vain oath. Consequently the oath would take effect and he would then be forbidden to sit in the *succah* to fulfill that *mitzvah* [and would have to get his oath annulled]. See *Lechem Mishneh* ad loc.

Rambam, however, rules that even the term matzah generally refers to matzos used for the *mitzvah,* the same as the term *succah.* Therefore, it would be considered an oath to annul a *mitzvah,* a vain oath, unless one swore not to eat matzah for a year or two, in which case it obviously includes both Pesach and ordinary matzah.

וְשֶׁלֹּא לִטּוֹל לוּלָב, וְשֶׁלֹּא לְהַנִּיחַ תְּפִלִּין. — *not to take a lulav, or not to put on tefillin.*

[I.e., if he swore not to fulfill the *mitzvah* of *lulav* on Succos or not to fulfill the *mitzvah* of *tefillin.*]

זוֹ הִיא שְׁבוּעַת שָׁוְא שֶׁחַיָּבִין עַל־זְדוֹנָהּ מַכּוֹת, וְעַל שִׁגְגָתָהּ פָּטוּר. — *These are the* [lit. *this is the*] *vain oaths for which one is liable to [a penalty of] lashes for their willful transgression and for whose inadvertent transgression one is exempt.*

I.e., all the aforementioned oaths constitute the category of vain oaths for which the intentional transgression brings a penalty of lashes and for which an inadvertent transgression brings no penalty. Thus, vain oaths stand in contrast to oaths of utterance, for which even inadvertent transgressions require the atonement of a sacrifice, as explained in mishnah 7 *(Tif. Yis.).*

[ט] „שְׁבוּעָה שֶׁאֹכַל כִּכָּר זוֹ," „שְׁבוּעָה שֶׁלֹּא אֹכְלֶנָּה" — הָרִאשׁוֹנָה שְׁבוּעַת בִּטּוּי, וְהַשְּׁנִיָּה שְׁבוּעַת שָׁוְא. אֲכָלָהּ, עָבַר עַל־שְׁבוּעַת שָׁוְא; לֹא אֲכָלָהּ, עָבַר עַל־שְׁבוּעַת בִּטּוּי.

[י] שְׁבוּעַת בִּטּוּי נוֹהֶגֶת בַּאֲנָשִׁים וּבְנָשִׁים, בִּרְחוֹקִים וּבִקְרוֹבִים, בִּכְשֵׁרִים וּבִפְסוּלִין, בִּפְנֵי בֵית דִּין וְשֶׁלֹּא בִפְנֵי בֵית דִּין, מִפִּי

יד אברהם

9.

The mishnah now delineates the rules for one who utters two conflicting oaths.

שְׁבוּעָה שֶׁאֹכַל כִּכָּר זוֹ," „שְׁבוּעָה שֶׁלֹּא אֹכְלֶנָּה" — *'I swear that I will eat this loaf,' 'I swear that I will not eat it'* —

[I.e., he first swore to eat the loaf and subsequently swore not to eat it.]

הָרִאשׁוֹנָה שְׁבוּעַת בִּטּוּי, — *the first is an oath of utterance,*

[The first oath is a valid oath of utterance, as in the first mishnah of our chapter.]

וְהַשְּׁנִיָּה שְׁבוּעַת שָׁוְא. — *and the second is a vain oath.*

Since he already swore to eat the loaf, he now has an obligation to uphold his oath by eating the loaf. The second, countermanding oath is therefore an oath to annul a *mitzvah,* which constitutes a vain oath *(Rashi).*

In mishnah 7 we learned that there is a difference between swearing in reference to a specific loaf, 'I will not eat *it*,' and swearing, 'I will not eat *this loaf*.' The latter means that he will not eat even an olive-sized piece of it. Accordingly, the oath, 'I swear that I *will* eat this loaf,' should also mean that he swears merely to eat one olive-sized piece of it. If this is true, the two oaths do not conflict, since the first oath requires him merely to eat an olive-sized piece of the loaf, while the second oath — 'I swear that I will not eat *it*' — only forbids him to eat the entire loaf, which in no way prevents him from eating an olive-sized piece of it. He can, therefore, fulfill both oaths by eating the minimum olive-sized piece, while making sure to leave over some of the loaf. Why, then, does the *Tanna* adjudge it a vain oath?

Tos. (29b) conclude, therefore, that we must distinguish between the negative of this oath — swearing *not* to eat *this loaf*, and its positive counterpart — swearing to eat *this loaf*. Even though the former refers only to an olive-sized piece, the latter refers to the entire loaf and requires him to eat all of it. Thus, his two oaths are mutually exclusive.

The distinction between the negative and positive versions of this oath can be explained in the following way. Many authorities rule that if one swears, 'I will not eat this loaf,' he is not only liable for eating the first olive-sized piece, but he is liable for every subsequent olive-sized piece that he eats as well. The reason for this is that the oath not to eat rests on the entire loaf. Similarly, if he swears, 'I will eat this loaf,' the oath to eat also rests on the entire loaf, and thus defines his intention to be that he will eat *every* olive-sized piece in the loaf. The second oath, therefore, is in direct conflict with the first oath, forbidding him to eat the entire loaf which the first oath had required him to eat every bit of it *(Rosh 16; Ritva; Ramban; Chiddushei HaRan* 27b; *Ran to Rif; Tos. R' Akiva).*

אֲכָלָהּ, עָבַר עַל־שְׁבוּעַת שָׁוְא; — *[If] he eats it, he transgresses [only the prohibition against] a vain oath;*

If he eats the entire loaf, he transgresses only the interdict against pronouncing a vain oath. This violation occurred as soon as the second oath was uttered *(Tif. Yis.)* [and thus has nothing to do with whether he eats the loaf or

3
9-10

9. 'I swear that I will eat this loaf', 'I swear that I will not eat it' — the first is an oath of utterance, and the second is a vain oath. [If] he eats it, he transgresses [only the prohibition against] a vain oath; [if] he does not eat it, he transgresses an oath of utterance [as well].

10. The oath of utterance applies to both men and women, non-relatives and relatives, qualified [persons] and disqualified [persons], [both] in court and out of court, [but only] by his own mouth. One is liable

YAD AVRAHAM

not]. The mishnah's point is that he violates *only* this prohibition *(Rav).*[1] He is not liable for violating his oath since the first oath was kept and the second one never took effect *(Rav* from *Gem.* 2a,b).

לֹא אֲכָלָהּ, — [*if*] *he does not eat it,*

[I.e., if he does not eat it in its entirety.]

עָבַר עַל־שְׁבוּעַת בִּטּוּי. — *he transgresses an oath of utterance* [*as well*].

By failing to eat the loaf he swore to eat he is guilty of transgressing an oath of utterance. As explained above, when he swore to eat the loaf, he became obligated to eat it. When he subsequently swore not to eat it, the second oath constituted an oath to annul a commandment and was therefore considered a vain oath. For this he incurs the penalty of lashes regardless of whether he eats the loaf. However, if he does not eat it, he incurs the penalty for transgressing the oath of utterance as well *(Rav* from *Gem.* 29b).

However, there is no penalty of lashes for this latter transgression, since it does not involve any action *(Gem.* 21a).

10.

Since the following chapter will state that the oath of testimony applies only to men, non-relatives, and to those qualified to testify, the Mishnah states here that the laws pertaining to the oath of utterance apply to everyone — even those to whom the oath of testimony does not apply *(Rav; Rashi).*

שְׁבוּעַת בִּטּוּי נוֹהֶגֶת בָּאֲנָשִׁים וּבְנָשִׁים, — *The oath of utterance applies to both men and women,*

[Women are also included in the laws and penalties of the oath of utterance.]

בִּרְחוֹקִים וּבִקְרוֹבִים, — *non-relatives and relatives,*

If someone swears, 'I will give so-and-so a loaf,' it is immaterial whether he is a relative or a non-relative *(Rav; Rashi; Tif. Yis.).*

בִּכְשֵׁרִים וּבִפְסוּלִין, — *qualified* [*persons*] *and disqualified* [*persons*],

I.e., both to those qualified to testify and to those disqualified from testifying *(Rav; Rashi).* As mentioned above, this distinction is relevant to the case of the oath of testimony given in chapter 4 *(Rambam Comm.).*

בִּפְנֵי בֵית דִּין וְשֶׁלֹּא בִפְנֵי בֵית דִּין — [*both*] *in court and out of court,*

[I.e., it makes no difference whether he swears before the court or elsewhere.]

מִפִּי עַצְמוֹ. — [*but only*] *by his own mouth.*

To be liable for transgressing an oath of utterance, the person must have sworn the oath himself. However, if others

1. Above (mishnah 7, s.v. אינו חיב אלא אחת), we learned that when an oath is repeated and the first oath is annulled, the second oath takes effect. From this it follows that the second oath was from the very beginning treated as a pending oath, not a vain one. That reasoning, however,

עַצְמוֹ. וְחַיָּבִין עַל־זְדוֹנָהּ מַכּוֹת, וְעַל־שִׁגְגָתָהּ קָרְבָּן עוֹלֶה וְיוֹרֵד.

[יא] **שְׁבוּעַת** שָׁוְא נוֹהֶגֶת בַּאֲנָשִׁים וּבְנָשִׁים, בִּרְחוֹקִים וּבִקְרוֹבִים, בִּכְשֵׁרִים וּבִפְסוּלִים, בִּפְנֵי בֵית דִּין וְשֶׁלֹּא בִפְנֵי בֵית דִּין, וּמִפִּי עַצְמוֹ. וְחַיָּבִין עַל־זְדוֹנָהּ מַכּוֹת, וְעַל־שִׁגְגָתָהּ פָּטוּר. אַחַת זוֹ וְאַחַת זוֹ, הַמֻּשְׁבָּע מִפִּי אֲחֵרִים, חַיָּב. כֵּיצַד? אָמַר: „לֹא אָכַלְתִּי הַיּוֹם,״ וְ„לֹא הִנַּחְתִּי תְפִלִּין הַיּוֹם״ — „מַשְׁבִּיעֲךָ אֲנִי,״ וְאָמַר: „אָמֵן,״ חַיָּב.

יד אברהם

וְחַיָּבִין עַל־זְדוֹנָהּ מַכּוֹת, וְעַל־שִׁגְגָתָהּ קָרְבָּן עוֹלֶה וְיוֹרֵד. — *One is liable for its willful transgression to [a penalty of] lashes, and for its inadvertent transgression, to a variable [sin-]offering.*

[In common with most laws requiring a sacrifice for their violation, the sacrifice is brought only for an unintentional transgression; deliberate ones are punished by the court — in this case with lashes.]

adjured him to swear that he ate or did not eat, and he responds, 'I did not eat,' while in fact he did eat, he is exempt since he personally uttered no oath *(Rav)*.

Nevertheless, the *Gemara* (19b) states that if he answers 'Amen' to their adjuration [rather than 'I did not eat'], it is tantamount to uttering the oath with his own mouth *(Rav)*. [See further, mishnah 11.]

11.

שְׁבוּעַת שָׁוְא נוֹהֶגֶת בַּאֲנָשִׁים וּבְנָשִׁים, — *The vain oath applies to [both] men and women,*

[As before in mishnah 10, the mishnah states this ruling to contrast the vain oath with the oath of testimony (chapter 4).]

בִּרְחוֹקִים וּבִקְרוֹבִים, — *non-relatives and relatives,*

Should one swear concerning a man that he is a woman, for example, he is liable for pronouncing a vain oath whether that person is his relative or not *(Rav; Rashi)*.

בִּכְשֵׁרִים וּבִפְסוּלִים, — *qualified [persons] and disqualified [persons],*

[I.e., it applies to persons qualified to testify, as well as to persons disqualified from testifying, unlike the oath of testimony.]

בִּפְנֵי בֵית דִּין וְשֶׁלֹּא בִפְנֵי בֵית דִּין, וּמִפִּי עַצְמוֹ. — *in court and out of court, but [only] by his own mouth.*

[As above, in regard to an oath of utterance.]

וְחַיָּבִין עַל־זְדוֹנָהּ מַכּוֹת, וְעַל־שִׁגְגָתָהּ פָּטוּר. — *One is liable for its willful transgression to [a penalty of] lashes, but for its inadvertent transgression one is exempt.*

[In contrast to an oath of utterance, there is no sacrifice required for a vain oath uttered inadvertently.]

אַחַת זוֹ וְאַחַת זוֹ, — *For both this and that,*

I.e., in the case of both a vain oath and an oath of utterance *(Rav)*.

applies only when the second oath repeats the first one and thus cannot take effect over it. In our case, in which it contradicts the first oath, it is not considered a pending oath but a vain one *(Tif. Yis.)*.

3 for its willful transgression to [a penalty of] lashes, and
11 for its inadvertent transgression, to a variable [sin-] offering.

11. The vain oath applies to [both] men and women, non-relatives and relatives, qualified [persons] and disqualified [persons], in court and out of court — but [only] by his own mouth. One is liable for its willful transgression to [a penalty of] lashes, but for its inadvertent transgression one is exempt. For both this and that, one who was adjured by others is liable. How so? [If] one said, 'I have not eaten today,' or, 'I have not put on *tefillin* today' — [and the other said,] 'I adjure you,' and he replied, '*Amen*,' he is liable.

YAD AVRAHAM

הַמֻּשְׁבָּע מִפִּי אֲחֵרִים, חַיָּב. — *one who was adjured by others is liable.*

[I.e., if one was charged in an oath to respond to assert the truth of a certain statement, his response can constitute an oath. Thus, if it was a vain one, he is held liable for a vain oath. Similarly, if he responded to an adjuration which was an oath of utterance, his response constitutes an oath of utterance and if it was false, he is liable as though he himself had pronounced a false oath. However, it is not in all cases of adjuration that one is held liable, only in the case delineated below.]

כֵּיצַד? — *How so?*

Did we not learn that one is liable for a vain oath or an oath of utterance only if he himself pronounces the oath (*Tif. Yis.*)?

The word כֵּיצַד does not appear in the mishnah printed with the *Gemara* (*Tif. Yis.*), nor in the editions of *Rif*, *Meiri*, and certain manuscripts.

אָמַר: „לֹא אָכַלְתִּי הַיּוֹם,״ וְ„לֹא הִנַּחְתִּי תְּפִלִּין הַיּוֹם״ — „מַשְׁבִּיעֲךָ אֲנִי,״ — *[If] one said, 'I have not eaten today,' or, 'I have not put on tefillin today' — [and the other said,] 'I adjure you,'*

[I.e., someone hears his statement and says to him, 'I adjure you' — i.e., I bind you to this statement by an oath.]

וְאָמַר: „אָמֵן,״ — *and he replied: 'Amen,'*

As mentioned above, *Amen*, meaning 'true,' represents an affirmation of the oath and is regarded as though the respondent himself had pronounced the oath. Thus, while an ordinary adjuration is ineffective in imposing an oath on the one responding to it, the special response of '*Amen*' is effective in imposing the oath upon him.

This is derived from the chapter in the Torah dealing with the *sotah*, the suspected adulteress.[1] The Torah states (*Num.* 5:19-22): וְהִשְׁבִּיעַ אֹתָהּ הַכֹּהֵן ... וְאָמְרָה הָאִשָּׁה אָמֵן אָמֵן, *And the Kohen shall adjure her ... and the woman shall say, 'Amen, amen'* (*Gem.* 29b).

Since she does not repeat the *Kohen's* statement by saying, 'I was not unfaithful' [the normal form of response to an adjuration, as will be explained in ch. 4], we cannot regard her as being adjured by

1. When a man suspects his wife of being intimate with another man, he may warn her in the presence of two witnesses not to seclude herself with this man. If subsequently two witnesses see her going into seclusion with that man, she becomes a *sotah* and must drink the bitter waters to prove her innocence (*Num.* 5:20). The above-mentioned oath is pronounced prior to her drinking the water; see *Sotah* 2:5 and *Yad Avraham* comm. there.

שבועות [א] **שְׁבוּעַת** הָעֵדוּת נוֹהֶגֶת בַּאֲנָשִׁים וְלֹא בְנָשִׁים, בִּרְחוֹקִין וְלֹא בִקְרוֹבִין, בִּכְשֵׁרִים וְלֹא בִפְסוּלִין; וְאֵינָהּ נוֹהֶגֶת אֶלָּא בִרְאוּיִין
ד/א

יד אברהם

חַיָּב. — *he is liable.*

If it was intentional, he is liable to lashes. If it was unintentional, he is liable to a variable sin-offering, since both the oaths used in the mishnah's illustration are oaths of utterance (*Tif. Yis.*).

others. Consequently, we must conclude that the declaration of *'Amen'* is more than just an adjuration, but is considered tantamount to a personal pronouncement of the oath (*Tos. Yom Tov* from *Ran*).

Chapter 4

The following chapter deals with the laws of שְׁבוּעַת הָעֵדוּת, *the oath of testimony.* This involves the case of witnesses who are in possession of knowledge which can be of benefit to a litigant in a monetary case, but who respond to his request to testify in his behalf by falsely swearing that they know nothing. For this false oath they are required to bring a קָרְבָּן עוֹלֶה וְיוֹרֵד, *variable sin-offering* — the sin-offering whose quality depends on the financial resources of the sinner (see above 1:2). This law is taught by the Torah in *Leviticus* chapter 5, the chapter dealing with the variable sin-offering. The very first verse there states: וְנֶפֶשׁ כִּי־תֶחֱטָא וְשָׁמְעָה קוֹל אָלָה וְהוּא עֵד אוֹ רָאָה אוֹ יָדָע אִם־לוֹא יַגִּיד וְנָשָׂא עֲוֹנוֹ — *And should a person sin and hear the voice of an adjuration, and he is a witness, having either seen or known; if he does not tell, he shall bear his iniquity.* The atonement of the variable sin-offering is then stated in verses 5-10 of that passage, together with that of all those who are subject to this form of sacrifice.

1.

שְׁבוּעַת הָעֵדוּת נוֹהֶגֶת בַּאֲנָשִׁים וְלֹא בְנָשִׁים, — *The oath of testimony applies to men but not to women,*

Concerning the oath of testimony the Torah states: וְהוּא עֵד, *and he is a witness,* implying that only those qualified to testify before the court are liable for swearing this oath falsely. Since under Torah law women are not eligible to serve as witnesses, even should a woman have knowledge of testimony and swear to the contrary, she is not held liable by the rule of the oath of testimony (*Rav; Rashi* from *Gem.* 30a).

בִּרְחוֹקִין וְלֹא בִקְרוֹבִין, — *to non-relatives but not to relatives,*

Since close relatives are disqualified from testifying concerning their kin, they too are not liable if they deny knowledge of testimony in a case in which their relative is involved. The list of disqualified relatives is to be found in *Sanhedrin* 3:4.

The disqualification of relatives applies to witnesses related either to the claimant, the defendant (*Sanhedrin* 27b), or to each other (*Shulchan Aruch, Choshen Mishpat* 33:17 from *Yerushalmi, Sanhedrin*). Some also disqualify them if they are related to the judges (ibid.; see commentators ad loc.). They are disqualified from testifying about their relatives whether their testimony would benefit them or harm them (ibid. 33:10 from *Bava Basra* 159a).

בִּכְשֵׁרִים וְלֹא בִפְסוּלִין, — *to those qualified but not to those disqualified,*

The term disqualified refers to people disqualified from testifying by virtue of their wickedness. According to the Torah, one who intentionally commits a sin punishable by death or lashes is

4 **1.** The oath of the testimony applies to men but not to
1 women, to non-relatives but not to relatives, to those qualified but not to those disqualified, and it applies only to those fit to testify; [both] in court and out

YAD AVRAHAM

disqualified from serving as a witness. Similarly, thieves are disqualified [though their crime is not subject to lashes] (see *Sanhedrin* 3:3). Consequently, should any such people swear that they have no knowledge of testimony, they are not held liable by the rule of the oath of testimony *(Rav; Rashi)*.

The seemingly redundant doubled expressions in the mishnah — *to men but not to women, to non-relatives but not to relatives, to those qualified but not to those disqualified* — can be accounted for as excluding women, relatives, and sinners even if both litigants to a civil case agree to accept them as witnesses. Although their testimony would be accepted in such a case (see *Sanhedrin* 3:2 and *Yad Avraham* comm. there) that is only because it is considered an agreement on the part of the one adversely affected to give away his money should these non-eligible witnesses testify against him. They are not, however, legally considered witnesses and they are thus not liable to the sacrifice of the oath of testimony *(Tif. Yis.* quoting his son *R' Boruch Yitzchak)*. See mishnah 11.

;וְאֵינָהּ נוֹהֶגֶת אֶלָּא בִּרְאוּיִין לְהָעִיד — *and it applies only to those fit to testify;*

This clause refers to a king, who is considered unfit to testify *(Sanhedrin* 2:2). This ruling is based on the commandment *(Deut.* 17:15): שׂוּם תָּשִׂים עָלֶיךָ מֶלֶךְ, *You shall invest a king over you,* meaning that you shall stand in awe of him. Since witnesses must stand when testifying while the judges sit, and since it would be disrespectful for anyone to be seated while the king stands, a king is not permitted to testify. Consequently, should the king deny knowledge of testimony and swear to that effect, although he is found to have known it, he is exempt from a variable sin-offering *(Rav, Tos. Yom Tov* from *Rashi* on *Gem.* 31a).

This clause also excludes persons Rabbinically disqualified from testifying, e.g., dice players and pigeon racers.[1] Although such people are eligible according to Torah law, since the Rabbis disqualified them, their testimony is in any case of no value *(Tos. Yom Tov* from *Rashi, Gem.* 31a).

⋄§ Personal and Adjured Oaths

There are two mechanisms by which a person's declaration becomes an oath. The first is by framing it in the language of an oath — 'I swear . . .' Such a personal oath is referred to by the mishnah as *an oath by his own mouth,* i.e., a personal oath. The second is by making the declaration in response to the adjuration of another. For example, if a litigant charges his counterpart with an oath to affirm his denial of the claim, and the latter responds to this adjuration by repeating his denial, the denial is considered an oath even though no oath was actually uttered by the respondent. This

1. מְשַׂחֵק בְּקוּבְיָא, literally, *a dice player,* is really any sort of gambler (see *Rambam, Eidus* 1:4). According to R' Sheshes *(Sanhedrin* 24b) this refers to a professional gambler. The Rabbis disqualified such a person because he does not engage in any profession of benefit to mankind, and so does not contribute to the maintenance of society. Since he is already somewhat of an outcast, he is not likely to feel embarrassed at taking a bribe to testify falsely and thus lacks credibility *(Meiri)*.

מַפְרִיחֵי יוֹנִים, *pigeon racers.* This translation follows the view in *Sanhedrin* 25a which explains this to mean those who race pigeons for money, similar to the dice players mentioned before *(Rav)*.

לְהָעִיד; בִּפְנֵי בֵית דִּין וְשֶׁלֹּא בִפְנֵי בֵית דִּין, מִפִּי עַצְמוֹ; וּמִפִּי אֲחֵרִים, אֵין חַיָּבִין עַד־שֶׁיִּכְפְּרוּ בָהֶן בְּבֵית דִּין; דִּבְרֵי רַבִּי מֵאִיר. וַחֲכָמִים אוֹמְרִים: בֵּין מִפִּי עַצְמוֹ וּבֵין מִפִּי אֲחֵרִים, אֵינָן חַיָּבִין עַד־שֶׁיִּכְפְּרוּ בָהֶן בְּבֵית דִּין.

[ב] **וְחַיָּבִין** עַל־זְדוֹן הַשְּׁבוּעָה, וְעַל־שִׁגְגָתָהּ עִם־זְדוֹן הָעֵדוּת, וְאֵינָן חַיָּבִין עַל־

יד אברהם

type of oath is referred to by the mishnah as *adjured by others.*[1]

In discussing the sacrifice of the witnesses who falsely swore the oath of testimony, the Torah refers explicitly only to an oath by adjuration. Furthermore, this oath is described as taking place in the presence of a court, teaching that the witnesses' liability for an adjured oath of testimony is only if their denial takes place in court. On the other hand, in regard to the sacrifice for the oath of deposit (see chapter 5), the Torah makes no stipulation that it take place in court, thereby indicating that the liability for this false oath is even for one taking place out of court. However, the Torah's discussion of that oath refers explicitly only to a personal oath, not an adjured one. By comparison of these two types of oaths, the Rabbis derived that there is liability for an oath of testimony even for a personal oath. There is, however, a dispute whether the personal oath of testimony must also take place in court to be liable for a sacrifice, the same as the adjured oath of testimony, or whether it follows the guidelines of the oath of deposit (having been derived from it) and incurs liability even for an oath outside of court.

בִּפְנֵי בֵית דִּין וְשֶׁלֹּא בִפְנֵי בֵית דִּין, מִפִּי עַצְמוֹ; — [*both*] *in court and out of court, by his own mouth;*

I.e., if he himself swore, 'I swear that I do not know any testimony for you,' he is liable, in the opinion of R' Meir, whether he swore in the presence of a *beis din*, or outside their presence *(Rav; Rashi).*

Similarly, if he answered 'Amen' to someone's adjuration, it is considered as if he personally uttered the oath, as explained above [3:10,11] *(Tos. Yom Tov)*, and he is liable both in and out of court.

וּמִפִּי אֲחֵרִים, אֵין חַיָּבִין עַד־שֶׁיִּכְפְּרוּ בָהֶן בְּבֵית דִּין; דִּבְרֵי רַבִּי מֵאִיר. — *but, if adjured by others* [*lit. from the mouth of others*], *they are not liable unless they deny* [*it*] *in court;* [*these are*] *the words of R' Meir.*

For example, if a litigant said to two prospective witnesses out of court, 'I adjure you to come and testify for me,' and they replied, 'We do not know any testimony for you,' even though their denial is considered an oath, they are not liable to the variable sin-offering sacrifice. Liability for an adjured oath of testimony is only when the witnesses deny their knowledge of testimony before a proper court *(Rav; Rashi).* This is derived from the verse *(Lev.* 5:1): אִם לוֹא יַגִּיד, *if he does not tell,* implying that if he were to tell, his testimony would be effective. This can refer only to testimony given in

1. As noted above (3:10,11), an adjured oath can become binding by a response of 'Amen,' without a repetition of the denial. However, the oath resulting from such a response is treated as a personal oath, not an adjured oath.

4 of court, by his own mouth; but if adjured by others,
2 they are not liable unless they deny [it] in court; [these are] the words of R' Meir. But the Sages say: Whether [he swears] by his own mouth or whether [he is adjured] by others, they are not liable unless they deny it in court.

2. They are liable for the willful transgression of the oath, as well as for its inadvertent transgression coupled with the willful transgression of the testimony;

YAD AVRAHAM

court, where it could exact money from the defendant.

However, the verse begins with וְשָׁמְעָה קוֹל אָלָה, *and hear the voice of an adjuration,* making the condition that the oath be in court apply only to an oath by adjuration. Should the potential witnesses swear on their own accord that they know no testimony, they are liable even for an oath which takes place outside of court. This is derived from the rule of the oath of deposit (see 5:1), for which one is liable even for an out-of-court oath *(Rav; Rashi* from *Gem.* 31a). Thus, according to R' Meir there is a difference between a personal oath, which need not take place in court to incur liability, and an adjured oath, for which there is liability only for an in-court denial.

וַחֲכָמִים אוֹמְרִים: בֵּין מִפִּי עַצְמוֹ וּבֵין מִפִּי אֲחֵרִים, אֵינָן חַיָּבִין עַד־שֶׁיִּכְפְּרוּ בָהֶן בְּבֵית דִּין. — *But the Sages say: Whether* [*he swears*] *by his own mouth or whether* [*he is adjured*] *by others, they are not liable unless they deny* [*it*] *in court.*

The Sages agree with R' Meir that we derive liability for a personal oath of testimony from the law of the oath of deposit. However, they reason that it must nevertheless follow the general guidelines outlined in the verse dealing with the laws of the oath of testimony. Since that verse talks only of an in-court oath — albeit an adjured one — we can only hold the witnesses liable for in-court oaths even when their oath was a personal one *(Tos. Yom Tov* from *Gem.* 31b).

The halachah is in accordance with the Sages *(Rav; Rambam Comm.).*

2.

וְחַיָּבִין — *They are liable*

Witnesses who swear falsely about their lack of knowledge are liable to a variable sin-offering for their offense *(Rav; Rashi).*

עַל־זְדוֹן הַשְּׁבוּעָה, — *for the willful transgression of the oath,*

Although they committed the transgression deliberately, they are nevertheless liable to a variable sin-offering. [This is in contrast to almost all other sins whose transgressions warrant a sacrifice, in which the sacrifice is brought only for an inadvertent transgression.] In discussing all the other cases for which one is liable to a variable sin-offering — viz., an oath of utterance and the *tumah*-contamination of the Temple and its hallowed things — the Torah uses the word וְנֶעְלַם, *and it be forgotten,* but it omits it in the case of the oath of the testimony. This indicates that even the witness who is completely aware of the sin he is committing by swearing falsely is liable to a sacrifice *(Rav; Rashi* from *Gem.* 31b, *Rashi* ad loc.).

וְעַל־שִׁגְגָתָהּ עִם־זְדוֹן הָעֵדוּת, — *as well as for its inadvertent transgression coupled with the willful transgression of the testimony,*

I.e., they remember the testimony and willfully deny it, and are also aware that

שִׁגְגָתָהּ. וּמָה הֵן חַיָּבִין עַל־זְדוֹן הַשְּׁבוּעָה? קָרְבָּן עוֹלֶה וְיוֹרֵד.

[ג] **שְׁבוּעַת** הָעֵדוּת כֵּיצַד? אָמַר לִשְׁנַיִם: „בּוֹאוּ וְהַעִידוּנִי," „שְׁבוּעָה שֶׁאֵין אָנוּ יוֹדְעִין לְךָ עֵדוּת"; אוֹ שֶׁאָמְרוּ לוֹ: „אֵין אָנוּ יוֹדְעִין לְךָ עֵדוּת," מַשְׁבִּיעַ אֲנִי עֲלֵיכֶם, וְאָמְרוּ: „אָמֵן" — הֲרֵי אֵלּוּ חַיָּבִין.

יד אברהם

this oath is prohibited; but they are unaware that its transgression must be expiated by a sacrifice *(Rav; Tos. Yom Tov; Rashi* from *Gem.* 31b). This may be considered a form of inadvertent transgression [since the sinner is unaware of the severity of his transgression]. In this manner it is possible to be liable for a sacrifice even for the inadvertent transgression of the law of the oath of testimony *(Gem.)*.

וְאֵינָן חַיָּבִין עַל־שִׁגְגָתָהּ. — *but they are not liable for its inadvertent transgression.*

I.e., they are not liable for a completely inadvertent transgression, such as occurs when at the time of their oath they really believed that they knew no testimony, and later reminded themselves that they did indeed have knowledge of it. In such a case they are deemed as having sinned accidentally, and they are therefore not liable for having sworn falsely. Consequently, they are exempt from a sacrifice *(Rav; Rashi)*.

Tos. question this interpretation on the grounds that since they were unaware that they had knowledge of the testimony at the time of the oath, the oath was indeed truthful, and they cannot even be characterized as having sinned accidentally, since they did not sin at all. *Tos.* therefore explain that the mishnah deals with the case of witnesses who swear that they *never* knew or saw testimony. Since at one time they did in fact know it or see it, the oath is false. They are exempt from the sacrifice only because they sinned accidentally, being unaware that they once knew the testimony.

Ran explains *Rashi's* view to be that since the witnesses were indeed aware of the testimony (which had merely slipped their mind at the time the oath was administered), had they concentrated on the matter they would have been able to refresh their memory. Consequently, their oath denying any knowledge is considered false. They are exempt only because they swore falsely by accident, not being consciously aware of the testimony at the time.[1]

In all other prohibitions, such as desecration of the Sabbath or eating prohibited fats, one is liable to a sin-offering even if he was unaware that the day was the Sabbath or that the fat he was eating was of the prohibited type. The same should hold true when swearing falsely — he should be liable even when he is unaware of the oath being false. There is, however, an inherent difference between the two.

If, for example, one cut grain on the Sabbath, the desecration lies in the act of cutting [i.e., *reaping*, one of the thirty-nine *melachos* (prohibited labors)]. It is a *melachah* whether he is aware of its being the Sabbath or not. In the case of the oath of testimony, however, the transgression is not in the utterance of these particular words, but in the lying. In order to be considered a liar, though,

1. *Tos.* offer yet another explanation, viz. that the witnesses were indeed aware of the testimony, but they were completely unaware that swearing falsely is prohibited. See also *Rambam, Hil. Shevuos* 1:13.

4 but they are not liable for its inadvertent transgression.
3 Now what are they liable for the willful transgression of the oath? A variable [sin-]offering.

3. What is the case of the oath of the testimony? [If] he says to two, 'Come and testify for me,' [and they reply,] 'We swear that we do not know any testimony for you'; or they say to him, 'We do not know any testimony for you,' [and he says,] 'I adjure you,' and they reply, 'Amen' — they are liable.

YAD AVRAHAM

one must have had knowledge of the truth. Thus, when they cannot remember the testimony, they cannot be held liable *(Ri Migash, Ramban, Meiri).*

וּמָה הֵן חַיָּבִין עַל־זְדוֹן הַשְּׁבוּעָה? קָרְבָּן עוֹלֶה וְיוֹרֵד. — *Now what are they liable for the willful transgression of the oath? A variable* [*sin-*]*offering.*

Should they intentionally deny the testimony, they are liable to a variable sin-offering. [The same applies to an inadvertent transgression of the oath with an intentional transgression of testimony, as explained above.]

Even if they were warned, there is never a penalty of lashes. According to *Rashi* (37a) this is because it is a doubtful warning,[1] i.e., the one who warns them of the penalty of lying is never sure that the witnesses do, indeed, know the testimony. According to *Tos.*, it is because the witnesses may always claim to have forgotten the testimony at the time of the oath, and it can never be proven that they perjured themselves intentionally.

3.

The following mishnah presents a number of examples of the oath of testimony and several details involved.

שְׁבוּעַת הָעֵדוּת כֵּיצַד? אָמַר לִשְׁנַיִם: „בּוֹאוּ וְהַעִידוּנִי," — *What is the case of the oath of the testimony?* [*If*] *he says to two, 'Come and testify for me,'*

[I.e., a litigant in a monetary suit demands of two people that they testify in his behalf.]

„שְׁבוּעָה שֶׁאֵין אָנוּ יוֹדְעִין לְךָ עֵדוּת"; — [*and they reply,*] *'We swear that we do not know any testimony for you';*

[Their mere denial of knowledge does not render them liable to a sacrifice unless it was made in the form of an oath. Thus, the mishnah states that they swore that they know no testimony.]

אוֹ שֶׁאָמְרוּ לוֹ: „אֵין אָנוּ יוֹדְעִין לְךָ עֵדוּת," — *or they say to him, 'We do not know any testimony for you,'*

I.e., they state this without an oath *(Rashi).*

„מַשְׁבִּיעַ אֲנִי עֲלֵיכֶם," — [*and he says,*] *'I adjure you,'*

The litigant responds to the denial by charging them with an oath to affirm it — 'I adjure you that what you said is true' *(Rashi).*

וְאָמְרוּ: „אָמֵן" — *and they reply, 'Amen'* —

[Though not actually uttering an oath themselves, they affirmed the oath by answering 'Amen,' thereby swearing falsely since, in reality, they did know testimony.]

הֲרֵי אֵלּוּ חַיָּבִין. — *they are liable.*

[They are liable to a sacrifice for a false

1. The courts can administer corporal punishment, such as lashes or execution, only if the transgressor was warned immediately prior to his act by two witnesses. It is considered a

הִשְׁבִּיעַ עֲלֵיהֶן חֲמִשָּׁה פְעָמִים חוּץ לְבֵית דִּין, וּבָאוּ לְבֵית דִּין וְהוֹדוּ, פְּטוּרִים. כָּפְרוּ, חַיָּבִים עַל־כָּל־אַחַת וְאַחַת. הִשְׁבִּיעַ עֲלֵיהֶן חֲמִשָּׁה פְעָמִים בִּפְנֵי בֵית דִּין וְכָפְרוּ, אֵינָן חַיָּבִין אֶלָּא אַחַת. אָמַר רַבִּי שִׁמְעוֹן: מַה־טַּעַם? הוֹאִיל וְאֵינָם יְכוֹלִים לַחֲזוֹר וּלְהוֹדוֹת.

יד אברהם

oath of testimony.] However, if they remain silent, neither affirming nor denying, then they are not deemed as having sworn, and they are exempt *(Rashi).*

We learned in mishnah 1 that according to R' Meir one who swears of his own accord is liable even if he swears falsely outside of court, while according to the Sages he is liable only if he swears in court. When adjured by others, even R' Meir agrees that he is liable only before the court. As mentioned above (3:10), if one replies, 'Amen' to another's oath, it is regarded as though he had sworn on his own accord. Consequently, according to R' Meir, they would be liable even if they reply 'Amen' outside of court. According to the Sages, however, they are liable only if they reply 'Amen' before the court.

The mishnah has thus far spoken only of personal oaths, not adjured oaths. However, in stating that they are not liable if they remain silent, *Rashi* implies that if they reply, 'We do not know any testimony for you,' it is considered an oath and they are liable. This constitutes being adjured by others (see mishnah 1), in which case, according to both R' Meir and the Sages they are liable only if they made their denial in court *(Tos. Yom Tov).*

If we are to attribute the mishnah to the Sages it must be qualified as referring to a denial in court. Consequently, the specification that they reply 'Amen' is not necessary, since the same rule applies even if they say, 'We do not know any testimony for you.' The mishnah states 'Amen' merely for the sake of brevity *(Tos. Yom Tov* from *Tos.). Tos.* also suggest that the mishnah may be qualified as referring to a case of witnesses denying out of court, in which case it would have to be attributed to R' Meir. This would have the advantage, however, of making the mishnah refer only to the case of the witnesses replying, 'Amen,' which constitutes swearing on their own accord. But should they reply, 'We do not know any testimony for you,' they would be exempt.

הִשְׁבִּיעַ עֲלֵיהֶן חֲמִשָּׁה פְעָמִים חוּץ לְבֵית דִּין, — *[If] he adjured them five times outside of court,*

I.e., if the litigant adjured them five times and they denied it every time out of court *(Tif. Yis.).*

וּבָאוּ לְבֵית דִּין וְהוֹדוּ, — *and they came to court and confessed,*

[They confessed their knowledge of testimony.]

פְּטוּרִים. — *they are exempt.*

They are exempt although they reiterated their denial each time he adjured them. Since those denials were outside of court, they do not render them liable *(Rav; Rashi* from *Gem.* 32a).

Even according to R' Meir who rules that if they swear of their own accord they are liable even outside of court, that refers only to the oath. However, the denial of knowledge of testimony must take place before a court, just as testimony itself is valid only before a court *(Ran).*

כָּפְרוּ, — *[If] they denied,*

[I.e., they remained silent until after he had adjured them five times and then

warning only if it is a definite warning, i.e., 'Don't commit this act since if you do, you will definitely be liable to lashes.' If, however, the warning is doubtful, it is not considered a warning *(Pesachim* 63b; see General Introduction to *Makkos).*

4 [If] he adjured them five times outside of court, and
3 they came to the court and confessed, they are exempt. [If] they denied, they are liable for each one. [If] he adjured them five times before the court, and they denied, they are liable only once. Said R' Shimon: What is the reason? Because they cannot retract and confess.

denied knowing any testimony.] This denial, however, took place in court (*Rav; Rashi*).

חַיָּבִים עַל־כָּל־אַחַת וְאַחַת — *they are liable for each one.*

The one denial applies to each adjuration separately and they are thus guilty of five false oaths (*Rashi*). This is derived from the verse (*Lev.* 5:5): וְהָיָה כִי־יֶאְשַׁם לְאַחַת מֵאֵלֶּה, *And it shall be, when he shall be guilty of one of these,* implying that there is an instance in which one can be liable for each one (*Rav* from *Gem.* 32a).

Even though the adjuration took place outside of court, as long as the denial took place in court, they are liable even according to the Sages. The important point is that the denial take place where the recitation of testimony would be valid — viz. in court (*Tos. Yom Tov* from *Ran*).

הִשְׁבִּיעַ עֲלֵיהֶן חֲמִשָּׁה פְעָמִים בִּפְנֵי בֵית דִּין וְכָפְרוּ, — *[If] he adjured them five times before the court and they denied,*

[I.e., whether they denied once after all five adjurations or after each one.]

אֵינָן חַיָּבִין אֶלָּא אַחַת. — *they are liable only once.*

In this case, we do not say that the one denial applies to all five adjurations, and that they should be liable for each one individually (*Tif. Yis.*).

אָמַר רַבִּי שִׁמְעוֹן: מַה־טַּעַם? — *Said R' Shimon: What is the reason?*

[I.e., why are they liable only once in this case?]

הוֹאִיל וְאֵינָם יְכוֹלִים לַחֲזוֹר וּלְהוֹדוֹת. — *Because they cannot retract and confess.*

If the witnesses denied each of the five adjurations in court, they can only be held liable for the first one, since once they do so their denial can never be retracted. This is because their denial in court of knowledge of testimony is itself treated as testimony, and the rule is that once witnesses state their testimony in court they can never retract or alter that testimony, even if they admit to having lied [כֵּיוָן שֶׁהִגִּיד שׁוּב אֵינוֹ חוֹזֵר וּמַגִּיד] (*Bava Basra* 31a). Therefore, the litigant cannot adjure them a second time, since they cannot testify even if they want to (*Rav; Rashi*).

The same is true, for example, if the witnesses remained silent in response to the first four adjurations, neither affirming nor denying them, and then denied knowledge after the fifth one. Their silence can be interpreted as denial or affirmation; either way there is only one oath. If it is considered a denial, then since it was in front of the court, it can never be retracted. On the other hand, if we take their silence as affirmation, then they already swore when he adjured them the first time and one oath does not take effect upon another oath. Perforce, then, the ruling of the verse that they are liable to five sacrifices for five oaths applies only to the case in which they were adjured outside of court and they denied before the court. Since their denial was made out of court, they could still have retracted that denial and testified in court. Consequently, each oath was a denial of valid testimony (*Rav; Rashi*).

According to *Rambam* (*Hil. Shevuos* 10:19) and *Meiri*, although they are not liable for a sacrifice for the other oaths under the rule of the oath of testimony, they are nevertheless liable for the other oaths under the rules of the oath of utterance.

[ד] **כָּפְרוּ** שְׁנֵיהֶן כְּאַחַת, שְׁנֵיהֶן חַיָּבִין; בְּזֶה אַחַר זֶה, הָרִאשׁוֹן חַיָּב וְהַשֵּׁנִי פָטוּר. כָּפַר אֶחָד וְהוֹדָה אֶחָד, הַכּוֹפֵר חַיָּב. הָיוּ שְׁתֵּי כִתֵּי עֵדִים, כָּפְרָה הָרִאשׁוֹנָה, וְאַחַר־כָּךְ כָּפְרָה הַשְּׁנִיָּה, שְׁתֵּיהֶן חַיָּבוֹת, מִפְּנֵי שֶׁהָעֵדוּת יְכוֹלָה לְהִתְקַיֵּם בִּשְׁתֵּיהֶן.

יד אברהם

4.

The following mishnah teaches us that one is liable for the oath of testimony only if his denial causes a monetary loss to the one on whose behalf he refused to testify.

כָּפְרוּ שְׁנֵיהֶן כְּאַחַת, שְׁנֵיהֶן חַיָּבִין; — *[If] they both denied simultaneously, both are liable;*

[If the two witnesses called to testify simultaneously denied any knowledge, both are liable to the sacrifice for the oath of testimony.] Since they were both in possession of testimony through which the claimant could exact money from the defendant, by their simultaneous denial they are deemed as having caused him monetary loss. If, however, first one denied and then the other, only the first is liable. Since the testimony of two witnesses is needed to collect money, once the first one denied knowledge, the second one's testimony would in any case no longer suffice. Therefore his denial caused no loss of money and he is exempt from a sacrifice *(Rav)*.

Since it is impossible that both of them speak at exactly the same instant, the *Gemara* explains the mishnah to mean that the second witness denied תּוֹךְ כְּדֵי דִבּוּר, *within the time of a brief statement (Rav; Rashi* from *Gem.* 32a). This is defined as the time it takes a disciple to greet his teacher and say, שָׁלוֹם עָלֶיךָ רַבִּי, *Peace upon you, my master.* Statements made this close together are legally considered simultaneous. Thus, as long as the second witness began his denial within this brief period following the first witness' statement, their denials are deemed simultaneous *(Tos. Yom Tov)*.

בְּזֶה אַחַר זֶה, — *consecutively,*

I.e., if there was a longer interval between their denials than the time it takes for a disciple to greet his teacher *(Rav)*.

הָרִאשׁוֹן חַיָּב וְהַשֵּׁנִי פָטוּר. — *the first one is liable, and the second one is exempt.*

Since the first one had already denied knowledge of testimony, the second one's testimony is no longer to any avail. Thus he causes no monetary loss by his denial *(Rav; Rashi)*.

In fact, the testimony of a single witness does avail to require an oath from the defendant contradicting the witness. Since most people will not swear falsely, the testimony of one witness is usually effective in exacting money. Therefore, the denial of testimony by even a single witness in effect causes a loss of money, and he should be liable. Nevertheless, since his testimony does not directly exact money but merely imposes an oath, his withholding of it does not make him liable to the sacrifice *(Tos. Yom Tov* from *Gem.* 32b).

כָּפַר אֶחָד וְהוֹדָה אֶחָד, הַכּוֹפֵר חַיָּב. — *[If] one denied and one admitted, the denier is liable.*

[If one of the two witnesses called to testify admitted to knowing testimony and the other denied it, only the one who denied is subsequently liable to a sin-offering.] The *Gemara* (32b) finds that this portion of the mishnah appears to be superfluous. We have seen that if both deny, one following the other, the first is liable while the second is exempt; so

4
4

4. [If] they both denied simultaneously, both are liable; consecutively, the first one is liable, and the second one is exempt. [If] one denied and one admitted, the denier is liable. [If] there were two pairs of witnesses, [and] the first one denied, and then the second one denied, both are liable, because the testimony could be upheld by either of them.

YAD AVRAHAM

surely, in our case, we may deduce that the one who denied is liable while the one who admitted is exempt. The *Gemara,* therefore, interprets this to mean that originally they both denied knowledge of the testimony, but within the time it takes to say three words one retracted his denial and confessed knowledge. The mishnah teaches us that he is exempt because the three-word time span can be used even to recant testimony from denial to confession *(Tos. Yom Tov).*

הָיוּ שְׁתֵּי כִתֵּי עֵדִים, — *[If] there were two pairs of witnesses,*

[I.e., if the claimant adjured two pairs of witnesses that they know no testimony in his favor.]

כָּפְרָה הָרִאשׁוֹנָה, וְאַחַר־כָּךְ כָּפְרָה הַשְּׁנִיָּה, — *[and] the first one denied, and then the second one denied,*

[I.e., the first pair he adjured denied knowledge of testimony and afterwards the second pair also denied knowledge.]

שְׁתֵּיהֶן חַיָּבוֹת, — *both are liable,*

[Both pairs of witnesses are liable to a variable sin-offering for their false oaths of testimony.]

מִפְּנֵי שֶׁהָעֵדוּת יְכוֹלָה לְהִתְקַיֵּם בִּשְׁתֵּיהֶן. — *because the testimony could be upheld by either of them.*

Since the testimony of the second pair would still have been effective even after the first pair had denied knowledge, they too are held liable for their denial. [This is in contrast to the earlier case of a single pair of witnesses, in which the denial of the first witness makes the issue of the second witness' testimony moot, thereby exempting him from liability.]

The question, however, is why the first pair is liable, since, at the time of their denial, the second pair could still testify. They could, therefore, argue that they did not cause the claimant any loss. To resolve this difficulty, the *Gemara* (33a) qualifies the mishnah as referring to a case in which the second pair was originally ineligible to testify by reason of kinship, being composed, for example, of two brothers-in-law, married to two sisters *(Rashi).* Their wives, however, were on their deathbed at the time the first pair denied knowledge of any testimony. Since their deaths would sever the kinship and thereby reinstate the eligibility of the two brothers-in-law to serve as one set of witnesses, and furthermore, since most deathbed patients die without recovering, it could be argued that the denial of the first pair caused the claimant no loss of money. The mishnah, however, teaches us that we judge their liability by the situation as it actually stood at the moment of denial. In reality the sisters were still alive, rendering the second pair of witnesses unfit to testify. Consequently, the first pair is causing him a loss *(Rav).* The liability of the second pair comes about when they deny knowledge of the testimony after the actual death of the wives, since at the time of their denial they are again eligible *(Tos. Yom Tov* from *Rambam Comm.).*[1]

1. They must also have been eligible [i.e., not yet married to their respective wives] at the time they witnessed the event to which they were called to testify. If they were related at that time as well, the subsequent dissolution of their kinship would not enable them to serve together as

[ה] „**מַשְׁבִּיעַ** אֲנִי עֲלֵיכֶם אִם־לֹא תָבוֹאוּ וּתְעִידוּנִי שֶׁיֶּשׁ־לִי בְּיַד פְּלוֹנִי פִּקָּדוֹן, וּתְשׂוּמֶת יָד, וְגָזֵל, וַאֲבֵדָה,״ „שְׁבוּעָה שֶׁאֵין אָנוּ יוֹדְעִין לְךָ עֵדוּת״ — אֵין חַיָּבִין אֶלָּא אַחַת. „שְׁבוּעָה שֶׁאֵין אָנוּ יוֹדְעִין שֶׁיֶּשׁ־לְךָ בְּיַד פְּלוֹנִי פִּקָּדוֹן, וּתְשׂוּמֶת יָד, וְגָזֵל, וַאֲבֵדָה״ — חַיָּבִין עַל־כָּל־אַחַת וְאַחַת.

„מַשְׁבִּיעַ אֲנִי עֲלֵיכֶם אִם־לֹא תָבֹאוּ וּתְעִידוּנִי שֶׁיֶּשׁ־לִי בְּיַד פְּלוֹנִי פִּקָּדוֹן חִטִּין, וּשְׂעוֹרִין וְכֻסְּמִין,״ „שְׁבוּעָה שֶׁאֵין אָנוּ יוֹדְעִין לְךָ עֵדוּת״ — אֵין חַיָּבִין

יד אברהם

Witnesses are disqualified by reason of kinship if they are related to either of the litigants or to each other (*Sanhedrin* 3:4; *Choshen Mishpat* 33:17). *Rav* follows *Rashi* in explaining the case here to be one in which the witnesses were related through marriage to each other. *Rambam* (*Hil. Shevuos* 10:15) explains that the witnesses were related through marriage to either the plaintiff or the defendant — not to each other.

However, both according to *Rav* and *Rambam*, there appears to be no reason for stating that both wives were near death. It would suffice to say that one of them was, since when she dies, the relationship is severed (*Tos. Yom Tov*).

Rashash answers that the mishnah refers to a case in which both are near death, to teach that even though the likelihood of their becoming eligible witnesses is correspondingly greater, since at the time of the denial both wives were still alive, making their husbands ineligible, the first pair is liable for causing the loss.

5.

The following mishnah explains that if one adjures witnesses to testify on his behalf concerning various claims and the witnesses do not specify these claims in their denial, but swear a generalized denial, they are liable to only one sacrifice.

„מַשְׁבִּיעַ אֲנִי עֲלֵיכֶם אִם־לֹא תָבוֹאוּ וּתְעִידוּנִי — *'I adjure you that you come and testify for me*

Literally translated this phrase would mean *if you do not come and testify for me,* though the intent is that he adjures them to testify. The negative formulation may perhaps refer to his invoking the curse for those who swear falsely (see mishnah 3) — i.e., 'may this curse befall you if you do not come and testify for me' (*Meleches Shlomo*).

שֶׁיֶּשׁ־לִי בְּיַד פְּלוֹנִי פִּקָּדוֹן, — *that I have in so-and-so's possession a deposit,*

[I.e., after the witnesses deny their knowledge of testimony, he charges them in an oath to affirm that they have no knowledge that he deposited an article in someone's possession.]

וּתְשׂוּמֶת יָד, — *a loan,*

The phrase literally means *something placed in the hand,* i.e., a loan — money placed into his hand by the lender (*Rav; Rashi*). A loan is given this name because the money is placed in the possession of the borrower to invest or use, unlike a deposit which cannot be used by the holder (*Tif. Yis.*).

witnesses concerning that matter (*Tos.* 33a). To be valid, witnesses must be eligible both at the time they witness the event and at the time they actually testify (*Bava Basra* 128a).

4
5 **5.** 'I adjure you that you come and testify for me that I have in so-and-so's possession a deposit, a loan, a stolen article, and a lost article,' [and they reply,] 'We swear that we do not know any testimony for you' — they are liable only once. [But if they reply,] 'We swear that we do not know that you have in so-and-so's possession a deposit, a loan, a stolen article, and a lost article' — they are liable for each one.

'I adjure you that you come and testify for me that I have in so-and-so's possession a deposit of wheat, barley and spelt,' [and they reply,] 'We swear that we do not know any testimony for you' — they are liable only

YAD AVRAHAM

״וְגָזֵל, וַאֲבֵדָה,״ — *a stolen article, and a lost article,'*

[In addition to adjuring the witnesses that they know nothing about the deposit and loan he made to this person, he further adjures them concerning his claim that this person also stole money from him as well as holds an article he lost which he refuses to return.]

״שְׁבוּעָה שֶׁאֵין אָנוּ יוֹדְעִין לְךָ עֵדוּת״ — [*and they reply,] 'We swear that we do not know any testimony for you' —*

[The witnesses respond with an oath swearing that they do not know any testimony, but they do not specify the various claims.]

אֵין חַיָּבִין אֶלָּא אַחַת. — *they are liable only once.*

[They are liable to only one sacrifice for their denial of knowledge of all four of these claims. Since they did not specify the various claims in their oath, their oath is treated as a single oath.]

Tos. Yom Tov questions the necessity of mentioning the word שְׁבוּעָה, *we swear*. Since he already said to them, 'I adjure you,' it should be sufficient for them to reply, 'We do not know any testimony for you,' and they would still be liable, as in mishnah 3. This, in fact, is the classic formula of the oath of testimony, as the Torah states: וְשָׁמְעָה קוֹל אָלָה, *and hear the voice of the adjuration.* He replies that the novelty of this may be that even in a case in which they state explicitly that they swear, they are liable but once. [See *Tos. Yom Tov* for other suggested solutions, as well as *Tif. Yis.* and *Meleches Shlomo.*]

״שְׁבוּעָה שֶׁאֵין אָנוּ יוֹדְעִין שֶׁיֶּשׁ־לְךָ בְּיַד פְּלוֹנִי פִּקָּדוֹן, וּתְשׂוּמֶת יָד, וְגָזֵל, וַאֲבֵדָה״ — [*But if they reply,] 'We swear that we do not know that you have in so-and-so's possession a deposit, a loan, a stolen article, and a lost article' —*

I.e., the witnesses specify each individual claim in their oath *(Tif. Yis.)*.

חַיָּבִין עַל־כָּל־אַחַת וְאַחַת. — *they are liable for each one.*

Since each is considered a separate oath *(Tif. Yis.)*.

״מַשְׁבִּיעַ אֲנִי עֲלֵיכֶם אִם־לֹא תָבֹאוּ וּתְעִידוּנִי שֶׁיֶּשׁ־לִי בְּיַד פְּלוֹנִי פִּקָּדוֹן חִטִּין, וּשְׂעוֹרִין, וְכֻסְּמִין,״ — *'I adjure you that you come and testify for me that I have in so-and-so's possession a deposit of wheat, barley, and spelt,'*

This is in essence a repetition of the previous ruling. The first case of the mishnah, however, deals with various types of claims, and this second case deals with various types of deposits *(Rav; Rashi)*.

״שְׁבוּעָה שֶׁאֵין אָנוּ יוֹדְעִין לְךָ עֵדוּת״ — [*and they reply,] 'We swear that we do not know any testimony for you' —*

[I.e., we have no knowledge of any

אֶלָּא אַחַת. „שְׁבוּעָה שֶׁאֵין אָנוּ יוֹדְעִין לְךָ עֵדוּת שֶׁיֵּשׁ לְךָ בְּיַד פְּלוֹנִי חִטִּין, וּשְׂעוֹרִין, וְכֻסְּמִין," חַיָּבִין עַל־כָּל־אַחַת וְאַחַת.

[ו] „**מַשְׁבִּיעַ** אֲנִי עֲלֵיכֶם אִם־לֹא תָבוֹאוּ וּתְעִידוּנִי שֶׁיֵּשׁ־לִי בְּיַד פְּלוֹנִי נֶזֶק," וַ„חֲצִי נֶזֶק," „תַּשְׁלוּמֵי כֶפֶל," „תַּשְׁלוּמֵי אַרְבָּעָה וַחֲמִשָּׁה," וְ„שֶׁאָנַס אִישׁ פְּלוֹנִי אֶת־בִּתִּי,"

יד אברהם

have in so-and-so's possession wheat, barley, and spelt,'

[They specified each type of deposit and denied knowledge of any testimony concerning it.]

חַיָּבִין עַל־כָּל־אַחַת וְאַחַת. — *they are liable for each one.*

[It is as though they swore separate oaths and they are, therefore, liable for each one.]

testimony concerning anything that you claim.]

אֵין חַיָּבִין אֶלָּא אַחַת. — *they are liable only once.*

[This is considered a single oath since they grouped all their denials into one.]

„שְׁבוּעָה שֶׁאֵין אָנוּ יוֹדְעִין לְךָ עֵדוּת שֶׁיֵּשׁ־לְךָ בְּיַד פְּלוֹנִי חִטִּין, וּשְׂעוֹרִין, וְכֻסְּמִין," — [*But if they reply,*] *'We swear that we do not know any testimony for you that you*

6.

As explained above, the obligation to bring a variable sin-offering for the oath of testimony applies only if the denial of knowledge of testimony leads to a monetary loss. The *Gemara* (33a) considers whether the witnesses' denial of knowledge of testimony which would have made the defendant liable to pay a fine to the plaintiff — e.g., the double payment for theft *(Exodus* 22:3), or the fourfold or fivefold payment for slaughtering or selling a stolen lamb or ox (ibid. 21:37) — is considered a monetary loss or not. The conclusion, according to *Rambam (Hil. Shevuos* 9:4), is that the obligation does not apply. He words it thus: 'And likewise, if one adjures witnesses of a fine and they deny, they are exempt from the oath of the testimony, since if the defendant had first confessed the fine, he would be exempt even if witnesses came later and testified. [The rule is that if one confesses to an act for which the punishment is the payment of a fine, he is exempt. However, once witnesses testify to the act he is not exempted by his subsequent admission.] Consequently, the witnesses did not convict him with their testimony alone; rather, their testimony in conjunction with the denial of the defendant convicted him. Had he confessed, their testimony would have been to no avail. Thus, if they deny and swear, they are exempt. We will now explain the mishnah in light of this decision.

„מַשְׁבִּיעַ אֲנִי עֲלֵיכֶם אִם־לֹא תָבוֹאוּ וּתְעִידוּנִי שֶׁיֵּשׁ־לִי בְּיַד פְּלוֹנִי — *'I adjure you that you come and testify for me that I have in so-and-so's possession*

[After denying knowledge of any testimony, the plaintiff adjured the witnesses with an oath to affirm that they have no knowledge of testimony for him regarding one of the following claims.]

נֶזֶק," — *damages,'*

[I.e., a claim of damages, viz. that the defendant owes him money for having damaged his person or his property.]

וַ„חֲצִי נֶזֶק," — *or 'half-damages,'*

There are instances in which the

once. [But if they reply,] 'We swear that we do not know any testimony for you that you have in so-and-so's possession wheat, barley, and spelt,' they are liable for each one.

6. 'I adjure you that you come and testify for me that I have in so-and-so's possession damages,' or 'half-damages,' 'double payment,' 'fourfold or fivefold payment,' or 'that so-and-so violated my daughter,' or

YAD AVRAHAM

Torah requires only half-damages to be paid. This occurs when an animal causes damage to an object without actually breaking it upon contact — e.g., if a stone shoots out from under its hoof as it is walking and strikes the object *(Bava Kamma* 19a). This is known as חֲצִי נֶזֶק צְרוֹרוֹת, *the half-damages of pebbles.* See *Bava Kamma* 2:1.

The half-damages usually mentioned in the mishnah refer to the half-indemnity paid for damage committed by a tame bull, i.e., one which is not a habitual gorer *(Bava Kamma* 1:4). There is, however, a dispute in the *Gemara* as to whether this payment is considered compensation, albeit only partial, or is actually a fine.[1] Since the halachah is that it is considered a fine, the law of the oath of testimony does not apply. We must, therefore, qualify the mishnah as referring to the half-damages of pebbles *(Rav* from *Gem.* 33a).

Having mentioned half-damages, in which the perpetrator does not pay the full amount of the damage, the mishnah goes on to list other types of payments in which the perpetrator must pay more than the amount of the damages *(Tos. Yom Tov* from *Rashi* 33a). Although each of these payments includes a fine as well as the actual restitution for the damage, there is, nevertheless, an obligation to bring a variable sin-offering for the false oath, because the denial of testimony caused the loss of actual restitution as well, as will be explained below *(Tif. Yis.* from *Gem.* ad loc.).

„תַּשְׁלוּמֵי כֶפֶל," — *'double payment,'*

[I.e., he called the witnesses to testify that the defendant stole money from him and is therefore liable to a double payment, as in *Ex.* 22:3: *If the theft be found in his possession . . . he shall pay double.*] Since this double payment consists of the principal, which is obviously restitution, even though it also includes the second payment, which is a fine, the witnesses are liable for their denial *(Rav* from *Gem.* 33a).

„תַּשְׁלוּמֵי אַרְבָּעָה וַחֲמִשָּׁה," — *'fourfold or fivefold payment,'*

The law is that if one steals a lamb or an ox and slaughters or sells it, he is liable to fourfold payment for a lamb and fivefold payment for the ox *(Exodus* 21:37). Should one adjure witnesses that they have no knowledge of such an incident, and they, in fact, have knowledge, they are liable for the oath of testimony. As above, this liability is because the claim includes the principal, which is restitution *(Rav* from *Gem.* ad loc.). Were he to admit that he stole the ox or lamb and slaughtered it, he would be exempt from the extra payment but would still be responsible for the principal *(Rav* from *Gem.* ad loc.).

וְ„שֶׁאָנַס אִישׁ פְּלוֹנִי אֶת־בִּתִּי," — *or 'that so-and-so violated my daughter,'*

The penalty for such an act is indem-

1. The logic of this latter position is that an ordinary bull is considered unlikely to gore intentionally and the owner therefore had no reason to take precautions to prevent it from

וּפִתָּה אֶת־בִּתִּי," וְ"שֶׁהִכַּנִי בְנִי," וְ"שֶׁחָבַל בִּי חֲבֵרִי," וְ"שֶׁהִדְלִיק אֶת־גְּדִישִׁי בְּיוֹם הַכִּפּוּרִים" — הֲרֵי אֵלּוּ חַיָּבִין.

[ז] "מַשְׁבִּיעַ אֲנִי עֲלֵיכֶם אִם־לֹא תָבוֹאוּ וּתְעִידוּנִי שֶׁאֲנִי כֹהֵן," "שֶׁאֲנִי לֵוִי," "שֶׁאֵינִי בֶן־גְּרוּשָׁה," "שֶׁאֵינִי בֶן־חֲלוּצָה," "שֶׁאִישׁ פְּלוֹנִי כֹּהֵן," "שֶׁאִישׁ פְּלוֹנִי לֵוִי," "שֶׁאֵינוֹ

יד אברהם

nity for disgrace, impairment, and pain, plus a fine of fifty *shekels*, as in *Kesubos* 3:4. As stated there in mishnah 3:9, all the aforementioned payments, with the exception of the fine, are considered restitution and are paid by the perpetrator to the girl's father even upon his own admission.[1] Consequently, if one adjures witnesses that they have no knowledge of testimony concerning such a case, they are liable for the oath of testimony sacrifice, since the claim includes indemnity for disgrace and impairment, which can be collected despite the confession of the perpetrator (*Rav* from *Gem.* 33a).

"וּ"פִתָּה אֶת־בִּתִּי, — *or 'seduced my daughter,'*

The penalty for this crime is also indemnity for shame, impairment, and a fine of fifty *shekels*. [There is, however, no indemnity for pain in the case of seduction] (*Kesubos* 3:4).

"וְ"שֶׁהִכַּנִי בְנִי, — *or 'that my son struck me,'*

I.e., that my son struck me without inflicting a wound, in which case there is no death penalty (*Sanhedrin* 11:1). Consequently, there is a monetary loss from denying knowledge of testimony (*Rav; Rashi*). Although no damage was inflicted, the son would have to pay for the shame and pain (*Rambam Comm.; Rashi*).

Had the son inflicted a wound, however, he would receive the death penalty and would, therefore, not incur the payment for shame and pain. This follows the principle of קִים לֵיהּ בִּדְרַבָּה מִנֵּיהּ, *he suffers the more severe punishment*, i.e., that one who is subject to the death penalty is absolved from lesser penalties incurred simultaneously (see *Yad Avraham* comm. to *Kesubos* 3:1).

"וְ"שֶׁחָבַל בִּי חֲבֵרִי, — *or 'that my neighbor wounded me,'*

For this, one pays indemnity for injury, pain, healing, loss of earnings, and disgrace (*Bava Kamma* 8:1).

— "וְ"שֶׁהִדְלִיק אֶת גְּדִישִׁי בְּיוֹם הַכִּפּוּרִים — *or 'that he ignited my stack of grain on Yom Kippur'* —

The phrase, 'on Yom Kippur,' refers to the preceding case as well. In both these cases, although the perpetrator is liable to *kares* (excision; Divinely imposed premature death), he is still liable to monetary payment. The principle that one suffers only the more severe punishment applies only when the severe punishment is execution at the hands of the courts, not

doing so. Thus, its occurrence must be classed an unforseeable damage, for which the owner cannot technically be held responsible. The Torah, however, adds a half-damage penalty to encourage the owner to exercise greater caution (*Bava Kamma* 15a).

1. Generally speaking, where there is liability for a fine, the fine is paid to the girl's father (*Kesubos* 3:9). See mishnah 3 there for an exception.

4
7

'seduced my daughter,' or 'that my son struck me,' or 'that my neighbor wounded me,' or 'that he ignited my stack of grain on Yom Kippur' — they are liable.

7. 'I adjure you that you come and testify for me that I am a *Kohen*,' 'that I am a Levite,' 'that I am not the son of a divorcee,' 'that I am not the son of a *chalutzah*'; 'that so-and-so is a *Kohen*,' 'that so-and-so

YAD AVRAHAM

when death is carried out by Heaven. In this respect, *kares* differs from capital punishment *(Rav; Tif. Yis.)*. See mishnah 7.

The *Tanna* of the mishnah differs with R' Nechunyah ben Hakaneh, who rules that even in cases of *kares*, he is free from monetary obligations incurred simultaneously, *kares* being equal to capital punishment *(Tos. Yom Tov* from *Rashi* 33a). Cf. *Megillah* 1:5, *Kesubos* 3:1, *Bava Kamma* 7:2, 8:3.

הֲרֵי אֵלוּ חַיָּבִין. — *they are liable.*

[The witnesses who denied knowledge of testimony in any of the above cases are liable to a variable sin-offering, because they caused the claimant a loss of principal by their denial, as explained above.]

7.

The following mishnah delineates various cases not involving monetary loss in which the plaintiff adjures the witnesses. In these cases the Torah does not mandate a variable sin-offering for the oath of testimony. This is derived exegetically from שְׁבוּעַת הַפִּקָּדוֹן, *the oath of deposit* (see chapter 5), in which the oath and resulting sacrifice always involve a claim of money *(Rav* from *Gem.* 34a).

„מַשְׁבִּיעַ אֲנִי עֲלֵיכֶם אִם־לֹא תָבוֹאוּ וּתְעִידוּנִי שֶׁאֲנִי כֹהֵן," — *'I adjure you that you come and testify for me that I am a Kohen,'*

I.e., testify for me that I am a *Kohen* and am entitled to receive *terumah (Tif. Yis.)*.

„שֶׁאֲנִי לֵוִי," — *'that I am a Levite,'*

I.e., testify for me that I am a Levite and am entitled to receive *maaser rishon* [the first tithe] *(Tif. Yis.)*.

„שֶׁאֵינִי בֶן־גְּרוּשָׁה," — *'that I am not the son of a divorcee,'*

[I.e., I am not the offspring of a *Kohen* and a divorced woman. Such offspring is disqualified from the *Kehunah*. See *Makkos* 1:1.]

„שֶׁאֵינִי בֶן־חֲלוּצָה"; — *'that I am not the son of a chalutzah';*

[I.e., I am not the offspring of a *Kohen* and a *chalutzah*, a woman who received *chalitzah* to release her from the *yibum*-bond. Such a union is forbidden Rabbinically, and the offspring thereof is disqualified from the *Kehunah* Rabbinically. See *Makkos* 1:1.]

In all these cases, the witnesses are not liable to the oath of testimony since no monetary loss is involved. Although if disqualified the *Kohen* will suffer the loss of *terumah* and the Levite the loss of the *maaser*, since he is not now involved in a monetary claim, the sacrifice does not apply. Furthermore, since the Israelite may in any case give the *terumah* or *maaser* to whichever *Kohen* or Levite he chooses, this particular individual suffers no direct monetary loss as a result of their failure to testify, merely a loss of potential gain. Consequently, they are exempt from the sacrifice of the oath of testimony *(Tif. Yis.)*.

„שֶׁאִישׁ פְּלוֹנִי כֹהֵן," „שֶׁאִישׁ פְּלוֹנִי לֵוִי," שֶׁאֵינוֹ בֶן־גְּרוּשָׁה," „שֶׁאֵינוֹ בֶן־חֲלוּצָה"; — *that so-and-so is a Kohen,' 'that he is not the son*

שבועות ד/ח

בֶּן־גְּרוּשָׁה," „שֶׁאֵינוֹ בֶּן־חֲלוּצָה," „שֶׁאָנַס אִישׁ פְּלוֹנִי אֶת־בִּתּוֹ," וּ„פִתָּה אֶת־בִּתּוֹ," וְ„שֶׁחָבַל בִּי בְנִי," וְ„שֶׁחָבַל בִּי חֲבֵרִי," וְ„שֶׁהִדְלִיק גְּדִישִׁי בַשַּׁבָּת," הֲרֵי אֵלּוּ פְטוּרִין.

[ח] **„מַשְׁבִּיעַ** אֲנִי עֲלֵיכֶם אִם־לֹא תָבוֹאוּ וּתְעִידוּנִי שֶׁאָמַר אִישׁ פְּלוֹנִי לִתֶּן־לִי מָאתַיִם זוּז וְלֹא נָתַן לִי," הֲרֵי אֵלּוּ פְטוּרִים,

יד אברהם

of a divorcee,' 'that he is not the son of a chalutzah';

[I.e., he adjures the witnesses to testify that a certain person is a *Kohen*, etc. This is in contrast to the previous case, in which he adjured them concerning his own status.]

This clause is superfluous, since even if he adjures them that someone has money in the possession of another, which constitutes a monetary loss, they are exempt, as long as the claimant himself did not adjure them (see mishnah 12). The purpose of this clause is to teach by implication that only in this case are the witnesses unequivocally exempt. In a case involving direct financial loss, however, even if the adjurer is not the claimant, the witnesses can sometimes be liable — viz. where the claimant gave the adjurer a power of attorney. In our case, however, which involves an intangible matter, power of attorney is irrelevant (*Tos. Yom Tov* from *Gem.* 33b).

„שֶׁאָנַס אִישׁ פְּלוֹנִי אֶת־בִּתּוֹ," וּ„פִתָּה אֶת־בִּתּוֹ"; *— 'that so-and-so violated his daughter,' or 'seduced his daughter';*

I.e., a certain man violated or seduced another man's daughter. Thus, it follows the pattern of the last case, in which the adjurer charges them concerning someone else's status, not his own. Since the witnesses are not being adjured by the claimant, they are exempt. Although the mishnah was qualified as dealing with the case of one who has the power of attorney, this does not make a difference in these cases, since the law is that one cannot give power of attorney to collect a claim for money he never had in his possession (*Rav; Rashi*).

Others explain that the subject of the accusation is charged with violating or seducing his own daughter. The witnesses to this are exempt from the sacrifice because this is a capital offense, and the defendant would be exempt from monetary obligations because of the rule that a person convicted of a capital crime suffers only the more severe punishment. *Rashi* rejects this interpretation, arguing that since the indemnity for shame and impairment belongs to the father, in a case in which the father is himself the perpetrator, he does not have to pay. Therefore, even if he were not liable to death there would be no loss of money. *Tosafos* (33a,b) resolve this difficulty by qualifying the mishnah to mean that the daughter was betrothed, divorced and then seduced. Once a girl is betrothed, she leaves her father's dominion and any money that accrues to her subsequently belongs to herself. Therefore, in this case the fine should be paid to her (see *Kesubos* 3:3). The only reason the father does not pay is because he is liable to the more severe punishment of execution (see further *Tos. R' Akiva*).

Rambam (Hil. Shevuos 10:4) explains the mishnah to refer to the daughter of the claimant in a case in which she was betrothed [and thus legally married but still a virgin]. Although the witnesses refused by oath to testify that the accused violated or seduced the betrothed daughter of the claimant, they are exempt from the sacrifice, because even if they had testified, the accused would have been exempt from any monetary obligations according to the principle that he can suffer

4 is a Levite,' 'that he is not the son of a divorcee,' 'that he
8 is not the son of a *chalutzah'*; 'that so-and-so violated his daughter,' or 'seduced his daughter'; or 'that my son wounded me,' 'that my neighbor wounded me,' or 'that he ignited my stack of grain on the Sabbath' — these are exempt.

8. 'I adjure you that you come and testify for me that so-and-so promised to give me two hundred *zuz,* but did not give me,' they are exempt, for one is not

YAD AVRAHAM

only the more severe punishment. Since relations with a betrothed woman are adulterous, he would be executed for this act *(Tos. Yom Tov).*

וְ,,שֶׁחָבַל בִּי בְּנִי,״ — *or 'that my son wounded me,'*

I.e., a wound leaving a bruise or causing blood to flow *(Sanhedrin* 11:1). Had the witnesses testified, the son would be liable to capital punishment *(Ex.* 21:15), and there would be no monetary obligation *(Bava Kamma* 8:5). Consequently, their refusal to testify does not cause monetary loss, and there is no liability to the oath of testimony *(Rav; Rashi).*

וְ,,שֶׁחָבַל בִּי חֲבֵרִי,״ וְ,,שֶׁהִדְלִיק גְּדִישִׁי בַּשַּׁבָּת״ — — *'that my neighbor wounded me,' or 'that he ignited my stack of grain on the Sabbath'* —

I.e., he wounded me on the Sabbath or he ignited my stack of grain on the Sabbath. In both cases, should the witnesses testify, the defendant would not be liable to pay, since he would suffer the more severe punishment, i.e., death, for desecrating the Sabbath. Therefore, there is no monetary loss involved, and the witnesses are exempt *(Rav; Rashi).*

This is true even if he desecrated the Sabbath without having been forewarned by the witnesses that his act was forbidden under penalty of death. Although he is not liable to the actual punishment of death without such a prior warning, since he committed a capital crime, there is still no monetary liability due to the more severe punishment rule *(Tif. Yis.* from *Bava Kamma* 35a).

הֲרֵי אֵלּוּ פְּטוּרִין. — *these are exempt.*

[In all of these cases their testimony would in any case not have lead to any monetary award. Therefore, they are exempt from having to bring the variable sin-offering for their false oath of testimony.]

As noted above (comm. at the end of mishnah 3), it is *Rambam's* view *(Hil. Shevuos* 9:14) that though exempted from the rule of testimony sacrifice, they may still be liable for a sacrifice for a false oath where the conditions for such a sacrifice have been met.

8.

,,מַשְׁבִּיעַ אֲנִי עֲלֵיכֶם אִם־לֹא תָבוֹאוּ וּתְעִידוּנִי שֶׁאָמַר אִישׁ פְּלוֹנִי לִתֶּן־לִי מָאתַיִם זוּז, וְלֹא נָתַן לִי,״ — *'I adjure you that you come and testify for me that so-and-so promised to give me two hundred zuz, but did not give me,'*

Thereupon, the witnesses replied, 'We do not know,' and they were found to be lying *(Tif. Yis.).*

הֲרֵי אֵלּוּ פְּטוּרִים, — *they are exempt,*

[They are exempt from bringing a

שֶׁאֵין חַיָּבִין אֶלָּא עַל־תְּבִיעַת מָמוֹן כַּפִּקָּדוֹן.

[ט] **„מַשְׁבִּיעַ** אֲנִי עֲלֵיכֶם, כְּשֶׁתֵּדְעוּן לִי עֵדוּת, שֶׁתָּבוֹאוּ וּתְעִידוּנִי," הֲרֵי אֵלּוּ פְּטוּרִים, מִפְּנֵי שֶׁקָּדְמָה שְׁבוּעָה לָעֵדוּת.

[י] **עָמַד** בְּבֵית הַכְּנֶסֶת וְאָמַר: „מַשְׁבִּיעַ אֲנִי עֲלֵיכֶם, שֶׁאִם אַתֶּם יוֹדְעִים לִי עֵדוּת, שֶׁתָּבוֹאוּ וּתְעִידוּנִי," הֲרֵי אֵלּוּ פְּטוּרִין, עַד־שֶׁיִּהְיֶה מִתְכַּוֵּן לָהֶם.

יד אברהם

sacrifice for the oath of testimony.]

שֶׁאֵין חַיָּבִין אֶלָּא עַל־תְּבִיעַת מָמוֹן כַּפִּקָּדוֹן. — *for one is not liable except for a claim of money, as [in the case of] a deposit.*

I.e., witnesses who denied their knowledge of testimony are not liable for a false oath of testimony unless it concerns a claim for money which is actually due him, such as money given to another as a deposit. In this case, even if it were true that this person promised him two hundred *zuz* as a gift, he is not legally bound by that promise. Thus, even if the witnesses had testified that he promised him that sum, the claimant would not have been able to exact it from him against his will *(Rav)*, and the donor could retract his promise [see *Kesubos* 101b] *(Rashi)*.

Not only are the witnesses exempt if the promised recipient is a rich man to whom there is no obligation to give money, they are exempt even if he is a poor man — in which case the one who promised is obligated by a *neder* (vow) in the cause of a *mitzvah* [viz., charity] to give the money. Since this *neder* does not create any lien on his property, should he neglect to pay, the courts cannot forcibly collect. Consequently, the witnesses' failure to testify cannot be considered a loss of money. *Beis din*, however, does place a ban upon him or inflicts lashes upon him to get him to fulfill his vow *(Tos. Yom Tov)*.

Others add that the vow can be annulled, thereby freeing him from keeping his promise. Consequently, the witnesses are not decisive in causing the alleged recipient any monetary loss *(Lechem Shamayim; Tif. Yis.)*.

9.

„מַשְׁבִּיעַ אֲנִי עֲלֵיכֶם, כְּשֶׁתֵּדְעוּן לִי עֵדוּת, שֶׁתָּבוֹאוּ וּתְעִידוּנִי," — *'I adjure you that, when you know testimony for me, that you will come and testify for me,'*

[I.e., he adjures them concerning the future, that if it should ever happen that they know something useful to him in regard to some future litigation, that they be bound by this oath to come and testify for him.] The witnesses responded to this adjuration by answering 'Amen' *(Rambam, Hil. Shevuos* 9:8). Later, they gain knowledge of testimony, but when the claimant demands that they come and testify in his behalf, they deny that they have any knowledge of testimony.

R' Akiva Eiger questions this, arguing that since at the time they affirmed the oath no testimony was involved, their oath cannot constitute an oath of testimony, merely an oath of utterance promising to testify when they will have that knowledge. Accordingly, their subsequent denial of any knowledge should be exempted from the oath of testimony sacrifice even apart from the reason

liable except for a claim of money, as [in the case of] a deposit.

9. 'I adjure you that, when you know testimony for me, that you will come and testify for me,' they are exempt, because the oath preceded the testimony.

10. [If] he stood in the synagogue and said, 'I adjure you that, if you know testimony for me, that you come and testify for me,' they are exempt, unless he directs himself to them.

YAD AVRAHAM

that the mishnah will give below. He therefore proposes that the mishnah may deal with a case in which the witnesses do not reply 'Amen' to the adjuration. Later, when they gain knowledge of testimony, the claimant confronts them with the demand, 'Did I not adjure you? Now come and testify for me.' At this point they reply, 'We have no knowledge of any testimony.' Since their response to the adjuration first takes place when they are called to testify and deny knowledge, the acceptance of the adjuration at that point constitutes an oath of testimony (*Tos. R' Akiva). Rabbeinu Chananel* also appears to explain the mishnah in this manner since he does not mention that they replied, 'Amen.' *Meiri*, however, adds: 'and they accepted the oath,' apparently following *Rambam.*

הֲרֵי אֵלּוּ פְּטוּרִים, מִפְּנֵי שֶׁקָּדְמָה שְׁבוּעָה לָעֵדוּת. — *they are exempt, because the oath preceded the testimony.*

I.e., they are exempt from the sacrifice for the oath of testimony, since the Torah states: וְשָׁמְעָה קוֹל אָלָה וְהוּא עֵד אוֹ רָאָה אוֹ יָדָע, *and hear the voice of an adjuration, and he is a witness, having either seen or known,* implying that for the obligation to take effect that he must already be a witness when he hears the voice of the adjuration (*Rav; Tif. Yis.* from *Gem.* 35a).

10.

עָמַד בְּבֵית הַכְּנֶסֶת וְאָמַר: — [*If*] *he stood in the synagogue and said,*

[I.e., he said to the entire congregation.]

„מַשְׁבִּיעַ אֲנִי עֲלֵיכֶם, שֶׁאִם אַתֶּם יוֹדְעִים לִי עֵדוּת, שֶׁתָּבוֹאוּ וּתְעִידוּנִי," — *'I adjure you that, if you know testimony for me, that you come and testify for me,'*

I.e., he said, 'Any of you who know testimony for me shall come and testify,' without specifying any individuals (*Rambam, Hil. Shevuos* 9:9).

הֲרֵי אֵלּוּ פְּטוּרִין, עַד־שֶׁיִּהְיֶה מִתְכַּוֵּן לָהֶם. — *they are exempt, unless he directs himself to them.*

Those who responded to this adjuration by falsely denying knowledge of testimony are exempt from the sacrifice required for the oath of testimony, because he did not direct his adjuration to them specifically.

This is derived from the Torah's statement: וְהוּא עֵד, *and he is a witness,* meaning that the adjurer directs himself to the witnesses, specifying which individual or group of individuals he is addressing (*Rav* from *Gem.* 35a). Should he specify, 'all those standing there,' then they are liable, since he specifically directed himself to all of them. The mishnah, however, deals with the case in which he does not know who can testify for him, and adjures the entire congregation in a general way (*Tif. Yis.* from *Gem.* 35a).

[יא] **אָמַר** לִשְׁנַיִם: „מַשְׁבִּיעַ אֲנִי עֲלֵיכֶם, אִישׁ פְּלוֹנִי וּפְלוֹנִי, שֶׁאִם אַתֶּם יוֹדְעִין לִי עֵדוּת, שֶׁתָּבוֹאוּ וּתְעִידוּנִי," „שְׁבוּעָה שֶׁאֵין אָנוּ יוֹדְעִין לְךָ עֵדוּת," וְהֵם יוֹדְעִין לוֹ עֵדוּת עֵד מִפִּי עֵד, אוֹ־שֶׁהָיָה אֶחָד מֵהֶן קָרוֹב אוֹ־פָסוּל, הֲרֵי אֵלּוּ פְּטוּרִין.

[יב] **שָׁלַח** בְּיַד עַבְדּוֹ, אוֹ־שֶׁאָמַר לָהֶן הַנִּתְבָּע: „מַשְׁבִּיעַ אֲנִי עֲלֵיכֶם שֶׁאִם אַתֶּם יוֹדְעִין לוֹ עֵדוּת, שֶׁתָּבוֹאוּ וּתְעִידוּהוּ," הֲרֵי אֵלּוּ פְּטוּרִין, עַד־שֶׁיִּשְׁמְעוּ מִפִּי הַתּוֹבֵעַ.

יד אברהם

11.

אָמַר לִשְׁנַיִם: „מַשְׁבִּיעַ אֲנִי עֲלֵיכֶם, אִישׁ פְּלוֹנִי וּפְלוֹנִי, שֶׁאִם אַתֶּם יוֹדְעִין לִי עֵדוּת, שֶׁתָּבוֹאוּ וּתְעִידוּנִי," — *[If] he said to two, 'I adjure you, so-and-so and so-and-so, that if you know testimony for me, that you come and testify for me,'*

[I.e., he charged them with the standard adjuration.]

„שְׁבוּעָה שֶׁאֵין אָנוּ יוֹדְעִין לְךָ עֵדוּת," — *[and they replied,] 'We swear that we do not know any testimony for you,'*

[They in turn denied knowing anything, thereby accepting the adjuration.]

וְהֵם יוֹדְעִין לוֹ עֵדוּת עֵד מִפִּי עֵד, — *and they know hearsay testimony* [lit., *testimony of one witness from the mouth of another witness*],

[I.e., they did not personally see the evidence but heard it from others. Such testimony is unacceptable (in most cases) since witnesses can testify only to what they saw themselves (*Sanhedrin* 3:6).]

אוֹ־שֶׁהָיָה אֶחָד מֵהֶן קָרוֹב אוֹ־פָסוּל, — *or one of them was a relative or a person ineligible [to testify],*

[I.e., one of the witnesses was related to the claimant or to the defendant, or he was ineligible to testify because of his sins, as in mishnah 1.]

הֲרֵי אֵלּוּ פְּטוּרִין. *they are exempt.*

Since their testimony would not have availed the claimant, they are exempt from bringing a sacrifice (*Rav*).

This mishnah appears to be superfluous since we learned in mishnah 1 that the law of the oath of testimony applies only to those eligible to testify. Similarly, unacceptability of hearsay testimony is already stated in *Sanhedrin* 3:6. *Ramban*, in order to solve this difficulty, explains that even if the defendant agreed to be bound by hearsay testimony or the testimony of the ineligible witnesses [which a litigant may do, see *Sanhedrin* 3:2], and they deny knowledge of the testimony thereby causing a litigant to lose money, they are still exempt (*Tos. Yom Tov*).

12.

We already learned in mishnah 7 that the witnesses are liable to the oath of testimony only if their testimony was demanded by the claimant himself. Should

4
11-12

11. [I]f] he said to two, 'I adjure you, so-and-so and so-and-so, that if you know testimony for me, that you come and testify for me,' [and they replied,] 'We swear that we do not know any testimony for you,' and they know hearsay testimony, or one of them was a relative or a person ineligible [to testify], they are exempt.

12. [I]f] he sent [the adjuration] through his slave, or [if] the defendant said to them, 'I adjure you that if you know testimony for him, that you come and testify for him,' they are exempt, unless they hear [it] from the claimant.

YAD AVRAHAM

anyone else adjure them that they testify for the claimant, they are not liable. However, should the adjurer be given power of attorney by the claimant, they are liable as though the claimant himself had adjured them. The following mishnah is the source of that ruling.

שָׁלַח בְּיַד עַבְדּוֹ, — *[If] he sent [the adjuration] through his slave,*

I.e., the claimant sent his slave to adjure the witnesses (*Rashi* 31b).

אוֹ־שֶׁאָמַר לָהֶן הַנִּתְבָּע: „מַשְׁבִּיעַ אֲנִי עֲלֵיכֶם שֶׁאִם אַתֶּם יוֹדְעִין לוֹ עֵדוּת, שֶׁתָּבוֹאוּ וּתְעִידוּהוּ," — *or* [*if*] *the defendant said to them, 'I adjure you that if you know testimony for him, that you come and testify for him,'*

[I.e., the defendant adjured the witnesses to testify on behalf of the claimant if they in fact know anything which would benefit him.]

הֲרֵי אֵלּוּ פְּטוּרִין, עַד־שֶׁיִּשְׁמְעוּ מִפִּי הַתּוֹבֵעַ. — *they are exempt, unless they hear* [*it*] *from the claimant.*

They are exempt from the oath of testimony sacrifice because their testimony was not demanded by the claimaint himself. The *Gemara* (35a) bases this ruling on the verse in *Lev.* 5:1 concerning the oath of testimony which states: אִם לוא־יַגִּיד, *if he will not tell his testimony.* The spelling here is a combination of both words לֹא, *not,* and לוֹ, *to him.* It is interpreted to mean: if to him (לוֹ) he does not (לֹא) tell, he shall bear his iniquity. Should he withhold testimony from someone else, however, he does not bear his iniquity (*Rav).*

Tos. Yom Tov explains that in the case of the slave this ruling holds true even if he gave him power of attorney. Although power of attorney generally suffices to validate a demand for testimony, since a Canaanite slave has no power of acquisition of his own (*Bava Metzia* 89a), the master cannot grant him power of attorney. This is because obtaining such a power is considered a type of acquisition. Thus, the slave remains like any other person who was not granted that power. This explains why the mishnah uses a slave as an example, since a slave must inevitably be considered an outsider.

Tos. R' Akiva and *Tif. Yis.* explain that, according to those authorities who rule that a Canaanite slave may be granted power of attorney, we must conclude that the mishnah deals with one who was not granted that power. The mishnah specifies a slave to teach us that not only is an outsider unable to adjure the witnesses to make them liable to the oath of testimony, but even a Canaanite

[יג] „**מַשְׁבִּיעַ** אֲנִי עֲלֵיכֶם," „מְצַוֶּה אֲנִי עֲלֵיכֶם," „אוֹסֶרְכֶם אֲנִי" — הֲרֵי אֵלּוּ חַיָּבִין. „בַּשָּׁמַיִם וּבָאָרֶץ" — הֲרֵי אֵלּוּ פְּטוּרִין. „בְּאָלֶ"ף דָּלֶ"ת," „בְּיוּ"ד הֵ"י," „בְּשַׁדַּי,"

יד אברהם

slave, whose hand is in a legal sense considered an extension of the master's hand [i.e., if he acquires anything, it is as though his master has acquired it], cannot be considered to serve in place of his master in regard to adjuring witnesses. Thus even his adjuration is of no significance unless he is granted power of attorney.

13.

The following mishnah delineates the various expressions and formulae accounted as oaths in regard to the sacrifice of the oath of testimony.

„מַשְׁבִּיעַ אֲנִי עֲלֵיכֶם," — *[If he says,] 'I adjure you,'*

[I.e., if one said to witnesses, 'I adjure you that you come and testify on my behalf.']

The *Gemara* (35a) qualifies this to mean that he says, 'I adjure you with an oath.' *Tif. Yis.* questions the redundancy of the expression, since to adjure means to charge with an oath. He points out that *Rashi* does not take this literally, but explains it to mean, 'I adjure you by the Name of HASHEM.' *Yerushalmi* states explicitly that the expression, 'with an oath,' is required only for the following two formulae, not for the formula, 'I adjure you.' *Rambam (Hil. Shevuos* 9:11), however, takes the *Gemara* literally, that he adjures them by uttering, 'I adjure you with an oath.'

„מְצַוֶּה אֲנִי עֲלֵיכֶם," — *'I command you,'*

I.e., I command you with an oath *(Rav* from *Gem.* 35a).

„אוֹסֶרְכֶם אֲנִי" — — *'I bind you'* —

I.e., I bind you with an oath *(Rav* from *Gem.* 35a). Without adding the words *with an oath,* neither of these expressions make any sense and cannot qualify as oaths *(Gem.).* According to *Rashi* (above), the *Gemara's* intention is not that he adds the words *with an oath* to these expressions, but that he charges them by these expressions with the Name of HASHEM (without necessarily mentioning an oath). *Rambam (Hil. Shevuos* 9:11), too, requires the mention of the Holy Name, but he requires the mention of *an oath* as well.

Ran explains that the oaths mentioned in the Torah are always accompanied by the name of God. See, for example, *(Lev.* 19:12): וְלֹא תִשָּׁבְעוּ בִשְׁמִי לַשָּׁקֶר, *And you shall not swear by My Name falsely;* and *(Ex.* 20:7) לֹא תִשָּׂא אֶת־שֵׁם ה׳ אֱלֹהֶיךָ לַשָּׁוְא, *You shall not take the Name of HASHEM your God in a vain oath.* In this context, he need not use the actual Name; any of the substitutes for *Hashem's* Name also suffice (see below). There is, however, a prohibition against swearing falsely even if one does not mention the Name of God. However, only swearing by the Name makes one liable for a sin-offering. Others rule that it is not necessary to mention God's Name in order to be liable for the oath of testimony, as long as he mentions 'oath' with one of the above expressions. However, if he swears by God's Name, he is liable even though he does not mention the word 'oath' *(Tos. Yom Tov).*

הֲרֵי אֵלּוּ חַיָּבִין. — *they are liable.*

[I.e., they are liable to a sacrifice for the oath of testimony.]

„בַּשָּׁמַיִם וּבָאָרֶץ" — — *'By heaven and earth'* —

[I.e., if he adjures them by reciting the following, 'I adjure you by heaven and earth that if you know testimony for me, you come and testify.']

הֲרֵי אֵלּוּ פְּטוּרִין. — *they are exempt.*

[They are exempt from the variable sin-offering of the oath of testimony.] We do not construe this to mean, 'I adjure you by the Master of heaven and earth,' in which case it would be swearing by the name of HASHEM; rather, we interpret it literally *(Gem.* 35b).

4
13 13. [If he says,] 'I adjure you,' 'I command you,' 'I bind you' — they are liable. 'By heaven and earth' — they are exempt. 'By *Aleph-dalet*,' 'by *Yud-hei*,' 'by *Shaddai*,' 'by *Tzevaos*,' 'by the Gracious

YAD AVRAHAM

◆§ Names of God

The Names of God found in the Torah are grouped by the Sages into three categories: (1) the Ineffable Name; (2) names which may not be erased (a mark of their great holiness); and (3) substitute names. As the mishnah explains, these groupings are relevant to the oath of testimony, the death penalty for blasphemy, the death penalty for cursing one's parents, and the penalty of lashes for cursing oneself or one's neighbor, all of which engender liability only if they include in some form the name of HASHEM.

The Ineffable Name, known in Hebrew as the שֵׁם הַמְיֻחָד, is the Tetragrammaton, written in Hebrew as *yud, keh, vav, keh,* which means: הָיָה הֹוֶה וְיִהְיֶה, *He was, He is, and He will be* — i.e., the Eternal One (*Shulchan Aruch, Orach Chaim* 5). This is the proper Name of God, which may not be uttered as it is written, but is pronounced instead as אֲדֹנָי. This Name may not be erased.

The second group is comprised of six other names in addition to the Ineffable Name. These, too, are Names of God, and may, therefore, not be erased. They are, however, not the principal Name. According to *Yoreh Deah* 276:9, they are as follows: אֲדֹנָי, *Lord;* אֱלֹהִים, אֱלוֹהַּ, אֵל, three variants meaning *God, the All-powerful One* (*Orach Chaim* 5); שַׁדַּי, *the Almighty;* צְבָאוֹת, [*the Lord of*] *Hosts,* i.e., of the hosts of heaven and earth. Some include אֶהְיֶה אֲשֶׁר אֶהְיֶה, *I will be that which I will be.* [It should be noted that due to the great sanctity of these Names, many people avoid pronouncing them during study discussions. Generally, they are pronounced on these occasions with one of their letters altered, e.g., *Kel, Elokim, Shakkai, Tzevakos.*]

The third group is comprised of other Names, describing God's attributes, e.g., הַגָּדוֹל, *the Great One;* הַגִּבּוֹר, *the Mighty One;* רַחוּם, *the Compassionate One;* אֶרֶךְ אַפַּיִם, *Slow to Anger;* רַב חֶסֶד, *Abundant in Kindness.* These are regarded as adjectives, and may be erased.

Note that the names in the second group are occasionally referred to as actual Names. This is done in order to contrast them with the names in the third group, which are merely adjectives. On other occasions, they are known as substitutes, in order to contrast them with the Tetragrammaton.

„בְּאָלֶ״ף דָּלֶ״ת," — *'By Aleph-dalet,'*

I.e., he says to the witnesses, 'I adjure you by *Adonay*,' the traditional reading of the Tetragrammaton (*Meiri*). *Rashi* seems to explain it to mean that he says, 'I adjure you by the Name written with *Aleph-dalet*,' without actually uttering the Name (*Tif. Yis.*).

„בְּיוּ״ד הֵ״י," — *'by Yud-hei,'*

This, too, may be explained in two ways. Either the claimant pronounced the Tetragrammaton, adjuring the witnesses thereby, or he said, 'I adjure you by the Name written with *Yud-hei*' (*Tif. Yis.*).[1]

„בְּשַׁדַּי," — *'by Shaddai,'*

This is one of the Names of God which may not be erased (35a). It is usually rendered, 'the Almighty.' (See *Ibn Ezra* to *Exodus* 6:3.) [As noted above,

1. *Shoshannim LeDavid* explains *Rashi* in the same manner as *Meiri*. He, however, comments that *Rashi* explains 'by *Yud-hei*' to mean that he pronounces God's Name in the traditional manner of *Aleph-dalet* etc., but his intention is to the spelling of the Tetragrammaton. By

שבועות „בִּצְבָאוֹת,״ „בְּחַנּוּן וְרַחוּם,״ „בְּאֶרֶךְ אַפַּיִם וְרַב
ד/יג חֶסֶד,״ וּבְכָל־הַכִּנּוּיִין — הֲרֵי אֵלּוּ חַיָּבִין.
הַמְקַלֵּל בְּכֻלָּן, חַיָּב; דִּבְרֵי רַבִּי מֵאִיר. וַחֲכָמִים פּוֹטְרִין. הַמְקַלֵּל אָבִיו וְאִמּוֹ בְּכֻלָּן, חַיָּב; דִּבְרֵי רַבִּי מֵאִיר. וַחֲכָמִים פּוֹטְרִין.

יד אברהם

many avoid pronouncing this Name (outside of the prayer or Torah readings), substituting a 'k' for the 'd' and pronouncing it as *Shakkai.*]

„בִּצְבָאוֹת,״ — *'by Tzevaos,'*

This, too, is one of the Names which may not be erased (*Shevuos* 35a). [It is translated as *Lord of Hosts*, meaning the Lord of the hosts of heaven and earth. Here too, the pronunciation *Tzevakos* is often substituted.]

These names are chosen as examples of the Names of God which may not be erased. Others are אֱלֹהִים, אֱלוֹהַ, אֵל, etc. (*Tif. Yis.*).

„בְּחַנּוּן וְרַחוּם,״ „בְּאֶרֶךְ אַפַּיִם וְרַב חֶסֶד,״ וּבְכָל־הַכִּנּוּיִין — הֲרֵי אֵלּוּ חַיָּבִין. — *'By the Gracious and the Compassionate,' 'by the Slow to Anger and Abundant in Kindness,' or with any of the substitutes — they are liable.*

Although he does not pronounce God's Name, since his intention is 'the One Who is gracious, the One who is compassionate,' he is deemed as adjuring by God. This is unlike 'by heaven and earth,' in which case we do not construe his intention as 'by the Master of heaven and earth,' since it is possible to interpret his words literally (*Tos. Yom Tov* from *Shevuos* 35b).

הַמְקַלֵּל בְּכֻלָּן, חַיָּב; — *Should one blaspheme any of them, he is liable;*

I.e., if one curses any of the Names of God, even these substitutes for His Name, he is liable to the death penalty by stoning (*Rav* as explained by *Tos. Yom Tov*). [To be liable for the penalty for blasphemy, the person must curse the Name of God with His Name. *See Sanhedrin* 7:5. Although the wording of the mishnah (בְּכֻלָּן, lit. *with any of them*) would indicate that the reference is to the Name being used to curse, *Tos. Yom Tov* demonstrates that the mishnah must be referring to the Name being blasphemed.]

דִּבְרֵי רַבִּי מֵאִיר. — *[these are] the words of R' Meir.*

R' Meir reasons that since the Torah states (*Lev.* 24:16): וְנֹקֵב שֵׁם ה׳ מוֹת יוּמָת, *One who blasphemes the Name of* HASHEM *shall be put to death*, why was it necessary to state: אִישׁ אִישׁ כִּי יְקַלֵּל אֱלֹהָיו וְנָשָׂא חֶטְאוֹ, *Should any man blaspheme his God, he shall bear his sin?* It should state simply: Should any man blaspheme the Name, he shall bear his sin and be put to death. We therefore deduce that he is liable for blaspheming any Name of God, even a substitute [i.e., the second and third categories of Names]. This is intimated by יְקַלֵּל אֱלֹהָיו, *blaspheme his God*, meaning any Name referring to God (*Tos. Yom Tov* from *Gem.* 36a, *Rashi*).

וַחֲכָמִים פּוֹטְרִין. — *But the Sages exempt [him].*

I.e., the Sages exempt from stoning one who blasphemes any Name of God but the actual Name. According to *Rashi*, this refers only to the Tetragrammaton. According to *Rambam* (*Hil. Avodah Zarah* 2:7), it includes the Name אֲדֹנָי, as well. However, he specifies that this

explaining the mishnah in this manner, he circumvents the difficulty of having the claimant pronounce the Tetragrammaton according to its spelling, a sin for which one loses his share in the World to Come (*Sanhedrin* 10:1). See *Tos.* 35a.

4
13

and the Compassionate,' 'by the Slow to Anger and Abundant in Kindness,' or with any of the substitutes — they are liable.

Should one blaspheme any of them, he is liable; [these are] the words of R' Meir. But the Sages exempt [him].

Should one curse his father or mother by any of them, he is liable; [these are] the words of R' Meir. But the Sages exempt [him].

YAD AVRAHAM

applies only to the Name being blasphemed. The Name invoked to blaspheme God may be any of the Names which may not be erased.

This is derived from (*Lev.* 24:16): בְּנָקְבוֹ שֵׁם יוּמָת, *when he blasphemes the Name, he shall be put to death.* Only if he blasphemes 'the Name' of God is he put to death. For blaspheming any other Name or substitute of God's Name, one transgresses the negative commandment (*Ex.* 22:27): אֱלֹהִים לֹא תְקַלֵּל, *You shall not curse God.* [Whether there is a penalty of lashes for transgressing this negative commandment, see *Minchas Chinuch, Mitzvah* 70.] According to *Tos.* (35a), there is also a penalty of *kares.* The *Gemara* means merely that there is no death penalty. *Rambam* does not mention this. See *Minchas Chinuch* ad loc.

As noted earlier in the mishnah, all three categories of Names suffice to render witnesses liable for an oath of testimony. In regard to this the Sages concur with R' Meir that one is liable not only for an oath containing the actual Name, but even for the substitutes. This is based on (*Lev.* 5:1), וְשָׁמְעָה קוֹל אָלָה, *and hear the voice of an adjuration,* which includes substitutes for God's Name (*Rav; Rambam Comm.* from *Gem.* 36a).

הַמְקַלֵּל אָבִיו וְאִמּוֹ בְּכֻלָּן, חַיָּב; דִּבְרֵי רַבִּי מֵאִיר. — *Should one curse his father or mother by any of them, he is liable;* [*these are*] *the words of R' Meir.*

[I.e., with any of these substitutes, he is liable to the death penalty of stoning (*Lev.* 20:9; *Sanhedrin* 7:8). Just as R' Meir rules that one who blasphemes any substitute for God's Name is liable, so too he rules that one who curses his father or mother by saying, 'May the Gracious One smite you,' or the like, is liable to the death penalty.]

וַחֲכָמִים פּוֹטְרִין. — *But the Sages exempt* [*him*].

The Sages derive this from (*Lev.* 24:16): בְּנָקְבוֹ שֵׁם יוּמָת, *when he blasphemes the Name, he shall be put to death.* This seemingly superfluous verse is taken by the Sages to teach that one who curses his father or mother is liable only if he curses them with the actual Name (*Gem.* 36a).

According to *Rashi's* view on the penalty of the blasphemer, the meaning is that he is liable only if he curses his parents by invoking the Tetragrammaton. *Rashi* to *Sanhedrin* 66a explains, however, that one is liable if he curses one of his parents by 'one of the actual Names.' The use of the plural would imply that he is liable also for invoking the Name אֲדֹנָי. He further states that he is exempt if he curses by one of the substitutes, e.g., חַנּוּן, רַחוּם, שַׁדַּי, צְבָאוֹת. This, too, implies that the Name אֲדֹנָי belongs in the first group.

Rav (*Sanhedrin* 7:8) explains that one is liable for cursing with any of the actual Names, but not for the Names: רַחוּם, חַנּוּן, *the Compassionate One, the Gracious One;* אֶרֶךְ אַפַּיִם, *the Slow to Anger* [i.e., the names of the third category]. From this it appears that he is liable for cursing with any of the Names which may not be erased (the second category). This appears to be *Rambam's* view as well. *Radbaz* (*Hil. Mamrim* 5:2) explains that *Rambam* derives this from the law of blasphemy, for which one is liable should he blaspheme the actual Name by invoking one of the Names that may not be erased (see *Hil. Avodah Zarah* 2:7).

הַמְקַלֵּל עַצְמוֹ וַחֲבֵרוֹ בְּכֻלָּן, עוֹבֵר בְּלֹא תַעֲשֶׂה. „יַכְּכָה אֱלֹהִים,״ „וְכֵן יַכְּכָה אֱלֹהִים״ — זוֹ הִיא אָלָה הַכְּתוּבָה בַּתּוֹרָה. „אַל יַכְּךָ,״ „וִיבָרֶכְךָ,״ וְ„יֵיטִיב לְךָ״ — רַבִּי מֵאִיר מְחַיֵּב, וַחֲכָמִים פּוֹטְרִין.

[א] **שְׁבוּעַת** הַפִּקָּדוֹן נוֹהֶגֶת בַּאֲנָשִׁים וּבְנָשִׁים, בִּרְחוֹקִים וּבִקְרוֹבִים, בִּכְשֵׁרִים

יד אברהם

הַמְקַלֵּל עַצְמוֹ וַחֲבֵרוֹ בְּכֻלָּן, — *Should one curse himself or his neighbor by any of these,*

[I.e., if one curses himself or his neighbor by one of these substitutes for God's Name.]

עוֹבֵר בְּלֹא תַעֲשֶׂה. — *he transgresses a negative commandment.*

Should he curse himself, he transgresses the negative commandment stated in *Deut.* 4:9: רַק הִשָּׁמֶר־לְךָ וּשְׁמֹר נַפְשְׁךָ מְאֹד, *Only beware and guard your soul exceedingly.* Wherever the Torah states הִשָּׁמֶר, *beware,* it is counted as a negative commandment. Should he curse his neighbor, he transgresses the negative commandment, stated in *Lev.* 19:14: לֹא־תְקַלֵּל חֵרֵשׁ, *You shall not curse a deaf person.* I.e., even a deaf person who cannot hear the curse, and, therefore, takes no offense you may not curse. Surely, one may not curse his neighbor who does hear *(Rav* from *Gem.* 36a).

„יַכְּכָה אֱלֹהִים,״ — *'May God smite you,'*

I.e., if one says to witnesses, 'May God smite you if you do not come and testify on my behalf' *(Rav).* [The singular form indicates that he spoke to each one individually.]

„וְכֵן יַכְּכָה אֱלֹהִים״ — — [*or*] *'So may God smite you'* —

I.e., he heard someone reading the verse in the Torah *(Deut.* 28:28) with the words: יַכְּכָה אֱלֹהִים, *May God smite you,* and he said to witnesses, 'So may God smite you if you do not testify on my behalf' *(Rav).*

[In fact, the Biblical verses *(Deut.* 28:28,29,35) all read: „יַכְּכָה ה, *may HASHEM smite you.* There are several other readings which appear to be more accurate. *Rif's* reading is: „יַכְּכָה ה׳,״ „וכן יַכְּכָה ה׳ ״ *'May HASHEM smite you,'* or *'So may HASHEM smite you,'* using the word ה׳, which is written in the verse instead of אֱלֹהִים. However, the reading found in our texts may also be correct. The mishnah alters the actual language of the verse to teach that although the reader reads, *'May HASHEM smite you,'* and he responds, 'So may *God* smite you,' it is regarded as the adjuration mentioned in the Torah even though he does not use the Name quoted in the verse *(Tos. Yom Tov* from *Chochmas Shlomo).*

זוֹ הִיא אָלָה הַכְּתוּבָה בַּתּוֹרָה. — *this is the curse written in the Torah.*

I.e., the Torah uses this expression in conjunction with the curses of the Torah delineated in that chapter. Consequently, these curses constitute the adjuration required for liability to the oath of testimony, also referred to as אָלָה *(Tif. Yis.).*

„אַל יַכְּךָ,״ — *'May He not smite you,'*

I.e., 'May God not smite you if you testify on my behalf' *(Rav; Rashi).*

וְ„יְבָרֶכְךָ,״ — *or 'May He bless you,'*

'May God bless you if you testify on my behalf' *(Rav; Rashi).*

וְ„יֵיטִיב לְךָ״ — — *or 'May He benefit you'*

'May God benefit you if you testify on my behalf' *(Rav).* I.e., he adjured the witnesses with one of these expressions and they denied knowledge of testimony *(Rashi).*

רַבִּי מֵאִיר מְחַיֵּב, — *R' Meir declares [him] liable,*

5
1 Should one curse himself or his neighbor by any of these, he transgresses a negative commandment. 'May God smite you,' [or] 'So may God smite you' — this is the curse written in the Torah. 'May He not smite you,' or 'May He bless you,' or 'May He benefit you' — R' Meir declares [him] liable, but the Sages exempt [him].

1. The oath of deposit applies to both men and women, non-relatives and relatives, those quali-

YAD AVRAHAM

In all these cases, R' Meir rules that the witnesses are liable. It is R' Meir's opinion that from the negative we can derive the affirmative — i.e., that framing a statement in the negative is tantamount to making the implied converse statement as well. Consequently, we understand him to mean, 'May God not smite if you testify, but may He smite you if you do not testify.' 'May He bless you if you testify, but may He curse you if you do not testify.' 'May he benefit you if you testify, but may He harm you if you do not testify' *(Rav; Rashi)*.

Although R' Meir usually does not subscribe to this theory (as in *Kiddushin* 3:4), that is only in monetary matters, but in matters pertaining to prohibitions, R' Meir does derive the affirmative from the negative *(Tos. Yom Tov* from *Gem.* 36b).

וַחֲכָמִים פּוֹטְרִין. — *but the Sages exempt [him]*.

Although the Sages usually hold that we derive the affirmative from the negative, they make an exception in this case. Since the Torah states: *And hear the voice of an adjuration*, they must actually hear that adjuration, not hear a blessing from which they deduce a curse *(Tos. Yom Tov, Tif. Yis.* from *Ran)*.

The halachah is not in accordance with R' Meir in any of the aforementioned controversies *(Rav; Rambam Comm.)*.

Chapter 5

The following chapter deals with שְׁבוּעַת הַפִּקָּדוֹן, *the oath of the deposit*. This involves one who has in his possession either a deposit, a loan, a stolen article, or the like, belonging to his neighbor, and swears that he does not have it. If he confesses, he must repay the principal, with the addition of a fifth, and bring an אָשָׁם, *guilt-offering*, as a sacrifice. This is stated in the text of *Lev.* 5:20-26. Although the oath applies to debts other than deposits, it is called the 'oath of the deposit' because the deposit is the first example mentioned in the verse.

1.

Following the precedent of the preceding chapter, the *Tanna* begins his delineation of the rules of the oath of deposit by outlining to whom the oath of the deposit sacrifice applies and to whom it does not *(Meiri)*.

שְׁבוּעַת הַפִּקָּדוֹן נוֹהֶגֶת בַּאֲנָשִׁים וּבְנָשִׁים, — *The oath of deposit applies to both men and women*,

Unlike the oath of testimony, which applies only to men, the oath of deposit applies to women as well. Women are excluded from the law of the oath of testimony only because they are ineligible to testify. This factor is irrelevant to the oath of deposit. Although this is obvious, the mishnah states this ruling to contrast the oath of deposit with the oath of testimony. Having stated this distinc-

שבועות ה/א

וּבִפְסוּלִים; בִּפְנֵי בֵית דִּין וְשֶׁלֹּא בִפְנֵי בֵית דִּין, מִפִּי עַצְמוֹ; וּמִפִּי אֲחֵרִים, אֵינוֹ חַיָּב עַד־שֶׁיִּכְפֹּר בּוֹ בְּבֵית דִּין; דִּבְרֵי רַבִּי מֵאִיר. וַחֲכָמִים אוֹמְרִים: בֵּין מִפִּי עַצְמוֹ בֵּין מִפִּי אֲחֵרִים, כֵּיוָן שֶׁכָּפַר בּוֹ, חַיָּב.

וְחַיָּב עַל־זְדוֹן הַשְּׁבוּעָה, וְעַל־שִׁגְגָתָהּ עִם־זְדוֹן הַפִּקָּדוֹן, וְאֵינוֹ חַיָּב עַל־שִׁגְגָתָהּ. וּמַה חַיָּב עַל־

יד אברהם

tion, the mishnah delineates all the other differences between them as well *(Rav; Rashi)*.

Tif. Yis. suggests that the inclusion of women may be because most women have no money of their own with which to pay their debts [since their earnings and property belong to their husbands]. We might thus be inclined to believe that claiming a debt from a married woman does not constitute a monetary claim, nor does her denial constitute a denial of money. There would, therefore, be no liability to a guilt-offering and an additional fifth. For this reason, the mishnah teaches that women *are* liable for the oath, since they do indeed owe the debt and may, at some future time, come into property with which to pay it (see *Bava Kamma* 8:4). Accordingly, it is deemed a monetary claim.

בִּרְחוֹקִים וּבִקְרוֹבִים, — *non-relatives and relatives,*

I.e., there is no difference whether the claimant and defendant are related to one another or not *(Rav; Rashi)*. This, too, is stated to contrast the oath of deposit with the oath of testimony, which applies only to non-relatives [4:1] *(Rav; Rashi)*.

Tif. Yis. suggests that the mishnah specifies relatives to teach that even in a case in which the defendant is a close enough relative to the claimant that he stands to inherit the money involved upon the latter's death, it is still considered a monetary claim. Even if the claimant is on his deathbed at the time of the oath, and will probably die before the defendant is able to make the payment, it is considered a monetary claim, and the defendant is liable to the sacrifice for the false oath of deposit.

בִּכְשֵׁרִים וּבִפְסוּלִים; — *those qualified and those disqualified;*

I.e., both those qualified to testify and those disqualified from testifying are liable to the oath of deposit. This clause, too, is to contrast the oath of deposit with the oath of testimony *(Rav; Rashi)*.

Here too *Tif. Yis.* suggests that this clause is inserted to teach that even in the case of a person whose oath is not accepted by a court to exempt him from payment of claims because he is a person suspected of swearing falsely, he is nevertheless liable for the oath of the deposit if he swears it falsely.

בִּפְנֵי בֵית דִּין וְשֶׁלֹּא בִפְנֵי בֵית דִּין, מִפִּי עַצְמוֹ; — *in court and out of court by his own mouth;*

I.e., if the defendant swears the oath himself, or he answers, 'Amen' to the adjuration of the claimant, which as we learned above (3:10) is equivalent to pronouncing the oath himself, and he then confesses that he owes the money, he is liable whether the oath was pronounced before the court or elsewhere. This is derived from *(Lev.* 5:21): וְכִחֵשׁ בַּעֲמִיתוֹ, *and he lied to his neighbor,* meaning that wherever he lies to his neighbor, whether before the court or elsewhere, he is liable *(Rav; Rashi)*.

וּמִפִּי אֲחֵרִים, — *but [if adjured] by others,*

I.e., he neither uttered an oath himself nor answered 'Amen' to the claimant's adjuration, but responded to the adjuration by repeating his denial, 'You have nothing in my possession' *(Rav; Rashi; Tif. Yis.)*.

אֵינוֹ חַיָּב — *he is not liable*

[I.e., he is not liable to an additional fifth and a guilt-offering. The principal, however, must obviously be returned.]

עַד־שֶׁיִּכְפֹּר בּוֹ בְּבֵית דִּין; דִּבְרֵי רַבִּי מֵאִיר. — *unless he denies it in court; [these are] the words of R' Meir.*

5
1

fied and those disqualified; in court and out of court by his own mouth; but [if adjured] by others, he is not liable unless he denies it in court; [these are] the words of R' Meir. But the Sages say: Whether by his own mouth or whether [adjured] by others, once he denies it, he is liable.

He is liable for a willful transgression of the oath, as well as for its inadvertent transgression coupled with a willful denial of the deposit; but he is not liable for its inadvertent transgression. Now what is he liable for its

YAD AVRAHAM

As explained in 4:1 (s.v. Personal and Adjured Oaths), the Torah mentions an adjured oath in regard to the oath of testimony and a personal oath ('by his own mouth') in regard to the oath of deposit. By analogy, we derive that both types of oaths apply to both categories. R' Meir reasons that since liability for an adjured oath in the case of an oath of deposit is derived from the oath of testimony, the liability for it cannot be greater than that of the oath of testimony. Since one is liable for the oath of testimony only if he denies before court, the same applies to the oath of the deposit (*Tos. Yom Tov* from *Rashi*, based on *Gem.* 31a).

וַחֲכָמִים אוֹמְרִים: בֵּין מִפִּי עַצְמוֹ בֵּין מִפִּי אֲחֵרִים, כֵּיוָן שֶׁכָּפַר בּוֹ, חַיָּב. — *But the Sages say: Whether by his own mouth or whether [adjured] by others, once he denies it, he is liable.*

The Sages reason that although the liability of one adjured by others is derived from the oath of testimony, once derived it must be applied in the context of the oath of the deposit. Since in the case of the oath of deposit mentioned explicitly in the verse — that of the personal oath — the Torah makes him liable even for an out-of-court denial, so too he is liable when adjured by others even out of court (*Tos. Yom Tov* from *Rashi*, based on *Gem.* 31a).

וְחַיָּב עַל־זְדוֹן הַשְּׁבוּעָה, — *He is liable for a willful transgression of the oath,*

Even if he remembered at the time of the oath that the deposit was in his possession and that there is an obligation of a guilt-offering for swearing falsely, he is still liable to a guilt-offering. This is unlike the rule for sin-offerings in general which are brought only for unintentional transgressions (*Shabbos* 69a). This is derived from the fact that the Torah does not specify וְנֶעְלַם, *and he forgot,* regarding the liability for a sacrifice when swearing a false oath of deposit (*Rav; Rashi*).

וְעַל־שִׁגְגָתָהּ עִם־זְדוֹן הַפִּקָּדוֹן, — *as well as for its inadvertent transgression coupled with a willful denial of the deposit,*

I.e., if he does not know that a false oath must be expiated by a guilt-offering, but he does know that the deposit is in his possession and that he is swearing falsely (*Rav; Rashi*). See above 4:2.

This is unlike other sins, for which one is exempt from a sin-offering if he commits a sin willfully, even if he is unaware that a sin-offering is required to expiate that sin (*Shabbos* 69a). [In the case of most sin-offerings, he is liable only if he errs concerning the substance itself; for example, if he is unaware that the fat he is eating is of the prohibited type (חֵלֶב) or he is unaware that certain fats are prohibited.] (*Tif. Yis.*).

וְאֵינוֹ חַיָּב עַל־שִׁגְגָתָהּ. — *but he is not liable for its inadvertent transgression.*

I.e., a transgression which is completely inadvertent, one in which he

וְדוֹנָהּ? אָשָׁם בְּכֶסֶף שְׁקָלִים.

[ב] **שְׁבוּעַת** הַפִּקָּדוֹן כֵּיצַד? אָמַר לוֹ: „תֶּן־לִי פִּקְדוֹנִי שֶׁיֶּשׁ־לִי בְּיָדְךָ," „שְׁבוּעָה שֶׁאֵין לְךָ בְּיָדִי"; אוֹ־שֶׁאָמַר לוֹ: „אֵין לְךָ בְּיָדִי," „מַשְׁבִּיעֲךָ אֲנִי," וְאָמַר: „אָמֵן" — הֲרֵי זֶה חַיָּב. הִשְׁבִּיעַ עָלָיו חֲמִשָּׁה פְּעָמִים, בֵּין בִּפְנֵי בֵית דִּין וּבֵין שֶׁלֹּא בִּפְנֵי בֵית דִּין, וְכָפַר — חַיָּב עַל־כָּל־אַחַת וְאַחַת. אָמַר רַבִּי שִׁמְעוֹן: מַה־טַּעַם? מִפְּנֵי שֶׁיָּכוֹל לַחֲזוֹר וּלְהוֹדוֹת.

יד אברהם

believes that what he is swearing is true. Such a false oath is deemed an אוֹנֶס, *unavoidable error (Rashi).* [See above, 4:2.]

וּמַה חַיָּב עַל־זְדוֹנָהּ? — *Now what is he liable for its willful transgression?*

[I.e., what is his liability when he intentionally transgresses the oath of deposit?]

אָשָׁם בְּכֶסֶף שְׁקָלִים. — *A guilt-offering worth [at least two] silver shekels.*

One liable for a guilt-offering must bring a ram worth at least two silver shekels, as in *Lev.* 5:14 *(Rav; Rashi).* Although that verse deals with אֲשַׁם מְעִילוֹת, *a me'ilah guilt-offering* — a guilt-offering for misusing consecrated objects — we derive the law of other guilt-offerings from there (*Tos. Yom Tov* from *Tos., Ran,* based on *Kereisos* 22b).

Of course, he must also repay the money he illegally withheld. In addition to this, he must also add a penalty payment of one-fifth the amount he denied (see below, mishnah 8:3; *Rambam, Hil. Shevuos* 1:9, *Gezeilah* 7:1,2). However, both this penalty payment and the guilt-offering are made only when the sinner admits his guilt. If he continues to deny that he swore falsely, even though witnesses have testified that he is lying, he repays only the principle but is exempt from the penalty and the guilt-offering (see mishnah 8:3). These last two items are for the purpose of atonement and they can therefore not be imposed by the testimony of witnesses where the defendant refuses to admit his guilt and repent (*Rambam, Gezeilah* 7:8).

2.

שְׁבוּעַת הַפִּקָּדוֹן כֵּיצַד? — *What is the case of the oath of deposit?*

[In what cases is one liable?]

אָמַר לוֹ, — *[If] someone said to him,*

[I.e., one person said to another.] The mishnah states this by way of example, but one is actually liable for an oath of deposit even if he swears of his own volition, with no one making any claim (*Tos. Yom Tov* from *Gem.* 32a).

„תֶּן־לִי פִּקְדוֹנִי שֶׁיֶּשׁ־לִי בְּיָדְךָ," — *'Give me my deposit that I have in your possession,'*

[I.e., my deposit with which I entrusted you.] Although one is liable for an oath of deposit even without a claim, he is liable only if he swears to someone who can say, 'Give me *my* deposit,' i.e., the owner of the money. Should he swear to someone other than the one to whom the money rightfully belongs, he is not liable to the sacrifice even though he swore falsely. However, should the claimant

5 willful transgression? A guilt-offering worth [at least
2 two] silver shekels.

2. What is the case of the oath of deposit? [If] someone said to him, 'Give me my deposit that I have in your possession,' [and he replied,] 'I swear that you have nothing in my possession'; or he replied, 'You have nothing in my possession,' [to which the other said,] 'I adjure you,' and he said, 'Amen' — he is liable. [If] he adjured him five times, either in court or out of court, and he denied [it] — he is liable for each one. Said R' Shimon: What is the reason? Because he can retract and confess.

YAD AVRAHAM

send an agent, he, too, as a representative, may say, 'Give me my deposit,' making the holder liable if he swears falsely to him.

Tos. Yom Tov insists that this applies only if he grants him power of attorney. Otherwise, an agent does not stand in place of his sender in matters of exacting money. *Tif. Yis*, following *Kesef Mishneh (Hil. Shevuos* 7:6), however, explains the mishnah to mean that even if he did not grant him power of attorney, but merely appointed him his agent, he represents him. Consequently, if the defendant swears in his presence, he is liable for a false oath of deposit. See 4:12.

"שְׁבוּעָה שֶׁאֵין לְךָ בְּיָדִי"; — *[and he replied,] 'I swear that you have nothing in my possession';*

[I.e., that you never entrusted a deposit to me.]

אוֹ־שֶׁאָמַר לוֹ: "אֵין לְךָ בְּיָדִי," — *or he replied, 'You have nothing in my possession,'*

[I.e., he did not swear, but merely stated, 'You have nothing in my hand.']

"מַשְׁבִּיעֲךָ אֲנִי," — *[to which the other said,] 'I adjure you,'*

[The claimant responds to the denial by adjuring the defendant with an oath that his denial is true.]

וְאָמַר: "אָמֵן" — הֲרֵי זֶה חַיָּב. — *and he said, 'Amen' — he is liable.*

[I.e., he is liable to a guilt-offering, as in mishnah 1.]

Answering 'Amen' constitutes an oath by his own mouth, as explained above (3:11). According to R' Meir, who rules that if he is adjured by others he is liable only if he denies the adjuration in court, we may say that the mishnah chooses the case of one who swears by his own mouth because one is liable for such an oath even if he denies the claim outside of court. According to the Sages, however, one who is adjured by others is liable even if he denies outside of court. Consequently, the mishnah could just as well have chosen a case in which he accepted the oath without saying 'Amen,' which would constitute being adjured by others. It chooses, however, to conform to the format established in mishnah 3 of the preceding chapter *(Tos. Yom Tov)*.

Beis David suggests that since the verse deals with the case of one who swears by his own mouth, the mishnah also chooses this case, rather than the case of one adjured by others.

הִשְׁבִּיעַ עָלָיו חֲמִשָּׁה פְּעָמִים, בֵּין בִּפְנֵי בֵית דִּין וּבֵין שֶׁלֹּא בִפְנֵי בֵית דִּין, וְכָפַר — *[If] he adjured him five times, either in court or out of court, and he denied [it]* —

I.e., either he swore a denial five times, or the claimant adjured him five times, and he denied each allegation, whether in court or out *(Rambam, Hil. Shevuos* 7:9).

חַיָּב עַל־כָּל־אַחַת וְאַחַת. — *he is liable for each one.*

[I.e., he is liable to a sacrifice for each false oath.]

[ג] **הָיוּ** חֲמִשָּׁה תוֹבְעִין אוֹתוֹ, אָמְרוּ לוֹ: „תֶּן־לָנוּ פִּקָּדוֹן שֶׁיֶּשׁ־לָנוּ בְּיָדְךָ,״ „שְׁבוּעָה שֶׁאֵין לָכֶם בְּיָדִי״ — אֵינוֹ חַיָּב אֶלָּא אַחַת. „שְׁבוּעָה שֶׁאֵין לְךָ בְיָדִי, וְלֹא לְךָ וְלֹא לְךָ — חַיָּב עַל־כָּל־אַחַת וְאַחַת. רַבִּי אֱלִיעֶזֶר אוֹמֵר: עַד־שֶׁיֹּאמַר „שְׁבוּעָה״ בָּאַחֲרוֹנָה. רַבִּי שִׁמְעוֹן אוֹמֵר: עַד־שֶׁיֹּאמַר „שְׁבוּעָה״ לְכָל־אֶחָד וְאֶחָד.

„תֶּן־לִי פִּקָּדוֹן, וּתְשׂוּמֶת יָד, גָּזֵל, וַאֲבֵדָה, שֶׁיֶּשׁ־לִי בְיָדְךָ,״ „שְׁבוּעָה שֶׁאֵין לְךָ בְיָדִי״ — אֵינוֹ חַיָּב אֶלָּא אַחַת. „שְׁבוּעָה שֶׁאֵין לְךָ בְיָדִי פִּקָּדוֹן, וּתְשׂוּמֶת

יד אברהם

אָמַר רַבִּי שִׁמְעוֹן: מַה־טַּעַם? מִפְּנֵי שֶׁיָּכוֹל לַחֲזוֹר וּלְהוֹדוֹת. — *Said R' Shimon: What is the reason? Because he can retract and confess.*

Why is he liable for each oath? Because he could have confessed after each denial, and he would then have been obligated to pay. Therefore, each oath is a new denial of a monetary obligation. This is in contrast to the ruling above (4:3) in regard to the oath of testimony. There the mishnah ruled that if they were adjured five times and denied knowledge of testimony in court, they are liable only once. The reason for this distinction is that in the case of testimony, once witnesses deny knowledge, they cannot retract their denial (see comm. to 4:3). Hence, after their initial denial they are ineligible to testify and their subsequent oath is not an oath of testimony *(Rav; Rashi; Meiri).* This reasoning does not apply to a deposit, where even after the defendant has denied holding the money, his confession to the contrary would be believed and accepted.

3.

This mishnah now delineates other instances in which one is liable to many guilt-offerings though he actually swore only once.

הָיוּ חֲמִשָּׁה תוֹבְעִין אוֹתוֹ, אָמְרוּ לוֹ: „תֶּן־לָנוּ פִּקָּדוֹן שֶׁיֶּשׁ־לָנוּ בְּיָדְךָ,״ — *[If] five [people] were pressing claims against him, [and] they said to him, 'Give us the deposits that we have in your possession,'*

[I.e., five people were pressing their separate claims for the return of their deposits which each claimed to have entrusted to the defendant.]

„שְׁבוּעָה שֶׁאֵין לָכֶם בְּיָדִי״ — *[to which he replied,] 'I swear that you have nothing in my possession'* —

[I.e., you never entrusted me with a deposit.]

אֵינוֹ חַיָּב אֶלָּא אַחַת. — *he is liable only once.*

[Since he swears but one oath to all of them, using the plural לָכֶם, *to you,* he is liable only once.]

„שְׁבוּעָה שֶׁאֵין לְךָ בְיָדִי, וְלֹא לְךָ וְלֹא לְךָ״ — חַיָּב עַל־כָּל־אַחַת וְאַחַת. — *[But if he replied,] 'I swear that you have nothing in my possession, nor you nor you' — he is liable for each one.*

[Since he addresses each claimant individually, it is considered as though he

3. [If] five [people] were pressing claims against him, [and] they said to him, 'Give us the deposits that we have in your possession,' [to which he replied,] 'I swear that you have nothing in my possession' — he is liable only once. [But if he replied,] 'I swear that you have nothing in my possession, nor you nor you' — he is liable for each one. R' Eliezer says: Not unless he says 'I swear' at the end. R' Shimon says: Not unless he says 'I swear' to each one.

[If someone said to him,] 'Give me the deposit, the loan, the stolen article, and the lost article that I have in your possession,' [and he replied,] 'I swear that you have nothing in my possession' — he is liable only once. [But if he replied,] 'I swear that you have in my possession neither a deposit, a loan, a stolen article nor a lost article'

YAD AVRAHAM

pronounces five oaths, and he is therefore liable to five guilt-offerings. See *Sifra* to *Lev.* 5:26 for the derivation.]

רַבִּי אֱלִיעֶזֶר אוֹמֵר: עַד־שֶׁיֹּאמַר „שְׁבוּעָה" בָּאַחֲרוֹנָה. — *R' Eliezer says: Not unless he says 'I swear' at the end.*

I.e., unless he says, 'You have nothing in my possession, nor you nor you, I swear.' Only in this case does R' Eliezer consider the oath to apply to each one individually [since his reply began as a series of differentiated statements to each one separately]. The opinion of the first *Tanna,* however, is that even if he says 'I swear' in the beginning, it is also considered a series of individual oaths *(Rav; Rashi).*

According to *Yerushalmi,* he is not liable for each one unless he says 'I swear' both at the beginning *and* at the end *(Yerushalmi* 5:3, quoted by *Ramban, Rashba,* et al.).

רַבִּי שִׁמְעוֹן אוֹמֵר: עַד־שֶׁיֹּאמַר „שְׁבוּעָה" לְכָל־אֶחָד וְאֶחָד. — *R' Shimon says: Not unless he says 'I swear' to each one.*

[Even if he says 'I swear' at the end, he is liable to only one guilt-offering, unless he says, 'I swear that you have nothing in my possession, and I swear that you have nothing, and I swear that you have nothing, etc.'] The halachah is in accordance with the first *Tanna (Rambam, Hil. Shevuos* 7:10).

„תֶּן־לִי פִּקָּדוֹן וּתְשׂוּמֶת יָד, גָּזֵל, וַאֲבֵדָה שֶׁיֶּשׁ־לִי בְּיָדְךָ," — [*If someone said to him,*] *'Give me the deposit, the loan, the stolen article, and the lost article that I have in your possession,'*

[I.e., a single plaintiff approached him with four separate claims. The claims used to illustrate this case are the ones mentioned in *Lev.* 5:20-26.]

„שְׁבוּעָה שֶׁאֵין לְךָ בְּיָדִי" — אֵינוֹ חַיָּב אֶלָּא אַחַת. — [*and he replied,*] *'I swear that you have nothing in my possession' — he is liable only once.*

[Since he answered all claims with one general denial, it counts as only one oath, and he is, therefore, liable only once.]

„שְׁבוּעָה שֶׁאֵין לְךָ בְּיָדִי פִּקָּדוֹן, וּתְשׂוּמֶת יָד, וְגָזֵל וַאֲבֵדָה," — [*But if he replied,*] *'I swear that you have in my possession neither a deposit, a loan, a stolen article nor a lost article' —*

[I.e., he directs his oath to each claim individually.]

יָד, וְגָזֵל, וַאֲבֵדָה״ — חַיָּב עַל־כָּל־אַחַת וְאַחַת.
„תֶּן־לִי חִטִּין, וּשְׂעוֹרִין, וְכֻסְּמִים שֶׁיֶּשׁ־לִי בְיָדְךָ,״
„שְׁבוּעָה שֶׁאֵין לְךָ בְיָדִי״ — אֵינוֹ חַיָּב אֶלָּא אַחַת.
„שְׁבוּעָה שֶׁאֵין לְךָ בְיָדִי חִטִּין, וּשְׂעוֹרִין, וְכֻסְּמִין — חַיָּב עַל־כָּל־אַחַת וְאַחַת. רַבִּי מֵאִיר אוֹמֵר: אֲפִילוּ אָמַר: „חִטָּה, וּשְׂעוֹרָה, וְכֻסֶּמֶת,״ חַיָּב עַל־כָּל־אַחַת וְאַחַת.

[ד] **„אָנַסְתָּ״** וּ„פִתִּיתָ אֶת־בִּתִּי,״ וְהוּא אוֹמֵר: „לֹא אָנַסְתִּי״ וְ„לֹא פִתִּיתִי,״
„מַשְׁבִּיעֲךָ אֲנִי,״ וְאָמַר: „אָמֵן״ — חַיָּב. רַבִּי שִׁמְעוֹן פּוֹטֵר, שֶׁאֵינוֹ מְשַׁלֵּם קְנָס עַל־פִּי עַצְמוֹ. אָמְרוּ לוֹ:

יד אברהם

חַיָּב עַל־כָּל־אַחַת וְאַחַת. — *he is liable for each one.*

[His denial is reckoned four separate denials — and oaths — one for each claim. Thus he is liable for each one separately.]

„תֶּן־לִי חִטִּין, וּשְׂעוֹרִין, וְכֻסְּמִים שֶׁיֶּשׁ־לִי בְיָדְךָ,״ — [*If someone said to him,*] *'Give me the wheat, barley, and spelt that I have in your possession,'*

In this case, it is one claim, consisting of various species (*Sifra* ibid.).

„שְׁבוּעָה שֶׁאֵין לְךָ בְיָדִי״ — אֵינוֹ חַיָּב אֶלָּא אַחַת. — [*and he replied,*] *'I swear that you have nothing in my possession' — he is liable only once.*

[Since he responds to the claim with a single, general denial, it is regarded as one oath, and he is, therefore, liable only once.]

„שְׁבוּעָה שֶׁאֵין לְךָ בְיָדִי חִטִּין, וּשְׂעוֹרִין, וְכֻסְּמִין,״ חַיָּב עַל־כָּל־אַחַת וְאַחַת. — [*But if he replied,*] *'I swear that you have in my possession neither wheat, barley, nor spelt' — he is liable for each one.*

Again, since in his oath he specifies each item, he is liable for each one. In these last two cases, too, R' Eliezer and R' Shimon differ, and declare him liable only once. According to R' Eliezer, he is liable for each species only if he says 'I swear' at the end. According to R' Shimon he is liable only if he says a separate 'I swear' concerning each species (*Tos. Yom Tov*, based on *Sifra* ibid.).

רַבִּי מֵאִיר אוֹמֵר: אֲפִילוּ אָמַר: „חִטָּה, וּשְׂעוֹרָה, וְכֻסֶּמֶת,״ חַיָּב עַל־כָּל־אַחַת וְאַחַת. — *R' Meir says: Even if he says, 'A wheat, a barley, and a spelt,' he is liable for each one.*

R' Meir asserts that if one claims that his neighbor owes him wheat (חִטָּה), barley (שְׂעוֹרָה), and spelt (כֻּסֶּמֶת), expressing himself in the singular form, and his neighbor replies, 'I swear that you have in my possession neither wheat (חִטָּה), barley (שְׂעוֹרָה), or spelt (כֻּסֶּמֶת), also in the singular, we do not construe this to mean that he claims one kernel of wheat, one kernel of barley, and one kernel of spelt, which do not equal the worth of a *perutah* [a small coin, the minimum amount considered money under Torah law in regard to transactions of any sort]; we say rather that he meant an amount of grain of wheat, barley, and spelt. The Sages, however, differ with R' Meir, and construe his speech to mean that he claims one kernel of wheat, etc. Since this

5 — he is liable for each one.
4 [If someone said to him,] 'Give me the wheat, barley, and spelt that I have in your possession,' [and he replied,] 'I swear that you have nothing in my possession' — he is liable only once. [But if he replied,] 'I swear that you have in my possession neither wheat, barley, nor spelt' — he is liable for each one. R' Meir says: Even if he says, 'A wheat, a barley, and a spelt,' he is liable for each one.

4. [If someone said to him,] 'You violated' or 'you seduced my daughter,' and he replied, 'I did not violate [her]' or 'I did not seduce [her],' [to which he said,] 'I adjure you,' and he replied, 'Amen' — he is liable. R' Shimon exempts [him], since he does not pay a fine by his own admission. They said to him: Although

YAD AVRAHAM

is not accounted as money, there is no liability to a guilt-offering for a false oath concerning it *(Rav; Tif. Yis.; Tos. Yom Tov)*. The halachah is not in accordance with R' Meir *(Rav; Rambam Comm., Hil. Shevuos* 7:13).

4.

The following two mishnahs are based on the principle that there is no guilt-offering required for denying a fine, since had the defendant admitted his obligation, he would not have been liable to pay the fine. One pays a fine only on the testimony of witnesses, not on his own admission. This has already been discussed in the context of the oath of testimony in the preceding chapter (mishnah 6).

„אָנַסְתָּ" ו„פִּתִּיתָ אֶת־בִּתִּי," — *[If someone said to him,] 'You violated' or 'you seduced my daughter,'*

[The claimant claims that the defendant violated his daughter, committing an offense punishable by a fine of fifty shekels, and indemnity for disgrace, impairment, and pain; or he claims that he seduced his daughter, for which he would also have to pay the fine, plus the indemnity for disgrace and impairment, as in *Kesubos* 3:4.]

וְהוּא אוֹמֵר: „לֹא אָנַסְתִּי" וְ„לֹא פִתִּיתִי," — *and he replied, 'I did not violate [her]' or 'I did not seduce [her],'*

[I.e., in the first case, he replies, 'I did not violate her,' and in the second case he replies, 'I did not seduce her.']

„מַשְׁבִּיעֲךָ אֲנִי," וְאָמַר: „אָמֵן" — *[to which he said,] 'I adjure you,' and he replied, 'Amen' —*

[The plaintiff then adjures the defendant with an oath that he did not commit the crime, and the defendant answers 'Amen.' As we saw above in 3:11, answering 'Amen' to an adjuration is equivalent to uttering the oath.]

חַיָּב. — *he is liable.*

[He is liable to a guilt-offering for the oath of deposit if he subsequently admits to lying.]

רַבִּי שִׁמְעוֹן פּוֹטֵר, שֶׁאֵינוֹ מְשַׁלֵּם קְנָס עַל־פִּי עַצְמוֹ. — *R' Shimon exempts [him], since*

אַף־עַל־פִּי שֶׁאֵינוֹ מְשַׁלֵּם קְנָס עַל־פִּי עַצְמוֹ, מְשַׁלֵּם בֹּשֶׁת וּפְגָם עַל־פִּי עַצְמוֹ.

[ה] ״**גָּנַבְתָּ** אֶת־שׁוֹרִי,״ וְהוּא אוֹמֵר: ״לֹא גָנַבְתִּי״ — ״מַשְׁבִּיעֲךָ אֲנִי,״ וְאָמַר: ״אָמֵן״ — חַיָּב. ״גָּנַבְתִּי, אֲבָל לֹא טָבַחְתִּי וְלֹא מָכַרְתִּי״ — ״מַשְׁבִּיעֲךָ אֲנִי,״ וְאָמַר: ״אָמֵן״ — פָּטוּר. ״הֵמִית שׁוֹרְךָ אֶת־שׁוֹרִי,״ וְהוּא אוֹמֵר: ״לֹא

יד אברהם

he does not pay a fine by his own admission.

Since had he admitted his seduction he would not be liable to pay the fine, denying it is not regarded as denying a monetary obligation *(Rav; Rashi)*. Accordingly, R' Shimon exempts him from the guilt-offering.

אָמְרוּ לוֹ: אַף־עַל־פִּי שֶׁאֵינוֹ מְשַׁלֵּם קְנָס עַל־פִּי עַצְמוֹ, מְשַׁלֵּם בֹּשֶׁת וּפְגָם עַל־פִּי עַצְמוֹ. — *They said to him: Although he does not pay a fine by his own admission, he pays the indemnity for shame and impairment by his own admission.*

Although the Sages agree that there is no guilt-offering for the false denial of a penalty claim, they dispute R' Shimon's ruling in this case because a father's claim regarding the violation or seduction of his daughter is not limited to a claim of fine money but includes a claim for damages — for impairment, shame and pain — as well. Accordingly, by his denial, he is denying restitution, for which there is an obligation to bring a guilt-offering.

The *Gemara* (38b) explains their disagreement in this way. If he claimed, 'You owe me a fifty *shekel* fine for seducing my daughter,' and the defendant swears falsely in denying it, both the Sages and R' Shimon agree that he is not liable. If he explicitly claimed indemnity for disgrace and impairment and not the fine, both the Sages and R' Shimon agree that he is liable for swearing falsely. If, however, he made a general accusation, 'You seduced my daughter,' the Sages feel his primary objective is the payment for disgrace and impairment, since that is an obligation that must and will be paid, whereas a fine is less definite since he can confess and then be exempt. The Sages, therefore, hold him liable. R' Shimon assumes the claimant is interested primarily in the fine, since that is a fixed amount, whereas the payment for disgrace and impairment must first be evaluated by the court. Therefore, R' Shimon holds him not liable *(Rav)*.

In the case of the violator, the indemnity for pain is payable by the admission of the perpetrator. It is regarded as restitution, rather than as a fine. The *Tanna* does not mention it since it does not apply to the seducer *(Tos. Yom Tov; Tif. Yis.)*.

The halachah is in accordance with the Sages *(Rambam, Hil. Shevuos* 8:3).

5.

The following mishnah continues to illustrate the various cases of restitution to which the oath of deposit pertains, and the various cases of fines to which it does not. Three groups are enumerated, each consisting of two contrasting cases, one concerning restitution, the other concerning a fine. They are cases of theft, damage inflicted by a bull, and wounds inflicted upon a person.

5 he does not pay a fine by his own admission, he pays
5 the indemnity for shame and impairment by his own
admission.

5. [If somone said to him,] 'You stole my ox,' and he replied, 'I did not steal [it],' [to which he said,] 'I adjure you,' and he replied, 'Amen' — he is liable. [But if he replied,] 'I stole [it], but I did not slaughter [it] and I did not sell [it],' [to which he said,] 'I adjure you,' and he replied, 'Amen' — he is exempt.

[If he said to him,] 'Your ox killed my ox,' and the other replied, 'It did not kill [it]' — [to which he said,] 'I

YAD AVRAHAM

„גָּנַבְתָּ אֶת־שׁוֹרִי," — *[If someone said to him,] 'You stole my ox,'*

[One says to the other, 'You stole my ox,' for which he is obligated to pay the principal plus a second payment (כֶּפֶל) as a penalty.]

וְהוּא אוֹמֵר: „לֹא גָנַבְתִּי," — *and he replied, 'I did not steal [it],'*

[The defendant denied stealing it.]

„מַשְׁבִּיעֲךָ אֲנִי," וְאָמַר: „אָמֵן" — *[to which he said,] 'I adjure you,' and he replied, 'Amen' —*

[The plaintiff adjured the defendant concerning his denial to which he replied 'Amen.' As explained above, answering 'Amen' is equivalent to personally uttering the oath.]

חַיָּב. — *he is liable.*

Although the double payment is a fine, not payable upon the admission of the perpetrator, he is nevertheless liable to a guilt-offering for denying the principal, which is restitution for the theft itself (*Tos. Yom Tov*).

In this case, even R' Shimon (mishnah 4) agrees that the plaintiff claims both the principal and the double payment since both are fixed amounts (*Tif. Yis.*).

„גָּנַבְתִּי, אֲבָל לֹא טָבַחְתִּי וְלֹא מָכַרְתִּי," — *[But if he replied,] 'I stole [it], but I did not slaughter [it] and I did not sell it,'*

I.e., in a case in which the plaintiff claimed that the defendant stole his ox and slaughtered it or sold it — in which case he is liable to a five-fold payment (*Ex.* 21:37; see *Bava Kamma* ch. 7) — and the defendant confessed the theft but denied having slaughtered the bull or having sold it (*Rambam, Hil. Shevuos* 8:1).

„מַשְׁבִּיעֲךָ אֲנִי," וְאָמַר: „אָמֵן" — *[to which he said,] 'I adjure you,' and he replied, 'Amen' —*

[The plaintiff adjured the defendant that he did not slaughter or sell it, to which the defendant answered 'Amen.']

פָּטוּר. — *he is exempt.*

[Since he previously admitted the theft, his denial pertained only to the slaughtering or the selling of the bull, for which the payment is a fine. For denying the obligation of paying a fine, there is no guilt-offering for the oath of deposit.]

„הֵמִית שׁוֹרְךָ אֶת־שׁוֹרִי," וְהוּא אוֹמֵר: „לֹא הֵמִית" — *[If he said to him,] 'Your ox killed my ox,' and he replied, 'It did not kill [it],'*

[I.e., he claimed that this person's ox, which was a מוּעָד *[muad], habitual gorer*, killed his ox. For this the owner of the goring animal is liable to נֶזֶק שָׁלֵם, *full damages*. The defendant denies this allegation.]

שבועות
ה/ה

הֵמִית" — „מַשְׁבִּיעֲךָ אֲנִי," וְאָמַר: „אָמֵן" — חַיָּב. „הֵמִית שׁוֹרְךָ אֶת־עַבְדִּי," וְהוּא אוֹמֵר: „לֹא הֵמִית"; „מַשְׁבִּיעֲךָ אֲנִי," וְאָמַר: „אָמֵן" — פָּטוּר.

אָמַר לוֹ: „חָבַלְתָּ בִּי וְעָשִׂיתָ בִּי חַבּוּרָה," וְהוּא אוֹמֵר: „לֹא חָבַלְתִּי בְךָ וְלֹא עָשִׂיתִי בְךָ חַבּוּרָה"; „מַשְׁבִּיעֲךָ אֲנִי," וְאָמַר: „אָמֵן" — חַיָּב. אָמַר לוֹ עַבְדּוֹ: „הִפַּלְתָּ אֶת־שִׁנִּי," וְ„סִמִּיתָ אֶת־עֵינִי," וְהוּא אוֹמֵר: „לֹא הִפַּלְתִּי" וְ„לֹא סִמִּיתִי"; „מַשְׁבִּיעֲךָ אֲנִי," וְאָמַר: „אָמֵן" — פָּטוּר. זֶה הַכְּלָל: כָּל־הַמְשַׁלֵּם עַל־פִּי עַצְמוֹ חַיָּב, וְשֶׁאֵינוֹ מְשַׁלֵּם עַל־פִּי עַצְמוֹ פָּטוּר.

יד אברהם

„מַשְׁבִּיעֲךָ אֲנִי," וְאָמַר: „אָמֵן" — חַיָּב. — [*to which he said,*] *'I adjure you,' and he replied, 'Amen' — he is liable.*

[He is liable to a guilt-offering for his false oath of deposit. Since payment of full damages when a *muad* kills is restitution, and is payable even upon the admission of the owner of the goring ox, it is regarded as a denial of a monetary claim, and the defendant is liable to a guilt-offering for swearing falsely.]

Should the bull be a תָּם [*tam*], *a bull which has not yet gored three times,* for which only half-damages are payable, he is not liable to a guilt-offering. As explained above (4:6), the half-damages payment is deemed a fine, not payable by the admission of the owner of the goring bull *(Tif. Yis.).* [These laws are discussed in *Bava Kamma* ch. 4.]

„הֵמִית שׁוֹרְךָ אֶת־עַבְדִּי," וְהוּא אוֹמֵר: „לֹא הֵמִית"; — [*But if he claimed,*] *'Your ox killed my slave,' and he replied, 'It did not kill* [*him*]*';*

The reference here is to an ox that is a habitual gorer and kills a Canaanite slave. The Torah *(Ex.* 21:32) prescribes a penalty of thirty shekels regardless of the value of the slave. Wherever the restitution one is obligated to pay is a fixed amount, not judged on a case-by-case basis for the actual damages, it is deemed a fine. Therefore this payment of thirty shekels is a fine *(Rav; Rashi).*

„מַשְׁבִּיעֲךָ אֲנִי," וְאָמַר: „אָמֵן" — פָּטוּר. — *'I adjure you,' and he said, 'Amen' — he is exempt.*

[Since this penalty is a fine, not payable by the admission of the owner of the goring ox, this does not constitute a denial of a monetary claim.]

אָמַר לוֹ: „חָבַלְתָּ בִּי וְעָשִׂיתָ בִּי חַבּוּרָה," — [*If*] *someone said to him, 'You injured and wounded me,'*

[If one person wounds another, he is obligated to pay indemnity for damage, pain, healing, idleness and shame] (see *Bava Kamma* 8:1).

וְהוּא אוֹמֵר: „לֹא חָבַלְתִּי בְךָ וְלֹא עָשִׂיתִי בְךָ חַבּוּרָה"; מַשְׁבִּיעֲךָ אֲנִי," וְאָמַר: „אָמֵן" — חַיָּב. — *and he replied, 'I did not injure* [*you*] *nor did I wound you'; 'I adjure you,' and he replied, 'Amen' — he is liable.*

[These payments are regarded as restitution, not as fines; therefore, the perpetrator is obligated to pay even on his own confession. Hence they are included in the rule of the oath of deposit.]

According to *Rambam (Hil. Chovel U'Mazik* 5:6,7), the injurer is liable by his own admission only to the indemnities for disgrace, idleness and healing, but not for damage and pain. Accordingly, he is liable to a guilt-offering because of those three.

5 adjure you,' and he replied, 'Amen' — he is liable. [But if
5 he claimed,] 'Your ox killed my slave,' and he replied, 'It did not kill [him]'; 'I adjure you,' and he replied, 'Amen' — he is exempt.

[If] someone said to him, 'You injured and wounded me,' and he replied, 'I did not injure [you] nor did I wound you'; 'I adjure you,' and he replied, 'Amen' — he is liable. [But, if] his slave said to him, 'You knocked out my tooth,' or 'You blinded my eye,' [and he replied,] 'I did not knock [it] out,' or 'I did not blind [it]'; 'I adjure you', and he replied, 'Amen' — he is exempt. This is the rule: Whoever pays by his own admission is liable, but whoever does not pay by his own admission is exempt.

YAD AVRAHAM

אָמַר לוֹ עַבְדּוֹ: „הִפַּלְתָּ אֶת־שִׁנִּי," וְ„סִמִּיתָ אֶת־עֵינִי," — *[But if] his slave said to him, 'You knocked out my tooth,' or 'You blinded my eye,'*

For destroying one of the limbs of one's Canaanite slave, the master must free the slave, as in *Ex.* 21:26. This is considered a fine, since the slave is his chattel *(Rav; Rashi).*

The mishnah places *tooth* before *eye,* while the Torah places *eye* before *tooth.* The *Tanna* wishes to teach us that not only is freeing the slave for the destruction of the tooth a relatively slight blemish — regarded as a fine — but even freeing him for the destruction of an eye — a serious blemish for which the punishment is more in line with the damage inflicted — is also a fine *(Hon Ashir).*

וְהוּא אוֹמֵר: „לֹא הִפַּלְתִּי," וְ„לֹא סִמִּיתִי" — „מַשְׁבִּיעֲךָ אֲנִי," וְאָמַר: „אָמֵן" — פָּטוּר. — *[and he replied,] 'I did not knock [it] out,' or 'I did not blind [it]'; 'I adjure you,' and he replied, 'Amen' — he is exempt.*

[If the master swore falsely to his slave's adjuration, he is nevertheless exempt from the oath of deposit since the claim constituted a fine, not damages.]

זֶה הַכְּלָל: כָּל־הַמְשַׁלֵּם עַל־פִּי עַצְמוֹ חַיָּב, — *This is the rule: Whoever pays by his own admission is liable,*

[I.e., in all cases of restitution in which the perpetrator pays even by his own confession, he is liable to a guilt-offering for a false oath. The fact that he pays even on his own admission demonstrates that the payment is restitution, not a fine.]

וְשֶׁאֵינוֹ מְשַׁלֵּם עַל־פִּי עַצְמוֹ פָּטוּר. — *but whoever does not pay by his own admission is exempt.*

[Claims which one does not pay on his own admission, but only on a conviction by the testimony of witnesses, are fines. Thus, they do not constitute a proper monetary claim in regard to the oath of deposit sacrifice.]

Chapter 6

The preceding three chapters dealt with the consequences of various false oaths uttered by an individual either spontaneously or in response to a litigant's claim. None of these, however, were oaths which the swearer was obliged to swear. The following chapter deals with oaths imposed by the court and the circumstances under which they are imposed.

According to Biblical law, there are only three types of oaths imposed by *beis din:* (1) שְׁבוּעַת מוֹדֶה בְּמִקְצָת, *the oath of one who admits part of the claim lodged against*

שְׁבוּעַת הַדַּיָּנִין — הַטַּעֲנָה שְׁתֵּי כֶסֶף וְהַהוֹדָאָה בְּשָׁוֶה פְרוּטָה; וְאִם

יד אברהם

him, (2) שְׁבוּעַת הַשּׁוֹמְרִים, *the oath of a shomer* (guardian) who claims exemption for loss of the deposit entrusted to him, or (3) שְׁבוּעַת עֵד אֶחָד, *the single witness oath,* i.e., the oath a defendant in a monetary case must swear to contradict the testimony of a single witness who testifies against him. This chapter deals with the oath of מוֹדֶה בְּמִקְצָת, *the one who admits part of the claim.*

All Biblical oaths are oaths imposed on the defendant, and they take the form of allowing the defendant to swear that he is telling the truth and thereby exempt himself from the claim lodged against him. There are cases, however, in which the Rabbis saw fit to institute an oath on the plaintiff to enable him to collect on his claim even without proof. They also instituted oaths to require various categories of people who manage other people's property to swear in certain circumstances that they did not abuse their trusts (see below, 7:8). These oaths are known as שְׁבוּעַת הַמִּשְׁנָה, *a mishnaic oath,* and they are discussed in the following chapter.

There is also a post-mishnaic oath, known as שְׁבוּעַת הֶסֵּת, *shevuas hesses.*[1] This oath is imposed on a defendant who denies the claim completely, as will be explained below. Since this oath was first initiated in Talmudic times *(Gem.* 40b; *Rambam, Hil. Toein* 1:3), the mishnah never refers to it. It should be understood, therefore, that in most of the cases in this chapter in which the mishnah exempts one from swearing an oath, he is exempt only from swearing the Biblical oath for a partial admission. In practice, however, he is still required to swear the less severe *hesses* oath.[2]

[It should also be noted that the terms *liable* and *exempt* in this chapter refer to liability for the oath, not for the claim. Only if he refuses to swear the oath for which he is liable is he required to pay the claim.]

1.

Before an oath of partial admission can be imposed, two basic conditions must be met: (1) the claim and denial must have a certain minimum value, (2) the admission must be of the same kind as the claim. The following mishnah delineates these two conditions and establishes the minimum value as two *maah.*

The *Gemara* (39b) records a fundamental controversy between Rav and Shmuel concerning the meaning of this requirement. Rav explains the two-*maah* minimum to refer to the denial — i.e., the part of the claim which the defendant denies must be at least two *maah;* the entire claim must obviously be for a larger sum. Shmuel, however, explains that the minimum refers to the actual claim — i.e., the claim as a whole must be for at least two *maah.* The denial, however, may be for a smaller amount as long

1. According to *Rashi* (40b), the meaning of the expression שְׁבוּעַת הֶסֵּת is an oath of imposition, i.e., an oath which the later Rabbis imposed upon the defendant. *Meiri* explains it to mean an oath of counsel, i.e., an oath concerning which the Rabbis took counsel and decided to innovate. *Hagahos Maimonios (Hil. Shevuos* 11, subpar. 4) quotes a *Gaon* who explains it as an expression of a burden; i.e., a burden imposed by the Sages, to compel the litigant to swear. *Aruch,* too, follows this view. *Rashi (Bava Metzia* 5a) explains it as an expression of persuasion, i.e., an oath which the Rabbis innovated in order to persuade the guilty party to admit his guilt.

2. There are various differences between a *hesses* oath and a Biblical one, such as the fact that, in line with all other Rabbinical oaths, one who refuses to swear a *hesses* oath can only be subjected to certain judicial penalties, but cannot have his property confiscated to pay the claim *(Gem.* 41a; *Choshen Mishpat* 87:9).

6
1

1. **T**he oath of the judges [is for] a claim of two silver and an admission of the value of a *perutah;* but if

YAD AVRAHAM

as it is not less than a *perutah (Tos. Yom Tov).* [There are 32 *perutos* in a *maah.*] This dispute will affect the interpretation of several cases in this mishnah and mishnah 3.

שְׁבוּעַת הַדַּיָּנִין — *The oath of the judges*

I.e., the oath which the judges impose upon the defendant who admits the validity of a portion of the claim, but denies that he owes the rest. This oath is derived from *(Ex.* 22:8): אֲשֶׁר יֹאמַר כִּי־הוּא זֶה, *Which he will say that this is it,* meaning that he admits to a portion of it. Concerning this, the Torah states (ibid. v. 7): וְנִקְרַב בַּעַל־הַבַּיִת אֶל־הָאֱלֹהִים, *And the householder approached the judges,* meaning that he must approach the judges to swear *(Rav, Rashi* from *Bava Kamma* 106b).

Unlike the preceding mishnayos dealing with oaths of utterance, vain oaths, the oath of testimony, and the oath of the deposit, this mishnah does not delineate those to whom this oath applies or does not apply. *Tos.* (38b) state that the absence of this pattern is due to the fact that it is self-evident that the oath of the judges applies to all. Although the mishnah does state in regard to the oath of deposit that it applies to all — even though this too is self-evident — it does so because the rule of the oath of deposit is in certain respects derived from that of the oath of testimony. Since the oath of testimony applies only to men, non-relatives, etc., it was necessary to state that the oath of deposit applies both to men and women, non-relatives and relatives, etc. In the case of the oath of the judges, however, there is no reason to believe that it should not apply to women, relatives, or those ineligible to testify.

Tos. Yom Tov questions this reasoning. He points out that the mishnah delineates all those to whom the oath of utterance and the vain oath apply although it is self-evident in those cases too that they apply to all. If so, why does the mishnah omit it in the case of the oath of the judges? To this *Shoshannim LeDavid* replies that, although it is self-evident that those oaths apply to all, the *Tanna* stated it since the verse dealing with these oaths is in the same section of the Torah as that dealing with the oath of the testimony. We could therefore erroneously assume that the same restrictions apply to the oath of the deposit as apply to the oath of testimony. In contrast, the oath of the judges is written in an entirely different section. Therefore, it is unnecessary to state it here. See *Tos. Yom Tov* for another reason for the omission.

Although the oath imposed on the *shomer* (guardian) who claims that the deposit was lost through an accident is also imposed by the judges, as is the oath required to contradict the single witness, our mishnah refers only to the oath of the partial admission, and the details mentioned further in the mishnah apply only to this oath, and not the other oaths administered by the judges *(Tos. Yom Tov* from *Ran).*

The reason the oath of the single witness does not require the details mentioned below is that a single witness imposes an oath whenever two witnesses would make the defendant liable to monetary payment. Since that is so even if the case involves only a *perutah,* one witness can impose an oath even in that case *(Tos. Yom Tov* from *Gem.* 40a).

In regard to the oath of the *shomer,* however, there is a dispute whether the two-*maah* minimum applies or not (see *Ran).*

הַטַּעֲנָה שְׁתֵּי כֶסֶף — [*is for*] *a claim of two silver*

I.e., in order for the judges to impose the oath for partial admission the claim must be for no less than two silver *maah.* A *maah* is a sixth of a *dinar,* making two *maah* a third of a *dinar.* Since a *dinar* equals ninety-six barleycorns of silver, two *maah* equal thirty-two barley-corns of silver [see table in mishnah 3] *(Rambam Comm.; Rav).*

As noted in the prefatory note, the *Gemara* (39b) cites a dispute between Rav and Shmuel concerning the subject of the two-*maah* requirement. Rav defines it as the amount of the claim the defendant must deny in order to be obliged to swear the oath of partial admission; the total claim, however, must

שבועות ו/א

אֵין הַהוֹדָאָה מִמִּין הַטַּעֲנָה, פָּטוּר. כֵּיצַד? „שְׁתֵּי כֶסֶף לִי בְיָדְךָ,״ „אֵין לְךָ בְיָדִי אֶלָּא פְרוּטָה״ — פָּטוּר. „שְׁתֵּי כֶסֶף וּפְרוּטָה לִי בְיָדְךָ,״ „אֵין לְךָ בְיָדִי אֶלָּא פְרוּטָה״ — חַיָּב.

יד אברהם

be for more (since he must also admit something; see below). Shmuel, however, understands the mishnah to mean that the amount of the claim must be two *maah;* the amount of denial need only be a *perutah (Rav* from *Gem.* 39b).

וְהַהוֹדָאָה בְּשָׁוֶה פְרוּטָה; — *and an admission of the value of a perutah;*

I.e., in order to impose upon the defendant the oath for the partial admission, the admission must equal at least the value of a *perutah (Rav).* A *perutah* equals the value of 1/2 barleycorn of silver, but the *perutah* itself was not made of silver but of copper *(Rambam Comm., Tos. Yom Tov* from *Rav* to *Kiddushin* 1:1).

Therefore, according to Rav, the claim must be for at least two *maah* and a *perutah,* since the denial must be for a minimum of two *maah* and the admission must equal at least a *perutah.* Should the denial be less than two *maah* or the admission less than a *perutah,* there is no Biblical oath imposed *(Rav).* According to Shmuel, the entire claim need only be a minimum of two *maah,* with the admission being at least a *perutah.* If these requirements are met, regardless of the amount of the denial [as long as it too is at least a *perutah*], the defendant is liable to a Biblical oath *(Tos. Yom Tov* from *Gem.* 39b).

As mentioned above, even where the amount involved is less than two *maah,* the defendant is exempt only from the Biblical oath; the Rabbinical oath called *shevuas hesses* is still imposed upon him.

Should the plaintiff claim utensils rather than money, e.g., two needles, and the defendant admits that he owes him one needle, he is liable to the oath of partial admission even though the value of the entire claim does not equal two *maah* of silver *(Tos. R' Akiva* from *Gem.* 40b). According to *Rambam (Hil. Toein Venitan* 3:5), in such a case the entire value need not equal even a *perutah.* Thus, if ten needles are sold for a *perutah* and the plaintiff claims two needles and the defendant admits to one, he is liable to an oath concerning the other one. This is the view of the *Geonim* and is accepted by *Rashba* [as mentioned in *Maggid Mishneh* ad loc.]. *Ramban,* however, rules that the two needles claimed must equal at least two *perutos (Tos. R' Akiva).*

When a Biblical oath is administered, the one swearing must grasp a sacred object, such as a Torah scroll or *tefillin* while he is uttering the oath. However, in the case of a *shevuas hesses,* the defendant does not hold a sacred object while swearing. Nevertheless, *Rambam (Hil. Shevuos* 11:3) states that it has become customary for the attendant of the synagogue or a member of the congregation [or the plaintiff *(Rav)*] to hold a Torah scroll when a *shevuas hesses* is administered in order to cast fear into the oath-taker's heart.

All Rabbinical oaths other than *hesses* are administered with the same ceremony as a Biblical oath *(Rav; Rambam, Hil. Toein Venitan* 1:2). [According to some authorities, all Rabbinical oaths are administered without grasping a sacred object, not just *hesses (Tur Choshen Mishpat* 87; see *Hagahos Maimonios, Hil. Shevuos* 11, subpar. 5). The halachah is in accordance with *Rav* and *Rambam (Choshen Mishpat* 87:13).]

Although Rabbinical oaths other than the *shevuas hesses* are administered in the same way as Biblical ones, there is, however, one distinction between them: In the case of a Biblical oath, should the defendant refuse to swear, the court can forcibly collect the amount in question from his property. In the case of a Rabbinical oath, however, they place a ban upon him until he pays or swears. Should he remain under the ban for thirty

6 the admission is not of the same kind as the claim, he is
1 exempt. How so? [If one claims,] 'Two silver of mine are in your possession,' [and the other replies,] 'You have in my possession only a *perutah'* — he is exempt. [But if he claims,] 'Two silver and a *perutah* of mine are in your possession,' [and the other replies,] 'You have in my possession only a *perutah'* — he is liable.

YAD AVRAHAM

days and still refuse to comply, the *beis din* punishes him with מַכַּת מַרְדּוּת, Rabbinically imposed lashes for disobedience. Then they release him from the ban, and he is free. They do not, however, collect from his property (*Rav* from *Gem.* 41a; *Choshen Mishpat* 87:9)

וְאִם אֵין הַהוֹדָאָה מִמִּין הַטַּעֲנָה, — *but if the admission is not of the same kind as the claim,*

[I.e., if the defendant admits to owing something other than what the plaintiff claims from him.]

.פָּטוּר — *he is exempt.*

[I.e., he is exempt from the oath of the partial admission.] The Torah's expression — כִּי הוּא זֶה, *that this is it* — conveys the idea that he admits to the charge in principle, merely denying the extent of the charge. The meaning of the verse is thus: כִּי הוּא, *it is so,* i.e., your accusation is a correct one, but only זֶה, i.e. it is limited to *this* (*Tos. Yom Tov* from *Gem.* 39b). See also *R' Hirsch's* comm. on *Chumash Ex.* 22:8.

?כֵּיצַד — *How so?*

According to the *Amora* Rav, the question *How so?* and the examples which follow illustrate the first rule of the mishnah that the minimum denial of a claim making the defendant liable to an oath is two silver *maah* (*Gem.* 39b). [Shmuel's interpretation of the mishnah will be explained below.]

„שְׁתֵּי כֶסֶף לִי בְיָדְךָ," „אֵין לְךָ בְיָדִי אֶלָּא פְרוּטָה" — [*If one claims,*] *'Two silver of mine are in your possession,'* [*and the other replies,*] *'You have in my possession only a perutah'* —

[I.e., the defendant replies that he owes only a *perutah* and not two *maah.*]

.פָּטוּר — *he is exempt.*

He is exempt from taking the oath of partial admission because the entire claim equaled only two *maah.* In order to be liable to an oath according to Rav, the denial itself must be for at least two *maah,* and the claim as a whole must therefore be for at least two *maah* and a *perutah* (see above s.v. וההודאה). Thus, this case fails to meet the minimum-value requirement necessary for an oath of partial admission (*Gem.* 39b).

The second condition necessary for this oath — viz. that the admission be of the same kind as the claim — is met, however, according to this view. This is because the claim of *two silver* is understood by Rav to be a claim for the value of two silver *maah* and not a claim for that amount of silver (*Gem.*).[1] Since it is common for people to refer to the value of things in such terms, we assume that the suit was for value, not silver (*Rashi* 39b, s.v. ליטרא). Therefore, even though the admission was for a *perutah* — a copper coin — the admission is of the same kind [value] as the claim (*Gem.* ibid.).

„שְׁתֵּי כֶסֶף וּפְרוּטָה לִי בְיָדְךָ," „אֵין לְךָ בְיָדִי אֶלָּא פְרוּטָה" — [*But if he claims,*] *'Two silver and a perutah of mine are in your possession,'* [*and the other replies,*] *'You have in my possession only a perutah'* —

[The plaintiff pressed a claim for two *maah* plus a *perutah,* and the defendant admitted to owing only the *perutah,* while denying the claim of two *maah.*]

.חַיָּב — *he is liable.*

The defendant is liable to swear the

1. There is also a third variation, where the claim is specifically for coins of certain denominations. This will be discussed in mishnah 3.

„מָנֶה לִי בְיָדְךָ," „אֵין לְךָ בְיָדִי" — פָּטוּר. „מָנֶה לִי בְיָדְךָ," „אֵין לְךָ בְיָדִי אֶלָּא חֲמִשִּׁים דִּינָר" — חַיָּב. „מָנֶה לְאַבָּא בְיָדְךָ," „אֵין לוֹ בְיָדִי אֶלָּא חֲמִשִּׁים דִּינָר" — פָּטוּר, מִפְּנֵי שֶׁהוּא כְמֵשִׁיב אֲבֵדָה.

יד אברהם

oath of partial admission, because now both the claim and the denial meet their minimum-value requirements *(Gem.* 39b).

At the same time, the admission is considered to be of the same kind as the claim, since both are for value, not metals, as explained above.

We have thus far explained the mishnah according to the view of the *Amora* Rav, that the two-*maah* minimum refers to the amount being denied, and the claim itself must be for at least two *maah* and a *perutah.* As noted above, however, the view of Shmuel *(Gem.* 39b) is that the two-*maah* sum refers to the claim as a whole, while the denial need only be a *perutah.* According to Shmuel, the mishnah's exemption of a two-silver claim and *perutah* denial from an oath of partial admission cannot be because of the insufficiency of the sums involved, since in his view they are sufficient. Accordingly, Shmuel explains that the mishnah's question, *How so?,* and the illustration which follows refer to the mishnah's second rule for the oath of partial admission — viz., the requirement that the admission be in the same kind as the claim. In Shmuel's view, the claim of *two silver* is not understood to mean two silver *maah* worth of debt, but two *maah* of silver — i.e., an amount of silver weighing two *maah.* [Coins were set at fixed weights of some precious metal; thus, two *maah* of silver meant silver weighing two *maah.*] Since the claim is specifically for silver, the admission of a *perutah* — copper — is not in the same kind as the claim and therefore does not result in the imposition of an oath *(Rav* from *Gem.* 39b; see *Ran).*

This is true only where the claim is strictly for silver. If the claim is for *two silver and a perutah* [the second case of the illustration], the admission of the *perutah* part of the claim is considered a partial admission in the kind of the claim. Since the claim was for both silver and copper, it is considered a single large claim of which the defendant admits to owing one *perutah.* Thus, his admission is of the same kind as the claim, and he is liable *(Rav* from *Gem.* 39b).[1]

„מָנֶה לִי בְיָדְךָ," — [*If he claims,*] *'I have a maneh in your possession,'*

[A *maneh* is equal to one hundred *zuz.*]

„אֵין לְךָ בְיָדִי" — — [*and the other replies,*] *'You have nothing in my possession'* —

[I.e., the defendant denies the claim entirely.]

פָּטוּר. — *he is exempt.*

He is exempt because there is no admission [and the Biblical oath applies only where the defendant admits to part of the claim] *(Rashi).*

„מָנֶה לִי בְיָדְךָ," „אֵין לְךָ בְיָדִי אֶלָּא חֲמִשִּׁים דִּינָר" — חַיָּב. — [*But if he claims,*] *'I have a maneh in your possession,'* [*and the other replies*], *'You have in my possession only fifty dinars' — he is liable.*

[I.e., in addition to having to pay the fifty *dinars* to which he admits, he is liable to the oath of partial admission and is required to swear that he does not owe

1. This case is analogous to the case in which one claims wheat and barley from another, with the defendant admitting to one while denying the other. In that case too, Shmuel deems it an admission of the same kind as the claim *(Rav* from *Gem.).* This, however, is itself subject to a dispute. According to other views cited in the *Gemara* (40a), a claim for wheat and barley is treated as two separate claims, and admission of one of them is therefore not considered a

6 [If he claims,] 'I have a *maneh* in your possession,'
1 [and the other replies,] 'You have nothing in my possession' — he is exempt. [But if he claims,] 'I have a *maneh* in your possession,' [and the other replies,] 'You have in my possession only fifty *dinars*' — he is liable. [If he claims,] 'A *maneh* of my father's is in your possession,' [and the other replies,] 'Only fifty *dinars* of his are in my possession' — he is exempt, because he is as one who returns a lost object.

YAD AVRAHAM

the remaining fifty *dinars.*]

Although we already learned this rule above in the case of the claim of two silver and a *perutah* in which the defendant admits to a *perutah*, the mishnah nevertheless repeats it in this form to contrast it with the next case (*Meleches Shlomo*).

Tif. Yis. conjectures that this may be added so that we not think that in this case he should be exempt because he could have admitted less than fifty *dinars*. By admitting to fifty *dinars* he has a *miggo*, i.e., the opportunity to advance a more advantageous claim (see comm. to next mishnah, s.v. אל תתנהו). Since if he had wished to lie, he would have chosen the more advantageous lie of a smaller admission, by admitting the larger amount he is showing his good faith and we should believe him without an oath. To preclude this line of reasoning, the mishnah states that he is nevertheless liable to the oath of partial admission.

„מָנֶה לְאַבָּא בְּיָדְךָ,״ „אֵין לוֹ בְּיָדִי אֶלָּא חֲמִשִּׁים דִּינָר״ — [*If he claims,*] *'A maneh of my father's is in your possession,'* [*and the other replies,*] *'Only fifty dinars of his are in my possession'* —

[I.e., the claim is made by the heir of the man who lent the defendant the money.]

פָּטוּר, מִפְּנֵי שֶׁהוּא כְּמֵשִׁיב אֲבֵדָה. — *he is exempt, because he is as one who returns a lost object.*

The defendant is exempt from the oath of partial admission because he could have denied the entire claim. Since children are usually not familiar with their father's affairs, had he completely denied the claim, the son would have had to accept it. Since he did not do so, he is considered the equivalent of one who returns a lost object and the loser claims that it is incomplete. In such a case, the Rabbis exempted him from an oath for the general good, so that people should not refrain from returning lost objects out of a fear of being accused of wrongdoing and being called upon to swear. The Rabbis therefore declared that one who returns an object he found need never swear to answer the owner's claims (*Rav; Rashi* from *Gittin* 5:3).

This is true only if the son does not lodge a definite claim, but claims, 'I think you may have owed my father a *maneh*.' Should he claim with certainty that this debt is owed his father — and thus him as the heir — the defendant is liable to swear since he is not deemed as one who returns a lost object (*Rav* from *Gittin* 42b).

Ran explains that the reference is not to the Rabbinical enactment exempting the one who returns a lost object from an oath. Rather the intention is that the defendant is believed by the rule of *miggo*, i.e., had he wanted to lie he would have denied the entire claim. In ordinary cases of partial admission,

partial admission, but a complete admission of one claim and a complete denial of the other. [According to some views, this issue is also a dispute of *Tannaim;* see below, mishnah 3, s.v. וחכמים אומרים.] The halachah, however, follows the view of Shmuel in this matter (*Choshen Mishpat* 82:12).

[ב] „מָנֶה לִי בְיָדְךָ," אָמַר לוֹ בִּפְנֵי עֵדִים: „הֵן." לְמָחָר אָמַר לוֹ: „תְּנֵהוּ לִי," „נְתַתִּיו לָךְ" — פָּטוּר. „אֵין לְךָ בְיָדִי" — חַיָּב.

„מָנֶה לִי בְיָדְךָ," אָמַר לוֹ: „הֵן"; „אַל תִּתְּנֵהוּ לִי אֶלָּא בְעֵדִים." לְמָחָר אָמַר לוֹ: „תְּנֵהוּ לִי," „נְתַתִּיו לָךְ" — חַיָּב, מִפְּנֵי שֶׁצָּרִיךְ לִתְּנוֹ לוֹ בְעֵדִים.

יד אברהם

the defendant has no credibility by the rule of *miggo* because there is counter-assumption that a person does not have the audacity to deny a claim completely when the plaintiff is fully aware that he is lying. In this case, however, since the heir is unaware of the true state of affairs, he could have denied the entire claim. Since he did not do so, he is believed with the rule of *miggo*. In this way, he is figuratively returning a lost object.

2.

„מָנֶה לִי בְיָדְךָ," אָמַר לוֹ בִּפְנֵי עֵדִים: „הֵן." — *'I have a maneh in your possession,'* [*and*] *he replied before witnesses, 'Yes.'*

[I.e., he admitted to the debt.] This admission is binding only if he says to the witnesses, 'Be my witnesses.' Otherwise, he can claim that his admission was said in jest *(Rav)*. I.e., he can say that since the claim was a complete fabrication he answered it in jest *(Tos. Yom Tov* from *Rashi* to *Sanhedrin* 29a).

לְמָחָר אָמַר לוֹ: „תְּנֵהוּ לִי," — *On the next day,* [*when*] *he said to him, 'Give it to me,'*

[I.e., on the next day, the creditor asked for payment of the debt.]

„נְתַתִּיו לָךְ" — — [*the other replied,*] *'I gave it to you' —*

[The debtor claims that he paid the debt subsequent to the previous day's admission.]

פָּטוּר. — *he is exempt.*

He is exempt from the Biblical oath for partial admission [because the defendant denies owing anything. Although the defendant admitted yesterday to owing the money, there is no way to prove that he did not pay it back in the interim].

The Rabbinical oath of *shevuas hesses,* however, is imposed upon him *(Rav* from *Gem.* 40b, 41a). As explained above, the *shevuas hesses* is a post-Mishnaic innovation imposed in cases in which the Biblical oath does not apply.

The *Gemara* notes two versions as to when this innovation applies. According to the first opinion, the *shevuas hesses* applies not only in this case but even in the case in the first mishnah in which the defendant denies ever having incurred the debt. Though the defendant denies ever owing anything, and the plaintiff offers no proof of his claim, the oath is nevertheless imposed based on the assumption that a person does not generally make a claim unless something is owed him. Though this assumption is not proof, it does create enough of a climate of doubt that the Rabbis required the defendant to exonerate himself by taking an oath. This oath applies all the more so in our case in which the defendant admits his previous indebtedness.

According to a second opinion, however, he must swear only in our case, i.e., the case in which he admits that he indeed owed the money but now claims that he paid it. The *Gemara* calls this דְּרָרָא דְּמָמוֹנָא, literally, *a connection to the money;* i.e., we see that there is some basis to his claim, since even the defendant admits to once owing the money. In the case of mishnah 1, however, in which the defendant denies the debt completely, not even a *shevuas hesses* is required. *Rif, Rambam (Hil. Toein Venitan* 1:3) and *Rosh* decide in favor of the first version, requiring the defendant to swear even when he denies the debt completely. See also *Choshen Mishpat* 87:1.

„אֵין לְךָ בְיָדִי" — חַיָּב. — [*But if he replied,*] *'You have nothing in my possession' — he is liable.*

If on the second day he does not say, 'I

6
2
2. 'I have a *maneh* in your possession,' [and] he replied before witnesses, 'Yes.' On the next day, [when] he said to him, 'Give it to me,' [the other replied,] 'I gave it to you' — he is exempt. [But if he replied,] 'You have nothing in my possession' — he is liable.

'I have a *maneh* in your possession,' [and] he replied, 'Yes'; [to which the other responded,] 'Do not give it to me except before witnesses.' On the next day, [when] he said to him, 'Give it to me,' [the other replied,] 'I gave it to you' — he is liable, because he is required to give it to him with witnesses.

YAD AVRAHAM

paid,' but rather, denies the indebtedness completely, he is liable to pay since he previously admitted his indebtness before witnesses. Even if he should claim later that he paid, he is no longer believed, even with an oath, since he is considered a confirmed liar *(Rav, Rashi* 42a).

Rosh qualifies this to mean that he states openly, 'You have nothing in my possession because I never borrowed from you.' Only then is he liable since that is a direct contradiction of his previous admission. If he merely says, 'You have nothing in my possession,' he can later justify his answer to mean that the claimant has nothing in his possession now, since he has already repaid him. Since this would correspond with his original statement, he would be believed and would not have to pay *(Tos. Yom Tov).*

The ruling of the mishnah applies only if the defendant denies the claim in *beis din.* Should he deny outside of *beis din,* his denial does not confirm him as a liar since people very often do not state their true claims outside of court so as not to divulge their tactics to their adversary *(Rav; Rashi; Tos. Yom Tov).*

„מָנֶה לִי בְיָדְךָ," אָמַר לוֹ: „הֵן"; — *'I have a maneh in your possession,' [and] he replied, 'Yes';*

[I.e., the defendant admitted the claim.]

„אַל תִּתְּנֵהוּ לִי אֶלָּא בְעֵדִים." — *[to which the other responded,] 'Do not give it to me except before witnesses.'*

[I.e., the lender stipulates with the borrower that the debt be repaid only in the presence of two witnesses.] Whether the lender said this to him at the time of the loan or afterwards, the borrower is required to comply with the request *(Choshen Mishpat* 70:3).

The mishnah deals only with the case in which the lender stated this before witnesses. If he did not — and we have only the borrower's admission to prove that such a stipulation was ever made — the borrower would be able to claim that he paid without witnesses and he would be believed, since he has a *miggo*[1] that he could have claimed that the creditor never told him to repay in front of witnesses.

— לְמָחָר אָמַר לוֹ: „תְּנֵהוּ לִי," „נְתַתִּיו לָךְ" — *On the next day, [when] he said to him, 'Give it to me,' [the other replied,] 'I gave it to you'* —

[On the next day, when the lender demanded payment of the debt, the borrower replied that he repaid the debt in the interim without witnesses.]

חַיָּב, — *he is liable,*

Since the borrower cannot produce

1. *Miggo* is a judicial principle which means that wherever a litigant who wished to lie could have invented a claim more advantageous to his case — one which the court would have been compelled to accept — his choice of a less advantageous claim indicates that he is telling the truth (see ArtScroll *Bava Basra* p. 62).

[ג] „לִטְרָא זָהָב יֶשׁ־לִי בְיָדְךָ," „אֵין לְךָ בְיָדִי אֶלָּא לִטְרָא כֶסֶף" — פָּטוּר.
„דִּינַר זָהָב יֶשׁ־לִי בְיָדְךָ," „אֵין לְךָ בְיָדִי אֶלָּא דִינַר כֶּסֶף," וּ„טְרִיסִית," וּ„פֻּנְדְּיוֹן," וּ„פְרוּטָה" — חַיָּב, שֶׁהַכֹּל מִין מַטְבֵּעַ אֶחָד.

יד אברהם

מַלְוֶה, *The borrower is a slave to the lender* [i.e., that a borrower is under a burden to satisfy the lender].

Ran, however, explains the reason to be not because the lender's subsequent stipulation creates a legal requirement to pay in the presence of witnesses. Rather, the reason is because once the creditor demands that the debtor pay before witnesses, it is unnatural for him to pay without witnesses, lest people believe that he does not pay his debts. The likelihood of this is so strong that it creates a judicial presumption that he did not, in fact, pay his debt without witnesses *(Tos. Yom Tov).*

Should the debtor claim that he paid the debt in the presence of two witnesses who are deceased or went abroad, he is believed *(Gem.* 41b). Nonetheless, should he claim that he paid without witnesses, he is not believed by the rule of *miggo* that he could have claimed that he paid before witnesses who are no longer here. One reason given for this is that this is considered a *miggo* contradicted by witnesses. Since it is highly unusual to pay without witnesses, it is as though we all are witnesses that his claim that he paid without witnesses is false. Therefore, even though he has a *miggo* to back his claim, the proof of witnesses is stronger and he is not believed.

witnesses to the repayment, he is liable to pay. The creditor need not even swear a *shevuas hesses* in order to collect his debt.

However, after collecting the money the borrower can sue the lender for the return of the 'excess' payment and thereby extract from him a *shevuas hesses* at that time that there had been only one repayment of the debt *(Tif. Yis.; Shach, Choshen Mishpat* 70:3 based on *Shulchan Aruch* ibid. 71:5).

.מִפְּנֵי שֶׁצָּרִיךְ לִתְּנוֹ לוֹ בְעֵדִים — *because he is required to give it to him with witnesses.*

[As mentioned above, this is true whether the lender made this stipulation at the time of the loan or at any time afterwards.]

Should he demand this at the time of the loan, the debtor is required to do so because he receives the money only under this condition. Should he add this stipulation subsequent to the loan, however, it is difficult to understand what obligates the borrower to comply with the creditor's demand that he pay only in the presence of witnesses.

Maggid Mishneh (Hil. Malveh 15:1) explains that the debtor is required to comply with the creditor's request based on the rule of *(Prov.* 22:7): וְעֶבֶד לֹוֶה לְאִישׁ

3.

In mishnah 1 we learned that the admission must be of the same kind as the claim in order for the oath of partial admission to apply. The following mishnah takes up various aspects of this rule.

In understanding this mishnah, it is necessary to bear in mind the dispute between Rav and Shmuel noted in mishnah 1. Arising out of their primary dispute concerning the meaning of the two-*maah* minimum, there emerged a second dispute as to whether a claim for *two silver* is to be understood as meaning a debt worth two silver *maah* [Rav] or whether it refers to a claim for silver weighing two *maah* [Shmuel]. (See comm. to mishnah 1, s.v. פטור and s.v. חיב.)

6
3 **3.** 'I have a *litra* of gold in your possession,' [and the other replies,] 'You have in my possession only a *litra* of silver' — he is exempt. [But if he claims,] 'I have a *dinar* of gold in your possession,' [and the other replies,] 'You have in my possession only a *dinar* of silver,' or 'a *trisis*,' or 'a *pundion*,' or 'a *perutah*' — he is liable, because all coins are of one type.

YAD AVRAHAM

„לִטְרָא זָהָב יֶשׁ־לִי בְיָדְךָ,״ — *'I have a litra of gold in your possession,'*

[The plaintiff claims a debt of a *litra* of gold.]

A *litra* is equivalent in weight to a *maneh*, and is thus worth one hundred *zuz* or *dinars* (*Aruch* from *Yerushalmi Terumos* 10:8). [However, the term is strictly a standard of weight, not a denomination of currency.]

„אֵין לְךָ בְּיָדִי אֶלָּא לִטְרָא כֶסֶף״ — [*and the other replies,*] *'You have in my possession only a litra of silver'* —

[I.e., the defendant admits to owing only a *litra* of silver.]

פָּטוּר. — *he is exempt.*

He is exempt from the oath of partial admission because the admission is not of the same kind as the claim (*Rav; Rashi* 42a).

According to the *Amora* Rav, when someone puts forth a claim for a debt of gold or silver, his claim is for their value, not their metal [see mishnah 1, s.v. פטור]. This renders the admission of a debt in a different type of metal a partial admission warranting an oath, since regardless of the metal mentioned, he is admitting part of the claim of a certain amount of money. Nevertheless, in the case under discussion here, since he mentions a weight, even Rav agrees that he means the gold itself, not merely its value. Thus, the admission of a debt of silver is not of the same kind as the claim (*Tos. Yom Tov* from *Gem.* 39b, *Rashi* ad loc.).

„דִּינַר זָהָב יֶשׁ־לִי בְיָדְךָ,״ — [*But if he claims,*] *'I have a dinar of gold in your possession,'*

A *dinar* of gold is the equivalent of twenty-five *dinars* of silver (see *Bava Kamma* 4:1).

„אֵין לְךָ בְּיָדִי אֶלָּא דִּינַר כֶּסֶף,״ וּ„טְרִיסִית,״ וּ„פֻּנְדְּיוֹן,״ וּ„פְרוּטָה״ — [*and the other replies,*] *'You have in my possession only a dinar of silver,' or 'a trisis,' or 'a pundion,' or 'a perutah'* —

The defendant admits to owing only a *dinar* of silver, or a *trisis*, or *pundion*, or *perutah* (*Rashi*).

A *trisis* is a small *maah* (*Tos. Yom Tov* from *Rashi* 40a), equivalent to three *issars* (*Musaf HeAruch*). A *pundion* is a coin equivalent to two *issars* or half a regular *maah* (*Rav, Rashi* to *Bava Metzia* 4:5; *Musaf HeAruch*). A *perutah* is one-eighth of an Italian *issar* (*Kiddushin* 1:2).

Table of Coins

8 *perutos* = 1 *issar*
2 *issars* = 1 *pundion*
3 *issars* = 1 *trisis*
2 *pundions* = 1 *maah*
6 *maah* = 1 *dinar*
2 *dinars* = 1 *shekel*
2 *shekels* = 1 *sela*
25 *selas* = 1 *maneh*
25 *dinars* of silver = 1 *dinar* of gold

חַיָּב, — *he is liable,*

[I.e., he is liable to a Biblical oath for partial admission.]

שֶׁהַכֹּל מִין מַטְבֵּעַ אֶחָד. — *because all coins are of one type.*

According to Rav, who explains a claim for silver or gold coins to mean that he claims the monetary value of the coins, the law of the mishnah is easily understood. Since the plaintiff claims the value of a *dinar* of gold and the defendant admits the value of a *dinar* of

„כּוֹר תְּבוּאָה יֶשׁ־לִי בְיָדְךָ,״ „אֵין לְךָ בְיָדִי אֶלָּא לֶתֶךְ קִטְנִית״ — פָּטוּר. „כּוֹר פֵּרוֹת יֶשׁ־לִי בְיָדְךָ,״ „אֵין לְךָ בְיָדִי אֶלָּא לֶתֶךְ קִטְנִית״ — חַיָּב, שֶׁהַקִּטְנִית בִּכְלַל פֵּרוֹת.

טְעָנוֹ חִטִּין, וְהוֹדָה לוֹ בִשְׂעוֹרִים — פָּטוּר. וְרַבָּן גַּמְלִיאֵל מְחַיֵּב.

יד אברהם

explicitly claims a minted *dinar* of gold and not gold the weight of a *dinar*. The mishnah teaches that admission of any type of coin is considered an admission since all currency is treated as one 'kind.' Thus, although one is of silver and one is of copper, admission of any of them warrants an oath.

Tos. explain the *Gemara's* statement to mean that the plaintiff's claim is that he gave the defendant a *dinar* of gold to change for him into smaller coins, and he now requests these coins. The defendant replies that the plaintiff gave him only a *dinar* of silver to change into smaller coins, of which he returned all but a *trisis*, or a *pundion*, or a *perutah*. Since the claim is for small coins of various kinds, the defendant's admission that he still owes one of them is an admission of the same kind as the claim. Although this is obvious, the mishnah teaches in passing that all these are acceptable types of coins and that one must accept even *perutos* as change for his *dinar*.

„כּוֹר תְּבוּאָה יֶשׁ־לִי בְיָדְךָ,״ — *'I have a kor of grain in your possession,'*

[The plaintiff claims he is owed a *kor* of grain.] A *kor* equals thirty *seah* (*Rav* to *Bava Metzia* 6:4).

„אֵין לְךָ בְיָדִי אֶלָּא לֶתֶךְ קִטְנִית״ — [*and the other replies,*] *'You have in my possession only a lesech of beans'* —

A *lesech* is half a *kor*, fifteen *seah* (*Rav; Rashi*).

פָּטוּר. — *he is exempt.*

Beans are not classified a type of grain. Therefore, the admission is not of the same kind as the claim (*Tif. Yis.*).

silver or an even smaller coin, it is a partial admission and he is obviously liable to an oath (*Gem.* 40a).

However, the meaning of this last line, *because all coins are of one type*, is obscure according to Rav since he explains the claim as being for value, not coins. The *Gemara* (as understood by *Rashi*) explains it to mean that all coins are treated as one — i.e., that the admission of even the smallest of them (the *perutah*) is sufficient in value to warrant an oath [though the claim and denial have higher minimum values]. Others understand the *Gemara's* explanation to mean that the mishnah means to make clear Rav's rule — that the claim of any type of coin is assumed to refer to value and not metal. The law is the same whether he claimed two silver coins as in the first mishnah, or a *dinar* of gold as in this mishnah, or a *trisis* or *perutah*. This is in contrast to the case in which he claims a weight, such as a *litra*, where it is assumed that the precious metal is being claimed, not the value (*Tos. Yom Tov* from *Ramban* and *Ran*).

This explains the mishnah according to Rav. According to Shmuel, however, who explains the mishnah to mean that when the claim is for a certain coinage of gold it is the gold itself that is being demanded, it should not be considered a partial admission, since the claim was for gold and the defendant admitted to silver, not gold. Accordingly, the *Gemara* (40a) explains that the mishnah according to Shmuel speaks of a case in which he demands of him a *dinar* of coins. *Rashi* explains this to mean that he

'I have a *kor* of grain in your possession,' [and the other replies,] 'You have in my possession only a *lesech* of beans' — he is exempt. [But if he claims,] 'I have a *kor* of produce in your possession,' [and the other replies,] 'You have in my possession only a *lesech* of beans' — he is liable, since beans are included in produce.

[If] he claimed from him wheat, and he admitted to him barley — he is exempt. But Rabban Gamliel declares [him] liable.

YAD AVRAHAM

„כּוֹר פֵּרוֹת יֶשׁ-לִי בְּיָדְךָ," „אֵין לְךָ בְּיָדִי אֶלָּא לֶתֶךְ קִטְנִית" — [*But if he claims,*] *'I have a kor of produce in your possession,'* [*and the other replies,*] *'You have in my possession only a lesech of beans'* —

[I.e., the claim was for the more generalized *produce* rather than *grain.*]

חַיָּב, שֶׁהַקִּטְנִית בִּכְלָל פֵּרוֹת. — *he is liable, since beans are included in produce.*

[He is liable to the Biblical oath of partial admission, because beans are included in the term *produce.* Consequently, the admission is of the same kind as the claim.]

טְעָנוֹ חִטִּין, וְהוֹדָה לוֹ בִשְׂעוֹרִים — פָּטוּר. — [*If*] *he claimed from him wheat, and he admitted to him barley — he is exempt.*

[Although the admission was for a smaller amount, it is not of the same kind as the claim. Thus, the oath of partial admission does not apply.]

The *Gemara (Bava Kamma* 35b) states that not only is the defendant exempt from an oath, but he is even exempt from paying for the barley to which he admitted. The reason according to *Tur (Choshen Mishpat* 88) is that the claimant, by claiming only the wheat and not the barley, admits that the defendant does not owe him barley. This admission exempts the defendant from paying the debt of barley which he says he owes. In the name of *Rosh,* he states that this applies only if the plaintiff states explicitly, 'I lent you wheat on such-and-such a day at such-and-such a time,' and the defendant replies, 'It was barley.' It follows that if he had lent him both, he would have claimed both, since the loan of both of them took place at the same time. Consequently, the claimant in effect admits that the defendant does not owe him barley. If, however, he claimed generally, 'I lent you wheat,' and he admits to barley, he must pay for the barley, since a person does not relinquish all other claims by lodging only one of them *(Tos. Yom Tov).*

Rama (loc. cit.) offers a different rationale. He explains that, since the plaintiff did not claim barley, the defendant can claim that he was jesting when he admitted owing what was not demanded of him. The difference between these two reasons is obviously where the defendant knows that he is indeed indebted to the plaintiff for barley. According to *Rama,* he is liable. According to the *Tur,* however, since we assume that the plaintiff has relinquished his claim, the defendant is exempt *(Rama* 88:12).

וְרַבָּן גַּמְלִיאֵל מְחַיֵּב. — *But Rabban Gamliel declares* [*him*] *liable.*

Rabban Gamliel does not require that the admission be of the same kind as the claim *(Rashi* 40a, 42a). Some commentators point out that although Rabban Gamliel holds the defendant liable to an oath that he does not owe the wheat, he is nevertheless exempt from payment for the barley, as explained in the preceding paragraph *(Tos. Yom Tov* from *Tos.* 40a, *Bava Kamma* 35b).

Although earlier parts of the mishnah are based on the principle that the admission must be of the same kind as the claim, as explained above, and Rabban Gamliel disagrees with all the cases, nevertheless the *Tanna* states Rabban Gamliel's divergent view at the very end, to indicate that he differs with all the previous rulings *(Tos.* 41a, s.v. אין).

שבועות
ו/ג

הַטּוֹעֵן לַחֲבֵרוֹ בְּכַדֵּי שֶׁמֶן, וְהוֹדָה לוֹ בְּקַנְקַנִּים — אַדְמוֹן אוֹמֵר: הוֹאִיל וְהוֹדָה לוֹ מִקְצָת מִמִּין הַטַּעֲנָה, יִשָּׁבַע. וַחֲכָמִים אוֹמְרִים: אֵין הַהוֹדָאָה מִמִּין הַטַּעֲנָה. אָמַר רַבָּן גַּמְלִיאֵל: רוֹאֶה אֲנִי אֶת־דִּבְרֵי אַדְמוֹן.

טְעָנוֹ כֵּלִים וְקַרְקָעוֹת, וְהוֹדָה בַּכֵּלִים וְכָפַר בַּקַּרְקָעוֹת, בַּקַּרְקָעוֹת וְכָפַר בַּכֵּלִים — פָּטוּר. הוֹדָה בְּמִקְצָת הַקַּרְקָעוֹת, פָּטוּר; בְּמִקְצָת הַכֵּלִים — חַיָּב,

יד אברהם

Tos. Yom Tov, however, conjectures that R' Yehudah HaNasi, the redactor of the mishnah, knew by tradition that the controversy between Rabban Gamliel and the Sages came about in the discussion of the case of one claiming wheat and the other answering that he owed him barley. Therefore, it is brought up in this case and not in the previous cases.

הַטּוֹעֵן לַחֲבֵרוֹ בְּכַדֵּי שֶׁמֶן, — *[If] one claims jars of oil from another,*

I.e., he claimed vessels full of oil *(Rav; Rashi).*

וְהוֹדָה לוֹ בְּקַנְקַנִּים — *and he admits to him the jars —*

I.e., he admits empty vessels, devoid of oil *(Rav; Rashi).*

The discrepancy between the expression of the claimant, כַּדִּים, *kaddim,* and that of the defendant, קַנְקַנִּים, *kankannim* — two types of jars — teaches us that the two terms are synonymous. Accordingly, if one sells *kaddim* to another, he may give him *kankannim,* although they are generally smaller, because the smaller vessel is also known as a *kad* *(Tos. Yom Tov; Meleches Shlomo, Kesubos* 13:4).

Others explain *kankannim* as meaning empty containers. This is the mishnah's way of stating that one claims full jugs of oil and the other one admits owing him empty jugs *(Tif. Yis.; Chiddushei Mahariach).*

[From the *Gemara* it appears that *kankannim* is either completely synonymous with *kaddim* or is a general term for all containers. Therefore, the mishnah must mean that the plaintiff claims containers of oil, and the other concedes that he owes him only empty containers.]

אַדְמוֹן אוֹמֵר: הוֹאִיל וְהוֹדָה לוֹ מִקְצָת מִמִּין הַטַּעֲנָה, יִשָּׁבַע. — *Admon says: Since he has admitted to him a part of the kind of the claim, he must swear.*

The claim is in effect for oil and jars. This is akin to one who claims wheat and barley, and the defendant admits owing one of them *(Rashi* 42a). Since he admits owing one of them [in this case the jars], he has admitted part of the claim and must therefore swear the oath of partial admission concerning the remainder which he denies.

וַחֲכָמִים אוֹמְרִים: אֵין הַהוֹדָאָה מִמִּין הַטַּעֲנָה. — *But the Sages say: The admission is not of the kind of the claim.*

They rule that if one claims wheat and barley, and the defendant admits one of them, he is exempt from swearing an oath on the one he denies *(Tos. Yom Tov* from *Gem.* 40b). [The Sages consider the claim for wheat and barley as two separate claims. When the defendant admits the barley and denies the wheat, he is admitting the one claim completely while denying the other entirely. It is therefore not considered a partial admission. Here, too, the claim for jars of oil is seen as two separate claims, to which the defendant admits the claim of the jars entirely, and denies the one for the oil entirely.]

This seems to be the explanation of the *Gemara* here [40a] *(Tos. Yom Tov).* However, the same mishnah appears in *Kesubos* 13:4. The *Gemara* there (108b) explains the controversy as follows: Admon construes the

6
3 [If] one claims jars of oil from another, and he admits to him the jars — Admon says: Since he has admitted to him a part of the kind of the claim, he must swear. But the Sages say: The admission is not of the kind of the claim. Said Rabban Gamliel: I see Admon's view.

[If] he claimed from him utensils and land, and he admitted the utensils but denied the land, [or he admitted] the land and denied the utensils — he is exempt. [If] he admitted part of the land, he is exempt;

YAD AVRAHAM

claim to include both the vessels and the oil. When the defendant concedes that he owes empty vessels, he is admitting to part of the claim, thus making himself liable to an oath. The Sages, however, interpret the plaintiff's claim for jars of oil to refer only to the oil; mention of the jars is merely to indicate how much oil. Therefore, when the defendant admits that he owes only empty vessels he is admitting to something that was not demanded of him, and he is exempt from swearing a Biblical oath *(Rav* to *Kesubos)*.

According to this understanding, the controversy between Admon and the Sages is only whether the claim is for both oil and jars. Should he explicitly claim both, and the defendant admit the jars, even the Sages would concur with Admon that he is liable *(Tos. Yom Tov)*. *Tos.* here (40b), however, attempt to reconcile the two different versions by showing that Admon and the Sages argue about both issues.

As noted in the commentary to mishnah 1 (fn. to s.v. חיב), whether or not it is a dispute of Admon and the Sages, the question of whether the admission of one part of a double claim (e.g., wheat and barley) warrants an oath of partial admission is certainly a dispute of *Amoraim*. The halachah follows the view that an oath is warranted *(Choshen Mishpat* 88:12).

אָמַר רַבָּן גַּמְלִיאֵל: רוֹאֶה אֲנִי אֶת־דִּבְרֵי אַדְמוֹן. — *Said Rabban Gamliel: I see Admon's view.*

The halachah is, indeed, in accordance with Admon *(Rav; Choshen Mishpat* 88:18).

טְעָנוֹ כֵּלִים וְקַרְקָעוֹת, וְהוֹדָה בַכֵּלִים וְכָפַר בַּקַּרְקָעוֹת, בַּקַּרְקָעוֹת וְכָפַר בַּכֵּלִים — *[If] he claimed from him utensils and land, and he admitted the utensils but denied the land, [or he admitted] the land and denied the utensils —*

[He admitted owing all the utensils claimed and denied owing any of the land. Or he admitted owing the land but not the utensils.]

פָּטוּר. — *he is exempt.*

He is exempt from a Biblical oath for partial admission [even according to Admon] because the Torah does not mandate oaths for cases concerning real estate. This is an example of the general rule stated in the next mishnah that one does not swear any oath concerning land. Even when he admits the land and denies the utensils — in which case his oath of partial admission would concern only the utensils which he denies — there is still no oath. Since the oath comes about through his admission of a claim of land, it is deemed an oath relating to land. Thus, if either the admission or the denial was for land, there is no liability for an oath *(Rav; Rashi)*.

הוֹדָה בְּמִקְצָת הַקַּרְקָעוֹת, פָּטוּר; — *[If] he admitted part of the land, he is exempt;*

[Since the claim is for land, it cannot warrant an oath.]

This part of the mishnah is seemingly superfluous. It is stated to make clear that the true reason for the just-mentioned law in the mishnah is because there is no oath in regard to matters involving real estate, and not because that *Tanna* follows the view that if one claims two kinds and the defendant admits one, he is

שֶׁהַנְּכָסִים שֶׁאֵין לָהֶם אַחֲרָיוּת זוֹקְקִין אֶת־הַנְּכָסִים שֶׁיֵּשׁ לָהֶן אַחֲרָיוּת לִשָּׁבַע עֲלֵיהֶן.

[ד] **אֵין** נִשְׁבָּעִין עַל־טַעֲנַת חֵרֵשׁ, שׁוֹטֶה, וְקָטָן; וְאֵין מַשְׁבִּיעִין אֶת־הַקָּטָן; אֲבָל נִשְׁבָּעִים לְקָטָן וְלַהֶקְדֵּשׁ.

יד אברהם

exempt from an oath of partial admission. By stating that he is exempt even if he admitted part of the land, thus making his claim and admission of the same kind, the mishnah makes it clear that the reason for the exemption from the oath is because there is no oath administered concerning land *(Tos. Yom Tov* from *Tos.* 40b, as explained by *Chochmas Shlomo).*

בְּמִקְצָת הַכֵּלִים — *part of the utensils* —

I.e., if the defendant admitted part of the utensils, thus making a claim and admission on movable property *(Rav).*

חַיָּב, — *he is liable,*

He is liable to the oath of partial admission that he does not owe the balance of the utensils. However, once *beis din* imposes an oath upon him for the utensils, an additional oath may be attached to it requiring him to swear that he does not owe the land, as the mishnah will now explain *(Rav* from *Gem.* 40a).

שֶׁהַנְּכָסִים שֶׁאֵין לָהֶם אַחֲרָיוּת — *because property which cannot have a lien on it*

[I.e., movables (personal property), for which an oath can be imposed.]

זוֹקְקִין אֶת־הַנְּכָסִים שֶׁיֵּשׁ לָהֶן אַחֲרָיוּת לִשָּׁבַע עֲלֵיהֶן. — *causes [one] to swear concerning property which can have a lien on it.*

[I.e., real estate. Although movable property can be collected for a debt, only real estate can be the subject of a lien.]

The principle of attaching oaths [גִּלְגּוּל שְׁבוּעָה] — i.e., attaching to an oath which a defendant is compelled to swear another oath concerning something to which he could ordinarily *not* be compelled to swear — is derived from the laws of the *sotah (Numbers* ch. 5). A *sotah* is a woman suspected of adultery on the basis of violating her husband's warning before witnesses not to be alone with a certain man. If she maintains her innocence from adultery, she is brought to the Temple and subjected to the test of the מֵי הַמָּרִים, *the bitter waters.*[1] As part of the test, the Torah states that the *Kohen* administers to her an oath that she did not commit adultery and she answers, *'Amen, amen' (Num.* 5:22). The double response denotes an oath that she had no intimacy with her alleged adulterer nor with any other man, as well as various other matters (see *Sotah* 2:4). Although there is no initial basis to require an oath regarding other acts of adultery (since she was not suspected of these), it is nevertheless imposed upon her as an adjunct to the primary oath *(Kiddushin* 27b). The mishnah there states that she can even be compelled to swear that she did not commit adultery during the stage of *erusin* (betrothal), although a woman suspected of adultery during this preliminary stage of marriage

1. A woman suspected of adultery need not undergo this test, which results in her death if she is indeed guilty of adultery. She may either confess her guilt or simply refuse to undergo the test, in which case she must be divorced (since a woman guilty of adultery is forbidden to continue her marriage to the husband she betrayed) with the loss of *kesubah* payments. She cannot, however, be executed on her own confession, because capital punishment can be imposed only on the testimony of two witnesses to the crime. Thus, she undergoes the test only if she wishes to prove her innocence and continue the marriage.

part of the utensils — he is liable, because property which cannot have a lien on it causes [one] to swear concerning property which can have a lien on it.

4. There is no oath in response to the claim of a deaf-mute, a mentally deranged person, or a minor; and we cannot impose an oath on a minor; but one swears to a minor and about consecrated property.

YAD AVRAHAM

cannot herself be subjected to the *sotah* test and accompanying oath (*Tos.* ibid.). From this we derive that in monetary issues too, an auxiliary oath can be attached even regarding those things which never require a primary oath — i.e., litigations involving real property (ibid. 28a).

4.

אֵין נִשְׁבָּעִין עַל־טַעֲנַת חֵרֵשׁ, שׁוֹטֶה, וְקָטָן; — *There is no oath* [lit. *one does not swear*] *in response to the claim of a deaf-mute, a mentally deranged person, or a minor;*

Although a deaf-mute cannot talk, he can lodge a claim by sign language. As is the case everywhere חֵרֵשׁ is mentioned, this rule applies only to a deaf-mute. A claim lodged by a deaf person who can speak requires an oath by the defendant (*Rav, Tos. Yom Tov* from *Terumos* 1:1).

The chapter dealing with the oath for the partial admission commences with the words (*Ex.* 22:6): *Should a man give to his neighbor money or utensils to watch* ... This indicates that if the one giving is a minor [who is not a *man*], the arrangement cannot lead to an oath. The deaf-mute and the mentally deranged person are equated with the minor because of their lack of mental capacity (*Rav* from *Gem.* 42a).

This applies only to the Biblical oath. One is liable, however, to take a *shevuas hesses*, the post-mishnaic oath imposed by the Sages of the Talmud (*Rav*). This was enacted to prevent people from taking monetary advantage of minors without ever being answerable for their actions (*Rambam, Hil. Toein* 5:10).

וְאֵין מַשְׁבִּיעִין אֶת־הַקָּטָן; — *and we cannot impose an oath on a minor;*

I.e., any oath whatsoever, since the minor lacks a proper awareness of the penalty for a false oath (*Rambam, Hil. Toein* 5:10).

אֲבָל נִשְׁבָּעִים לַקָּטָן — *but one swears to a minor*

I.e., if someone wishes to collect a debt from the property of a minor, he cannot do so unless he swears that the debt was not yet paid (*Rav* from *Gem.* 42b). This was enacted to protect minors.

וְלַהֶקְדֵּשׁ. — *and about consecrated property.*

A property encumbered by a lien can be sold or consecrated by the debtor; however, if the debtor is unable to repay the debt when it falls due, the creditor can collect the encumbered property in payment for his debt. Should a debtor with a lien on his property consecrate it to the Temple, a creditor with a deed of indebtness that predates the consecration can step forward and take it in payment for his debt. In such a case, however, the creditor must swear that the debt was not previously collected before collecting from the Temple treasury (*Rav* from *Gem.* ad loc.).

Furthermore, although the consecration was not effective, the creditor must nevertheless pay a small sum of money to redeem the property (by Rabbinical law), so that people not think that consecrated objects can be released without redemption (as in *Arachin* 6:2).

וְאֵלּוּ דְּבָרִים שֶׁאֵין נִשְׁבָּעִין עֲלֵיהֶן: הָעֲבָדִים, וְהַשְּׁטָרוֹת, וְהַקַּרְקָעוֹת, וְהַהֶקְדֵּשׁוֹת; אֵין בָּהֶם תַּשְׁלוּמֵי כֶפֶל, וְלֹא תַשְׁלוּמֵי אַרְבָּעָה וַחֲמִשָּׁה. שׁוֹמֵר חִנָּם אֵינוֹ נִשְׁבָּע, נוֹשֵׂא שָׂכָר אֵינוֹ מְשַׁלֵּם. רַבִּי שִׁמְעוֹן אוֹמֵר: קָדָשִׁים שֶׁחַיָּב

יד אברהם

5.

וְאֵלּוּ דְּבָרִים שֶׁאֵין נִשְׁבָּעִין עֲלֵיהֶן: — *These are the things for which no oath is imposed* [lit. *for which one does not swear*]:

I.e., when litigating any of the following items, the three Biblical oaths — שְׁבוּעַת מוֹדֶה בְּמִקְצָת, *the oath of partial admission*, שְׁבוּעַת הַשּׁוֹמְרִים, *the oath of the shomer*, שְׁבוּעַת עֵד אֶחָד, *the oath to contradict the single witness* — are never imposed *(Tif. Yis.)*.

The Torah *(Exodus* 22:8) illustrates the matters over which litigation can result in an oath as follows: עַל־כָּל־דְּבַר פֶּשַׁע עַל־שׁוֹר עַל־חֲמוֹר עַל־שֶׂה עַל־שַׂלְמָה עַל־כָּל־אֲבֵדָה, *Over any matter of liability — over a bull, a donkey, a sheep, or a garment — over any loss . . .* The opening phrase of the verse, *Over any matter of liability*, is a general statement including all types of litigation, as is the later phrase, *over any loss*. The middle phrase, however, cites specific examples — a bull, donkey, sheep and garment. Following the hermeneutic principle of כְּלָל וּפְרָט וּכְלָל, *generalization, specification and generalization* (see above 3:5, s.v. אמר לו אם רבה), the verse is expounded to teach that only those matters similar in nature to the four specific examples cited here are subject to the laws of oath, as the mishnah will now define *(Rav)*.

הָעֲבָדִים, וְהַשְּׁטָרוֹת, וְהַקַּרְקָעוֹת, וְהַהֶקְדֵּשׁוֹת; — *slaves, legal documents, land, and consecrated property;*

The four items mentioned in the verse in regard to an oath have in common that they are movable and have intrinsic value. Thus we exclude from the law of oaths land, which is not movable; slaves, which the Torah classifies as real property and thus legally equivalent to land; legal documents, which although movable, have only extrinsic, not intrinsic, value [i.e., their value is not for their paper, but for their legal value in proving a debt or transaction]. Furthermore, since the section commences with the words (v. 6): *Should a man give his fellowman . . .* we deduce that the obligation to swear mentioned in the section deals only with a man and his fellowman, not a man and the Temple treasury. Thus, if a man was guarding consecrated [i.e., Temple] property, for example, the Biblical oath of the *shomer* cannot be imposed upon him *(Rav* from *Gem.* 42b).

אֵין בָּהֶם תַּשְׁלוּמֵי כֶפֶל, — *neither is there twofold payment,*

We have learned previously that if one steals something and is caught he must give a twofold payment — the first being the object or its value and a second payment as a fine. The Torah teaches this principle in the same section that deals with the oath of the *shomer* (guardian), where the bull, donkey, etc. are specified. We therefore learn that should one kidnap a slave, steal a loan document, or change the boundary on his neighbor's property [thereby stealing his land], he is not liable to the twofold payment for this theft *(Rav)*. [He must, of course, return what he has stolen; it is only the penalty payment that is exempted.]

Another manner in which theft of real estate is possible is where one entrusts vines laden with grapes to someone, and he later claims that the grapes were stolen. [Since the grapes were still growing from the vines, they are classified as real estate under the rule

6 5. **T**hese are the things for which no oath is imposed:
5 slaves, legal documents, land, and consecrated property; neither is there twofold payment, nor fourfold nor fivefold payment. An unpaid *shomer* does not swear, a paid *shomer* does not pay. R' Shimon says:

YAD AVRAHAM

that whatever is attached to the ground is legally treated like the land itself (see next mishnah).] If he swears to that effect and is subsequently discovered to have taken them himself, he is not liable to twofold payment for his theft (*Tos.* 42b).

וְלֹא תַשְׁלוּמֵי אַרְבָּעָה וַחֲמִשָּׁה. — *nor fourfold nor fivefold payment.*

We learned in the preceding chapter that if one steals a bull or sheep and then proceeds either to sell or slaughter it, he must pay four or five times the value of the stolen item; i.e., he pays the twofold payment that any thief pays, plus an additional twofold payment for a sheep and threefold payment for a bull. If one stole a consecrated bull and then sold or slaughtered it, however, since he is exempt from the initial twofold payment, there is no four or fivefold payment. Since the four and fivefold payments apply only to cattle and sheep, this part of the mishnah obviously deals only with consecrated objects, not slaves, documents and land (*Rav* from *Gem.* 42b; *Tos.* 42b).

שׁוֹמֵר חִנָּם אֵינוֹ נִשְׁבָּע, — *An unpaid shomer does not swear,*

An unpaid *shomer* (guardian) is obligated to pay for the object entrusted to him only if it was lost or stolen due to his negligence. If the loss or theft did not result from his negligence, he does not have to reimburse the owner. He does, however, have to swear that the loss was not due to his negligence (*Ex.* 22:7). The mishnah here teaches us that if the owner entrusted him with land, documents, slaves or consecrated objects, and these were lost or stolen, the *shomer* is exempt from swearing the oath of the *shomer* (*Rav*).

Tos. (42b) assert that not only is he exempt from an oath if he claims that their theft was not due to his negligence, but he is even exempt from paying in a case where he was negligent, since these items are not included in the section of the Torah dealing with watchmen.

Rambam, however, rules that where he was negligent he is liable to pay. The rationale for this is that negligence is akin to damaging, and that liability to pay for negligence is therefore not as a *shomer*, but as any person who damages another's property. In the laws of damages there are no exclusions for non-movables and items having no intrinsic value (*Rambam, Hil. Sechirus* 2:3).

נוֹשֵׂא שָׂכָר אֵינוֹ מְשַׁלֵּם. — *a paid shomer does not pay.*

[Lit. one who receives pay. This is synonymous with שׁוֹמֵר שָׂכָר, *a paid shomer* (guardian). The reason for this term will be discussed below (8:1).]

A paid *shomer* is generally liable for theft or loss, even those not resulting from his negligence (see below, 8:1). Nevertheless, he is exempt from those liabilities in the case of slaves, documents, land, and consecrated objects. This is derived from the first verse in the section dealing with a paid *shomer* (*Ex.* 22:9): *And should a man give to his fellowman a donkey, bull, sheep, or any beast to watch, etc.* The common denominator of all these is that they are movable and have intrinsic value, as explained above. Here too consecrated objects are excluded from the expression, רֵעֵהוּ, *his fellowman* (*Rav* from *Gem.* 43a).

As above, in the case of the unpaid *shomer*, the paid *shomer* is also exempt from negligence according to *Tosafos* and others, and liable for negligence according to *Rambam*.

Should the paid *shomer* claim that the animal died, broke a limb, or was captured — accidents from which even a paid *shomer* is exempt from paying by swearing to that effect (8:1) — if it was a

בְּאַחֲרָיוּתָן, נִשְׁבָּעִין עֲלֵיהֶן; וְשֶׁאֵינוֹ חַיָּב בְּאַחֲרָיוּתָן, אֵין נִשְׁבָּעִין עֲלֵיהֶן.

[ו] **רַבִּי** מֵאִיר אוֹמֵר: יֵשׁ דְּבָרִים שֶׁהֵן בַּקַּרְקַע, וְאֵינָן כְּקַרְקַע; וְאֵין חֲכָמִים מוֹדִים לוֹ. כֵּיצַד? „עֶשֶׂר גְּפָנִים טְעוּנוֹת מָסַרְתִּי לָךְ," וְהַלָּה אוֹמֵר: „אֵינָן אֶלָּא חָמֵשׁ" — רַבִּי מֵאִיר מְחַיֵּב שְׁבוּעָה; וַחֲכָמִים אוֹמְרִים: כָּל־הַמְחֻבָּר לַקַּרְקַע הֲרֵי הוּא כְּקַרְקַע.

יד אברהם

consecrated animal he is exempt from the oath as well.

The mishnah's failure to mention that the borrower and the hirer [the other two types of *shomerim* (8:1)] are also exempt from paying or swearing when they borrow or hire the aforementioned items is puzzling. *Rav*, based on *Rambam Comm.*, explains that the reason for this omission is that there is no way to borrow land, that borrowing legal documents is unusual, while renting does not apply to them, and that consecrated objects may not be lent or hired.

Tos. Yom Tov takes issue with *Rav's* reasoning since lending does apply to land. He quotes numerous instances mentioned in the *Gemara* and *Rambam* where lending applies to land. He therefore agrees with *Nimmukei Yosef*, who states that since lending and hiring are not applicable to consecrated objects, the mishnah omits mention of them entirely.

Some rule that a house is judged as movable property, since it was once detached and only later became attached to the earth. Consequently, it is subject to the laws of *shomerim*, and should one borrow a house, for example, and it burns down, he is liable *(Rama* 95:1, quoting *Tur* in the name of *Ittur)*. See *Shach* who contests this view.

רַבִּי שִׁמְעוֹן אוֹמֵר: קָדָשִׁים שֶׁחַיָּב בְּאַחֲרָיוּתָן, — *R' Shimon says:* [*Concerning*] *consecrated things for which one is responsible,*

I.e., if one said: הֲרֵי עָלַי, *'I take upon myself* to bring a sacrifice,' and then designated a particular animal for that sacrifice, since the vow was to bring a sacrifice, if something happens to the designated animal, even though it was through no fault of his, he must replace it with another animal. Thus he is responsible for the security of the sacrifice *(Tif. Yis.; Rav, Megillah* 1:6).

נִשְׁבָּעִין עֲלֵיהֶן; — *an oath is imposed;*

R' Shimon rules that, since a loss of this animal causes a loss to the one who consecrated it, it is treated as if it was his money [not the Temple's], and an oath is imposed concerning it *(Tif. Yis.)*.

וְשֶׁאֵינוֹ חַיָּב בְּאַחֲרָיוּתָן, — *but* [*concerning*] *those for which one is not responsible,*

I.e., he said: הֲרֵי זוּ, *'This animal* shall be a sacrifice.' In this case he did not obligate himself to bring a sacrifice, merely to bring this particular animal as a sacrifice. Therefore, if something should happen to it, he is not obligated to replace it *(Tif. Yis.)*.

אֵין נִשְׁבָּעִין עֲלֵיהֶן. — *no oath is imposed.*

These are treated as consecrated objects, which are excluded from Biblical oaths.

The halachah is not in accordance with R' Shimon. Rather, no oath is imposed concerning any consecrated object regardless of whether the consecrator is responsible for its security or not.

In all the cases mentioned in this mishnah the exemption is from the Biblical oath; a *shevuas hesses*, however, is imposed *(Rambam Comm.)*.

6
6 [Concerning] consecrated things for which one is responsible, an oath is imposed; but [concerning] those for which one is not responsible, no oath is imposed.

6. R' Meir says: Some things are attached to the ground, but are not treated as land; but the Sages do not concur with him. How so? [If one claims,] 'I delivered to you ten fruit-laden vines,' and the other one says, 'They were only five' — R' Meir declares him liable to an oath; but the Sages say: Anything attached to the ground is treated as land.

YAD AVRAHAM

6.

רַבִּי מֵאִיר אוֹמֵר: יֵשׁ דְּבָרִים שֶׁהֵן בַּקַּרְקַע, — *R' Meir says: Some things are attached to the ground,*

Other editions read: שֶׁהֵן כְּקַרְקַע, *which are like land (Gem.; Rav; Rashi; Rif).*

וְאֵינָן כְּקַרְקַע; — *but are not treated as land;*

I.e., they are adjudged as movables insofar as an oath is imposed concerning them *(Rashi).*

וְאֵין חֲכָמִים מוֹדִים לוֹ. — *but the Sages do not concur with him.*

[I.e., the Sages account them as land, and no oath is imposed concerning them, as taught in mishnah 5.]

כֵּיצַד? „עֶשֶׂר גְּפָנִים טְעוּנוֹת מָסַרְתִּי לָךְ," — *How so?* [*If one claims,*] *'I delivered to you ten fruit-laden vines,'*

[I.e., he claims that he entrusted this person with ten fruit-laden vines.] These trees were then picked and their owner now demands payment for the fruit *(Ran;* but see *Rashba* cited below).

וְהַלָּה אוֹמֵר: „אֵינָן אֶלָּא חָמֵשׁ" — — *and the other one says, 'They were only five' —*

I.e., the recipient claims to have been entrusted with only five fruit-laden vines. These he admits having picked, but claims the other five were never entrusted to him and were therefore not picked by him *(Ran).* [Thus, their dispute does not concern the vines but only their fruit.]

רַבִּי מֵאִיר מְחַיֵּב שְׁבוּעָה; — *R' Meir declares him liable to an oath;*

Should the grapes be ripe and ready to pick [at the time they were entrusted *(Ran)*], no longer requiring the nourishment of the vine, R' Meir considers them to have the legal status of grapes already picked. Since they are considered as movables, he is liable to the oath of partial admission for the five he denies *(Rav* from *Gem.* 43a).

וַחֲכָמִים אוֹמְרִים: כָּל־הַמְחֻבָּר לַקַּרְקַע הֲרֵי הוּא כְּקַרְקַע. — *but the Sages say: Anything attached to the ground is treated as land.*

The Sages rule that though the grapes were ready to be picked, since they were still physically attached to the ground they are legally classified as land, and the oath can therefore not be imposed concerning them *(Rav).* Although the grapes have since been picked, and it is only the payment for them that is in question, since the liability derives from something which, according to the Sages, was classified as land, an oath of partial admission cannot be imposed regarding reimbursement for them *(Ran).*

Ran also cites the opinion of *Rashba* who asserts that a claim for reimbursement for the grapes would be considered a claim for movables (i.e., money), not land. Accord-

אֵין נִשְׁבָּעִין אֶלָּא עַל־דָּבָר שֶׁבְּמִדָּה, וְשֶׁבְּמִשְׁקָל, וְשֶׁבְּמִנְיָן. כֵּיצַד? „בַּיִת מָלֵא מָסַרְתִּי לָךְ,״ וְ„כִיס מָלֵא מָסַרְתִּי לָךְ,״ וְהַלָּה אוֹמֵר: „אֵינִי יוֹדֵעַ, אֶלָּא מַה־שֶׁהִנַּחְתָּ אַתָּה נוֹטֵל״ — פָּטוּר. זֶה אוֹמֵר: „עַד הַזִּיז,״ וְזֶה אוֹמֵר: „עַד הַחַלּוֹן״ — חַיָּב.

[ז] **הַמַּלְוֶה** אֶת־חֲבֵרוֹ עַל־הַמַּשְׁכּוֹן, וְאָבַד הַמַּשְׁכּוֹן; אָמַר לוֹ: „סֶלַע הִלְוִיתִיךָ

יד אברהם

of a *shomer*, however, since they were entrusted to the *shomer* for safekeeping while they were attached to the ground, with the intention that they remain in that state, they are accounted as land *(Tos. Yom Tov).*

אֵין נִשְׁבָּעִין — *There is no oath*

No oath is imposed on the defendant who admits part of the claim *(Meiri).*

אֶלָּא עַל־דָּבָר שֶׁבְּמִדָּה, וְשֶׁבְּמִשְׁקָל, וְשֶׁבְּמִנְיָן. — *except in regard to something defined by measure, weight, or number.*

I.e., he must admit part of a number if the claim was something defined by number; part of the weight if the claim was something defined by weight; or part of the measure if the claim was something defined by measure *(Rambam Comm.).*

כֵּיצַד? „בַּיִת מָלֵא מָסַרְתִּי לָךְ,״ וְ„כִיס מָלֵא מָסַרְתִּי לָךְ,״ — *How so?* [*If one claims,*] *'I delivered to you a full house,' or 'I delivered to you a full purse,'*

I.e., a house full of grain or a purse full of money to watch *(Meiri).*

וְהַלָּה אוֹמֵר: „אֵינִי יוֹדֵעַ, אֶלָּא מַה־שֶּׁהִנַּחְתָּ אַתָּה נוֹטֵל״ — *and the other one says, 'I do not know, but whatever you put down you are taking'* —

The person entrusted claims not to know whether it was full or not *(Meiri),* insisting only that whatever remains is all that he was given.

פָּטוּר. — *he is exempt.*

[Since the claim and the admission were not defined by measure, weight, or volume, he is exempt from the oath.]

ingly, *Rashba* explains the mishnah as referring to a case in which only five of the ten trees have been picked. The defendant admits to having picked these five of the plaintiff's vines but asserts that the five still-laden trees belong to him, not the plaintiff. As regards the grapes, therefore, the plaintiff claims payment for the five picked vines, as well as the return of the grapes still attached to the other five vines. The defendant admits part of this claim — viz. the produce of five vines — but denies owing the still-attached fruit. Consequently, according to R' Meir who considers these ready-to-pick grapes as already picked, the entire claim is for movable property and the partial admission therefore necessitates an oath. According to the Sages, however, the still-attached grapes are treated as land and their denial cannot form the basis of an oath. [The dispute over the trees obviously does not give rise to an oath since according to all opinions they are legally classified as real estate.]

As regards the law of the *shomer* the halachah is in accordance with the Sages. In regard to the oath of the partial admission, as well as the laws applying to such matters as commercial transaction and overcharges, the halachah is that anything ready to be picked is accounted as already picked *(Rav; Rambam, Hil. Toein* 5:4; *Choshen Mishpat* 95:2).

This ruling is shared by *R' Yosef HaLevi (Ri Migash)* cited by *Tur*. The reason for this distinction is given in *Tur Choshen Mishpat* 95. When one sells grapes ready to pick, since they are sold and bought for the purpose of being picked, they are deemed as picked and are adjudged as movables in all regards, e.g. overcharging, oaths, and the like. In the case

6
7

There is no oath except in regard to something defined by measure, weight, or number. How so? [If one claims,] 'I delivered to you a full house,' or 'I delivered to you a full purse,' and the other one says, 'I do not know, but whatever you put down you are taking' — he is exempt. [If] this one says, 'Up to the projecting beam,' and this one says, 'Up to the window' — he is liable.

7. [If] one lends another on security, and the security was lost; [if] he says to him, 'I lent you a *sela* on it,

YAD AVRAHAM

Tos. Yom Tov explains that although the volume of a house has a definite measure, the term *full house* is a relative term, e.g., it can be used for a house almost full as well as completely full. Therefore, since no actual measure was mentioned either in the claim or in the admission, he is exempt.

"וְזֶה אוֹמֵר: „עַד הַזִּיז — [*If*] *this one says, 'Up to the projecting beam,'*

If the plaintiff claims that he delivered a house full of produce extending as far as the beam projecting from the second story *(Rav)*.

"וְזֶה אוֹמֵר: „עַד הַחַלּוֹן — *and this one says, 'Up to the window'* —

The defendant admits receiving produce extending up to the window *(Meiri)*.

.חַיָּב — *he is liable.*

[Since both the claim and admission were for an exact, measurable amount, it is considered admitting to a measure, and he is therefore liable to a Biblical oath.]

The *Gemara* in *Bava Metzia* (4a, 5a) discusses the rule of הֵילָךְ, *here it is.* This refers to a case in which the plaintiff claims that the defendant owes him one hundred *zuz*, and the defendant admits to fifty and pays him immediately. Since the case between them now concerns only the remaining fifty, it is considered a complete denial rather than a partial denial and no Biblical oath is imposed. In our mishnah, if the produce *up to the window* to which he admits is intact, it would be a case of הֵילָךְ, *here it is,* since the produce to which he admits immediately reverts to the possession of the claimant. We must therefore explain our mishnah to refer to a case in which the produce to which he admits spoiled due to his negligence, and thus the portion to which he admits must now be paid for. It is thus considered a partial admission and he is liable to a Biblical oath *(Tos. Yom Tov)*.

7.

If a person lends money to another and receives a valuable from him as security [מַשְׁכּוֹן], either at the time of the loan or later, he is considered a paid *shomer* on that security, as taught in *Bava Metzia* 6:7. Should the security be lost or stolen, the lender is liable for it. Thus if the value of the security equaled the loan, the borrower is released from the loan. Should the loan exceed the value of the security, the borrower is liable only for the difference. Should the value of the security exceed the loan, the lender must pay the borrower the difference. Should the security be lost through an accident for which a paid *shomer* is exempt (see below, 8:1), the lender is exempt. He must swear that it was lost accidentally (in line with the law of the paid *shomer)* and then collect the entire loan *(Rav)*.

,הַמַּלְוֶה אֶת־חֲבֵרוֹ עַל־הַמַּשְׁכּוֹן — [*If*] *one lends another on security,*

Thus making him a paid *shomer* *(Rav)*.

;וְאָבַד הַמַּשְׁכּוֹן — *and the security was lost;*

It was either lost or stolen. Since a paid *shomer* is liable for entrusted items

שבועות ו/ז

עָלָיו, וְשֶׁקֶל הָיָה שָׁוֶה,״ וְהַלָּה אוֹמֵר: ״לֹא כִי, אֶלָּא סֶלַע הִלְוִיתַנִי עָלָיו, וְסֶלַע הָיָה שָׁוֶה״ — פָּטוּר. ״סֶלַע הִלְוִיתִיךָ עָלָיו, וְשֶׁקֶל הָיָה שָׁוֶה,״ וְהַלָּה אוֹמֵר: ״לֹא כִי, אֶלָּא סֶלַע הִלְוִיתַנִי עָלָיו, וּשְׁלֹשָׁה דִינָרִים הָיָה שָׁוֶה״ — חַיָּב.

״סֶלַע הִלְוִיתַנִי עָלָיו, וּשְׁתַּיִם הָיָה שָׁוֶה,״ וְהַלָּה אוֹמֵר: ״לֹא כִי, אֶלָּא סֶלַע הִלְוִיתִיךָ עָלָיו, וְסֶלַע הָיָה שָׁוֶה״ — פָּטוּר. ״סֶלַע הִלְוִיתַנִי עָלָיו, וּשְׁתַּיִם הָיָה שָׁוֶה,״ וְהַלָּה אוֹמֵר: ״לֹא כִי, אֶלָּא סֶלַע הִלְוִיתִיךָ עָלָיו, וַחֲמִשָּׁה דִינָרִים הָיָה שָׁוֶה״ — חַיָּב. וּמִי

יד אברהם

which are lost or stolen (even when he was not negligent), the lender is in this case responsible for the security *(Rav).*

אָמַר לוֹ: — [*if*] *he says to him,*

[If the lender says to the borrower.]

״סֶלַע הִלְוִיתִיךָ עָלָיו, וְשֶׁקֶל הָיָה שָׁוֶה,״ — *'I lent you a sela on it, and it was worth a shekel,'*

I lent you a *sela* on this security while the security was worth only a *shekel,* which is half a *sela (Rav; Rashi).* [Hence, the lender claims the balance of the loan, which equals a *shekel.*]

וְהַלָּה אוֹמֵר: — *and the other one says,*

[I.e., the borrower replies.]

״לֹא כִי, אֶלָּא סֶלַע הִלְוִיתַנִי עָלָיו, וְסֶלַע הָיָה שָׁוֶה״ — *'Not so; you lent me a sela on it, and it was worth a sela'* —

[Consequently, the borrower owes nothing.]

פָּטוּר. — *he is exempt.*

[Since the debtor denies any indebtedness, he is exempt from the Biblical oath of partial admission.]

״סֶלַע הִלְוִיתִיךָ עָלָיו, וְשֶׁקֶל הָיָה שָׁוֶה,״ — [*But if he says,*] *'I lent you a sela on it, and it was worth a shekel,'*

[The lender's claim is unchanged from the previous case.]

וְהַלָּה אוֹמֵר: ״לֹא כִי, אֶלָּא סֶלַע הִלְוִיתַנִי עָלָיו, וּשְׁלֹשָׁה דִינָרִים הָיָה שָׁוֶה״ — *and the other one says, 'Not so, you lent me a sela on it, and it was worth three dinars'*

[A *sela* equals four *dinars.* The borrower's reply is therefore that he owes only one *dinar.*]

חַיָּב. — *he is liable.*

The borrower is liable to the oath of the partial admission *(Rav).*

The *Gemara (Bava Metzia* 34b) states that both litigants must swear. The borrower must swear how much the security was worth, while the lender must swear — the same as any *shomer* — that it is not in his possession. Although he cannot be suspected of stealing the security — since its value is in any case deducted from the loan payment — we nevertheless fear that he may have taken a liking to it and wishes to purchase it against the will of its owner.

Ran points out that even if the lender admits to having the security in his possession, keeping it against the will of the borrower, the latter must nevertheless pay the part of the loan to which he admitted. In this case, however, since the lender transgresses the negative commandment of לֹא תַחְמֹד, *You shall not covet,* the courts will not force the borrower to pay his debt, since by doing so they would be aiding a person in his transgression *(Tos. Yom Tov).*

6 and it was worth a *shekel*,' and the other one says, 'Not
7 so, you lent me a *sela* on it, and it was worth a *sela*' — he is exempt. [But if he says,] 'I lent you a *sela* on it, and it was worth a *shekel*,' and the other one says, 'Not so, you lent me a *sela* on it, and it was worth three *dinars*' — he is liable.

[If he says to him,] 'You lent me a *sela* on it, and it was worth two,' and the other one says, 'Not so, I lent you a *sela* on it, and it was worth a *sela*' — he is exempt. [But if he says,] 'You lent me a *sela* on it, and it was worth two,' and the other one says, 'Not so, I lent you a *sela* on it, and it was worth five *dinars*' — he is liable.

YAD AVRAHAM

„סֶלַע הִלְוִיתַנִי עָלָיו, — *[If he says to him,] 'You lent me a sela on it,*

[In this case it is the borrower who presses a claim against the lender, claiming that the lost security was worth more than the loan.]

וּשְׁתַּיִם הָיָה שָׁוֶה," — *and it was worth two,'*

[Therefore, you owe me a *sela*.]

וְהַלָּה אוֹמֵר: „לֹא כִי, אֶלָּא סֶלַע הִלְוִיתִיךָ עָלָיו, וְסֶלַע הָיָה שָׁוֶה" — *and the other one says, 'Not so, I lent you a sela on it, and it was worth a sela'* —

[Therefore, the lender owes nothing.]

פָּטוּר. — *he is exempt.*

[Since the lender denies *any* indebtedness to the borrower, he is exempt from a Biblical oath.]

As mentioned above, the *Gemara (Bava Metzia* 34b, 35a) states that a lender who claims the security was lost must swear that it is not in his possession. [Thus the mishnah means only to say that he is exempt from swearing how much it was worth.] This being the case, the *Gemara* questions why the lender cannot also be compelled to swear the oath concerning its worth by attaching an oath (see above, mishnah 3) about the worth to the oath concerning its loss.

The conclusion is that normally such an oath could be attached and he would indeed have to swear how much it was worth. However, the mishnah is qualified as referring to the case in which the borrower believes the lender in his claim that the security is lost but does not believe him as to its value. The difference is that the borrower believes that he knows the value of the article better than the lender, but in other matters he believes him. Since he believes him in regard to the loss of the security, there is no primary oath, and without the primary oath that it is not in his possession, there can be no auxiliary oath concerning its value.

„סֶלַע הִלְוִיתַנִי עָלָיו, וּשְׁתַּיִם הָיָה שָׁוֶה," — *[But if he says,] 'You lent me a sela on it, and it was worth two,'*

[Here too the borrower is seeking compensation from the lender. His claim is identical to the one in the previous case.]

וְהַלָּה אוֹמֵר: „לֹא כִי, אֶלָּא סֶלַע הִלְוִיתִיךָ עָלָיו, וַחֲמִשָּׁה דִינָרִים הָיָה שָׁוֶה" — *and the other one says, 'Not so, I lent you a sela on it, and it was worth five dinars'* —

[The lender agrees that he owes compensation for the lost security, but only one *dinar*, not a *sela*, as the borrower claims.]

חַיָּב. — *he is liable.*

I.e., the lender is liable to a Biblical oath since he admits part of the borrower's claim *(Gem.* 43b).

נִשְׁבָּע? מִי שֶׁהַפִּקָּדוֹן אֶצְלוֹ, שֶׁמָּא יִשָּׁבַע זֶה, וְיוֹצִיא הַלָּה אֶת־הַפִּקָּדוֹן.

[א] **כָּל־הַנִּשְׁבָּעִין** שֶׁבַּתּוֹרָה נִשְׁבָּעִין וְלֹא מְשַׁלְּמִין. וְאֵלּוּ נִשְׁבָּעִין וְנוֹטְלִין: הַשָּׂכִיר, וְהַנִּגְזָל, וְהַנֶּחְבָּל, וְשֶׁכְּנֶגְדּוֹ חָשׁוּד

יד אברהם

וּמִי נִשְׁבָּע? — *Now who swears?*

This query cannot be referring back to the case immediately preceding this, since it is obvious that in that case the lender must swear since he is the defendant. The *Gemara* (43b), therefore, interprets the mishnah to be referring back to the second case, in which both the lender and the borrower must swear. The question is: Who swears first? *(Rav).*

מִי שֶׁהַפִּקָּדוֹן אֶצְלוֹ, — *The one who had the deposit,*

I.e., the lender, who had the security in his possession, must be the first to swear that it is no longer in his possession but lost *(Rav).*

Although we are dealing with security, not with a deposit, the mishnah uses the term deposit to indicate that the same ruling applies to a deposit, viz., that the *shomer* must swear that it was lost even if he pays for it *(Tos. Yom Tov).*

שֶׁמָּא יִשָּׁבַע זֶה, וְיוֹצִיא הַלָּה אֶת־הַפִּקָּדוֹן. — *lest this one swear, and the other one produce the deposit.*

I.e., lest the borrower swear first concerning the value of the security, perhaps not stating the exact value, and then the lender will produce it, proving him a liar and thereby render him ineligible for testimony and oaths *(Rav; Rashi).*

Tos. object to this interpretation since this would constitute an enactment for the benefit of a liar. [If he doesn't swear falsely he has nothing to lose from swearing first.] They prefer, therefore, to explain that when the lender produces the security we see the value of the article. Consequently, the borrower's oath although true was in vain. Thus, the Name of Heaven is profaned *(Rif).*

Although we stated above that the mishnah deals with the case in which the borrower trusts the lender, nevertheless, *beis din* will force him to swear. The reason is that since the borrower must swear, there is always the danger that the lender will produce the security and render his oath a vain one *(Tos. Yom Tov* from *Ran).*

As we learned above from the *Gemara* in *Bava Metzia* (34b), the reason a *shomer* must swear that the deposit is not in his possession even when he is willing to pay is that we fear he took a liking to the object and wants to purchase it against the wishes of the owner. Therefore, *Rambam* explains that he need only swear in a case in which the deposit or security was something unusual and not readily available. If it was something readily available for purchase, however, he would have no reason to covet just this item and therefore he does not have to swear that it is not in his possession *(Rambam, Hil. She'elah).*

Chapter 7

1.

In the preceding chapter it was explained that the Torah prescribes three instances of oath: (1) in the case of the partial admission, (2) to assert one's claim against the testimony of a single witness who testifies for the plaintiff, and (3) in the case of the *shomer* who claims exemption from paying for the item entrusted to him. In all these

7 Now who swears? The one who had the deposit, lest
1 this one swear, and the other one produce the deposit.

1. All those required to swear by the Torah swear and do not pay. But the following swear and collect: the hired laborer, the one who was robbed, the one who was wounded, the one whose opponent is not trusted to

YAD AVRAHAM

cases, the oath is incumbent upon the defendant to exempt him from payment. There are, however, several oaths instituted by the Rabbis, some of which were imposed on the plaintiff to enable him to receive payment. These Rabbinical oaths are the topic of this chapter.

כָּל־הַנִּשְׁבָּעִין שֶׁבַּתּוֹרָה — *All those required to swear by the Torah*

I.e., the *shomer* who claims exemption, the one who admits part of a claim, and the one against whom a single witness testifies *(Meiri).*

נִשְׁבָּעִין וְלֹא מְשַׁלְּמִין. — *swear and do not pay.*

Biblical oaths are never imposed on the plaintiff to enable him to collect what he claims is due him. All instances of oath are cases of the defendant swearing in order to be exempt from paying. This is derived from *(Ex.* 22:10): *The oath of* HASHEM *shall be between the two of them, that he did not extend his hand into his fellowman's property; and the owner shall accept* [*it*] *and he shall not pay.* This implies that in the instances involving Biblical oaths, it is the one who would have to pay who must take the oath [in order to exempt himself] *(Rav* from *Gem.* 45a).

Although this verse deals with the paid *shomer* who claims that the animal deposited in his trust died, broke a limb, or was captured — claims which exempt him but to which he must swear — the *Gemara* takes this as a general rule for all oaths imposed by the Torah.

Ran explains that we can know that the oaths for partial admission and against a single witness are also incumbent upon the defendant from the text of the verse. The verse begins by saying: *The oath of* HASHEM *shall be between the two of them, that he did not put his hand into his fellowman's property.* From this it is obvious that we are discussing a *shomer* who swears that he took nothing. Why then does the verse end by saying: *And he shall not pay?* The entire point of having him swear must certainly be to enable the court to accept his claim that he properly discharged his duties as guardian of the property, and if he did, he is obviously exempt from paying. We understand therefore that the final clause is written to teach the general rule of Biblical oaths — that in the cases of the partial confession and the single witness, it is also the defendant who must swear in order to exempt himself, not the plaintiff who swears to collect.

וְאֵלּוּ נִשְׁבָּעִין וְנוֹטְלִין: — *But the following swear and collect:*

All those mentioned in this chapter *(Tos. Yom Tov* from *Ran* and *Ramban)* are instances in which the Rabbis imposed an oath upon the plaintiff in order to collect what he claims is due him, as will be explained below *(Rav; Rashi).*

הַשָּׂכִיר, וְהַנִּגְזָל, וְהַנֶּחְבָּל, — *the hired laborer, the one who was robbed, the one who was wounded,*

[I.e., a laborer whose employer claims he already paid him, a debtor whose creditor entered his house without permission and unlawfully took security for the debt (thereby robbing the debtor), and one who emerged from another's house battered. These three are discussed in the following three *mishnayos.*]

וְשֶׁכְּנֶגְדּוֹ חָשׁוּד עַל־הַשְּׁבוּעָה, — *the one whose opponent is not trusted to swear,*

[I.e., one whose opponent in a litiga-

עַל־הַשְּׁבוּעָה, וְהַחֶנְוָנִי עַל־פִּנְקָסוֹ.

הַשָּׂכִיר כֵּיצַד? אָמַר לוֹ: „תֵּן־לִי שְׂכָרִי שֶׁיֶּשׁ־לִי בְּיָדְךָ,״ הוּא אוֹמֵר: „נָתַתִּי,״ וְהַלָּה אוֹמֵר: „לֹא נָטַלְתִּי״ — הוּא נִשְׁבָּע וְנוֹטֵל. רַבִּי יְהוּדָה אוֹמֵר: עַד שֶׁתְּהֵא שָׁם מִקְצָת הוֹדָאָה. כֵּיצַד? אָמַר לוֹ: „תֵּן־לִי שְׂכָרִי חֲמִשִּׁים דִּינָר שֶׁיֶּשׁ־לִי בְּיָדְךָ,״ וְהוּא אוֹמֵר: „הִתְקַבַּלְתָּ דִּינָר זָהָב.״

יד אברהם

tion is obligated to swear a Biblical oath but whom the court will not allow to swear because of his untrustworthiness, as explained in mishnah 4.]

וְהַחֶנְוָנִי עַל־פִּנְקָסוֹ. — *and the storekeeper over his account book.*

[As will be explained in mishnah 5.]

הַשָּׂכִיר כֵּיצַד? — *The hired laborer, how so?*

[I.e., in which case did the Rabbis permit him to swear in order to collect his wages?]

אָמַר לוֹ: „תֵּן־לִי שְׂכָרִי שֶׁיֶּשׁ־לִי בְּיָדְךָ,״ — [*If*] *he says to him, 'Give me my wages which are in your possession,'*

[After completing his work, the laborer asked his employer for his wages.]

הוּא אוֹמֵר: „נָתַתִּי,״ — [*and*] *he replies, 'I gave* [*them to you*],*'*

[I.e., the employer replies that he already paid him for the work.]

וְהַלָּה אוֹמֵר: „לֹא נָטַלְתִּי״ — *but this one says, 'I did not receive* [*them*]*' —*

[I.e., the worker claims that he has not yet received his wages.]

הוּא נִשְׁבָּע וְנוֹטֵל. — *he swears and collects.*

[The laborer swears that he has not been paid and collects his wages.] This oath is sworn holding a sacred object, as explained in the last chapter *(Tif. Yis.)*.

The Rabbis enacted that the hired laborer take an oath and receive payment because an employer is usually busy directing the work of his laborers, and it is likely that he does not remember whether he paid each of them his wages *(Rav* from *Gem.* 46a). The *Gemara* explains further that actually the laborer should receive his wages without an oath, since we believe that the employer, because of his preoccupation with his laborers, is uncertain of his claim, and the laborer is certain that he did not receive his wages. An oath was nevertheless imposed to appease the employer.

Many authorities explain that the oath was instituted primarily to protect the laborer's livelihood. Theoretically, it should have been imposed upon the employer requiring him to swear that he paid his worker, just as Biblical oaths are imposed on the defendant. Because of the many affairs occupying the employer, however, the Rabbis transferred it to the laborer allowing him to swear and collect *(Rif; Ran; Rosh; Rambam, Hil. Sechirus* 11:6).

The mishnah's ruling applies whether the employer has many laborers or whether he has just one. The Rabbis did not differentiate in their enactments and granted the oath to the laborer in all cases. *Yerushalmi* adds that since the householder is busy with numerous affairs, although he has just one worker, he is deemed as advancing an uncertain claim *(Tos.* 46a).

The *Gemara* does, however, qualify this ruling as applying only when the hired laborer demands his wages within the time allotted an employer to pay his workers, as taught in *Bava Metzia* (9:12). There the mishnah states that one hired for the day must be paid during the night following his employment, and one hired for the night must be paid during the day following his

7 swear, and the storekeeper over his account book.

1 The hired laborer, how so? [If] he says to him, 'Give me my wages which are in your possession,' [and] he replies, 'I gave [them to you],' but this one says, 'I did not receive [them]' — he swears and collects. R' Yehudah says: Only if there is a partial admission. How so? He says to him, 'Give me my wages of fifty *dinars* which are in your possession,' while he replies, 'You have [already] received a gold *dinar*.'

employment. Should he demand his wages after this period, we assume that the employer would not transgress the Biblical injunction against keeping the wages of a hired worker until morning (*Lev.* 19:13), nor would the worker neglect to collect his wages for that length of time. We therefore assume that the employer has indeed paid him his wages, and the laborer cannot collect his wages merely by taking an oath. Instead, the employer swears a *shevuas hesses* and is then exempt from paying (*Rav* from *Gem.* 45b).

Another exception to this rule is the case in which the laborer was hired without witnesses. In that case, the employer is always believed, since had he wanted to cheat the laborer out of his wages, he could have denied ever hiring him. This follows the rule of *miggo*, as discussed above [6:1] (*Rav* from *Gem.* 45b). The employer must, however, swear a *shevuas hesses*, as in all cases of complete denial (*Rambam, Hil. Sechirus* 11:6).

Furthermore, should the laborer produce witnesses that he was hired, but they do not know whether he actually performed the work for which he was hired, the employer is similarly believed that he paid the wages by the rule of *miggo*, since he could have denied that the laborer performed the labor for which he was hired (*Maggid Mishneh* ad loc.). Should the controversy concern only the amount of pay stipulated and not whether the wages were actually paid, e.g., the laborer claims that the employer agreed to pay him two *selaim* and the employer claims that he agreed to pay only one, the employer must swear the Biblical oath of partial admission to exempt himself from paying the difference (*Rav* from *Gem.* 46a). In this case, the Rabbis did not enact an oath for the benefit of the laborer, since the preoccupation of the employer does not cause him to forget something as basic as the amount stipulated. Consequently, we have no reason to believe the laborer's claim over the employer's (*Gem.* 46a).

רַבִּי יְהוּדָה אוֹמֵר: עַד שֶׁתְּהֵא שָׁם מִקְצָת הוֹדָאָה. — *R' Yehudah says: Only if there is a partial admission.*

[The Rabbis did not impose an oath on the hired laborer unless the employer admits to part of the claim advanced by the laborer.]

כֵּיצַד? אָמַר לוֹ: „תֶּן־לִי שְׂכָרִי חֲמִשִּׁים דִּינָר שֶׁיֵּשׁ לִי בְּיָדְךָ," — *How so? He says to him, 'Give me my wages of fifty dinars which are in your possession,'*

[The hired laborer demands from the employer his entire wages of fifty *dinars.*]

וְהוּא אוֹמֵר: „הִתְקַבַּלְתָּ דִּינָר זָהָב." — *while he replies, 'You have [already] received a gold dinar.'*

[A gold *dinar* is the equivalent of twenty-five silver *dinars*, as above (6:3). Thus, the employer claims that he already paid half the wages.]

R' Yehudah holds that the Rabbis did not enact a new oath for the laborer. Rather, in a case in which the employer would in any case have had to swear the Biblical oath of partial admission, the Rabbis transferred it to the employee. However, where the employer claims to have paid completely, thereby exempting himself from any Biblical oath, the employee does not swear and cannot collect

[ב] **הַנִּגְזָל** כֵּיצַד? הָיוּ מְעִידִין אוֹתוֹ שֶׁנִּכְנַס לְבֵיתוֹ לְמַשְׁכְּנוֹ שֶׁלֹּא בִרְשׁוּת. הוּא אוֹמֵר: „כֵּלַי נָטַלְתָּ," וְהוּא אוֹמֵר: „לֹא נָטַלְתִּי" — הֲרֵי זֶה נִשְׁבָּע וְנוֹטֵל. רַבִּי יְהוּדָה אוֹמֵר: עַד שֶׁתְּהֵא שָׁם מִקְצָת הוֹדָאָה. כֵּיצַד? אָמַר לוֹ: „שְׁנֵי כֵלִים נָטַלְתָּ," וְהוּא אוֹמֵר: „לֹא נָטַלְתִּי אֶלָּא אֶחָד."

יד אברהם

swear and collect regardless of whether the employer admitted part of the claim or denied it all *(Rav; Rambam, Hil. Sechirus* 11:6).

without proof *(Tos. Yom Tov* from *Rashi).*

The halachah is not in accordance with R' Yehudah, and the laborer may

2.

הַנִּגְזָל כֵּיצַד? — *The one who was robbed, how so?*

[I.e., in which case does the victim swear and collect?]

הָיוּ מְעִידִין אוֹתוֹ שֶׁנִּכְנַס לְבֵיתוֹ — *They testified about him that he entered his house*

Two witnesses testify that he entered the house of the alleged victim with nothing hidden under his clothes *(Rif).*

לְמַשְׁכְּנוֹ שֶׁלֹּא בִרְשׁוּת. — *to take a security from him without authorization.*

I.e., the person seen entering the house said that he was doing so for the purpose of taking some valuables as security for the debt owed him by the householder *(Tif. Yis.).* However, he did not receive authorization, either from the owner or from the *beis din (Tos. Yom Tov* from *Maggid Mishneh, Hil. Gezeilah* 3:16, quoting *Ri Migash).* He is thus treated as a thief.

Accordingly, the ruling given below, that the victim may swear to the value of the objects taken and collect, would certainly apply in the case of an ordinary thief *(Tif. Yis.).*

The *Gemara* (46a) emends the mishnah to read: וּמִשְׁכְּנוֹ, *and he took a security from him.* I.e., they testify that they saw him remove something from the plaintiff's house. Should he merely state his intention to do so, however, the ruling would not apply since it is possible that he was only threatening but did not actually do so. This is, indeed, the reading in *Yerushalmi.*

הוּא אוֹמֵר: „כֵּלַי נָטַלְתָּ," וְהוּא אוֹמֵר: „לֹא נָטַלְתִּי" — *He says, 'You took my utensils,' and he replies, 'I did not take [them]'*

The householder claims that certain utensils were taken from him, while the thief claims either that he did not enter, or entered but took nothing, or took only utensils belonging to him, or that he took only one utensil, whereas the householder claims that he took two *(Meiri).*

הֲרֵי זֶה נִשְׁבָּע וְנוֹטֵל. — *he swears and receives payment.*

[Since witnesses refute his claim that he took nothing,[1] the householder swears that such-and-such utensils were taken by the thief, who is then compelled to pay that amount.]

If they could identify the objects taken, there would be no question as to what was owed. The *Gemara* therefore explains that the witnesses saw him leaving the house with objects concealed

1. The claim that he took only articles actually belonging to him is never believed (else it would never be possible to convict a thief), and whenever there are witnesses to someone's removing something from someone else's possession without authority, there is a legal

7
2 **2.** The one who was robbed, how so? They testified about him that he entered his house to take a security from him without authorization. He says, 'You took my utensils,' and he replies, 'I did not take [them]' — he swears and receives payment. R' Yehudah says: Only if there is a partial admission. How so? He says to him, 'You took two utensils,' while he replies, 'I took only one.'

YAD AVRAHAM

under his clothes, which they could not identify. Subsequently, the householder lodged a claim against him for small articles which could indeed have been concealed under his garments *(Rashi)*. The claimant swears to what was taken and collects.

Tosafos (46a) and *Rosh* suggest that the witnesses must have seen that the alleged thief took at least some of the disputed articles. Otherwise, the householder would not be believed even with an oath, because it is possible that he took out stones or earth or pretended to take something but actually took nothing *(Tos. Yom Tov)*.

The Rabbis instituted this procedure to make it easier to collect from thieves, so that people would refrain from harming their fellow men *(Tos. Yom Tov* from *Rambam Comm.* to mishnah 3).

This ruling applies only where the householder is wealthy enough to have owned the articles he is claiming. However, if a man with the householder's means would normally not own such items, the defendant swears and is exempt *(Rav; Tur* 90, quoting *Rav Hai Gaon)*.

However, the question arises why the defendant is eligible to take an oath in this case. Since witnesses testify that he took something out of the house, his denial of it directly contradicts witnesses, making him a confirmed liar and ineligible to swear. *Perishah* (ad loc.) explains that he does not directly contradict the witnesses since he merely claims that he did not take more than was due him, or that he took his own utensils. He therefore does not become ineligible to take an oath in *beis din.*

Others rule that the defendant is indeed suspect and is ineligible to take an oath in *beis din.* Instead, a *cherem* (general ban) is placed upon all who illegally hold other people's money and do not pay them *(Tur* 90, quoting *Rabbenu Yeshayah). Shach* (90:10) states that such a defendant is never allowed to swear. Since the rule is that one who takes an object as security without the authorization of the debtor or the *beis din* is a thief *(Rambam, Gezeilah* 3:16), this defendant is always ineligible to swear *(Shulchan Aruch Choshen Mishpat* 90:5).

Ravad (Hil. Gezeilah 3:16), however, rules that one who takes a security without authorization is deemed a thief only if it is discovered that there was no debt entitling him to this pledge; otherwise, he is not deemed a thief and is thus eligible to take an oath in *beis din.*

רַבִּי יְהוּדָה אוֹמֵר: עַד שֶׁתְּהֵא שָׁם מִקְצָת הוֹדָאָה. — *R' Yehudah says: Only if there is a partial admission.*

[The plaintiff does not swear unless the defendant admits part of the plaintiff's claim.]

כֵּיצַד? אָמַר לוֹ: „שְׁנֵי כֵלִים נָטַלְתָּ," וְהוּא אוֹמֵר: „לֹא נָטַלְתִּי אֶלָּא אֶחָד." — *How so? He says to him, 'You took two utensils,' while he replies, 'I took only one.'*

As explained above in mishnah 1, R' Yehudah is of the opinion that the oath the Rabbis delegated to the plaintiff is the Biblical oath of partial admission normally incumbent upon the defendant. In

presumption that it belonged to the one in whose possession it was originally found *(Bava Basra* 33b, 34a; *Choshen Mishpat* 90:15; see *Gem.* 46a,b here for various qualifications of this rule).

[ג] **הַנֶּחְבָּל** כֵּיצַד? הָיוּ מְעִידִים אוֹתוֹ שֶׁנִּכְנַס תַּחַת יָדוֹ שָׁלֵם וְיָצָא חָבוּל, וְאָמַר לוֹ: „חָבַלְתָּ בִּי,” וְהוּא אוֹמֵר: „לֹא חָבַלְתִּי” — הֲרֵי זֶה נִשְׁבָּע וְנוֹטֵל. רַבִּי יְהוּדָה אוֹמֵר: עַד שֶׁתְּהֵא שָׁם מִקְצָת הוֹדָאָה. כֵּיצַד? אָמַר לוֹ: „חָבַלְתָּ בִּי שְׁתַּיִם,” וְהַלָּה אוֹמֵר: „לֹא חָבַלְתִּי בְךָ אֶלָּא אַחַת.”

יד אברהם

a case in which there would not have been any oath placed upon the defendant, the plaintiff does not swear and cannot collect. Here too the halachah is not in accordance with R' Yehudah *(Rav; Rambam, Hil. Gezeilah* 4:2).

3.

הַנֶּחְבָּל כֵּיצַד? — *The one who was wounded, how so?*

[I.e., in which case does a wounded person swear and collect damages?]

הָיוּ מְעִידִים אוֹתוֹ שֶׁנִּכְנַס תַּחַת יָדוֹ שָׁלֵם — *They testified about him that he entered his domain uninjured* [lit. *whole*]

Two witnesses testify that they saw the plaintiff enter the premises of the defendant uninjured, and that the defendant was present at the time *(Tif. Yis.).*

וְיָצָא חָבוּל, — *and emerged wounded,*

[When the plaintiff emerged, he was wounded.] However, the witnesses did not see the defendant actually wound the plaintiff *(Rambam, Hil. Chovel* 5:4).

וְאָמַר לוֹ: „חָבַלְתָּ בִּי,” — *and he says to him, 'You wounded me,'*

The plaintiff claims that the defendant inflicted these wounds and is liable for the five categories of compensation enumerated in *Bava Kamma* 8:1 *(Rambam, Hil. Chovel* 5:6).

וְהוּא אוֹמֵר: „לֹא חָבַלְתִּי” — — *while he says, 'I did not wound* [*you*] *—'*

[I.e., the defendant claims that the plaintiff inflicted the wounds upon himself.]

הֲרֵי זֶה נִשְׁבָּע וְנוֹטֵל. — *he swears and collects.*

Although the rule is that in order to collect money from another it is necessary to have the testimony of two witnesses, in this case the Rabbis decided to penalize violent people to deter them from performing further acts of violence and injuring people. They therefore instituted the law that in instances in which circumstances strongly indicate that the defendant wounded the plaintiff — viz., where he entered the defendant's premises uninjured and emerged wounded — the plaintiff may swear that the householder whose premises he entered wounded him, and collect *(Rambam Comm., Hil. Chovel* 5:4).

Ravad (ad loc.) differs, maintaining that this was instituted because it is unusual for one to inflict a wound upon himself. The Rabbis therefore believed the injured person with an oath, even though no testimony was given *(Tos. Yom Tov).*

The oath is necessary only if the wound could have been inflicted by the victim himself. If it is obvious that it could not have been self-inflicted, e.g., if there was a bite on his back, and there was no one else in the house who could possibly have inflicted it, the victim collects without an oath *(Rav* from *Gem.* 46b).

Rama states that if a third person was with the plaintiff, and it is obvious that he did not inflict the wounds, it is deemed as though only the householder was present, and the

7 **3.** The one who was wounded, how so? They testified
3 about him that he entered his domain uninjured
and emerged wounded; and he says to him, 'You
wounded me,' while he says, 'I did not wound [you]' —
he swears and collects. R' Yehudah says: Only if there is
a partial admission. How so? He says to him, 'You
inflicted two wounds on me,' while he replies, 'I inflicted
only one wound on you.'

YAD AVRAHAM

wounded party collects without an oath. Likewise, if it is obvious that he did not go near a wall or any obstruction, and it was thus impossible for him to inflict the wounds on himself, he also collects without an oath. He writes further that he receives payment by taking an oath only if the two were previously quarreling, and subsequently, one of them went into the other's house uninjured and came out wounded. In that case, it is apparent that the defendant wounded him, since they were quarreling. Otherwise, he does not collect even if it is clear *(Tur)* that he was not wounded through anything else, and that he did not wound himself. In such a case, the plaintiff does not swear and collect; rather the defendant must swear, and exempt himself. Since there was no quarrel, there is nothing to indicate that he wounded him any more than anyone else *(Bach* ad loc.).

Sema (ibid. 46) and *Shach* (ibid. 28), however, dispute this reading of *Tur* and rule that if it is clear that no one else could have inflicted the wounds, then even if there was no previous quarrel, the plaintiff collects without an oath.

רַבִּי יְהוּדָה אוֹמֵר: עַד שֶׁתְּהֵא שָׁם מִקְצָת הוֹדָאָה. — *R' Yehudah says: Only if there is a partial admission.*

[He may not collect with an oath unless the defendant admits part of the allegation.]

כֵּיצַד? אָמַר לוֹ: „חָבַלְתָּ בִּי שְׁתַּיִם,״ וְהַלָּה אוֹמֵר: „לֹא חָבַלְתִּי בְךָ אֶלָּא אַחַת.״ — *How so? He says to him, 'You inflicted two wounds on me,' while he replies, 'I inflicted only one wound on you.'*

[Since the defendant admits to inflicting one wound — and therefore to the compensation owed for that assault — he is liable to the Biblical oath of partial admission in regard to the injury he denies inflicting. As explained above, it is R' Yehudah's opinion that only in cases in which a Biblical oath should be imposed on the defendant did the Rabbis transfer it to the plaintiff and allow him to swear and collect. In cases in which there is no Biblical oath on the defendant, there is no Rabbinical oath to allow the plaintiff to swear and collect.]

The halachah is not in accordance with R' Yehudah *(Rambam, Hil. Chovel* 5:4).

4.

The fourth category of Rabbinically instituted oaths in which a plaintiff swears and collects (mishnah 1) is when an oath is actually incumbent upon the defendant in the case but he is someone whose oaths are not accepted by the court because there is reason to suspect that he is capable of transgressing the terrible sin of swearing falsely.[1]

1. The prohibition to swear falsely is the third of the Ten Commandments and is considered one of the most severe of the Torah prohibitions. So terrible a crime is it, that the entire world trembled when *Hashem* declared this prohibition at Mt. Sinai *(Gem.* 39a). Its transgression brings retribution not only upon the person, but upon his family and, to some measure, upon the world as a whole. In contrast to other sins, even repentance cannot expiate it and retribution must nevertheless come his way (ibid., *Rashi).*

וְשֶׁכְּנֶגְדּוֹ חָשׁוּד עַל־הַשְּׁבוּעָה כֵּיצַד? אַחַת שְׁבוּעַת הָעֵדוּת, וְאַחַת שְׁבוּעַת הַפִּקָּדוֹן, וַאֲפִלּוּ שְׁבוּעַת שָׁוְא; הָיָה אֶחָד

יד אברהם

The following mishnah cites several categories of people whose oaths are considered suspect and therefore unacceptable. The first of these is one known to have sworn falsely on some previous occasion. In this respect it makes no difference what the subject of his false oath concerned; having sworn falsely once, his oaths can no longer be considered reliable.

וְשֶׁכְּנֶגְדּוֹ חָשׁוּד עַל־הַשְּׁבוּעָה כֵּיצַד? — *The one whose opponent is not trusted to swear, how so?*

[What grounds cause a person to become disqualified from swearing because of untrustworthiness, thereby transferring the oath and the right to collect to his opponent?]

אַחַת שְׁבוּעַת הָעֵדוּת, — *No matter whether [he had falsely sworn] an oath of testimony,*

[I.e., no matter whether it was an oath of testimony, delineated in ch. 4; viz., that he swore that he had no knowledge of certain testimony, when in fact he was aware of that testimony.]

Rashba questions how it is possible to know that he was aware of the testimony at the time of the oath when it is possible that he merely forgot it at that time? Thus, even if it should be shown that he witnessed the event, he cannot be considered ineligible for an oath for having sworn that he did not know. Even if he should confess that he did remember the testimony at the time he swore that he did not, this confession would be valid only in obligating him to bring a variable sin-offering (see ch. 4), but it would not be valid in disqualifying him from future oaths. This is because of the general rule that a person cannot declare himself a wicked person, i.e., he cannot be convicted of a crime (swearing falsely) on the basis of his own testimony, as explained in *Kesubos* 2:3.

Ran, in order to solve this difficulty, qualifies the mishnah in two alternative manners. First, the mishnah may refer to an event so recent that we do not take into consideration the possibility that he had forgotten the testimony at the time of the oath, since that is unlikely.

Second, it may refer to a case in which the present defendant confesses to having intentionally sworn falsely on some previous occasion. The rule that a person cannot be convicted on the basis of his own testimony does not apply to admissions of monetary liability, only to those of criminal liability. Thus, a defendant in a monetary case who admitted that he had once sworn falsely would lose his right to swear in this case, because the effect of his confession is to increase his liability to pay by invalidating his oath and transferring the right to swear (and collect) to the plaintiff. In regard to this liability his confession is acceptable, though it could not be used to invalidate him in general.

Tos. Yom Tov points out that this Rabbinic enactment transferring the oath of the suspect to his opponent can be unfair to the plaintiff. If the defendant knows he is guilty and perceives his opponent, the claimant, to be a person who is afraid to swear even to the truth [a proper attitude], he has merely to 'admit' that he is suspect and thereby force the plaintiff to swear to collect what is rightfully his — something he will not do. The *Rama* therefore rules that the transfer of oaths is done only with the consent of the plaintiff. In the event the plaintiff refuses, the defendant is told either to swear and clear himself or pay (*Tur* 92). *Rambam* (*Hil. Toein* 2:3), however, rules that one does not become suspect for an oath unless witnesses testify that he has committed a transgression by which he becomes ineligible. Should he confess to committing a transgression by which he becomes ineligible, we say to him, 'If you are telling the truth, swear. Just because you once committed a sin, you are not prohibited from swearing truthfully. And if you are lying, confess to your opponent.'

וְאַחַת שְׁבוּעַת הַפִּקָּדוֹן, — *or an oath of*

4. The one whose opponent is not trusted to swear, how so? No matter whether [he had falsely sworn] an oath of a testimony, or an oath of deposit, or even a vain oath; [or if] one of them was a dice-player,

YAD AVRAHAM

deposit,

[I.e., he swore that he had never been entrusted with the deposit, or never received the money in question, and it was later discovered that he had. As a result of this false oath, he becomes disqualified from swearing.]

Without having sworn falsely, however, the fact that he denied receiving the deposit, thereby attempting to steal it, would not render him ineligible. This is because there is a possibility that he did not really intend to steal it, but that he had misplaced the article and wished to put off the owner until he could find it and return it. If, however, witnesses testify that he had the article in his possession at the time of denial, he is obviously a thief and he becomes suspect even without swearing falsely (*Tif. Yis.* from *Gem.* 40b, *Bava Metzia* 5b).

וַאֲפִלּוּ שְׁבוּעַת שָׁוְא; — *or even a vain oath;*

[The vain oath has been delineated in 3:8. Since he is not above deliberately violating the Torah's prohibitions on oaths, his oath is unacceptable.] Thus, a person becomes disqualified not only by transgressing the oath of testimony or the oath of deposit — in which by being untruthful he sins both against God and man — but even if he once swore vainly, in which case he sins only against God, he is suspect, and is consequently ineligible for an oath before *beis din* (*Rav, Rashi* from *Gem.* 46b).

The mishnah does not mention the oath of utterance, delineated in 3:1, since that oath includes both swearing to a future act and swearing on a past act. Should he swear that he would eat a certain loaf of bread or not eat it, and subsequently violate his oath, he does not become disqualified because at the time he pronounced the oath he may have intended to keep it, but was later tempted to violate it. However, should he swear that he ate or did not eat a certain loaf of bread, it is equivalent to a vain oath, since he utters a patently false oath, and he would indeed become disqualified (*Rav, Rashi* to *Gem.* 46b, 47a; *Rambam; Rashba).*

Others, however, rule that the transgression of an oath of utterance concerning a future act does, indeed, render the transgressor ineligible to swear. The *Gemara* means only that the mishnah does not include in its list an oath which is not false at the time of its utterance. But if one swears that he will or will not eat a certain loaf of bread, or the like, and he willfully violates his oath, he is in fact rendered ineligible to take an oath before the *beis din* (*Tos.* quoting *Rabbeinu Tam; Maggid Mishneh, Hagahos Maimonios, Hil. Toein Venitan* 2:3).

This ruling includes anyone guilty of swearing any oath falsely. Even if he perjured himself regarding a *shevuas hesses,* he is disqualified from swearing any other oaths (*Meiri; Rambam, Hil. Toein Venitan* 2:11).

Once a person has been disqualified because of a false oath, he does not regain his eligibility for oaths and testimony until he receives lashes from the court for his transgression and repents his sin (*Choshen Mishpat* 92:14; *Sema* ad loc.).

◆§ The Ineligibility of Robbers and Wicked People

In addition to those found guilty of swearing falsely, many of those ineligible to testify because of their status as רְשָׁעִים, *wicked people,* are deemed suspect and their oaths are not trusted. This includes both those disqualified by the Torah and by the Rabbis (*Meiri).*

Those disqualified by the Torah from testifying as a result of their wickedness include such sinners as robbers, those involved in usurious loans, and those who eat non-kosher food. Those disqualified by the Rabbis include gamblers, such as dice

מֵהֶן מְשַׂחֵק בְּקֻבְיָא, וּמַלְוֶה בְרִבִּית, וּמַפְרִיחֵי יוֹנִים, וְסוֹחֲרֵי שְׁבִיעִית — שֶׁכְּנֶגְדוֹ נִשְׁבָּע וְנוֹטֵל. הָיוּ

יד אברהם

players and pigeon flyers, as will be explained in the mishnah (*Rambam, Hil. Toein Venitan* 2:2).

Although the ineligibility of a dishonest person to testify is definitely Biblical, as the *Gemara* (*Sanhedrin* 27a) explains, it is questionable whether he is similarly disqualified from swearing. The *Gemara* (*Bava Metzia* 5b, 6a) cites a dispute whether חָשׁוּד אַמָּמוֹנָא חָשׁוּד אַשְׁבוּעֲתָא, *one whose integrity is suspect in monetary matters is similarly suspect in regard to oaths.* One opinion is that he is not because even someone who would steal would not readily violate the more severe prohibition of swearing falsely (*Rashi*). Support for this view may be seen in the many instances in which people are asked to swear that they do not have or owe the money being claimed by a plaintiff. In all these cases the defendant is suspected of taking or keeping what is not his and yet the court asks him to swear that what he says is true. By this reasoning, even a confirmed robber should not be Biblically disqualified, and his ineligibility is due to a Rabbinical enactment (*Tos.* ibid. 5b; but see opinion of *R' Yehudah HaChassid* cited there). The opinion of Abaye (ibid. 6a), however, is that anyone known to be dishonest in monetary matters is considered similarly untrustworthy in regard to his oaths.[1] Thus, a confirmed thief is Biblically ineligible to swear. However, his dishonesty must be known to us by the testimony of witnesses (*Rosh*). If it is merely suspected but has not been established, his oaths are acceptable.[2] This is the view accepted as halachah (*Choshen Mishpat* 92:3).

הָיָה אֶחָד מֵהֶן — [*or if*] *one of them was*

[I.e., if one of the litigants, viz., the defendant, who is always obligated to swear in order to exempt himself from paying.]

The *Tanna* first dealt with those who are Biblically disqualified, and now he lists those disqualified by Rabbinical enactment (*Rav* from *Gem.* 47a).

מְשַׂחֵק בְּקֻבְיָא, — *a dice-player,*

[This includes any sort of gambler (see *Rambam, Eidus* 10:4).]

According to R' Sheshes (*Sanhedrin* 24b), this refers to a professional gambler. His ineligibility is caused by the fact that he does not engage in any profession of benefit to mankind, and so does not contribute to the maintenance of society. Such a person lacks credibility; since he is already somewhat of an outcast, he is not likely to feel embarrassment at taking a bribe to testify falsely (*Meiri*).

Rami bar Chama (ibid.) is of the opinion that any gambler is ineligible, even if he has another profession. According to his view, money won at gambling is considered stolen money [since the loser does not part with it willingly (having received nothing in

1. Although even Abaye would grant that there are certainly many people who are dishonest in their financial affairs who would nevertheless refrain from swearing falsely, this cannot be said to be a general rule and thus the courts cannot rely on it to accept the oaths of such people (*Aruch HaShulchan* 92:4).

2. According to this view, the reason people are asked to swear that their claims are true is not because we suspect them of being completely dishonest and attempting to steal what is not theirs, since in that case their oaths would be just as suspect. Rather, we suspect them of holding the money because of a possible previous debt which may be owed them (*Bava Metzia* 6a). Although this too is forbidden, it does not show them to be unscrupulous in money matters and we thus have no reason to disqualify their oaths. Similarly, they may be denying their debt to put off their creditor until they can put together the money to repay it. For this reason, even if it is proven that someone had lied about a debt, he is not yet disqualified from swearing in future litigations (ibid. 5b).

7 or one who lends on interest, or [they were] pigeon
4 flyers, or *Sheviis*-merchants — his opponent swears and

return), but only to avoid the shame and censure of his friends]. The winner is thus considered a גַּזְלָן, *robber*. But he is not disqualified as a witness by Torah law since the loser pays him of his own free will and the gambler does not look upon his activity as robbery *(Tosafos; Rav, Sanhedrin* 3:3).

The first view is the generally accepted one. *Rambam*, however *(Hilchos Gezeilah* 6:10; see also *Hilchos Eidus* 10:4 with *Kesef Mishneh)*, appears to favor the second view (cf. *Sema, Choshen Mishpat* 34:49).

וּמַלְוֶה בְּרִבִּית, — *or one who lends on interest,*

One who lends on interest is Biblically ineligible *(Meiri)*; see prefatory remarks. *Rav (Rosh Hashanah* 1:8) states that although usury is prohibited by the Torah *(Ex.* 22:24, *Lev.* 25:36, *Deut.* 23:20), a usurer is disqualified only under Rabbinic law. Torah law does not consider him a knowing thief since he justifies the act by claiming that the interest is given him willingly. [Thus, his sin cannot be taken as a token of his general willingness to violate any prohibition for financial gain.]

Others explain that the mishnah refers to usurers who practice forms of usury prohibited only under Rabbinic law (e.g., a lender who lives on the borrower's property without paying rent) [*Bava Metzia* 5:2] *(Tif. Yis., Rosh Hashanah* 1:8).

Both the lender and the borrower (who pays the interest) are ineligible, as the prohibition against usury applies to both *(Sanhedrin* 25a).

Some rule, however, that in the case of usury prohibited only under Rabbinic law, only the lender becomes ineligible *(Choshen Mishpat* 34:10).

וּמַפְרִיחֵי יוֹנִים, — *or [they were] pigeon flyers,*

One view in *Sanhedrin* 25a explains this to mean those who race pigeons for money, similar to the dice-players mentioned above *(Rav)*.

Another view is that it refers to people who use specially trained pigeons to lure other pigeons from their owners' coops, thereby stealing them from their owners.

This is not considered theft under Torah law since the owners of the coops do not really *own* the pigeons, which can come and go as they please. The Sages, however, prohibited the luring away of these pigeons מִפְּנֵי דַרְכֵי שָׁלוֹם, *in order to maintain the peace* (see *Chullin* 139b). One who transgresses this Rabbinical prohibition of theft is thereby disqualified as a witness *(Rav)*.

וְסוֹחֲרֵי שְׁבִיעִית— — *or Sheviis-merchants—*

[The agriculture laws of Eretz Yisrael are governed by a seven-year cycle, in which every seventh [*sheviis*] year is a *Shemittah* [Sabbatical] year. During this year the land may not be cultivated *(Lev.* 25:4). While the produce that grows in this year uncultivated may be eaten, it is forbidden to engage in סְחוֹרָה, *commerce*, with these fruits (see *Tosafos* to *Succah* 39a for a definition of what constitutes commerce in this respect). This is a Torah prohibition derived from the verse in *Leviticus* 25:6: לְאָכְלָה, *for eating purposes*, from which the *Gemara (Avodah Zarah* 62a) infers: וְלֹא לִסְחוֹרָה, *but not for commercial purposes.*]

Those who deal in the produce of *Sheviis* are disqualifed as witnesses only by Rabbinic decree, although they have transgressed a Scriptural prohibition. Numerous explanations for this are given:

(a) *Tosafos (Rosh Hashanah* 22a) state that our mishnah is speaking of *Shemittah* in post-Temple times. In their view, in the absence of the Temple the observance of *Shemittah* is a Rabbinic requirement. [See General Introduction to

שְׁנֵיהֶן חֲשׁוּדִין, חָזְרָה הַשְּׁבוּעָה לִמְקוֹמָהּ; דִּבְרֵי רַבִּי יוֹסֵי. רַבִּי מֵאִיר אוֹמֵר: יַחֲלֹקוּ.

[ה] **וְהַחֶנְוָנִי** עַל־פִּנְקָסוֹ כֵּיצַד? לֹא שֶׁיֹּאמַר לוֹ: „כָּתוּב עַל־פִּנְקָסִי שֶׁאַתָּה חַיָּב לִי מָאתַיִם זוּז." אֶלָּא, אָמַר לוֹ: „תֵּן לְבָנַי

יד אברהם

ArtScroll *Sheviis* p. 13 for an elaboration.]

(b) *Ran* explains that the dealers are unaware that they are transgressing a Torah law since they use the money gained from their transactions for the purchase of food which they then eat in conformity with the halachic restrictions of *Shemittah* food (see *Sheviis* 8:2).

(c) *Meiri* says that since the prohibition against doing business with the produce of *Sheviis* is not stated clearly in the Torah but is only implied, those who transgress are treated as if they had transgressed a Rabbinic law only.

(d) *Rambam (Hil. Eidus* 10:4) interprets our mishnah as referring to people who did not engage in business except before *Shemittah*, leading to the strong suspicion that they are engaged in forbidden commerce with the year's produce. Since, however, we cannot be certain of this, their ineligibility is only Rabbinical.

שֶׁכְּנֶגְדּוֹ נִשְׁבָּע וְנוֹטֵל. — *his opponent swears and collects.*

[I.e., the plaintiff. In all the above cases, since the defendant is not permitted to swear, the plaintiff must swear in order to collect.]

Generally, the rule is that if a defendant cannot swear the oath to which he is obligated, he must pay. For example, if he admits owing part of the claim and is uncertain of the rest of the claim, since he cannot swear that he does not owe it, he is liable. The Rabbis, however, changed this rule in regard to those who are ineligible to swear in order to protect them from unscrupulous people who would take advantage of this situation by lending them a *perutah*, and then claiming to have lent an amount equal to all their possessions. The defendant would have to admit to the *perutah* and thereby become obligated to swear the oath of partial admission that he does not owe any more than a *perutah*. Since his oath would be unacceptable, he would be obligated to pay everything. In order to rescue them from this predicament, the Rabbis declared that when the defendant is ineligible to swear, the plaintiff must swear that he owes him the amount he claims in order to collect [which, as explained above, even unscrupulous people would hesitate doing] *(Tos. Yom Tov* from *Tos.* 47a, s.v. מתוך).

הָיוּ שְׁנֵיהֶן חֲשׁוּדִין, — *[If] they were both suspect,*

[I.e., if both litigants are ineligible to take an oath.]

חָזְרָה הַשְּׁבוּעָה לִמְקוֹמָהּ; דִּבְרֵי רַבִּי יוֹסֵי. — *the oath returns to its place; [these are] the words of R' Yose.*

The *Gemara* (47a) cites a dispute about the meaning of this ruling. Some *Amoraim* explain this to mean that the oath returns to Sinai; i.e., it reverts to the oath with which God adjured Israel to keep the *mitzvah* of לֹא תִגְזֹל, *You shall not steal,* and it is left to God to punish whoever illegally holds money belonging to another. The *beis din*, however, does not compel the defendant to pay, but issues a general ban on him if his claim should be false *(Tos. Yom Tov).* Others explain that the oath returns to the one who was originally liable, viz.,

collects. [If] they were both suspect, the oath returns to its place; [these are] the words of R' Yose. R' Meir says: They divide.

5. The storekeeper over his account book, how so? Not that he says to him, 'It is written in my account book that you owe me two hundred *zuz*.' Rather, he said to him, 'Give my sons two *seahs* of

YAD AVRAHAM

the defendant, who admitted part of the claim. Since he cannot swear, he must pay *(Rav; Rashi)*. [Since it is really the defendant's responsibility to attest to his claim by swearing to its truth, and the shift to the plaintiff where the defendant is ineligible was only done as a favor to him, if the plaintiff is also ineligible, the oath reverts to its primary party — the defendant.]

רַבִּי מֵאִיר אוֹמֵר: יַחֲלֹקוּ. — *R' Meir says: They divide.*

[I.e., the defendant pays half the claim.] According to the conclusion of the *Gemara* (47a), the positions are reversed. It is R' Yose who rules that they divide, while R' Meir rules that the oath returns to its place. *Rambam (Hil. Toein* 2:4) decides in favor of R' Meir, that the oath returns to its place and the defendant must pay since he cannot swear. *Tur (Choshen Mishpat* 92), however, decides that they divide. This decision is based on the ruling of *R' Hai Gaon* and *Rosh (Tos. Yom Tov)*.

5.

The following mishnah takes up the last category of those who swear and collect — the storekeeper over his account book. This refers to a storekeeper who supplies a householder with his needs on credit and allows the debt to accumulate till an agreed upon amount, when the householder must pay *(Rambam, Hil. Malveh* 16:5).

וְהַחֶנְוָנִי עַל־פִּנְקָסוֹ כֵּיצַד? — *The storekeeper over his account book, how so?*

[What is the case of the storekeeper over his account book, who can swear and collect what he claims is due him?]

לֹא שֶׁיֹּאמַר לוֹ: „כָּתוּב עַל־פִּנְקָסִי שֶׁאַתָּה חַיָּב לִי מָאתַיִם זוּז.״ — *Not that he says to him, 'It is written in my account book that you owe me two hundred zuz.'*

This is not to be taken to mean that a storekeeper is believed with an oath any time he claims that he has recorded in his account book that someone owes him a sum of money, two hundred *zuz*, for example. Since we have no real indication that he owes him the two hundred *zuz*, he cannot collect with just an oath *(Rashi)*.

In this case, however, the householder would still be liable to a *shevuas hesses* (see chapter preface). If he claims that he is uncertain whether he owes or not, he must swear that he is uncertain. Even if the storekeeper should make this claim without the evidence of the account book, the ruling would still be the same *(Meiri)*.

אֶלָּא, אָמַר לוֹ: — *Rather, he said to him,*

I.e., the householder had previously said to the storekeeper *(Tif. Yis.)*.

„תֵּן לְבָנַי סָאתַיִם חִטִּין,״ — *'Give my sons two seahs of wheat,'*

I.e., the householder admits to having placed an order and the point of contention is whether the storekeeper in fact gave the wheat to the householder's sons. Since there is an indication of indebted-

סָאתַיִם חִטִּין,״ „תֵּן לְפוֹעֲלַי בְּסֶלַע מָעוֹת.״ הוּא אוֹמֵר: „נָתַתִּי,״ וְהֵן אוֹמְרִים: „לֹא נָטַלְנוּ״ — הוּא נִשְׁבָּע וְנוֹטֵל, וְהֵן נִשְׁבָּעִין וְנוֹטְלִין. אָמַר בֶּן־נַנָּס: כֵּיצַד? אֵלּוּ בָאִין לִידֵי שְׁבוּעַת שָׁוְא וְאֵלּוּ בָאִין לִידֵי שְׁבוּעַת שָׁוְא! אֶלָּא הוּא נוֹטֵל שֶׁלֹּא בִשְׁבוּעָה, וְהֵן נוֹטְלִין שֶׁלֹּא בִשְׁבוּעָה.

יד אברהם

הוּא אוֹמֵר: „נָתַתִּי,״ — [*If*] *he* [*now*] *says, 'I gave,'*

[I.e., the storekeeper says I gave the wheat or the money as you instructed me.]

וְהֵן אוֹמְרִים: „לֹא נָטַלְנוּ״ — *but they say, 'We did not collect'* —

[The sons or the workers deny receiving the wheat or the money from the storekeeper. Thus, in the case of the workers, both they and the storekeeper claim compensation from the householder. The workers claim their wages, while the storekeeper claims the money he advanced to the workers.]

הוּא נִשְׁבָּע וְנוֹטֵל, — *he swears and collects,*

[The storekeeper swears and collects from the householder what he claims to have advanced on his behalf. Even if the workers had already sworn and received their wages from the householder (see below), the storekeeper is not affected by their oath. The reason is that a person does not have to accept the oath of another unless he previously indicated a trust in that person. The householder trusted the workers, as evidenced by the fact that he did not instruct the storekeeper to pay them before witnesses; therefore, the householder must accept their oath and pay them. The storekeeper, on the other hand, is not so obligated *(Rav; Rashi)*.

וְהֵן נִשְׁבָּעִין וְנוֹטְלִין. — *and they swear and collect.*

[I.e., the workers swear that they did not receive their wages from the store-ness, the Rabbis instituted that the storekeeper swears and collects *(Rashi)*.

Furthermore, even if the storekeeper does not recall filling the order and the sons of the householder are certain that they never received the wheat, if the account book states explicitly that the order was indeed filled, we rely on the written record and the householder must pay *(Tos. Yom Tov* from *Tur Choshen Mishpat* 91, quoting *Rosh)*. The storekeeper swears that he found this transaction recorded in his account book and then collects *(Rama* 91:4 from *Rosh)*.

„תֵּן לְפוֹעֲלַי בְּסֶלַע מָעוֹת.״ — [*or*] *'Give my workers a sela's worth of maos.'*

I.e., I will give you a *sela*, and you give my workers that amount in smaller coins [see table in mishnah 6:3] so that they will be able to spend them little by little. *Rambam (Hil. Malveh* 16:5) and *Tur* 91, however, state merely: Give my workers a *sela (Tos. Yom Tov)* [i.e., that the storekeeper advanced the householder money by paying his workers' salaries].

In the case of the workers the householder will ultimately have to pay twice, once to the workers (who deny having been paid) and again to the storekeeper (who insists he paid; see further in mishnah). Had the mishnah stated only the case of the workers, we might have assumed that the storekeeper need only swear in that case because of the householder's double payment; but in the case of the sons, to whom the householder is not obligated, the storekeeper collects without an oath. The *Tanna*, therefore, states that even in the case of the sons, the storekeeper must take an oath in order to collect his claim *(Tos. Yom Tov* from *Ran)*.

7 wheat,' [or] 'Give my workers a *sela's* worth of *maos*.'
5 [If] he [now] says, 'I gave,' but they say, 'We did not
collect' — he swears and collects, and they swear and
collect. Said Ben Nannas: How can this be? These come
to a vain oath and these come to a vain oath! Rather, he
collects without an oath, and they collect without an
oath.

keeper and receive payment from the householder.] Other editions read: אֵלּוּ וְאֵלּוּ נִשְׁבָּעִין וְנוֹטְלִין מִבַּעַל הַבַּיִת, *they both swear and collect from the householder* (*Rav; Rashi* 47b).

The workers, too, may argue that they are not required to believe the oath of the storekeeper (*Rav, Rashi* from *Bava Metzia* 2b).

Ran compares this ruling to that of *Bava Kamma* 10:7: *[If] one says to another, 'I robbed you,' [or] 'You lent me,' [or] 'You deposited with me,' 'but I do not know whether I returned [it] to you'* — he is obligated to pay, since a liability surely existed and he himself is doubtful whether it was satisfied. Accordingly, *Ran* questions why the householder should not be obligated to pay his workers without their having to swear an oath, since he was surely liable to pay his workers and he himself is doubtful whether they were paid. He replies that since the householder must pay the storekeeper as well, the Rabbis enacted the ruling that the workers cannot receive payment without first taking an oath that they did not yet receive their wages (*Tos. Yom Tov*).

When the workers and the storekeeper swear to receive payment from the householder, each must swear in the presence of the other in order that the lying party be embarrassed to lie in the presence of those who know it is a lie (*Rav* from *Gem.* 47b). This increases the likelihood that they will confess (*Meiri*).

אָמַר בֶּן־נַנָּס: כֵּיצַד? אֵלּוּ בָאִין לִידֵי שְׁבוּעַת שָׁוְא וְאֵלּוּ בָאִין לִידֵי שְׁבוּעַת שָׁוְא! — *Said Ben Nannas: How can this be? These come to a vain oath and these come to a vain oath!*

How can *beis din* require them all to swear and thereby insure that either the storekeeper or the workers will swear falsely, thereby profaning the Name of Heaven (*Rav, Meiri*)? The *Tanna* uses the expression, שְׁבוּעַת שָׁוְא, *a vain oath*, rather than שְׁבוּעַת שֶׁקֶר, *a false oath*, because it is obvious that one party is swearing falsely. Thus, it is equivalent to swearing to something that is known to be false (see above, 3:8).

אֶלָּא הוּא נוֹטֵל שֶׁלֹּא בִשְׁבוּעָה, וְהֵן נוֹטְלִין שֶׁלֹּא בִשְׁבוּעָה. — *Rather, he collects without an oath, and they collect without an oath.*

I.e., the storekeeper as well as the workers collect from the householder without an oath (*Rav*).

Ran's reading is אֶלָּא הוּא נוֹטֵל בִּשְׁבוּעָה, *Rather, he collects with an oath.* I.e., only the storekeeper swears to collect, since it is not known whether he fulfilled his commitment to pay the workers. However, the workers receive payment without an oath, since the householder's indebtedness to them is definite. [I.e., he was indebted to them previously because of their work, and he is not certain that he paid them] (*Tos. Yom Tov* from *Ran*).

The halachah is not in accordance with Ben Nannas (*Rav; Rambam Comm.*).

[ו] **אָמַר** לְחֶנְוָנִי: "תֶּן־לִי בְדִינָר פֵּרוֹת," וְנָתַן לוֹ; אָמַר לוֹ: "תֶּן־לִי אֶת־הַדִּינָר," אָמַר לוֹ: "נְתַתִּיו לְךָ, וּנְתַתּוֹ בְאַנְפָּלִי" — יִשָּׁבַע בַּעַל הַבַּיִת. נָתַן לוֹ אֶת־הַדִּינָר, אָמַר לוֹ: "תֶּן־לִי אֶת־הַפֵּרוֹת," אָמַר לוֹ: "נְתַתִּים לְךָ, וְהוֹלַכְתָּן לְתוֹךְ בֵּיתְךָ" — יִשָּׁבַע הַחֶנְוָנִי. רַבִּי יְהוּדָה אוֹמֵר: כָּל־שֶׁהַפֵּרוֹת בְּיָדוֹ, יָדוֹ עַל־הָעֶלְיוֹנָה.

יד אברהם

6.

Unlike the previous mishnah which dealt with a dispute over a credit account, this mishnah deals with a cash transaction in which a dispute arises whether the customer paid or not.

אָמַר לְחֶנְוָנִי: "תֶּן־לִי בְדִינָר פֵּרוֹת," — *[If] one said to a storekeeper, 'Give me produce for a dinar,'*

[This is a simple case of a customer asking to buy merchandise.]

וְנָתַן לוֹ; — *and he gave it to him;*

The storekeeper gives the customer the produce, but in such a way that neither of them currently has legal possession of the produce. Should either of them have such possession, any dispute arising over payment would be resolved in favor of the one holding it unless the other could prove his case. This follows the rule that the burden of proof (in monetary litigations) lies with the one seeking to exact property from the possession of another (*Bava Kamma* 46b). Accordingly, the *Gemara* explains the mishnah to be referring to a case in which the storekeeper piled up produce in a public domain, so that neither the storekeeper nor the householder has it in his legal possession (*Rav* from *Gem.* 48a).[1]

אָמַר לוֹ: "תֶּן־לִי אֶת־הַדִּינָר," אָמַר לוֹ: "נְתַתִּיו לְךָ וּנְתַתּוֹ בְאַנְפָּלִי" — *[but when] he said to him, 'Give me the dinar,' he replied, 'I gave it to you and you put it into the till'* —

[When the storekeeper asked the customer for the *dinar* payment, he claimed that he had already paid the storekeeper,] who had taken it and put it into the case made for keeping money (*Rav*).

יִשָּׁבַע בַּעַל הַבַּיִת. — *the householder swears.*

The customer takes an oath similar to that of the Torah, in that it is made while holding a sacred object, and he receives the produce. As explained above, the produce is not in the legal possession of the storekeeper [and thus he has no intrinsic legal claim to it]. Since the storekeeper admits that he sold the produce and demands only the money for it, the householder's claim to the produce is seen as stronger. Consequently, the Rabbis assigned to the householder the right to swear and keep the produce (*Rav, Ran* citing *Rif*, as quoted by *Tos. Yom Tov*).

נָתַן לוֹ אֶת־הַדִּינָר, — *[If] he gave him the dinar,*

1. An alternate explanation is that the purchaser picked them up, thereby performing the *kinyan* (act of acquisition) of *hagbahah* (lifting up; see General Introduction to ArtScroll *Bava Basra*), and then placed them in the public domain (*Maggid Mishneh* to *Rambam, Hil. Mechirah* 20:7). It appears, however, that *Ran* and *Rav* explain simply that the produce was lying in a public domain and the purchaser did not perform a *kinyan* (*Tos. Yom Tov*). This is the view of *Rif* as cited by *Ran*.

7
6 **6.** [If] one said to a storekeeper, 'Give me produce for a *dinar,*' and he gave it to him; [but when] he said to him, 'Give me the *dinar,*' he replied, 'I gave it to you and you put it into the till' — the householder swears. [If] he gave him the *dinar,* [and] said to him, 'Give me the produce,' [and] he replied, 'I gave it to you and you took it home' — the storekeeper swears. R' Yehudah says: Whoever has the produce in his possession has the upper hand.

YAD AVRAHAM

[I.e., if the householder gave a *dinar* to the storekeeper.]

אָמַר לוֹ: „תֶּן־לִי אֶת־הַפֵּרוֹת," — *[and] said to him, 'Give me the produce,'*

[I.e., the householder asks the storekeeper to give him the produce for which he paid.]

אָמַר לוֹ: „נְתַתִּים לְךָ וְהוֹלַכְתָּן לְתוֹךְ בֵּיתְךָ" — — *[and] he replied, 'I gave it to you and you took it home'* —

The storekeeper claims that the householder came to him without money and asked for a *dinar's* worth of produce, promising to return soon with the money. The *dinar* that he just received from him he claims is payment for that produce, and the produce lying in the public domain is not his but additional produce that the storekeeper took out to sell. The householder claims that he never took any produce before this, and the *dinar* he now gave him was a payment for the produce lying in the public domain, which he is now buying *(Rav; Ran; Tos. Yom Tov).*

יִשָּׁבַע הַחֶנְוָנִי. — *the storekeeper swears.*

[I.e., the storekeeper must swear that the householder took the produce away previously and did not pay for it until now.] *Ran,* quoting *Rif,* explains that in this case, the storekeeper's claim possesses more validity than that of the householder. Since he claims that the householder has no connection with this produce at all, and the householder admits that he has not yet purchased it, only that he gave a *dinar* in order to purchase it,[1] the storekeeper's claim carries greater weight and he is given the option to swear and keep the produce *(Tos. Yom Tov).*

רַבִּי יְהוּדָה אוֹמֵר: כָּל־שֶׁהַפֵּרוֹת בְּיָדוֹ, יָדוֹ עַל־הָעֶלְיוֹנָה. — *R' Yehudah says: Whoever has the produce in his possession has the upper hand.*

R' Yehudah dissents with the ruling in the second case and rules that in both cases the householder may swear and take the produce. He reasons that since the produce is outside the store, it is as though it is in the possession of the householder, and it therefore makes more sense to give him the option to swear and take possession of the produce *(Rav).* Although the produce is in the public domain, since it is unusual for a storekeeper to pile it there prior to a sale, it is viewed by R' Yehudah as being more in the householder's possession *(Ran* from *Rif).*

Rashi explains R' Yehudah's view in a different manner. He explains that R' Yehudah differs with the *Tanna Kamma* in the ruling of the first case. Whereas the *Tanna Kamma* rules that the householder swears and takes possession of the produce, R' Yehudah argues that a storekeeper who does not usually sell on credit would not have given the produce without being paid. Therefore the money given by the house-

1. Movable property cannot be legally acquired merely by payment but must be acquired by one of the various formal acts of acquisition in which the purchaser takes physical possession of the item *(Bava Metzia* 47b). See General Introduction to ArtScroll *Bava Basra.*

אָמַר לְשֻׁלְחָנִי: „תֶּן־לִי בְדִינָר מָעוֹת," וְנָתַן לוֹ; אָמַר לוֹ: „תֶּן־לִי אֶת־הַדִּינָר," אָמַר לוֹ: „נְתַתִּיו לְךָ וּנְתַתּוֹ בְּאַנְפָּלִי" — יִשָּׁבַע בַּעַל הַבַּיִת. נָתַן לוֹ אֶת־הַדִּינָר, אָמַר לוֹ: „תֶּן־לִי אֶת־הַמָּעוֹת," אָמַר לוֹ: „נְתַתִּים לְךָ וְהִשְׁלַכְתָּם לְתוֹךְ כִּיסְךָ" — יִשָּׁבַע הַשֻּׁלְחָנִי. רַבִּי יְהוּדָה אוֹמֵר: אֵין דֶּרֶךְ שֻׁלְחָנִי לִתֵּן אִסָּר עַד־שֶׁיִּטֹּל דִּינָרוֹ.

[ז] **כְּשֵׁם** שֶׁאָמְרוּ הַפּוֹגֶמֶת כְּתֻבָּתָהּ לֹא תִפָּרַע אֶלָּא בִשְׁבוּעָה; וְעֵד אֶחָד מְעִידָהּ

יד אברהם

holder must be for this produce now in dispute, and he may therefore take possession without an oath.

אָמַר לְשֻׁלְחָנִי: — *[If] one said to a moneychanger,*

The mishnah now repeats the above ruling for the case of a moneychanger; i.e., one who changes large coins into smaller ones. [Before banks, this existed as a separate trade.]

„תֶּן־לִי בְדִינָר מָעוֹת," — *'Give me a dinar's worth of maos,'*

I.e., change a *dinar* of silver into smaller copper coins *(Tos. Yom Tov).*

וְנָתַן לוֹ; — *and he gave [them] to him;*

[I.e., the moneychanger gave the householder the copper coins. In this case as well, the copper coins are now in the possession of neither of them, but are lying in the public domain, as was the case with the produce above.]

אָמַר לוֹ: „תֶּן־לִי אֶת־הַדִּינָר", אָמַר לוֹ: „נְתַתִּיו לְךָ, וּנְתַתּוֹ בְּאַנְפָּלִי" — *[but when] he said to him, 'Give me the dinar,' he replied, 'I gave it to you and you put it into the till' —*

[When the moneychanger asked for the *dinar,* the householder claimed to have already given it.]

יִשָּׁבַע בַּעַל הַבַּיִת. — *the householder swears.*

[I.e., the householder swears that he gave the *dinar,* and he takes the *maos* that are piled up in the public domain.]

נָתַן לוֹ אֶת־הַדִּינָר, — *[If] he gave him the dinar,*

[I.e., if the householder already gave the moneychanger the *dinar* before receiving the coins.]

אָמַר לוֹ: „תֶּן־לִי אֶת־הַמָּעוֹת," אָמַר לוֹ: „נְתַתִּים לְךָ, וְהִשְׁלַכְתָּם לְתוֹךְ כִּיסְךָ" — *[and] said to him, 'Give me the maos,' [and] he replied, 'I gave them to you and you threw them into your purse' —*

[When the householder asked for the small coins the moneychanger replied that he had given them to him already, and the coins lying in the public domain are others.]

יִשָּׁבַע הַשֻּׁלְחָנִי. — *the moneychanger swears.*

[The moneychanger swears that the householder has already received the change and that these coins are others.]

רַבִּי יְהוּדָה אוֹמֵר: אֵין דֶּרֶךְ שֻׁלְחָנִי לִתֵּן אִסָּר עַד־שֶׁיִּטֹּל דִּינָרוֹ. — *R' Yehudah says: It is not customary for a moneychanger to give an issar until he receives his dinar.*

It is unusual for a moneychanger to place the smaller coins in the public domain before receiving the *dinar* he is to change *(Tif. Yis.).*

According to *Rambam (Comm.),* R' Yehudah differs with the *Tanna Kamma* in the second case, and rules that in that case too, the householder swears and

7 [If] one said to a moneychanger, 'Give me a *dinar's*
7 worth of *maos*,' and he gave [them] to him; [but when] he said to him, 'Give me the *dinar*,' he replied, 'I gave it to you and you put it into the till' — the householder swears. [If] he gave him the *dinar*, [and] said to him, 'Give me the *maos*'; [and] he replied, 'I gave them to you and you threw them into your purse' — the moneychanger swears. R' Yehudah says: It is not customary for a moneychanger to give an *issar* until he receives his *dinar*.

7. Just as they said [that] a woman who impairs her *kesubah* is not paid except with an oath; and [that]

YAD AVRAHAM

takes the *maos*. According to *Rashi* and *Rosh*, R' Yehudah differs in the first case, ruling that the householder takes the *maos* without an oath *(Tif. Yis.)*.

The mishnah repeats the controversy between the *Tanna Kamma* and R' Yehudah in both these cases although they are basically the same. The *Gemara* (48a) accounts for this repetition in the following manner. Should the mishnah state the controversy only in regard to the storekeeper, we would be inclined to believe that only in this case does the *Tanna Kanna* rule that the storekeeper swears and takes the produce, since it is customary for the storekeeper to give the produce before receiving the money. However, in the case of the moneychanger, they would concur with R' Yehudah that the moneychanger does not give an *issar* until he receives his *dinar*. Should the mishnah state only the instance of the moneychanger, we would be inclined to believe that only in this case does R' Yehudah rule that the moneychanger swear and keeps the money because it is not customary for a moneychanger to give an *issar* until he receives his *dinar*. But in the case of the storekeeper, who sometimes gives the produce before receiving the money, we might assume that R' Yehudah concurs with the *Tanna Kamma* that the storekeeper swears and takes the produce. Therefore, the mishnah states both cases *(Rav; Tos. Yom Tov)*.

7.

Generally speaking, when a claimant produces a valid legal document attesting to the debt he claims, he collects his debt without having to swear any oath. The document is considered the equivalent of testimony upholding the claim, and the debtor is not believed to claim that he paid [since in that case, he would have demanded the document back before paying the debt].

There are, however, instances in which the testimonial power of the document is impaired with the result that, despite the document, the claimant must swear before being allowed to collect his claim. This rule was previously defined in *Kesubos* 9:7 in regard to a divorcee or widow who wishes to collect the money promised her in her *kesubah* (marriage contract) from her former husband or his estate. Citing this precedent, the mishnah here defines a similar rule for the heirs of a creditor who attempt to collect that debt from the heirs of the debtor.

כְּשֵׁם שֶׁאָמְרוּ — *Just as they said*

I.e., just as they said in *Kesubos* 9:7 *(Rashi)*.

הַפּוֹגֶמֶת כְּתֻבָּתָהּ — *[that] a woman who impairs her kesubah*

Following her divorce, a woman came

שֶׁהִיא פְרוּעָה, לֹא תִפָּרַע אֶלָּא בִשְׁבוּעָה; מִנְּכָסִים מְשֻׁעְבָּדִים וּמִנִּכְסֵי יְתוֹמִים, לֹא תִפָּרַע אֶלָּא בִשְׁבוּעָה; וְהַנִּפְרַעַת שֶׁלֹּא בְפָנָיו לֹא תִפָּרַע אֶלָּא בִשְׁבוּעָה — וְכֵן הַיְתוֹמִים לֹא יִפָּרְעוּ אֶלָּא בִשְׁבוּעָה: „שְׁבוּעָה שֶׁלֹּא פִקְּדָנוּ אַבָּא, וְלֹא אָמַר לָנוּ

יד אברהם

to court and pressed a claim for the money to which she was entitled under the terms of her *kesubah* (marriage contract). The former husband denies owing her anything, claiming that he already paid her. To prove her claim, she produces her *kesubah* document. Under ordinary circumstances this would suffice to prove her claim, as explained above. However, in this case, she admits to receiving part of the payment, and her claim is for the balance *(Rav; Rashi* from *Kesubos* 9:8).

;לֹא תִפָּרַע אֶלָּא בִשְׁבוּעָה — *is not paid except with an oath;*

I.e., she cannot collect the balance of her *kesubah* without swearing an oath that it is still owed to her *(Tif. Yis.)*. [Since the husband claims that she received the entire *kesubah*, and even she admits to receiving part of it, she must swear that her claim for the balance is valid and that she was not already paid that amount as well.]

One who receives partial payment of a debt does not always pay attention to exactly how much is being paid. The Rabbis therefore imposed an oath on a woman who comes to collect the balance of her *kesubah*, since by being aware that she may have to swear she will take careful note of how much she is receiving *(Kesubos* 87b).[1]

The *Gemara* (41a) explains that actually when a wife seeks to collect her *kesubah*, and the husband claims that it has already been paid, she must in all cases swear to the contrary — even if she does not admit to having received part of it. Since that is so, why does our mishnah single out the case of a woman who impairs her *kesubah?* The *Gemara* answers that generally she must swear only if the husband demands an oath. In the case of one who impairs her *kesubah*, *beis din* requires her to swear even if the husband did not demand an oath.

,וְעֵד אֶחָד מְעִידָהּ שֶׁהִיא פְרוּעָה — *and* [*that*] *one against whom a single witness testifies that it is paid,*

A woman comes to collect her *kesubah* and one witness testifies that she has already received it, thereby corroborating the husband's claim that it has been paid *(Kesubos* 9:8).

;לֹא תִפָּרַע אֶלָּא בִשְׁבוּעָה — *is not paid except with an oath;*

According to Biblical law, the testimony of one witness, though insufficient to exact payment, requires that the one against whom he testified swear to uphold his claim in the face of the witness' testimony. However, as taught in mishnah 1, Biblical oaths are always in the form of one swearing to exempt himself from payment, not swearing to collect. Thus, the Biblical oath applies only if the witness testifies against the defendant, not when he testifies against the claimant as in this case. Nevertheless, the Sages

1. As noted above (footnote to mishnah 6:2), the principle of *miggo* gives credence to a litigant's claim, since if she had wished to lie, a more effective lie was readily available. Seemingly, this woman should be believed with a *miggo* that she could have claimed that she had received nothing. Since she admits receiving part of the *kesubah*, we should accept her claim in regard to the balance without an oath. *Tos.* reply that the reason *miggo* is not applied here is because the primary concern is not that she is lying, but that she simply does not clearly remember how much she collected. Thus, we wish to compel her to swear so that she will claim only the amount of which she is absolutely sure *(Tos., Kesubos* 87b; *Tif. Yis.)*.

7 one against whom a single witness testifies that it is paid
7 is not paid except with an oath; [and that] from
mortgaged property or from the property of orphans, she is not paid except with an oath; and [that] one who receives payment in his absence is not paid except with an oath — so too orphans are not paid except with an oath, [viz.]: 'We swear that our father did not enjoin us,

YAD AVRAHAM

instituted this oath to appease the husband (*Kesubos* 87b).

מִנְּכָסִים מְשֻׁעְבָּדִים — [*and that*] *from mortgaged property*

I.e., if her husband sold his property, and she comes to collect from the purchasers (*Kesubos* 9:8). [In Torah law, mortgaged property can be sold, but it remains subject to collection by the seller's creditors if he has no funds to pay his debts. When a man marries, all his property is subject to a lien deriving from the *kesubah.*]

וּמִנִּכְסֵי יְתוֹמִים, — *or from the property of orphans,*

I.e., a widow who wishes to collect her *kesubah* from the property of her husband's orphans (*Kesubos* 9:8).

לֹא תִפָּרַע אֶלָּא בִשְׁבוּעָה; — *she is not paid except with an oath;*

In chapter 6 (mishnah 4) we learned that one must swear in order to collect from minors. Our mishnah tells us that in order to collect from orphans, even those who have reached their majority, one must swear that the debt was not paid by the father (*Gem.* 42b).

וְהַנִּפְרַעַת שֶׁלֹּא בְּפָנָיו — *and* [*that*] *one who receives payment in his absence*

I.e., a woman who produces her bill of divorce and her *kesubah* for collection from his estate while her former husband is away in a distant place.

If, however, he is close enough for us to send a messenger to him who can return within thirty days, we do so and notify him. If the husband does not come, the wife swears and collects the *kesubah* from his property (*Tos. Yom Tov* to *Kesubos* 7:7 from *Rosh*).

לֹא תִפָּרַע אֶלָּא בִשְׁבוּעָה — *is not paid except with an oath —*

Had the husband been present, he might have denied her claim by claiming that he had already paid her. This would have forced her to swear in order to collect, as part of the general rule taught by the *Gemara* (41a) that whenever a defendant is forced to pay because of a document of indebtedness which he claims to have paid, he may demand an oath before paying. Since he is unavailable to contest the claim, the court demands it on his behalf (*Rashi, Kesubos* 87a).

All the aforementioned are a continuation of the opening clause, *Just as they said.* Just as the Sages said in *Kesubos* 7:8 that in all these cases a woman cannot receive payment of her *kesubah* without first swearing an oath that she did not yet receive it, so the Rabbis said that ... [see below] (*Rav; Rashi*).

וְכֵן הַיְתוֹמִים — *so too orphans*

I.e., if the creditor and the debtor both died, and the creditor's heirs come to collect from the debtor's estate (*Rav* from *Gem.* 48a).

לֹא יִפָּרְעוּ אֶלָּא בִשְׁבוּעָה: — *are not paid except with an oath,*

If the debtor's heirs claim that they do not know whether their father paid the debt, the creditor's heirs cannot collect without swearing the following oath (*Rav* from *Gem.* 48a).

However, should they claim that their father told them that he had never borrowed money from this party, since the creditor's heirs produce a document proving their claim, they can collect

אַבָּא, וְשֶׁלֹּא מָצִינוּ בֵּין שְׁטָרוֹתָיו שֶׁל־אַבָּא שֶׁשְּׁטָר זֶה פָּרוּעַ.״ רַבִּי יוֹחָנָן בֶּן־בְּרוֹקָה אוֹמֵר: אֲפִילוּ נוֹלַד הַבֵּן לְאַחַר מִיתַת הָאָב, הֲרֵי זֶה נִשְׁבָּע וְנוֹטֵל. אָמַר רַבָּן שִׁמְעוֹן בֶּן־גַּמְלִיאֵל: אִם יֵשׁ עֵדִים שֶׁאָמַר הָאָב בִּשְׁעַת מִיתָתוֹ: ,,שְׁטָר זֶה אֵינוֹ פָּרוּעַ,״ הוּא נוֹטֵל שֶׁלֹּא בִשְׁבוּעָה.

יד אברהם

without an oath. The reason for this is that when one claims he didn't borrow any money it is tantamount to admitting that he didn't repay any money. Therefore, since the heirs have a document to prove that a loan took place, and the debtor, by his denial of the loan, admitted to not having paid it, his heirs must now pay *(Rav)*.

Another qualification made by the *Gemara* (48b) is that the mishnah's ruling applies only if the creditor predeceased the debtor. If, however, the debtor predeceased the creditor, the creditor would have been required to swear before receiving payment from the debtor's estate. Therefore, when that debt is bequeathed to his children, it is bequeathed under the same legal condition, viz., with the obligation to swear that the money was not yet paid. Being unable to swear with certainty, because children are usually not fully aware of their father's dealings, they cannot collect *(Rav from Gem.)*.

,,שְׁבוּעָה שֶׁלֹּא פִקְּדָנוּ אַבָּא, — [*viz.*]: *'We swear that our father did not enjoin us,*

I.e., he did not leave instructions at the time of his death that this debt was paid *(Rav; Rashi)*.

וְלֹא אָמַר לָנוּ אַבָּא, — *neither did our father tell us,*

I.e., neither did he tell us at any earlier date that this debt was paid *(Rav; Rashi)*.

Rambam (Hil. Malveh 17:1) explains these two stipulations to mean that he neither left instructions with a third party nor did he inform us directly.

וְשֶׁלֹּא מָצִינוּ בֵּין שְׁטָרוֹתָיו שֶׁל־אַבָּא — *nor have we found among our father's documents*

I.e., we have not found among our father's legal papers a receipt on this note *(Tos. Yom Tov* from *Rashi)*.

שֶׁשְּׁטָר זֶה פָּרוּעַ.״ — *that this note is paid.'*

In order to assume that the note was paid, there must be two indications, viz., that they find a receipt to that effect and that the document is found among other of the creditor's documents that have already been paid, as *Rav* states in *Bava Metzia* 1:8 *(Tos. Yom Tov* from *Maggid Mishneh, Hil. Malveh* 17:2).

רַבִּי יוֹחָנָן בֶּן־בְּרוֹקָה אוֹמֵר: אֲפִילוּ נוֹלַד הַבֵּן לְאַחַר מִיתַת הָאָב, הֲרֵי זֶה נִשְׁבָּע וְנוֹטֵל. — *R' Yochanan ben Berokah says: Even if the son is born after the father's death, he swears and collects.*

[I.e., if the son of the creditor was born after his father had died, and thus he cannot swear that his father did not enjoin him before his death or at any other time, he can still collect by swearing that he did not find a receipt among his father's papers *(Tur Choshen Mishpat* 108).

Rambam Comm. states that the halachah is in accordance with R' Yochanan ben Berokah. However, in *Hil. Malveh* 17:2, he states that 'even if the heir was an infant lying in a cradle when his father, who bequeathed him his property, died, he may swear and collect.' Since he does not state that even if the heir was born after his father's death, *Maggid Mishneh* deduces that he does not decide the halachah in favor of R' Yochanan ben Berokah. *Tos. Yom Tov*, however, differs, and this appears to be the view of *Hagahos Maimonios* as well.

Other editions read: הֵעִיד רַבִּי יוֹחָנָן בֶּן־

7
7

neither did our father tell us, nor have we found among our father's documents that this note is paid.' R' Yochanan ben Berokah says: Even if the son is born after the father's death, he swears and collects. Said Rabban Shimon ben Gamliel: If there are witnesses that the father said at the time of his death, 'This note is not paid,' he collects without an oath.

YAD AVRAHAM

בְּרוֹקָה, *R' Yochanan ben Berokah testified.* [I.e., he testified to a precedent.] (*Mishnah* in *Yerushalmi; Rif; Rosh; Hagahos Maimonios, Hil. Malveh* 17:2; *Cambridge Ms.; Naples print.*)

According to the latter reading, the halachah is surely in accordance with R' Yochanan ben Berokah according to the rule that every 'testimony' is a halachah. This appears to be the view of *Tur* (*Beis Yosef* 108, quoting *R' Meir*).

אָמַר רַבָּן שִׁמְעוֹן בֶּן־גַּמְלִיאֵל: אִם יֵשׁ עֵדִים שֶׁאָמַר הָאָב בִּשְׁעַת מִיתָתוֹ: „שְׁטָר זֶה אֵינוֹ פָּרוּעַ,״ הוּא נוֹטֵל שֶׁלֹּא בִשְׁבוּעָה. — *Said Rabban Shimon ben Gamliel: If there are witnesses that the father said at the time of his death, 'This note is not paid,' he collects without an oath.*

The *Tanna Kamma*, however, rules that, even in that case, the heirs must take an oath in order to receive payment. We fear that the father made this statement in order to lend prominence to his sons so that people should think that he left them a large inheritance (*Tos. Yom Tov* from *Tos.* 48b).

The halachah is in accordance with Rabban Shimon ben Gamliel (*Rav; Rambam, Hil. Malveh* 17:3).

8.

The following mishnah delineates a new class of Rabbinical oaths. The Rabbinical oaths listed until this point are all oaths which are invoked only by a litigant's definite claim of debt, damages, or ownership. Similarly, the Biblical oaths listed in the previous chapter are also imposed only for a definite claim.[1] The Rabbis, however, also instituted oaths which may be imposed even by a litigant's uncertain claim. These apply to situations in which persons handle other people's money in a position of trust, in which, by the very nature of the matter, the owner of the estate cannot definitely say whether the trust was faithfully executed or abused.

---

1. There is, however, a dispute concerning the oath to negate the testimony of a single witness. *Ran* (to *Gem.* 40a) cites the view of *Ri Migash* and *Rabbeinu Ephraim* that this oath, too, is only invoked if the claim which the single witness' testimony supports is a definite claim, not an uncertain one. *Ran*, however, disputes this and rules that even a plaintiff's uncertain claim supported by the testimony of a single witness necessitates an oath on the part of the defendant. Unlike other oaths, the impetus for the single-witness oath does not come from the claims and counter-claims of the litigants, but from the witness' testimony. Now the rule is that wherever the testimony of two witnesses would obligate a defendant to pay, the testimony of one witness obligates him to swear (*Gem.* 40a). Since the testimony of two witnesses obligates him to pay even if the plaintiff is personally uncertain of the debt, the testimony of the single witness similarly obligates the defendant to swear even if the plaintiff is uncertain of his claim. This latter view is shared by *Rif* and *Rambam*, as cited by *Rosh*, and is the accepted halachah (*Choshen Mishpat* 75:23).

וְאֵלּוּ נִשְׁבָּעִים שֶׁלֹּא בְטַעֲנָה: הַשֻּׁתָּפִין, וְהָאֲרִיסִין, וְהָאַפּוֹטְרוֹפִּין, וְהָאִשָּׁה הַנּוֹשֵׂאת וְהַנּוֹתֶנֶת בְּתוֹךְ הַבַּיִת, וּבֶן־הַבַּיִת. אָמַר לוֹ: „מָה אַתָּה טוֹעֲנֵנִי?" „רְצוֹנִי שֶׁתִּשָּׁבַע לִי" — חַיָּב.

חָלְקוּ הַשֻּׁתָּפִין וְהָאֲרִיסִין, אֵין יָכוֹל לְהַשְׁבִּיעוֹ. נִתְגַּלְגְּלָה לוֹ שְׁבוּעָה מִמָּקוֹם אַחֵר, מְגַלְגְּלִין עָלָיו אֶת־הַכֹּל. וְהַשְּׁבִיעִית מְשַׁמֶּטֶת אֶת־הַשְּׁבוּעָה.

יד אברהם

וְאֵלּוּ נִשְׁבָּעִים שֶׁלֹּא בְטַעֲנָה: — *The following must swear although no claim is lodged:*

I.e., they swear although there is no certain claim being lodged against them. Rather, without knowing whether anything of his was misappropriated, the claimant demands that the defendant swear that he did not keep anything belonging to him. All those listed here have a tendency to rationalize their appropriation of the property since they worked hard taking care of it. Consequently, the Rabbis required them to swear an oath though the claimant does not definitely claim that they took anything (*Rav* from *Gem.* 48b).

הַשֻּׁתָּפִין, — *partners,*

I.e., a partner who held common money or merchandise in his possession whose exact value or measure had not been previously determined (*Tif. Yis.* from *Choshen Mishpat* 93:5). [The partners are now dividing the property.]

וְהָאֲרִיסִין, — *sharecroppers,*

I.e., one who undertook to sow a field and to share the produce with the owner (*Tif. Yis.*). [At the end of the harvest, he must make an accounting with the landowner.]

וְהָאַפּוֹטְרוֹפִּין, — *administrators,*

I.e., administrators who were appointed to manage some person's property (*Rav*).

Where one administers the property of orphans, his status in regard to this oath depends on who appointed him. If he was appointed by *beis din* he must swear, but if he was appointed by the father he need not swear, since he obviously trusted him (*Rav; Rashi*). See *Gittin* 5:4.

וְהָאִשָּׁה הַנּוֹשֵׂאת וְהַנּוֹתֶנֶת בְּתוֹךְ הַבַּיִת, — *the wife who manages the affairs of the house,*

I.e., a woman whose husband installed her as a storekeeper, or as an administrator over his property (*Rav; Rashi*).

וּבֶן־הַבַּיִת. — *and the son of the house.*

I.e., one of the brothers who managed the affairs of the estate after the death of the father (*Rav; Rashi*).

אָמַר לוֹ: „מָה אַתָּה טוֹעֲנֵנִי?" — [*If*] *he said to him, 'What claim do you lodge against me?'*

This is an explanation of the beginning of the mishnah. If one of the aforementioned said to the claimant, 'What claim do you lodge against me?' (*Tif. Yis.*).

„רְצוֹנִי שֶׁתִּשָּׁבַע לִי" — — [*and he replied,*] *'I want you to swear to me'* —

The claimant replies, 'I want you to swear to me that you did not keep anything' (*Rashi*).

חַיָּב. — *he is liable.*

He is required to swear. People in these positions tend to rationalize taking what is not theirs by the fact that in their own eyes they worked above and beyond what they were paid for (*Rav*).

חָלְקוּ הַשֻּׁתָּפִין וְהָאֲרִיסִין, אֵין יָכוֹל לְהַשְׁבִּיעוֹ. — *Once the partners or the sharecroppers divided, he cannot make him swear.*

I.e., if they have already divided the

7 **8.** The following must swear although no claim is
8 lodged: partners, sharecroppers, administrators, the wife who manages the affairs of the house, and the son of the house. [If] he said to him, 'What claim do you lodge against me?' [and he replied,] 'I want you to swear to me' — he is liable.

Once the partners or the sharecroppers divided, he cannot make him swear. [If] an oath was imposed upon him from elsewhere, they impose upon him an oath for the entire claim. The *Shemittah* year releases [one from] an oath.

YAD AVRAHAM

property and no oath was demanded at the time of the division *(Rav; Rashi)*, he can no longer demand an oath from him for an uncertain claim. The silence at the time of the division is seen as a waiver of the right to demand an oath from the partner or sharecropper *(Tif. Yis.)*.

This applies not only to the partners and sharecroppers, but to all those enumerated in the mishnah *(Tos. Yom Tov* from *Rif)*.

נִתְגַּלְגְּלָה לוֹ שְׁבוּעָה מִמָּקוֹם אַחֵר, — [*If*] *an oath was imposed upon him* [lit. *rolled to him*] *from elsewhere,*

I.e., if he became liable to swear to him concerning another transaction which occurred after the division *(Rav; Rashi)*.

מְגַלְגְּלִין עָלָיו אֶת־הַכֹּל. — *they impose upon him an oath for the entire claim.*

Since the partner or landowner did not relinquish his right explicitly, if the defendant becomes liable to him for another oath, he may attach to that oath an additional oath concerning their previous partnership or sharecropping division *(Rav)*. [The principle of גִּלְגּוּל שְׁבוּעָה, *attaching oaths*, has been explained above, at the end of mishnah 6:3.]

Just as an auxiliary oath may be attached to the Biblical and Rabbinic oaths of the mishnah, so an auxiliary oath may be attached to a *shevuas hesses* *(Rav* from *Gem.* 48b).

וְהַשְּׁבִיעִית מְשַׁמֶּטֶת אֶת־הַשְּׁבוּעָה. — *The Shemittah year releases* [*one from*] *an oath.*

[This begins a new case and does not refer back to the previous case of this mishnah.]

In addition to the agricultural laws affecting the *Shemittah* (seventh year, the Sabbatical year — see above, mishnah 4), the Torah also decrees that it cancel all debts. Thus, if one borrowed money and the *Shemittah* year then canceled the debt, he cannot be made to swear about that debt anymore. Just as the *Shemittah* year releases him from the loan, so it releases him from the oath involved with it *(Rav; Rashi)*.

The *Gemara* (49a) derives the release from the oath from the first verse of the Torah's passage detailing the cancellation of debts. The verse begins: וְזֶה דְּבַר הַשְּׁמִיטָּה, *And this is the matter of the release (Deut.* 15:2). This is literally, 'the word of the release,' meaning that the seventh year releases the obligation of speech, i.e., the obligation of uttering an oath *(Tos. Yom Tov)*.

Ran questions the necessity for this derivation to release him from the oath. Since the borrower is released from paying the loan, how can there be any oath in regard to it? He replies that the case in question is one in which the creditor advanced his claim prior to the onset of the Sabbatical year, and the debtor made a partial confession. Based on *Yerushalmi Sheviis*, if one denies a loan before the time of cancellation, he is not released from paying it. This halachah is

שבועות
ח/א

[א] **אַרְבָּעָה** שׁוֹמְרִין הֵן: שׁוֹמֵר חִנָּם, וְהַשּׁוֹאֵל, נוֹשֵׂא שָׂכָר, וְהַשּׂוֹכֵר.
שׁוֹמֵר חִנָּם נִשְׁבָּע עַל־הַכֹּל; וְהַשּׁוֹאֵל מְשַׁלֵּם אֶת־הַכֹּל; נוֹשֵׂא שָׂכָר וְהַשּׂוֹכֵר נִשְׁבָּעִין עַל־

יד אברהם

stated by *Rambam* in *Hil. Shemittah* 9:8. The result is that the money he denied, if it indeed existed, was not released by the *Shemittah*. Since that part of the claim was not released, he should also be liable to swear the oath of the partial admission about it even after the completion of the *Shemittah* year. It is in regard to this oath that the Torah must tell us that he is released from the obligation to take the oath. Since the part of the claim that the debtor admitted is released, it is as though he denied the entire claim, and when one denies the entire claim, there is no oath *(Tos. Yom Tov)*.

Chapter 8

The following chapter expounds the section of the Torah dealing with the four *shomerim* [guardians] *(Exodus* 22:6-14); i.e., the four categories of custodianship for those who have been entrusted with other people's property, and their corresponding levels of liability. The Biblical section consists of three paragraphs, each of which defines a level of liability for an item which was lost, stolen or destroyed. The first (vs. 6-8) prescribes that the *shomer* swear should he claim that the article with which he was entrusted was stolen, and thereby exempt himself from paying for it. The Sages understood this paragraph to be dealing with a שׁוֹמֵר חִנָּם, *an unpaid shomer.* Since he receives no remuneration for his services, he is not liable for anything that happens to the article in his care unless he is guilty of negligence.

The second paragraph (vs. 9-12) prescribes that the *shomer* is liable for theft, and that he must swear should he claim that an unavoidable accident had occurred to the article in his care (if there are no witnesses to substantiate his claim). The Sages understood this paragraph to be referring to a שׁוֹמֵר שָׂכָר, *paid shomer.* Since he is remunerated for his services, he has additional responsibilities and liabilities.

The third paragraph (vs. 13,14) deals with the borrower, who is liable even if the animal in his care dies a natural death or breaks a limb. Since he has full use of the animal or the article without paying for it, he is liable for everything, even for unavoidable accidents, as will be discussed further. He is exempt only if the loss of the object resulted from its proper and normal use in the task for which he borrowed it [see *Bava Metzia* 96b].

The renter, too, is mentioned in this paragraph, but the Torah is not explicit concerning his liabilities. There is, therefore, a dispute whether he has the liabilities of an unpaid *shomer* or a paid *shomer.* Our mishnah follows the view that he is treated as a paid *shomer (Gem.* 49b).

1.

This mishnah appears also in *Bava Metzia* (7:8). It is repeated here in conjunction with the following mishnah, which deals with liability to and exemption from the guilt-offering for swearing falsely in the case of the oath of deposit. That liability is contingent upon his having exempted himself from paying for the deposit with the false oath. If, however, he would have been exempt from paying even had he said the truth, he is not liable to a guilt-offering for making a false claim and swearing to it, because his false oath does not constitute a denial of money. The mishnah therefore repeats the liabilities of the four *shomerim* to enable us to judge which claim constitutes a denial of money and which does not *(Tos. Yom Tov* from *Rashi).*

8 1 **1.** There are four [types of] *shomerim:* the unpaid *shomer*, the borrower, the paid *shomer*, and the renter. The unpaid *shomer* swears for everything; the borrower pays for everything; the paid *shomer* and the renter swear concerning an animal that broke a limb, an

YAD AVRAHAM

אַרְבָּעָה שׁוֹמְרִין הֵן: — *There are four* [*types of*] *shomerim:*

There are four classes of guardians entrusted with the care of other people's property. However, between them there are only three levels of liability, since a paid *shomer* and a renter have the same liabilities (*Rav* from *Gem.* 49b).

שׁוֹמֵר חִנָּם, — *the unpaid shomer,*

[I.e., one who undertakes to watch money, utensils, or anything else without receiving remuneration.]

וְהַשּׁוֹאֵל, — *the borrower,*

[I.e., one who borrows any animal or utensil without paying for its use.]

נוֹשֵׂא שָׂכָר, — *the paid shomer* [lit. *he who receives payment*],

The mishnah often uses the term נוֹשֵׂא שָׂכָר, *he who receives payment*, instead of the more explicit שׁוֹמֵר שָׂכָר, *paid shomer*, to indicate that not only one who accepts an article as a watchman and receives his pay directly is subject to this level of liability, but even one who accepts an article as a broker, with the intention of profiting by its sale, has the responsibilities of a paid *shomer*, since he expects to derive a benefit from it (*Tif. Yis.* to *Bava Metzia* 7:8).

Tif. Yis. to our mishnah explains that the *Tanna* also wishes to include the one who benefits indirectly by watching the article, such as the *shomer* entrusted with loose money which he may use, thereby rendering him a paid *shomer*, as in *Bava Metzia* 3:11.

וְהַשּׂוֹכֵר. — *and the renter.*

[I.e., one who pays for the use of the article.]

שׁוֹמֵר חִנָּם נִשְׁבָּע עַל־הַכֹּל; — *The unpaid shomer swears for everything;*

I.e., the unpaid *shomer* is exempt from all liabilities mentioned in conjunction with the other types of *shomerim*. In order to substantiate his claim, however, he must swear (*Rav; Rashi*). The Sages deduce this from the words in the first paragraph, וְנִקְרַב בַּעַל־הַבַּיִת אֶל־הָאֱלֹהִים, *and the householder shall come near to the judges* (*Ex.* 22:7), the intention of which is that he shall come near to the judges to swear that the article was stolen as he claims (*Bava Metzia* 41b).

This generality does not include negligence, for which all *shomerim* are liable (*Tos. Yom Tov* to *Bava Metzia* 7:8 from *Tos.* 94b). Therefore, he must swear that he did not neglect to watch the article, in addition to swearing what actually befell the article (*Rav; Rashi*).

וְהַשּׁוֹאֵל מְשַׁלֵּם אֶת־הַכֹּל; — *the borrower pays for everything;*

In contrast with the unpaid *shomer*, who can exempt himself with an oath, the borrower is liable for everything (*Tos. Yom Tov*, referring to *Bava Kamma* 4:9).

This includes all occurrences mentioned in this section, viz., theft, loss, natural death, capture, and broken limbs [in the case of an animal]. However, this does not include the eventuality that the article breaks or the animal dies during normal usage. Since that is what he borrowed it for, and he was permitted to use it, he is exempt (*Rav* from *Bava Metzia* 96b).

נוֹשֵׂא שָׂכָר וְהַשּׂוֹכֵר — *the paid shomer and the renter*

[The paid *shomer* and the renter have the same regulations, as explained below.]

נִשְׁבָּעִין עַל־הַשְּׁבוּרָה, וְעַל־הַשְּׁבוּיָה, וְעַל־הַמֵּתָה, — *swear concerning an animal that broke a limb, an animal that was captured, and an animal that died,*

[Upon swearing they are exempt from

שבועות ח/ב

הַשְּׁבוּרָה, וְעַל־הַשְּׁבוּיָה, וְעַל־הַמֵּתָה, וּמְשַׁלְּמִים אֶת־הָאֲבֵדָה וְאֶת־הַגְּנֵבָה.

[ב] **אָמַר** לְשׁוֹמֵר חִנָּם: „הֵיכָן שׁוֹרִי?" אָמַר לוֹ: „מֵת" — וְהוּא שֶׁנִּשְׁבַּר, אוֹ־נִשְׁבָּה, אוֹ־נִגְנַב, אוֹ־אָבַד; „נִשְׁבַּר" — וְהוּא שֶׁמֵּת, אוֹ־נִשְׁבָּה, אוֹ־נִגְנַב, אוֹ־אָבַד; „נִשְׁבָּה" — וְהוּא שֶׁמֵּת, אוֹ־נִשְׁבַּר, אוֹ־נִגְנַב, אוֹ־אָבַד; „נִגְנַב," וְהוּא שֶׁמֵּת, אוֹ־נִשְׁבַּר, אוֹ־נִשְׁבָּה, אוֹ־אָבַד; „אָבַד," וְהוּא שֶׁמֵּת, אוֹ־נִשְׁבַּר, אוֹ־נִשְׁבָּה, אוֹ־נִגְנַב — „מַשְׁבִּיעֲךָ אֲנִי," וְאָמַר: „אָמֵן," פָּטוּר.

יד אברהם

paying for the damages to an animal that broke a limb while in their custody, or the loss of an animal that died or was captured.] *Captured* means that it was taken by force by an armed brigand, in contrast to *theft*, in which the article was not taken by force (*Rashi* to *Exodus* 22:9; *Rambam, Sechirus* 1:2). The same is true for any article which is lost through some completely unavoidable accident [אוֹנֶס גָּדוֹל] (*Rambam*, ibid.).

As explained above, the second paragraph deals with the paid *shomer*. This paragraph states (*Exodus* 22:9,10): כִּי יִתֵּן אִישׁ אֶל־רֵעֵהוּ חֲמוֹר אוֹ־שׁוֹר אוֹ־שֶׂה וְכָל־בְּהֵמָה לִשְׁמֹר וּמֵת אוֹ נִשְׁבַּר אוֹ נִשְׁבָּה אֵין רֹאֶה: שְׁבֻעַת ה׳ תִּהְיֶה בֵּין שְׁנֵיהֶם ... וְלָקַח בְּעָלָיו וְלֹא יְשַׁלֵּם — *Should a man give his neighbor a donkey, a bull, a lamb or any animal to watch, and it die, break a leg, or be captured, with no one seeing it; an oath of God shall be between them both . . . and the owner shall accept* [*it*] *and shall not pay.*

וּמְשַׁלְּמִים אֶת־הָאֲבֵדָה וְאֶת־הַגְּנֵבָה. — *but they pay for loss or theft.*

The Torah states (*Exodus* 22:11): וְאִם־גָּנֹב יִגָּנֵב מֵעִמּוֹ יְשַׁלֵּם לִבְעָלָיו, *and if it is stolen from him, he shall pay to its owner.* Since he must pay for theft, which is close to being an unavoidable accident, he must surely pay for loss, which is closer to negligence (*Rav* to *Bava Metzia* 7:5 from *Gem.* 94b).

The renter, too, has the same liabilities as the paid *shomer*. Since the hired article is in his possession primarily for his benefit, although he pays for it, he is judged as a paid *shomer*. The fact that he pays for its use is effective only in distinguishing him from the borrower, who has all the benefit, and consequently has more liabilities.

As noted above, this matter is the subject of a Tannaitic dispute. The view of our mishnah is R' Yehudah's. R' Meir rules that a renter is judged as an unpaid *shomer* because the renter pays for his use of the article and thus watches it without pay (*Gem.* 49b, *Rashi, Bava Metzia* 80b). One opinion in the *Gemara* reverses the positions of R' Yehudah and R' Meir. In any case the halachah follows the view of our mishnah that a renter is treated the same as a paid *shomer* (*Rambam, Sechirus* 1:2; *Choshen Mishpat* 307:1).

2.

אָמַר לְשׁוֹמֵר חִנָּם: „הֵיכָן שׁוֹרִי?" אָמַר לוֹ: „מֵת" — — [*If*] *one said to an unpaid shomer, 'Where is my bull?'* [*and*] *he replied, 'It died'* —

8 animal that was captured, and an animal that died, but
2 they pay for loss or theft.

2. [If] one said to an unpaid *shomer*, 'Where is my bull?' [and] he replied, 'It died' — whereas [in fact] it broke a limb, was captured, stolen, or lost; [or he replied,] 'It broke a limb' — whereas [in fact] it died, was captured, stolen, or lost; [or he replied,] 'It was captured' — whereas [in fact] it died, broke a limb, was stolen, or lost; [or he replied,] 'It was stolen' — whereas [in fact] it died, broke a limb, was captured, or lost; [or he replied,] 'It was lost' — whereas [in fact] it died, broke a limb, was captured, or stolen — [and he said to him,] 'I adjure you,' and he replied, 'Amen,' he is exempt.

YAD AVRAHAM

[Thus, the unpaid *shomer* seeks to exempt himself from having to make restitution.]

וְהוּא שֶׁנִּשְׁבַּר, אוֹ־נִשְׁבָּה, אוֹ־נִגְנַב, אוֹ־אָבַד; — *whereas [in fact] it broke a limb, was captured, stolen, or lost;*

[I.e., the truth of the matter is that the bull broke its leg or disappeared in any of these manners, for all of which an unpaid *shomer* is exempt.]

„נִשְׁבַּר" — *[or he replied,] 'It broke a limb'* —

[Or in answer to the query, 'Where is my bull,' he claimed that the bull broke a limb, something for which an unpaid *shomer* is exempt.]

וְהוּא שֶׁמֵּת, אוֹ־נִשְׁבָּה, אוֹ־נִגְנַב, אוֹ־אָבַד; — *whereas [in fact] it died, was captured, stolen, or lost;*

[I.e., the truth of the matter is that it did not break a limb, but was lost in one of these other manners. For any of these, an unpaid *shomer* is similarly exempt.]

„נִשְׁבָּה" — וְהוּא שֶׁמֵּת, אוֹ־נִשְׁבַּר, אוֹ־נִגְנַב, אוֹ־אָבַד; — *[or he replied,] 'It was captured' — whereas [in fact] it died, broke a limb, was stolen, or lost;*

[Or the unpaid *shomer* claimed that the bull was taken by force by armed brigands (*Rashi* to *Exodus* 22:9), whereas the truth of the matter was that it was not captured but lost in some other manner for which an unpaid *shomer* is exempt.]

„נִגְנַב" — וְהוּא שֶׁמֵּת, אוֹ־נִשְׁבַּר, אוֹ־נִשְׁבָּה, אוֹ־אָבַד; „אָבַד" — וְהוּא שֶׁמֵּת, אוֹ־נִשְׁבַּר, אוֹ־נִשְׁבָּה, אוֹ־נִגְנַב — *[or he replied,] 'It was stolen' — whereas [in fact] it died, broke a limb, was captured, or lost; [or he replied,] 'It was lost' — whereas [in fact] it died, broke a limb, was captured, or stolen* —

[All these afford exemption to an unpaid *shomer*, but not the one he claimed.]

„מַשְׁבִּיעֲךָ אֲנִי," — *[and he said to him,] 'I adjure you,'*

[I.e., I adjure you that this is what really happened, and that you were not negligent in watching my bull.]

וְאָמַר: „אָמֵן," — *and he replied, 'Amen,'*

[The unpaid *shomer* responded to the adjuration by saying *'Amen.'* [As explained above (3:10), when one is adjured and responds by answering *'Amen,'* it constitutes acceptance of the oath and is equivalent to pronouncing it.]

פָּטוּר. — *he is exempt.*

He is exempt from a guilt-offering, even if he subsequently confesses that he swore falsely. Since he would have been

שבועות [ג] **„הֵיכָן** שׁוֹרִי?" אָמַר לוֹ: „אֵינִי יוֹדֵעַ מָה
ח/ג אַתָּה סָח" — וְהוּא שֵׁמֵת, אוֹ־
נִשְׁבַּר, אוֹ־נִשְׁבָּה, אוֹ־נִגְנַב, אוֹ־אָבַד — „מַשְׁבִּיעֲךָ
אֲנִי," וְאָמַר: „אָמֵן" — פָּטוּר.
„הֵיכָן שׁוֹרִי?" אָמַר לוֹ: „אָבַד"; „מַשְׁבִּיעֲךָ אֲנִי,"
וְאָמַר: „אָמֵן" — וְהָעֵדִים מְעִידִין אוֹתוֹ שֶׁאֲכָלוֹ —
מְשַׁלֵּם אֶת־הַקֶּרֶן. הוֹדָה מֵעַצְמוֹ, מְשַׁלֵּם קֶרֶן,
וְחֹמֶשׁ, וְאָשָׁם.

יד אברהם

He is, however, liable to a variable sin-offering for a false oath of utterance; see chapter 3 (*Tos. Yom Tov* from *Rambam Comm.* at the end of the chapter).

exempt from payment even if he had told the truth, his denial was not a denial of money. Consequently, there is no guilt-offering *(Rav; Rambam Comm.).*

3.

„הֵיכָן שׁוֹרִי?" אָמַר לוֹ: „אֵינִי יוֹדֵעַ מָה אַתָּה סָח" — *[If he said to him,] 'Where is my bull?' [and] he replied, 'I don't know what you are talking about'* —

[The depositor asked the unpaid *shomer* to return his bull to him.] The *shomer*, however, denied ever becoming a *shomer*, thereby attempting to exempt himself from an oath as well as monetary payment *(Tif. Yis.).*

וְהוּא שֵׁמֵת, אוֹ־נִשְׁבַּר, אוֹ־נִשְׁבָּה, אוֹ־נִגְנַב, אוֹ־אָבַד — *whereas, [in fact,] it died, broke a limb, was captured, stolen, or lost* —

[The truth of the matter was that he had accepted responsibility to guard this bull, but an accident occurred for which an unpaid *shomer* is exempt.]

„מַשְׁבִּיעֲךָ אֲנִי," וְאָמַר: „אָמֵן" — *[and he said to him,] 'I adjure you,' and he replied, 'Amen'* —

[The depositor adjured the *shomer* with an oath that he had never undertaken to guard the bull. The *shomer*, though not bound to swear in such a case,[1] answered *'Amen'* to this adjuration, thereby accepting upon himself the oath. As explained above, this is tantamount to swearing with his own mouth.]

פָּטוּר. — *he is exempt.*

[I.e., he is exempt from a guilt-offering, since whether he was never engaged as a *shomer*, or whether he was, but one of the above-mentioned calamities befell the bull, he would not be obliged to pay. He must, however, bring a variable sin-offering for a false oath of utterance, as above.]

„הֵיכָן שׁוֹרִי?" — *[If he said to him,] 'Where is my bull?'*

This, too, refers to an unpaid *shomer* *(Rav).*

אָמַר לוֹ: „אָבַד"; — *[and] he replied, 'It was lost';*

[An unpaid *shomer* is not liable to pay for non-negligent loss.]

„מַשְׁבִּיעֲךָ אֲנִי," וְאָמַר: „אָמֵן" — וְהָעֵדִים מְעִידִין אוֹתוֹ שֶׁאֲכָלוֹ — *[and he said to him] 'I adjure you,' and he replied, 'Amen' — but witnesses testify against him that he ate it* —

1. According to the law of the Mishnah, a *shomer* is obligated to swear only for claiming exemption as a *shomer,* not if he denies being a *shomer* at all. In such a case, he would only be required to swear the post-Mishnaic oath of *shevuas hesses.*

3. [If he said to him,] 'Where is my bull?' [and] he replied, 'I don't know what you are talking about' — whereas, [in fact] it died, broke a limb, was captured, stolen, or lost — [and he said to him,] 'I adjure you,' and he replied, 'Amen' — he is exempt.

[If he said to him,] 'Where is my bull?' [and] he replied, 'It was lost'; [and he said to him,] 'I adjure you,' and he replied, 'Amen' — but witnesses testify against him that he ate it — he must pay the principal. [If] he confessed on his own, he must pay the principal, plus a fifth, and a guilt-offering.

YAD AVRAHAM

[Witnesses came and testified that the *shomer* had eaten the animal entrusted to him.]

.מְשַׁלֵּם אֶת־הַקֶּרֶן — *he must pay the principal.*

An unpaid *shomer* who, after claiming that the deposit was lost and swearing to that effect, is refuted by witnesses who testify that he took it for himself, is liable only for the article itself, or its value, but not the twofold payment imposed upon a thief. Having received the animal as a *shomer*, he cannot become subject to the legal penalties attendant on a thief [גַּנָּב] except under the circumstances delineated below (*Maggid Mishneh* in explanation of *Ravad, Hil. Geneivah* 4:10; see, however, *Rambam* and commentators ibid.).

He is also exempt from the guilt-offering for a false oath of deposit, which is only brought by someone who confesses his guilt; see below.

,הוֹדָה מֵעַצְמוֹ — [*If*] *he confessed on his own,*

I.e., if he confessed to having sworn falsely in the absence of witnesses (*Rashi*), or at least before any witnesses came forward (*Rav*).

,מְשַׁלֵּם קֶרֶן, חֹמֶשׁ — *he must pay the principal, plus a fifth,*

[I.e., he must add a fifth of the value of the principal as a penalty (*Lev.* 5:24). However, this fifth is not calculated as twenty percent of the principal, but rather as one-fifth of the total payment that will be made. I.e., when the principal-plus-penalty payment is made, the penalty must equal one-fifth of that sum. This makes it actually a fourth of the value of the principal. For example, if the principal amounted to twenty *zuz*, the one-fifth penalty comes to five *zuz* [rather than four] so that of a total payment of twenty-five *zuz*, the penalty portion (five) represents one-fifth of the total. See *Bava Kamma* 65b.

.וְאָשָׁם — *and a guilt-offering.*

In addition to the payments, he must bring a guilt-offering according to the law of the oath of deposit, as delineated above (5:1).

The guilt-offering [as well as the one-fifth additional payment] is brought only by someone who confesses, repents and wishes to atone for his sin, not by someone who is convicted on the basis of witnesses' testimony (*Rav*). This is learned from the passage that deals with robbing a convert (see *Bava Kamma* 9:11), where the Torah states (*Num.* 5:7): *and they confess* (*Rav* to *Bava Kamma* 9:7).

This applies only if he continues to deny his guilt even after the witnesses testified against him. Since he does not repent, he cannot atone for what he did.

„הֵיכָן שׁוֹרִי?" אָמַר לוֹ: „נִגְנַב"; „מַשְׁבִּיעֲךָ אֲנִי," וְאָמַר: „אָמֵן" — וְהָעֵדִים מְעִידִין אוֹתוֹ שֶׁגְּנָבוֹ — מְשַׁלֵּם תַּשְׁלוּמֵי כֶפֶל. הוֹדָה מֵעַצְמוֹ, מְשַׁלֵּם קֶרֶן, וְחֹמֶשׁ, וְאָשָׁם.

[ד] **אָמַר** לְאֶחָד בַּשּׁוּק: „הֵיכָן שׁוֹרִי שֶׁגָּנַבְתָּ?" וְהוּא אוֹמֵר: „לֹא גְנַבְתִּי" — וְהָעֵדִים מְעִידִין אוֹתוֹ שֶׁגְּנָבוֹ — מְשַׁלֵּם תַּשְׁלוּמֵי כֶפֶל. טָבַח

יד אברהם

However, should he confess his guilt even after the witnesses' testimony, he would be subject to the one-fifth payment and guilt-offering (*Rambam Comm.* and *Hil. Gezeilah* 7:8).

Although the mishnah actually speaks of a case in which he confessed in the absence of witnesses, as noted above, the mishnah does so only because this point is relevant to the ruling which follows. As far as the present ruling is concerned, there is no difference whether he confessed before or after witnesses arrived (*Tos. R' Akiva Eiger* to *Bava Kamma* 9:7 from *Tos.* ibid. 108a).

„הֵיכָן שׁוֹרִי?" אָמַר לוֹ: „נִגְנַב," — [*If he said to him,*] *'Where is my bull?'* [*and*] *he replied, 'It was stolen,'*

[An unpaid *shomer* is exempt for paying for a stolen deposit.]

„מַשְׁבִּיעֲךָ אֲנִי," וְאָמַר: „אָמֵן" — וְהָעֵדִים מְעִידִין אוֹתוֹ שֶׁגְּנָבוֹ — — [*and he said to him,*] *'I adjure you,' and he replied, 'Amen' — but witnesses testify against him that he stole it —*

[Witnesses testify that the *shomer* himself stole the bull.]

מְשַׁלֵּם תַּשְׁלוּמֵי כֶפֶל. — *he must pay the twofold payment.*

[By making a false claim of theft and swearing to it, the *shomer* earns for himself the status of a thief, and he is thus liable to the twofold payment.] This is derived from the verse (*Ex.* 22:7f): *If the thief is not found, and the householder has approached the judges ... whomever the judges condemn shall pay twofold to the other.* The intention is: *If the thief is not found* — i.e., his claim that the article was stolen is found to be false, *and the householder* — i.e., the *shomer, has approached the judges* — i.e., had already sworn that the item was stolen, he pays the twofold payment.[1]

The Torah's rule equating a dishonest *shomer* who swears falsely with a thief applies only to one who falsely swore that the deposit had been stolen. Should he seek to retain possession of the deposit by claiming that the item was lost, if he is found guilty of swearing falsely, he is liable only to the principal, not to the twofold payment (*Rav, Bava Kamma* 63b).

The mishnah here chooses a case in which the witnesses testify that the *shomer* himself stole the bull, whereas in the previous case, in which the *shomer* claimed that the animal was lost, the witnesses testified that he had 'eaten the animal.' Actually, there is no difference in regard to this law whether he killed the animal or merely stole it; the difference between the two cases depends solely on whether he falsely swore that it had been lost or whether he swore that it had been stolen. The different examples are given to point out that if the *shomer* claims that the bull was lost, even if witnesses testify that it no longer exists — e.g., he ate it — he pays only the principal. Should he claim that it

1. Should he subsequently confess and wish to atone for his sin, he would *not* have to add an additional fifth (*Bava Kamma* 65a,b).

[If he said to him,] 'Where is my bull?' [and] he replied, 'It was stolen'; [and he said to him,] 'I adjure you,' and he replied, 'Amen' — but witnesses testify against him that he stole it — he must pay the twofold payment. [If] he confessed on his own, he must pay the principal, plus a fifth, and a guilt-offering.

4. [If] he said to someone in the street, 'Where is my bull that you stole?' and he replied, 'I did not steal [it] — but witnesses testify against him that he stole it — he pays the twofold payment. [If] he slaughtered [it] or

was stolen, however, even if the witnesses testify that the stolen animal still exists, he must nevertheless pay twofold (*Tos. Yom Tov* to *Bava Kamma* 9:8 from *Tos.* 63b).

Just as a *shomer* becomes liable to the twofold payment of a thief by falsely swearing that the deposit was stolen, so too if he should slaughter or sell the bull, he must pay the fourfold or fivefold payment of a thief [see above, 5:5] (*Tif. Yis.* from *Bava Kamma* 106b).

הוֹדָה מֵעַצְמוֹ, מְשַׁלֵּם קֶרֶן, וְחֹמֶשׁ, וְאָשָׁם. — *[If] he confessed on his own, he must pay the principal, plus a fifth, and a guilt-offering.*

Since he confesses his own guilt, he does not pay the twofold payment because that is a fine, and one does not pay a fine on his own confession (*Rav*). We derive this principle from *Exodus* 22:8: *Whomever the judges condemn shall pay twofold to the other* — that is, only if the *judges* condemn him must he pay the fine, but not if he admits the crime himself (*Rav* to *Bava Kamma* 9:8 from *Gem.* 64b).

It is for this reason that the mishnah chooses a case in which he confesses in the absence of witnesses. Had their testimony preceded his confession, he would have to pay the twofold payment.

He does, however, pay the principal plus the fifth, and must bring a guilt-offering as in the previous case. He pays the fifth since that payment is not considered a criminal fine but rather an atonement for his sin (*Tif. Yis.* to *Bava Kamma* ibid.).

4.

אָמַר לְאֶחָד בַּשּׁוּק: „הֵיכָן שׁוֹרִי שֶׁגְּנַבְתָּ?" וְהוּא אוֹמֵר: „לֹא גְנַבְתִּי" — *[If] he said to someone in the street, 'Where is my bull that you stole?' and he replied, 'I did not steal [it]* —

[This case does not deal with a *shomer*, but with an ordinary thief.]

וְהָעֵדִים מְעִידִין אוֹתוֹ שֶׁגְּנָבוֹ — *but witnesses testify against him that he stole it* —

[Two witnesses testify in court that he stole the bull.]

מְשַׁלֵּם תַּשְׁלוּמֵי כֶפֶל. — *he pay the twofold payment.*

Although he did not swear that he did not steal it, he must, nevertheless, pay the twofold payment, since he is a common thief (*Ex.* 22:6). It is only the *shomer* who falsely claims that an article entrusted to him was stolen who must swear in order to be liable for the twofold payment (*Rav* from *Bava Kamma* 64b).

This is according to *Rashi's* reading, which omits the usual formula of the adjuration and the acceptance of the oath. *Tos.* (49a), however, include that formula in this case. In their view, the mishnah wishes to teach that only if the thief admits of his own volition is he liable to a fifth and a guilt-

וּמָכַר, מְשַׁלֵּם תַּשְׁלוּמֵי אַרְבָּעָה וַחֲמִשָּׁה. רָאָה עֵדִים שֶׁמְּמַשְׁמְשִׁין וּבָאִין, אָמַר: „גָּנַבְתִּי, אֲבָל לֹא טָבַחְתִּי וְלֹא מָכַרְתִּי" — אֵינוֹ מְשַׁלֵּם אֶלָּא קֶרֶן.

[ה] **אָמַר** לְשׁוֹאֵל: „הֵיכָן שׁוֹרִי?" אָמַר לוֹ: „מֵת" — וְהוּא שֶׁנִּשְׁבַּר, אוֹ־נִשְׁבָּה, אוֹ־נִגְנַב, אוֹ־אָבַד; „נִשְׁבַּר" — וְהוּא שֶׁמֵּת, אוֹ־נִשְׁבָּה, אוֹ־נִגְנַב, אוֹ־אָבַד; „נִשְׁבָּה" — וְהוּא שֶׁמֵּת, אוֹ־נִשְׁבַּר, אוֹ־נִגְנַב, אוֹ־אָבַד; „נִגְנַב" — וְהוּא שֶׁמֵּת, אוֹ־נִשְׁבַּר, אוֹ־נִשְׁבָּה, אוֹ־אָבַד; „אָבַד" —

יד אברהם

offering. Should he confess after the witnesses testify, and after he has become liable to twofold payment, he is not liable to pay the fifth.

טָבַח וּמָכַר, — [*If*] *he slaughtered* [*it*] *or sold* [*it*],

[I.e., if he slaughtered the bull or sold it, and witnesses testified to that effect.]

מְשַׁלֵּם תַּשְׁלוּמֵי אַרְבָּעָה וַחֲמִשָּׁה. — *he must pay a fourfold or fivefold payment.*

[I.e., fivefold payment for the bull and a fourfold payment if it was a sheep, as in *Exodus* 21:37.]

רָאָה עֵדִים שֶׁמְּמַשְׁמְשִׁין וּבָאִין, — [*If*] *he saw witnesses approaching,*

If, after the thief had denied the theft, he saw witnesses on their way to *beis din* to testify that he had stolen the animal, and he quickly returned to *beis din* (*Meiri*).

אָמַר: „גָּנַבְתִּי, אֲבָל לֹא טָבַחְתִּי וְלֹא מָכַרְתִּי" — — [*and*] *he said, 'I stole, but I did not slaughter or sell'* —

He quickly returned to court to confess his theft and thereby exempt himself from the second (penalty) payment. He continued to deny, however, that he had butchered or sold the animal. Later, these witnesses testified that he both stole and slaughtered or sold the bull or the sheep (*Meiri*).

As we learned above, if one confesses to committing a crime for which there is a fine he is exempt. From this mishnah it is evident that even if witnesses come after his confession and testify to the same effect, he has, nevertheless, been exempted by his earlier confession and is not liable. Cf. *Bava Kamma* 7:4.

אֵינוֹ מְשַׁלֵּם אֶלָּא קֶרֶן. — *he pays only the principal.*

Although his confession was inspired by his fear of the approaching witnesses, it is nevertheless valid, and he is exempt from the twofold payment. There still remains the payment of the principal and the fourfold payment for slaughtering the sheep and the fivefold payment for slaughtering the bull. However, the four or fivefold payment includes the double payment for the theft itself. Since by virtue of his confession he is exempt from the double payment, his maximum payment would be three or fourfold. Since the Torah does not prescribe any such payment, he is completely exempt from the payment of any fine for the theft or the slaughter or sale of the animal (*Rav; Rashi*).

Should the witnesses testify only that he slaughtered or sold the animal but know nothing of the theft, it is self-evident that he is exempt from fourfold or fivefold payment, since we have no evidence of the theft except through his confession. Otherwise, the ani-

sold [it], he must pay a fourfold or fivefold payment. [If] he saw witnesses approaching, [and] he said, 'I stole, but I did not slaughter or sell' — he pays only the principal.

5. [If] one said to a borrower, 'Where is my bull?' [and] he replied, 'It died' — whereas [in fact] it broke a limb, was captured, stolen, or lost; [or he replied,] 'It broke a limb' — whereas [in fact] it died, was captured, stolen, or lost; [or he replied,] 'It was captured' — whereas [in fact] it died, broke a limb, was stolen, or lost; [or he replied,] 'It was stolen' — whereas [in fact] it died, broke a limb, was captured, or lost; [or he replied,]

YAD AVRAHAM

mal he slaughtered could have been his own. However, the witnesses testifying concerning the slaughter or sale need not be the same ones who testify concerning the theft *(Bava Kamma* 7:2).

The explanation of the mishnah given above follows the *Amora* Rav, who rules that if one confesses to an act whose punishment is a fine and then witnesses come, he is exempt. According to Shmuel, however, confession exempts one from paying a fine only so long as it is the sole basis for the court's knowledge of the crime, but if witnesses subsequently arrive to convict him by their testimony, he is liable. Shmuel therefore qualifies the mishnah to mean that he is exempt only if the witnesses retreat and never appear in the beis din to testify *(Tos.* 49a from *Bava Kamma* 75a).

5.

אָמַר לְשׁוֹאֵל: „הֵיכָן שׁוֹרִי?" — *[If] one said to a borrower, 'Where is my bull?'*

[I.e., a lender asked the borrower to return the bull he had lent him.]

אָמַר לוֹ: „מֵת" — *[and] he replied, 'It died'* —

The borrower replied that the bull had died of natural causes, unrelated to its work. [Thus, the borrower admits to his liability.] Should it die because of its work, however, the borrower would be exempt, as noted in the preface to our chapter *(Tos. Yom Tov).*

וְהוּא שֶׁנִּשְׁבַּר, אוֹ־נִשְׁבָּה, אוֹ־נִגְנַב, אוֹ־אָבַד; — *whereas [in fact] it broke a limb, was captured, stolen, or lost;*

[The truth of the matter is that it did not die but broke a limb. In all of these cases, he would also be liable.]

„נִשְׁבַּר" — *[or he replied,] 'It broke a limb'* —

[I.e., or the borrower claimed that the animal broke a limb, for which he is liable.]

וְהוּא שֶׁמֵּת, אוֹ־נִשְׁבָּה, אוֹ־נִגְנַב, אוֹ־אָבַד; — *whereas [in fact] it died, was captured, stolen, or lost;*

[I.e., for any of these incidents, he would also be liable.]

„נִשְׁבָּה" — וְהוּא שֶׁמֵּת, אוֹ־נִשְׁבַּר, אוֹ־נִגְנַב, אוֹ־אָבַד; „נִגְנַב" — וְהוּא שֶׁמֵּת, אוֹ־נִשְׁבַּר, אוֹ־נִשְׁבָּה, אוֹ־אָבַד; „אָבַד" — וְהוּא שֶׁמֵּת, אוֹ־נִשְׁבַּר, אוֹ־נִשְׁבָּה, אוֹ־נִגְנַב — *[or he replied,] 'It was captured' — whereas [in fact] it died, broke a limb, was stolen, or lost; [or he replied,] 'It was stolen' — whereas [in fact] it died, broke a limb, was captured, or lost; [or he replied,] 'It*

וְהוּא שֶׁמֵּת, אוֹ־נִשְׁבַּר, אוֹ־נִשְׁבָּה, אוֹ־נִגְנַב — „מַשְׁבִּיעֲךָ אֲנִי," וְאָמַר: „אָמֵן," פָּטוּר.

[ו] „הֵיכָן שׁוֹרִי?" אָמַר לוֹ: „אֵינִי יוֹדֵעַ מָה אַתָּה סָח" — וְהוּא שֶׁמֵּת, אוֹ־נִשְׁבַּר, אוֹ־נִשְׁבָּה, אוֹ־נִגְנַב, אוֹ־אָבַד — „מַשְׁבִּיעֲךָ אֲנִי," וְאָמַר: „אָמֵן," חַיָּב.

אָמַר לְנוֹשֵׂא שָׂכָר וְהַשּׂוֹכֵר: „הֵיכָן שׁוֹרִי?" אָמַר לוֹ: „מֵת" — וְהוּא שֶׁנִּשְׁבַּר אוֹ־נִשְׁבָּה; „נִשְׁבַּר" — וְהוּא שֶׁמֵּת אוֹ־נִשְׁבָּה; „נִשְׁבָּה" — וְהוּא שֶׁמֵּת אוֹ־נִשְׁבַּר; „נִגְנַב" — וְהוּא שֶׁאָבַד; „אָבַד" — וְהוּא שֶׁנִּגְנַב — „מַשְׁבִּיעֲךָ אֲנִי," וְאָמַר: „אָמֵן," פָּטוּר.

יד אברהם

was lost' — whereas [in fact] it died, broke a limb, was captured, or stolen —

[In all of these cases, the borrower admitted to his liability but lied about the specific cause of the animal's loss.]

„מַשְׁבִּיעֲךָ אֲנִי," — *[and he said to him,] 'I adjure you,'*

Although the borrower admits his liability, the lender nevertheless requests that he swear to substantiate his assertion *(Tos. Yom Tov)*.

The oath referred to in the mishnah, however, cannot refer to an oath that the bull is not in his possession, which he is, in fact, required to swear, because if that were in fact the case the mishnah's ruling would be self-evident since that oath is true *(Tos. Yom Tov)*.

וְאָמַר: „אָמֵן," — *and he replied, 'Amen,'*

[He accepted the adjuration which, as explained above, is tantamount to swearing by himself.]

פָּטוּר. — *he is exempt.*

Although he swore falsely, his oath did not exempt him from payment, since his claim was not one for which he would be exempt. Therefore, he is not liable to a guilt-offering *(Rav; Rashi)*.

However, he is still liable to the variable sin-offering for a false oath of utterance, as explained in the previous mishnayos.

6.

„הֵיכָן שׁוֹרִי?" — *[If he said to him,] 'Where is my bull?'*

This too refers to a lender asking the borrower to return his animal *(Tif. Yis.)*.

אָמַר לוֹ: „אֵינִי יוֹדֵעַ מָה אַתָּה סָח" — *[and] he replied, 'I don't know what you are talking about' —*

[I.e., he denies ever having borrowed the bull.]

וְהוּא שֶׁמֵּת, — *whereas [in fact] it died,*

[The truth of the matter was that he had indeed borrowed the animal, and it died of natural causes, for which he is liable.]

אוֹ־נִשְׁבַּר, אוֹ־נִשְׁבָּה, אוֹ־נִגְנַב, אוֹ־אָבַד — *or broke a limb, was captured, stolen, or lost —*

[For any of these, he would be liable.]

„מַשְׁבִּיעֲךָ אֲנִי," וְאָמַר: „אָמֵן," — *[and he said to him,] 'I adjure you,' and he replied, 'Amen,'*

[The lender adjured the borrower with an oath that he never borrowed the bull, an oath the borrower accepted by reply-

8 'It was lost' — whereas [in fact] it died, broke a limb,
6 was captured, or stolen — [and he said to him,] 'I adjure you,' and he replied, 'Amen,' he is exempt.

6. [If he said to him,] 'Where is my bull?' [and] he replied, 'I don't know what you are talking about' — whereas [in fact] it died, broke a limb, was captured, stolen, or lost — [and he said to him,] 'I adjure you,' and he replied, 'Amen,' he is liable.

[If] one said to a paid *shomer* or to a renter, 'Where is my bull?' [and] he replied, 'It died' — whereas [in fact] it broke a limb or was captured; [or he replied,] 'It broke a limb' — whereas [in fact] it died or was captured; [or he replied,] 'It was captured' — whereas [in fact] it died or broke a limb; [or he replied,] 'It was stolen' — whereas [in fact] it was lost; [or he replied,] 'It is lost' — whereas [in fact] it was stolen — [and he said to him,] 'I adjure you,' and he replied, 'Amen,' he is exempt.

ing, '*Amen.*']

חַיָּב. — *he is liable.*

Had he admitted the truth he would have been liable. Therefore his claim is a denial of a monetary obligation, for which he is liable to a guilt-offering for his false oath *(Rav; Rashi; Rambam Comm.).*

As above, if the borrower admitted his guilt he is liable to a fifth in addition to the principal and guilt-offering *(Meiri).*

אָמַר לְנוֹשֵׂא שָׂכָר וְהַשּׂוֹכֵר: — *[If] one said to a paid shomer or to a renter,*

[As explained previously, they are governed by the same rules.]

„הֵיכָן שׁוֹרִי?" — *'Where is my bull?'*

[I.e., where is the bull I entrusted you with, or that I rented you?]

אָמַר לוֹ: „מֵת" — *[and] he replied, 'It died' —*

[This is a claim which exempts a paid *shomer* or renter from payment.]

וְהוּא שֶׁנִּשְׁבַּר אוֹ־נִשְׁבָּה; — *whereas [in fact] it broke a limb or was captured;*

[In all these cases, they would also be exempt.]

„נִשְׁבַּר" — וְהוּא שֶׁמֵּת אוֹ־נִשְׁבָּה; „נִשְׁבָּה" — וְהוּא שֶׁמֵּת אוֹ־נִשְׁבַּר; — *[or he replied,] 'It broke a limb' — whereas [in fact] it died or was captured; [or he replied,] 'It was captured' — whereas [in fact] it died or broke a limb;*

[In all these cases, they would be exempt.]

„נִגְנַב" — וְהוּא שֶׁאָבַד; „אָבַד" — וְהוּא שֶׁנִּגְנַב — — *[or he replied,] 'It was stolen' — whereas [in fact] it was lost; [or he replied,] 'It is lost' — whereas [in fact] it was stolen —*

[In contrast to the previous cases, these are all cases in which the paid *shomer* admits his liability but lies about the particular cause, claiming that it was stolen when it was in fact lost or vice versa.]

„מַשְׁבִּיעֲךָ אֲנִי," — *[and he said to him,] 'I adjure you,'*

[I adjure you that your claim is true. In the first three cases, he adjured him with

„מֵת," אוֹ „נִשְׁבַּר," אוֹ „נִשְׁבָּה" — וְהוּא שֶׁנִּגְנַב אוֹ אָבַד — „מַשְׁבִּיעֲךָ אֲנִי," וְאָמַר: „אָמֵן," חַיָּב. „אָבַד," אוֹ „נִגְנַב" — וְהוּא שֶׁמֵּת, אוֹ־נִשְׁבַּר, אוֹ נִשְׁבָּה — „מַשְׁבִּיעֲךָ אֲנִי," וְאָמַר: „אָמֵן," פָּטוּר. זֶה הַכְּלָל: כָּל־הַמְשַׁנֶּה מֵחוֹבָה לְחוֹבָה, וּמִפְּטוּר לִפְטוּר, וּמִפְּטוּר לְחוֹבָה, פָּטוּר; מֵחוֹבָה לִפְטוּר, חַיָּב. זֶה הַכְּלָל: כָּל־הַנִּשְׁבָּע לְהָקֵל עַל־עַצְמוֹ חַיָּב, לְהַחְמִיר עַל־עַצְמוֹ — פָּטוּר.

יד אברהם

the oath of the *shomerim*, since he claims exemption. In the last two cases, he adjures him merely to verify his claim, although he is liable to pay even according to his own claim.]

וְאָמַר: „אָמֵן," — *and he replied, 'Amen,'*

[I.e., he accepted the oath.]

פָּטוּר. — *he is exempt.*

In all the aforementioned cases, the oath does not constitute a denial of money. In the first three cases, he would have been exempt even if he had confessed the truth, since the paid *shomer* is exempt in cases of natural death, breaking a limb, and capture by armed brigands. In the last two cases, even his false claim did not exempt him. Therefore, there was no denial of a monetary debt *(Rav).*

„מֵת," אוֹ „נִשְׁבַּר," אוֹ „נִשְׁבָּה" — *[But if he replied,] 'It died,' 'It broke a limb,' or 'It was captured' —*

If the paid *shomer* or the renter claimed that the bull died, broke a limb, or was captured [in which case he would be exempt] *(Tif. Yis.).*

וְהוּא שֶׁנִּגְנַב אוֹ אָבַד — *whereas [in fact] it was stolen or lost —*

[In these cases, the paid *shomer* and renter are liable.]

„מַשְׁבִּיעֲךָ אֲנִי," וְאָמַר: „אָמֵן," — *[and he said to him,] 'I adjure you,' and he replied, 'Amen,'*

[In this case, he is liable to an oath since he claims exemption.]

חַיָּב. — *he is liable.*

Since, in fact, he is liable to pay, and he claimed to be exempt, his oath constitutes a denial of a monetary debt. Therefore, if he confesses his guilt he is liable to pay the principal plus a fifth, and to bring a guilt-offering *(Tif. Yis.).*

„אָבַד," אוֹ „נִגְנַב" — *[If he replied,] 'It is lost,' or 'It was stolen' —*

[If the paid *shomer* or renter claimed that the bull was lost or stolen, in which cases he would be liable.]

וְהוּא שֶׁמֵּת אוֹ נִשְׁבַּר אוֹ נִשְׁבָּה — *whereas [in fact] it died, broke a limb, or was captured —*

[In each of these cases, the paid *shomer* is exempt.]

„מַשְׁבִּיעֲךָ אֲנִי," וְאָמַר: „אָמֵן," — *[and he said to him,] 'I adjure you,' and he replied, 'Amen,'*

[I.e., I adjure you that the bull was stolen or lost. Although the *shomer* made himself liable, the owner wished to verify his claim that the bull was, indeed, stolen or lost.]

פָּטוּר. — *he is exempt.*

Since the *shomer* made himself liable while he was, in fact, exempt, and brought loss to himself, rather than gain, he is exempt from a guilt-offering *(Rav; Rashi).*

זֶה הַכְּלָל: — *This is the rule:*

I.e., this is the general rule governing all the aforementioned cases *(Shoshannim LeDavid).*

[But if he replied,] 'It died,' 'It broke a limb,' or 'It was captured' — whereas [in fact] it was stolen or lost — [and he said to him,] 'I adjure you,' and he replied, 'Amen,' he is liable.

[If he replied,] 'It is lost,' or 'It was stolen' — whereas [in fact] it died, broke a limb, or was captured — [and he said to him,] 'I adjure you,' and he replied, 'Amen,' he is exempt. This is the rule: Whoever changes from one liability to another liability, from one exemption to another exemption, or from an exemption to a liability, is exempt; from a liability to an exemption, is liable. This is the rule: Whoever swears to make it more lenient for himself is liable, to make it more stringent for himself — is exempt.

YAD AVRAHAM

כָּל־הַמְשַׁנֶּה מֵחוֹבָה לְחוֹבָה, — *Whoever changes from one liability to another liability,*

E.g., the borrower who swears that the bull died, when in fact it broke a limb, for which he is liable either way (*Shoshannim LeDavid*).

וּמִפְּטוּר לִפְטוּר, — *from one exemption to another exemption,*

[E.g., the paid *shomer* who claims that the bull was captured, when in fact it died a natural death.]

וּמִפְּטוּר לְחוֹבָה, — *or from an exemption to a liability,*

[E.g., a paid *shomer* who claims that the animal was lost, when in fact it died.]

פָּטוּר; — *is exempt;*

I.e., he is exempt from the guilt-offering required for violating the oath of deposit. However, he is liable to a variable sin-offering for a false oath of utterance (*Rambam Comm.* from *Gem.* 49b, according to Rav).

מֵחוֹבָה לִפְטוּר, — *from a liability to an exemption,*

[E.g., if a paid *shomer* swears that the animal was captured, when in fact it was stolen or lost.]

חַיָּב. — *is liable.*

I.e., he is liable to pay the principal, add a fifth, and bring a guilt-offering, as delineated above in chapter 4 (*Rambam Comm.*).

זֶה הַכְּלָל: — *This is the rule:*

I.e., the general rule of the oath of deposit (*Shoshannim LeDavid*).

כָּל־הַנִּשְׁבָּע לְהָקֵל עַל־עַצְמוֹ חַיָּב, — *Whoever swears to make it more lenient for himself is liable,*

I.e., anyone who swears to deny a debt is liable to pay the principal, add a fifth, and bring a guilt-offering (*Rambam Comm.*).

לְהַחֲמִיר עַל־עַצְמוֹ — — *to make it more stringent for himself —*

I.e., if he swears that he owes money, which in fact he does not (*Shoshannim LeDavid*).

פָּטוּר. — *is exempt.*

I.e., he is exempt from a guilt-offering, but must bring a variable sin-offering (*Rambam Comm.*).

This latter clause is difficult insofar as the implication of the first clause contradicts the implication of this second clause. The first clause states that whoever swears to make it more lenient for himself is liable, implying

that if he swears to make the same degree of stringency, e.g., from one exemption to another, or from one liability to another, he is exempt. The second clause states that if he swears to make it more stringent for himself, he is exempt. This implies that if he swears to make the same degree of stringency, he is liable. This contradicts not only the implication of the first clause, but the ruling of the mishnah as well, as delineated above. *Tos. Yom Tov*, therefore, explains that this final rule must be taken to mean that whoever swears to make the same degree of stringency upon himself is deemed as though swearing to make it more stringent for himself, and he is exempt.

Toras Chayim explains that the second rule of the mishnah alludes to a paid *shomer* who stipulated that he should be exempt from liability for theft and loss, but liable for accidents (see *Bava Metzia* 7:10).[1] Should an accident occur and he claims that the animal was stolen or lost, although he changes from a claim which is usually an exemption to one which is usually a liability, since he had stipulated to reverse their roles, it is considered that he makes it more lenient for himself, and he is liable to a guilt-offering. Should the animal be stolen, and he claims that an accident occurred and swears to that effect, although he changes from a claim which is usually a liability to one which is usually an exemption, since he swears to make it more stringent for himself according to his stipulation, he is exempt from a guilt-offering.

סליקא לה מסכת שבועות

1. That mishnah explains that a *shomer* and depositor may agree between themselves to any system of liability or exemption even though it is not the same as that of the Torah. Since this money is their own to dispose of as they see fit, their agreements are valid.